Armenia
with Nagorno Karabagh

the Bradt Travel Guide

Deirdre Holding

edition
4

www.bradtguides.com

Bradt Travel Guides Ltd, UK
The Globe Pequot Press

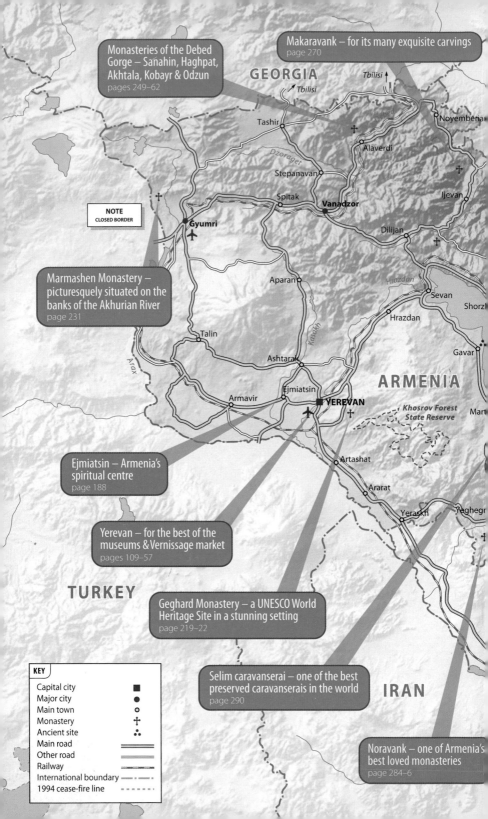

Makaravank – for its many exquisite carvings
page 270

Monasteries of the Debed
Gorge – Sanahin, Haghpat,
Akhtala, Kobayr & Odzun
pages 249–62

GEORGIA

Tbilisi

Tbilisi

Noyemberia

Tashir

Alaverdi

Dzoraget

NOTE
CLOSED BORDER

Stepanavan

Spitak

Vanadzor

Ijevan

Gyumri

Dilijan

Marmashen Monastery –
picturesquely situated on the
banks of the Akhurian River
page 231

Aparan

Hrazdan

Sevan

Shorz

Hrazdan

Talin

Kasakh

Gavar

Ashtarak

Akhurian

ARMENIA

Armavir

Ejmiatsin

YEREVAN

Khosrov Forest
State Reserve

Mart

Ejmiatsin – Armenia's
spiritual centre
page 188

Artashat

Ararat

Yerevan – for the best of the
museums & Vernissage market
pages 109–57

Yeraskh

Yaghegr

Araks

TURKEY

Geghard Monastery – a UNESCO World
Heritage Site in a stunning setting
page 219–22

KEY

Capital city   ■
Major city   ●
Main town   ○
Monastery   †
Ancient site   ∴
Main road
Other road
Railway
International boundary
1994 cease-fire line

Selim caravanserai – one of the best
preserved caravanserais in the world
page 290

IRAN

Noravank – one of Armenia's
best loved monasteries
page 284–6

ARMENIA & THE SELF-DECLARED REPUBLIC OF NAGORNO KARABAGH

Goshavank – home to one of Armenia's most famous khachkars
page 276

Field of khachkars, Noratus – site of Armenia's largest collection of khachkars
page 205

Tigranakert – site of an ancient fortified city on a dramatic escarpment together with its museum in a medieval castle
page 336

AZERBAIJAN

Dadivank – the final resting place of 1st-century apostle & martyr St Thaddeus
pages 338–40

nbarak

NOTE
CLOSED BORDER

NOTE
1994 CEASE-FIRE LINE
CLOSED BORDER

Vardenis

Tartar

Martakert

NAGORNO KARABAGH
(Self-declared Republic)

NOTE
1994 CEASE-FIRE LINE
CLOSED BORDER

Jermuk

Aghavnaget

Stepanakert

Shushi

Sisian

Vorotan

Goris

Hadrut

NOTE
CLOSED BORDER

Tatev Monastery – one of Armenia's most famous sites, now served by the world's longest cable car
pages 307–10

NAKHICHEVAN
(Azerbaijan)

Kapan

Voghji

Kajaran

Shikahogh Reserve

Arax

Petroglyphs of Mount Mets Ishkhanasar – hundreds of ancient carvings are scattered on this extinct volcano
page 303

Meghri

↘ Teheran

N

Bradt

0   50km
0   25 miles

Armenia
Don't
miss...

Monasteries
The monastery of Hovhannavank, perched right on the edge of the cliff above the deep gorge of the River Kasakh, is just one of Armenia's many fascinating monasteries in beautiful surroundings (JS/AWL) page 163

People
Good food, such as this tasty hand-made cheese, plays a very important part in the life of the Armenian people (SS) pages 33–4

Mountains

Armenia's mountains provide many magnificent settings. Mount Khustup in southern Armenia forms a stunning backdrop to the town of Kapan (DH) pages 313–14

Exquisite stone carvings

Khachkars, carved memorial stones, such as this one at Noravank, are an important, conspicuous and beautiful feature of Armenian decorative art (JS/AWL) page 43

Apricots

Armenians claim, with some justification, that their apricots are the best in the world page 88 (VA/S)

Armenia in colour

above   Yerevan's Republic Square is certainly one of the finest central squares created anywhere in the world during the 20th century (E/S) pages 128–9

left   Yerevan's thriving outdoor café culture comes to life from spring right through to autumn (SS) pages 99–100

below   The view from Yerevan's Cascade, over the Tamanian Sculpture Park to the Spendiarian Opera House and Khachaturian Concert Hall (f/S) pages 137–9

above   Yerevan is a city of many statues and sculptures such as this one of *The Men*, depicting characters from a Soviet-era film of the same name popular with Armenians (DH) page 138

right   Men playing draughts or chess is a common sight in Yerevan and throughout Armenia (MN) page 55

below left   This wonderfully imaginative lion is just one of many fascinating exhibits in the eclectic collection of Yerevan's Cafesjian Centre for the Arts (DH) page 154

below right   The Genocide Memorial is an impressive and poignant reminder of the 1915 Armenian genocide. On 24 April, Genocide Memorial Day, thousands of people come to lay flowers. (J/S) pages 145–6

We're 40...
how did that happen?

How did it all happen? George (my then husband) and I wrote the first Bradt guide – about hiking in Peru and Bolivia – on an Amazon river barge, and typed it up on a borrowed typewriter. We had no money for the next two books so George went to work for a printer and was paid in books rather than money.

Forty years on, Bradt publishes over 200 titles that sell all over the world. I still suffer from Imposter Syndrome – how did it all happen? I hadn't even worked in an office before! Well, I've been extraordinarily lucky with the people around me. George provided the belief to get us started (and the mother to run our US office). Then, in 1977, I recruited a helper, Janet Mears, who is still working for us. She and the many dedicated staff who followed have been the foundations on which the company is built. But the bricks and mortar have been our authors and readers. Without them there would be no Bradt Travel Guides. Thank you all for making it happen.

Hilary Bradt

AUTHOR

Born in Liverpool, **Deirdre Holding** moved to Scotland in 1963 and graduated with a degree in medicine from University of St Andrews. It was at university that she met her husband, Nicholas, and they married in 1970. Among many shared interests was one in the communist world and they made their first visit to the Soviet Union in 1973. The downfall of communism enabled them to travel more freely around the former Soviet bloc, and sparked their interest in Armenia. Deirdre retired early, in 2003, after a career in the Scottish National Health  Service as a consultant eye surgeon. Nicholas wrote the first two editions of the Bradt guide to Armenia. After his death in 2008, Deirdre took over the authorship, having always been closely involved with the guide. She updated the book for the third edition (2011) and has now written this fourth edition. She continues to visit Armenia regularly and tries to learn a little of the Armenian language. She still lives in Scotland.

NICHOLAS HOLDING

Author of the first two editions of the Bradt guide to Armenia, Nicholas Holding was born in Wigan (then in Lancashire, but now part of Greater Manchester). He moved to Scotland in 1965 and graduated from the University of St Andrews with a degree in electrical engineering. Nicholas and Deirdre met at university and they married in 1970. After a career in the Scottish electricity supply industry, Nicholas took early retirement in 2000. This enabled him to devote more time to his many interests among which were music (especially opera and in particular Russian opera), literature of the 18th and 19th centuries, wine and food (he became an excellent cook after retirement). He was by nature a forward planner. That, combined with a facility with timetables, made him an efficient organiser of trips to many parts of the world. His ease with timetables stemmed from a childhood interest in trains. A continuing fascination with natural history also started early in life; as a child he spent many hours familiarising himself with the contents of his local ponds. During the last 15 years of his life he developed a particular interest in moths and became County Moth Recorder for two counties in Scotland. Nicholas had an extraordinarily good memory. During his life he amassed a vast fund of knowledge on many subjects, including what he liked to call 'useless information', enabling him to hold forth on any number of disparate subjects.

When asked to write the guidebook to Armenia he applied his characteristic thoroughness to the task, seeking out information and occasionally revealing in his writing his dry sense of humour and his delight in the obscure and esoteric. Nicholas wrote the first two editions of the guidebook to Armenia, the first published in 2003, the second in 2006. He became ill not long after the second edition was published and although he always hoped to write the third edition his death prevented that. He died in 2008. Nicholas's original work forms much of the backbone on which this guide is built; those who knew Nick can still glimpse his personality in that part of the text which is his.

PUBLISHER'S FOREWORD   *Adrian Phillips*

When we published the first edition of this groundbreaking guide I noted that Armenia seemed to have everything: a fascinating history, vibrant culture and rewarding natural history. And in Nicholas Holding we had an author who could do justice to this marvellous yet little-known country. Sadly, Nicholas passed away after the second edition was published. Since then, Deirdre Holding – who travelled with Nicholas, her husband, during his journeys around the country – has picked up the reins and ensured that each subsequent edition is scrupulously updated. Armenia remains well off the beaten track, and adventurous travellers have the benefit of Deirdre's latest discoveries in this fascinating land.

Fourth edition published September 2014
First published 2003
Bradt Travel Guides Ltd, IDC House, The Vale, Chalfont St Peter, Bucks SL9 9RZ, England
www.bradtguides.com
Print edition published in the USA by The Globe Pequot Press Inc, PO Box 480, Guilford, Connecticut 06437-0480

Text copyright © 2014 Deirdre Holding
Maps copyright © 2014 Bradt Travel Guides Ltd
Photographs copyright © 2014 Individual photographers (see below)
Project Managers: Laura Pidgley & Anna Moores
Cover research: Pepi Bluck, Perfect Picture

ISBN: 978 1 84162 555 3 (print)
e-ISBN: 978 1 84162 877 6 (e-pub)
e-ISBN: 978 1 84162 876 9 (mobi)

British Library Cataloguing in Publication Data

A catalogue record for this book is available from the British Library

Photographs Adrian Chan (AC); Alamy: Paul Carstairs (PC/A), Rastislav Kolesar (RK/A), Sérgio Nogueira (S/A); AWL Images: Jane Sweeney (JS/AWL); Deirdre Holding (DH); Dreamstime: Salajean (S/D), Graphics. vp (G/D); Maria Oleinik (MO); Michael Nyholm (MN); Shutterstock: Asaf Eliason (AE/S), Aubord Dulac (AD/S), Emena (E/S), fpolat69 (f/S), HANA (H/S), Maros Markovic (MM/S), Magdalena Paluchowska (MP/S), Marc Venema (MV/S), Piotr Sitnik (PS/S), ruzanna (r/S), VahanN (V/S), Vahan Abrahamyan (VA/S); SuperStock (SS)

Front cover Norovank (S/A)
Back cover Amberd Fortress on the southern slope of Mt Aragats (JS/AWL), the heroic statue of Mother Armenia, Yerevan (H/S)
Title page Mesrop Mashtots statue outside the Matenadaran, Yerevan (AD/S), freshly baked *gata* at Geghard (SS), carved stone portico of Ejmiatsin Cathedral (MO)

Maps David McCutcheon FBCart.S (base mapping, modified by Bradt Travel Guides, provided by ITMB Publishing Ltd (*www.itmb.com*) 2014); colour map base by Nick Rowland FRGS; some town plan maps include data © OpenStreetMap contributors (under Open Database License)

Typeset from the author's disc by Ian Spick, Bradt Travel Guides
Production managed by Jellyfish Print Solutions; printed in India
Digital conversion by the Firsty Group

My husband and I first went to Armenia in 2001, on holiday. We were enthralled by the country: its landscapes, the wild flowers, the many medieval monasteries and churches, its unique alphabet, the welcome given to us, its complex history at so many crossroads – geological, historical, political and religious. But there were frustrations. There was virtually no information in Armenia itself. Even road signs were in short supply. Yes, there was internet information but how many printouts can be packed before a suitcase is overweight? Many times we bewailed the absence of a practical and informative guidebook, such as the Bradt guides we had used elsewhere.

So when, after our return, Nick was asked to write the first Bradt guide to Armenia he accepted willingly. We enjoyed getting to know the country better and feeling that we were making some contribution. It was also hard work! It wasn't just the journeys on dreadfully pot-holed roads but also the research involved. I remember Nick once spent the whole day researching an apparently authoritative statement that a certain cave held a colony of fruit bats. Fruit bats? In Armenia? It turned out that the species of bat referred to wasn't fruit-eating at all and it was in fact quite another species which actually inhabited the cave!

Armenia has been one of the things which has helped me to cope with the enormous gap left in my life by Nick's death. I continue to find the country endlessly fascinating and have come to realise how much more there is to be known than we ever grasped during our early visits. I hope this edition reflects at least some of this increased appreciation of what Armenia was and is, and what it has to offer the visitor.

From the start our hope was that the Bradt guide to Armenia would inform and make a visit there even more enjoyable than it is bound to be. That continues to be my hope for this edition.

Acknowledgements

My greatest debt is to my late husband, Nicholas, whose original work for the first and second editions still comprises a significant part of this present edition, the fourth. Indeed, much of the background and descriptive information remains his text although with deletions, changes and additions as required. Without his foundation I could not have contemplated writing this guidebook.

Special thanks are due to Saro Boick who has continued to drive me cheerfully and safely the length and breadth of Armenia, on roads both good and bad, and who also assisted greatly as interpreter.

Thanks are also due to the staff at Armenia Travel + M in Yerevan, particularly Kristina Gharibyan and Nina Dadayan, for their willing efficiency when making arrangements; to Hasmik Shahverdyan for giving me so much of her time and company in Yerevan and for finding the answers to innumerable questions; to Carl Meadows of Regent Holidays for his help; to Raffi Youredjian for advice about cycling in Armenia; to Andrew Selkirk, Editor-in-Chief of *Current Archaeology*, who allowed some reciprocal cribbing from his writing on archaeology in Armenia; to Tina Walkling, also for archaeological insights particularly in relation to petroglyphs; to David Sayers (author of the Bradt guide to the Azores) for continued use of his guidance on botanical matters; to Anahit Shahverdyan, our original adviser, interpreter and guide to all things Armenian, whose past contribution to the language section was invaluable and who has continued to assist.

I would also like to thank the very many other people in Armenia, and in Nagorno Karabagh, who gave freely of their time, knowledge and practical help, so contributing much to this guidebook.

In their dealings with me the staff at Bradt have encouraged and helped, shown patience and understanding, all laced with cheerfulness and humour.

DEDICATION

In memory of Nick.

Contents

LIST OF MAPS

Introduction

This is a guidebook to the present-day Republic of Armenia together with the territory of Nagorno Karabagh. In the English-speaking world, an individual's knowledge of this fascinating country generally falls into one of two categories. Most people know nothing about it at all, not even where it is. The others, a small minority, not only speak the Armenian language, although neither they nor their parents were born in Armenia, but also have some knowledge of Armenian culture and Armenia's often tragic history. When it comes to who actually visits Armenia nowadays the numbers in the two categories are more evenly balanced. The explanation is that Armenia has one of the most successful and supportive diasporas in the world and that present-day Armenia is very dependent on them. So far as Nagorno Karabagh is concerned, the contrast is even more stark with the diaspora being wholly familiar with its recent past while few others would claim even to have heard of it, apart from those who are well informed politically and might recall its name as the scene of some half-remembered conflict around the time that the Soviet Union disintegrated.

This book is aimed primarily at the general tourist who is interested in seeing the country and understanding something of its long and complex history. Nevertheless, even fairly knowledgeable members of the diaspora should also find it useful as they, like virtually all other visitors to Armenia, unfortunately often confine themselves to only half a dozen of the more popular places which are not always the most interesting ones. It appears that few visitors know anything about the many other sights in Armenia which warrant a visit. As a consequence, only a handful of visitors to Armenia spend more than a week in the country and many visits last a mere four or five days. This book seeks to rectify that regrettable situation and demonstrate that Armenia has huge potential for visitors. Not just for general sightseeing, although its spectacular gorges and medieval buildings certainly provide plenty of excellent opportunities for that, but also for activities such as hiking, cycling, birdwatching, architectural and archaeological tours, historical visits, botanical trips, horseriding and caving. Although many visitors will probably continue to combine a visit to Armenia with one to neighbouring Georgia, there is quite enough in Armenia alone to occupy several holidays without ever going to the same place twice.

Armenia is actually a very easy country to visit. Its people are overwhelmingly friendly, helpful and welcoming: I have only ever once encountered an unhelpful and unwelcoming attitude in my travels around the country. Many tourists no longer need a visa to enter the country, and those who do can easily get one either over the internet, paying for it by credit card, or on arrival in Armenia. There is relatively little crime and the risk of theft or being short-changed is much less than in most other European countries.

Is Armenia in Europe? It certainly feels far more like a southern European country than an Asian one and it is a member of the Council of Europe and the

Organisation for Security and Co-operation in Europe. In addition, the Armenian people have been Christian for 1,700 years and from 1828 to 1991 they were ruled by another country whose culture, the Bolshevik Revolution notwithstanding, was fundamentally Christian. On a more practical level, Armenia has an international telephone dialling code (374) in the European sequence and the British post office charges the European rate for letters sent to Armenia from Britain.

By contrast to these factors making it easy to visit Armenia, the main drawback is the language barrier, although even this is becoming less of a concern in places used to dealing with tourists. However, outside the main tourist locations in Yerevan and the larger hotels in the regions, few people speak English or any other western European language. The main second language is, and is likely to remain, Russian so visitors travelling on their own may well find it convenient to consider employing an English-speaking guide or driver or else arranging accommodation in advance. Either can be done through one of the Yerevan travel agents or an overseas agent who specialises in the country.

The infrastructure continues to improve with good hotel accommodation now available in most places. However, there are still parts of the country where homestays remain the best option, providing an insight into Armenian family life. Roads are also improving. Most main routes now have a good asphalt surface although secondary roads can still be poor. While all villages can be reached by minibus there are many places of interest which are not served by public transport. For these, one of Armenia's cheap taxis is a viable alternative. If hiring a car, it is generally cheaper to hire one with a driver than to drive oneself, although the car may then be older. Depending on the expected destinations a 4x4 vehicle can be requested, essential for getting to some places and quite helpful for many others. Good road maps are available but the lack of detailed maps for walking, such as the British Ordnance Survey maps, means that Armenia's vast potential for hiking remains relatively difficult to access for the independent visitor.

As well as the improvement in hotels and roads most towns, especially the capital, have seen much new building and a significant improvement in the reliability of the water supply. On the other hand, many villages remain largely unaltered. Huge advances have been made on the technological side with Armenia leap-frogging from an antiquated and cumbersome Soviet-era telephone system to one of the most advanced mobile phone and internet systems. Armenia is changing rapidly and it is likely that some comments made in this book will quickly be superseded.

The amount of information available to tourists has increased almost unbelievably. At many historic sites welcome information boards, in several languages, have sprung up and there has been an improvement in museum displays and labelling, although much remains to be done. A significant amount of restoration of historic sites has been, and is being, carried out, some of it good, some of it questionable.

Political and economic problems remain for Armenia. Perhaps the most obvious to visitors is the unresolved question of the status of Nagorno Karabagh, resulting in the continued closure by Azerbaijan and Turkey of their respective borders with Armenia. The refusal of Turkey to recognise as genocide the 1915 massacre of Armenians in the Ottoman Empire continues to influence Armenia's relations with Turkey. There is also the question of how far Armenia can develop closer links with Europe in the light of the 2013 agreement to participate in the planned formation of a Russia-led economic union of former Soviet states, the Eurasian Union.

Armenia has so much to offer visitors. It will never become a mainstream tourist destination like Mallorca or Florida but few visitors to Armenia leave disappointed, apart from wishing that they had had more time in the country. The author very much hopes that this guide will encourage others to explore not only the popular sites but also more of the off-the-beaten-track places. They will be rewarded by seeing enthralling sights in a country in transition. After centuries of foreign domination Armenia is now once again an independent nation preserving for future generations its unique heritage. Many of the best things in Armenia have not changed: the hospitality of the people, the wonderful quality of seasonal fruit and vegetables, its magnificent landscapes and the abundant ancient sites, both prehistoric and medieval. It remains a country well worth visiting.

AN IMPORTANT WORD OF WARNING Do not try to take a copy of this book into Azerbaijan. It will be confiscated at the border.

NOTE ON TRANSLITERATION There is no standard transliteration from the Armenian alphabet into English. For example, the principal city of northwest Armenia can appear in English as Gyumri, Gyumry, Giumri, G'umri or even Kyumrï, while the province of which it is the capital is Shirak in English, Schirak in German or Chirak in French. Some transliteration schemes even resort to letters borrowed from Czech and Slovak such as č, š and ž, which few English speakers know how to pronounce anyway.

For place names in this guide the author has usually followed those used by Brady Kiesling and Raffi Kojian in *Rediscovering Armenia* (see page 357). Occasionally this does result in combinations of consonants appearing such as those in Smbataberd, Aghjkaghala and Ptghni but these are actually quite close to the Armenian pronunciation. So far as surnames are concerned, the ending '...ian' has been preferred to '...yan' for the many which end this way (eg: Abovian rather than Abovyan) except where this would result in the ending '...aian' or something similar, and there '...ayan' has been used (eg: Babayan rather than Babaian). In this guide the transliteration Karabagh has usually been preferred to Karabakh, except where an organisation itself uses the latter form.

HOW TO USE THIS GUIDE

MAPS

Keys and symbols: Maps include alphabetical keys covering the locations of those places to stay, eat or drink that are featured in the book. Note that regional maps may not show all hotels and restaurants in the area: other establishments may be located in towns shown on the map.

Grids and grid references: Some maps use grid lines to allow easy location of sites. Map grid references are listed in square brackets after the name of the place or sight of interest in the text, with page number followed by grid number, eg: [103 C3].

LISTINGS

Accommodation is marked with a price code and listed alphabetically in descending price code order (**$$$$$–$**); the few hotels where a standard double including breakfast is over AMD100,000 are highlighted. As **restaurants** vary very little in price across the country, they are not marked with price codes, although the very expensive and very cheap are noted within their individual entries.

HISTORIC SITES

Prices and opening hours are included where they apply. Otherwise assume the site is free and always open.

FEEDBACK REQUEST AND UPDATES WEBSITE

At Bradt Travel Guides we're aware that guidebooks start to go out of date on the day they're published – and that you, our readers, are out there in the field doing research of your own. You'll find out before us when a fine new family-run hotel opens or a favourite restaurant changes hands and goes downhill. So why not write and tell us about your experiences? Contact us on ☎ 01753 893444 or e info@bradtguides.com. We will forward emails to the author who may post updates on the Bradt website at www.bradtupdates. com/armenia. You can also add a review of the book to www.bradtguides. com or Amazon.

Part One

GENERAL INFORMATION

Location A landlocked country in the southern Caucasus between the Black Sea and the Caspian Sea bordered by Georgia, Azerbaijan, Iran and Turkey. The border with the self-declared Republic of Nagorno Karabagh is not recognised internationally. Yerevan, the capital, is on the same latitude as Naples, Madrid and New York. It is on the same longitude as Volgograd, Russia, Baghdad and Sana'a, Yemen. It is five hours' flying time from London.

Area 29,800km^2 – similar to Belgium and the US state of Maryland. Note, however, that following the 1994 ceasefire the territory administered is 31,200km^2.

Status Presidential parliamentary republic with universal adult suffrage.

Population 3.02 million resident in the country at the date of census (October 2011); 97.9% are ethnic Armenians, 1.3% Yezidis, 0.5% Russians, 0.05% Kurds. The balance comprises a wide range of nationalities.

Major cities Yerevan (the capital, population 1.1 million); Gyumri (146,500); Vanadzor (104,800). Note that the Yerevan population figure covers only those living within the city. Urban sprawl into the surrounding provinces results in a much larger figure for the Yerevan conurbation.

Administrative divisions The country is divided into the capital (Yerevan) and ten provinces (*marz*): Shirak, Lori, Tavush, Aragatsotn, Gegharkunik, Kotayk, Armavir, Ararat, Vayots Dzor and Syunik.

Language Armenian, an Indo-European language. Russian is also widely understood but western European languages are not, although English is becoming a little better known, mainly in the capital.

Alphabet The unique Armenian alphabet, currently with 39 letters, was devised around AD400.

Religion Very predominantly Armenian Apostolic. There are a few Roman Catholics, mostly in Shirak province, and there are several sects seeking converts. The Yezidis are Zoroastrian and the Kurds are Muslim.

Currency Dram (AMD) divided theoretically into 100 luma.

Exchange rate £1 = AMD691, US$1 = AMD423, €1 = AMD562 (May 2014).

International telephone code +374.

Time GMT + 4 hours.

Electricity 220V AC; European two-pin plug.

Weights and measures Metric system.

National flag Three horizontal stripes: red, blue, orange.

National anthem 'Land of Our Fathers, Free, Independent' (*Mer Hayreniq, azat, ankakh*); words adapted from a poem by Mikayel Nalbandian (1829–66); music by Barsegh Kanachian (1885–1967).

Symbols of Armenia The classical symbol is the *khachkar* ('cross stone'). The grape and pomegranate are also used as symbols as is the eagle which appears on the country's coat of arms.

Public holidays See page 95.

1

Background Information

GEOGRAPHY AND CLIMATE

GEOLOGICAL FEATURES Visitors to Armenia can hardly fail to be aware of two key geological features of the country: the **Lesser Caucasus** mountain range that projects into the country, with the **dormant volcano of Mount Aragats** being the highest peak at 4,090m; and the frequency of earthquakes. The two are both accounted for by the theory of plate tectonics. Under this theory, which has been generally accepted internationally since the 1960s, the outermost shell of the earth or lithosphere is formed of a dozen or so large, rigid slabs of rock together with many smaller ones. These slabs, called tectonic plates, are around 75km thick and comprise the thin outer crust plus the solid part of the mantle. The plates float on the liquid part of the mantle or asthenosphere, which is several hundred kilometres thick, and the slow movement of the plates is due to convection currents in the asthenosphere caused by heat escaping from the earth's core. As the enormous plates move, they grind against each other and stress builds up until there is a sudden movement of one plate against another resulting in an earthquake when rocks break along fault lines. Armenia is on the line where the Arabian plate, moving at about 2.5cm per annum, is colliding with the larger Eurasian plate, and it is consequently very prone to earthquakes. About 25 million years ago the Caucasus Mountains themselves were formed as a consequence of this collision. Quite young as mountain ranges go, they are largely volcanic rocks such as basalt, andesite and tuff, all three of which have been used as building materials in Armenia. **Basalt and andesite** are magma (liquid material from the asthenosphere) which escaped to the surface during the collision of the plates and then solidified. The difference between the two is in the relative proportions of silica, iron and magnesium. **Tuff** by contrast is formed when small rock fragments (less than 2mm across) which have spewed out from a volcano become fused together on the ground. Tuff has long been the building material of choice in Armenia when it is available and it is highly characteristic of the country. Today the biggest working tuff quarry is close to the town of Artik in Shirak province. Another consequence of the volcanic past is that the semiprecious stone obsidian can be found here. **Obsidian**, which occurs in a range of colours and is used to make jewellery, is a glassy rock formed through the very rapid solidification of lava. In Armenia it occurs most commonly in the Hrazdan region. Apart from these volcanic rocks, Armenia also has substantial deposits of the sedimentary rock **limestone** and in some of these are extensive though little-known cave systems. The most important mineral deposits are of copper (7.4 million tonnes, of which 4.5 million tonnes are at Kajaran), molybdenum (711,000 tonnes, of which 600,000 tonnes are at Kajaran) and gold (268 tonnes, of which 97 tonnes are at Sotk).

GEOGRAPHICAL FEATURES Armenia is a very high country. The lowest part, the Debed Valley at the Georgian border in the northeast, lies at 400m above sea level while the average altitude is 1,370m and only 10% of the land is under 1,000m. Although mountainous in parts, much of Armenia is more a high plateau fissured by deep gorges. The volcanic soil in the valleys means that the ground is highly fertile but irrigation is essential because of the low rainfall and about 10% of the entire land is irrigated. Even so, Armenia is a net importer of food. The growing of food crops is obviously unfeasible in the mountainous areas but is equally unfeasible on much of the plateau because of the lack of water, although some of the alpine meadows are used for the production of hay. The mountains do support a surprisingly large population of cattle as well as sheep and goats, and livestock can often be encountered at unexpected elevations in fairly inaccessible places. About 20% of the land is arable, while 24% is pasture and about 15% is forest. **Fruit growing** is important. Fruits as diverse as pomegranates, grapes, strawberries, peaches, persimmons and apples are grown but two fruits native to Armenia and which were consequently first eaten here remain important although they have now spread to the rest of the world. One is the **apricot** – its scientific name reflects this – *Armeniaca vulgaris* – and Armenians claim with some justification that their apricots are the best in the world. Apricot stones 6,000 years old have been found at archaeological sites and today there are about 50 varieties in the country. The other is the **sweet cherry** or mazzard, *Prunus avium*, from which all the world's 900 varieties of sweet cherry have been cultivated. It spread to the West very early and was known in Greece by 300BC. Walnuts, pistachios, almonds and hazelnuts grow wild in Armenia and they too are now extensively cultivated. Also of great importance is that Armenia is possibly the country where wheat was first cultivated, perhaps about 10,000 years ago. Two native species of wheat *Triticum urartu* and *T. araraticum* still grow in protected fields in the Arax Valley. The importance of both culinary and medicinal herbs, collected from the hillsides, can be seen in any Armenian market.

A major feature of the country is **Lake Sevan** whose surface area was formerly 1,416km^2, but this has been reduced by abstracting water for hydro-electric and irrigation purposes. It is one of the world's largest high-altitude lakes with its surface originally 1,915m above sea level. By 2001, it had fallen to 1,896m but it has now started to rise again. There is commercial exploitation of fish stocks although the introduction of alien species has led to the virtual extinction of the endemic trout.

Armenia has a number of **significant rivers** which all flow east into the Caspian Sea. **Hydro-electric schemes** on these rivers are important as the only indigenous energy resource within the country which has been developed apart from a small wind farm on the top of the Pushkin Pass in Lori province. Hydro-electric schemes provide around one third of electricity requirements and small hydro-electric schemes are under construction throughout the country. Another third of electricity is generated using **nuclear power** and the balance is **thermal generation** mostly using imported gas. Electricity is exported to Georgia and there are seasonal exchanges with Iran. Gas is mostly imported from Russia by pipeline through Georgia although the Armenian and Iranian gas networks are also linked. Armenia itself has no known reserves of coal, oil or gas but geological and seismic surveys for oil and gas have started.

CLIMATE Armenia has a highland continental climate with hot, dry summers (June to September) and cold winters (December, January and February being the coldest months). However, this simple statement masks the fact that the weather can vary greatly within short distances because of differences in altitude and other factors affecting local microclimates. Variation in altitude often has more influence on the weather than north–south distances. For example, Gyumri can be much cooler than Yerevan even although the distance between them is only 122km, and Amberd, about an hour's drive from Yerevan, can be snowbound until late May (see also pages 57 and 109 for Yerevan's weather). April and May are the wettest months: although this usually means heavy showers the rain can be continuous for long spells. Spring can be very short, the weather changing from wintery to summery in just a few days. During the hottest months of June, July and August low humidity mitigates the high temperatures. Autumn is relatively long and often very pleasant.

ARMENIA'S BORDERS Prior to the war with Azerbaijan, landlocked Armenia was bordered to the north by Georgia, to the east by Azerbaijan, to the south by Iran and to the west by Turkey and by the detached part of Azerbaijan known as Nakhichevan. The borders totalled 1,254km: 164km with Georgia; 566km with Azerbaijan; 35km with Iran; 268km with Turkey; and 221km with Nakhichevan. The area of the country was 29,800km², slightly smaller than Belgium or slightly larger than the American state of Maryland. An additional complication was that five small detached enclaves within Armenia were actually part of Azerbaijan while Azerbaijan had a small Armenian enclave within its borders. The ceasefire in 1994 has led to a considerable change. First, all these small enclaves were occupied by the surrounding power. Secondly, Nagorno Karabagh, which had been an autonomous region within Azerbaijan, declared itself an independent republic; the present-day republic of Nagorno Karabagh does not incorporate all the territory of the former autonomous region since Azerbaijan holds the northern part. Thirdly, Armenia was left in control of a considerable area of the territory of Azerbaijan and much of this is now administered by the self-declared Republic of Nagorno Karabagh. A noticeable change in 2002 was that for the first time maps were starting to show the occupied territories either as a part of Armenia or as a part of the Republic of Nagorno Karabagh. Relatively few people live in them since the Azeri population has fled and Armenian refugees have not chosen these territories in which to settle. The international community still recognises the pre-1991 boundaries. Since 1989 the long western border with Turkey and Nakhichevan and the eastern border with Azerbaijan have been closed. The border with the self-declared Republic of Nagorno Karabagh is open, and is, in fact, the only way of entering the latter. Although the northern border with Georgia is open at major border crossings, the exact position of the border in some places, especially in Lori province, is disputed. This has led to the closure of several minor border crossings previously used by local people. It also means that two monasteries (Khuchap and Khorakert) in the border area can no longer easily be visited from Armenia.

NATURAL HISTORY AND CONSERVATION

The number of species of animals and plants in Armenia is very high for a country of its size which lies wholly outside the tropics. This is largely accounted for by the great altitudinal variation and the diversity of vegetation zones. Armenia is normally described as having **six distinct zones**: semi-deserts, dry steppes, mountain steppes, forest, subalpine and alpine. **Semi-deserts** account for about 10% of the country and occur in the Ararat Valley and adjacent mountain slopes up to altitudes of 1,200–1,300m, as well as in the Arpa Valley around Vayk, and in the Meghri region. The land has generally been cultivated for millennia except for a few patches where sand has accumulated and a semi-desert landscape has resulted.

Cultivation has required extensive irrigation and these irrigated areas now account for most of the fruit, vegetable and wine production. **Dry steppes** are found at higher altitudes than semi-deserts (above 1,500m) in the Ararat Valley and some other areas, but are also found at lower altitudes (above 800m) in the northeast in areas which were originally forested. A range of soils is found and in the Ararat Valley these are mostly stony. Irrigation of dry steppes has allowed some cultivation of crops and fruit. **Mountain steppes** are the dominant landscape for most of the country, particularly at altitudes above 1,500m. In the northeast of the country and also in the south, ridges among these highland meadow steppes often contain patches of forest. Elsewhere **forests** are usually found on the mid-zone of mountains though in some regions the forests were much affected by the cutting of trees for fuel during the energy shortages of the early 1990s. The most extensive forested areas are now in the northeast. **Subalpine meadows** occur at higher altitudes than steppes and forests, including highland mountain ranges. **Alpine meadows** occur higher still and are important pasture lands even though climatic conditions are severe with long cold winters and snow cover lasting up to nine months. So-called **azonal landscapes** (meaning that the soil type is determined by factors other than the local climate and vegetation) cover the remaining 10% of the territory of the country and include wetlands, as well as saline and alkaline areas in the Ararat Valley where the underground waters are close to the earth's surface, resulting in water vaporisation and salt precipitation.

MAMMALS Armenia's mammal list was recently increased from 76 to 83 when seven additional species of bat were identified. However, one of the mammals on the list, striped hyena (*Hyaena hyaena*), is probably extinct in the country and the status of Caucasian birch mouse (*Sicista caucasica*) is unknown. Another six are officially classified as endangered: the distinctive Armenian subspecies of mouflon (*Ovis orientalis gmelini*), Persian ibex or wild goat (*Capra aegagrus*), marbled polecat (*Vormela peregusna*), otter (*Lutra lutra*), Pallas's cat (or manul) (*Felis manul*) and brown bear (*Ursus arctos*) (or grizzly bear as the same species is known in North America). Despite bears being classified as endangered, their droppings can often be encountered while walking in the mountains, sometimes surprisingly close to habitation. Other interesting mammals include leopard (*Panthera pardus*), now the subject of a WWF protection programme in Armenia, lynx (*Felis lynx*), wild cat (*Felis silvestris*), wolf (*Canis lupus*), Bezoar ibex (*C.a. aegagrus*), porcupine (*Hystrix indica*), roe deer (*Capreolus capreolus*) and wild boar (*Sus scrofa*). However, no mammals in Armenia can be described as easy to see and, apart from a wolf disturbed from its daytime retreat and a few unidentified bats, I have only ever observed red fox (*Vulpes vulpes*), brown hare (*Lepus capensis*), European souslik (*Citellus citellus*) and Vinogradov's jird (*Meriones vinogradovi*), the jird being one of five species of gerbil found in Armenia.

BIRDS The standard guide, *A Field Guide to the Birds of Armenia* (see page 356), lists 346 species of bird as having been recorded in Armenia up to 1997. However, as there are only a few observers many vagrants and casuals must go unrecorded. Armenia is at the boundary of two faunal zones and the north sees northern species at the southern limit of their range while the south sees southern species and those from the eastern Mediterranean at their northern limit. Raptors are surprisingly common and easy to see. Five species of eagle breed in Armenia: lesser spotted, golden, booted, steppe, and short-toed snake-eagle. This is in addition to osprey, four vultures, two harriers and a good selection of buzzards and falcons. Other large and conspicuous birds include white and black storks, the former mainly in the Arax Valley where their nests are conspicuous in some places on top of electricity poles. The Dalmatian pelican breeds in the country and great white pelicans are year-round visitors. Specialities of the Caucasus include Caucasian grouse and Caspian snowcock, both of which are endangered and difficult to see without a knowledgeable local guide in their subalpine and alpine meadows. Smaller birds of note include both eastern and western rock nuthatches, white-tailed lapwing, Persian wheatear, Armenian gull, white-throated robin and Finsch's wheatear. Raptor migration in autumn is very rewarding as Armenia is on a major flightway between the Black and Caspian seas with the most numerous species being steppe buzzard, steppe and lesser spotted eagles, and Montagu's and pallid harriers, honey buzzard, Levant sparrowhawk, lesser kestrel and black kite. September sees migrating demoiselle cranes at Lake Sevan with daily totals of up to 4,500 being recorded.

Anyone interested in Armenia's birds is strongly recommended to join the **Ornithological Society of the Middle East, Caucasus and Central Asia** (*c/o The Lodge, Sandy, Bedfordshire, SG19 2DL, UK; e secretary@osme.org; www.osme.org*) who can assist with birdwatching trips to the country as well as funding small projects such as the survey of Armash fish ponds.

AMPHIBIANS AND REPTILES Armenia's dry climate is reflected in the paucity of **amphibian species** and lack of specialities. All eight species in the country have a wide distribution even though only one is also native to the UK. Widespread European species are marsh frog (*Rana ridibunda*), green toad (*Bufo viridis*), eastern spadefoot toad (*Pelobates syriacus*), European tree frog (*Hyla arborea*) and smooth newt (*Triturus vulgaris*). The others, not included in most field guides, are banded frog (*Rana camerani*), lemon-yellow tree frog (*Hyla savignyi*) and banded newt (*Triturus vittatus*).

By contrast, Armenia is very rich in **reptile species** with a total of 50 although some are now threatened by denudation of the habitat as a result of overgrazing. The Mediterranean tortoise (*Testudo graeca*) may occasionally be encountered as one crosses a track. Ponds may contain one of two species of terrapin, European pond terrapin (*Emys orbicularis*) and stripe-necked terrapin (*Mauremys caspica*).

The **geckos** which can frequently be seen on the outside walls of buildings in the countryside are Caspian rock geckos (*Tenuidactylus caspius*). The Caucasian agama (*Laudakia caucasia*) is a lizard with a decidedly prehistoric dragon-like appearance. Like all agamas, it has a plump short body with a long thin tail, a triangular head and long legs. Agamas are capable of some colour change to match their background. Two **legless lizards** which might be mistaken for snakes (though being lizards rather than snakes they have eyelids and they can shed their tails to escape a predator, a practice known as autotony) are the slow worm (*Anguis fragilis*) and the European glass lizard (*Ophisaurus apodus*). **Skinks** are lizards which, while not usually completely legless, generally in Europe only have vestigial legs of little or no apparent value for locomotion. The Armenian fauna includes several skinks: two-streaked lidless skink (*Ablepharus bivittatus*); Chernov's lidless skink (*Ablepharus chernovi*); golden grass skink (*Mabuya aurata*); and the Berber skink (*Eumeces schneideri*). The other lizard species are typical lizards belonging to the large family Lacertidae. Ones of particular interest are those with a limited range outside Armenia such as stepperunner (*Eremias arguta*), Balkan green lizard (*Lacerta trilineata*) and Caucasian green lizard (*Lacerta strigata*). Even more unusual is the Armenian lizard (*Lacerta armeniaca*) in which a proportion of the females practise parthenogenesis – in other words without fertilisation by a male they lay eggs which hatch and produce a daughter that is an exact genetic copy of the mother.

Snakes are very well represented with 23 species and they are more commonly seen than in many countries. Interesting snakes include the sand boa (*Eryx jaculus*), one of Europe's few snakes which kill their prey by constriction, mostly small lizards and rodents in this case. Largely nocturnal it rests by day in rodent burrows or under large stones. Unusually the snake is viviparous, the female giving birth to about 20 live young which feed on small lizards. The Montpellier snake (*Malpolon monspessulanus*) belongs to the family Colubridae, snakes whose fangs are at the back of the mouth. Such snakes find it difficult to inject their venom into large objects. Unusually for a snake this diurnal species possesses good vision and, when hunting, it sometimes rises up and looks around rather resembling a cobra. The Montpellier snake reaches 2m in length. A much smaller colubrid is the Asia Minor dwarf snake (*Eirenis modestus*) which grows to only 15cm and feeds on insects. Dahl's whip snake (*Coluber najadum*) is another diurnal snake. Very slender, it is extremely fast moving but rarely exceeds 1m in length. Another whip snake is the secretive and weakly venomed mountain racer (*C. ravergieri*). Caucasian rat snake (*Elaphe hohenackeri*) is one of Europe's smaller snakes, growing up to about only 80cm. Very unusually for a snake it is often found in the vicinity of human habitations where it frequents piles of stones and holes in old stone walls.

Vipers are among the snakes which, unlike the colubrids, have fangs at the front of their mouth. They are consequently much more dangerous because they do not need to get their mouth round the victim in order to inject poison. There are several interesting species in Armenia which have a very limited distribution. Armenian viper (*Vipera raddei*) is now seriously threatened in the country through pasturing and overgrazing while Darevsky's viper (*V. darevskii*), described as recently as 1986, also has a very limited range and is similarly threatened. Bites from these species can be fatal as can those from Armenia's more widely distributed vipers. Perhaps the most dangerous of all is the blunt-nosed viper (*V. lebetina*), at 2.5m one of the largest of its genus. An able climber of trees, the danger from this snake lies mainly in the extreme speed of its attack and the method of biting: rather than bite and withdraw, it keeps its teeth lodged in its target and works its jaws to pump more venom in. It is not a snake to be approached lightly, although it generally makes a loud hissing before attacking, thus giving some warning (see page 72 for what to do in the event of a snakebite).

FISH Of the 31 species of fish found in Armenia, six have been introduced. Common whitefish (*Coregonus lavaretus*) was introduced into Lake Sevan from Lake Ladoga in Russia with a view to increasing commercial fish production and this was followed by goldfish (*Carassius auratus*) from eastern Asia. Fish farms are responsible for introducing silver carp (*Hypophthalmichthys molitrix*) from China and Pacific salmon (*Salmo gairdneri*). Presumably Pacific salmon was preferred to the native Caspian salmon (*S. caspius*) because of the ease of obtaining stock. Grass carp (*Ctenopharyngodon idella*) came from China with the hope of improving water quality in irrigation systems and marshy lakes as it is herbivorous and so helps to control aquatic vegetation. By contrast mosquito fish (*Gambusia affinis*) was brought from the southeast part of the USA because, as its name implies, it eats mosquito larvae and hence assists in the control of malaria.

Apart from these exotics there has been some stocking of waters with common carp (*Cyprinus carpio*) which has been introduced to lakes in Lori province as well as Dilijan and Ijevan reservoirs. On the other hand, overfishing of rivers has led to a decline in the abundance of trout (*Salmo trutta*) and European catfish or wels (*Silurus glanis*). However, chub (*Leusciscus cephalus*) remains common in lakes. Drastic reduction in the water level of Lake Sevan has led to the virtual extinction in Armenia of the endemic Sevan trout (*Salmo ischchan*) (see page 200). Paradoxically its successful translocation into Lake Issyk-kul in Kyrgyzstan, although having negative consequences for the indigenous Issyk-kul fish fauna, has probably saved this fish from extinction. Stocks in Lake Sevan of Sevan khramulya (*Varicorhinus capoeta*) have also seriously declined but it survives in some of the lake's tributaries.

OTHER FAUNA About 17,000 species of **invertebrate** have been identified in Armenia but this must only represent a small fraction of the total. Two groups may be of particular interest to visitors but for very different reasons. Armenia has three species of **scorpion** which fortunately are rarely encountered. That said, they occur on the rocky and stony ground such as that which surrounds many monasteries and form an additional reason to wear robust footwear as well as taking care when scrambling up slopes. Far more conspicuous is the abundance of **butterflies**. About 570 species of lepidoptera (moths and butterflies) have been identified in Armenia but that is clearly only a small percentage of the total since it compares with a figure of 2,600 for the UK which, although larger, has a much less suitable climate. A well-illustrated guide to the butterflies of the whole of the former Soviet Union including Armenia (*Guide to the Butterflies of Russia and Adjacent Territories*) is available – it was published in Sofia, Bulgaria, and is obtainable from specialist booksellers worldwide – but unfortunately its two enormous heavy volumes make it difficult even to take to Armenia let alone carry around. More portable is *A Field Guide to the Butterflies of Turkey* published in 2007. Obviously it does not cover Armenia specifically but there is enough overlap to make it more useful than no guide at all. For details of these books see pages 356–7. The American University of Armenia, which published *A Field Guide to the Birds of Armenia,* promised a field guide to the butterflies of Armenia. The original planned publication date was 2012 but at the time of writing it had not yet appeared. A 2004 checklist of the dragonflies and damselflies (Odonata) of Armenia can be found at www.armenodon.org.

FLORA Identified so far in Armenia have been 388 species of algae, 4,166 fungi, 2,600 lichens and 430 mosses in addition to the very large total of 3,200 species of vascular plants, including some endemics – plants found only in Armenia. Since Armenia's flora is very large it is perhaps surprising that gymnosperms (basically conifers) should be poorly represented by a mere nine species: five junipers, one pine, one yew and two shrubby members of the family Ephedraceae whose American relatives include Nevada joint fir and desert tea.

One third of the forests are oak and they are widely distributed across the country. Of the four species found in Armenia, two are typical of these forests, Caucasian oak (*Quercus macranthera*) and Georgian oak (*Q. iberica*). Caucasian oak is the more frost-tolerant species and is found throughout the country at altitudes as high as 2,600m. By contrast, Georgian oak is typically restricted to altitudes between 500 and 1,400m, and is mostly found in the north and the extreme south. Other species found in oak forests are ash (*Fraxinus excelsior*), hornbeam (*Carpinus betulus*), Georgian maple (*Acer ibericum*), cork elm (*Ulmus suberosus*) and field maple (*Acer campestre*). A third oak species – Arax oak (*Q. araxina*) – is now declining, probably because of agricultural development.

1

Another third of the forest are the beech forests of northern Armenia. They are dominated by Oriental beech (*Fagus orientalis*). They are mostly on north-facing slopes at an altitude of 1,000–2,000m. Other species in beech forests include small-leaved lime (*Tilia cordata*), Litvinov beech (*Betula litwinow*) and spindle-tree (*Euonymus europaeus*). Hornbeam forests occur at altitudes of 800–1,800m. Other trees found in these forests include the various oaks, field maple, ash, Caucasian pear (*Pyrus caucasicum*) and Oriental apple (*Malus orientalis*). Scrub forests are found in both the north and south of the country occurring at altitudes of 900–1,000m in the north, but at much higher altitude in the south (1,800–2,000m). These forests support around 80 species of xeric trees and shrubs, all of which are drought tolerant and light-loving. As well as thorn forest dominated by juniper, broad-leaved forests also occur, characterised by species such as Georgian maple, various cherries, pistachio (*Pistacia mutica*), almond (*Prunus dulcis*), buckthorn (*Rhamnus catharticus*) and wild jasmine (*Jasminum fruticans*). There are groves of virgin yew (*Taxus baccata*) in Dilijan National Park and a relict plane (*Platanus orientalis*) grove in Shikahogh Reserve in the south of the country.

A number of Armenia's plants will be familiar to visitors because they have become popular cultivated plants of temperate gardens such as the florist's scabious, the flamboyant oriental poppy, the ubiquitous catmint, burning bush and grape hyacinth. Different types of vegetation can be seen within relatively limited areas, often accessed easily from the principal roads. Many flowers are to be found in the dry mountain habitats typical of central Armenia. It is here, for example, that the almost impossible to cultivate, but striking and often bizarre Oncocyclus iris, can be found. The extensive grasslands surrounding the high passes crossed by the main highways, the river gorges and the broad-leaved deciduous forests are all worth exploring for interesting and attractive plants. One of the great joys of Armenia is that botanical excursions and visits to ancient churches and monasteries so often happily coincide.

CONSERVATION AND ENVIRONMENTAL ISSUES Conservation has not been a priority in Armenia, a country still coping with the aftermath of the severe earthquake in 1988, the war over Nagorno Karabagh and the associated closure of borders by Azerbaijan and Turkey, and the loss of most of its industrial base following the collapse of the Soviet Union. The loss of heavy industry did at least have the beneficial result of a reduction in atmospheric pollution. The economic crisis resulted in overexploitation of natural resources and it is probably fair to say that awareness of environmental issues is not generally high, although it is increasing. Even where awareness exists, the priority for those who are poor is, understandably, simply to survive. There are many active environmental NGOs and international foundations which support conservation activities, large investments are made to support environmental education programmes and action for particular species but there is little positive result to be seen on the ground, in spite of considerable relevant expertise in Armenia. The reasons for this include bureaucracy, corruption and political manoeuvring.

The main environmental issues facing Armenia include pollution and land preservation, with **mining-associated problems** a particular concern. The Armenian government has made mining a key part of its economic development strategy but there is widespread anxiety, both within Armenia and internationally, on environmental and social grounds. There are more than 400 active mines in Armenia and 19 tailings dumps. The Teghut mine in the north of Lori province exemplifies many of the concerns: a licence to extract copper and molybdenum in one of Armenia's preserved forest areas has been granted. Some 82% of the land allocated (1,491ha) for the mine is forested – the project involves felling 364ha of virgin forest which is home to six species of flora and 29 species of fauna listed in Armenia's Red Book as endangered. According to the World Bank, Armenia's forests have already shrunk from 20% to 7% of total land area in the last 20 years; the country is in danger of losing all its forests in the next 20–30 years. Some 1,100 tons of waste material will be produced, some containing lead, arsenic, zinc and sulphurous compounds. Tailings will be disposed of into the gorge of the Dukanadzor River. Riverine Tailings Disposal (RTD) is no longer considered an environmentally sound practice in most situations and has led to significant environmental damage in other parts of the world. The Dukanadzor River is a tributary of the Shnogh which flows into the Debed River so the Teghut mine creates pollution implications not only for the population of northern Lori but also for Georgia. Already there is significant pollution in the Debed Valley caused by the copper smelter in Alaverdi. In January 2012 the Parliamentary Assembly of the Council of Europe (PACE) issued a written declaration, signed by 44 parliamentarians representing 27 countries, which referred to the Teghut mining project as a manmade ecological disaster, asserting that the Armenian government had violated its international obligations and Armenian legislation.

Desertification, often triggered by deforestation, is a significant problem. Loss of tree cover predisposes to landslides and leads to thin soil layers being washed away. The Armenian National Plan to Combat Desertification estimates that 26.8% of the total territory of Armenia faces the threat of extremely severe desertification and only 13.5% is not exposed to any threat of desertification. The loss of forests makes Armenia more susceptible to the consequences of climate change. In 2009 the United Nations Development Programme (UNDP) published a study which looked at the likely effects on Armenia of climate change (*Socio-Economic Impact of Climate Change in Armenia* by Stanton, Ackerman and Resende, Stockholm Environment Institute). The study predicted a rise in temperature; reductions in precipitation, river and lake levels; and an increased risk of heat waves, droughts, landslides and floods. They suggested that Armenia's future economic development depends on investment to adapt to climate change.

There is a **Ministry of Nature Protection** responsible for protecting the environment but it also sells mining and logging concessions. Powerful businesses seem to be able to operate even in protected areas and the status of a protected area may be downgraded to allow such activity. There are four main **protected areas** in Armenia: Shikahogh State Reserve (see page 316), Khosrov Forest State Reserve (pages 181–4), Dilijan National Park (page 275), which was reduced from reserve to park status in 2002, and Sevan National Park (pages 199–202), as well as a number of smaller sites. Until now Shikahogh has been the best protected, mainly because of its isolation. The fear is that the new road to the south of the country, built through the reserve, will alter this. The problems of Lake Sevan are being addressed (see pages 199–202).

Voluntary organisations exist; for example, the **Armenia Tree Project** (*www. armeniatree.org*) aims to repair the damage done to forests during the years of power shortages in the early 1990s (see page 226). The **American University of Armenia** has a research centre, the Acopian Center for the Environment (ACE) (*www.acopiancenter. am*). There is evidence of a small but growing awareness of environmental issues, particularly among younger people. In 2011 Trchkan Waterfall (see page 238) was the focus of a successful campaign, probably the first of its kind in Armenia, by **civic activists** to save it after work had started to dam the river above the waterfall for a

1

hydro-electric scheme. Permission for the scheme had been granted even though the waterfall was deemed a preserved natural area. Plans and licences were never made publicly available as was required by Armenian law. The activists made use of the internet to draw attention to their cause, to organise a 10,000 signature petition and to publicise demonstrations in Yerevan and at the waterfall.

Waste management is a significant issue which has only recently begun to be tackled. Most rubbish goes to landfills, but in rural areas there is no governmental waste-disposal management and people have to dispose of waste as best they can. The first waste processing scheme was established only in 2011 with sorting plants in Gyumri, Vanadzor and Yerevan. Waste management problems are particularly acute in Yerevan and the Lake Sevan area, where the problem is being addressed with the help of the European Union and the European Bank for Reconstruction and Development. There is no recycling industry in Armenia. Visitors will unfortunately see examples of a lack of concern for the environment such as litter, vehicles with high exhaust emissions (although Armenia also leads the world in the use of clean natural/bottled gas to run cars) and the loss of much of Yerevan's green space.

Some issues transcend national boundaries, and these mainly relate to rivers and water catchment areas – the Kura River, for example, flows through Turkey, Georgia and Azerbaijan and is partly fed by rivers which originate in Armenia. Likewise Turkey, Iran, Azerbaijan and Armenia have a common interest in the Arax River. Although not much has been achieved, the countries of the region do try to find points of contact on environmental protection, focusing on border water resources, biodiversity and the impact of conflicts on the ecological situation.

HISTORY

Visitors to Armenia are confronted by the country's history everywhere they look, and not just in the prehistoric sites or splendid medieval monasteries that are a major attraction of Armenia for most visitors. Other aspects of Armenia's history are reflected in the legacy of Soviet-era apartment blocks identical to those in Kaliningrad or Omsk, and in the huge investment in modern Armenia funded by the country's large, important and successful diaspora. Further observations soon strike the visitor: that the oldest surviving building in the country, at Garni, looks Greek rather than Armenian and quite different from any other; that there are no Roman remains; that the old churches and monasteries were built within certain very restricted time periods interspersed with long periods from which nothing seems to have survived; that different foreign influences seem to have been significant at different epochs. Visitors will also see everywhere signs written in a distinctive and unique alphabet, the use of which is a large factor in determining what it means to be Armenian. Beginning to make sense of all this jumble of impressions necessitates gaining some understanding of Armenia's long and varied history.

During this history there were periods of independence as an Armenian nation, though often with the nation divided into separate kingdoms because of internal struggles for supremacy by individual families. These periods were separated by much longer spells of foreign rule, by a whole host of different peoples at different times. The 20th-century regaining of independence after centuries of foreign rule, briefly at first from 1918 to 1920 but then lastingly since 1991, owes little to the nations, notably Britain, which repeatedly let down the Armenian people between 1878 and 1923. However, perhaps the West can take some of the responsibility for the Soviet Union's bankruptcy and collapse.

THE LEGENDARY ORIGINS OF THE ARMENIAN PEOPLE Although all foreigners call the country Armenia, Armenians themselves call it Hayastan: literally the 'Land of Haik'. Chapter 8 of Genesis states that Noah's ark grounded on Mount Ararat. Chapter 10 records that Togarmah was a son of Gomer who was a son of Japheth who had accompanied his father Noah on the Ark. According to Armenian legend the Armenian people are the descendants of Haik who was the son of Togarmah and therefore the great-great-grandson of Noah. Their name for their country records this.

According to the legend, of the three sons of Noah, Japheth and Ham settled with their families in the Ararat region while Shem subsequently moved away to the northwest. Ham's and Japheth's sons gradually spread out to the various regions of the Armenian Plateau. When Japheth's great-grandson Haik was 130 years old, he travelled south to the city of Shinar (probably what we know as present-day Babylon in Iraq) and worked on the building of the Tower of Babel (Genesis 11). After the Tower eventually collapsed, Haik, a handsome man and a strong warrior (despite his age) with curly hair and good eyesight, was able to defy even Nimrod (or Bel as he is known in the legend), the tyrannical ruler of Assyria. Nimrod had ordered that he should be worshipped by his people but Haik refused and moved back north with his family (including his 300 sons) to the lands around Ararat. Nimrod resented Haik's departure, and ordered him back, even seeking to lure him by reminding him that Armenia had a less favourable climate than Assyria. When

ARCHAEOLOGY IN ARMENIA

Armenia has an amazing wealth of archaeological sites. Some of the most important include the Early Bronze Age trans-Caucasian Kura-Araxes-culture site of **Shengavit** (3500–2000BC); the Middle Bronze Age (2500–1000BC) site of **Metsamor** (a copper-mining and major bronze-production site; also a site with ritual rock-carvings and where the cemetery revealed rich burials containing looted Babylonian jewellery); the Late Bronze Age (1500–900BC) site of **Lchashen** (where the wheeled wagons in the State History Museum were discovered) and the 9th–7th century BC Iron Age Urartian cities of **Erebuni** and **Teishebaini** (Karmir Blur). These are simply a few, albeit an important few, of the many sites throughout the country. Other places are detailed in this guidebook.

Much excavation was carried out in the Soviet period with results published in Russian-language scientific journals. The amount of information available to non-professional but interested visitors was until recently very limited. This is changing with excellent displays in Yerevan's State History Museum (pages 150–2) and Erebuni Museum (page 147), the promise of upgrading the museums at Metsamor and, maybe, at Shengavit, and with a small number of attractive publications.

Visiting these ancient sites can leave the visitor feeling less than impressed because after excavation the area often has to be reburied to preserve it. Some imagination is required to clothe the low walls or mounds with their original splendour. Good places to start are the State History Museum in Yerevan, where many of the rich finds from excavations are on display, and Erebuni, where walls were reconstructed in Soviet days to a height of about one metre. While this has drawbacks it does allow an impression of what the citadel looked like.

1

Haik refused, Nimrod marched north with his army (which outnumbered Haik's) and battle was joined on the shores of Lake Van. Nimrod, according to the legend, wore iron armour but Haik drew his bow, and shot him with a three-feathered arrow which pierced the armour killing the king. Seeing this happen, the Assyrian army turned and fled. Haik returned to Ararat and died at the age of 400. The discovery of boundary stones and of Babylonian writings dating from Nimrod's reign confirm the battle and the manner of Nimrod's death as described in the legend.

The name Armenia by which everybody else knows the country was first used by Greek historians about 3,000 years ago, although in legend the name commemorates the great leader of the country, Aram, who was sixth in line of descent from Haik.

ANCIENT HISTORY Crudely worked stone tools found in caves and river gorges and on mountain slopes, including Mount Aragats, have been dated to around 600,000 to 800,000 years ago and more sophisticated ones such as knives to the period between 40,000 and 100,000 years ago. The transition from hunting and gathering to a more settled way of life sustained by agriculture and pastoralism had begun in Armenia in the Arax Valley by about 6000BC. However, the first people to leave significant traces on the Armenian landscape did so in the form of **petroglyphs**, or images carved on rock, which can be found in various regions of Armenia. Those in the Geghama Mountains west of Lake Sevan have been studied in some detail but the carvings in other regions are similar. They are believed to date mainly from the 5th to 2nd millennium BC. They depict both wild animals such as mountain goats, deer, wild boar, wolves, foxes, snakes, storks and water birds as well as domestic animals such as yoked oxen and dogs. Images of hunters using bows are fairly common, some hunters accompanied by their dogs. Humans are depicted, usually in a highly schematic style.

There are also carvings of celestial bodies: the sun, moon and stars. Some of the later carvings show carts and chariots drawn by oxen or bulls with stellar symbols on their fronts and these may be connected with a cult of the sun.

Little is known about those who created the rock art but during the Early Bronze Age, when some of the earlier carvings were created, a series of villages and fortified settlements developed in the Arax Valley based on agriculture and herding but also practising **metalworking**. Local high-quality supplies of ore led to the forging of copper and bronze and later the smelting of iron by around 1000BC. Artefacts found in these settlements include red-black burnished pottery with geometric patterns. Burial goods from the Middle and Late Bronze Ages also suggest a religious belief centred on the sun. Armenia has two monuments from this period which some believe to be astral observatories. At Metsamor (Armavir province) there is a series of stone platforms dated to 2800BC oriented towards Sirius, the brightest star visible, and there are also numerous carvings said to show the position of stars in the night sky together with a compass pointing east. At Karahunj (near Sisian in Syunik province) there is an elaborate arrangement of stones in which holes are bored. Some authorities suggest they had an astronomical purpose, possibly enabling the tracking of solar and lunar phases, while other authorities dispute such astronomical theories for both sites. It has even been suggested that it was in Armenia at this period that the signs of the zodiac were named: certainly the animal signs are all of creatures which would have been familiar in Armenia with no obvious omissions apart possibly from the leopard.

URARTU These early peoples spoke a variety of languages but, probably around 1165BC, another people migrated into Armenia and they spoke the language from which present-day Armenian is descended. Their close affinity to the Phrygians (who lived in the north of present-day Turkey) is attested by classical writers such as Herodotus and Eudoxus and this suggests that they came into Armenia from the west.

During the 9th century BC the empire of Urartu developed eventually to incorporate much of Anatolia and most of present-day Armenia. Co-operation under central leadership may have been the result of increasing Assyrian aggression. By the reign of the Urartian king Sarduri I (reigned c840–c825BC) the capital had been established at Tushpa, present-day Van in Turkey. Expansion was achieved through a series of military campaigns with Argishti I (reigned c785–c763BC) extending Urartian territory as far as present-day Gyumri and his successors taking the land west and south of Lake Sevan. Urartian expansion provoked Assyrian concern and in 735BC the Assyrian king Tiglath Pileser III invaded as far as Van. It was not, however, until 715BC that Urartu began to suffer a series of catastrophic defeats, not just against the Assyrians but also against other neighbours, and in 714BC King Rusa I committed suicide on hearing news of the sack of the temple at Musasir. The 7th century BC was to become a period of irreversible decline with Urartu finally disappearing around 590BC: it did, however, outlive Assyria which had fallen to Babylon in 612BC and its name survives to this day in the form of Mount Ararat.

This first state on Armenian territory, Urartu's regional importance briefly rivalled that of its powerful neighbours. An inscription reveals that it had 79 gods of whom 16 were female. Clearly the most important was Tushpa, god of war: he had over three times the volume of sacrifices offered to his nearest rival. Seventeen bulls and 34 sheep were specified, presumably on some regular basis. The accumulation of animal remains in temples must have been a problem: a room at one site yielded to archaeologists 4,000 headless sheep and calves sacrificed over a 35-year period. Armenia's metalworking skills were important in sustaining Urartu and irrigation works supplied water to vineyards, orchards and crops. The empire was more or less self-sufficient in most goods with the exception of tin (needed to make bronze) which was probably imported from Afghanistan. However, fragments of Chinese silk have been found, providing evidence of foreign trade.

Urartu's cities, linked by a network of good roads, were well developed with high walls, moats, and towers at their entrance gates. One Assyrian opponent claimed that the walls reached to 240 cubits – around 120m – but this looks suspiciously like exaggeration to prove his own valour. Van probably had a population of around 50,000 while Armavir had around 30,000. Numerous forts were built throughout the country for defence and as bases for future attacks. They were built in defensible sites and surrounded by walls whose height may have reached 20m and whose walls were 2–3m thick. They were constructed of massive stone blocks up to a height of 2m. Above this level construction was in mud brick.

FOREIGN RULE AFTER URARTU The Medes dealt the final blow to Urartu in 590BC. What happened to the Armenians subsequently is not clear but during the 6th century BC the Persian Achaemenids under Darius extended their empire to include the country. Political autonomy vanished, a situation that prevailed until the Persians were defeated by Alexander the Great in 331BC. However, the Persians did not seek to impose their culture or religion on their subject peoples though there was in practice probably some influence on Armenian religion – it is thought that the Persians followed an early form of Zoroastrianism which involved belief in a supreme creator God opposed by an uncreated evil spirit. The Armenians did not follow Zoroastrianism absolutely: whereas this disapproved of animal sacrifice the Armenians continued to practise it, notably by sacrificing horses to the sun god. The defeat of the Persians in 331BC did not lead to Greek rule over Armenia, which in fact achieved a greater degree of independence. Alexander's policy in the captured Persian Empire was to continue the existing administrative system under Iranian satraps. For Armenia he appointed Mithrenes who was probably the son of the deposed Persian king Orontes. Mithrenes took the title of King of Armenia. The Greek Empire did not long outlive Alexander's death in 323BC as there was a period of rivalry and war between his erstwhile successors. By 301BC, Seleucus had become satrap of Armenia but his dynasty was to control Armenia only nominally and sporadically with real power in the hands of the Orontid kings, the successors of Mithrenes. The impact of Greek civilisation was, however, increasingly felt and there was a partial revival of urban life which had largely disappeared under the Persians. In around 200BC the satrap Antiochus III was probably involved in the removal of the last Orontid king, Orontes IV, but ten years later he provoked the wrath of Rome through his invasion of Greece. Defeated at the Battle of Magnesia, his own generals then switched sides to Rome and for this they were rewarded by Rome in 189BC with the title of kings of independent Armenia.

EMPIRE The settlement with Rome compromised the territorial integrity of Orontid Armenia but also marked the start of a period of territorial expansion which saw the reacquisition, for the first time since defeat by the Medes in 590BC, of much of present-day Armenia. In particular the area south of Lake Sevan as far as the present-day Iranian border was taken back from the Medes. The acquisition of empire reached its apogee under Tigranes the Great who came to power in c95BC, but Tigranes's success clearly created a hindrance to further Roman expansion in the east. Tigranes's father-in-law was Mithridates VI, King of Pontus, and Tigranes unwillingly got dragged into the (third) war between Rome and Pontus when he refused to surrender his father-in-law to the brusque and offensive Roman envoy. Tigranes's new capital Tigranocerta, which he had modestly named after himself, consequently fell to a Roman siege in 69BC and, although Tigranes subsequently made good some of the losses, his son deserted him for Rome and formed an alliance with Pompey. Tigranes was forced to make peace and Pompey rearranged the political geography. Armenia suffered considerable territorial losses and Antiochus I, a distant descendant of Darius the Great, became king. For the next 80 years Armenia, although independent, had kings appointed by Rome and it became increasingly dependent on Rome for keeping them in power. In due course Roman authority weakened and by the 50s AD Rome was unable to prevent the Parthians imposing their choice of king, Trdat I, on Armenia. After a period of instability reflected in further fighting it was agreed by Parthians and Romans in AD63 that Trdat would be king of Armenia but crowned by the Roman emperor Nero.

There then began a fairly stable period for the Armenian kingdom with the kings holding the throne with Roman approval. This was punctuated by the Roman emperor Trajan's policy of expansion which saw Armenia conquered in AD114 only for the Romans to suffer defeat and withdraw after a rebellion in AD116. In AD253, Armenia was captured by the Persian Sasanians and it remained under Persian rule until a Roman victory over Persia in AD298. There were Christians elsewhere in the region from around AD100 and by AD300 there were Christians in Armenia, albeit in small numbers and with few in the elite. Zoroastrianism remained the main religion and animal sacrifice continued to be practised.

CONVERSION TO CHRISTIANITY The adoption of Christianity as the state religion of Armenia, the first country in which this happened, is perhaps the single most important event in Armenian history. Although traditionally said to have happened in AD301 there is debate over the precise date, but it had certainly happened by 314. King Trdat III held power, like his predecessors, with the support of Rome against the continuing threat from Persia. The precise date of Armenia's conversion is interesting as it reflects differently on Trdat's motives depending on when it was: 301 was before the persecution of the Christians by the Roman emperor Diocletian in 303 and it was also before the Roman edict of toleration of Christianity in 311 and the conversion of the Emperor Constantine in 312. A later date for Armenia's conversion suggests a much closer alignment with imperial thinking, as adopting Christianity in 314 would have been more than likely to please an emperor who had himself just become a Christian. There is an account of Armenia's conversion which claims to have been written by a contemporary but in reality it was written c460, a century-and-a-half after the events. In this account, well known and much quoted in Armenia, Trdat had St Gregory the Illuminator, who was in his service, tortured to persuade him to give up Christianity. Gregory refused and Trdat additionally realised that Gregory's father had murdered his, Trdat's, father. As a consequence Trdat then had Gregory imprisoned in a snake-infested pit for 12 years at a place now occupied by the monastery of Khor Virap, and he also persecuted other Christians including the nuns Hripsime (whom Trdat tried to rape) and Gayane who were refugees fleeing from Rome. Divine punishment was sent: Trdat is said to have behaved like a wild boar (though in what respect he imitated these rather engaging animals is not clear), while torments fell on his household and demons possessed the people of the city. Eventually Trdat's sister had a vision after which Gregory was released, the martyrs were buried and the afflicted were cured. Trdat himself proclaimed Christianity the state religion, and Gregory became Bishop of Caesarea.

Conversion required much change in social customs and this change did not happen quickly. In particular Zoroastrianism permitted polygamy and it promoted consanguineous marriages between the closest of relatives as being particularly virtuous. A Church council in 444 needed to condemn the apparently continuing practice of consanguineous marriage, while as late as 768 another needed to emphasise that a *third* marriage is detestable adultery and an inexpiable sin.

PARTITIONED ARMENIA By c387 Rome and Persia had decided to abolish Armenia as an independent state and to divide the country between them, a move which was finally accomplished with the removal of the last Armenian king in 428. The intervening 40 years were ones of weakness, decline and foreign domination though with a strengthening Christian presence. Present-day Armenia lies in the part which came under Persian rule after 428. A major hindrance to the acceptance of Christianity was removed through the creation in c400 of the Armenian alphabet by Mesrop Mashtots. This permitted the Scriptures to be made available in Armenian for the first time and for other religious works to be published. Although this important education programme was centred in Persian-controlled Armenia, permission was obtained from the Roman Empire (whose capital had by this time been moved to Constantinople) to set up schools there as well. However, the Persian monarchy's increasing dependence on the Zoroastrian religious establishment led to pressure on Armenian Christians under Persian rule to convert to Zoroastrianism. The first crisis occurred in 450 when taxes were imposed on the Church and the nobility was ordered to convert. The Armenians, in alliance with some Huns, inflicted heavy casualties on a much larger Persian force at the Battle of Avarayr in 451. Although the Armenians were ultimately defeated and their leader Vardan Mamikonian killed, Armenians see it as a moral victory because continuing resistance subsequently resulted in the taxes being removed and freedom of religion granted, although the patriarch and some clergy were executed and many nobles were imprisoned. Persia continued to discriminate in favour of Zoroastrians in making important appointments, a situation which prevailed until the death of the Persian king in 484.

Roman expansion finally restarted in the 6th century but it was to make little headway despite several campaigns against Persia until 591, after which the frontier was redrawn to place some of the western parts of present-day Armenia under Roman rule: the new border ran just west of Garni. However, neither Rome nor Persia was prepared for a new wave of invaders – Arabs who, from the 630s, invaded, fighting in the name of Islam. The Persians were soon defeated and the Romans lost major provinces. By 661, Armenia was under Arab rule though there were promises of religious freedom. Armenian revolts in the early 8th century gave rise to some temporary Arab repression but it was only from the rule of Caliph Umar I (717–20) onwards that Armenian Christianity was seriously threatened. Orders were given that Christian images should be torn down, financial levies were increased and pressure was applied to convert to Islam. This stimulated the creation of a cycle of rebellion, harsher treatment, another rebellion, even harsher treatment, until by c800 annual taxation on Armenia amounted to 13 million dirhams, 20,000 pounds of fish, 20 carpets, 200 mules, 30 falcons and 580 pieces of cloth. Under these conditions many Armenians chose to leave the country for Roman areas.

RESTORATION OF MONARCHY Conditions eased in the 9th century to the extent that the caliph agreed in 884 to the restoration of the Armenian monarchy for the first time in 456 years and Ashot I was crowned King of Armenia, the first ruler of the Bagratid dynasty. For the next 40 years, however, Armenia went through a period of continued unrest as different leaders struggled with each other for power and territory. In addition, a prolonged rebellion against the caliph led by his governor in Azerbaijan, who was responsible for collecting Armenian taxes, led to both caliph and governor presenting their own separate tax bills. Armenia was not a united nation but this time was one of a great flourishing of Armenian scholarship, literature and church building. This was particularly the case during the reign of King Abas (928–52) who succeeded in establishing a degree of security, but during the 960s and 970s after his death, the renewed struggle for succession led to increasing fragmentation of the country and by the end of the 10th century there were five separate Armenian kingdoms – three Bagratid (based at Kars, Ani and Lori); one Artsruni based in Vaspurakan east of Lake Van, and one Syunian in the south of present-day Armenia. Armenia's political fragmentation, however, inevitably left it unable to cope with renewed expansion by the Roman Empire's successors in Byzantium during the 11th century, though Byzantine rule was to be benign in comparison with the new invaders from the south, the Seljuk Turks, who ravaged cities and brought political and economic disruption even to the Byzantium-controlled areas after 1045. The victory of the Seljuk Turks over the Romans in 1071 led to the latter's demise as a significant power and to the establishment of Seljuk rule over Armenia. The immediate consequence of the Seljuk conquest was another period of migration: this time to areas such as Georgia, Ukraine and Syria. A new separate Armenian kingdom arose in Cilicia (on the Aegean coast of Turkey) which was to last until it was overrun in 1375 by the Mamluks, the Turkish military dynasty which then ruled Egypt. Although important in Armenian history, Cilicia lies wholly outside present-day Armenia and is therefore not relevant to this guidebook.

Seljuk power in turn waned and in a series of campaigns culminating in 1204, a Georgian army which included many Armenians defeated the sultan's forces. Georgian influence increased, reflected in the style of a number of Armenia's finest churches in present-day Lori province, only for Armenia to be conquered yet again, this time by the Mongols in a series of campaigns culminating in 1244. High taxation created the usual resentment and rebellion. In 1304 matters worsened for Armenians when Islam became the official religion of the Mongol Empire and religious persecution became a matter of policy. In turn Mongol power declined and between 1357 and 1403, following a series of invasions by the Mamluks, tens of thousands of Armenians were transported as slaves. By 1400, most of Armenia had passed to a Turkmen dynasty called the Black Sheep which ruled for about 50 years before a second Turkmen dynasty, called the White Sheep, became dominant.

RUSSIA VERSUS TURKEY The end of the Byzantine Empire came in 1453 when the Ottomans took Constantinople (Istanbul). Further Ottoman aggression saw Armenia itself conquered and taken from the White Sheep, who were now ruling it, by the 1530s. Yet again Armenia became a battleground as hostility grew between the Ottomans and Persia, until in 1639 the two powers agreed that western Armenia would be controlled by Turkey and eastern Armenia by Persia. A further wave of emigration from the Persian territories began around 1700 because of taxation and persecution; this time many went to India. A local rebellion in southern Armenia led by David Bek, together with invasion in 1722 by Russian forces under Peter the Great, saw Persian rule largely end and in 1724 most Persian territory was divided between the Ottomans and Russia although Persia retained Nagorno Karabagh. David Bek died in 1728 and in 1730 his successor Mkhitar Sparapet was betrayed by Armenian villagers as a result of Turkish threats. That same year David Bek's territory, centred at Tatev, fell to Turkey. Russian expansionism in the area restarted under Catherine the Great. In the conquered lands, largely Muslim, Russian policy was to encourage Christians to settle and Muslims to leave. Starting in 1796 the Russians began a further series of campaigns conquering the west Caucasian khanates. These khanates were effectively autonomous Turkish principalities (although nominally vassals of the Persians under the 1724 treaty) and they occupied an area roughly equivalent to present-day Armenia and Azerbaijan.

At that time Armenians, having been subject to so many varieties of foreign rule, and often persecution, for so long, were scattered throughout the Caucasus and eastern Anatolia rather than concentrated in the Armenian heartland. However, in 1826 Russia began a forced exchange of population which resulted ultimately in the creation of an Armenian-dominated state in the khanate of Yerevan. Russia gained dominance in the south Caucasus by defeating Persia in the war of 1826–28 and the Ottomans in the war of 1828–29, and these victories further encouraged Armenians to migrate into Russian-controlled areas of Armenia while they simultaneously continued to encourage Turks to leave. Conditions in Ottoman-controlled regions were certainly difficult for Christians. Muslim courts did not even allow testimony from them until 1854 and even after that it was usually discounted. Christians paid higher taxes than Muslims, and they were not allowed to bear arms to defend themselves whereas Muslims were. The conditions within Ottoman-controlled Armenia became known in the West through exiles, travellers' publications and official reports, and started to cause wide concern.

BRITAIN AND ARMENIA Britain and Turkey were on the opposite side to Russia in the Crimean War. The treaty which ended the war in 1856 required Russia to evacuate some Armenian areas which it had occupied during the war. Although this was put into effect, British officers on the spot, especially in the 1870s, were still stressing the risk to the trade routes across the Ottoman Empire which they believed were threatened by Russia's renewed interest in southerly expansion. In 1877, the British ambassador in Constantinople went so far as to write (considerably exaggerating) that in the event of a Russian conquest of Armenia: 'The consequence would be the greatest blow ever struck at the British Empire.' Britain therefore supported Turkey against Russia though there was a simultaneous British realisation that Turkey's chance of retaining Armenia would be greater if it treated the native Armenian population better. The British government's concern, however, was with who controlled Armenia and hence the trade routes. It was not with the Armenian people except insofar as their support for Russia would weaken Turkey's hold on the region.

Russia again defeated the Ottomans in 1877–78, thereby gaining control of eastern Anatolia. The three treaties of 1878 are crucial to understanding subsequent British concern over Armenia. The first was signed between Russia and Turkey in March. In it Turkey ceded large areas to Russia and this, of course, increased British concern about the threat to trade routes. In the second, signed in June, Britain promised to defend Turkey against further Russian aggression in exchange for two commitments by Turkey: one was to hand Cyprus over to Britain; and the other was to agree with Britain reforms which would improve the lot of Christians in the Ottoman territories – principally Armenia. The third treaty, signed in July, restored to Turkey large areas which had been ceded in March. In it Turkey also promised to introduce reforms to improve the lot of the Armenians. Crucially those reforms no longer had to be agreed with Britain, and Russia was to evacuate the specified areas even before the reforms had been introduced. What had been in June 1878 Britain's responsibility to enforce became in July nobody's. Moreover in July the sultan lost any real threat of action being taken if he did not comply, as the power best able to make him do so, Russia, was the last which Britain wished to see involved. It was this crucial abandonment of British influence on the plight of the Armenians, together with the increasingly harsh and cruel treatment of the Christian Armenians by the Muslim Turks and Kurds, which led the devoutly Christian and humane Gladstone to make the Armenians' plight the subject of the last major speech of his career in 1896. His speech to an audience of 6,000 in his home city of Liverpool led to the resignation of the leader of his party, Lord Rosebery, a fortnight later. There is no doubt that the removal of pressure on the sultan by Britain between June and July 1878 led to the disastrous consequences culminating in the genocide of 1915.

The Muslim Ottoman government saw Christian Armenians as likely supporters of the Christian Russian conquerors: other Christian parts of the Ottoman Empire such as Greece and Bulgaria had already experienced revolution with foreign support. The Armenians meanwhile saw the Ottomans as oppressors of their increasingly nationalistic feelings just as the Greeks and Bulgarians already had. Consequently the migration of both Christian Armenians and Muslim Turks increased after the Russian victory in 1878. Demonstrations by Armenians for greater autonomy and against the imposition of tribute demanded by local Kurds were violently suppressed (over 1,000 demonstrators were massacred on one occasion) and a refusal to pay the tribute demanded by the Kurds in addition to government taxes led to weeks of slaughter. Western ambassadors protested about the excessive violence used against the demonstrators but took no other action, not even when 300,000 Armenians died in the pogroms of 1894–96. Conditions grew even worse when the Young Turk movement, which had previously promulgated a programme of reform and courted the Armenian population, changed tack and adopted in 1909 a policy of Turkisation of all Ottoman subjects. This was strengthened by a growing pro-Islam movement. Twenty thousand were massacred among the Armenian community in Cilicia that year, ostensibly to prevent an Armenian uprising.

Meanwhile in the Russian-controlled areas, the climate of liberalism was in recession. The Russian government was no more enthusiastic about Armenian nationalism than the Ottoman, and a policy of Russification, similar to that adopted at the time in other parts of the Russian Empire such as Finland, came into being. Armenian schools, societies and libraries were closed. References in print to the Armenian nation or people were banned and Armenian Church property was taken over by the Tsar. Not surprisingly many Armenians emigrated, principally to the USA.

WORLD WAR I AND GENOCIDE The Ottoman Empire entered World War I on the German side but it was already in a state of rapid decline: between 1908 and 1912 it had lost 33% of its territory and the Armenians were the only significant Christian people to remain under Ottoman rule. In 1915, Russia, which had joined the Allied side, inflicted a disastrous defeat on the Ottomans. The Ottomans saw Russians and diaspora Armenians fighting against them and this inflamed their existing suspicions concerning the loyalty of their Armenian subjects: their knowledge of how they had treated the Armenians would in any case hardly have reassured them concerning their likely loyalty. The 60,000 Armenians serving in the Ottoman forces were quickly demobilised and organised into labour groups in February 1915, only to be massacred by April. It was also ordered that Armenians living in regions near the war front should be moved to the Syrian Desert and the Mesopotamian Valley with the clear expectation that, even if they survived the forced marches under difficult conditions, they would not survive the inhospitable terrain and hostile tribesmen of these regions for long. In reality, not only those Armenians in the frontier regions but also those living nowhere near the frontier regions were deported and then either massacred or left to starve in the desert. Large-scale massacres of Armenians developed, including the Armenian intelligentsia in Constantinople and other cities who were arrested on 24 April and then murdered. There is some dispute as to the authenticity of evidence, which suggests that it was the central Ottoman government which ordered the massacres, though they were evidently carefully planned as they were carried out simultaneously in all regions of the Ottoman Empire, but there is no doubt at all that around 1½ million Armenians died in the first genocide of the 20th century. It was recognised as such by the European Parliament in 1987. It is recognised by 21 countries, including Germany, Switzerland, Italy, France, the Vatican, Sweden, Belgium, Argentina, Chile and Canada (but not the UK, although Scotland, Wales and Northern Ireland do) and by 42 US states. However, no Turkish government has ever accepted that these very well-attested events happened. The message of the genocide was not lost on Adolf Hitler, a keen student of history, who, on the eve of his invasion of Poland in 1939 rallied his generals with the words: 'Who still talks nowadays of the extermination of the Armenians?'

THE FIRST ARMENIAN REPUBLIC Following the Russian Revolution in November 1917, Russian forces began withdrawing from the areas of Ottoman Armenia which they had occupied: Lenin was well aware that disillusion with the war was rampant in the Russian army and that withdrawal was necessary to ensure the soldiers' loyalty.

Consequently in Anatolia, Armenians were fighting the Ottomans virtually alone. There was a short respite from fighting following the formation in Moscow of a Caucasian federation on 24 April 1918 uniting Armenia, Georgia and Azerbaijan, but ethnic and religious differences quickly led to its demise. Turkey then started a new offensive attacking Armenia from the west while Russian Menshevik and Turkish forces based in Azerbaijan attacked from the north and east. The Turks advancing from the west were initially successful, retaking the territory west of the Arax River and capturing Alexandropol (Gyumri) on 15 May. They invaded the Arax Valley, occupying the village and railway station of Sardarapat on 21 May from which they launched an offensive towards Yerevan the following day. It was to be a decisive defeat for Turkey. For three days the Turks attacked the Armenian forces under Daniel-Bek Pirumian but were repelled and on 24 May the Armenians went over to the offensive and routed the Turks. The victory at Sardarapat followed by others at Bash-Aparan and Gharakilisa between 24 and 28 May led to a declaration of independence on 28 May 1918 when the first Republic of Armenia was established under the Dashnak Party. The territories of Nakhichevan and Nagorno Karabagh were incorporated into the Armenian republic but were excluded from Armenia only a week later when Armenia and Turkey signed a peace treaty at Batum on 4 June. However, Turkey's involvement in World War I ended with its capitulation on 30 October and the question of Nakhichevan and Nagorno Karabagh was automatically reopened.

The Armenians hoped that the victorious Allies would keep their promises and enlarge the borders of the new Armenian state after the armistice in November. Eventually the Treaty of Sèvres in August 1920 granted Armenia borders which were adjudicated by President Woodrow Wilson of the USA in November of that year. Meanwhile, Turkey had invaded Armenia in September and seized part of the country. In parallel to these events the Bolsheviks had invaded Armenia in April 1920 and the combined pressure of Turks and Bolsheviks caused the collapse of the Armenian government, notwithstanding the deliberations about its borders taking place far away in France. In reality, acceptance of Bolshevik rule was for the Armenians the only real defence against the Turks. Armenia was formally incorporated into the Transcaucasian Soviet Federated Socialist Republic on 29 November 1920.

The Bolsheviks made large territorial concessions to Turkey, notably by handing over areas which had been under Russian rule even prior to 1914, including the historic Bagratid capital of Ani and the city of Kars. Soviet historians have claimed that the Bolsheviks wanted a quick agreement with Turkey because they believed that a Turkish delegation was in London where David Lloyd George, much more in favour of newly secularised Turkey under Ataturk than Bolshevik Russia under Lenin, was offering Turkey rule over the Caucasus as a protectorate. This protectorate, the Bolsheviks believed, would include Armenia but, much more important from both Russian and Western perspectives, the Baku oilfields in Azerbaijan. It is, however, more likely that Lenin's real motive was to encourage Ataturk whom he (mistakenly) believed would be an ardent supporter of the communist cause. He probably also believed that Turkey was militarily too strong for Russia to be able to win a campaign in Armenia and these two factors led to Russia's concurrence with Turkey's proposals for the border. Had any Armenians been involved in the Moscow discussions between Russia and Turkey it is inconceivable that Ani would have been relinquished. The Treaty of Sèvres was formally replaced in 1923 by the Treaty of Lausanne, effectively abandoning any pretence of Western support for an independent Armenia and reconfirming the message of 1878 that the Western powers, whatever their feelings about the sufferings of the Armenian people, would relegate action to the 'too difficult' pile.

SOVIET ARMENIA From 1921 Lenin made overtures to the new Turkish government, led by Ataturk, which was under attack by Greek forces, Turkey having reneged on its promise to return historic Greek lands in Asia Minor in return for Greek support during the war. By 1921, Greek troops were approaching Ankara. Soviet Russia initially helped Turkey, Lenin still believing that Ataturk was intent on building a socialist state on the Soviet model. Lenin also agreed with Turkey that Nagorno Karabagh, Nakhichevan, Syunik and Zangezur would be incorporated into Azerbaijan. However, Lenin eventually came to realise that Ataturk had no intention of building a socialist state and withdrew support. Meanwhile, led by Garegin Nzhdeh, an Armenian who had fought successful guerrilla campaigns against the Turks during Bulgaria's struggle for independence, Armenian forces fought a successful campaign in Syunik and Zangezur (southern Armenia) against the Red Army and the Turks simultaneously. Stalemate developed and Nzhdeh forced Lenin to compromise and accept his terms that Syunik and Zangezur would be incorporated into the Republic of Armenia rather than into Azerbaijan. He can thus be seen as the person who saved the south of Armenia for the country. Subsequently he went into exile and, after Hitler's coming to power, pursued fruitless negotiations with Nazi Germany in an attempt to regain for Armenia the lands occupied by Turkey. He died in a Soviet prison in 1955 but his remains were secretly returned to Armenia in 1983. In 1987 he was buried at beautiful (but little-visited) Spitakavor Monastery in Vayots Dzor province. In 2005 he was buried for a third time on the slopes of Mount Khustup in Syunik province.

Between 1921 and 1924 Armenia witnessed a resurgence of intellectual and cultural life and Armenian intellectuals, believing that they at last had a homeland, came from abroad, notably the architect Alexander Tamanian who had drawn up ambitious plans for the creation of a fine capital for the First Republic and who returned to complete his plans. These resulted in the creation of the buildings around Republic Square, possibly the finest of all Soviet architectural ensembles, admittedly not a field in which the competition is stiff. He also planned green belts, gardens and residential areas for a city capable of housing a then unimaginable population of 150,000. Yerevan State University was also constructed and professors were recruited from the West. This was also the era of Lenin's New Economic Policy, forced on him by the failure of communist orthodoxy to deliver material benefit, and limited private enterprise was consequently tolerated.

In 1923, Stalin, who was then Commissar for Nationalities, adopted a divide and rule policy which led to Nagorno Karabagh (whose population was largely Armenian, according to most sources, although this is disputed by Azerbaijan) and Nakhichevan (which had a substantial Armenian minority) being placed in Azerbaijan. Additionally the new Soviet republics were created in such a way that they did not have continuous boundaries: for example, isolated villages deep inside Armenia were designated part of Azerbaijan. This was a deliberate, conscious attempt by Stalin to encourage ethnic tensions between Armenians and Azeris so as to discourage them from uniting together against Soviet rule. The Transcaucasian Federation was abolished in 1936 and Armenia became a Soviet republic in its own right though still with the artificial 1923 boundaries.

Economic growth was impressive but the abolition of the New Economic Policy caused considerable resentment, especially among farmers. Although Armenia did not suffer deliberate mass starvation during the forced collectivisation of agriculture in the same way as Ukraine did in 1932–33, it did suffer along with other parts of the Soviet Union during Stalin's purges between 1934 and 1939. At least 100,000 Armenians were victims. Persecution of Christians also reached a height in the mid to late 1930s and all churches except Ejmiatsin were closed by 1935. The head of the Church was murdered in 1938 and the entire Armenian political leadership along with most intellectuals was condemned to death for the crime of bourgeois nationalism (ie: being perceived by Stalin as a threat to himself).

Stalin's pact with Hitler in August 1939 did not save the Soviet Union from attack for long and Germany invaded on 22 June 1941. German troops never reached Armenia: they approached no closer than the north Caucasus where the oilfields around Grozny were a principal objective as Hitler simultaneously wanted to secure their output for Germany and to deprive the Soviet Union. About 630,000 Armenians out of a then population of two million fought during World War II (or the Great Patriotic War as it is called throughout the former Soviet Union) of whom about half died.

Armenia experienced rapid growth after 1945 with Yerevan's population increasing from 50,000 to 1.3 million. Huge chemical plants were established in Yerevan, Leninakan (Gyumri) and Kirovakan (Vanadzor) and Armenia became one of the most highly educated and most industrialised of the Soviet republics. By contrast, a new wave of repression began in 1947 with the deportees being exiled to the infamous gulag camps of Siberia. After Stalin's death, probably by poisoning at the instigation of the secret police chief Lavrentii Beria, conditions relaxed and during the Brezhnev era (1964–82) dissenters were merely certified insane and kept among the genuinely mentally ill in mental hospitals.

The coming to power of Gorbachev in 1985 saw an upsurge in Armenian nationalism, especially over the question of the enclave of Nagorno Karabagh. Gorbachev refused to allow its transfer from Azerbaijan to Armenia. There were demonstrations in both republics and, especially following Soviet government inaction after the killing in February 1988 of 30 (some estimates claim up to 120) Armenians by their Azeri neighbours at Sumgait, an industrial city north of Baku, many Armenians fled from Azerbaijan to Armenia while at the same time many Azeris fled in the opposite direction. This unprecedented killing shocked the Soviet Union; the perpetrators were tried and sentenced in Moscow. Thereafter ethnic tensions continued to rise and during the fighting over Nagorno Karabagh there were civilian deaths on both sides. Perhaps the incident which gained most international notice and condemnation was the deaths of 161–613 (numbers are disputed) Azeri civilians, fired on by Armenian forces in February 1992, as they tried to leave Khojaly, near Aghdam, as it was about to be occupied by Armenian forces. (Khojaly was used as a military base by the Azeris to shell Stepanakert.) In July 1988, Nagorno Karabagh declared its secession from Azerbaijan and in December the pressure group known as the Karabagh Committee, which had meanwhile broadened its objectives to include democratic change within Armenia itself, was arrested and held in Moscow without trial for six months. In early 1989, Moscow imposed direct rule on Nagorno Karabagh and rebellion broke out. In November that year Armenia declared that Nagorno Karabagh was a part of Armenia (a claim it no longer makes) as a result of which Turkey and Azerbaijan closed their borders with Armenia and imposed an economic blockade: the problems this caused were greatly exacerbated because of the closure, as a precautionary measure, of Metsamor nuclear power station following the major earthquake in December 1988.

THE THIRD REPUBLIC In July 1990, elections were won by the Armenian National Movement which had developed from the Karabagh Committee. Its leader, Levon Ter-Petrosian, became president of the Armenian Supreme Soviet which declared independence from the Soviet Union in August. (This was quite legal as, under

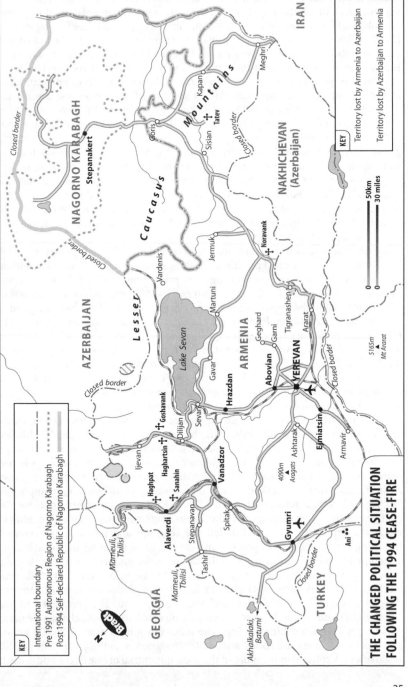

the Soviet constitution, all republics were nominally free to secede.) The new government took a moderate line over the Nagorno Karabagh dispute and tried to distance itself from the fighting. The collapse of the Soviet Union in August 1991, following the failed putsch against Gorbachev, was followed by a referendum on 21 September in which the population of Armenia overwhelmingly voted in favour of independence. Meanwhile Azerbaijan likewise declared itself independent. However, after Armenia signed a mutual assistance treaty with Russia and certain other members of the Confederation of Independent States (CIS) in May 1992, Russia started supplying arms to Armenia which was able to drive Azerbaijan out of most of Nagorno Karabagh, the area between Armenia and Nagorno Karabagh, as well as border areas with Iran. After the death of around 25,000 combatants a ceasefire was declared in 1994 and largely holds firm at the time of writing. During the conflict the closure of the Turkish and Azerbaijan borders together with frequent sabotage of the gas pipelines in southern Georgia (used to supply gas to Armenia) resulted in Armenia becoming heavily dependent on Iran for supplies. It might now be possible to resolve the dispute if Armenia were willing to give up the southernmost part of its territory bordering Iran in exchange for Nagorno Karabagh, but the Armenian government's understandable wish to retain this direct link with Iran makes any short-term settlement of the dispute unlikely. Meanwhile Azerbaijan apparently hopes that Russia will lose interest in the area and cease supporting Armenia.

Armenia adopted a new presidential constitution in 1995 and in September 1996 Ter-Petrosian was re-elected president. Ter-Petrosian appointed Robert Kocharian, a former leader of Nagorno Karabagh, as prime minister and he was elected president in turn when Ter-Petrosian resigned in 1998. Parliamentary elections in May 1999 brought the opposition Unity Alliance to power with Vazgen Sargsian of the nationalist Republican Party (HHK) as prime minister and Karen Demirchian (loser of the presidential election) as speaker, but on 27 October 1999 both of them, along with six others, were assassinated when gunmen stormed into parliament. The trial of the killers in late 2001 has not clarified the motives behind the attack. On 22 March 2000, Arkady Gukasian, the president of the self-declared Republic of Nagorno Karabagh, narrowly escaped an assassination attempt for which the former defence minister Samuel Babayan was jailed for 14 years.

A bitter struggle for power within the Armenian government led to some senior ministers being ousted and by mid-2001 the People's Party of Armenia (HZhK, led by Stepan Demirchian, son of the assassinated speaker) was becoming unhappy with its role as junior partner in the ruling coalition. Some of its members joined communists and the Hanrapetutian (Republic) party of former prime minister Aram Sargsian (the assassinated prime minister's brother) in blocking an important bill on civil service reform. In August 2001, Kocharian proposed controversial changes to the constitution while the opposition predictably called on him to resign. In September 2001, HZhK left the coalition and joined the opposition in calling for Kocharian's impeachment on charges of violating the constitution, condoning terrorism, and causing a political and economic crisis. A further scandal blew up that month when an Armenian resident of Georgia, a member of the pro-Kocharian Dashnak Party, was beaten to death in the gentlemen's toilet of Yerevan's Aragast jazz club by members of Kocharian's bodyguard. The president had just left the club and the bodyguard apparently objected to anti-Kocharian remarks which they had heard him making. The following month around 25,000 joined anti-Kocharian demonstrations and 400,000 signed a petition demanding his resignation. A conspicuous feature of the subsequent trial of one of the bodyguards on the fairly minor charge of involuntary manslaughter was the unwillingness of any of the several dozen people who had witnessed the events to come forward and testify, apparently because of fear of what might happen to them at the hands of the police.

THE PRESENT In the first round of the presidential election held on 19 February 2003, there were nine candidates, all male, including the incumbent Robert Kocharian. The official result was that Kocharian had received 49.48% compared with 28.22% for Stepan Demirchian and 17% for Artashes Geghamian in third place. Since a candidate must achieve 51% of the vote for an outright victory a second round of voting was required. The entire campaign had been conducted with a great deal of mud-slinging, little discussion of important issues such as education, taxation and welfare, and little in the way of specific proposals for constitutional or legislative change. Neither Demirchian nor Geghamian even mentioned Nagorno Karabagh with all its implications for the country. However, both advocated closer ties with Russia and, though Demirchian was non-specific, Geghamian advocated joining the rouble zone, and changing Armenia's legislation in the fields of customs and taxation to match Russia's. One of Demirchian's few concrete proposals was to abandon the 1996 local government reforms and revert to the Soviet-era divisions.

Two invited teams of international observers spent six weeks in the country prior to the election. The reports of those from the Organisation for Security and Co-operation in Europe (OSCE) differ markedly from those of the CIS observers. Among the shortcomings, the OSCE observers noted that there had been pre-election intimidation and incidents of disruption of campaign events, including one instance of violence, pre-election manipulations including schemes to impersonate voters, and the heavy use of public resources in support of the incumbent. The international observers on polling day assessed the voting process positively in 90% of polling stations but noted that there were unauthorised people including government officials in 23% of polling stations who often acted in an intimidatory manner. Irregularities noted at some stations included cases of ballot-box stuffing, individuals voting more than once, a policeman carrying a box of at least 50 passports (used in the election as evidence of identity) out of a polling station and intimidation of candidates' proxies, two of whom were seen being assaulted. (In Armenian elections a proxy is the appointed representative of a candidate in a polling station, who acts as an observer on the candidate's behalf; if he notices any irregularity his report must be attached to the result of the count submitted by the returning officer.) The count itself was negatively assessed by the international observers in 20% of polling stations, some of whose results showed a striking disparity both in voter turnout and outcome from the otherwise consistent pattern of results.

The second round with two candidates was held on 5 March and resulted in a win for Kocharian with 67.44% of the vote as opposed to 32.56% for Demirchian. The OSCE observers were even more condemnatory of the process. Indeed, this time some polling stations recorded more votes than there were registered voters. Between the rounds the police arrested 142 of Demirchian's supporters on charges of hooliganism, of whom 77 were given short prison sentences and the others fined. Publicly funded television and radio made no attempt to fulfil their legal obligation to report even-handedly and the state-funded newspaper *Hayastani Hanrapetutian* also gave overwhelming support to the incumbent. The extent of all this election fraud led the observers to conclude that the election 'fell short of international standards for democratic elections'. All this was in complete contrast to the CIS observers who considered the elections to be 'democratic and legitimate' with 'no mass violations of the Electoral Code'. As one local newspaper commented it was rather a 'dialogue of civilisations' with the (mostly western) European observers having different expectations from those from former Soviet republics.

The parliamentary election held on 25 May 2003 resulted in a similar clash of views although, as on previous occasions, there was less actual malpractice than in the presidential election. The Western observers referred to 'serious incidents and shortcomings' and hoped that 'there will be no return to the sense of impunity evident in the recent presidential election'. The CIS observers thought the election 'transparent and democratic' and praised the Armenian authorities for 'ensuring fair elections'. Turnout in the poll was 52% with six of the 21 parties and blocs breaking the 5% threshold required to gain seats in the new parliament. The largest share of the vote, 24.5% of the votes cast, went to the Republican Party which is supportive of the president. The next largest share of the vote, 14.2%, went to the Justice bloc led by Stepan Demirchian who had been runner-up in the presidential election in March. The Communist Party gained a mere 1.6% of the votes.

As a result of the May 2007 parliamentary elections, in which the Republican Party led by Serzh Sarkisian swept to power, and with the decision in February 2008 of the Rule of Law Party to join the governing coalition, 113 seats in the National Assembly, out of a total of 131, were held by pro-government parties. The only opposition faction in parliament, the Heritage Party, held seven seats while the remaining 11 seats were held by independents who were mostly aligned with pro-government parties.

Presidential elections were held in February 2008. Serzh Sarkisian (previously Defence Minister) was declared the winner with 52.9% of votes in the first round. The election was followed by ten days of street protests by thousands of opposition supporters claiming that voting was rigged. Clashes between demonstrators and security personnel left ten dead and hundreds injured. Dozens of opposition supporters, and some innocent bystanders, were imprisoned. A 20-day state of emergency was declared. International groups criticised the detentions as being politically motivated. OSCE observers reported that the vote had mostly met international standards, although later it was found to be marred by similar problems as previous elections such as ballot stuffing, intimidation and vote buying. Sarkisian eventually took office as president in April 2008.

Western observers, from OSCE, the European Parliament and the Council of Europe's Parliamentary Assembly (PACE), gave Armenia's 2012 parliamentary elections a mixed assessment, saying that while the election campaign was open and respected fundamental freedoms, and the media offered broad and balanced coverage, there were still significant irregularities in polling stations on voting day. These included the inaccuracy of voting lists, widespread interference with the running of polling stations and vote buying. Isolated cases of serious violations such as the falsification of results and ballot box stuffing were also reported. Armenia's largest vote-monitoring organisation, the NGO It's Your Choice, said that the election was largely democratic despite noted irregularities. The overall conclusion was that while there was a significant improvement from previous elections further progress was needed before Armenia met internationally recognised democratic standards. The turnout was 62.35%. Six political parties gained seats plus two independent candidates. Once again the Republican Party (HHK) swept to power with 69 seats (an increase of five seats); second was the Prosperous Armenia Party with 37 seats (an increase of 12 seats). The Armenian National Congress (HAK), an opposition coalition, came third with seven seats. Three other parties accounted for the remaining 16 seats. Out of a total of 131 seats in the National Assembly, 90 are distributed among the parties using a proportional system; the remaining 41 seats are elected from constituencies by majority vote. Before the election there was a proposal to abolish the constituency seats and go to a full proportional representation system. Most political parties, including three of the (then) five parliamentary parties supported the initiative but two months before the election the National Assembly voted against the proposal. After the election there were again claims that the result did not reflect the real picture of popular support. Although thousands attended post-election street demonstrations organised by the Armenian National Congress there were not the same violent clashes which marked previous elections. The Armenian National Congress applied to the Constitutional Court demanding the annulment of the proportional election results but the Court rejected the appeal.

The presidential election was held in 2013. There were six candidates, only two of whom received any substantial proportion of the votes. Serzh Sarkisian, Republican Party, was re-elected with 59% of the vote; Raffi Hovhannisian of the Heritage Party came second with 36.75%. Three of the major non-government parties, the Prosperous Armenia Party, the Armenian National Congress and Armenian Revolutionary Federation, did not field candidates. The opinions of Western observers were much the same as they had been for the parliamentary elections in 2012 with the additional concern of 'implausibly high' voter turnout recorded for some precincts. Hovhannisian refused to recognise the legitimacy of the election, claiming that it was rigged. Once again there were post-election mass protests. No violence was reported during these demonstrations but the pre-election period was marred by the shooting of one of the candidates, Paruyr Hayrikian, leader of one of the smaller political parties. He survived and continued as a candidate, coming fourth with 1.23% of the votes. Armenia's Constitutional Court rejected claims by two of the unsuccessful candidates and upheld Sarkisian's election; he was inaugurated for a second term as president in April 2013.

The next parliamentary elections are due in 2017 and presidential elections in 2018. Armenia is a presidential parliamentary democracy. The constitution adopted in 1995 and amended in 2005 gives sweeping powers to the president, making him the most powerful state official. In September 2013 the president set up a commission to draft constitutional amendments, one option being a change to a parliamentary republic led by a powerful prime minister. The commission is headed by the chairman of the Constitutional Court and will have eight other members, almost all of whom are government officials or others loyal to the president. The 2005 constitution bars Sarkisian from seeking a third term of presidential office in 2018. It is reported that Sarkisian would like to extend his rule beyond 2018. He could possibly become prime minister, so retaining power if there is a change to a parliamentary republic. The commission has to produce a 'concept' of reform by April 2014. It will then have ten months to draft specific constitutional amendments after the concept is approved by the head of state.

Transparency International is a non-governmental organisation, with headquarters in Berlin, which monitors and publicises corporate and political corruption. It publishes an annual Corruption Perceptions Index (CPI), a comparative listing of corruption worldwide, defining corruption as the abuse of entrusted power for private gain which eventually hurts everyone who depends on the integrity of people in a position of authority. Armenia's relative position declined steadily, from 88th place in 2005 to 129th in 2011. For the first time in 2012 it showed an improvement, to 105th place. It is still rated as better than two of

1

its neighbours, Azerbaijan (137th in 2005, 139th in 2012) and Iran (joint 88th with Armenia in 2005, 133rd in 2012). Turkey continues to beat Armenia, its position having improved to 54th place (65th in 2005). Georgia overtook Armenia in 2007 and has shown a fairly consistent improvement since then being ranked in 51st place in 2012.

In October 2009, after what has been termed 'football diplomacy' (their presidents meeting during football matches between the two countries), Armenia and Turkey signed an accord agreeing to establish diplomatic ties and to reopen the border between the two countries, but the agreement was never ratified by either parliament. There were and still are obstacles in both countries to the agreement although it is generally perceived that both would benefit from a reopening of the border. The main Armenian objection is the continuing refusal of Turkey to recognise as genocide the massacres of 1915. The agreement called for a joint commission of independent historians to study the genocide issue but Armenians said that ratifying the accord would hinder international recognition of the Armenian genocide. Difficulties for Turkey included an undertaking to its ally Azerbaijan that it will not open the border with Armenia until the Nagorno Karabagh dispute is resolved and Armenia has withdrawn its forces from what Azerbaijan considers occupied territory, a move unacceptable to Armenians. However, that was not included as a condition in the protocol for establishing diplomatic ties between Turkey and Armenia, Turkey viewing it as a parallel process which is under the auspices of the OSCE. Meanwhile the border remains closed.

ECONOMY

Between 1960 and 1988 Soviet Armenia achieved growth of 30% in GNP (during the same period, growth of GNP in the USA was 135%) but the following years were catastrophic for the economy. First, the devastating earthquake in northwest Armenia in December 1988 resulted in 25,000 deaths, 20,000 injured and 500,000 made homeless and caused huge damage to infrastructure. This was to be followed by the break-up of the Soviet Union and war with Azerbaijan so that between 1989 and 1994 GNP fell from US$4,500m to US$652m. By 1994, however, the Armenian government had launched an ambitious economic programme sponsored by the International Monetary Fund (IMF) which resulted in positive growth rates of about 6% or more, until the global financial crisis led to a decline in 2008 and a severe fall in 2009 (to −19.7%), since when the rate has gradually recovered, reaching 3.8% in 2012. The IMF expects a stable growth rate of 4% during 2013–15.

Armenia is regarded as a lower middle-income country by the World Bank. Economic growth is driven mainly by the mining sector, which the Armenian government has prioritised. Also important are remittances from migrant workers which reached 12.1% of GDP in 2011. The financial crisis affected both rural and urban poverty; the poverty rate increased from 27.6% in 2008 to 35.8% in 2010. Even this figure is better than a 1998 estimate of 60–70% of the population living below the poverty line. The support of the diaspora has been and continues to be of considerable importance to the Armenian economy.

Armenia had made a full switch to a market economy by 2009 and in 2013 was rated the 38th most economically free nation in the world by the Heritage Foundation. Inflation too has been brought under control, falling from a horrific 4,964% in 1994 to as low as 2% in 2002 although there has since been an increase, standing at 7.7% in 2013. The country receives support from international organisations such as the IMF, the World Bank and the European Bank for

Reconstruction and Development. Armenia was one of the first to benefit from a special fast-track facility set up by the World Bank to help the poorest countries cope with the impact of the global financial crisis. As of June 2012 the World Bank was supporting 14 projects in Armenia which include improving rural roads to link villages with highways; reforming the energy sector, especially the use of safe, clean and affordable heating and renewable energy generation; improving access to water; modernising health care; and improving agriculture through irrigation.

Prior to the Soviet collapse in 1991, Armenia had developed a large industrial sector, supplying machine tools, textiles and other manufactured goods to the other Soviet republics in exchange for raw materials and energy. By 1994, most of this had closed. Given the state of the plants, the privatisation of industry has inevitably been slow. There has been a reversion to small-scale **agriculture** away from the large agro-industrial complexes of the Soviet era, but the sector has considerable need for investment and updated technology. Armenia remains a net food importer. This, combined with the lack of energy resources, ensures that Armenia runs a current account deficit. Agriculture employs around 46% of the working population while 15% work in industry and 38% in services – this last figure has increased considerably as the economy has restructured. Unemployment is estimated at 17% by the Armenian statistical service. Another source cites 7% of the working population as unemployed although both of these figures are somewhat misleading as perhaps 70% of the population isn't actually paid wages: the many subsistence farmers, tradesmen and owners of small businesses receive no salary as such.

The main **exports** are cut diamonds (which are imported uncut – Armenia has no sources of diamonds of its own), brandy and, increasingly, minerals: copper, molybdenum, ferro-alloys and gold. By value the main export trading partners are Russia at 15%, Bulgaria 14%, Germany 13%, Netherlands 9%, Belgium 8.5% (to which the diamonds go) and the US at 8%. The principal **imports** are natural gas, petroleum, diamonds, cars, telephones and automatic data processing media. The main import trading partners are Russia at 25%, Georgia 14%, China 11%, Belgium/Luxembourg 8% and UAE 5%.

In September 2013 President Sarkisian announced that Armenia would join the **Russia-led Customs Union** and would participate in the formation of the Eurasian Economic Union. The Customs Union of Belarus, Kazakhstan and Russia came into being in January 2010 as a first step towards forming, in 2015, an integrated economic union of former Soviet states, the Eurasian Union, which Russian leaders see as a counterbalance to the European Union. Although it was known that meetings had also been taking place with Russia, Sarkisian's announcement surprised European diplomats because for four years Armenia had been engaged in negotiations with the EU and the following month was expected to initial (along with Georgia, Moldova and Ukraine, which also failed to sign at the last moment) an Association Agreement with the EU, strengthening trade relations while committing Armenia to democratic changes. A year previously when Armenia ratified the Commonwealth of Independent States (CIS) free trade zone agreement President Sarkisian had stated that EU, CIS and Eurasian integration need not be mutually exclusive and, on announcing Armenia's decision to join the Customs Union, he said that it was not a rejection of dialogue with European institutions. However, EU diplomats have said that membership of the Customs Union is incompatible with a free trade agreement with another jurisdiction. Russia has considerable leverage on Armenia; it supplies natural gas to Armenia and is also Armenia's main safeguard in relation to Azerbaijan. Officials in Brussels have no doubt that this leverage was significant in Armenia's decision.

The long periods of foreign rule, often accompanied by religious persecution, led to the Armenian people becoming widely scattered and not comprising a majority in any territory. What distinguished them as Armenians was their Church and their language. During the 19th century this changed as a result of the Russian conquest of eastern Armenia. There was a deliberate Russian policy of encouraging Christian immigration and Muslim emigration. Although the Tsarist regime was initially tolerant of Christians who were not Orthodox believers, this changed as a consequence of increasing Armenian nationalism as well as more general concern about national feelings and socialism in the Russian Empire. By the end of the century a policy of deliberate Russification of subject people was being applied. The movement of population resulted, at the start of the Bolshevik regime, in the new Armenian Soviet Socialist Republic having an Armenian majority but with a significant Azeri minority. Similarly Azerbaijan had many Armenians within its boundaries, a number increased through the boundaries being deliberately gerrymandered. There was little Russian immigration to Armenia in either Tsarist or Soviet periods but the large population movements during the conflict with Azerbaijan between 1988 and 1994 resulted in massive emigration of Azeris and immigration of ethnic Armenians from Azerbaijan.

The population at the 1979 census was 3.8 million of whom 91% were ethnic Armenians. The census in February 1989 gave a population of 3.3 million but is regarded as unreliable since it took place only two months after the devastating earthquake in northwest Armenia which made obtaining data within the region almost impossible. The most recent census in October 2011 gave a figure of 3.02 million, although the real figure, once those temporarily present are deducted and those absent are added, is estimated to be about 2.9 million. At present about 98% of the population is ethnically Armenian, 1.3% Yezidi and 0.5% Russian.

During the preceding ten years 173,000 people left Armenia and, at the time of the census, 12.6% of citizens were out of Armenia, a figure which includes those who have sought work abroad. The birth rate showed a steady fall from 1991 (from a previously steady rate around 25/1,000) to a low of 9.9/1,000 in 2001. Since then there has been a gradual rise to 14/1,000 at the 2011 census. The fertility rate of women plummeted to less than half its 1990 rate but has shown a small rise in recent years; however, not to a level which allows the population to reproduce itself. The current total fertility rate is 1.38 (2012 estimate). Experts say that Armenia is facing a serious demographic problem because of the low birth rate and outward migration. In the Soviet Union abortion was the primary method of birth control. Although the abortion ratio (the number of abortions per 1,000 live births) has fallen since independence it remains relatively high at 274, compared with 222 for the EU. Abortion is legal up to 12 weeks gestation. The number of abortions is probably higher than official statistics suggest as many women choose to end pregnancies using over-the-counter abortifacients. The average number of abortions per woman is eight and some women may have as many as 20. Both surgical abortion and medical abortion are far cheaper methods of birth control than the contraceptive pill, which costs about USD15–20/month, a price totally beyond reach of many women. In 2010 only 27% of married women used modern methods of contraception.

A skew in the birth ratio of boys to girls has appeared in recent years, the second worst ratio in the world after China. (The average ratio at birth is boys:girls 106:100. In Armenia it is 112:100.) For economic reasons selective abortion of female foetuses is being practised. Because girls traditionally move to the husband's parental home on marriage, boys are viewed as a greater security for parents' old age. This loss of potential future mothers also has implications for Armenia's demography. The government has announced that from January 2014 parents will receive a lump sum of a million drams for a third and each subsequent child (and a one-off sum of AMD50,000 for a first and second child at the time of writing). Most regions have recorded a drop in population, the highest drop being in Lori province. Only Kotayk and Armavir provinces recorded an increase. Some 36.7% of the population lives in villages and 63.3% in towns; 55% of the urban population is in Yerevan.

One rural feature, not only in Armenia but the whole region, is that of villages being predominantly of one ethnicity. This is most evident in the Russian villages east of Vanadzor and in northern Lori. Other villages still have significant Greek or Assyrian-speaking populations. It is also the reason why some villages are completely abandoned – they were Azeri.

LIFE IN ARMENIA Life for many ordinary Armenians is still far from easy and the global financial crisis made life even harder with the poverty rate increasing from 27.6% in 2008 to 35.8% in 2010. Many, perhaps even most, people in what was in Soviet times a fairly heavily industrialised country have either reverted to subsistence agriculture if they live in rural areas or else have sought to become small-scale vendors of some kind of goods or other if they live in towns. For parents it is their hope that education will help their children to escape the widespread poverty. The population has fallen by about 20% since the 1980s as a result of emigration in search of work, and the low birth rate. Yet it cannot really be said that Armenians look either despairing or unhappy. They cope with the problems and family members help each other out. It has to be said that the vast majority of those old enough to have worked in the Soviet era look back on it as a golden age – they are generally too young of course to remember Stalin's terror and overlook the failure of the Soviet Union to deal with the civil war which broke out between Armenia and Azerbaijan in 1989. Younger people see things differently and to an observer their preoccupations appear much the same as their contemporaries in the West, their mobile phones in constant use. However, they are also to be seen lighting candles in churches and on Genocide Memorial Day it is striking to see the large number of young people joining the commemoration in Yerevan.

One of the big changes has been the improvement in the **water supply**. Ten years ago it was a significant problem. Leaking mains meant that the water supply in most towns and cities had to be restricted to a few hours a day to prevent large quantities running away to waste. Sometimes it could even be cut off for days and in both urban and rural areas water had to be stored in quantity for use when needed. Considerable progress has been made in the reliability and quality of water and its infrastructure. Now in the towns, at least, there is usually running water 24 hours a day. The situation in villages has also improved greatly although in remoter areas water may still have to be obtained from the village spring or a well in the garden. Improvement in waste-water management and sewerage has also begun but much remains to be done. The European Bank for Reconstruction and Development and the European Union have given grants to help upgrade water and sewerage systems, most notably in Yerevan and the Lake Sevan areas. Irrigation networks are also being upgraded.

Virtually every family except for those living in flats grows as much **food** as it can with all the family members, children included, working hard planting and harvesting potatoes and other vegetables by hand. In late summer, women can be encountered in the villages winnowing grain, preserving fruit for the winter by drying it in the sun, and making fruit juices and homemade vodkas to last through the winter. Throughout the year they also join their neighbours in the baking of *lavash*, Armenia's classic flatbread (see box, page 90). Keeping the home clean is difficult for women; not all have domestic appliances. The level of dirt is increased by the wood-burning stoves which are very common and the seas of mud which almost engulf villages particularly in late winter at the time of snow melt and which are aggravated by the numbers of livestock kept in the villages.

Very many families keep their own **livestock** and even in towns cattle and sheep can often be seen being tended by a family member. (Unlike western Europe even sheep have to be taken back to the house at night because of the danger from wolves.) In some areas free-range pigs wander through the village foraging for food. Armenians are very hard working, even more important now when so much work has to be done by hand because machinery, fertilisers, weedkillers and pesticides are all unaffordable. (This has the incidental benefit of making much Armenian food organic, albeit unofficially.) Even so, lack of suitable land makes Armenia a net importer of food, which results in a permanently adverse trade balance. For well-educated Armenians, life is not necessarily much easier. Salaries are low, there is serious underfunding of education and health, and career prospects are limited. Many such people seek work abroad, mostly in Russia, although the global economic recession of recent years has made even this option less available.

The **Christian faith** is important to very many Armenians, their Church binding them together as a community as it has for over 1,700 years while simultaneously uniting them internationally with Christians elsewhere. It is the Armenian Christians of the diaspora who pay for most of the very necessary infrastructure investment in Armenia. Few countries are so heavily dependent on help from abroad. Yet despite all these difficulties, Armenians are generous to a fault. Desperately poor people welcome you into their homes and provide refreshments, often unintentionally embarrassing Western visitors who feel awkward about accepting from those who obviously have so much less. Especially in rural areas, people are fascinated by the few Westerners who appear and are genuinely touched that people from so far away could even have heard of Armenia let alone be interested enough to come. Having said that, pride in the country's history and language is intense, with Armenians well aware of the artistic and spiritual achievement of their great monasteries and of the contributions made by many distinguished Armenians in history.

LANGUAGE

Armenian is an Indo-European language with its own branch, thus not closely related to any other language. It has its own unique alphabet created in AD405, originally with 36 letters, three more being added later. It is a so-called synthetic language – the construction of one word with declensions and various endings gives as much information as a whole phrase in English. There are two forms of Armenian, eastern Armenian (as spoken in Armenia) and western Armenian (as formerly spoken in Anatolia and still spoken by the diaspora). Although different the two are mutually intelligible. For further information see pages 345–54.

The second language is **Russian**, which is spoken virtually everywhere. **English** is becoming more common but can only be relied upon in places popular with tourists. Outside Yerevan, apart from the larger hotels, it is common to find that no English is spoken. Other European languages are even less well known although of course interpreters can be employed. Independent travellers can hire an English-speaking guide and an increasing number of drivers of hired cars also speak some English.

CHURCH NAMES

The great majority of Armenian churches are dedicated to a small number of people or events. Although this guidebook uses English names throughout, visitors will often see an English transliteration of the Armenian name used on the spot. Apart from a few dedicated to Armenian saints, the common ones are:

Sourb Amenaprkich	Holy Redeemer
Sourb Astvatsatsin	Holy Mother of God
Sourb Astvatsnkal	Holy Wisdom of God
Sourb Arakelots	Holy Apostles
Sourb Grigor Lusavorich	St Gregory the Illuminator
Sourb Hakob	St Jacob
Sourb Hovhannes	St John (usually the Evangelist)
Sourb Haratyun	Holy Resurrection
Sourb Karapet	Holy Forerunner (ie: St John the Baptist)
Sourb Nshan	Holy Sign (of the cross)

Learning the Armenian alphabet and a few common words certainly enhances a visit to Armenia and Armenians are delighted if a foreigner makes even a small effort with their language.

RELIGION

Ethnic Armenians are overwhelmingly members of the Armenian Apostolic Church, whose head, the Katholikos, has his seat at Ejmiatsin. The Katholikos is elected, following the death of his predecessor, by an electoral college of around 400 delegates comprising members of the senior clergy and representatives of all branches of the Armenian Church worldwide. The present Katholikos, Karekin II, was elected in 1999. The Church is called Apostolic because Christianity is believed to have been brought to Armenia by Jesus's disciples Bartholomew and Thaddeus (or Lebbaeus as he is called in St Matthew's gospel). It is also sometimes called the Gregorian Church because it was founded in Armenia by St Gregory the Illuminator. Most visitors to Armenia will visit several of the churches. The layout and form of worship are quite different from that in the West. They are more similar to the Orthodox Church but there are even here some major differences in that Armenian churches do not have an iconostasis with its royal doors and, doctrinally, the Armenian Church has not adopted the views of the Council of Chalcedon (AD451) concerning the duality of Christ's nature. The Armenian Church did not participate in the Council of Chalcedon, which met on 8 October. It was not convened until after the Battle of Avarayr (see pages 17–18) on 26 May, a battle which left Armenia in confusion with her patriarch and bishops either in prison or exile. The Armenian Church maintains as lawful the decrees of the first three ecumenical councils, Nicaea (AD325), Constantinople (AD381) and Ephesus (AD431). These three councils were equally recognised by both the Western and Eastern Churches; their decisions could thus be seen as emanating from the Universal Church. The split between eastern and western Christianity came later. The seemingly interminable controversies over the nature of Christ (still unresolved some 16 centuries later!) concerned the closeness of the two natures of Christ (the divine and the human), with the theological debates taking place amidst political and hierarchical dissentions. In simplistic terms the council of Ephesus affirmed a close union of the two natures; the council of Chalcedon inclined to a distinctness and separateness of the two natures.

At one end of the church will be a raised altar dais called a *bema*. In active churches a curtain can be drawn across it during parts of the service (see below) and during Lent. A legacy of the Soviet period was a shortage of priests, but numbers are increasing as are seminaries to train priests. (Training for the priesthood lasts seven years.) New churches are being built and old ones renovated although in some places there is still a shortage of money to pay priests and repair churches. Accordingly, many churches do not have regular worship and an individual priest might have to look after several churches.

When visiting any Armenian church it is normal to buy candles on entry and then to light them (matches are provided), placing them upright in the trays of sand. The only exception to this rule is the new cathedral in Yerevan where candles are forbidden (there is a special chapel for them to the southeast of the cathedral). Women do not need to wear headscarves unless taking communion. It is correct to leave a church walking backwards so as not to turn one's back on God. It is still common for an animal (and more particularly, the salt with which the animal will be seasoned), always male and usually a ram or a cock, to be presented by a family for sacrifice. Sacrifice is usually carried out by the priest outside the church after the Sunday service. First, the priest blesses the animal and salt at a special stone called the *orhnakar* ('blessing stone') and then he sacrifices the animal at the *mataghatun* ('sacrifice house'). The animal will have been given in thanksgiving for some event, such as recovery from a serious illness, or as a particular request to God. It is partly a form of charity since some of the meat from the slaughtered animal will be given to the poor although the donor's family and friends will eat the rest, always boiled and never roasted or barbecued. The animals destined for slaughter are beautifully groomed before being offered to God in this way. Families will sometimes slaughter a cock themselves and evidence of such sacrifice is not uncommon at small shrines and churches. Another frequent sight outside churches is a tree or shrub to which numerous scraps of cloth are tied. Each scrap is attached by a person making a private prayer.

WORSHIP Worship usually lasts for about 2½ hours, the service having been extended by additional prayers at various times over the centuries. Despite its length there were traditionally no seats but pews are now becoming more common. Worship is quite different from that in Western churches. Visitors need not attend the whole service (which usually starts at 10.30) and can come just for part except that at some churches (notably Sevan) the building is so crowded that it is difficult either to enter or to leave. (Geghard is a good option on a Sunday morning for those staying in Yerevan with access to transport.) Even for those with no knowledge of the Armenian language the beauty of the singing is deeply impressive.

The devout fast on Sunday mornings before going to church. For the celebrant priest the liturgy begins in the vestry. He acknowledges his sinfulness and how privileged he is to be able to lead the people in worship. The deacon then hands him in turn the various items of the vestments and he puts each of them on with a brief prayer. The priest and deacon now enter the nave but do not go immediately up to the *bema*. At first they remain among the congregation where the priest symbolically washes his hands and then asks the congregation to pray for his forgiveness. Once they are up on the *bema*, the curtain is drawn across it to avoid distracting the congregation with the preparations. After the elements have been prepared the curtain opens and the deacons lead the priest in a procession round the altar and down into the nave, walking round the whole church offering incense and inviting the faithful to kiss the cross which the priest carries.

After two hymns the deacon symbolically holds the Gospel book over the priest's head and there is a further procession around the altar accompanied by another hymn. This is followed by readings from the Bible and more prayers. The main part of the service, the liturgy of the Eucharist, starts with the priest removing his crown and slippers in obedience to God's command to Moses at the burning bush. The deacon processes around the altar holding the veiled chalice above his head. At the end of the procession the deacon hands the elements to the celebrant. The so-called kiss of peace which follows is a ritualised greeting everyone makes to their neighbours. A long sequence of prayers and hymns concludes with the curtain being again closed, this time for the priest to receive communion while hidden from view – it is traditional in all Eastern Churches for the celebrant to receive communion out of sight of the congregation. Communion is now distributed: as communicants stand before the priest they make the sign of the cross and say 'I have sinned against God.' Thereupon the priest places a small part of the bread which has been dipped into the wine directly into the mouth of the communicant who again makes the sign of the cross. (The sign is made in the same way as in the Orthodox Church – right breast before left – but the opposite way from the Roman Catholic practice which is left breast before right.) This is followed by more prayers and hymns during part of which the curtain is closed while the priest and deacons reorganise the altar. The priest then raises his right hand to bless the congregation in Armenian style – with the thumb and ring finger forming a circle to represent the world and the other fingers pointing upward to represent the persons of the Trinity. The service ends with the congregation kissing the Gospel book.

MARRIAGE IN ARMENIA Traditional marriage in Armenia differs somewhat from that in many other European countries and in North America. Tourists are almost bound to see weddings unless visiting during either Lent, when weddings cannot be held in church, or during May, Armenians having adopted the old Russian custom of considering that weddings in May will lead to an unhappy marriage. Weddings are particularly common on Saturdays.

The first point to note is that fewer young people than formerly are getting married, but not because they are simply living together as in many Western countries. In general Armenian couples do not do this. Young Armenian couples marry and then expect to have their first child a year or so after the wedding and the wife will stay at home to look after it. A young Armenian man will often not make a proposal of marriage unless he feels confident that he will be able to support his wife and child. In the uncertain economic climate (after decades of Soviet predictability) many young men felt unsure that they would be able to support a family and hence stayed single. Armenia's marriage rate fell by 50% after the Soviet collapse. However, since 2007 there has been a gradual increase in the marriage rate. The problem of housing also arises. Economic uncertainty means that young people are reluctant to borrow money to buy a house or flat and the alternative of living with the husband's parents may or may not be feasible.

A second point to note is that Armenians tend to have quite small families. A couple will generally only have further children if they believe that they can support them. This is similar to the view of many Western couples but economic uncertainty, or at least the perception of it, is greater in Armenia than in the West and this impacts on family size.

As traditionally happened in the West, if a man wishes to marry a woman he will go to her father to ask for her hand in marriage. A difference in Armenia is that he will usually be accompanied by his parents and possibly by other very close relatives such as his brother or sister. Unlike the West, wedding ceremonies are not planned long in advance: rarely more than a month ahead and sometimes only a few days, although this is changing as churches and reception venues become busier; it can now be as long as two or three months. On the wedding day the bride will be helped to get ready by her maid of honour (the equivalent of chief bridesmaid): this is always one of her unmarried sisters if she has any and only a close friend if she has no unmarried sister. It is never a married woman: the concept of a matron of honour doesn't exist in Armenia. The bridegroom's family provides and pays for the bride's dress, the bridegroom and the brother of the cross (the equivalent of best man) bringing it to her family's house on the day of the wedding. The bridegroom will normally also be accompanied by members of his family and friends (though not by his mother) and they, together with the bride's relatives and friends, eat and drink at the house while the bride is putting on her dress and being helped to get ready. Traditionally the bride would have worn a gown of red silk with a headpiece, often made of cardboard, shaped into wings and decorated with feathers. Nowadays she usually wears a long white dress similar in style to those worn throughout the West. The bridegroom often wears a suit, though in a rather more interesting colour than one bought for sober office wear. Relatives and friends, including the maid of honour, tend to dress much as in the West although pale suits for all the prominent younger men are common.

Eventually the bride and bridegroom set off for the church together (no bridegroom waiting for the bride at the altar!) accompanied by their relatives and friends. Traditionally the bride's mother stays at home and does not attend her daughter's wedding: for her to do so is considered to bring bad luck upon the couple. However, this tradition is changing and nowadays the bride's mother often does attend the wedding. The bridegroom's mother has always attended. The couple may have either a church service, a civil ceremony or both. If they opt to have a church service but no civil ceremony their marriage is valid in the eyes of God although it is not recognised in Armenian law and the couple are, in theory at least, both free to remarry. Nevertheless many couples do in fact have only a church service: the subsequent rate of separation is in practice low. The wedding party enters the church with a large decorated basket containing wedding favours to be distributed to the guests: in the past these might have been small ceramic containers with almonds in them but many modern brides choose something much less traditional and there is a demand for such exotica as glass containers decorated with sea shells. During the service the officiating priest puts a ring on the finger of the bridegroom and then of the bride before joining their hands. The bridegroom then makes his vows followed in turn by the bride.

After the ceremony, all present, though still without the bride's mother (if she has stayed at home), traditionally go to the bridegroom's family house for the reception although nowadays a room in a hotel or restaurant is sometimes hired for the occasion. *En route* there is likely to be a motorcade with blaring horns and in Yerevan driving three times round Republic Square is an essential and audible part of the proceedings. On arrival at the reception the groomsmen and bridesmaids, holding their flowers aloft, form arches through which the young couple walk and two white doves are traditionally released to symbolise their love and happiness. There is more eating and drinking, this time at the expense of the bridegroom's family (although this too is changing with costs being shared), accompanied by dancing in an amalgam of traditional Armenian and more modern styles. The food will almost certainly be the menu invariably eaten on all Armenian celebratory occasions: *khorovats* – barbecued meat, most commonly pork but sometimes lamb or chicken, accompanied by salads and vegetables together with *lavash*, Armenia's flatbread. There will be the inevitable toasts. Friends, neighbours, and indeed almost anyone passing, drop in to wish the newlyweds well. The party goes on until everyone has had enough.

That isn't quite the end of marriage customs. Trndaz (Purification) day, 13 February, commemorates the purification of Mary 40 days after the birth of Jesus, as laid down in the rules given in Leviticus, chapter 12. After a church service during the evening, the priest blesses a fire. Candles lit in this fire are then taken to the homes of couples who have been married in the previous year and also to the homes of young women who have become engaged. A fire is kindled at the house using the candles lit from the fire at the church which the priest blessed. Then the couples jump over it to get rid of the small devils hanging from the edge of their clothes. The ceremony is the pretext for a large family celebration.

In some years Trndaz coincides with St Sargis's Day whose date is variable (between 11 January and 15 February) and fixed by the Church calendar. As with so many Armenian customs the actual details vary from family to family but traditionally young people fast on the eve of St Sargis's Day. They then eat unleavened salt bread which has been baked either by their grandmother or by a happily married middle-aged woman, and retire to bed without either drinking or speaking. Their inevitable thirst will supposedly make them dream of the person whom they will marry. If a footprint appears in the bowl of flour left outside the house overnight then the young man of the house will marry in the coming year. On St Sargis's Day itself there is a service of blessing for young people at the church.

ST SARGIS

St Sargis, often called St Sargis the Warrior, is remembered for his martyrdom in AD362. Why then is he also known as the Armenian patron saint of love and youth? One legend about St Sargis may explain why.

There was a poor bard, named Gharib, who loved Shah-Sanam, the daughter of a wealthy man. Shah-Sanam returned Gharib's love but her father would not let them marry because he wanted to marry his daughter to a rich man. Bard Gharib decided to go to foreign countries to seek his fortune. Before leaving he asked Shah-Sanam to promise to wait for him for seven years, saying that if he were even one day late she would be free to marry as her father wished.

The seven years were difficult for Gharib. He worked hard day and night to amass a fortune, all the time thinking of his beloved and looking forward to the day when they could meet again. Eventually when the seven years were almost up he had enough money and he started back on the perilous journey but he encountered so many hardships and delays that he feared he would not arrive in time. He prayed and begged St Sargis to help him. St Sargis, seated on his white horse, immediately appeared and, lifting Gharib on to the horse beside him, brought him in a trice to Shah-Sanam's house. Seeing the bard's strength of character and the young couple's love for each other, Shah-Sanam's father gave their union his blessing.

St Sargis is often portrayed on his white horse, a small figure seated beside him. He is buried at Ushi Monastery (see page 164).

EDUCATION

The Soviet education system was successful in producing a well-educated population, and a literacy rate of 100% was reported as early as 1960. In the Soviet period, Armenian education followed the standard Soviet programme with control from Moscow of curricula and teaching methods. After independence Armenia made changes. Curricula were altered to emphasise Armenian history and culture while Armenian became the dominant language of instruction. Russian is still widely taught now as a second language but the former compulsory clutter – subjects such as History of the Communist Party of the Soviet Union, Dialectical Materialism, Historical Materialism, Foundations of Marxist-Leninist Aesthetics, and Foundations of Scientific Communism – was rapidly jettisoned.

Children formerly started compulsory education at the age of seven, but after independence the starting age was changed to six, giving 12 years of compulsory education. There is also day-care for two to three-year-olds and kindergarten for three to six-year-olds. The school year normally begins on 1 September ('Welcome Back to School' day) – as in most parts of the former Soviet Union children in all classes can be seen making their way to school immaculately dressed and clutching bunches of flowers for their class teacher. University courses last five years or more, four years for a basic Bachelor's degree and typically another two years for a Master's. Education has suffered from lack of funding since independence and the low salaries paid to teachers have discouraged young people from entering the profession. As well as school leaving exams there are additional university entrance exams. A particular difficulty is the gap which has developed between what children have learned during their 12 years at school and what they are required to know to pass the universities' entrance exams. It was hoped that the extension of schooling to 12 years would remove the gap in knowledge but that has not yet happened. The only way to bridge this gap is to pay for extra tuition and so important is their children's education to parents that almost all are willing to pay for it. So highly is education regarded that Yerevan's 12 state universities have, despite the falling population, been augmented by 25 private ones since independence. Armenians who do not seek a university education are very much in a minority despite recent figures showing that only 20% of university graduates find jobs after graduation. The ministry is keen to reduce the number of graduates and to increase the extent of vocational training as there are significant shortages of trained specialists such as hairdressers and construction workers. The most highly regarded degrees and diplomas are those from the state institutions, and especially those of students who scored so well in the entrance examination that they gained a free place.

CULTURE

ARCHITECTURE
Church building For some members of the diaspora, to experience Armenia's culture and language on its home territory will be their overriding memory of a visit to Armenia, but for the majority of visitors it is the historic buildings which will make the greatest impression, above all the monasteries but also to a lesser degree the secular medieval buildings such as fortresses and caravanserais. Only a very few buildings survive from the pre-Christian era: little more than the foundations can be observed of the cities of the Kingdom of Urartu such as Erebuni. By far the best known pre-Christian building is the sole-surviving example of Graeco-Roman architecture in Armenia, built at Garni sometime in the first two centuries AD at a

ARMENIAN SUNDIALS

Sundials can be seen on the walls of many Armenian monasteries and churches. The details of some are easily seen, such as that on the eastern façade of the small St Stephen's Church at Haghartsin Monastery. By contrast, the elaborately carved sundial at Harichavank is positioned so high up on the eastern wall of the Mother of God Church that binoculars are almost needed to appreciate the detail. Sundials were sometimes placed high up on a wall to avoid them being shaded from the sun by surrounding trees but, if this was originally the case at Harichavank, it is certainly not a problem now. The sundials themselves are not dated and it is not always possible to ascertain if they are contemporaneous with the building they adorn or if they were added later.

Armenian sundials are of the vertical type, with a horizontal gnomon at right angles to the wall. They are semicircular and usually divided into 12 (occasionally 11) equal petal-like divisions, each division representing an hour. Such dials show unequal hours, daylight being divided into 12 periods regardless of the length of daylight so an 'hour' in winter will occupy less time than an 'hour' in summer. The hours are counted from one at sunrise on the horizontal line at the left, to 12 at sunset on the horizontal line at the right. Visitors may be more familiar with sundials showing equal hours, with their divisions of variable width and gnomons at an angle to the vertical, the angle determined by the sundial's latitude.

The divisions of some Armenian sundials carry letters of the Armenian alphabet. Armenian letters were (and sometimes still are) used to represent numbers. The first nine letters of the Armenian alphabet represent the units one to nine, the next nine letters represent the tens (ten, 20 … 90), the next nine letters the hundreds (100, 200 … 900), etc. The first ten divisions on a sundial bear the first ten letters of the alphabet, 11 and 12 usually being represented by a repeat of the first two letters. Very occasionally, as seen on a more recently carved sundial at Zvartnots, 11 is shown, correctly, as a combination of the tenth letter (representing ten) and the first letter (representing one). Similarly 12 is shown as the tenth letter plus the second letter of the alphabet.

time when the country was an ally of Rome. The Greek style was widely employed in contemporary Roman buildings throughout the empire and the survival of no other buildings in Armenia from this era is largely the consequence of Christians destroying pagan temples after the conversion of the country. Almost certainly others would have been constructed. However, the influence of the Greek style, and before that of the elongated halls of Urartian buildings, can be seen in the early hall or basilica churches.

The early churches were often built on the site of pagan shrines employing the same foundations, and hence they had the same dimensions as the temple which they replaced; moreover the Christian altar was usually placed directly over the previous pagan one as at Ejmiatsin. From the earliest times the churches were built in stone, most commonly the volcanic tuff which is easily carved and tends gradually to harden when exposed to the atmosphere. The need to build in stone was dictated by the unavailability of suitable timber, even for roofing, and the weight of the heavy vaulted stone roof in turn dictated the need for thick walls to support it with few windows. Where tuff was unavailable, most commonly in border areas, other volcanic rocks such as basalt or andesite were used.

From fairly early days almost all churches, apart from the earliest basilicas, were built with a cupola supported by a cylindrical structure called a tambour. Tambours are usually circular in cross-section when viewed from the interior of the church but are often polygonal on the outside. The preference for churches to have a cupola supported by a tambour is one of Armenian architecture's most abiding features and makes its churches very distinctive. Such domed churches first appeared in the 4th century, the simplest being essentially a dome on a cube with one to four apses. These central dome churches had exclusively local roots: centrally focused sanctuaries are known from Urartian temples. The dome may have developed from domestic dwellings which used the *hazarashen* method of construction in which stones are progressively added across angles to make an aperture of decreasing size. (This construction is most easily appreciated in some *gavits* (see page 45) which have a central opening or *yerdik*.) The domed style rapidly developed after the conversion to Christianity and continued until the Arab invasion and conquest in the mid-7th century. Thereafter no churches were built for over 200 years until the establishment of the Bagratid dynasty in the late 9th century. Under this re-established regime new churches began to be built, initially copying the old style but gradually starting to develop this style to provide greater height and space. Once again church building ceased after foreign invasion, this time by the Seljuk Turks after the middle of the 11th century. Domes were also incorporated into the basilica style churches, the dome supported by either free-standing pillars or wall piers. Most domed basilicas date from the 9th to 14th centuries.

The establishment of Georgian independence together with the Armenian Zakarid dynasty in the late 12th century led to a renewal of church building and, in particular, to the development of the large monastic complexes with their multiple churches and ancillary buildings which are probably nowadays the most visited tourist sights in the country. Again the traditional style was used but the quest for greater space was now satisfied by building several churches on the same site rather than by increasing the size of each structure. Inevitably, construction ceased at the end of the 13th century after the Mongol invasions and the Armenian kingdom of Cilicia also ceased to exist in 1375 following the Mamluk invasions. No more churches were built until the 17th century when construction, still in the traditional style, restarted at a time when Armenia was ruled by the Safavid Shahs of Iran. Church building increased in the 19th century as Armenian national consciousness grew, only to come to a complete stop with the genocide of 1915 in western Armenia and the Bolshevik Revolution in the east. Independence has led to a resurgence in church building, largely with funds provided by the diaspora, with the traditional style and hallmark tuff generally retained. This can make it difficult for the visitor to know what is new and what is renovated old.

Church construction Two overriding practical constraints influenced early church architects: the need to use stone for roofs because of the lack of suitable timber, and the need to withstand fairly frequent earthquakes. The necessary strength was provided by the use of an early type of concrete in a method probably copied from Roman architects. The earliest churches were built of massive stone blocks, with mortar separating them, forming the outer and inner surfaces of the walls; between them was a thin layer of concrete. This concrete was compounded of broken tuff and other stones, lime mortar and eggs. During the 5th and 6th centuries the technique evolved, the slabs of the stone shell becoming thinner and the cement core thicker. The method of construction was then to erect finely cut slabs of tuff or other stone a few rows at a time and without mortar to form the

Khachkars, carved memorial stones, are an important, conspicuous, and beautiful feature of Armenian decorative art. The word khachkar literally means 'cross stone'. In quiet streets in central Yerevan it is possible to see even today the stone carvers at work, using traditional methods to create these endlessly varied monuments in a revival of this ancient tradition. The earliest khachkars date from the 9th and 10th centuries, a period when Armenia had gained effective independence from the Arab caliphate and separate Armenian kings each ruled their individual states. This flowering of Armenian craftsmanship under independence was paralleled in architecture: some of Armenia's finest monasteries date from this period.

The earliest datable khachkar is one erected at Garni by Queen Katranide, wife of King Ashot Bagratuni I, in 879 in mediation for her person. Securing the salvation of the soul was the most common reason for erecting khachkars but some were put up to commemorate military victories or the completion of churches, bridges, fountains and other constructions. Even unrequited love might be commemorated in this way. The dominant feature of the design is generally a cross, occasionally a crucifix, resting on a rosette or sun disc design, often with a stylised tree of life encompassing the lower vertical of the cross. The four limbs of the cross usually terminate in two triple-loops, perhaps a reference to the Trinity. The remainder is covered with complex patterns of leaves, bunches of grapes or abstract geometrical patterns. Occasionally the whole was surmounted by a cornice showing biblical characters or saints and there is sometimes an inscription recording when, by whom and for what reason the khachkar was erected. The absolute peak of khachkar design was probably between the 12th and 14th centuries. Amazingly elaborate and delicate patterns were created using the same elements of design. Depiction of the Crucifixion and Resurrection become more common and at this time some khachkars came to be erected as a spiritual protection against natural disasters. The supreme masterpieces include that at Geghard created by Timot and Mkhitar in 1213, the Holy Redeemer khachkar at Haghpat Monastery which was created by Vahram in 1273, and that at Goshavank created by Poghos in 1291. Some good examples have been transported to the Historical Museum in Yerevan and the cathedral at Ejmiatsin. There can, however, be no substitute for seeing them where they were originally erected.

The Mongol invasion at the end of the 14th century led to a decline of the tradition and although there was a revival in the 16th and 17th centuries, the artistic heights of the 14th were never regained.

Some khachkars, often recording donations, are embedded in the walls of monasteries but the majority are free-standing. Armenia has over 40,000 surviving khachkars. An amazing sight is the so-called field of khachkars at Noratus, the largest of several groupings of khachkars in Armenia. This is an old graveyard with 900 khachkars marking graves and the endless variations of design make a visit there particularly rewarding. Noratus is especially interesting because examples there span the whole period from the 10th to the 17th century. Note that at Noratus, as at all places where khachkars are still in their original location, they face west. This means that they are best photographed in the afternoon.

Since 2010, khachkars, their symbolism and craftsmanship are inscribed in the UNESCO list of Intangible Cultural Heritage.

Background Information CULTURE

1

43

surfaces of the outer and inner walls after which concrete was poured into the cavity between them. This concrete adhered to the facing slabs and formed a solid strong core and it is this core, rather than the thin slabs of tuff, which forms the building's major support. The slabs were varied in size and height to break up the vertical and horizontal rows and thus provide protection against parts of the concrete core falling out during earthquakes. Great thought was given to enhancing the artistic appearance of churches, and different churches had the tuff slabs erected in different ways. In some churches the slabs were carved and either different colours of slab might be employed to provide a contrast or else a uniform colour might be used, sometimes with mortar applied between the slabs to give a completely uniform appearance. As the technique evolved the largest stone blocks gradually came to be reserved for the lowest courses of stonework as well as for corners, and smaller ones were used elsewhere. Although windows were, from structural considerations, never a significant feature of Armenian church architecture, their size and number did tend to increase over time.

Styles of church All the earliest-known churches were of basilica construction (ie: rectangular with an apse at the east end) with either a single aisle or three aisles. They sat on a stepped base, or stylobate. The more spacious three-aisle basilicas were built in cities or important religious centres and had pylons, or pillars, dividing the space and supporting the roof. The three vaults of the aisles were covered by a single gable roof with pediments on the short façades. Sometimes the middle aisle, which was wider than the side aisles, was also higher and had a separate roof. Some basilica churches had outside galleries, around the north, south and west walls, used when the congregation was too large for the main building, for liturgy on weekdays and for the repentant. St Gregory the Illuminator spoke of the need for repentance beyond the church walls. Galleries arose in the 4th century, were widespread in the 5th and 6th centuries and fell out of use by the 7th century. A variation was a covered porch at the west end. In the late 4th century, rooms each side of the altar apse, or corner rooms at both east and west ends, became a feature of Armenian churches and have remained so.

The incorporation of a cupola as a central feature caused changes to church layout and the basilica style gave way to a more centrally planned church built around the cupola, sometimes with four apses or else with four arms of equal length, or sometimes with three apses and one extended arm. This resulted in what was essentially a cross-shaped church but the addition of corner rooms between the arms of the cross resulted in many church buildings being more or less rectangular in plan when seen from the outside but with the church itself cross-shaped in plan when on the inside. Churches with a cupola and four arms are often referred to as cross-dome churches although cross-cupola would perhaps be less misleading as most English speakers think of domes as being hemispherical. The ultimate exemplar of this centrally planned style, the church of St Hripsime at Ejmiatsin, is still further developed. Four semicircular apses are separated from each other by four circular niches each of which leads to a square corner room, all this being incorporated within the basic rectangular shape. Another variant of the centrally planned church was to make the entire building circular; most are not strictly circular but polygonal. The best known, the ruined 7th-century church at Zvartnots, has 32 sides.

The basic style of Armenian church architecture has remained to this day the centrally planned church, built around its cupola and with two or more corner rooms. However, two later developments were the additions of a narthex, or *gavit* as it is known in Armenia, and the building of a bell tower. Both *gavit* and bell tower came into being during the great upsurge in monastery building from the 10th century onwards. A *gavit* is a square room usually attached to the west end of the church and serving as a vestibule, a room for meetings, and a burial place for notables. Apart from the relatively few free-standing ones *gavits* could also house the overflow when the congregation was too large for the main church. They were sometimes very large with massive walls and, like the other parts of the church, were frequently elaborately carved. Bell towers appeared at monastery complexes from the 13th century onwards and were often detached from the church building itself. The walls of later churches, both the exterior and the interior ones, sometimes incorporate *khachkars*. There are also occasionally carvings of the donors, often holding a model of the church.

Inside Armenian churches there may or may not be carving but the most conspicuous feature is the altar dais or *bema* at the eastern end with steps leading up to it. The entire dais forms the altar and in an active church it can be shut off by a curtain though the curtain is never closed except during parts of services and during Lent. Unlike the Orthodox Church there is never an iconostasis. A few churches have a decorated wooden or stone altar screen, as at Sevanavank or Mughni, but this never obscures the holy table as does the iconostasis in the Orthodox Church.

In the Middle Ages churches were sometimes fortified. An extra, high wall was added to the outside of the church. Most of these walls were demolished in the 19th century but remnants can still occasionally be seen. For example, the church of St John at Byurakan, Tsiranavor Church at Parpi and Tsiranavor at Ashtarak.

Some small churches or shrines seem to emerge from the hillside, the eastern end of the roof almost level with the higher ground. This is thought to indicate that the site may originally have been a pagan spring shrine. Flowing water can still occasionally be seen, in the first cave church in Geghard and in the mausoleum at Kobayr.

A word which visitors might hear when any small church is being referred to is *zham*, as opposed to *vank* for a monastery and *yekeretsi* for a church. *Zham* is the Armenian word for 'hour' or 'time'. Using it to mean a church dates from when the church was the (only) means of telling the time, either by bell or sundial. *Zham* is also often used to refer to simple hall-like village churches without a dome and often with wooden rather than stone pillars supporting the roof. They are rarely thought worthy of being pointed out to tourists but they are widespread and often have interesting older khachkars incorporated into their walls.

While the vegetation on some church roofs is the result of centuries of disrepair, on some small basilica churches it is a traditional, deliberate technique to protect the roof. The roof of stone tiles is covered with a layer of turf which gives a grass-covered roof and, in spring, an attractive church-top meadow. Such turf or sod roofs have historically been used in Iceland, the Faroe Islands and northern Scotland to increase both insulation and watertightness. Modern variations are becoming an increasingly popular eco-friendly option. Most turf roofs are flat or with only a gentle incline but in Scotland, in 2006–12, trials found that turf was just as effective on the steeply pitched roof of a 15th-century tower-house.

Secular medieval architecture
Two types of secular medieval building will attract the attention of visitors: castles and caravanserais. Unlike the churches, neither is distinctively Armenian. Essentially Armenia's **castles** were sited and built according to the general thinking in castle design of the day and followed the same principles as applied throughout Europe. **Caravanserais** were built along the main east–west trade routes to provide secure lodging for merchants and their pack

Vishaps are menhirs or large carved stones from the first two millennia BC, usually associated with water and thought to have religious significance. Vishap is Armenian for 'dragon' and such stones have a dragon or serpent head carved near the top. These tall stones tend to be somewhat cylindrical or cigar-shaped and are often grey in colour. There are also fish-like vishaps which are usually recumbent. Vishaps are sometimes so weathered, or altered, that the carving can be difficult to make out. A good example stands outside the ethnographical museum at Sardarapat. They were sometimes reused. One at Garni has an 8th-century BC cuneiform inscription carved on it. Much later, crosses were added to some, as if to Christianise them. They were probably the forerunners of stelae, tetragonal columns on a cube-shaped base erected on a stepped stylobate, which functioned as memorials or gravestones. Stelae often have carvings depicting religious subjects such as the madonna and child, angels, saints, or biblical scenes eg: Old Testament stories of Abraham and Isaac, the three youths in the burning, fiery furnace and Daniel in the lions' den. There is a good array of stelae in Talin, near the small Mother of God Church. Vishaps may also have been the forerunners of the unusual funerary monuments at Aghdzk and Odzun. The latter is particularly interesting, not only for the wealth of carving on each side of the two obelisks but also etymologically. The name of Odzun probably derives from *odz*, the Armenian for 'snake', and legends relating to Ardvi, not far from Odzun, involve two snakes or dragons (see box, page 253). In Armenian mythology vishaps are dragons which live in the mountains, especially on Mount Ararat.

animals. They are generally rectangular and sometimes surprisingly large, reflecting just how important this trade was. Only a single, fairly small, door was provided so that the caravanserai would be easily defensible against robbers. Inside there were rows of stalls with feeding troughs for animals and booths for the merchants. Ordinary domestic architecture has not survived, apart from the low stone walls and foundations seen clustered around buildings such as castles and monasteries. Excavations have unearthed important palaces at Dvin, Aruch and Zvartnots. Their architecture parallels that of the church, with large halls divided into aisles by columns, and galleries along outside walls.

THE ARTS

Illuminated manuscripts If khachkars are the symbol of Armenia, the painting of illuminated manuscripts is undoubtedly Armenia's other great contribution to the art world. The beauty and skill represented in the many surviving examples are rarely equalled and seldom surpassed in other cultures. Extensive sets of pictures were used to illustrate manuscripts of the books of the Bible and obviously books such as Genesis or Exodus, where there is plenty of physical action, lent themselves particularly to this art form, with some manuscripts having up to 750 illustrations. The most elaborate manuscripts tended to be those of the four Gospels which were frequently bound with sumptuous covers of ivory or metalwork. A characteristic feature of these copies of the Gospels is the set of canon tables which were designed to show which passages of the individual Gospels were in agreement with any of the other three. They were arranged with columns of figures under decorative arches, often highly elaborated and usually accompanied by scenes or symbols of the evangelists. Before the Gospel itself there is a picture of the evangelist, again within an architectural structure and also with writing desk, lectern and writing implements.

The purpose of these books was to aid worship. They were made to be displayed on the altar as well as to be used by the priest reading to the congregation. A very few examples survive which predate the Arab conquest in 640. The subsequent repression of Christianity by the Muslims led to the suspension of artistic activity until after the end of Arab occupation in the 9th century. From then the art flourished. The importance of manuscripts to the Armenian Church is comparable to that afforded to icons by the Orthodox Church. The large number that has survived testifies to how valuable they were considered to be and how closely they were guarded in times of war. Manuscripts, particularly those believed to be endowed with miraculous powers, were given special names such as Saviour of All or Resurrector of the Dead. The manuscripts were also thought of as pledges for the salvation of the donors, as treasures in heaven, and they are therefore rarely anonymous productions. The names of the sponsor and the creators are carefully recorded so that they might be recalled by those who used the manuscripts. Given the importance of manuscripts and their beauty, it is unfortunate that the only place in Armenia where manuscripts can readily be seen is the Matenadaran ('Manuscript library') in Yerevan where a handful are on display in the five exhibition rooms. In 1997 the Mantenadaran Ancient Manuscript Collection was added to UNESCO's Memory of the World Register in recognition of its world significance.

Music Both traditional folk music and classical music have fallen on hard times since 1991 with the reductions in state funding. **Folk music** can now most often be heard on national holidays but a more convenient option is to go to one of the Yerevan restaurants where a folk ensemble plays each evening. The *oud* is a 12-stringed (two strings for each note) ancestor of the lute and guitar with a distinctive bent neck. The *tarr* is another lute-like instrument but smaller than the *oud*. The *kemenche* is a three-stringed violin played with the instrument held vertically resting on the lap. The *duduk* makes the sound most often associated with Armenian music. It is a low-pitched woodwind instrument, with a large double reed, made from apricot wood. The *shvi* ('whistle') by contrast is a high-pitched woodwind instrument without a reed and with eight holes, seven for playing and a thumb hole. The *dhol* is a cylindrical drum with one membrane being thicker to give a low pitch and the other thinner to give a higher pitch. Other distinctive instruments which may be encountered include the *zurna*, a higher-pitched wind instrument than the *duduk* but also with a double reed and made from apricot wood; the *kanun*, a plucked box zither, trapezoid in shape, which is played resting on the player's knee or on a table, the strings being plucked by plectra attached to the fingers; and the *dumbeg* which is an hourglass-shaped drum with a membrane made of lamb skin at only one end, the other end being open.

It was the Russian conquest in the 19th century which brought Western **classical music** to Armenia and the fusion of the folk-inspired Russian nationalistic composers such as Rimsky-Korsakov and Borodin with the existing Armenian traditional music was to result in distinctively Armenian style. Full of bright colours and rhythms it is vigorous rather than cerebral, music of the heart rather than the head. The best known Armenian composer outside the country is undoubtedly **Aram Khachaturian** (1903–78), though broadcasters frequently and incorrectly refer to him as Russian. In particular his violin and piano concerti are regularly encountered in concert and the ballets *Spartacus* and *Gayaneh* have often been staged outside Armenia. Most people would probably recognise the Sabre Dance from *Gayaneh*. Armenian **opera** has made little impact abroad but in recent years there have been American stagings of *Arshak II* by **Tigran Chukhadjian**, first heard (incomplete) in Italian at Constantinople in 1868, and *Anoush* by **Armen Tigranian** which was first performed at Alexandropol (present-day Gyumri) in 1912. To make these acceptable to Stalinist censors both had to have their plots changed during Soviet times: the alterations required to *Arshak II* in 1945 at the end of the Great Patriotic War included changing the character of Arshak from that of a tyrannical leader to that of a virtuous and unselfish one, and changing the composer's tragic ending into a hymn of rejoicing. Presumably this was in the hope that the audience would identify Stalin with the now virtuous, unselfish and victorious Arshak. *Arshak II* is considerably influenced by Verdi but *Anoush* aims at a fusion of classical Western music with distinctive Armenian melody and harmony. In Yerevan the **Armenian Philharmonic Orchestra** gives regular concerts and opera and ballet are staged in the Spendiarian Opera and Ballet Theatre except during the summer break.

Another distinctive Armenian form is that of **liturgical music**. It is sung without instrumental accompaniment and is based on a so-called Phrygian scale rather than the major and minor scales familiar in Western music. The number of surviving compositions is considerable: more than 1,000 from the Middle Ages survive on parchment and the range is diverse, sometimes quick and sprightly, sometimes solemn, sometimes dramatic. Only later did composers start to write polyphonically. The best known more recent composer is **Komitas** (1869–1935) who wrote many wonderful chants as well as other compositions in traditional Armenian style. To listen to this beautiful music in any of Armenia's churches on a Sunday morning is an experience which every visitor should seek out.

Dance Dance in Armenia can broadly be divided into traditional dance and classical ballet, the latter considerably influenced by the Russian school. The **traditional dances** which are encountered in Armenia today are those of eastern Armenia and as such differ in some respects from the dances of Armenian groups abroad which usually represent the western Armenian tradition. The energetic men's dance *Jo Jon* (also called *Zhora Bar*) comes from Spitak province. *Mom Bar*, meaning 'Candle Dance', was originally from the Lake Sevan region and is now traditionally the last dance at wedding parties. The candles are blown out at the end of the dance signalling that it is time for guests to leave. Women's solo dances called *Naz Bar*, meaning 'Grace Dance', are improvisatory with intricate hand gestures used to tell stories of love, betrayal, conflict and triumph. In Yerevan in particular choreographic schools and song and dance ensembles preserve the tradition in a form suitable for stage presentation, although funding is more difficult than in the Soviet era.

The musical accompaniment can be played on traditional instruments or sung (or both). **Costumes** for women are invariably sumptuous, whether based on medieval court dress or on simpler peasant dress. Brightly coloured shimmering dresses are decorated with gold embroidery and pearls. A light lace veil surmounts the embroidered hat. For men costume is simpler. Full trousers and embroidered tunics or else the *cherkessa*, traditional Caucasian dress similar to Cossack style, with red, white or black silk trousers, leather boots, woollen or fur hat, and a dagger in the belt. Men's dances are martial and vigorous; women's are graceful with elaborate gestures.

Funding is also more difficult for **classical ballet**, performed at the Spendiarian Opera and Ballet Theatre. The standard of dance remains high but numbers of

Armenian dancers are making successful careers in western Europe and North America and the pool of talent remaining in Yerevan has diminished.

Drama In ancient times **Greek drama** was popular in Armenia and several amphitheatres were built during the Hellenistic age including one at Tigranakert, the new capital which Tigran II built. When the Romans sacked the city in 69BC the actors were killed during the celebration games which followed. After the conversion of Armenia to Christianity in the 4th century, drama was suppressed by the Church and there is no record of any Armenian theatre until the 18th century when plays were put on by the Armenian community in Venice. The first recorded performance of a play in Armenia proper since the 4th century is often said to have been of **Alexander Griboyedov's** *Woe from Wit* in 1827 at the palace of the Yerevan Fortress, with members of the Imperial Russian Army as the cast. That seems highly unlikely as this scathing satire on corruption, ignorance and bribery in Tsarist society was banned during the author's lifetime and not staged until 1831.

The **first regular theatre** in Yerevan opened in 1865 and in that year **Gabriel Sundukian** (1825–1912) published *Khatabala* which may be said to represent the foundation of a realistic Armenian drama. Theatres were established in several Armenian communities both in Armenia and among the diaspora in cities such as Teheran and Tbilisi, but those in Ottoman-controlled areas were repressed after anti-Armenian action started in earnest in 1894. During the Soviet period drama blossomed with a healthy diet of Armenian and Russian works as well as Armenian translations of foreign classics, particularly Shakespeare, who translates very well into Armenian. Since 1991, as with all the arts, the curtailment of government subsidies has led to considerable retrenchment although several theatres survive at Yerevan and Gyumri.

Literature Written Armenian literature could clearly not develop until the creation of the alphabet by Mesrop Mashtots in the early 5th century and any early pagan oral tradition would almost certainly have been suppressed after the conversion to Christianity. Apart from the Bible, other theological works were soon translated from both Greek and Syriac after the creation of the alphabet. Some of Mesrop Mashtots's pupils also wrote original works: **Eznik** wrote a treatise on the origins of evil and the subject of free will called *Refutation of the Sects* while **Koriun** wrote a biography of Mashtots in about AD443. The *Epic Histories* were written in the 470s by an anonymous cleric and give an account of Armenian history between about 330 and 387 bringing together traditional stories about kings from Khosrov III to Arsaces II, as well as about patriarchs. The author sought to draw parallels between historic and contemporary events, and, when he wrote about a dying ruler urging his son to die bravely for their Christian country since by doing so he would be dying in the service of God and the Church, it was undoubtedly meant to apply to his readers.

This tradition of martial resistance and martyrdom was continued in the *History* written by **Lazarus of Parp** (or Ghazar Parpetsi as he is known in Armenia), abbot of the monastery of Vagharshapat (modern Ejmiatsin), which continues the story after 387, when the *Epic Histories* break off, as far as 485. In describing the events of 451, the author shows the Armenians finding the Persians unprepared at Avarayr and then holding off since they wanted martyrdom more than victory. He wrote that the face of one martyr was illuminated before his death as a sign of his imminent transformation into an angel. Widows of martyrs and women whose husbands were imprisoned by the enemy were considered to be living martyrs.

From the late 5th century onwards, **translations from the Greek** were made of secular works including the writings of philosophers such as Aristotle and Plato and of the medical writers Hippocrates and Galen. Meanwhile the writers of histories continued to stress martyrdom. In the *History* by **Yeghishe**, probably written in the late 6th century, the account of the revolt in 451 goes even further than had Lazarus of Parp in emphasising martyrdom and justifying armed resistance as well as giving the clergy a leading role. The Armenians are depicted as treating Persian promises of religious freedom as deceitful.

The period after the Arab conquest was a low point for Armenia generally and it was the 10th century before a literary revival took place. Competition between monasteries for endowments led to an interesting forgery. The *History of Taron* (Taron is the area north of Lake Van) was written sometime between 966 and 988 but claims to have been started in the 4th century by Zenob of Glak, the first Bishop of Taron, and then continued by John Mamikonyan, the 35th Bishop of Taron, in the 7th century. The book states that Glak was St Gregory the Illuminator's first foundation, earlier even than Ejmiatsin, while the truth was that Glak was a new foundation in the 10th century. The supposed history includes a completely bogus story of Glak's possession of miracle-working relics of John the Baptist which had produced divine intervention in war. The purpose of all this monastic skulduggery was twofold. First, it was an attempt to show that Glak, being Armenia's oldest monastery, was worthiest of endowment, more so even than Ejmiatsin and Dvin. Secondly, and even more explicitly, in the book some ascetics pray that anyone who makes generous gifts to the monastery from their 'sinful' wealth should be delivered from tribulation; they are answered by a voice from heaven which assents. Rather more prosaic is the description of the cutting off of enemy noses: 24,000 on one occasion.

The 10th century produced several rather more **reliable histories** while the *Book of Lamentations* by **Gregory of Narek** (c950–1010), a long poem comprising prayers about the wretchedness of the soul, the sinfulness of mankind and the certainty of salvation, remains a classic of Armenian literature. It is the earliest written work still to be widely read and was completed in 1002. Its author is usually considered to be Armenia's greatest poet and has been translated into 30 languages. Armenia's national epic, *David of Sassoun*, also dates from the 10th century although it was not committed to print until 1873. It recounts the story of David's family over four generations with Sassoun, its setting, symbolising Armenia. David in particular incarnated a symbol of the Armenians who fought foreign oppression in the 7th and 8th centuries.

Nerses Shnorhali ('Nerses the Gracious') (1100–73) was a great **lyrical poet**, musician, theologian and philosopher who became Katholikos Nerses IV in 1166. His greatest poem *Lament on the Fall of Edessa* (present-day Urfa in Turkey) records the capture of that city in 1144 by the Turks who slaughtered most of its inhabitants together with the archbishop. Nerses is also the author of several hymns still used in the Armenian communion service. By the late 13th century, poems on love and other secular themes began to appear and grow as an important force in Armenian literature. The greatest of these poets, **Constantine of Erznka**, wrote poetry of springtime, love, beauty and light, allegorically exalting the Christian mysteries. Constantine broadened the scope of Armenian poetry, moving away from religious terminology towards the imagery of the natural world. This was taken even further until in the 15th and 16th centuries pure love poetry came to Armenia. Its first great exponent was **Nahapet Kuchak**, who is thought to have lived near Lake Van in the 16th century but may have lived earlier and elsewhere. His poems have deep, often erotic, emotional passion, stunning imagery and wit, and are as vividly alive today as when they were written. **Sayat Nova** (1712–95) was perhaps the culmination of this tradition. Poet and composer in Georgian and Persian as well as Armenian, he wrote of courtly love and the beauty of his unattainable beloved.

The development of the **novel** throughout the Western world in the late 18th century inevitably impacted upon Armenia. The first great Armenian novelist was **Khachatur Abovian** (1805–48). He was the first author to abandon the classical Armenian language and use modern spoken Armenian for his works. His most famous novel is *Armenia's Wounds*, set during the Russian conquest of Armenia from Persia in 1826–28 and dealing with the Armenian people's suffering under foreign domination. Abovian was also a noted translator of Homer and Schiller. Further impetus to the quest for Armenian identity was given in the novels of the other great 19th-century Armenian novelist, **Raffi** (pen name of Hakop Melik-Hakopian) (1835–88). The grandeur of Armenia's historic past was recalled in novels such as *The Madman* (1881), *Samvel* (1886) and *The Spark* (1887).

The writings of **Hovhannes Tumanian** (1869–1923) encompass **fables and epic poetry**. An admirer of Shakespeare and translator of Byron, Goethe and Pushkin, it is regrettable that his work is not better known outside Armenia. He wrote patriotic verse with titles such as *In the Armenian Mountains*, *Armenian Grief* and *With My Fatherland* but also legends such as *A Drop of Honey* in which the eponymous drop is the cause of a war. The work, based on a medieval legend, concludes with the few terrified survivors asking themselves what caused the worldwide conflagration. Tumanian moralised without preaching, notably in works such as *My Friend Nesso*, a story about how the most handsome boy in the village turns into an evil, dishonest man and ends up dragging out a deprived life at the bottom of society. Similarly, *The Capture of Fort Temuk* traces the criminal path which leads from simple ambition to treason. Most Armenians consider that Tumanian's masterpiece is *Anoush*, a tragic story of village life in which Anoush's brother kills her lover for breaking a village taboo. The work is much more than a simple story, the author expressing his philosophy of life, his ideas about the existence of man and the world of human passions. His ardently expressed love for Armenia led to his being tried in 1908 for anti-Tsarist activities and he was later very active in seeking to help victims of the genocide.

Tumanian appears on the AMD5,000 banknote while the figure on the AMD1,000 note is the poet **Eghishe Charents** (1897–1937). Born in Van, then under Turkish rule, Charents was involved in anti-Turkish activity as part of the Armenian self-defence corps as early as 1912. His early work reflects this in pieces such as *Three Songs to a Pale Girl* (1914) and *Blue-Eyed Homeland* (1915). In 1915, he moved to Moscow to continue his education at the university thereby witnessing the Bolshevik Revolution and becoming greatly influenced by its ideology. In 1918, he joined the Red Army. Returning to Yerevan an enthusiastic supporter of communism in 1919, at this stage of his life his writings covered topics such as civil war in Russia and Armenia, world communism, famine, poverty, World War I and the Bolshevik Revolution. From the mid-1920s there is a gradual change in his work as he became disillusioned with communist rule and increasingly nationalistic. His satirical novel *Land of Nairi* (1925) starts to reflect this but his last published collection of poems, *Book of the Road*, published in 1933, was to make him notorious. One poem called 'The Message', ostensibly in fulsome praise of the genius of Stalin, contains a second message hidden in the second letter of each line: *Oh! Armenian people, your salvation lies only in your collective power*. Inevitably deemed nationalistic by the Soviet authorities he was arrested shortly afterwards

AVETIK ISAHAKIAN

The poet, writer and public activist Avetik Isahakian (1875–1957), whose image appears on the AMD10,000 note, was an establishment figure in Soviet days. Born in Alexandropol (Gyumri) he studied philosophy and anthropology in Leipzig. On his return in 1895 he joined the committee of the Armenian Revolutionary Federation which supported armed groups and sent financial aid to Western Armenia. After twice being arrested and imprisoned by the Tsarist authorities he left the Caucasus. Fearing that pan-Turkism was aimed at the extinction of the Armenians and believing that Germany, Turkey's ally, could prevent it he went to Berlin and participated in the German-Armenian movement. The massacres of the genocide confirmed his fears. In his social and political articles he wrote about the Armenian cause, putting forward genocide accusations. At the same time his poetry was coloured by images of the massacres. Between 1930 and 1936 he again lived abroad, acting as a friend of the Soviet Union. On his return to Armenia he continued to be involved with social matters and was elected to the Academy of Sciences and was president of the Writers' Union of the Armenian SSR. He was twice awarded the Order of Lenin. His poems are filled with sorrow and lament for humanity and are permeated with love for his homeland and the Armenian struggle for freedom. He is buried in Yerevan's Pantheon.

by the NKVD (forerunner of the KGB). He died in prison, an early victim among the tens of millions killed at Stalin's behest, although it was claimed by the Soviet authorities that he had committed suicide while on hunger strike. All his works were banned until his rehabilitation in 1954, the year after Stalin's death.

Later Armenian writers could inevitably have no personal experience of a pre-Soviet world or even of the genocide. **Hovhannes Shiraz,** born Hovhannes Karapetian (1915–84), however, came much closer than most since his mother was widowed by the genocide shortly before his birth. Growing up in considerable poverty, he attracted attention when his first work *Beginning of Spring* was published in 1935. He acquired the name Hovhannes Shiraz, by which he is better known, because one writer commented that his 'poems have the fragrance of roses, fresh and covered with dew, like the roses of Shiraz' (Shiraz is a town in Iran). His work includes parables and translations as well as a great deal of poetry and is immortalised for Armenians by such lines as: 'Let all nations reach the moon, but Armenians reach Ararat.' A critic of Armenia's corrupt Soviet government, his protests included publicly urinating one evening on the statue of Lenin in Yerevan.

Gevorg Emin was born in 1919, slightly later than Shiraz. Qualifying as a hydraulic engineer in 1940, his knowledge of the technological world of dams, pipelines and power stations is reflected in the concrete images and complex relationships between people and technology which he employs metaphorically. Subtle and witty, his work was translated into Russian by Boris Pasternak. A more establishment figure than Shiraz, his book *Land, Love, Era* was awarded the Soviet State Prize for Literature in 1976.

Paruyr Sevak (1924–71) was another staunch critic of the corrupt Soviet government to the extent that most Armenians believed that his death was murder at the hands of the KGB rather than the result of a road accident – and certainly the spot where the alleged accident took place is a straight unobstructed section of road with little traffic. The tenor of his writings is conveyed in titles such as *The*

Unsilenceable Belfry (1959) and *Let There be Light* (1971). He is considered one of the greatest Armenian poets of the 20th century.

Not all Armenian writers spoke Armenian as their native language. The novelist **Gosdan Zarian** (1885–1969) was the son of a staunchly Armenian father who was a general in the Tsarist army and he was brought up speaking Russian and French but not Armenian. His youth was spent in various Western countries where he frequently ate with Lenin in Geneva and knew Picasso in Paris. He started to learn Armenian only in 1910, studying with the Mekhitarists on the island of San Lazarro in Venice. He moved to Constantinople in 1913 and two years later was one of the few Armenian intellectuals who managed to escape the genocide, in his case by fleeing via Bulgaria to Rome. He returned to Istanbul in 1920 and in 1922 moved to Yerevan. Thoroughly disappointed with the Soviet regime, he left in 1925 and spent a nomadic existence including spells in the USA and Lebanon before returning to Armenia in 1961. His poem *The Bride of Tetrachoma*, first published in Boston in 1930, was republished in Yerevan in 1965 while a bowdlerised edition of his novel *The Ship on the Mountain*, first published in Boston in 1943, appeared in Yerevan in 1963.

Probably the best known Armenian writer outside Armenia is **William Saroyan** (1908–81). Born to Armenian parents at Fresno, California, he sprang to fame in 1934 with his first book *The Daring Young Man on the Flying Trapeze*. His first successful Broadway play *My Heart's in the Highlands* was first performed in 1939. He was awarded both the New York Drama Critics' Circle Award and the Pulitzer Prize for *The Time of Your Life* (1939) but he refused to accept the latter since he believed that 'Commerce should not patronise art.' A prolific writer, Saroyan acknowledged Armenian culture as an important source of his literary inspiration and his work gave international recognition to Armenia. A year after his death, half of his cremated remains were interred in the Pantheon of Greats in Yerevan, while the other half remained in Fresno.

Painting Russian expansionism into Armenia and subsequent greater contact with western European painting greatly influenced the development of Armenian realistic painting in the 19th century. The first notable painter to break away from the medieval manuscript tradition was **Hakop Hovnatanian** (1806–81) whose family had been painters for nearly 200 years. (His grandfather's grandfather had contributed to the decoration of Ejmiatsin Cathedral in the late 17th century.) He painted portraits of his contemporaries in an original manner which fused elements of the painting of illuminated manuscripts with European traditions of portraiture: everything in these portraits is expressed through the face, above all the eyes, and the hands of the conventionally posed sitter.

By contrast **Hovhannes Aivazovsky** (1817–1900), often referred to as Ivan Aivazovsky – its Russian equivalent – shows little Armenian influence. He was born to an Armenian father at Feodosia in the Crimea and painted wonderful seascapes, calm seas with beautiful lighting effects, violent storms sometimes with men struggling to survive (over half his seascapes) or surprisingly vivid pictures of the historic sea battles of the Russian navy. Though with few equals to his ability to capture the many moods and colours of the sea, his non-marine pictures are decidedly more pedestrian. His achievements were probably more recognised internationally than is the case with any other 19th-century Armenian painter and he was even awarded the Légion d'Honneur in 1857.

Another recipient of the Légion d'Honneur was **Zakar Zakarian** (1849–1923) who left his home in Constantinople to train as a doctor in Paris but later turned to painting. His still lifes with their careful composition and interplay of light and dark frequently incorporate a glass of water, interpreted by his contemporaries as expressing his feeling from his Paris home of the tragic events in his homeland. **Gevork Bashinjaghian** (1857–1920) developed the painting of landscapes with his calm, serene views, mostly of Armenia although he also travelled. **Vardghez Sureniants** (1860–1921) was a much more versatile artist. Like Bashinjaghian a painter of landscapes, he also painted many Armenian subjects and his 1895 painting *Desecrated Shrine* was a response to the massacres of the Armenians by the Turks. He additionally painted historical subjects; he was a gifted book illustrator and in 1899 was chosen to illustrate Pushkin's *Fountain of Bakhchisarai* as part of the centenary celebrations; and as a stage designer he was chosen by Konstantin Stanislavsky in 1904 to design his Moscow production of Maurice Maeterlinck's symbolist drama *Les Aveugles* (*The Blind*).

The landscapes of **Eghishe Tatevosian** (1870–1936) reflect the strong influence of French painters as well as of his teachers in Moscow, and the French influence is even stronger in the works of **Edgar Shaheen** (1874–1947) who studied in Paris. **Vano Khodjabekian** (1875–1922) was a complete contrast: a primitivist who on his arrival in Yerevan in 1919 created some moving scenes of the plight of the refugees who had escaped the Turkish massacres. **Hovsep Pooshman** (1877–1966) was another painter of still lifes, mostly incorporating oriental statuettes with titles such as *The Golden Decline of Life* and *The Murmur of Leaves*.

Probably the most brilliant and certainly the most influential Armenian artist of the early 20th century was **Martiros Sarian** (1880–1972) whose works mirror the creative intellectual ferment in the artistic world of the day and show an amazing feel for colour and form. He was born near Rostov-on-Don in Russia and studied in Moscow. His first visit to Armenia in 1901 resulted in the cycle *Stories and Dreams* which shows much symbolist influence. From 1909 he turned towards a more representational style using large areas of single colour with great attention to shapes and contrasts and the qualities of light. Another artist working through the revolutionary period was **Hakop Kojoyan** (1883–1959). He produced haunting landscapes as well as works which take a stylised medieval approach and book illustrations for authors such as Gorki. His *Execution of Communists at Tatev*, however, seems likely to have been painted for political reasons.

The Soviet period saw those Armenian painters who remained in the country and were approved by the regime supported, while others were harassed regardless of their talent. **Gyorgy Yakulov** (1884–1928) worked as a stage designer in Tiflis and Yerevan before being invited to Paris by Diaghilev where his work had immense success. He travelled in both China and Italy and his paintings reflect an attempt to combine traditional orientalism with the Italian high Renaissance. **Sedrak Arakelian** (1884–1942) was a follower of Sarian whose own lyrical landscapes successfully capture ephemeral moments in the Armenian countryside. Another follower, **Arutiun Galents** (1908–67), was one of the children who escaped the genocide of 1915. His parents both died and he was brought up in an orphanage in Beirut. Not surprisingly his work reflects the tragic circumstances of his childhood. **Minas Avetissian** (1928–75) is regarded particularly highly in Armenia. His work came to prominence in 1962 at the *Exhibition of Five* in Yerevan. Again a follower of Sarian, much of his work was destroyed either in a fire at his studio in 1972 (widely believed in Armenia to have been deliberately started by the Soviet security forces) or in the 1988 earthquake which destroyed his frescoes at Leninakan (present-day Gyumri) and the museum dedicated to his work at Jajur, his native village. He himself was tragically killed when he was knocked down by a car which had mounted the pavement. According to some sources this was the work of the KGB.

For a small country of only three million inhabitants Armenia has a remarkably high standing in the world of chess, being ranked fourth by the World Chess Federation (FIDE) behind Russia, Ukraine and China (September 2013). It has one of the highest per capita number of chess grandmasters. As of August 2013 FIDE listed 24 active (male) Armenian grandmasters, four women grandmasters, 17 international (male) masters and four women international masters. At the time of writing, Armenia's number one player, Levon Aronian, was ranked as world No. 2 by FIDE. He won the world cup in 2005 and was a World Champion candidate in 2007, 2012 and 2013. Five Armenians are in FIDE's top 100 players. At the international Chess Olympiads Armenia's men's team won the gold medal in 2006 and 2008 and the bronze in 1992, 2002 and 2004. Armenia was the World Team champion in 2011. The country has hosted many international competitions including the 32nd Chess Olympiad in 1996 and the 5th World Team Championship in 2001.

Chess has a long history in Armenia, being known since the 9th century and mentioned in manuscripts from the 12th and 13th centuries. It was popularised during the Soviet era and competitions started in 1927 with the founding of the Armenian Chess Federation. Its popularity increased with the successes of Tigran Petrosian who was World Champion from 1963 to 1969 and a member of the Soviet team which won the Chess Olympiad nine times between 1958 and 1974.

The Yerevan Chess House (*50 Khanjian St, Yerevan;* \10 554 923) was opened in 1970 and since 1984 has been named after Tigran Petrosian whose statue stands in front of the building. It is home to the Armenian Chess Federation (*www.chessfed.am*) whose current president is Serzh Sarkisian, President of the Republic of Armenia. The Chess House publishes a weekly magazine, in Armenian, whose name translates as *Chess in Armenia*. The magazine's website (*www.armchess.am*) has details of competitions and live coverage of games. The Federation's website also has live coverage. The Chess Academy of Armenia (*www.chessacademy.am*) was founded in 2002 under the auspices of the Armenian Chess Federation. Supported by the government, it organises chess tournaments and is the leading centre for chess training. In 2011 Armenia became the first country to make chess a mandatory part of the school curriculum for all seven to nine-year-olds, allocating funds to the Chess Academy to draw up courses, create textbooks and train instructors. Funds have also been allocated to equip chess classrooms in every school.

A complete contrast to these followers of Sarian is **Alexander Bazhbeuk-Melikian** (1891–1966) who can be regarded more as a follower of Degas. He painted women. In warm clear colours, whether exercising on a swing or combing their hair, they are elegant and at ease.

Ervand Kochar (1899–1979) was a sculptor and designer as much as a painter and his best known work in Armenia is perhaps the striking statue of David of Sassoun on horseback which stands outside Yerevan railway station, while the works most noticed by visitors may be the statue of Vardan Mamikonian, also on horseback, which stands on Yerevan's green belt at the southern end of Buzand Street; his *Melancholy* on Buzand Street itself, outside the Centre for Contemporary Experimental Art, opposite Vernissage; and the eagle which stands at the gates of

Background Information   CULTURE   1

Zvartnots Cathedral. The three-dimensional quality of his paintings tends to express his interest in sculpture and he created some amazing three-dimensional paintings, examples of which are in the Kochar Museum, Yerevan, and the Pompidou Centre, Paris. An immensely gifted artist, he had lived and worked in Paris from 1923 until 1936 but then, although highly successful there, he returned to Soviet Armenia. After his return he was accused of the Soviet crime of formalism and suffered periods of imprisonment. While in Paris in 1930 he married Melineh Ohanian, his second wife. (His first wife, Vardeni – whom Kochar married in Paris in 1925 – and their daughter died of TB in 1928.) Although Melineh was of Armenian descent, she had been born in France and the Soviet government would not allow her to enter the Soviet Union. Neither was Kochar ever allowed to leave, not even during the period of the Khrushchev thaw. In 1966 an exhibition was held in Paris of the works Kochar had produced in France. Melineh and a group of prominent Parisians petitioned the Soviet authorities to allow Kochar to travel to attend the exhibition but neither he nor the pieces of his post-Paris period were allowed to leave. Melineh committed suicide in 1969. Kochar married his third wife, Manik Mkrtchian, in 1945.

Petros Konturajian (1905–56) was another child who was orphaned by the genocide of 1915. He went to Paris and became a successful painter of the city under the influence of Cézanne and the Cubists. In 1947, he returned to Armenia but he failed to come to terms with Soviet conditions and committed suicide. **Hakop Hakopian** (1928–75) also moved to live in Armenia at a similar age to Konturajian but was able to adapt, perhaps because life under Brezhnev was less intolerable than under Stalin. His still lifes and landscapes have a dramatic quality expressing deep anxiety. **Girair Orakian** (1901–63) is another painter who was driven from his home city of Constantinople. He spent most of the rest of his life in Rome. His paintings expressing the struggles between life and death for the poor can again be understood against his childhood background.

If Ivan Aivazovsky is Armenia's best known 19th-century painter outside the country, the best known 20th-century one is probably **Garnik Zulumian**, also known as Carzou (1907–2000). He worked as a stage designer as well as a painter and engraver and his paintings do often reflect a decorative and theatrical quality. Claiming that Picasso was no painter at all, he alleged the only truly great painters were Claude Lorrain, Watteau and Dalí. Carzou's response to the Armenian earthquake of 1988 was the painting *Armenia: Earthquake. Hope*, in which a naked woman is shown standing over ruins against a background of Armenian buildings and mountains.

Foremost among artists born after the establishment of Soviet power is **Sergei Parajanov** (1924–90). Although better known as a film director, he also created a wide range of extraordinary works of art including collages and mosaics which were frequently made using everyday materials – perhaps he developed this technique during his involuntary periods in Siberian labour camps. Many of his works display strong egocentricity. Of the artists alive today, the one whose work visitors are most likely to notice is **Ara Shiraz** (b1941), as his 9m-high sculpture of Andranik Ozanian riding two horses is at the foot of the slope leading up to Yerevan Cathedral.

2

Practical Information

WHEN TO VISIT

Winter in Armenia can be bitterly cold and should be avoided by visitors if at all possible. Also, many of the sights outside the Arax Valley are inaccessible because of snow (however, there are those who relish the adventure and beauty of Armenia in the snow – see box, page 58). That apart, the timing of any visit has to be a compromise because of the altitudinal variation in the weather. The best times to go are generally late May and June or else **late September** and **October**. The former sees the flowers at their very considerable best and is the nesting season for birds. The latter is drier but of course there are few flowers and much of the country is parched and brown. As compensation, this does make the brilliant autumn colours of the trees even more striking. Particularly amazing are the apricot trees whose leaves turn bright yellow before becoming a wonderfully warm apricot colour. These periods of late spring and late summer are also when visibility is better with frequent views of Mount Ararat. It is usually invisible in **summer** because of heat haze.

HIGHLIGHTS

I am particularly fond of medieval buildings such as monasteries or fortresses in spectacular scenic settings and having a pleasant walk to get there adds to the enjoyment. Despite its accessibility by a good road and despite the number of tourists who go there, **Noravank** with its splendid setting and wonderful carvings is a must-see. **Khor Virap** is worthwhile if the visibility is good for giving the best views of Ararat. Other fine sites accessible by good roads are the monasteries of **Haghpat**, **Goshavank** and **Amberd** (together with its adjacent castle), **Selim caravanserai**, the field of khachkars at **Noratus** and the prehistoric stones at **Karahunj**. The UNESCO World Heritage List monastery of **Geghard** is another must-see. **Tatev** in its dramatic setting gives a good idea of the layout of monasteries and can now be reached by the world's longest cable-car ride.

However, my favourites are the wonderful **carvings at Makaravank**, the fortress of **Smbataberd** on its ridge (which makes a fine walk combining it with **Tsakhatskar Monastery**), **Spitakavor Monastery** (another fine walk), **Akhtala Monastery** (with its wonderful frescoes), **Kobayr Monastery** (short uphill walk), the petroglyphs on Mount Mets Ishkhanasar (4x4) and the monastery of **Harichavank** (together with the other small churches of the area). Some of Yerevan's museums and art galleries are also must-sees, especially the **State History Museum** and the **National Gallery** (both in the same building) and the **Matenadaran** for a glimpse of Armenia's wonderful illuminated manuscripts.

I thank Jehu Molina for sharing his delight in a Christmas trip to Armenia, together with some of his advice.

Most tourists will wish to avoid visiting Armenia in winter but for a few the adventure of travelling at this time of year appeals. Winter is bitterly cold but many places remain accessible despite the snow and ice. Apart from during snowstorms the major routes are largely kept open. Thermal clothing and an off-road vehicle (SUV or 4x4) with tyres in perfect condition are essential. The driver must know how to drive in snow and when to stop and turn back. Drive only during daylight and go well equipped for the conditions.
    The advantages of Armenia in winter include:

* Lower air fares and hotel prices
* You are alone (no crowds, no tourist buses) and have the monasteries, churches and museums to yourself
* Excellent light for photography; superb sunrises and sunsets
* The breathtaking beauty and silence of frozen trees, rivers and lakes

Jehu drove up to Selim caravanserai, down to Marmashen, over mountain passes to Goris and into Nagorno Karabagh. However, many places may not be accessible and minor routes are not cleared. The author has failed to reach the popular site of Amberd, because of snow, as late as May.

SUGGESTED ITINERARIES

A minimum of two or three days should be devoted to **Yerevan's museums** though check carefully the opening hours and days they are closed when planning your trip. Try to be in Yerevan at the weekend so as to get to **Vernissage market**. (An extra two or three days in Yerevan would allow visits to some of the worthwhile sites which can be reached as day trips from the capital.) In planning a trip round the rest of the country, there are three major factors to consider: whether or not to hire a car and, if so, whether to hire a 4x4; whether or not one wishes to do any walking; and whether some of the chosen places to visit will be inaccessible because of snow. The following would show a great deal of the country and could be tailored to suit individual requirements:

DAYS 1–3 Yerevan (or split time in Yerevan between start and end of tour).

DAY 4 Drive to Gyumri (pages 226–31) visiting Talin (page 175), Mastara (page 176) and Harichavank (page 237) *en route*. Visit Marmashen (pages 231–3) from Gyumri. Overnight Gyumri.

☞ **Note** that some of the places mentioned are not served by public transport or only by infrequent public transport. If using a mixture of public transport and taxis more time would be required.

DAY 5 Drive via Spitak (pages 244–5) and the Pushkin Pass tunnel (page 246) to Stepanavan (page 247). Visit Lori Berd (pages 247–8). Then drive via Kurtan (visit Hnevank, page 263) to the Dzoraget/Alaverdi area for overnight (pages 239 and 241–2).

DAY 6 Visit the monasteries of the Debed Gorge: Akhtala (pages 259–62), Haghpat (pages 257–9), Sanahin (pages 255–7) and Kobayr (pages 251–2). Overnight in the Dzoraget/Alaverdi area (pages 239 and 241–2).

DAY 7 Drive via Noyemberian (page 272) to Dilijan (pages 273–5) visiting Makaravank (pages 270–1) *en route* and also Haghartsin (pages 275–6). Visit Goshavank (pages 276–7). Alternatively, drive via Vanadzor (pages 243–4) visiting Goshavank and Haghartsin. Overnight in Dilijan or Ijevan (pages 265–7).

DAY 8 Visit Sevanavank (pages 203–4), the field of khachkars at Noratus (page 205) and Selim caravanserai (pages 290–1) before descending into Vayots Dzor (page 279). Overnight in Vayots Dzor (pages 281–2).

DAY 9 Walk to Tsakhatskar (pages 287–8) and Smbataberd (pages 288–9). Overnight in Vayots Dzor.

DAY 10 Walk to Spitakavor (pages 292–3). Overnight in Vayots Dzor.

DAYS 9 AND 10 If not wishing to walk visit Yeghegis (pages 289–90), Tanahat Monastery (pages 293–4) and Jermuk (pages 297–8).

DAY 11 Visit Tatev (pages 307–10). Then return to Sisian for overnight (page 302).

DAY 12 Visit Karahunj (pages 303–5). Then drive via Gndevank (page 296) to Vayots Dzor for overnight.

DAY 13 Drive via Noravank (pages 284–6) and Khor Virap (page 180) to Yerevan for overnight.

DAY 14 Visit Garni Temple (pages 218–19) and Geghard (pages 219–22). Visit Ejmiatsin (pages 188–93). Overnight in Yerevan.

NAGORNO KARABAGH If you want to visit the self-declared Republic of Nagorno Karabagh then on the eleventh day, after visiting Tatev, continue to Stepanakert (see pages 328–9). Registering with the Nagorno Karabagh Foreign Ministry, either in Yerevan or Stepanakert (see pages 327–8) is essential before visiting other parts of the territory. Gandzasar and Dadivank (see pages 337 and 338 respectively) can be combined in a single day and the opportunity should be taken to visit Shushi (see pages 340–2). If there is time, Khndzoresk (see pages 312–13) is not far off the Goris to Stepanakert road.

THE EXTREME SOUTH Anyone wishing to travel to the extreme south of the country could do so on the twelfth day after visiting Karahunj. Travel via Goris (see pages 310–11), stay overnight in either Kapan (pages 313–14) or Kajaran (page 317) and visit Meghri (pages 317–19) for the day, or stay overnight in Meghri, possibly driving there on the older road via Kajaran and back on the newer one through the Shikahogh Reserve (see page 299).

TOURIST INFORMATION

Sadly, the once excellent Armenian Tourism Development Agency no longer exists. The old website (*www.armeniainfo.am*) can still be accessed. Although it is not kept up to date it is still a source of useful information.

The best **internet source** of information is www.armeniapedia.org which is reasonably comprehensive on sites (including those in Nagorno Karabagh) but patchy on practical information. There is practical information on www.tacentral. com (including useful guides to the State History Museum in Yerevan and to Metsamor) but some of the country is not covered and it is out of date in places. The Armenian Monuments Awareness Project (AMAP) (*www.armenianmonuments. org*; see page 104) is behind the information boards now appearing at many sites in Armenia. The developing website has some useful information, including a guide to Noratus. For more websites see pages 358–9.

The most useful **maps** of the country are published in Yerevan by Collage Ltd (*4 Sarian St, Yerevan;* ✆ +374 10 *520217; e collage@arminco.com; www.collage.am*). The pocket atlas *The Roads of Armenia*, costing AMD2,500, covers the country together with Nagorno Karabagh at a scale of 1:300,000. It has small street plans of Yerevan, Gyumri and Vanadzor. Roads, rivers, railways, mountain summits and historical sites are shown, and names are given in both Armenian and English. The atlas does not appear to be available outside Armenia.

Collage Ltd also publishes *Armenia & Mountainous Karabakh*, at a scale of 1:400,000 costing AMD2,500. Place names on the most recent edition are in both English and Armenian. There is also a version in English and Russian. Both the above maps show distances between towns and road numbers. Collage Ltd also publishes the best map of *Yerevan* (AMD2,500), greater Yerevan at a scale of 1:17,000 and the city centre at 1:7,000. Unlike the road atlas, the other two maps are available from Stanfords (*12 Long Acre, London WC2E 9LP, UK;* ✆ *020 7836 1321; e sales@stanfords.co.uk; www.stanfords.co.uk*) but at several times what they cost in Yerevan. Collage Ltd also produces a *Yerevan Guide Map* (AMD1,500) to a slightly smaller scale (greater Yerevan 1:20,000, city centre 1:8,000) than its main Yerevan map but this smaller one usefully includes building numbers (see box, page 87). There are occasional minor inaccuracies on the Collage maps; where relevant to descriptions in this guidebook these are noted.

TOUR OPERATORS

INTERNATIONAL OPERATORS
The following tour operators can make arrangements to travel to Armenia or else operate group tours themselves.

UK
Birdquest Two Jays, Kemple End, Clitheroe, Lancs BB7 9QY; ✆ 01254 826317; e birders@ birquest.co.uk; www.birdquest-tours.com. Specialists for serious, in-depth birdwatching. Sometimes includes Armenia in regional tours.
Birdwatching Breaks Cygnus Hse, Gordons Mill, Balblair, Ross-shire IV7 8LQ; ✆ 01381 610495; e enquiries@birdwatchingbreaks.com; www. birdwatchingbreaks.com. A serious birdwatching company which sometimes includes Armenia.
Explore Worldwide Nelson Hse, 55 Victoria Rd, Farnborough, Hants GU14 7PA; ✆ 0845 291 4541; e res@explore.co.uk; www.explore.co.uk.

Offers a Land of the Golden Fleece trip (the fleece was kept at Colchis, near present-day Batumi on the Black Sea coast of Georgia). The 16-day trip spends 5 nights in Armenia & a 4-day Azerbaijan extension is available.
Kudu Travel 3 Midland Close, Bradford on Avon, Wiltshire BA15 1DB; ✆ 01225 436115; e kuduinfo@kudutravel.com; www.kudutravel. com. Offers a 13-day tour which includes some walking.
Martin Randall Travel Voysey Hse, Barley Mow Passage, London W4 4GF; ✆ 020 8742 3355; e info@ martinrandall.co.uk; www.martinrandall.com. Specialises in high-brow cultural holidays. Offers an 8-day historical group tour, with lecturer.
Naturetrek Cheriton Mill, Hamps SO24 0NG; ✆ 01962 733051; e info@naturetrek.co.uk; www.naturetrek.co.uk. Offers a 9-day tour in spring concentrating on birds & flowers. In 2014,

As indicated on page 62, Armenia has huge potential for hiking. Apart from private property (where there may be fierce guard dogs) and the State Reserves of Khosrov and (parts of) Shikahogh, where an accompanying guide is obligatory, one is free to wander almost everywhere. However, there are no detailed maps, equivalent to the British Ordnance Survey maps, showing footpaths. There are a few marked trails but finding out about these in advance of happening to come across them has eluded me and often the detail given is inadequate for those who do not already know the route. It is usually easy to find a local person who will show you the way to a local site but long distances will obviously require advance notice.

Detailed information on long-distance hikes is beyond the scope of this guidebook and author but I have enjoyed many walks in Armenia (some of them fairly long and strenuous!) and I have tried throughout the book to indicate pleasant walks. Many minor roads and tracks are eminently suitable for walking, with the advantage that getting lost is unlikely. If intending to go cross-country the same precautions and equipment are needed as anywhere else. Remember, Armenia is a high country and hills which are no problem at home can feel surprisingly difficult. It is also sunny; sunburn can easily occur. When the sun goes in it can suddenly become very cold.

operated their first butterfly tour for the Butterfly Conservation organisation. Aims to donate 10% of the proceeds of the tour to be invested in the conservation of British & European butterflies.

Regent Holidays 6th Floor, Colston Tower, Colston St, Bristol BS1 4XE; 020 7666 1244; e regent@regent-holidays.co.uk; www.regent-holidays.co.uk. Can organise any itinerary in Armenia & Nagorno Karabagh (combined with Georgia & Azerbaijan if required) for individuals or groups. They also offer group tours to Armenia & Georgia & short city-break tours to Yerevan. The author has had personal experience of this firm's efficiency, flexibility & helpfulness over many years.

Silk Road Tours 8 Oak Cottages, Green Lane, London W7 2PE; 020 728 2478; e info@silkroadtours.co.uk; www.silkroadtours.co.uk. Offers a 9-day tour to Armenia; 14-day tour to Armenia & Georgia; 14-day tour to Armenia, Georgia & Azerbaijan. See ad, page 106.

The Traveller 51 Castle St, Cirencester, Glos GL7 1QD; 01285 880931; e info@the-traveller.co.uk; www.the-traveller.co.uk. Offers tailor-made itineraries & a 14-day group tour to Armenia & Georgia.

Undiscovered Destinations Ltd PO Box 746, North Tyneside NE29 1EG; 0191 296 2674; e travel@undiscovered-destinations.com; www.

undiscovered-destinations.com. Offers 13-day group tours to Armenia & Georgia. Also tailor-made tours.

Wild Frontiers Adventure Travel Ltd Unit 6, Hurlingham Business Park, 55 Sulivan Rd, London SW6 3DU; 020 7736 3968; e info@wildfrontierstravel.com; www.wildfrontierstravel.com. Can organise any itinerary for individuals but also offers a 9-day tour to Armenia inc 2 nights in Nagorno Karabagh.

USA

In the USA, 2 companies which offer arrangements to Armenia are based in Glendale, California, & another in Pennsylvania. Each also has an office in Yerevan.

Levon Travel 408 East Broadway, Glendale, CA 91205; +1 818 552 7700, +1 800 445 3866; e sales@levontravel.com; wwwlevontravel.com. Also an office at 10 Sayat Nova Bd, Yerevan; +374 10 525210, 525284; e sales@levontravel.am; www.levontravel.am.

Sidon Travel 428 S Central Av, Glendale, CA 91204; +1 818 553 0777, +1 800 826 7960; e info@sidontravel.com; www.sidontravel.com. Yerevan office 14 Sayat Nova Av; +374 10 522967; e yerevan@sidontravel.com.

Practical Information TOUR OPERATORS

2

Sima Tours 2064 Sproul Rd, Broomall, PA 19008; ✆+1 610 359 7521; m +1 610 304 5948; e info@simatours.com; www.simatours.com. It also has an office at 50 Terian St, Yerevan; ✆+374 10 589954, 548715.

Austria

Biblische Reisen Stifsplatz 8, 3400 Klosterneuburg; ✆+43 2243 353 770; e info@biblische-reisen. at; www.biblische-reisen.at. Runs group tours concentrating on churches & monasteries.

Georgia

Georgica Travel 22 Shanidze St, Tbilisi; ✆+995 32 25 21 99; e georgica@caucasus.net; www. georgicatravel.ge. Arranges Caucasus combination tours to Armenia, Georgia & Azerbaijan.

Germany

Biblische Reisen Silberburgstrasse 121, D-70176, Stuttgart; ✆+49 7116 19250; e info@

biblische-reisen.de, info@biblical-tours.com; www.biblische-reisen.de, www.biblical-tours. com. Runs group tours concentrating on churches & monasteries.

Ventus Reisen Krefelder Strasse 8, D-10155 Berlin; ✆+49 3039 100 332/3; e office@ventus. com; www.ventus.com. Group tours & individual arrangements.

Israel

Breeza Tours 27 Lishanski St, Rishon Letzion; ✆+972 3 9625020; e info@breeza.co.il; www. breeza-tours.co.il. Group & individual tours.
Eco-Field Trips 11 Nes Ziona St, Tel-Aviv; ✆+972 3 5100454; e mail@eco.co.il; www.eco.co.il. Group & individual arrangements.

Italy

Metamondo Via Ca' Rosso 21a, 30174 Mestre (VE); ✆+39 41 8899 211; e info@metamondo.it; www.metamondo.it. Group tours.

SPECIAL-INTEREST VISITS

Armenia lends itself to special-interest visits and several agents offer hiking, trekking, camping, winter sports, archaeological and other special-interest tours. See pages 63–4.

A good website for information on **activity holidays** is the section on ecotours on www.tacentral.am.

Anyone interested in **birdwatching** should contact the Ornithological Society of the Middle East, Caucasus and Central Asia (see page 7) and visit www. armeniabirding.info. See page 60 for two specialist birdwatching British companies which sometimes include Armenia in regional tours.

The diversity of accessible vegetation zones means that **botanical tours** are very rewarding. These can be arranged either via the Botanical Institute in Yerevan (✆+374 10 568690) or the Yerevan tour operator Armenia Travel + M (see page 63 and ad, 2nd colour section). Tours to **watch mammals** such as wolves and bears do not exist but local arrangements may be possible through local agents (pages 63–4).

Horseriding holidays are also available at a number of locations such as the southern slopes of Mount Aragats and near Ijevan. See page 125 for details of a Yerevan riding school and pages 272–3 for information about the riding school near Ijevan, Tavush province. Hire of horses can be arranged when visiting Khosrov and Shikahogh state reserves (see pages 181 and 316).

Most of the country away from the Ararat Valley has huge **hiking** potential and visitors are free to wander almost wherever they like, the only problems being the complete absence of detailed maps and the difficulty of avoiding hospitality at every cottage. *Adventure Armenia* (see page 357) describes 22 day-hikes. A number of signboards indicating trails have appeared at some sites, for example at Haghartsin Monastery, at Jukhtakvank and a 19km trail from Verishen to Shativank in Vayots Dzor, but it is difficult to get information

Netherlands

Koning Aap Reizen Entrada 223, 1096 EG Amsterdam; ✆ +371 20 788 7700; e info@ koningaap.nl; www.koningaap.nl. Offers 8-day tour to Armenia & 23-day tour to Armenia (10 days) & Georgia.

LOCAL OPERATORS

All tour operators in Armenia are based in Yerevan. (Some hotels in the provinces can organise local excursions; noted under individual entries.) Apart from the American agents mentioned on pages 61–2, there are around 130 more travel agents in Yerevan. Visitors who do not speak Armenian are strongly recommended to deal with those who have experience in making ground arrangements for tour operators from the UK since they will have staff who speak reasonable English. Tour operators dealing mainly with the diaspora may not speak as good English since the members of the diaspora usually speak Armenian. Tour operators can arrange all types of accommodation, guides & interpreters, car hire with or without driver, special-interest & general tours. They can also help with theatre tickets & virtually anything else a visitor may want. Armenians are very flexible & most things are possible.

Armenia Travel + M 4 Vardanants St; ✆ +374 10 563667, 545330; e incoming@armeniatravel. am; www.armeniatravel.am. Can organise almost anything for groups & individuals. The author has had personal experience of this company's efficiency & flexibility over many years.
Hyur Service 50 & 96 Nalbandian St; ✆ +374 10 546040, 546080; e contact@hyurservice.com; www.hyurservice.com. Offers a wide range of services, such as apartments & tours.
Saberatours-Sevan 32–38 Hanrapetutyan St (at Europe Hotel); ✆ +374 10 525555; e incoming@saberatours.am; www.saberatours. am. Offers tours, car hire, apartments etc in Armenia but is also a specialist in travel to &

about these beforehand. **Mountain climbing and hiking** can apparently be arranged through Ajdahag Mountain Hiking Club (contact details given but website not helpful: e *ajdahag@yahoo.com; www.ajdahag.narod.ru*). Armenia has superb **caving** with more than 10,000 caves in most regions of the country often concentrated along the river gorges. Most of the caves are little known although there is an active Armenian Speleological Society (✆ *+374 10 582254, 10 620248*). The proprietor of the Vayots Dzor Tourism Centre and Hotel at Vayk leads caving expeditions. Reportedly some of the best caving, though only for the experienced, is in Vayots Dzor province. Magili Cavern is in the gorge which leads to Noravank and is 1.7km deep. Stone tools and artefacts have been discovered in the cave, as well as more recent ceramic fragments from the 9th century onwards. The cave is home to thousands of insectivorous bats. The passageway is horizontal and varies from just enough for a person to crawl through to a spacious 10–15m in width. Because of damage in recent years this cave is no longer as freely open to visitors as it once was. Other caves are strictly for the expert. At 3.3km, Archeri ('Bear') cave near Yeghegnadzor is Armenia's longest with some of the most spectacular stalactites and stalagmite formations in Europe. Unlike Magili it is far from horizontal with a vertical range of 145m. The cave gets its name from the remains of bears found here. Mozrovi, about 7.6km west of Arpi, has fine speleothems (mineral deposits of calcium carbonate precipitated from solution).

Winter sports are available at Tsaghkadzor (see pages 215–16) and Jermuk (see pages 297–8). Cross-country skiing can be arranged via Berlin Art Hotel, Gyumri. (Byurakan Astrophysical Observatory (see pages 169–70) offers events for amateur **astronomers** (m *091 195903*; e *director@bao.sci.am, observ@bao.sci.am; www.bao. am*). Visits can be arranged by local tour operators.

from Iran, being the sales agent for Iran Aseman Airlines, the Iranian company which flies between Tehran & Yerevan. It can also arrange land transportation to & from Iran & Iranian visas.

Special interest operators

AdvenTour 125a Arshakuniats Av; ☎+374 10 539609, 482271; m 091 426745; e adventour@ netsys.am, info@dubbed-adventurer.com; www. dubbed-adventurer.com

Armenia Holidays (Elitar Ltd) 7 Abovian St; ☎+374 10 582292 (+374 10 543311); e info@ armeniaholidays.com (info@tourism.am); www. armeniaholidays.com (www.tourism.am). Offers a wide range of tours including camping, hiking/ trekking, cycling, 4x4 tours.

Armenia Travel Bureau 24b Baghramian Av; ☎+374 10 563321; m 093 885642, 077 563321; e info@atb.am; www.atb.am. Offers a wide range of tours including biking, eco-tours, wine, spa, archaeological, faith-based & even casino tours!

Avarayr 1 Buzand St; ☎+374 10 563681,

524042; e avarayr@arminco.com; www.avarayr. am. A long-established company offering camping, hiking/trekking tours as well as cultural visits.

Exotic Armenia Tours Apt 63, 10/1 Shinararneri St; ☎+374 60 448712; m 094 448712/5; email: info@exoticarmeniatours.com; www. exoticarmeniatours.com. Offers both hiking & winter tours.

Jeep Tour Armenia Apt 16, 54a Tigran Mets St; m +374 77 131504, +374 99 131504; e jeeptourarmenia@gmail.com; www. jeeptourarmenia.com. A new enterprise offering 1-day, 7-day & tailor-made jeep tours to off-the-beaten track Armenia & Nagorno Karabagh. Offers cultural-historical, trekking & off-road tours. Future plans include caving, camping, extreme sports, fishing & even diving in Lake Sevan.

Seven Springs Tour 45/15 Komitas St, Yerevan; ☎+374 10 232440; m +374 94 912008; e info@7springstour.am, incoming@7springstour. am; www.7springstour.am. Offers hiking, birdwatching & botanical tours.

RED TAPE

Since 10 January 2013 citizens of EU member states and the Schengen Agreement member states are entitled to enter and stay in Armenia for up to 180 days per year without a visa. Foreigners must have a valid passport. Passport holders of Argentina, Azerbaijan, Belarus, Georgia, Kazakhstan, Kyrgyzstan, Moldova, Russian Federation, Tajikistan, Ukraine and Uzbekistan also do not require a visa. Holders of all other passports require a visa. Tourist visas are easy to obtain and there are three ways of so doing. The easiest and now the most common way is **on arrival in Armenia**. At Zvartnots Airport, where most visitors arrive, it is straightforward and quick. Single-entry tourist visas are available for 21 or 120 days. The fee must be paid in Armenian drams (AMD3,000 for a 21-day visa, AMD15,000 for a 120-day visa). It is easy to change money in the airport, but a considerable commission is charged, so only change the minimum required and get a better deal later at one of the many bureaux de change in the city centre. When coming down into the arrivals hall the exchange kiosk is straight ahead. To the left is an area where visa application forms can be completed. The visa issuing desks, usually well staffed, are opposite the form-filling area. Visas can also be obtained at the following border checkpoints with Georgia: Ayrum railway station, Bavra, Bagratashen and Gogavan crossings and at the Agarak land border with Iran near Meghri. The procedure here may be slower, especially for those last off the bus. Border crossing points can only issue single-entry visas (3-day transit, 21-day or 120-day tourist visas).

The second method is to apply for a conventional visa through an **Armenian embassy**. The application form for a conventional visa can be downloaded from the Armenian Foreign Ministry website (*www.mfa.am*) and applications should be made to the appropriate embassy. Residents of the USA can also apply to the Consulate General in Los Angeles where payment must be by money order. Visas are normally issued in two to three working days. Since 1 January 2010 the fees for a conventional visa are the same as for those obtained on arrival (see opposite). Visas for children under 18 are issued free of charge. Multiple-entry visas are only available through an embassy.

A third way of obtaining a tourist visa is to obtain **an electronic visa** over the internet. Simply go to the web page of the Armenia Foreign Ministry (see page 359), complete the application page and pay the fee by credit card. (The electronic-visa site www.evisa.mfa.am has useful information.) The visa is normally issued within two working days and confirmation that it has been issued is sent electronically. It can then be collected on arrival. A valid e-visa allows entry through Zvartnots Airport, Shirak Airport in Gyumri and the same land border crossing points as opposite. E-visas are currently US$15 for a 21-day visa and US$60 for 120-days (so more expensive than obtaining either a visa on arrival or a conventional visa through an embassy). It has the advantage that no paper is inserted into one's passport, a consideration if you intend to visit Azerbaijan in the future. Payment must be by credit card.

For any type of visa other than a tourist visa an invitation is required. In the case of **business trips** it must be certified by the Consular Department of the Ministry of Foreign Affairs or for private trips by the Passport and Visa Department of the Ministry of Internal Affairs. Multiple-entry visitor visas are available and transit visas are required for stops in Armenia *en route* to other countries. (For full details see the website of the appropriate Armenian embassy below.)

Tourist visas can be extended at the Passport and Visa Department of Police of Republic of Armenia in Yerevan (*13A Mashtots Av;* +374 10 530182) for AMD500 per extra day. Failure to extend on time now carries a fine of AMD50,000–100,000 and prohibition of return to Armenia for one year. Previously, due to the inconvenience of the several visits needed to extend a visa, the advice given was to pay, on departure, the US$3 (approx AMD1,000) per day fine for overstaying, now a much less financially attractive option.

ARMENIAN EMBASSIES ABROAD

E Argentina J A, Pacheco de Melo 1922, C1126AAD Buenos Aires 1035; +54 114 816 8710; e armargentineembassy@mfa.am

E Austria 28 Hadikgasse, 1140 Vienna; +43 1 5227479; e office@armembassy.at; www.austri.mfa.am

E Bahrain Embassies District (al-Safarat), 24 Al Karamah St, Zone 2, PO Box Number 6358; +9712 4444196; e armemiratesembassy@mfa.am

E Belarus 50 Bumazhkov St, 220037 Minsk; +375 17 2979257; e armbelarusembassy@mfa. am; www.belarus.mfa.am

E Belgium Rue Montoyer 28, 1000, Brussels; +32 2 348 4400/2; e armbelgiumembassy@ mfa.am; www.belgium.mfa.am

E Brazil SHIS QL 28, Conjunto 3, Casa 4, CEP: 71665-235; e armbrazilembassy@mfa.am; www. brazil.mfa.am

E Bulgaria 3 Zagorichane S, 1111 Sofia; +359 2 9461272; e armembsof@omega.bg; www.bulgaria.mfa.am

E Canada 7 Delaware Av, Ottawa, Ontario K2P 0Z2; +1 613 234 3710; e armcanadaembassy@ mfa.am; www.canada.mfa.am

E China 9 Tayuan Nanxiaojie, Chaoyang District, Beijing, 100600; +86 10 653 25677; e armchinaembassy@mfa.am; www.china.mfa.am

E Czech Republic Na Piskách 1411/95, 160 00 Prague 6, Dejvice; +420 220 518 175; e armembassy.cz@mfa.am; www.cz.mfa.am

E Denmark Ruvangs Alle 50, 2900 Hellerup, Copenhagen; +45 35822900; e armembdk@ mfa.am; www.denmark.mfa.am

E Egypt 20 Mohamed Mozhar St, Zamalek, 11211 Cairo; +202 27374157/59; e armegyptembassy@mfa.am; www.egypt.mfa.am

E France 9 Rue Viète, 75017 Paris; +33 1 42 12 98 00; e ambarmen@wanadoo.fr; www.france. mfa.am

E Georgia 4 Tetelashvili St, Tbilisi; +995 32 2951723; e armgeorgiaembassy@mfa.am; www. georgia.mfa.am

Germany 4 Nussbaumallee, 14050 Berlin; +49 30 405 0910; e armgermanyembassy@ mfa.am; www.germany.mfa.am

Greece 95 Konstantinou Paleologou Av, Khalandri 15232, Athens; +30 210 683 1130; e embassy.athens@mfa.am; www.greece.mfa. am

India Armenia St, D-133 Anand Niketan, New Delhi 110021; +9111 24112851/52; e armindiaembassy@mfa.am

Iran 1 Ostad Shahriar Street Corner of Razi, Jomhouri Eslami, Teheran; +98 21 66704833; e armiranembassy@mfa.am

Iraq House 5, Street 11, Sect.215, International Zone, Baghdad; +964 78 08306424; e armiraqembassy@mfa.am; www. iraq.mfa.am

Italy Via XX Settembre, 98/E-00187 Rome; +39 06 329 6638; e info@ambasciatarmena.it; www.italy.mfa.am

Japan #230 Residence Viscountess 11-36 Akasaka, 1-chome, Minato-ku, Tokyo; +81 362 777453; e armembjapan@mfa.am; www.japan. mfa.am

Kazakhstan 19 Kiz Zhibek St, Komsomolski Microdistrict Astana, Kazakhstan; +7 7172 402015; e armkazakhstanembassy@mfa.am; www.kazakhstan.mfa.am

Kuwait Jabriya, Block 8, Street 3, House 8, Al Kuwait; +965 25322175; e embassy.kuwait@ mfa.am; www.kuwait.mfa.am

Lebanon 28 Rue des Jasmins, Mtaileb, Beirut; +961 4 418860; e armlebanonembassy@mfa.am; www.lebanon. mfa.am

Lithuania Lenktoji g.17, 08124 Vilnius; (370-5) 2075040; e armlithuaniaembassy@ mfa.am; www.lithuania.mfa.am

Netherlands Lan Van Meerdervoort 90, 2517 AP, The Hague; +31 703106436; e armembnl@ mfa.am; www.netherlands.mfa.am

Poland 50 Bekasow St, 02-803 Warsaw;

+48 22 8990940; e armpolandembassy@mfa. am; www.poland.mfa.am

Romania 27 Intrarea Poiana St, Sector 1, 014136, Bucharest; +40 21 2332452; e armromaniaembassy@mfa.am; www.romania. mfa.am

Russia 2 Armianskiy Pereulik, Moscow 101000; +7 495 6241269; e incom@armem.ru; www.russia.mfa.am

Spain Calle Mayor 81, 28013 Madrid; +34 915 422627; e embajada@armenia.e.telefonica. net; www.spain.mfa.am

Switzerland 28 Av du Mail, 1205 Geneva; +41 22 320 1100; e mission.armenia@bluewin. ch; www.switzerland.mfa.am

Syria 2 Saad Ben Abi Uakksi, Building 2, West Mezze, Damascus; +963 11 613 3617; e armsyriaembassy@mfa.am

Turkmenistan 53 Gorki St, 744001 Ashgabad; +993 12 971418; e armturkmenembassy@mfa.am; www. turkmenistan.mfa.am

Ukraine 45 Volodimirska St, Kiev 01901; +38044 234 9005, 235 1004; e armukraineembassy@mfa.am; www.ukraine. mfa.am

United Arab Emirates Al Karamah 24 Str., Zone 2, Embassies Area, Abu Dhabi; +971 2 4444196; e armemiratesembassy@mfa.am; www. uae.mfa.am

UK 25A Cheniston Gdns, London W8 6TG; +44 207 938 5435; e armukembassy@mfa.am; www.uk.mfa.am

USA 2225 R St, NW Washington, DC 20008; +1 202 319 1976; e contact@armembassy.org; www.usa.mfa.am. Consular Section: +1 202 319 2983; e consul@armembassy.org. Consulate General also at 364 North Central Av, Glendale, CA 91203; +1 818 265 5900; e info@armeniaconsulatela.org; www. armeniaconsulatela.org

For a list of embassies and consulates in Armenia, see pages 126–7.

For a list of embassies and consulates in Armenia, see pages 126–7.

GETTING THERE AND AWAY

BY AIR Yerevan has two airports, at **Zvartnots** 10km west of the city and **Erebuni** (now used only by the military) closer to the centre on the south side. A new terminal has brought Zvartnots fully up to international standards with signage in English as well as Armenian. Trolleys are available; rates are AMD500 for a trolley or AMD2,500 for a trolley and a porter who will carry up to three items of baggage. Additional items of baggage are extra. Porters can be recognised by their distinctive red tops with 'CART SERVICE' written in English on the back. **Note** that on leaving the airport the tag on your luggage will be checked against that on your ticket or boarding pass, so do not discard it. There is a duty-free area in arrivals after passport control and a small tourist information desk (not always staffed in the middle of the night) just before leaving arrivals.

The departure hall has a well-stocked **duty-free** area where there are typical Armenian specialities such as crafts, dried-fruit sweetmeats, coffee and herbal teas as well as the usual alcohol (including brandy which is cheaper than in central Yerevan), perfume, clothes, luggage, etc. There is a small range of books mostly in Armenian.

Airlines flying to Yeravan
Armenia's carrier, Armavia Airlines, filed for bankruptcy and stopped operating in April 2013, having failed to cope with the 2008 world economic crisis. In October 2013 **Air Armenia**, established in 2003 as a cargo air company, started passenger flights to destinations in Russia. At the time of writing it was operating from Yerevan to Krasnodar, Moscow, Nizhny Novgorod, Rostov-on-Don, St Petersburg, Samara and Sochi.

The following European airlines fly to Yeravan, but please note: as airlines change schedules frequently, the listings are intended only as an indication of the situation at the time of writing. A **full timetable** for Zvartnots Airport is available at www. zvartnots.am.

✈**Aeroflot** 12 Amirian St, Yerevan; ✆10 532131; www.aeroflot.ru. Flies 4 times daily from Moscow to Yerevan with good connecting flights throughout Europe.

✈**Air France** 9 Alek Manukian St, Yerevan; ✆10 512277; www.airfrance.com. Offers 2 flights a week from Paris.

✈**Alitalia** Festatour, sales agent in Yerevan for Alitalia, 31/114 Moskovian St, Yerevan; ✆10 530608, 10 539752; www.festatour.am; www.alitalia.com. Schedule inc 2 flights a week from Rome.

✈**Austrian Airways** 9 Alek Manukian St, AUA Business Centre, Yerevan; ✆10 512201/2/3; Zvartnots Airport office 60 373029; www.austrian.

com. Operates 4 flights a week from Vienna.

✈**LOT Polish Airlines** 7 Argishti St, Yerevan; ✆10 510284; www.lot.com. Flies twice a week from Warsaw.

✈**Transaero** 54 Mashtots Av, Yerevan; ✆60 488080, 60 400303; Zvartnots Airport office ✆60 373030; www.transaero.com, www.transaero. ru. Operates 11 flights a week from Moscow with reasonable connections throughout Europe.

✈**Ukraine International** 15 Mashtots Av, Yerevan; ✆10 531800; Zvartnots Airport office ✆60 373002; www.flyuia.com. Flies 5 times a week from Kiev with good connections throughout Europe.

Most **passengers transiting** via Moscow, Ukraine or Georgia no longer require transit visas as was the case in the past. Note, however, that passengers must have a connecting through ticket and must not leave the airport. While Russian transit visas are not needed for foreigners spending less than 24 hours at the airport, they are required for a longer transit. They can be obtained from the consular office at the airport (⊕ *06.00–01.00 daily*) although anyone who needs a Russian transit visa is strongly advised to obtain one before travelling.

A number of CIS airlines also fly to Yerevan, but many of them have no offices in either the city or at the airport and, while tickets can readily be booked through a travel agent, it is not possible to easily contact many of these airlines direct. Some services operate only weekly. Most flights to CIS destinations are on Russian-built aircraft. These aircraft were once banned from western European airports on environmental grounds (too noisy). They can now fly in parts of Europe but not usually in the UK. They are used almost exclusively by the plethora (around 350–400) of airlines operating within the CIS.

All air fares change frequently; the following is only an indication of cost at the time of writing. As flights fill over time and departure dates draw near prices go up. By booking very early a return fare of around £400 (economy fare, including taxes) from London can usually be found. This figure can rise to £600–800 for travel in high season at short notice. Aeroflot and Ukraine International tend to have the most reasonable prices. Austrian Airlines tends to be relatively expensive. From the UK, for those not within easy reach of London, Air France tends to be a good option. Travel agents and tour operators normally have cheaper contracted fares but these can only be sold as part of a package holiday.

Airport transfer The **city centre** can be reached by **minibus 17, 18 or 37** (cost AMD250; see page 114 for routes), but this is of no use to passengers arriving on flights from western Europe since minibuses do not operate at night. However, Yerevan's **taxis** are cheap – expect to pay around AMD5,000 to the centre. **Aerotaxi** (✆ 10 771100; m 055 319050; e info@aerotaxi.am; www.aerotaxi.am) is the official taxi service of Zvartnots Airport. It has a desk in the arrivals hall after passing through customs. It accepts credit cards. To Yerevan there is a service fee of AMD400 plus AMD250/km. The journey takes about 15 minutes. To the regions there is a service fee of AMD600 then AMD200/km.

Other international airports Yerevan Zvartnots is not the only Armenian airport with international services. Shirak Airport (page 231) at Gyumri has flights to and from Russia operated by VIM Airlines (*23, blg 1 Novokhokhlovskaya St, 109052 Moscow;* ✆ *+7 499 271 0333;* e *info@vim-avia.com; www.vim-avia.com*). At the time of research there was a flight from and to Moscow on Tuesdays, Fridays and Sundays and a flight to and from Leningrad on Sundays. Anyone thinking of flying to or from Gyumri should contact the airline directly: Shirak Airport is only staffed during flight arrivals and departures.

BY TRAIN It is quite possible to arrive in Armenia by train. Overnight trains operate between **Tbilisi** in Georgia and Yerevan. In summer (*15 Jun–1 Oct*) the service is extended to Batumi and runs every day, taking 16 hours. It leaves Yerevan at 15.25 and costs AMD11,000–27,000 depending on class (see below). In winter the service between Yerevan and Tbilisi runs alternate days. From Yerevan it departs 21.30, takes 10½ hours and costs AMD9,000–18,000. Because the alternate days are continuous (so are neither odd nor even dates) it is necessary to check departure days at the station. The train from Tbilisi leaves at 20.20 and arrives in Yerevan at 07.00 but check times as well as days if intending to travel. *En route* the train calls at 12 intermediate stations, including Ayrum, Sanahin, Vanadzor, Gyumri and Armavir, but mostly at inconvenient hours of the night. Trains have four classes: *obshi* (open seating on wooden benches), *plas* (reserved seats, possibly on wooden seats, more often on padded ones) and two types of compartments: *coupé* (compartments with sleeping berths for four), and *CB* (SV in English) or Luxe, a compartment for two. Toilets on the train are not noted for their cleanliness, and food is not available so bring some with you. The ride is highly scenic but the best bits are hidden in the dark except, to some extent, in midsummer. Tickets, one-way, are bought at the stations and can be purchased up to about ten days in advance; seats can also be booked.

BY BUS It is easy to travel by bus from either Georgia or Iran. There are also services from Turkey which operate via Georgia, but note that it is currently not possible to travel from Russia to Armenia via Georgia, as was previously the case. It is now illegal under Russian law for foreigners to enter or leave Georgia via land borders with Russia. Citizens of EU countries and USA are among those who do not need visas to visit Georgia so should not need transit visas. In theory a Georgian transit visa should not be required for holders of Armenian visas spending less than 72 hours in Georgia. If you need a Georgian transit visa they can now be obtained at the border. Tickets should be bought in advance if at all possible. The baggage allowance on buses is 20kg with excess being charged at AMD250 per kilo. Most buses to destinations outside Armenia leave from Kilikia Central Bus Station (*6 Isakov Av, just past the brandy factory on the road to Ejmiatsin;* \ *+374 10 565370*).

From Georgia direct buses leave Tbilisi at 08.00 and 10.00 daily, taking seven hours for the journey to Yerevan via Stepanavan and Ashtarak at a cost of about GEL44 (Georgian lari) (US$25). The return service also operates at 08.00 and 10.00; the cost is about AMD10,000. Minibuses also travel between Tbilisi and Yerevan, approximately two-hourly 10.00–16.00, leaving when full. In both countries tickets are purchased at the bus stations (Ortachala bus station and at the main train station in Tbilisi; Kilikia Central Bus Station in Yerevan) and can be bought a few days in advance. (**Note:** times can change so check locally if intending to use these routes.)

From Iran the bus leaves from Tehran daily at 13.00 and is scheduled to arrive in Yerevan 26 hours later. The fare is about US$50. The southbound service leaves Yerevan at 10.00 daily; cost AMD17,000. Saberatours-Sevan (see pages 63–4) can arrange transport between Iran and Armenia.

Coming **from Turkey**, a number of companies operate buses between Yerevan and Istanbul, via Georgia, all apparently leaving Istanbul's Emniyet Garaji bus terminal on Thursdays between 09.00 and 10.00. From Yerevan buses depart on Saturdays at 10.00 or 11.00 or 'when it is full'. The journey is scheduled to take 41 hours and the fare is about US$60. The advice is to check details before travelling and to book a ticket three to seven days in advance either personally at the bus station or via a tour operator. See above about Georgian transit visas. Some travellers report being asked for an additional US$10 'entry fee' at the Georgian border at Batumi.

HEALTH   *with Dr Felicity Nicholson*

All travellers to Armenia should ensure that they are up to date with **immunisation** against tetanus, polio and diphtheria (now given as an all-in-one vaccine, Revaxis, which lasts for ten years), and hepatitis A. Hepatitis A vaccine (Havrax Monodose or Avaxim) comprises two injections given about a year apart. The course costs about £100 (but may be available on the NHS), it protects for 25 years and can be given even close to the time of departure. Travellers to more remote areas may be advised to be vaccinated against typhoid fever. In addition, some visitors, depending on what they are likely to be doing, may be advised to have protection against hepatitis B and rabies (see pages 70–1). Visitors should ensure that they take any essential medications with them as drugs can be difficult to access. Consider also taking antibiotics with you (available only on prescription in the UK). **Tuberculosis** is very common in Armenia, with an incidence of 73 cases per 100,000 people in 2008. The disease is spread through close respiratory contact and occasionally through infected milk or milk products. The vaccine is usually only recommended for those aged 16 or younger who will be spending three months or more living and working with the local population. For those aged 17–35, a case-by-case assessment needs to be done. The vaccine is less effective the older you are, so it would only be used for those over the age of 35 if they had never been vaccinated and were going to Armenia as health care workers.

MALARIA   In 2011, the WHO granted Armenia a malaria-free status. Previously it occurred in the Ararat Valley, roughly between Khor Virap and Yeraskh, with the Armash fishponds (an area popular with birdwatchers) being especially implicated. Anyone planning to spend significant time at the Armash fishponds is advised to check the current status of malaria in Armenia.

HEPATITIS B   Vaccination against hepatitis B can take six months to become effective and as the disease is most likely to be picked up through inadequately sterilised needles or syringes the best way of avoiding it may be to take an emergency medical kit which contains these items. Do note, however, that a shorter course is available if there is no time for the full course. Three injections are needed for the best protection and can be given over a three-week period if there is time for those aged 16 or over. The shortest course for those under 16 is two months. **Hepatitis A** vaccine can be given in combination with hepatitis B, as Twinrix, although two doses are needed at least seven days apart to be effective for the hepatitis A component and three doses are needed for the hepatitis B. Hepatitis B vaccine is always recommended when working in medical settings and also with children.

RABIES   Vaccination is essential for anyone likely to be in close contact with animals or for those who are going to be more than 24 hours from medical help. Pre-exposure vaccination comprises three doses over a minimum of 21 days, and all three doses are required to change the treatment needed should you be exposed. If you have had all three pre-exposure doses, then you still need two more doses of vaccine if you are bitten or otherwise exposed, the first ideally on the day of exposure (or as soon afterwards as possible) and the second post-exposure dose three days later. If you have not had the pre-exposure doses you will need rabies immunoglobulin (RIG), which is expensive (around US$800 a dose) and is often unavailable. Vaccine alone when you have not had the pre-exposure doses of vaccine is not effective. Post-exposure prophylaxis should be given as soon as possible although it is never too late to seek help as the incubation period for rabies can be very long.

Rabies is spread through an infected bite, scratch or lick over an open wound from any warm-blooded animal. Dogs are the most likely source in Armenia. If you think you have been exposed then wash the wound immediately and thoroughly with soap and running water for about ten minutes. Then douse the wound with iodine or a strong alcoholic solution (vodka may be the most immediately available) and go straight to medical help.

Note that it is important to seek medical help even if you have had the full three-dose course of pre-exposure immunisation, as explained above. Inform the medical staff of exactly what immunisation you have, or have not had – this can save a lot of worry, and unnecessary expense. Medications, including vaccines, have to be paid for in Armenia.

TRAVELLERS' DIARRHOEA Like anywhere else, travellers' diarrhoea can occur in Armenia and visitors should take the usual sensible precautions such as handwashing before eating. Tap water should not be drunk unless boiled (remember to avoid ice cubes) but the water from Armenia's many springs (see page 94) is safe. Bottled water is easily available. Where the water quality is dubious, brush your teeth with bottled or boiled water. Food such as fruit and cheese bought at markets for picnics should be well washed in the spring water which flows at most picnic sites. Food you have washed and peeled yourself, and hot foods, should be safe. Raw foods, cold cooked foods, salads which have been prepared by others and ice cream are potentially risky, and foods kept lukewarm in hotel buffets may be dangerous, but do keep a sense of proportion. In many lengthy visits to Armenia, eating in all sorts of places and enjoying vast quantities of delicious Armenian fruit, vegetables, salads and ice cream, I have only been afflicted twice.

TREATING TRAVELLERS' DIARRHOEA

Should diarrhoea occur it is important to maintain hydration by drinking plenty of fluids. Sachets of oral rehydration salts give a perfect biochemical replacement but other, less expensive, mixtures will do. Any dilute mixture of sugar and salt in water is beneficial; for example, Coke with a three-finger pinch of salt in a glass. Or make a solution of eight level teaspoons of sugar (18g) and one level teaspoon of salt (3g) to one litre (five cups) of safe water. A squeeze of lemon juice or orange juice improves the flavour and adds potassium which is also lost in diarrhoea. Drink two large glasses after each bowel action and more if you are thirsty. These solutions are still absorbed well if you are vomiting, but you will need to take just sips at a time. If you are not eating you need to drink three litres a day plus whatever is pouring into the toilet. If you feel like eating, take a bland, high carbohydrate diet.

If the diarrhoea is bad, or you are passing blood or slime, or you have a fever, you will probably need antibiotics in addition to fluid replacement. A dose of norfloxacin or ciprofloxacin repeated twice a day for three days may be appropriate. Note that antibiotics are only available on prescription in the UK.

SUN Remember that Armenia is a sunny country and that the temperature at the higher altitudes can mask the strength of the sun. Sunscreen, hat and sunglasses should not be forgotten.

SNAKEBITE Snakes rarely attack unless provoked, usually preferring to get out of the way of humans as soon as they detect any vibration. Wear stout shoes and long trousers in areas where there may be snakes. Most snakes are harmless and even venomous species will dispense venom only in about half of their bites so even if you are bitten you are unlikely to have received venom. Many so-called first-aid techniques such as cutting into the wound or applying a tourniquet are dangerous and do not work. The only effective treatment is antivenom. If you are bitten by a snake which you think may be venomous:

- Keep calm. It is likely that no venom has been dispensed.
- Prevent movement of the bitten limb by applying a splint.
- Keep the bitten limb below heart height to slow the spread of any venom.
- If you have a crêpe bandage wrap it round the whole limb (eg: toes to thigh) as tightly as you would for a sprained ankle.
- Evacuate to a medical facility which has antivenom. If within an hour's drive of Yerevan go to the Republican Hospital, Department of Toxicology, 6 Makarian Street (☏ *reception: +374 10 340020; toxicology dept +374 10 343166*) or, for children, to the Muratsan Hospital Complex, 144 Muratsan Street. All main hospitals in the regions have antivenom.
- NEVER cut or suck the wound.
- NEVER give aspirin. Paracetamol is safe.
- DO NOT apply ice packs.
- DO NOT apply anything to the wound.

Treatment with antivenom requires identification of the snake. Ideally the snake should be killed, if that can be done safely, and taken to show the doctor. Beware! A dead or even a decapitated snake can still exhibit a bite reflex and can leak venom through its fangs. It is wise to handle it with a stick and transport it in a leak-proof container.

HIV/AIDS The CIA World Factbook estimates the prevalence rate at about 0.1% of the adult population. This compares with the prevalence rate in the UK of around 0.2% and in the USA of 0.6%. If you must indulge, use condoms or femidoms, which help to reduce the risk of transmission.

TRAVEL CLINICS AND HEALTH INFORMATION A full list of current travel clinic websites worldwide is available on www.istm.org. For other journey preparation information, consult www.nathnac.org/ds/map_world.aspx (UK) or http://wwwnc. cdc.gov/travel/ (US). Information about various medications may be found on www.netdoctor.co.uk/travel. All advice found online should be used in conjunction with expert advice received prior to or during travel.

IN ARMENIA The health care system in Armenia has been undergoing significant reforms and improvement although there remains much to be done. The focus has been on strengthening Primary Health Care: rebuilding or modernising local outpatient units and providing them with new equipment; merging outdated, dilapidated and inefficient hospitals; retraining doctors and nurses and aiming to provide specialist services in the regions, not just in Yerevan. The World Bank (through the Health System Modernisation Project) is assisting the Armenian government in their aim to modernise the health system and improve the key health indicators of the population.

A **reciprocal health agreement** exists for British citizens which means that health treatment (excluding drugs but including dental) is free on producing a UK passport. Many US health insurance policies do not include Armenia so special cover needs to be purchased. In spite of improvements, the UK Foreign Office and the US State Department still advise that medical facilities are generally poor, especially outside Yerevan. It is prudent for all visitors to ensure that their insurance will cover repatriation, or at least evacuation, in the event of serious illness or accident.

Visitors at present still do a fair amount of **passive smoking** in spite of anti-smoking legislation. From the end of 2005 separate non-smoking areas were meant to have been designated in restaurants, while public organisations and state institutions had to allocate a separate room for smokers with the rest of the premises smoke-free. In 2006 smoking in hospitals, public transport, schools and colleges, and sports facilities was banned. Observation of the ban is variable and enforcement minimal apart from in public transport. Certainly in smaller restaurants it seems non-existent. Cigarettes are consumed in large quantities; around 58% of men over 20 smoke, one of the highest rates in Europe. Public awareness of the risks of smoking is low despite health warnings on cigarette packets and the fact that advertising is banned except at point of sale. Surveys show that 35% of Armenian smokers believe that smoking will do them no harm while 45% believe that passive smoking is harmless. Around 39% of Armenian doctors smoke, although no longer perhaps in front of their patients as was the case in the past! Nevertheless life expectancy remains among the highest in the CIS at 70.5 years for men and 74.5 for women (according to official statistics), but 69 and 77 respectively according to the American CIA.

SAFETY

Most visits to Armenia are trouble free. Crime is increasing in Yerevan especially (though from a very low base level) and visitors should take sensible precautions. The risk of being a victim is, however, much less likely than in most western European and American cities. Far greater risks after dark are either tripping up on pavements in need of repair or else falling into holes dug during the pavement's reconstruction. Watch out, too, for missing manhole covers. These risks have reduced, at least in the centre of Yerevan, but can still be a problem elsewhere.

The military situation does mean that some areas along the 1994 ceasefire line should definitely be avoided because of the risk from occasional snipers on the Azerbaijan side. The old road from Ijevan to Noyemberian is a particular problem but there is no need to use it as a new road has been built further from the ceasefire line. There is a problem, particularly in Nagorno Karabagh, from minefields. To the best of the author's knowledge all places mentioned in this guide are perfectly safe to visit and sights where the unresolved conflict means that safety is problematic have been excluded. However, visitors to Nagorno Karabagh should note that consular services are unavailable there if they do encounter difficulties.

Given the disputed border with Georgia in the north (see page 260), especially in Lori Province, visitors are advised not to attempt to cross the border apart from at the recognised border crossings. Visitors are unlikely to be in great physical danger but may be arrested by the Georgian authorities.

Armenia's death rate in road-traffic accidents has historically been proportionately much higher than that in the UK despite considerably lower traffic levels. The Armenian

2

figure is likely to deteriorate even further as the improved roads tempt drivers to higher speeds and increasing traffic levels mean that it is even more dangerous than it was previously to drive round blind bends on the wrong side of the road. In fact the old pot-holed tracks, where speeds were perforce low as drivers sought to avoid the deepest ruts, have undoubtedly helped to keep the accident rate down. The legislation dating from Soviet days making the wearing of seat belts compulsory is now actively enforced by the traffic police, as are speed limits (see page 83).

Pedestrians should be extremely careful at pedestrian crossings. Often vehicles do not give pedestrians priority at such crossings, even though there is a hefty fine if caught disobeying. Be especially aware of traffic turning right.

Telephone numbers for the **emergency services** are: **Ambulance** ⟍ 103; **Fire** ⟍ 101; **Police** ⟍ 102.

WOMEN TRAVELLERS There are no particular safety problems for women as the strongly traditional family values ensure that they will not receive unwelcome attention. It is true that a woman walking alone in the late evening is an uncommon sight but it does not imply that she would be vulnerable if she did. Women drivers are now seen in Armenia but they are still a small minority.

OTHER TRAVELLERS Armenia has very few facilities for the **disabled** although ramps for wheelchair access have appeared in one or two hotels.

Travelling with children is not a problem from the social aspect. They are welcome anywhere. Family life is important to Armenians – they would find the concept of a child not being allowed into a restaurant, for example, very strange. Nappies and baby food are available in Yerevan and other major towns, often from pharmacies. Most restaurants and hotels will respond to parents' requests about food preparation. In Yerevan, the Grand Candy café (see page 137) is specifically geared towards children and some other cafés have play areas. There are funfairs near the cathedral and in Victory Park and amusements for smaller children in Children's Park on Beirut Street. Some swimming pools have facilities for children, for example Waterworld, and good weather brings out street amusements in a number of towns. See page 75 for advice on taking children to historical sites.

Homosexuality was decriminalised in 2003 but is still an unacceptable lifestyle in Armenian society. The British Foreign Office advises homosexual travellers to exercise discretion in Armenia. It is common in Armenian culture to see a mother and daughter or two female friends holding hands in the street and not uncommon to see two men hug and kiss each other in greeting; these signs of affection are not an indication of sexual orientation.

OTHER DANGERS AND ANNOYANCES The **traffic police** who used to spend much of their time stopping motorists for 'routine checks' (and who were reputed to seek bribes) are now more usefully employed enforcing the seat belt laws and speed limits. They do still sometimes stop cars for routine checks of documents (see page 83), but I was assured by my driver that bribery is now much less common.

As mentioned elsewhere in this guide, there is danger from earthquakes, poisonous snakes, deep holes concealed by long grass at several monasteries and various other hazards ranging from the potential for dehydration when it's hot to the possibility of frostbite when it's cold. The vast majority of visitors suffer none of these, although it is rather difficult always to take precautions against earthquakes. (The US Federal Emergency Management Agency gives advice on what to do during an earthquake at www.ready.gov/earthquakes.) Another precaution, not always

As Armenia is a former republic of the Soviet Union, attitudes towards disabled travellers are still very much entrenched in the communist era. However, like other countries in the region, it is slowly changing to reflect outside influences as it tries to increase its tourist trade for those with disabilities.

PLANNING AND BOOKING There are few specialist travel agencies running trips to Armenia. Companies such as Visit Armenia (*www.visitarm.com*) may be able to offer trips to the area.

GETTING THERE The main airport in Armenia is Zvartnots International Airport and it has facilities for those in wheelchairs including disabled toilets and other amenities. However, Shirak Airport may lack the same facilities.

ACCOMMODATION A number of hotels in Armenia have wheelchair access, such as the Royal Tulip Hotel (*14 Abovian St, Yerevan;* ✆ *+374 10 591600; www.royaltulipgrandhotelyerevan.com; see page 119*) or Best Western Congress Hotel (*1 Italia St, Yerevan;* ✆ *+374 10 591199; www.congresshotelyerevan.com; see page 118*).

VISITING PLACES Armenia has a number of historical sites and many will be difficult for wheelchair users to gain access to. The Garni temple, for example, has a number of steps and may cause problems for those who struggle on their own unless they are accompanied by an assistant.

Unfortunately, public transport does not have full access which may cause problems if you are unable to board buses unaided.

TRAVEL INSURANCE There are a few specialised companies that deal with travel to Armenia. A number of operators deal with pre-existing medical conditions such as Orbis Plus (✆ *0845 338 1638; www.orbisplus.co.uk*) and Insure for All (✆ *0800 082 1265; www.medicitravel.com*).

Medical facilities within Armenia are limited. The main hospitals in Yerevan, such as the University Clinic, are somewhat basic but are able to cater for those travellers who are in wheelchairs or have impediments. Hospitals in other parts of the country, however, lack the facilities of those in the capital.

feasible, is to avoid Soviet-era flats. If visiting such flats, note that the staircases are often in poor condition with limited illumination.

It is, however, necessary to **supervise children** very closely at many historic sites. Apart from the deep holes concealed by long grass, and the snakes, which find convenient lairs in the piles of fallen stones, much of the masonry of less frequented buildings is precarious and Armenian castle builders were adept at siting their fortresses on the top of precipices. Even at touristy places like Noravank the cantilevered steps which give access to the second floor of the mausoleum require considerable care – especially descending. Just to reach a few of the sites requires hill-walking skills and appropriate footwear – it may not be a long walk to Baghaberd for example but it is extremely steep and made difficult by unstable scree.

At one or two sites, notably Kirants, beware of giant hogweed *Heracleum mantegazzianum*. This is a tall plant of the family Umbelliferae whose white flowers are held in flat-topped umbels. Do not touch it with bare skin as it causes painful weals. Its hollow stems sometimes tempt children to use them as peashooters with the result that their lips and hands become affected and require treatment.

WHAT TO TAKE

Apart from obvious items like **walking boots** and a compass if you're going hiking or **binoculars** if you're birdwatching, there are a few other items which are best brought into the country. Any **medications** that you may need should be brought as these may be difficult to obtain, particularly away from Yerevan. Bring a small **torch** and carry it around, as it is needed when visiting the subterranean rooms at a few sites and may also be useful on the stairs of Soviet-era flats, in poorly lit subways and in bedrooms where the light switch is sometimes a long way from the bed. Film for prints is readily obtainable and processing is usually of good quality. **Memory cards** are likewise easily obtainable and printing of digital images readily available. **Digital camera batteries** are hard to find – the best place to look for them is at Zig Zag photographic chain, see page 126. **Clothing** is largely dependent on the time of year, the altitude of the places visited and activities planned, but do note that Armenians recognise foreign tourists by their casual clothes. Armenians regularly dress much more smartly and stylishly than most Westerners. If there is any likelihood of being invited for dinner into somebody's home, or going to an orchestral concert or the opera, it is worth taking something smarter. Note that Armenian women do not have pierced parts of their body other than their ear lobes, men do not wear earrings, and neither sex sports tattoos. The temperature can change rapidly during late April/early May going from chilly conditions to warm summer in a couple of days. Likewise, in October I have walked around Yerevan one day in short sleeves and sandals and the next day have been wishing for gloves. At these times of year it is as well to take layers of clothing and a jacket for cool mornings and evenings.

Armenia's **electricity** supply is at a voltage of 220V and a frequency of 50Hz. It uses standard continental European plugs with two round pins. This means that British and Irish appliances need only a simple cheap **adaptor** to match their plugs with Armenian sockets. Such adaptors are easily bought at home but cannot easily be found in Armenia so they should be taken. However, in North America electricity is supplied at 110V and 60Hz. This means that American appliances require not only an adaptor (to cope with the different shape of the pins of the plug) but also a **transformer** to cope with the different voltage. These should be bought before leaving home. In addition American devices where the mains frequency is important (such as electric clocks) will not work correctly in Armenia. Also in the case of computers and hi-fi equipment it is necessary to check whether or not particular components will function correctly on frequencies of both 50Hz and 60Hz.

Very few Armenian sinks have **plugs**, even in Western-style, modern hotels. If you want to be able to fill a sink with water take a one-size-fits-all plug with you.

MONEY AND BUDGETING

MONEY Armenia's own economic problems, coupled with the disintegration of the financial markets of the former Soviet Union, reinforced the need for Armenia to have an independent monetary policy. The introduction of the dram (officially abbreviated to AMD) as a national currency on 29 November 1993 made an independent monetary policy possible. Each dram, which is simply the Armenian word for money, is made up of 100 luma, the Armenian word for a small part of anything. Initially the exchange rate was US$1 = AMD14. By the end of March 1994 it had reached US$1 = AMD230 and at the end of 1994 stood at US$1 = AMD400. It subsequently drifted down to US$1 = AMD585 and £1 = AMD850 but then appreciated, and in June 2006 stood at US$1 = AMD417 and £1 = AMD767. In May 2014 the rate was US$1 = AMD423, £1 = AMD691 and €1 = AMD562. There were originally five denominations of banknotes: AMD10, 25, 50, 100 and 200. Inflation subsequently forced the addition of AMD500, 1,000 and 5,000 notes. In 1997, these were superseded by a completely different design of banknote depicting famous Armenian males. The notes currently in use depict: AMD1,000 – the poet Eghishe Charents (1897–1937; see pages 51–2); AMD5,000 – the writer and poet Hovhannes Tumanian (1869–1923; see page 51); AMD10,000 – the poet Avetik Isahakian (1875–1957; see page 52) and AMD20,000 – the painter Martiros Sarian (1880–1972; see page 54). Recently an AMD50,000 note was introduced, dedicated to the 1,700th anniversary of the adoption of Christianity, which depicts Ejmiatsin. Over the years notes up to and including AMD500 have been replaced by coins.

Armenia is still very much a **cash-based society**. Some hotels and shops aimed at Western visitors accept credit cards but many do not, cash or bank transfer being the only accepted form of payment in many hotels, especially outside Yerevan. Although the larger hotels outside Yerevan are increasingly accepting cards this is by no means universal. Armenia now has **ATMs** in all major towns operated by various banks, although not all accept Western cards. Look for the symbols by the machine advising what cards will work there. With the increased prevalence of ATMs it is no longer as essential as it was for visitors to Armenia to bring most of their funds in cash US dollars, regarding other forms solely as an emergency reserve, but this is still an option. Even if relying on cash machines in Yerevan it is as well to remember that in more remote places you will need to take cash with you. The lack of crime makes carrying more cash than you would normally do at home safer than might be imagined. It is very easy to change US dollars at one of the innumerable exchange offices in the country. Euros and roubles are widely accepted and a few places, mostly in Yerevan, will take British pounds. It is usually possible to exchange other currencies in the centre of Yerevan. There is less concern than formerly about accepting notes in less than pristine condition but it can still prove difficult to get rid of ones which are torn or marked.

Travellers' cheques can most easily be exchanged at HSBC branches in Yerevan, but they charge a significant fee for doing so on any cheques but their own. You will need to show your passport. Travellers' cheques issued by Thomas Cook or American Express are easiest to cash; ones denominated in US dollars are preferred, but those denominated in euros are also accepted.

Although all purchases in Armenia should be paid for in drams, there are a few places where dollars are welcome. Vernissage market is one: most of the stallholders even quote prices in dollars (though they will of course accept drams).

There seems to be a constant shortage of change in Armenia; small establishments may not be able to change the higher denomination notes.

BUDGETING Apart from Western-style hotels, which charge Western prices as indicated in the body of the text, and international phone calls, most things of interest to visitors are cheap. In particular, other than in establishments aimed at Westerners it is difficult to spend more than AMD5,000 on a meal, and a snack at a stall in the street will only cost AMD150–1,000. In a café an Armenian coffee will

2

cost AMD200 or so, a cappuccino AMD1,500 while a half-litre of beer costs up to AMD500. When thirsty in the countryside, patronise free one of the excellent springs, but you can buy a litre bottle of water for under AMD400. A 100g block of chocolate to keep you going will set you back about AMD480 while an imported Mars bar is AMD350. A loaf of bread or some sheets of *lavash* for your picnic will cost AMD300–500. Fruit and salad ingredients bought in markets or at roadside stalls are cheap by Western standards eg: tomatoes AMD400/kg.

Other tourist essentials: postcards cost between AMD300 and AMD500 with an additional AMD240 for postage; a 36-exposure 35mm film costs up to AMD4,000; memory cards for digital cameras start at AMD7,000 for a 4GB card, AMD260,000 for 16GB; a digital camera battery (difficult to find) costs AMD6,600, a battery plus charger is AMD14,000; and the T-shirt to prove that you've been to Armenia is priced between AMD3,000 and AMD6,000.

Public transport fares are low and the longest minibus journey from Yerevan (to Meghri) costs AMD6,000. The longest train journeys, such as Yerevan to Gyumri, cost AMD1,000. Car hire with driver is cheaper than without, but don't necessarily expect a new vehicle. Typical rates are AMD25,500–27,300 per day for a private car or AMD32,760–59,000 for a 4x4 including fuel; prices will depend on the cost of fuel. The driver's expenses such as meals and accommodation must also be met if he is away from home.

CYCLING IN ARMENIA

I am indebted to Raffi Youredjian, who has cycled enthusiastically through Armenia and Nagorno Karabagh, for advice on this topic.

In much of Armenia riding a bicycle is regarded as being only for children. Attitudes are slowly changing but cycling is currently something of a fashion trend, not a serious alternative to the car. However, the number of cyclists – especially foreign tourists – is increasing so, although you may still be viewed with some amazement, you will not be the only one. There are no set cycle routes; decide for yourself what interests you and go for it. See page 57 for when to go, remembering that altitude can have a significant influence on the temperature.

EQUIPMENT Bring your own bike and all your equipment with you; you won't find well-stocked bike shops. Airlines will allow a well-packed bike for a one-off sports equipment fee; check with individual airlines. Choice of bike depends on the type of trip. A mountain or touring bike is best for a long journey. A racing bike should only be considered if travelling very light. Tough tyres are essential, as well as spare inner tubes. Don't forget the puncture repair kit. Armenians are good at fixing nearly everything so ask for help if you encounter serious mechanical problems.

ROADS Cyclists say that avoiding pot-holes is probably easier on a bike than in a car. Nearly all roads provide adequate shoulder lane for cycling. Cycling in Yerevan is not recommended; the roads are congested and drivers are not used to cyclists. See warnings on page 74 for pedestrians; cyclists are liable to be just as invisible. For further information on the state of road surfaces, see page 82.

FITNESS A good level of fitness is highly recommended. Remember that Armenia is a high country; you may well get breathless going up hills that would be no

A standard antibiotic might cost AMD3,000 for 14 tablets, paracetamol AMD180 for 20 tablets and a tube of acyclovir, should you develop an unexpected cold sore, AMD1,500–3,240 depending on the manufacturer.

Tipping is discretionary, but the etiquette is much the same as in the West with approximately 10% being added to the bill in restaurants and taxis. In Yerevan city centre where taxi journeys usually cost under AMD1,000 it is the norm to at least round up the amount given to AMD1,000. If you have engaged the services of a guide, interpreter or driver and are pleased with their performance you may wish to show appreciation with a tip – again 10% is standard.

GETTING AROUND

Note that all fares quoted are for a single journey unless stated otherwise. Return tickets are not sold; a notable exception is the cable-car to Tatev.

BY TRAIN Virtually the whole of Armenia's rail network is electrified at 3,000V DC. The track has the standard Soviet gauge of 1.524m rather than 1.435m which is the norm in western Europe and North America. Apart from the passenger services round Yerevan, which are operated by multiple units, other trains are hauled by twin-unit locos of class VL10: VL stands for Vladimir Lenin. They were built at

problem at home. Apart from the Arax plain in the south you will always be going either uphill or downhill. A daily distance of 50–60km is reasonable (according to Raffi), unless you are a professional athlete in training when 100km a day is achievable. Armenia is small enough for a day's ride to let you reach a destination before dark.

SAFETY The standard of driving is variable. Make sure you are visible and wear bright colours. Lighting in tunnels is often dim so make sure your own lights are good. The main route to the south carries a lot of heavy lorry traffic to and from Iran.

Fairly scary dogs will be encountered at steady intervals and most will give you a good chase. A loud shout of *khelok* (behave!) will usually put some fear into them and soon you'll be left alone.

FOOD AND WATER Take plenty of water with you before starting any ride. Almost every village has a small well-stocked shop as do many petrol stations. On more popular routes there will be wayside stalls selling seasonal produce.

ACCOMMODATION See pages 85–7 for types of accommodation available. Camping (page 87) is possible if you bring a tent with you. Out of experience Raffi suggests the best option is to follow the recommendations in this guidebook and use them as daily destination points. Asking around in any village will usually produce someone who is willing to provide homestay accommodation for a suitable price, but this of course involves an element of potluck.

As explained on page 34 local people will be fascinated to find out about you and may well invite you into their home for coffee. The main problem is that if you accept every invitation you will never get anywhere!

Tbilisi, Georgia, and Novocherkassk, Russia, between 1967 and 1977. A timetable, in Russian, is available on request at Yerevan's main railway station (see pages 142–3). To reach the main railway station take the metro to Sasuntsi Davit which adjoins the railway station. The station is open 24 hours; the international ticket office is open 09.00–18.00, the local ticket office 07.30–19.30. Some timetable and ticket price information is available at www.UKZHD.am but as this is not exactly the same as the information given to me by the station director, and as timetables change from year to year (and according to season), do check times before travelling.

There are only a handful of internal train services but some of them may be of use to visitors. Travelling by train is cheap with the longest journeys, such as Yerevan to Gyumri, costing AMD1,000. Tickets are bought at stations and are always for a single journey. Trains are, on the whole, efficient although relatively slow. It is possible to book tickets and seats a few days in advance although trains are rarely so busy that seats can't be found. Trains leaves the main railway station in **Yerevan for Gyumri** (*AMD1,000*) at 08.00 and 18.10 daily; journey time three hours. Return departure times are the same. Another useful route is that from **Yerevan to Hrazdan** (*AMD300*), extended in summer (*15 Jun–30 Sep*) to Sevan (*AMD600*) and to Shorzha (*Sat–Sun only, AMD1,000*). Trains run daily. They do not, however, leave from the main railway station but from Kanaker station in Yerevan's northeast suburb of the same name. The station is hidden down a narrow winding lane which goes eastwards off the northern part of Zakaria Kanakertsi Street. A small sign, in Armenian and Russian and attached to a gas pipe, points the way. (The train actually starts at Almast station in Yerevan's Zeytoun district but Almast consists simply of a platform whereas Kanaker station is staffed.) Trains leave Kanaker at 08.30 and 19.25 (ten minutes earlier from Almast) and arrive in Hrazdan 1½ hours later. (The summer morning extension arrives in Sevan at 10.50 and Shorzha at 12.10. The return train leaves Shorzha at 16.30 and Sevan at 18.00.) Trains leave Hrazdan for Kanaker at 07.15 and 18.40. Dates of the extension to Sevan are decided on an annual basis and times can change so check beforehand if intending to use the route.

The daily summer (*15 Jun–1 Oct*) train from Yerevan to Batumi on Georgia's Black Sea coast, via Tbilisi, leaves Yerevan at 15.25 (see page 68). Intermediate stations include Gyumri, Vanadzor, Sanahin and Ayrum. In winter the train is replaced by an overnight Yerevan to Tbilisi train on alternate days (see page 68). Unfortunately the timings of these trains means that the spectacularly scenic ride along the Debed Gorge is mostly in the dark. Unless the early morning train from Gyumri to Ayrum is reintroduced, those wishing a scenic ride on public transport will have to rely on minibuses.

BY BUS Bus services proper have declined and no longer serve all main towns direct from Yerevan. All places are, however, linked by minibus (*marshrutka*) services. The maximum bus fare from Yerevan by bus is to Tashir (AMD1,500). Generally speaking minibuses cost around 50% more than buses. The maximum minibus fare is to Stepanakert or Meghri, both of which cost AMD6,000. Minibuses are driven more recklessly than buses and are consequently considerably quicker. When travelling between the north and south of the country, it is invariably necessary to change at Yerevan. While it is probably possible to go almost anywhere you might want to go by minibus, the problem for the visitor is finding out where the bus leaves from and at what time. Timetables, as such, are not available and although many routes leave from the Kilikia Central Bus Station which is about 800m from Victory Bridge in the Zvartnots direction, many leave from other places and there are about 16 bus stations in Yerevan. The Armenians themselves, if they

Note that you are advised to check bus times a day or two before travelling. Places of departure are also subject to change.

14/3 Gai Street   Near Mercedes Benz showroom – formerly called Haik Av. Departures to: Garni (bus/minibus)

28 Isahakian Street   In front of Drama Theatre. Departures to: Dilijan (minibus), Sevan (bus/minibus)

Abovian Square   Departures to: Zvartnots Airport (minibus)

Agatangeghos/Khorenatsi streets corner   Behind Rosia trade centre. Departures to: Alaverdi (minibus), Artik (minibus), Gyumri (minibus), Vanadzor (minibus)

Arshakuniats Avenue   Rd south from south end of Grigor Lusavorich St. Departures to: Yeghegnadzor (minibus)

Kilikia Central Bus Station   6 Admiral Isakov Av; +374 10 565370. Departures to: Armavir (minibus), Artik (bus), Gyumri (bus), Jermuk (minibus), Noyemberian (minibus), Sisian (minibus), Stepanakert (minibus), Stepanavan (bus/minibus), Tashir (minibus), Vanadzor (bus/minibus), Vardenis (minibus)

Khorenatsi Street   Behind Rosia trade centre. Departures to: Artashat (minibus), Dvin (minibus), Goris (minibus), Kapan (minibus), Meghri/Agarak (minibus)

Mashtots Avenue/Sarian Street corner   Departures to: Ejmiatsin (bus/minibus)

Northern Bus Station   1 Tbilisian Rd; +374 10 621670. Has a timetable posted on the door. Departures to: Berd (minibus), Chambarak (minibus), Dilijan/Ijevan (minibus), Martuni (minibus), Vanadzor (bus), Vardenis (minibus)

Paronian Street/Mashtots Avenue corner   Departures to: Ashtarak (bus/minibus)

Raykom Station   24 Azatutian Av. Departures to: Gavar (minibus), Hrazdan (minibus)

Tigran Mets Avenue   Departures to: Spitak (minibus)

want to find out something such as where a bus goes from, will ask someone who knows or who knows someone else who knows. A visitor may be best to follow their example and ask at their hotel or homestay. The Northern Bus Station in Yerevan and some regional bus stations have a timetable on the door; in many, however, including the Kilikia Central Bus Station in Yerevan (where there was a timetable over the ticket office but staff told me it was wrong!) the expected course of action is to go to the bus station a day or two before you want to travel and say where you want to go. The website (*www.armeniainfo.am*) of the now defunct Armenian Tourism Development Agency still has details of routes and frequencies – it may be out of date, but it gives an idea of what is available. Transport to a single destination can leave from several sites in the city. The Central Bus Station can be reached by

Practical Information   GETTING AROUND

2

many minibus routes including 13, 15, 23, 27, 54, 67, 68, 75, 77, 90, 94 and 99. It is a large A-frame building which functions from 07.00 to 17.00, with left-luggage lockers available 07.00–17.00. There is also a café (⏰ *09.00–20.00*).

The details on page 81 of the stations from which buses/minibuses of possible interest to tourists depart are an indicative guide only; changes are frequent. Note also that bus routes sometimes become minibus routes.

Other towns have minibus services to local villages – again, ask locally. Minibuses do not serve tourist sites per se: a taxi is often the best way to reach such sites.

BY TAXI Taxis in Armenia are plentiful and relatively cheap and are often a reasonable alternative to public transport, even for intercity journeys. Bus stations usually have plenty of waiting taxis, they can be flagged down in the street and if you see a taxi stationary at the side of the road then it is probably

ROADS

The publisher has requested that roads on the maps be marked according to whether they are tarmac or dirt roads. This distinction undoubtedly has some value but it can also be misleading: tarmac roads are not always good roads, likewise a dirt road is not necessarily synonymous with a bad road. There are four main categories of road surface in Armenia; good

KEY TO ROADS

═══	Asphalt
═══	Secondary road
═══	Broken asphalt
═══	Dirt
═════	4x4/track

tarmac (often extremely good), bad tarmac (occasionally appallingly bad), dirt (which can sometimes be good but which is much more likely to be difficult) and minor roads which are really no more than rough tracks which should only be tackled with a 4x4, in good weather and with a driver who is used to such terrain. The tarmac/dirt distinction is useful in wet conditions. Some dirt roads become seas of mud after rain. This applies especially to roads within villages, where the daily passage of animals from their accommodation within the village to the fields and back ensures that village streets end up like farmyards.

Armenia's roads have improved enormously in the past 15 years. Most major routes have good tarmac. There can be problems with pot-holes, especially after the severe winters which are the norm in Armenia. Perhaps even more difficult than the pot-holes themselves are the stretches of road where pot-hole repair is under way and rectangles of road surface have been removed but not yet made good.

Some tarmac roads have had no maintenance for many years and are in a bad condition, sometimes so bad that local drivers have created multiple alternatives by going off-road. These 'off-road' dirt tracks may be noticeably better than the road itself. Occasionally one comes across a bad stretch on a road which is otherwise good. The transition can be disconcertingly abrupt.

As soon as one turns off a main road one is likely to encounter a dirt road; but not always as there is a programme of upgrading rural roads. Regard such surfaced side-roads as a bonus! There is a handful of really good dirt roads but these are exceptions.

Throughout the book I have tried to indicate where road conditions are other than standard. Of course a road surface can change quickly, for the better with upgrading or for the worse with adverse weather conditions.

available. Although there are no designated taxi ranks they do tend to wait in roadside bays. You should have no difficulty in finding a taxi! On the whole taxi firms and drivers do not speak English so if phoning for a taxi it is best to ask your hotel or host to do it for you. After the minimum charge of a few hundred drams, prices are in the order of AMD70–200/km. If you are hiring a private taxi for a long journey, be sure to agree the price before starting. In 2013 a taxi from Vanadzor to Yerevan, for example, cost AMD10,000, as did one from Goris to Tatev. Registered taxis in Yerevan charge AMD100/km. Most journeys within central Yerevan cost less than AMD1,000. Telephone numbers of some Yerevan taxi firms are given on page 115.

DRIVING Much improvement in the state of the roads has taken place in recent years but many dirt roads remain and pot-holes continue to be a problem (see opposite). Drivers will also encounter assorted livestock, either going out to pasture in the morning, returning in the evening or simply grazing on the roadside. The latter are not usually much of a problem being either tethered or looked after by a family member.

Vehicles drive on the right and drivers must give way to the right, even on roundabouts unless the road you are on is signed as the through road by the main-artery yellow-square sign.

On dual carriageways it is not permitted to turn left across the carriageways. The procedure is to carry on past the turn-off you want, do a U-turn at the next signed U-turn position, drive back to the junction you want and turn right. The same procedure is followed when turning left after exiting a side road on to a dual carriageway. Turn right until you can make a U-turn on to the desired carriageway. This procedure means that you must be aware that vehicles may be slow or stationary in the outside lane.

Name signs for entering/leaving a village or town relate to the administrative area of the settlement; it may be some way to the actual built-up area. Conversely, if the village is off the main road, the village cancellation sign may be just a few metres after the entry sign.

Speed limits are 60km/h within towns, 90km/h on rural roads and 40km/h in tunnels. Speed cameras have been installed in Yerevan. The traffic police have become very active in stopping drivers who break speed limits. Police are obliged to show a driver photographic proof, which should include the number plate, place and time of the alleged speeding offence. The size of any fine relates to how much over the speed limit the car was travelling, starting at AMD10,000. **Seat-belt compliance** is also being enforced, with fines for any driver or front-seat passenger not wearing one. Rear seat belts are not compulsory. For infringements the driver is issued with a note of the fine which must be paid at a bank within 30 days.

Drivers must carry their licence and proof of car ownership at all times. You can drive in Armenia on an **International Driving Permit**.

Petrol is available in three categories: regular (93 octane), premium (95 octane) and super (97 octane). At the time of writing regular cost AMD500 per litre, premium AMD700 and super AMD900. Unleaded fuel is unavailable but diesel is widely sold. Gone are the days when much fuel was dispensed in cans from parked roadside tankers although this can still occasionally be seen in the more remote areas. Many vehicles in Armenia are dual-fuel, petrol and gas (CNG, compressed natural gas), gas being significantly cheaper at AMD200 per cubic metre. When filling up with gas all occupants must leave the vehicle: a waiting area, of varying comfort, is usually provided. Petrol and gas are readily available in towns and on main routes leading out of towns but stations are less frequent when off the main roads. As everywhere, it is sensible to fill up before embarking on a long journey.

Practical Information   GETTING AROUND

2

Parking With the increase in traffic, on-street parking in central Yerevan can be a problem. It is free except in private areas (where a fee of AMD100–200 will be collected, usually by an elderly man, on leaving) and in the red-line areas. These on-road red lines, together with yellow notice boards (Armenian and English boards) detailing fees and how to pay, were introduced in central Yerevan in 2013 and there are plans to extend the system to all administrative areas of the city. The privatisation of parking spaces has caused controversy and accusations of corruption. The company which won the tender, Parking City Service (*2 Adonts Av, Yerevan;* \ *060 606 606; www.pcs.am – in Armenian*), was the only contender and is owned by a close ally and friend of President Serzh Sarkisian. The city did not receive any payment for the parking areas; the company plans to retain 70% of collected fees, the other 30% going to local taxes and 'other expenses'. The company's director says that US$10 million will be invested in the project. Red-line parking fees are charged 09.00–24.00. The first five minutes are free; thereafter it is AMD100/hour; 500/day; 1,000/week; 2,000/month; 12,000/year. Hourly and daily payments can only be made via SMS, the fee being taken from a prepaid mobile phone account. Other rates are made via banks. Clear instructions are given on the yellow boards. The system is policed by both fixed and mobile surveillance cameras and there is a fine of AMD5,000 for non-payment.

Pedestrians Especially in Yerevan it can feel as if drivers are completely oblivious to pedestrians. Great care should be taken when crossing roads, even at 'green man' crossings. Vehicles approach at high speed with apparently no intention of stopping. Drivers turning right are allowed to proceed at pedestrian crossings if there is no-one crossing but should otherwise give priority to pedestrians. Failure to do so carries a fine, if caught, of AMD30,000 but the risk of being caught must be slight, given the number of drivers who flout this law. A new ruling allows a pedestrian to be fined AMD3,000 for jaywalking.

Car hire Cars can be hired with or without a driver. Many local tour operators (see pages 63–4) can arrange private car hire, tailoring car and driver to particular requirements. For all car rentals, a valid driving licence and passport must be presented, a refundable deposit is required and payment is by credit card. Other terms and conditions, including minimum age, vary between firms.

Several **international car-hire companies** are established in the country and have offices in Yerevan. Only one has an office at the airport although pick-up and drop-off at the airport can be arranged in advance. Rates range from AMD22,000–100,000 per day and 4x4 is available. **Local** competition is provided by an increasing number of companies. All are based in Yerevan and are geared to foreign visitors. It is very rare for Armenians to hire a car. All firms must ensure that their cars comply with regulatory standards including MOT. Some local companies are included below.

International companies

🚗 **Europcar** 8/1 Abovian St; \ +374 10 544905; m 091 404201, 099 4112285; e info@europcar.am; www.europcar.am

🚗 **Hertz** 7 Abovian St; \ +374 10 584818; m 096 584818; e info@hertz.am; www.hertz.am. Website covers terms & conditions clearly.

🚗 **Sixt** 42 Acharian St, 6/36 Zakian St, Zvartnots International Airport arrivals hall; \ +374 60 373366; e info@sixt.am; www.sixt.am

Local firms

🚗 **ArTourRent** 10/6 Pushkin St; \ +374 10 566359; m 094 383890; e info@artourrent.am; www.artourrent.am

🚗 **Avanguard** 7/3 Mashtots Av; \ +374 10 500809; m 099 806010; e info@avanguard.am; www.avanguard.am

🚗 **Caravan** 50a Mashtots Av (next to Nairi cinema, entrance from Isahakian St); \ +374 10 529292; m 098 559292; e info@caravan.am;

www.caravan.am. Car hire with or without driver. 🚗 **Hyur Service** 96 Nalbandian St; ✆+374 10 546040; 19 Sayat Nova Av (in lobby of Ani Hotel); ✆+ 374 10 541903; m 093 504040; e contact@

hyurservice.com; www.hyurservice.com 🚗 **Tourorent** 4 Tigran Mets; ✆+374 10 541025; m 093 462212; e tourorent@gmail.com; www.tourorent.am

ACCOMMODATION

Yerevan is well provided with upmarket hotels. There is a wide choice of hotels within the central area although some visitors might prefer, particularly in midsummer, to stay outside the central district. Expect to pay Western prices at these hotels. There are also some less expensive hotels, mostly built in the Soviet era for tourist groups and since renovated. Small mid-range hotels are appearing. Budget travellers have a small number of hostels to choose from. An alternative is a homestay (bed and breakfast). For those staying longer than a few days renting an apartment is an economical option. Information about Yerevan accommodation is given on pages 115–21.

Outside Yerevan accommodation has now improved enormously and good hotels are available in most of the places tourists are likely to want to stay. Some of these hotels are new-builds while others are **renovated Soviet-era hotels**. The latter vary from very acceptable to excellent. There are still some Soviet-era hotels that were used to house refugees in the early 1990s, have never recovered, and are not recommendable. Soviet-era hotels tend to be renovated floor by floor. Renovated floors are usually fine, but avoid those which are not. A chain of upmarket **Tufenkian hotels** (*www.tufenkian.am*) aimed at Western tourists is being developed in restored buildings. They aim to showcase Armenian history and culture with furnishings handmade by Armenian artisans from local materials in a modern yet distinctively Armenian style. There are Tufenkian hotels on Lake Sevan, in the Debed Valley, at Dilijan and in Yerevan.

Some hotels have **self-catering facilities**. These may be in the form of so-called **cottages** – separate small buildings which can accommodate between four and eight persons, although the number is flexible as extra beds can often be erected. Such cottages in Soviet times tended to be in hotels with large grounds and were originally for families spending the whole of their holiday in one place. However, the concept of cottages has been happily adapted to new establishments and it is quite common for a hotel to comprise several small buildings rather than one large building. This preference for individual units can also be found in restaurants where instead of one large dining room there are multiple rooms with a single table.

Another feature of the Soviet era was the **guesthouses** run by various bodies to provide accommodation for their members while on holiday. They are therefore usually in pleasant surroundings. Some of these have been sold off, while in other cases they remain in the hands of the original owner. It is possible to stay at most of them and they are generally inexpensive. The standard varies enormously. The privatised ones are usually well managed, some having been upgraded, some still needing a lot of new investment. Soviet-era guesthouses were usually large establishments offering a variety of activities as well as accommodation. Now renovated, such establishments often call themselves '**hotel resorts**'. This slightly puzzling term usually means that the hotel offers a number of facilities (such as sauna and swimming pool) as well as activities (various sports, horseriding, etc) all within the hotel complex.

Yet another feature of the Soviet era was the **spa hotels** which provided various therapeutic treatments for their guests. More and more of these are being upgraded, most noticeably in the town of Jermuk. They combine their medical and hotel functions and are often relatively inexpensive for the facilities offered. It is perfectly possible to stay there without being a patient but prices usually include treatment (and full board) whether you take it or not.

Motel-type accommodation, often associated with roadside eating places on the main routes, is increasing rapidly. Such accommodation is often newly built and pleasant. **Hostel** accommodation in Armenia is limited. There are a few hostels in Yerevan (see page 120) and a small amount of YMCA accommodation in Spitak. **Homestays** (Armenia's term for bed and breakfast establishments) are available throughout the country and provide a real insight into Armenian family life particularly as generally excellent meals can be organised. The one real snag is, of course, the language barrier but many visitors enjoy homestays in spite of this. Homestays, invariably safe and usually very comfortable, can be arranged through one of the Yerevan travel agents (see pages 63–4) or one of the few regional information centres. (It is not unknown for tourists simply to ask around when they arrive in a village, but of course there is an element of potluck in this method.) There will be only one bathroom for everyone, both you and the household. Expect to pay about AMD10,000 per person for a twin room including breakfast plus about AMD4,000 per person for dinner – including drinks. You will need to give the hostess enough time to prepare an evening meal (eg: requesting it at breakfast time or the previous day) but you'll get a feast. A lighter meal of salads, cheese, etc can usually be provided at much shorter notice. Also, it's usually best to buy some wine yourself, or you'll probably end up with a choice of vodka or sweet red wine. Even if you cannot manage to stay, do try to fit in one or two home-cooked meals. As with homestay accommodation, such meals can be organised through one of the Yerevan travel agents. While the water situation (see page 33) has improved greatly in most parts of Armenia, some rural places still face difficulties and water may only be available for limited periods each day. Occasionally you may have to fill the WC cistern by ladling water stored in the bath. Hot water may not be continuously available everywhere.

Rented accommodation can be arranged through Yerevan travel agents and is a good option for those wishing to stay for more than a day or two. The price varies according to the standard and size of apartment; expect to pay AMD14,000–27,000 per day for a one-bedroom apartment. Many Soviet-era flats have an unpromising approach, with dark, dilapidated stairways and lifts that do not always function, but

FINDING AN ADDRESS

Addresses in Armenia can be confusing, at least to visitors from the UK. It is the whole building, sometimes covering a large area, which is numbered rather than individual premises or entrances. Thus, several shops may all have the same address because they are in the same building and two addresses, eg: numbers 2 and 6 on the same street which look as if they will be fairly close together, can be a surprising distance apart. If a building occupies a corner site with wings on two (or more) streets the whole building has a number relating to one of the streets on which it stands. Premises in that building, even if their entrance is from another street, will still give the first street as their address. It is quite common therefore to have to go round the corner to get in. For example, the Jazzve café with an address of 8 Moskovian Street in Yerevan is actually on parallel Isahakian Street, as the building stretches round three sides of a square. If an address number has a suffix, such as 4a or 4/1, it is possible that it is round the back of the building. Most large blocks have courtyards round the back and many premises are entered via these courtyards, particularly residential apartments in buildings where shops occupy the ground floor. The address may even be in a separate building within a courtyard or in a row of buildings behind the row which fronts on to the street.

However, the familiar pattern of even and odd numbers on opposite sides of the street is used, as is numbering buildings from the town centre outwards.

the flats themselves are usually spacious and comfortable. Hyur Service (see page 63) can arrange rented accommodation.

It is possible to **camp** anywhere except on private property and in the national reserves (see page 11). There are no permanent campsites as found in the West. Some tour operators (see page 64) do include camping during their treks and one enterprise (see page 267) in Tavush province offers a riverside campsite.

The **accommodation price codes** (see box, page 86) used in this guide are based on the price of a double room in peak season, usually late May/June to the end of October, although for accommodation in winter sports areas winter is the peak season (and here, at weekends, it can be very busy). Even in the peak summer season it should not be difficult for individual visitors to find accommodation although the choice is obviously greater if you book in advance. Groups do need to book in peak season. Prices usually include **breakfast** although in a significant minority of establishments, both small and large, breakfast is extra. Where this is the case the cost is stated in individual accommodation entries. Breakfast rarely costs more than AMD2,000. A few hotels do not include **tax** in their price; this is noted in the listings. As explained on page 77, Armenia is a cash-based society and, although cards are becoming more widely accepted, most accommodation (apart from big hotels in Yerevan and some other towns) has to be paid for in cash or by bank transfer. Establishments which accept **cards** are noted under individual entries. Although the position may change, it should be assumed that cards are not accepted unless it is positively stated that they are. Some hotels offer lower prices outside their peak season. One person occupying a double room will usually pay less than two people occupying the same room – the iniquitous single-occupancy surcharge has not reached Armenia. Often there will be a range of prices for double/twin rooms in hotels. The price depends on the size of room and whether there is a separate sitting room.

EATING AND DRINKING

Two points need to be made about eating in Armenia. First, Armenian cuisine has much more in common with Turkish, Persian or Arab cooking, all of which countries at one time ruled Armenia, than it does with the cooking of Russia, which also ruled Armenia, or that of western Europe. Secondly, given the range and interest of dishes which can be experienced in an Armenian household, the menus of restaurants and hotels tend to be repetitive and predictable. Very sadly, almost all restaurant menus, especially away from Yerevan, have been reduced to a few salads followed by grilled or barbecued meat and vegetables. Armenian thinking is quite different from that in Britain or France, for example, where one goes to a restaurant for a good meal. In Armenia one goes to a restaurant to give the wife of the family a rest and accepts that the food will be worse than at home. The only way most tourists can begin to appreciate the range of Armenian cookery is to get a travel agent to organise for them some homestays with dinner included or else to book a meal in a private house – this can be arranged at houses which provide homestays as long as notice is given. The hostess is highly likely to outshine any restaurant in the vicinity. I personally have never eaten better in Armenia than in private houses. Having said that, it is also true that the quality and variety of restaurants, especially in Yerevan, has improved out of all recognition since Soviet days when surly staff glumly informed customers that everything they asked for from the menu was unavailable and meals took hours as the staff frequently vanished to enjoy a long rest. Nowadays one problem for foreigners who are not used to it is quite the reverse: meals are served quickly with the second course arriving before the first is half eaten. (It is the normal Armenian custom to serve everything at once. Avoid this if you wish by only ordering one course at a time.) It is perfectly acceptable to order a number of main dishes and have these placed in the middle of the table so everyone can sample a little of each.

The quality of the ingredients is extremely high because Armenia produces a wide range of excellent fruit and vegetables as well as meat: pork, chicken and lamb. The only exception is beef which tends to be less satisfactory because it is predominantly from Caucasian brown cattle, a breed developed between 1930 and 1960 by crossing Swiss brown bulls with cows of the local lesser Caucasus breed. The resulting beef does not compare to Aberdeen Angus, Beef Shorthorn or Hereford. Also the Armenian practice of eating beef and lamb fresh rather than hanging it for up to three weeks after slaughter tends to make it tougher and less flavoursome than in the West.

The quality of Armenia's **fruit and vegetables** is so high, partly because the climate favours them, partly because they have not been bred to survive transport to a supermarket in another continent and partly because they do not have to appear absolutely identical to every other example of that fruit or vegetable which the supermarket sells. Probably apricots, native to Armenia, are the most famous produce, but in season markets and the ubiquitous roadside vendors pile their stalls with peaches, cherries, apples, pears, quinces, grapes, figs, pomegranates, plums, oranges, lemons, melons, watermelons, tomatoes, squashes, aubergines, peppers, asparagus, cucumbers, courgettes, onions, potatoes, carrots, peas, beans, cabbages, okra, a whole range of mushrooms, almonds, walnuts and hazelnuts.

A staple ingredient of Armenian cookery is **bulghur**. Traditionally it is made by boiling whole grains of wheat in large cauldrons until they begin to soften, upon which they are removed and dried in the sun. The grains are cracked open and the kernels divided into categories depending on size. This process ensures that they will keep for years without deteriorating. Fine bulghur is preferred for *keufteh* (see page 92) while coarse bulghur is preferred for pilaffs and soups.

Warning to **vegetarians**: although it is extremely easy to have a meat-free diet in Armenia some Armenian dishes may not be what they seem from the menu. For example, mushroom salad may contain as much chicken as mushroom and, because the ingredients may be chopped fine and mixed up together, it will be impossible to avoid the chicken. Always ask before ordering.

BREAKFAST Most Armenians make do with a cup of coffee (*soorj*) or tea (*tay*) together with bread (*hats*), butter (*karag*), jam (use the English word), honey (*merr*) and possibly cheese (*paneer*). Another preserve which may appear at breakfast is *muraba*, various whole fruits in a thick syrup, although it can also be offered as a sweetmeat with coffee. Occasionally a **tomato omelette** (*loligov dzu*) will be offered, in the Armenian version of which onions are first gently fried, then chopped tomatoes are added and finally whipped eggs are poured on (sometimes with a little cream and curry powder added) for the final cooking. Yoghurt (*madzoon*) is also likely to be offered. In smaller establishments you will be asked the evening before what you will want and when. In homestays the uneaten food from the night before (of which there will be a great deal since Armenian cooks greatly overestimate visitors' appetites) will also be laid out. It is not unknown for the evening's undrunk brandy also to be proffered at breakfast. The main **Yerevan hotels** offer something considerably more than this (though minus the brandy) with a whole buffet breakfast available and a variety of omelettes but this is pandering to Western hotel eating habits rather than being authentically Armenian. Nor can one or two Soviet-style guesthouses which offer semolina and boiled beef be regarded as remotely Armenian. Breakfast is often served relatively late by Western standards, rarely before 08.00 and frequently not until 09.00. In fact the whole day is shifted somewhat towards evening.

For breakfast in winter visitors may encounter **khash**, which can perhaps be translated as 'cowheel soup'. Most visitors detest it, but a *khash* party is a unique Armenian ritual. Apart from the (acquired?) taste, it also makes the breath smell foul! *Khash*, which traditionally is never eaten by one person dining alone, is sometimes served in restaurants but usually it is a ritual for a group of friends who will have fasted the previous evening. The cowheels (and sometimes other parts of the animal such as the head or stomach) are boiled all night with neither salt nor herbs. By morning a thick broth has been produced and the meat has flaked off the bones. Just before serving at breakfast time, crushed garlic and salt are added. The broth is then eaten by dipping *lavash* in it. The soaked *lavash* is transferred to the mouth using hands alone. It is always accompanied by greens, radishes, yellow chilli peppers, mineral water, and sometimes by red chillies and pickles as well. It is also accompanied by vodka, ideally mulberry vodka, of which considerable quantities are drunk in a series of toasts, the first of which is '*Bari luys*' ('Good morning') and the last of which is to the maker of the *khash*.

LUNCH Many restaurants start serving meals by 12.00 and service is continuous until late evening. Armenians argue that one should eat when one is hungry rather than be guided by the clock. Traditionally though, lunch is a fairly light meal with the main meal being taken after work. For visitors, lunch is often an excuse to buy some fresh produce at the market. The basis for the picnic is **lavash**, Armenia's classic flatbread (see box, page 90) which is traditionally unleavened. It is baked rapidly in an oven set into the ground called a *tonir* and comes in the form of thin sheets which can be readily stored since *lavash* is successfully freshened even after it has dried out by sprinkling a little water on it. In villages where there is no market people still bake it in their own houses, often several women saving on fuel and having a social morning by baking bread together, each making enough to last her family for a few days or longer.

Tomatoes and cucumbers together with cheese and sour cream make an excellent filling. Other possibilities obtainable at any market are the spiced dried meats such as *basturma*, which is dried, salted and flattened beef surrounded by a dried mixture of paprika, garlic and cumin, or *sojuk*, which is spiced and salted minced beef (sometimes mixed with pork or lamb) formed into a sausage and then dried. In the Sevan area smoked fish can be bought to make another variant.

An alternative lunch would be to call at one of the roadside **barbecue** stalls which are common on the main roads in summer. They offer the ubiquitous Armenian menu of *khorovats* (barbecued meat, usually pork but sometimes chicken or lamb, together with salads, vegetables and *lavash*). Seeing and smelling the food cooking and then eating it either in the open air or under an awning is one of the pleasures of travelling in Armenia. Prices are usually a little less than you would pay for a similar meal in a restaurant. Of course, the restaurants are open if it's either raining or else too hot. In towns it might be possible to find a café selling the traditional Armenian fast food **lahmadjoun**. This tasty speciality comprises a thin dough base covered, in similar style to a pizza, with tomato, herbs, spices and very small pieces of meat. It's normally rolled up and eaten like a sandwich.

DINNER The main meal is eaten in the evening. **Bread** will certainly be provided, usually *lavash*, but some restaurants, particularly in Yerevan, have taken to giving foreigners ordinary bread and reserving the *lavash* for Armenians unless

MAKING *LAVASH* – ARMENIA'S FLATBREAD

The *tonir*, or oven, in which *lavash* is baked is a large cylindrical clay structure sunk into the ground. A fire is lit in the bottom of the *tonir* and baking begins when the walls of the oven are hot enough, as *lavash* is cooked on the actual wall of the oven. When meat is being cooked it is suspended within the *tonir* over the glowing fuel.

Traditionally *lavash* dough consists simply of flour, salt and water although nowadays some cooks add yeast or other ingredients such as buttermilk. When several women from the same family or same village join together to make a large batch an efficient mini production line ensues, with one woman rolling out pieces of dough on a floured baking board, a second skilfully stretching the dough into very thin sheets by throwing it to and fro in the air and then laying it on a special padded implement, a *batat*, which has a handle on the non-padded side. It is said that the dough should be stretched to about 24 by 12 inches (30x60cm) and should be no more than $1/16$-inch (1½mm) thick. The dough is then swiftly and firmly applied by means of the *batat* to the wall of the *tonir* to cook. This takes only a brief time. It is then removed from the *tonir* with a long metal hook, often by a third member of the group, and added to the pile of cooked *lavash*. The skill lies in judging the correct moment to remove the *lavash* from the *tonir* and the oldest member of the group is often granted this important task. The surface of the blisters which form when the dough comes in contact with the heat should be nicely browned.

foreigners specifically ask. The meal usually begins with a selection of **salads** which can incorporate both raw and cooked vegetables, peas, beans, herbs, fruits, nuts, bulghur, eggs and meat. In season romaine lettuce is used but in winter cabbage is substituted. Often the salads will double up as an accompaniment to the main course. Popular salads include cucumber and tomato salad (*varounki yev loligi aghtsan*), green bean salad (*kanach lobov aghtsan*), kidney bean salad (*karmir lobov aghtsan*), aubergine salad (*simpoogi aghtsan*) and potato salad with sour cream (*titvaserov kartofili aghtsan*).

The second course would traditionally have been **soup**, although this is not now commonly served in summer, and restaurants frequently have none available. Some of the soups are actually so substantial as to be main courses while others are cold concoctions for summer. Armenian soups are excellent so take any opportunity to try one – if you can manage yet more food. A popular summer soup is *jajik*, chilled yoghurt and cucumber soup, which can either accompany the main course or precede it. Other cold soups made with apricots, cornelian cherries *Cornus mas*, currants, mulberries, or sweetbrier *Rosa rubiginosa* can be served as either a first course or a dessert. More substantial soups for winter include *targhana abour* made with yoghurt, mint and onion, *shoushin bozbash* (lamb soup with apple and quince) and *missov dziranabour* (lamb soup with apricots). More homely soups, often offered in homestays, are *spas* (yoghurt and bulghur) and *aveluk* (wild sorrel). *Harissa*, a thick soup of bulghur and chicken which is filling if rather unexciting, may be offered in homestays.

The main course would usually be based on meat or fish. **Fish** is obviously less common than in countries which are not landlocked but whitefish from Lake Sevan is sometimes available and also trout from Armenia's rivers. Trout and sturgeon are available from the Armash fish ponds. Beware some of Yerevan's restaurants which offer sea fish, smoked salmon or shellfish imported from goodness knows where. Leave such dishes to the expatriates who want to be reminded of home.

Unfortunately restaurants rarely offer dishes which have been cooked by braising or casseroling although such dishes certainly form part of traditional Armenian cookery. **Chicken** is far more likely to be roasted, perhaps with a stuffing (*pilavov letzvadz hav*) based on rice or bulghur and with some vegetables or dried fruit, or else it might be barbecued (*khorovats varyag*) or fried (*tapakatsi*). A really upmarket restaurant might offer a more imaginative stuffing such as would be used in Armenia on festive occasions. **Game** is very rarely offered, probably because so little of it survives. **Lamb** is immensely popular and a huge variety of lamb stews are cooked in the country with ingredients from quinces (*missov sergevil*) and apricots (*missov dziran*) to artichokes (*missov gangar*) and leeks (*missov bras*). They are fascinating, delicious dishes, usually served with a rice pilaff (*printzi pilaff*) or bulghur pilaff (*tzavari pilaff*), but the chance of finding one on a restaurant menu is slight. You will, however, find lots of **barbecues** (*khorovats*) using lamb (*gar*), pork (*khoz*), beef (*tavar*), chicken (*hav*) or, occasionally, veal (*hort*). The meat will come with vegetables, of very high quality but not prepared or cooked with the flair and imagination shown in an Armenian household. A popular way of cooking green vegetables, such as asparagus and beans, is to fry them and then add whipped eggs. The result is rather like scrambled eggs with vegetables and could form a meal in itself although it is usually served as a side dish.

Other dishes occasionally encountered include *dolma* of which there is a whole range. They comprise vegetables or occasionally fruits which have been stuffed with meat or rice. Vine leaves or cabbage leaves are most commonly used depending on the season but the range of vegetables used in Armenian homes is staggering: artichokes, chard, aubergines, peppers, courgettes, onions, tomatoes, apples, melons and quinces. The stuffing could be made from some combination of minced beef or lamb, rice, bulghur, dried fruits, chopped vegetables, yoghurt, and a mixture of herbs and spices. Needless to say a visit to an Armenian home is necessary to encounter this kind of range but some restaurants do include one of the more common ones on the menu.

Keufteh is another classic style of Armenian cookery. It is bulghur which has been mixed with finely chopped vegetables and herbs and often with lamb as well. Again there are innumerable variations depending on the cook and the availability of seasonal ingredients. It can be cooked or uncooked, hot or cold, and some have two separate mixtures, one for the core and one for an outer shell. In the popular *sini keufteh* the inner stuffing is made from butter, onions, minced lamb, pine nuts and spices while the outer shell comprises bulghur, more lamb, onion and other spices. It is prepared in a baking dish before being cut into squares and then baked. It can be eaten hot or cold with vegetables or salad.

DESSERT AND PASTRIES Dessert as often as not consists of **fresh fruit** accompanied by cheese (*paneer*). In summer **ice cream** (*parrparrak*) is served but is always factory rather than artisan produced. **Pastries** are more often eaten with a cup of afternoon tea or coffee or in the late evening. Armenia's best pastries, and very good they are too, are those which exploit its fruit and nuts. *Baklava* is widely available and exists in many forms. Layers of buttered filo pastry stuffed with some combination of nuts, apples, cheese and cream is formed into rolls or diamonds and then baked. Afterwards it is covered either with honey or with a sugar and water syrup that has been flavoured with lemon. Another popular pastry is *gata*, a bun-like cake baked with a mixture of butter, flour, sugar and (sometimes) ground almonds inside.

EATING OUT IN ARMENIA

It is relatively cheap to eat out in Armenia except for the few places in Yerevan aimed at the more expensive end of the tourist trade which charge Western prices. Main courses usually cost somewhere between AMD2,500 and AMD4,000 and it is easy to have a full meal (which in Armenia usually comprises salads and a main course) for AMD5,000 per person. A bottle of wine will add somewhere between AMD2,500 and AMD5,000, half a litre of beer AMD500 and two coffees AMD400. There is not usually a significant price differential between restaurants and cafés. Restaurants which fall outside this price range are noted under their individual entries. A light course, such as an omelette, may well cost under AMD1,000 and a savoury street snack can be had for as little as AMD150. Most restaurants open at noon and cafés about 10.00. Most will stay open until midnight or until the last customer has gone. For picnics or for those self-catering, markets provide a wide range of food at budget prices. Another option is to patronise the roadside stalls which sell seasonal fruit and vegetables (see page 88).

Particularly outside Yerevan, many cafés and restaurants do not have a printed menu. You are simply asked what you would like – somewhat disconcerting when you have no idea what is available! The standard fare of salads, cheese, bread, barbecued meat (*khorovats*) and vegetables is usually available. Other staples such as an omelette and fried potatoes can probably be provided but it is worth asking what they suggest. In cold weather soup may be on offer.

Freshly baked, the large flat rounds (looking more like bread than cake) are often sold at tourist sites such as Geghard. Also excellent are the **dried fruits** such as apricots, peaches or plums which have been stuffed with nuts. Another interesting and enjoyable novelty is **fruit or sour** *lavash*, thin sheets of dried fruit *purée*. Plum was the classic fruit to use but nowadays a wide range of fruits is employed.

DRINKS Armenia is justly renowned for its **brandy**, its **coffee** and its **spring water**. Other drinks, such as some of the **herbal teas** – particularly the thyme tea – are well worth trying and certainly some of the **wines** are passable without quite threatening the industries of Chile or Australia just yet. Armenian alcohol consumption is at the bottom end of the European range. Although beer can be drunk freely, social etiquette has established formal rules for the drinking of wine and spirits. They may only be drunk when eating and each table has its *tamada* who is responsible for making toasts: no-one drinks without a toast. Toasts can be extremely long, with persons around the table requesting the *tamada* to be allowed to toast. The theory is that the *tamada* is able to regulate the alcohol intake of those present and stop people getting drunk. Unfortunately it doesn't always work because the *tamada* himself sometimes ends up inebriated forcing everyone else to keep going. For most Westerners anyway this ritual is irksome since they are both forced to swig a glass of brandy or vodka when they don't want one just because a toast is proposed or else they are forbidden to enjoy a sip of wine with the food because no toast is then coming to an end. Women will be let off drinking at every toast but it is considered unacceptable for men not to drink every time. Armenians themselves often prefer to drink brandy or vodka with meals rather than drink wine, quite contrary to Western habits. Indeed, drinking even Armenian wine is largely the prerogative of foreigners.

Armenia's drinks industry suffered from two heavy blows in the late 1980s. First, Soviet president Gorbachev launched a strong anti-alcohol campaign and then during the blockade years in the early 1990s goods could not get to the main market in the rest of the CIS. As markets could not import Armenian products other, often inferior, suppliers were only too happy to step into the void. As a result of both these factors production and sales fell considerably, bottoming out in 1996 before recovering. The range and quality of Armenian wines continues to improve. There are specialist wine and brandy shops but a good selection is also available in supermarkets.

Armenian **brandy** (*konyak*) sprang to prominence at the Yalta conference in 1945 when Stalin plied Winston Churchill, the British prime minister, with it and Churchill declared that it was better than any French brandy. Many would still agree. Although called cognac in Armenia and the rest of the former Soviet Union, this is forbidden under Western trade rules which specify that cognac must be produced in the Cognac region of France. Armenian brandy comes in a variety of qualities. At the bottom of the range is three star, so called because it has been kept (in oak casks) for three years after fermentation. Up to six years the number of stars indicates age, but for six years and beyond special names are given. The Ararat factory in Yerevan, founded in 1887 and now owned by Pernod Ricard, offers Ani (six years old), Select (seven years old), Akhtamar (ten years old), Celebratory (15 years old), Vaspurakan (18 years old) and Nairi (20 years old). Prices range from AMD5,200 for a 500ml bottle of three star, AMD8,400 for Ani, AMD14,300 for Akhtamar to AMD39,500 for Nairi. Prices in the duty-free at Yerevan Zvartnots Airport are lower – for example AMD11,000 for a bottle of Akhtamar (my favourite) and AMD30,400 for Nairi (but note the caution about airline regulations on liquids, see page 97). About 70% of production is exported to Russia. Other quality producers are Great Valley and MAP and they also export a large proportion of their production. There are around a dozen smaller firms producing inferior products.

Vodka (*vodka* or *oghi*) is distilled by more than 45 small and medium-sized companies in Armenia, including Avshar, Vedi-Alco, SGS (based in Nagorno Karabagh), Garib and Artashat-Vincon. Production has been increasing steadily since 1996 and in 2000 Armenia began exporting its vodka, mainly to the United States and Cyprus. As well as ordinary vodka, several traditional Armenian varieties are made in people's homes, such as mulberry (*t'ti*) vodka, grape (*khagho*) vodka and apricot (*tseeran*) vodka. Many of the vodkas are pleasant enough but they do not compare in quality to the brandy though they are popular in Armenia. The price of vodka (AMD990–10,000 for 500ml) depends on the quality and what it is made from. Armenian vodka is cheaper than Russian and fruit vodkas more expensive than ordinary vodka. You can buy a 500ml bottle of decent fruit vodka for AMD5,000–7,500.

Armenia grows a range of grape varieties but the climate does not lend itself to the 'cool climate' grape growing such as is becoming more popular in the New World, and the **wineries** (more than 15 in Armenia) have had insufficient funds to be able to invest in temperature-controlled fermentation. A considerable number of different white and red wines are available, many of the reds being sweet or semi-sweet. Although the best known grape variety in Armenia is Areni, used for making dry red wines, the most enjoyable white Armenian wines are those made by the Ijevan winery from the Georgian Rkatsiteli grape. Although some very cheap wine is available, the more drinkable bottles cost about AMD1,800 to AMD2,000 and a good red wine about AMD4,000, slightly more in a restaurant whose mark-ups, other than in Western-style hotels, rarely exceed 25%. The Armenian for wine (*ginee*) can be preceded by the appropriate adjectives: red (*karmir*); white (*spitak*); dry (*chor*); or sweet (*kaghtsr*).

Although imported **beer** (*garejoor* but mostly people use the name of the brand they want rather than the generic word for beer) is available, usually from Heineken or Russia's Baltika brewery, two indigenous brands are ubiquitous throughout the country: Kilikia (brewed in Yerevan) and Kotayk (brewed in Abovian). Local connoisseurs tend to prefer the Kilikia brand but many visitors opt for Kotayk. A third brand, Erebuni, is in fact brewed at the Kotayk brewery and a fourth, Gyumri, is brewed in Gyumri. Beer costs around AMD390–450 for a 500ml bottle bought from a supermarket but this rises to AMD750 for one in a popular pavement café in central Yerevan.

Haikakan soorj, **Armenian coffee** (also called *sev soorj*, black coffee), is excellent and the perfect end to a meal, ideally accompanied by a glass of brandy. It is brewed in small long-handled copper pots using very finely ground beans and served in small cups in a similar way to Turkish coffee. It is usually served slightly sweetened (called *normal* with the stress on the second syllable) and even visitors who drink coffee without sugar at home may prefer it this way. If coffee is desired without any sugar then ask for it *soorj arants shakari*. In a café, coffee costs around AMD200. Instant coffee is also available and tastes just like it does everywhere else. **Tea** (*tay*) in Armenia can be either a standard brand of tea bag dunked in a cup or herbal. Some wonderful teas, especially thyme tea (*oortsi tay*), may be encountered made from a whole gamut of different herbs collected from Armenia's hillsides during the summer and then dried.

Water (*joor*) is another joy in Armenia. The water from Armenia's springs is delicious and always safe to drink. Many of these springs are located by the sides of roads or tracks or at monastic sites and, quite often, picnic tables are provided. It may seem bizarre to recommend spring water but all visitors should make an effort to try it. **Bottled water** (*hankayeen joor* – literally mineral water) is also available. Jermuk is the most common source but Dilijan, Bjni, Byurakan, Byureg and Noy may also be encountered. Carbonated and still are both widely sold. If you ask for bottled water it will be assumed that you want sparkling; if you want still water ask for it without gas (*arants gazi*).

A drink popular with Armenians and often drunk with meals is *tan*, a mixture of yoghurt, sparkling or still mineral water and salt. I am told it is most refreshing.

Pasteurised fruit juices are generally available, normally in cartons, as is the usual international range of bottled soft drinks together with some local competitors. A particular joy which might be encountered during a homestay is fruit juice made from the family's own fruit trees. Cornelian cherry juice is especially recommended. Occasionally one of the more traditional restaurants will have a novel juice on offer: sea buckthorn juice is one possibility. Despite its name, sea buckthorn *Hippophae rhamnoides*, a small tree of the oleaster family, grows in Armenia. Supermarkets stock a wide variety of good locally produced fruit juices.

PUBLIC HOLIDAYS AND FESTIVALS

PUBLIC HOLIDAYS

New Year's Day	1 January
Christmas Day	6 January
Army Day	28 January
International Women's Day	8 March
Good Friday	March/April
Easter Monday	March/April
Day of Motherhood and Beauty	7 April
Genocide Memorial Day	24 April
Victory and Peace Day	9 May
First Republic Day	28 May
Constitution Day	5 July
Independence Day	21 September
Earthquake Memorial Day	7 December
New Year's Eve	31 December

Genocide Memorial Day and Earthquake Memorial Day are called 'commemoration days' rather than public holidays. On Genocide Memorial Day everything is shut as on a public holiday. Earthquake Memorial Day is now a working day, although with civic commemoration ceremonies.

FESTIVALS

Vardevar The Vardevar Festival, held on a Sunday in summer, is a date for which visitors should be well prepared. The precise date is fixed according to the church calendar and varies from year to year. Being 14 weeks after Easter, it usually falls in July. Vardevar nowadays commemorates the Transfiguration, the incident described in St Matthew's Gospel, chapter 17, when Christ took three disciples up Mount Sinai where his appearance was transfigured as he talked with Moses and Elijah. Its origins, however, are pre-Christian: Vardevar was formerly associated with Aphrodite (Anahit) and rose petals were scattered on the worshippers (*Vard* is the Armenian word for 'rose'). Nowadays in place of rose petals the festival involves children collecting water, stalking passers-by, and then throwing it over them. That the more water-affluent children will have managed to stockpile many buckets' worth means that nobody that day should wear smart clothes or indeed any clothes which might be damaged by water. Inevitably Vardevar is therefore a risky day to get married. It is also most unwise, despite the temperature in summer, to drive around with car windows open unless certain that no children are lurking out of sight behind a tree or wall. Adults can and do retaliate against the water throwers, for example by using their own stockpiled supplies to effect revenge on the miscreants below by aiming at them from the safety of the balconies of their apartments. Armenia is not the only country to have such a festival – Thailand and Myanmar (Burma) both have similar festivals to celebrate the Buddhist New Year. In Poland and Hungary water throwing is practised on Easter Monday when the boys throw it on the girls – the more gallant married men spray perfume on their wives but this variant has not yet reached Armenia. If you get soaked, and foreigners are not immune although the police do sometimes try to keep the area in front of the State Museum relatively water-free, enter into the spirit of the festival: it can actually be refreshing to be soaked in the July heat and you will soon dry off.

New Year and Christmas In Armenia, as in all Eastern churches, Christmas (which falls on 6 January) is celebrated after New Year. In fact the two weeks from 31 December are a period of continuous family and church-centred celebration. In the weeks before New Year the shops are busy with people shopping – principally for food although also for presents. Food, especially family meals, forms the important focus of the festivities. For three days before New Year's Eve so much food is prepared that you would think there was going to be a two-month siege! Everyone wants to make sure that there are generous helpings for all the extended family members who will visit. Everyone visits everyone else. Even if your aunt has visited you one day, you will still go and see her the next. On New Year's Eve a large piece of meat is cooked, often roast leg of pork, as well as numerous accompanying dishes and desserts, in preparation for visitors who start to arrive after the midnight bells.

THE ORIGINS OF KAGHAND PAPI

In Russia, and some other Slavic cultures, the traditional character of Ded Moroz (the literal meaning of the Russian being 'Grandfather Frost' but often translated as 'Father Frost') played a similar role to that of Santa Claus or Saint Nicholas in the West. Ded Moroz has his roots in pagan beliefs and was originally a wicked sorcerer who stole children, but under the influence of Christian Orthodox tradition he became a kind person who gave gifts to children at New Year. In the officially atheist Soviet Union the celebration of Christmas was discouraged and New Year celebrations, which included the arrival of Ded Moroz with gifts, were promoted. He, or a local counterpart, was introduced into other parts of the Soviet Union and into eastern European counties in the Soviet bloc, despite his being alien to them. Since the collapse of the Soviet Union countries such as Slovenia, Bulgaria, Poland and Romania have reverted to their traditional characters associated with Christmas.

In Armenia it was Dzmer Papi (literally 'Grandfather Winter' but usually more euphoniously translated as 'Father Frost') who was introduced during the Soviet period. There seems not to have been a pre-Soviet equivalent. Since independence, Dzmer Papi has been replaced by Kaghand Papi (Grandfather New Year) – possibly based on a figure from ancient mythology.

A small gift is always taken for whoever you are visiting, often a box of chocolates or a bottle of wine or vodka. Presents are given on New Year's Eve rather than at Christmas and it is Kaghand Papi, Grandfather Kaghand (see box, opposite), who brings them for small children. Both the birth of Jesus and his baptism are remembered on 6 January. At the church service water is blessed, consecrated oil (chrism or, in Armenian, *meron*) is poured into the water and a cross is dipped into the water to symbolise Christ's baptism. This water is then distributed to the faithful who will either drink it or wash their hands and faces in it.

Christmas is a religious festival. The family goes to church on either Christmas Eve or Christmas Day, the main family meal taking place on the other day. Again large amounts of food are prepared for the many visitors who will come. A pilaff and baked fish are always included.

Easter A night-time Easter Eve church service is attended followed by a family meal on Easter Sunday. As with Christmas, fish forms the centrepiece of the meal and there will also be green vegetables cooked with whipped eggs and a sweet pilaff. There are egg fights for the children, with hard-boiled eggs which they have painted or dyed the previous day. The pointed ends of the eggs are engaged first then, when they have all cracked, the blunt ends are tested. The winner is the one whose egg lasts the longest without breaking. The eggs are then made into an Easter sandwich with *lavash*, greens (usually tarragon) and cheese.

SHOPPING

In town centres most shops open at 09.30 or 10.00 and then remain open until 19.00. Shops rarely close for lunch. Some, especially food shops and markets, open daily but many specialist shops such as bookshops remain closed on Sundays. In residential areas small shops and kiosks are open for very long hours – often till after midnight – while roadside stalls on main routes are sometimes open 24 hours.

Also open 24 hours are branches of the supermarket chains which have appeared in recent years. These supermarkets, and indeed all shops in Armenia, are well stocked and visitors should be able to buy most of what they need, especially in the towns. (See page 76 for items which should be brought from home.) Shopping, apart from the Western designer shops on Northern Avenue in Yerevan which charge Western prices, is relatively inexpensive.

The widest range of **souvenirs** is to be found in Yerevan. Obvious items to take home include the increasing number of books of photographs of Armenia (see page 126 for bookshops), Armenia's highly regarded brandy (easily obtainable in markets, shops and specialist brandy outlets) but remember airline restrictions on liquids in hand-luggage and buy whatever you want to carry on to an aircraft *after* going through security; anything bought beforehand will be confiscated. Remember too, if your flight is not to your final destination, that even liquids bought after security on the initial leg of your flight will almost certainly be confiscated at security during transit checks. Craft items are also obvious souvenirs. There is no doubt that the best place to buy crafts is at Vernissage in Yerevan (see page 132), but they can also be found on souvenir stalls at some of the more popular tourist sites and in other outlets in Yerevan (see pages 125–6). The cathedral shop at Ejmiatsin also has a good range of articles. Typically Armenian are carpets (and for those who want something cheaper than a full-sized floor covering, bags and waistcoats made from carpet offcuts), wood and

TAKING SOUVENIRS HOME

By law, exporting any work of art which is more than 75 years old from Armenia requires approval from the government's Department of Cultural Heritage Preservation at 51 Komitas Avenue, third and fourth floors. For those without linguistic skills, it is advisable to get the dealer to sort it out. You need to take the item, together with two photographs, to the third floor – the Department of Expertise – and pay a small initial fee. You then go to the fourth floor – the permit department – with the photographs and the papers issued on the third floor. You pay a further sum which depends on the valuation of the expertise department. The sums due are variable but in the past they have been around 3–5% of the valuation. Generally the permit is then issued on the spot. However, if the item is considered to be of national importance museums and art galleries have a month to exercise the option to buy it. If none want it an export permit will be issued. This procedure is not required for items less than 75 years old, but the date, name of the author and his/her signature should be appended.

This may be rigorously enforced in the case of paintings (sometimes even those painted last week by an unknown artist and bought at Vernissage) and handmade carpets, but often less so in the case of other items such as carvings or embroideries. In the past, there were reports of customs officers at the airport citing rules written and unwritten and refusing to allow the export of paintings in particular, despite the purchaser having the correct paperwork. Bribery was reported to work in these cases.

stone carving, embroidered articles (from large tablecloths to handkerchiefs; see page 133) and jewellery incorporating Armenia's semiprecious obsidian (see page 3). Paintings for sale are displayed at weekends in the small park to the northwest of the opera house in Yerevan and at Vernissage.

Both large and small towns in the provinces have all the basic facilities such as shops, banks, post offices, etc. Almost every village has a well-stocked shop and many petrol and gas stations have a small shop attached.

ARTS AND ENTERTAINMENT

As in most countries, but perhaps more so than in many, access to the arts and to formal entertainments is concentrated in the capital. All the major **museums and art galleries** are in or near Yerevan (see pages 150–7). Other towns do have small museums and art galleries, many of which are worth visiting, but they do not compare to those in Yerevan. Labelling in English has improved enormously but many museums, even important Yerevan museums, make no concession to non-Armenian speakers.

Entrance fees are low by Western standards, rarely being more than AMD1,000 and often much less. The entrance fee for children is usually lower than the adult rate. If an English-speaking guide is available, this costs about an extra AMD2,500–5,000. The most commonly encountered foreign-language guided tours are English and Russian. Other languages are much rarer; if available they are noted under individual entries. Most museums are closed on Mondays, a few on other days. Opening hours and days are stated in individual entries.

Theatres and concert halls are also concentrated in Yerevan (see page 124). Performances are usually in Armenian, apart from opera which may be sung in the original language. Theatre tickets cost AMD1,500–15,000 and are usually bought from the venue although tickets for one venue, especially if it is not in the town centre, may sometimes be sold at another. Box offices display posters showing which tickets they are selling. Tour operators can arrange tickets.

In Soviet days most towns had a **cinema** but this is no longer the case; only Yerevan has cinemas, including two refurbished ones (see page 124) which show films in English. Tickets cost AMD1,500–5,000 for evening screenings; AMD500 for matinées. The annual **Golden Apricot International Film Festival** (*3 Moscovian St, Yerevan;* \ *10 521042;* e *info@gaiff.am; www.gaiff.am*) takes place in Yerevan during July. The first festival in 2004 attracted 148 films by 70 film-makers from 20 countries – it has since grown exponentially with the tenth festival in 2013 attracting 1,200 submissions from 94 countries. The festival takes as its theme 'Crossroads of Cultures and Civilisations' and welcomes films representing various nations, ethnicities and religions, collectively depicting the richness of the human experience. The opening of the festival is marked by a traditional blessing of Armenia's famous apricots.

Armenia is a country of **statues**. This is an active art form, perhaps not surprising in a land with such a long history of carving; witness the thousands of khachkars. New statues appear regularly throughout the country. Some statues are described in this guide (see pages 128–44 and 151) but visitors are likely to see many more. Khachkar carving continues to be an active art form.

More modern forms of entertainment such as **casinos** and **nightclubs** are on offer in Yerevan (see page 124), as are some **sports** (see page 125). The Armenians are good at entertaining themselves. They have certainly taken to the café culture;

A NOTE ABOUT SITE NAMES

English versions of Armenian site names sometimes result in tautology if the Armenian name incorporates the type of place it is. The names of two of Armenia's most visited monasteries, Tatev and Noravank, illustrate the problem. In Armenian the former is called Tatev Vank; two words, the first being the name of the place, the second being the Armenian word for monastery. It is therefore correctly called, in English, Tatev Monastery. The other monastery is, in Armenian, Noravank; one word with two parts, *nor* (new) and *vank* (monastery). Usually it is, correctly, referred to just as Noravank but occasionally the tautological Noravank Monastery appears. While this has the merit of indicating what sort of a place is being referred to, it can grate on the ears of purists. (Strictly speaking it should be translated as New Monastery but it never is.)

A similar dilemma arises with names which have the suffix *berd* (fortress), *ler* or *sar* (mountain), *get* (river), *dzor* (gorge) and *lich* (lake).

The following compromise has been adopted for headings **in this guide** in the cause of clarity. Where a name incorporates one of these descriptive suffixes, the heading is given in the form Noravank (monastery). Where the descriptive term is a separate word in Armenian it is translated and given as part of the full name eg: Tatev Monastery.

A related problem is caused by the fact that some places are habitually referred to in a translated form eg: Arpi Lake (not Arpi Lich), while others usually retain their Armenian form eg: Parz Lich (not Parz Lake). In such cases the name most commonly used in English is employed.

2

witness the large numbers of busy cafés in Yerevan's city centre. Bars (see page 123), apart from those in international hotels, are a relatively recent phenomenon; cafés and restaurants are the places to relax, have a drink and enjoy company. Strolling, a pastime which seems to have disappeared from much of Western life, is alive and well in Armenia and visitors may enjoy rediscovering this art.

HISTORIC SITES

In this guide, prices and opening hours are included where they apply. Otherwise assume the site is free and always open.

There may appear to be some confusion between the terms **church** and **monastery** at times. This is because at some sites only the church of a monastery survives but the site is still referred to as a monastery. With more and more churches becoming active places of worship, it is now common for the church itself to be locked at night although the site as a whole may still be accessible. Larger churches, and especially those in well-known historic sites, will be open all day, at least 09.00–18.00 and often longer. Active churches in small villages are now sometimes kept locked unless there is a service taking place but it is often possible to gain entrance. The caretaker, having seen visitors arriving, may well just appear. If not, it is often possible to contact the key-holder, who usually lives nearby, by asking anyone who happens to be around. The key-holder will also sell candles to visitors: it is customary on entering an Armenian church to light candles (see page 36). Most other sites (**fortresses**, **caravanserais**, **prehistoric monuments**) are always open.

MEDIA AND COMMUNICATIONS

MEDIA Armenia has two **television** stations: Armenia First (public television) and Armenia TV (commercial) and over 40 private television companies, mostly owned by wealthy individuals with government connections. They are of little interest to those who do not speak Armenian and, indeed, many Armenians themselves prefer to watch Russian television. The independent television station A1+ is closed down from time to time by the government but posts news on its website (*www.A1plus.am*) in both Armenian and English. The **press** is likewise almost entirely in Armenian with the exception of the weekly *Noyan Tapan Highlights* (*Noah's Ark Highlights*) which gives an English-language résumé of contemporary events as well as listings of what's on at the theatres. It isn't particularly easy to obtain but it is on sale at Artbridge bookshop (*20 Abovian St*) and Salt Sack (*3/1 Abovian St*). Investigative journalists in Armenia are periodically assaulted by thugs employed by those who have vested interests to protect. Censorship was prohibited under a 2004 media law but libel and defamation are punishable by prison terms and journalists have been sentenced under these laws. The US-based NGO Freedom House reports that self-censorship is common, particularly in regard to reporting corruption and the Nagorno Karabagh situation. **Radio** does not play a large part in the life of Armenians, being mostly listened to in the car. Public Radio of Armenia is the national, state-run station. There are also many private radio stations; I am told that the quality is not good. The **internet** is now the main source of news for many Armenians.

TELEPHONE In 2006 the large Russian **mobile** telephone operator VimpelCom acquired the 90% share of Armentel which had been owned since 1998 by the Hellenic Telecommunications Organisation; the remaining 10% remained in the

Alaverdi 253	Goris 284	Spitak 255
Aparan 252	Gyumri 312	Stepanavan 256
Armavir 237	Hrazdan 223	Talin 2490
Artik 244	Ijevan 263	Tsaghkadzor 223
Ashtarak 232	Jermuk 287	Vayk 282
Chambarak 265	Kapan 285	Vanadzor 322
Dilijan 268	Meghri 2860	Vardenis 269
Ejmiatsin 231	Sevan 261	Yeghegnadzor 281
Gavar 264	Sisian 2832	Yerevan 10

For Karabagh phone codes, see page 333. There are several codes for mobile phones but people will give you this with their phone number.

hands of the Armenian government. There had been widespread dissatisfaction with Greek-owned Armentel which levied high charges for poor service. Enormous strides have now been made in modernising the outdated Soviet-era system. In 2008 Armentel was rebranded as Beeline. Beeline (*www.beeline.am*) holds all landlines and 18% of the cellular network. There are two other phone companies, VivaCell-MTS (*www.mts.am*) which holds 61% of the cellular market and Orange (*www.orangearmenia.am*), a relative newcomer, which holds 21%. Mobile phones are ubiquitous and there is good coverage throughout the country. If you need to hire a mobile phone this can be done through Hyur Service (see page 63) for AMD500 per day. Either VivaCell or Orange are recommended for tourists due to the variety of tariffs and languages offered. Beeline's website is only in Armenian and Russian, the other two have an English option. A comparison of tariffs and prices can be found at www.itel.am.

Both Beeline and VivaCell-MTS have 24-hour desks in the arrivals hall at Zvartnots Airport where an Armenian SIM card can be obtained. Note that an identification document is required of both Armenians and foreigners when registering a SIM card so your passport will be needed. All companies have multiple outlets in Yerevan and throughout the country where prepaid or post-paid cards are available and they can also be bought at numerous supermarkets, shops and kiosks.

Your own mobile phone will work in Armenia on a roaming basis if you arrange this with your provider before leaving home. The advantage is that you can keep your own mobile number; the disadvantage is that it is significantly more expensive than using an Armenian SIM card and number. To use an Armenian SIM card in your own phone it will first have to be unlocked. If staying in the country for more than a few days a cheaper and convenient option may be to buy a mobile phone in Armenia. The mobile companies have some very reasonable packages. Telephone numbers starting 60 are starting to appear. These belong to U-com (*www.ucom. am*) an Armenian company which is developing a fibre optic system with the support of the Swedish technology company, Ericsson. They offer TV, internet and mobile phone packages. Being relatively expensive by Armenian standards they are currently used mainly by large commercial companies.

Dialling Armenia from abroad the country code is 374 followed by the local city code. If **dialling within Armenia**, insert an additional 0 before the city code. **In this guide**, town codes are given, where relevant, with the entry for the town and a list of the main ones appears above. Elsewhere, the appropriate code is included

Practical Information MEDIA AND COMMUNICATIONS

2

with the individual phone number, except for Yerevan phone numbers in *Chapter 3*, where the code (10) is omitted from individual numbers.

International calls from Armenia can of course be made from landlines or mobiles as elsewhere. If using a landline, a cheaper option than direct dialling is to purchase an **international call card** available from shops, kiosks, newspaper stands, etc. Instructions are on the card but essentially you dial the number on the card, followed by the scratch number then follow the voice instructions.

In Yerevan and a few other places calls can be made from **public card phones** in the streets, these cards being on sale at post offices and kiosks.

INTERNET Internet services have also improved greatly in recent years to a high standard. All types of connection are available including via the three mobile companies. Wi-Fi is widely available in hotels and cafés. Although not as numerous as they used to be there are still plenty of internet cafés, charging about AMD500 per hour. A curious feature of previous Armenian use of the internet was that it could not cope with the Armenian alphabet and, surprisingly, not even the Cyrillic alphabet with any reliability. Therefore Armenians emailing each other tended to transliterate these languages into Roman letters. Having got used to doing this many Armenians continue to do so, although using the Armenian alphabet is no longer a problem. Problems can arise, however, if you're carrying out internet searches because of the lack of standardisation of transliteration (see page ix).

POSTAL SERVICES The national postal service Haypost (*www.haypost.am*) is now under Dutch management. Post offices throughout the country are being modernised and new services introduced. Post offices, in Haypost's blue, white and orange colours, are widespread; even quite small villages have one. At last postal services to Armenia appear to be improving. Recent letters from the UK have arrived three to four weeks after being posted, much better than the past when they often never arrived at all. Postal services from Armenia to the West are usually reliable. Items have taken as little as six days from Yerevan to Scotland but two weeks is average. It can be slower from the provinces. There is a standard charge of AMD240 for postcards sent abroad. Letters are charged by weight; for those going abroad the cost is AMD375 for letters up to 20g, AMD875 for 20–100g, etc.

BUSINESS

Even after over 70 years of Soviet rule, Armenians have maintained an entrepreneurial spirit. However, corruption in official bodies is widespread, though less of a problem than in Russia, for example. Business practices as such are not widely different from those in the West but it is absolutely vital to be certain of the competence of interpreters when translating between Armenian and Western languages: many problems arise because what is apparently the same word or phrase does not mean precisely the same in two different languages. Business hours are 09.00–17.00. At work men and women are on an equal footing although, as explained on page 37, it is customary for a married woman to stay at home to look after the couple's children while they are young. On a semi-social level, most business visitors find themselves being taken out to restaurants by their hosts for lengthy meals and numerous toasts (see page 93 for the rules on toasting). They may also be taken to historic sites, particularly at the weekend.

BUYING PROPERTY

It is easy to purchase property in Armenia. Foreigners can buy an apartment or house outright although they cannot buy land outright unless they are either of Armenian descent or else buy it through a company (which can be foreign-owned). Foreigners can only lease land, which can be for up to 99 years. Prices are highest in central Yerevan at about US$5,000/m^2, while one of the newly built apartments on Northern Avenue currently costs US$2,500/m^2. Prices drop gradually the further from the centre one travels, with suburban prices being about half this. Prices in towns near Yerevan tend also to be relatively high with prices in other towns considerably lower. The smallest house in the new Vahakni residential community on the northwest outskirts of Yerevan will cost you 141 million drams plus a 'homeowner's fee' of AMD45,000 per month. When looking for anywhere to buy, only ever consider stone-built property: the poor quality of Soviet prefabricated construction was demonstrated vividly in the 1988 earthquake. Property is widely advertised in the local press, including the English-language *Noyan Tapan Highlights*, or you could use a broker to find you something though they rarely speak English. A broker's fee is typically 3% of the purchase price. Brokers will also handle the paperwork, whether or not you purchase through them, for a fee of around US$250.

Sound advice on buying a property in Armenia can be found at www.armeniapedia.org together with recommended brokers and websites.

CULTURAL ETIQUETTE

As is made clear throughout this guide, Armenians are extremely hospitable and, especially in rural areas, visitors will often be invited into people's houses for coffee. Accept with good grace, however poor the family; the invitation is sincere and the family will be genuinely pleased to see you. If dining with a family, including on a homestay, expect to be plied with far more food than it is humanly possible to eat. It is polite to at least try every dish. See the section on drinks (page 93) for the rules on toasting and the section on breakfast (page 89) if you have the (mis)fortune to be invited to a *khash* party.

If invited to someone's home for a meal a small gift for the hostess, who will have spent very many hours preparing the meal, is appropriate – a box of chocolates or flowers (but always an odd number of flowers, an even number is for the cemetery).

When visiting churches it is customary to buy candles (expect to pay AMD60–100 each) and then light them before sticking them in the trays of sand. Matches are provided. There is no particular need to dress more conservatively than elsewhere in Armenia, but women should wear a headscarf if intending to take communion. It is correct to leave a church walking backwards (so as not to turn one's back on God) but some people don't.

Armenians do tend to dress more smartly than Westerners and also more formally. In particular going to someone's house for dinner, or to the theatre, is an occasion for formality (suit or dress) rather than for dressing down. Shorts are worn by both sexes in summer in Yerevan but are much less common elsewhere.

It is normal to greet people any time you meet them outside a town. Just say '*Barev dzez*' – 'Hello'. Expect people in rural areas to be very curious about where you come from, what you are doing, and what you think about Armenia. It is very hard not to interact with local people, although the language barrier is considerable unless you speak either Armenian or Russian. Very few people speak English and even those who do, including English-language teachers, may not understand what is said to them since they are unaccustomed to hearing English spoken by native speakers of the language.

With very few exceptions, Armenians of all ages love having their photograph taken, although it is of course polite to ask before taking a portrait shot. In general, people will happily pose. You may well be remonstrated with by old ladies if you fail to take their photograph while photographing the monument by which they are sitting, and children will quite often pester you to take their picture.

In the West, although we are not necessarily conscious of it, we often smile at someone we are speaking to, even if we do not know them and are encountering them in a superficial business situation, as in a bank or enquiry office. However, this is not always the case in Armenia and it can be surprisingly disconcerting for a foreigner. It is not that the person is surly or doesn't want to see you, it is just that Armenians tend not to smile unless they know you or there is something to smile at, such as a joke.

Again, in the West, we are accustomed to think that if a door is firmly shut it probably means that the place is either closed or one is not meant to enter. This is not the case in Armenia. If the place looks shut it is worth trying the door: the premises may well be fully open for business. For example, the ticket office for the Matenadaran can look shut when it is in fact open. Even in the National Gallery the large forbidding doors to some of the rooms may be firmly shut (sometimes for so prosaic a reason as to keep out the cold) but one is meant to open them to continue the tour of the art gallery.

Some large hotels have an entry hall devoid of furnishing or people. Go up to the next floor and you will find a fully functioning hotel. There may be a couple of burly men sitting in the entrance hall: they will direct you to where you need to go. If a hotel looks deserted when you arrive, don't panic, someone will soon appear.

TRAVELLING POSITIVELY

Armenia's economic situation means there is much poverty, although this is not always evident. The country is very dependent on assistance from outside and help is always welcome, both large and small scale.

Armenian Monuments Awareness Project (AMAP) 101 Pavstos Buzand St, Door 1, Apt 6, Yerevan; ☎+374 10 532455; e contact@armenianheritage.org; www.armenianmonuments.org. An NGO which aims to stimulate sustainable economic development arising from tourism at Armenia's historical, cultural & natural monuments. It also aims to assist in monument preservation & is the body behind much of the welcome recent increase in information at historic sites. Contact them by email if you wish to consider a donation.

HALO Trust Carronfoot, Thornhill, Dumfries DG3 5BF, UK; ☎+44 1848 331100; e mail@halotrust.org; www.halotrust.org. A non-political, non-religious NGO & the largest humanitarian mine-clearance organisation in the world undertakes mine clearing in Nagorno Karabagh (see box, page 326). Some governments are withdrawing funding from the Nagorno Karabagh sphere of operation, eg: the UK's Department for International Development excluded Nagorno Karabagh from its mine-action strategy for 2011–14, despite previously funding mine clearing there, & it has been excluded from the follow-on strategy covering 2014–17. Governmental monies can only be used within the pre-1991 boundaries of Nagorno Karabagh so mine clearance outwith these boundaries is entirely dependent on other sources. All donations, whatever the size, are welcome & can be made via the website (*www.halotrust.org/donate*) or sent to the HALO Trust's headquarters. Anyone wishing their money to be used specifically for Nagorno Karabagh should state this.

Hayastan All-Armenian Fund Hayastan All-Armenian Fund Great Britain, c/o Armenian Vicarage, Iverna Gardens, Kensington, London W8 6TP; www.himnadram.org. Founded in 1992 as a means whereby all Armenians worldwide could contribute to the development & stability of newly independent Armenia. Help is given where it is most needed whether that be infrastructure, economic development, job creation or humanitarian relief. Projects range in size from a new classroom for a village school to 150km of new road, & they also cover green projects such as the planting of trees to replace those cut down for firewood during the electricity shortages of 1992–95. All contributions to programmes great & small are welcome, & not only from members of the diaspora. Donations can be made via the website or through one of the local branches. Donors can be certain that their money will be used to fund the project specified. It will not end up in some corrupt politician's pocket: the diaspora go to see how their money has been spent & would never tolerate corruption.

Orran 6 First Yekmalian St, Yerevan; 10 535167; e orran@orran.am; www.orran.am. A charity established in 2000 with its headquarters in Yerevan. It aims to help the poorest in society, mainly children & the elderly. Visitors are welcome. Donations can be made via their website or by cheque in US dollars to 2217 Observatory Avenue, Los Angeles, CA 90027, USA.

Oxfam Oxfam has worked in Armenia since 1998 to support refugees who fled to Armenia during the Karabagh conflict & the communities in which they settled. It now assists small farmers & women's groups & monitors the impact of government policies on the poor. A visit to Oxfam's projects can be arranged via Margarita Hakobyan at Oxfam's office in Yerevan (*Apt 10, 3a Terian St;* +374 10 538418, 501464). Donations can be sent to Oxfam House (*John Smith Drive, Cowley,*

Oxford OX4 2JY, UK). Anyone who wishes their donation to go specifically to Armenia should state this when donating.

Stuff Your Rucksack www.stuffyourrucksack. com. A website set up by television's Kate Humble which enables travellers to give direct help to small charities, schools or other organisations in the country they are visiting. Although there are no Armenian organisations listed on this website at present the sorts of gifts envisaged would be welcome in Armenia. Some of the other charities listed here may be able to give information about the best means of directing help to where it is needed.

Tekeyan Centre 50 Khanjian St, Yerevan; +374 10 573057; e info@tekeyancentre.am; www.tekeyancentre.am. The stated aim of the organisation, a British-Armenian charity based in London & Yerevan, is to unite all Armenians to develop & spread Armenian culture, science & art all over the world. On a practical level it has provided free textbooks to schools in Armenia & Nagorno Karabagh &, together with the British Embassy in Yerevan, raised funds to install a heating system in the Lord Byron School (see page 231) in Gyumri. Anyone wishing to donate, either specifically for the Lord Byron School or more generally, can contact the British Embassy (*enquiries.yerevan@fco.gov.uk*) or the Tekeyan Centre itself.

World Vision International Head Office, Opal Drive, Fox Milne, Milton Keynes, MK15 0ZR, UK; 919 2nd Avenue, 2nd Floor, New York, NY 10017, USA; e info@worldvision.org.uk; www.wvi.org/armenia. An organisation which includes Armenia in its worldwide aim of working with children, families & their communities to enable them to reach their full potential by tackling the causes of poverty & injustice. Often works by sponsoring individual children. Sponsors receive annual reports about the child/family they sponsor.

UPDATES WEBSITE

You can post your comments and recommendations, and read the latest feedback and updates from other readers online at www.bradtupdates.com/armenia.

Part Two

THE GUIDE

ARMENIA PROVINCES

3

Yerevan

Telephone code: 10

Armenia's capital stands on the Hrazdan River which flows south from Lake Sevan to join the Arax south of the city. The river in its deep gorge skirts the centre of the city on its western side and consequently many visitors only ever see it as they cross Victory Bridge (so called because it was built in 1945) on the drive into the city from Zvartnots Airport. Yerevan's lower parts are at an altitude of around 900m above sea level but the higher parts up on the plateau are around 1,200m. Precipitation is light at 277mm per annum with May being the wettest month (43mm) and August the driest (8mm). The average temperature (measured over 24 hours) varies from –3°C in January to 26°C in July though these averages mask considerable diurnal variation: night-time lows in January are around –15°C while daytime highs in July reach 44°C. Yerevan is a very sunny place with an average of 2,579 hours of sunshine annually (there are 8,760 hours in a year) and only 37 days classed as non-sunny.

Yerevan's centre, Republic Square, boasts some of the finest Soviet-era buildings in the whole of the former USSR and there is a surprising range of architectural styles within the whole central area owing largely to the fusion of Armenian and Russian styles. Outside the central core of the city, Soviet influence is rampant owing to the rapid expansion of the city during that epoch when its population increased 30-fold.

HISTORY

Although Yerevan's fortunes have waxed and waned considerably over time, and it was never the capital of Armenia prior to 1918, it is actually a very old city. The Urartian king Argishti I (ruled c785–c763BC) established a garrison of 6,600 troops at Erebuni in the southeast part of the present city in 782BC, thus making Yerevan older even than Rome which is traditionally claimed to have been founded in 753BC. About a century later, the Urartian king Rusa II (ruled c685–c645BC) chose a different site, Teishebai Uru ('City of [the God] Teisheba') overlooking the Hrazdan River which he believed would be less vulnerable to attack by the Scythians. It is now known as Karmir Blur ('Red Hill') in the western part of the modern city. Erebuni had grown within 100 years to be a substantial settlement but the establishment of Teishebai Uru caused its rapid decline.

Proximity to the fertile plain ensured that Yerevan remained a significant settlement as, along with the rest of Armenia, it was caught up over the centuries of turmoil, its size fluctuating considerably as the degree of urbanisation in the country varied. Eventually it was almost totally destroyed by an earthquake in 1679. The collapsed bridge over the Hrazdan was quickly replaced by a new four-arch structure and Yerevan's importance began to rise again as it found itself close to the frontier line where the Persian, Turkish and Russian empires were jostling for supremacy. At the time of the earthquake, Yerevan itself was under Persian rule,

3

with a mixed Christian and Muslim population. In 1684, at the request of the French king Louis XIV, Shah Suleiman II permitted French Jesuits to establish a mission there to try to persuade the Katholikos to accept the supremacy of the Pope and bring the Armenian Church into the Roman Catholic fold. The missionaries achieved little and greatly lamented the loss of the excellent Yerevan wine when Shah Hussein, who had succeeded his father, banned all wine throughout the Persian Empire in 1694. A new main church to replace those destroyed in the earthquake was erected in 1693–94 and a new central mosque in 1765–66.

Russian southward expansion into the Caucasus began under Peter the Great in 1722, ostensibly with the object of protecting Orthodox believers. It was a fairly gradual process. In 1801, Russia formally annexed eastern Georgia as the new Russian province of Tiflis and installed Prince Paul Tsitsianov, Georgian born but Russian educated, as governor. In 1804, Tsitsianov led a 5,000-strong Russian army south and attacked Yerevan on 1 May. Despite besieging the town from 2 July until 3 September he was forced to withdraw but the following year he was asked by two Armenian notables to try again so as to save the Christian population of Yerevan from Muslim oppression. His haughty reply was to the effect that he did not care even if the Christians at Yerevan were 'dying in the hands of unbelievers' because 'unreliable Armenians with Persian souls' deserved in his view to 'die like dogs' since they had done nothing to help him when he was besieging the city. Tsitsianov was killed at Baku in 1806 and in 1808 Russia made a second attempt, this time under Field Marshal Ivan Vasilievich (1741–1820) but had no more success. Eventually General Ivan Paskevich (1782–1856), a veteran of the Battle of Borodino, succeeded and led victorious Russian troops into Yerevan on 2 October 1827. On this occasion the Tsar awarded him the title Count of Yerevan but he subsequently gained the additional title Prince of Warsaw as a further token of the Tsar's appreciation when he was responsible for killing 9,000 Poles during the second Polish uprising against Russian rule in 1831.

The Russian conquerors found a town which in 1828 had 1,736 low mud-brick houses, 851 shops, ten baths, eight mosques, seven churches, seven caravanserais and six public squares all set among gardens surrounded by mud walls. On the one and only visit to Yerevan by a Tsar, Nikolai I in 1837 described the city as a 'clay pot'. Matters changed only slowly in what was still a garrison town; the principal Russian settlement in Armenia was Alexandropol (Gyumri) rather than Yerevan. Occasional traces of 19th-century Yerevan can still be found, although Yerevan's importance was to change out of all recognition with its proclamation as capital of the First Armenian Republic on 28 May 1918. The brilliant Armenian architect Alexander Tamanian (1878–1936) drew up a master plan in 1924–26 for what was now the capital of Soviet Armenia. It envisaged the creation of a large central square surrounded by imposing buildings constructed of tuff. From this square would lead broad avenues, and encircling the whole central area would be a green ring of parkland. Quite a large part of this did in fact come to pass and is described in the following section.

Tamanian did not, of course, foresee the 30-fold expansion of the city's population during the Soviet era to an estimated 1.2 million with its dreary urban sprawl of apartment blocks. There was in practice considerable local enthusiasm for expanding the city since any Soviet city with a population exceeding one million was considered to be of 'all Union importance' and entitled to benefits which included a metro system and a crematorium. Economic problems since independence have resulted in a fall in Armenia's population so the main focus in building, apart from the new cathedral, is on luxury houses for the new elite together with the paraphernalia of hotels, embassies and accommodation for expatriates which any capital city attracts. There is also under way considerable necessary and welcome refurbishment of the infrastructure, such as roads and pavements, which is largely being paid for by the diaspora. By contrast the erosion of the green belt by an amazing number of cafés is rather sad.

GETTING THERE AND AWAY

Most visitors to Armenia begin their stay in Yerevan, the vast majority arriving **by air** at Yerevan's Zvartnots Airport. For information about arriving by air, including airlines, the airport and transport to the city centre, see pages 66–8. Even those arriving **by bus** from Iran, Georgia or Turkey (via Georgia) (page 69) or **by train** from Georgia (pages 68–9) usually start their tour in Yerevan. Apart from the fact that most transport delivers passengers to the city, there is much to be said for starting in the capital, which has the best sources of information, much of the cultural life and is where bookings (for accommodation, hire cars, etc) can most easily be made if not arranged in advance. Many of the important historical sites can be reached in day trips from the capital and all transport to the provinces goes through Yerevan.

Hiring a car, with or without driver, gives most flexibility, especially if wishing to reach off-the-beaten-track places (see pages 58 and 84). Rates range from AMD22,000 to AMD75,000 per day. For some sites 4x4 is essential; these are noted under individual entries.

It is possible to reach most places by **public transport** but note that the transport serves local communities, so if a tourist site is not near a town or village it will not be served per se. Most public transport is in the form of buses or minibuses (see pages 80–2) which are cheap, the longest journeys in the country costing AMD6,000. Trains are even cheaper, the most expensive journey costing only AMD1,000, but much of Armenia is not covered by rail. There are, however, some routes which may be useful to visitors (see pages 79–80).

Taxis (pages 82–3) are also relatively cheap, are abundant and can provide a viable alternative to a hire car or public transport. For example, a taxi for the 120km from Vanadzor to Yerevan costs around AMD10,000. They are the only option for getting to some places not served by public transport, apart from walking or cycling.

GETTING AROUND

BY METRO The metro consists of one line together with a short branch in the southern suburbs. It is safe, efficient and cheap. The main line runs from the north side of the city across the central district and out to the south. The stations most likely to be of interest to visitors are, from north to south: Marshal Baghramian [116 C1] (near the British embassy); Yeritasardakan ('Youth') [117 G2] on the green belt east of the Cascade; Hanrapetutian Hraparak ('Republic Square') [117 F5] which is not actually on Republic Square but is behind the art gallery at the west end of Vernissage; Zoravar Andranik ('Commander Andranik') [117 E7] opposite the foot of the slope leading up to the cathedral; and Sasuntsi Davit ('David of Sassoun') [112 D5] adjacent to the main railway station. The first section from Barekamutyun ('Friendship') [112 D3] in the north to Sasuntsi Davit was opened on 7 March 1981. The system was then extended south to Gortsaranain ('Factory') [112 D6] in 1983, Shengavit [112 D6] in 1985 and Garegin Nzhdehi Hraparak ('Garegin Nzhdeh Square') [112 C6] in 1987. The branch to Charbakh [112 C6] was opened after independence in 1996 to make a total of 13.4km of route with ten stations. An extension into the northwestern suburbs is

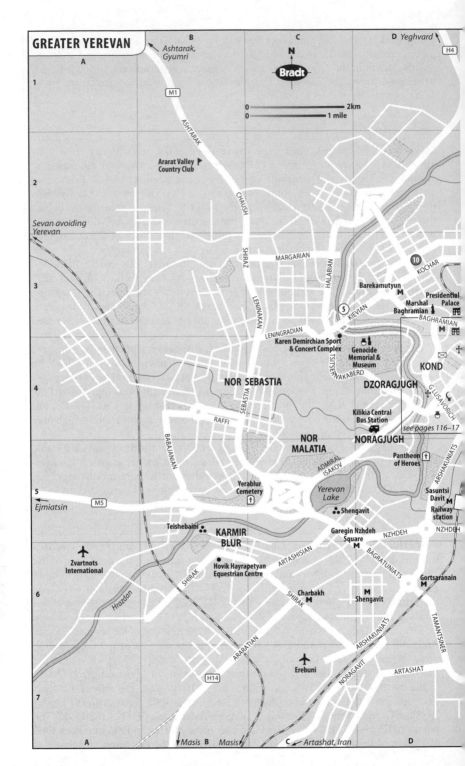

GREATER YEREVAN

Ashtarak, Gyumri

N

Bradt

0 ——————— 2km
0 ——————— 1 mile

M1

ASHTARAK

Ararat Valley
Country Club

CHAUSH

Sevan avoiding
Yerevan

SHIRAZ

MARGARIAN

HALABIAN

KOCHAR

10

Barekamutyun
M

Marshal
Baghramian M

Presidential
Palace

5 KIEVIAN

BAGHRAMIAN

M

LENINAKAN

LENINGRADIAN

Karen Demirchian Sport
& Concert Complex

TSITSERNAKABERD

Genocide
Memorial &
Museum

KOND

NOR SEBASTIA

SEBASTIA

DZORAGJUGH

G LUSAVORICH

RAFFI

Kilikia Central
Bus Station

NORAGJUGH

see pages 116–17

BABAJANIAN

NOR
MALATIA

ADMIRAL
ISAKOV

Pantheon
of Heroes

ARSHAKUNIATS

Yerablur
Cemetery

Yerevan
Lake

Sasuntsi
Davit M

Ejmiatsin

M5

Shengavit

Railway
station

NZHDEH

Teishebaini

KARMIR
BLUR

Garegin Nzhdeh
Square M

NZHDEH

BAGRATUNIATS

Gortsaranain
M

Zvartnots
International

SHIRAK

Hovik Hayrapetyan
Equestrian Centre

ARTASHISIAN

SHIRAK

Charbakh
M

Shengavit
M

ARSHAKUNIATS

TAMANTSINER

Hrazdan

ARARATIAN

H14

Erebuni

NORAGAVIT

ARTASHAT

Masis

Masis

Artashat, Iran

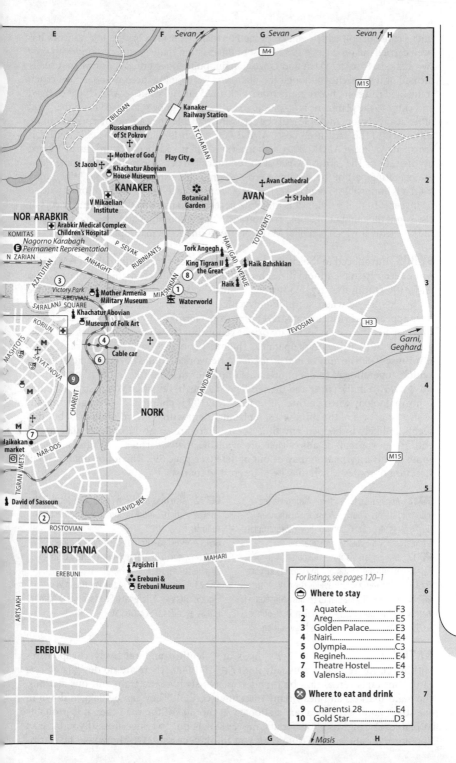

E F Sevan G Sevan H Sevan H

M4

M15

1

TBILISIAN ROAD

Kanaker
Railway Station

ATCHARIAN

Russian church
of St Pokrov

Mother of God Play City ●

St Jacob Khachatur Abovian
House Museum

KANAKER

Botanical
Garden

AVAN Avan Cathedral

St John

2

V Mikaelian
Institute

NOR ARABKIR

Arabkir Medical Complex
Children's Hospital

KOMITAS
Nagorno Karabagh
Permanent Representation
N ZARIAN

P SEVAK

ANHAGHT

RUBINIANTS

HAIK (GAI) AVENUE

TOTOVENTS

Tork Angegh

King Tigran II
the Great

8

Haik

Haik Bzhshkian

3

AZATUTIAN

3

Victory Park

SARALANJ SQUARE ABOVIAN

MIASNIKIAN

Mother Armenia
Military Museum

1

Waterworld

Khachatur Abovian
Museum of Folk Art

TEVOSIAN

H3

Garni,
Geghard

KORIUN

4

Cable car

DAVID-BEK

4

MASHTOTS

SAYAT-NOVA

M

M

9

CHARENT

6

NORK

Haikakan
market

7

M

NAR-DOS

METS

TIGRAN

M15

5

David of Sassoun

DAVID-BEK

2

ROSTOVIAN

NOR BUTANIA

EREBUNI

MAHARI

Argishti I

Erebuni &
Erebuni Museum

ARTSAKH

For listings, see pages 120–1

🛏 **Where to stay**

1 Aquatek......................F3
2 Areg...........................E5
3 Golden Palace............E3
4 Nairi..........................E4
5 Olympia......................C3
6 Regineh.....................E4
7 Theatre Hostel...........E4
8 Valensia.....................F3

6

EREBUNI

✖ **Where to eat and drink**

9 Charentsi 28...............E4
10 Gold Star...................D3

7

E F G Masis H

under construction which will cross the Hrazdan River on a bridge, but no work has been carried out on it since 1989. Most of the existing route is underground with only two stations, Sasuntsi Davit and Gortsaranain, built above ground. Trains are usually formed of two coaches although the platforms were built to accommodate five-coach trains, and run every five minutes from 06.30 to 23.00. A flat fare of AMD100 is charged and entry to the platforms is by plastic tokens which can be purchased from the ticket office at any station. Multiple journey cards are available; they are no cheaper, just more convenient. (The card itself costs AMD1,000 which is refundable when the card is returned. An initial AMD2,000 (20 journeys) is purchased then the card can be topped up thereafter.) The card is swiped at the entrance barrier. The maps of the route show the operating part of the system in red and projected extensions in blue. When on a train it is impossible to read the names of stations since the signs are positioned so as to be invisible from the trains. It is therefore necessary to listen to the announcements or else count the number of stops. The entrances to stations are marked on the surface by the blue letter Մ which is capital M (for Metro) in the Armenian alphabet.

BY BUS Introduced to the city in 1949, **trolleybuses** charge a flat fare of AMD100. More recently conventional diesel **buses** have been added for which the fare is also AMD100 within the city. No further vehicles were purchased after independence until 2003, since when secondhand vehicles from Marseille, Lyon and Florence have appeared as well as new MAN buses from Germany and smaller Isuzu vehicles from Japan. The new vehicles are bright yellow but the secondhand ones still sport the livery of their previous operator. The most conspicuous means of transport is **minibuses** (*marshrutny* or *marshrutkas*). A network of routes covers the city with the vehicles operating at frequent intervals until the small hours. To board one simply wave it down in the street and then indicate to the driver when you wish to alight. It is normal to pay when getting off. A flat AMD100 is charged. The city government wishes to get rid of the minibuses, replacing them with conventional ones, but this seems unlikely to happen any time soon. There are some 125 *marshrutka* routes within Yerevan; full details of each are available at www.armeniainfo.am, although some of this information may be out of date (see page 59). The following is a small selection of routes which may be of interest to tourists:

🚌 **18** Abovian Sq to Zvartnots Airport via the following streets: Abovian, Moskovian, Khanjian, Tigran Mets, Artsakh, Garegin Nzhdeh, Bagratuniats, Admiral Isakov & Ejmiatsin crossroads.

🚌 **17** Mergelyan Institute, Hakobian St (near Barekamutyun metro station) to Zvarnots Airport, via a westerly route which avoids the city centre.

🚌 **11** Central Bus Station to Erebuni Museum via Victory Bridge, Mashtots Av, Amirian St, Republic Sq, Tigran Mets Av & the main railway station.

🚌 **72** Also runs between Erebuni Museum & the railway station, before heading into the western suburbs.

🚌 **37** Proshyan Brandy Factory (Ashtarak Highway, north of Ararat Valley Country Club) to Zvartnots Airport.

🚌 **23** Railway station to the Pantheon via Tigrans Mets Av, Khorenatsi St, Mashtots & Admiral Isakov avenues & Sebastia St.

BY TAXI (See also pages 82–3.) Taxis are plentiful and relatively cheap. Fares within central Yerevan are usually under AMD1,000. There are no designated taxi ranks but taxis can always be found at places such as the train and bus stations, the main markets and near many road intersections. They can be flagged down in the street and if you see a taxi stationary at the side of the road then it is probably available. During rush hour, traffic moves slowly due to congestion. If you have an appointment allow more time than you think necessary. On the whole taxi firms and drivers do not speak English so if phoning for a taxi it is best to ask your hotel or host to do it for you. There are dozens, if not hundreds, of reliable taxi firms in Yerevan including the following:

🚕 **Aerotaxi** ✆10 771100; m 055 319050; e info@aerotaxi.am; www.aerotaxi.am. Official taxi service of Zvartnots Airport (see page 68).
🚕 **Alex** ✆10 209090

🚕 **Busy** ✆10 211000, 222222
🚕 **Pink** ✆10 209999. A taxi service for women only.
🚕 **Super** ✆10 534110, 531410

ON FOOT For those who are reasonably fit central Yerevan is best explored on foot, not least because it can be quicker and pleasanter than sitting in a vehicle (especially a crowded minibus in the heat of summer) in a traffic jam. Those unaccustomed to walking may find that some of the distances, especially when going uphill, stretch them. Personally, I have found it perfectly easy to cover the whole of the area within the circular green belt and somewhat beyond (the area shown as central Yerevan on most maps) on foot.

Envoy Hostel (*www.envoyhostel.com*) organises free daily (morning and evening) guided walking tours of Yerevan (see page 120).

TOURIST INFORMATION

Sadly, the once excellent Armenian Tourism Development Agency (and its tourist information office) no longer operates. A website still exists (*www.armeniainfo.am*) which has some information although much is out of date. A number of maps and free leaflets are available from most hotels. Two booklets are particularly useful: *Yerevan Scope* (*www.yerevanscope.am*) has information about Yerevan and the provinces as well as a wealth of practical information. *TourInfo* (*www.ati.am*), published monthly, also provides practical information, including details of what is on in theatres and concert halls.

For a list of local tour operators in Yerevan, see pages 63–4. Note that some agents offer a variety of services which may be of use to visitors, such as Hyur Service (page 63) which offers apartment and house accommodation, house cleaning and laundry, interpreter services (*1hr/1 day AMD20,000/120,000*) and cell-phone rental (*AMD500/day*) as well as organising tours and car rental.

WHERE TO STAY

The development of new hotels in Yerevan, particularly upmarket ones, has been considerable in recent years, but there are fewer available at the lower end of the market. In February 2006 a new official voluntary grading system (from one to five stars) for hotels, motels and spas was introduced by the Ministry of Trade and Economic Development, shown either as five-pointed stars or in Roman numerals. During the winter many hotels charge a lower rate. It is now required by law that hotels quote their prices in AMD but note that a few tend to quote their prices excluding Armenia's 20% VAT. Some hotels away from the central area provide free transport to and from the centre. This can be quite a pleasant option in the heat and humidity of midsummer but the inconvenience would probably outweigh the bonuses for most visitors.

In October 2005, Armenia's first backpacker hostel, Envoy (see page 120), opened charging US$15 per night – it became understandably popular. For some years it was Yerevan's only hostel but others have now opened.

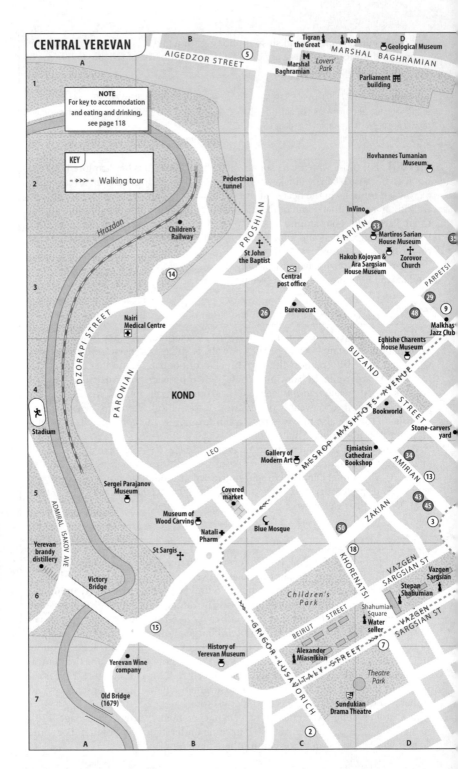

CENTRAL YEREVAN

A B C D

AIGEDZOR STREET

MARSHAL BAGHRAMIAN

Tigran the Great
Noah
Geological Museum

Marshal Baghramian
Lovers' Park

Parliament building

NOTE
For key to accommodation and eating and drinking, see page 118

KEY
- >>> - Walking tour

Hovhannes Tumanian Museum

Pedestrian tunnel

InVino

Hrazdan

Children's Railway

PROSHIAN

SARIAN

Martiros Sarian House Museum

St John the Baptist

Hakob Kojoyan & Ara Sargsian House Museum

Zorovor Church

PARPETSI

Central post office

DZORAPI STREET

Nairi Medical Centre

Bureaucrat

Eghishe Charents House Museum

Malkhas Jazz Club

PARONIAN

KOND

BUZAND STREET

MESROP MASHTOTS AVENUE

Bookworld

Stone-carvers' yard

Stadium

LEO

Gallery of Modern Art

Ejmiatsin Cathedral Bookshop

AMIRIAN

Sergei Parajanov Museum

Covered market

Museum of Wood Carving

ZAKIAN

ADMIRAL ISAKOV AVE

Natali Pharm

Blue Mosque

St Sargis

KHORENATSI

VAZGEN SARGSIAN ST

Yerevan brandy distillery

Victory Bridge

Children's Park

Vazgen Sargsian

Stepan Shahumian

BEIRUT STREET

Shahumian Square
Water seller

VAZGEN SARGSIAN ST

History of Yerevan Museum

GRIGOR LUSAVORICH

ITALY STREET

Alexander Miasnikian

Theatre Park

Yerevan Wine company

Sundukian Drama Theatre

Old Bridge (1679)

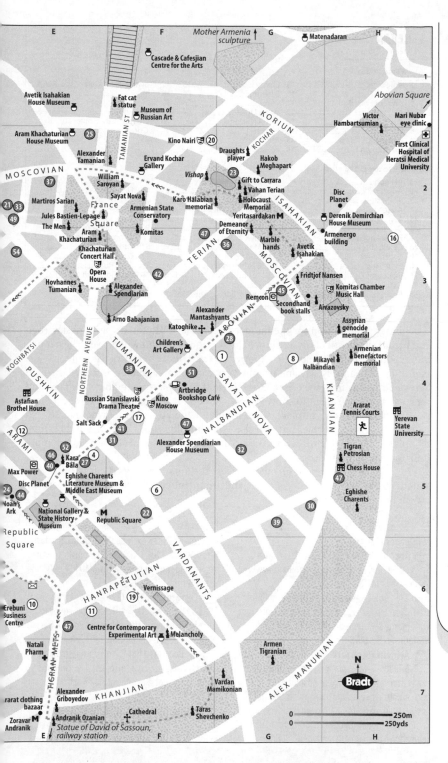

Mother Armenia sculpture

Matenadaran

Cascade & Cafesjian Centre for the Arts

Abovian Square

Avetik Isahakian House Museum

Fat cat statue

Museum of Russian Art

Victor Hambartsumian

Mari Nubar eye clinic

Aram Khachaturian House Museum

25

Kino Nairi 20

First Clinical Hospital of Heratsi Medical University

Alexander Tamanian

Ervand Kochar Gallery

Draughts player

Hakob Meghapart

MOSCOVIAN

37

William Saroyan

Vishap

23

Gift to Carrara

Vahan Terian

Disc Planet

Martiros Sarian

France Square

Sayat Nova

Karo Halabian memorial

Holocaust Memorial

Derenik Demirchian House Museum

21 33

49

Jules Bastien-Lepage

Armenian State Conservatory

Yeritasardakan M

Armenergo building

16

The Men

Komitas

Demeanor of Eternity

Marble hands

54

Aram Khachaturian

47

36

Avetik Isahakian

Khachaturian Concert Hall

Fridtjof Nansen

Opera House

Alexander Spendiarian

42

Komitas Chamber Music Hall

Hovhannes Tumanian

Remcon

45

Secondhand book stalls

Aivazovsky

Arno Babajanian

Alexander Mantashyants

Katoghike ✝

28

Assyrian genocide memorial

Children's Art Gallery

1

8

Mikayel Nalbandian

Armenian benefactors memorial

Astafian Brothel House

38

51

Artbridge Bookshop Café

Ararat Tennis Courts

Yerevan State University

Russian Stanislavski Drama Theatre

Kino Moscow

17

Salt Sack

41

47

12

31

Alexander Spendiarian House Museum

32

Tigran Petrosian

46

52

Kara Bala

4

27

Chess House

Max Power

40

47

Disc Planet

Eghishe Charents Literature Museum & Middle East Museum

6

Eghishe Charents

24 44

Noah's Ark

National Gallery & State History Museum

M

Republic Square

22

30

39

Republic Square

Vernissage

Erebuni Business Centre

10

19

Natali Pharm

11

47

Centre for Contemporary Experimental Art

Melancholy

Armen Tigranian

N

Bradt

rarat clothing bazaar

Alexander Griboyedov

Vardan Mamikonian

0   250m
0   250yds

Zoravar Andranik M

Andranik Ozanian

Cathedral ✝

Taras Shevchenko

Statue of David of Sassoun, railway station

⌂ Where to stay

1	Ani Plaza......................G4	9	Envoy Hostel................D3	17	Royal Tulip Yerevan...............F4
2	Ararat...........................C7	10	Erebuni........................E6	18	Shirak...C6
3	Armenia Marriott......D5	11	Europe.........................E6	19	Tufenkian Historic
4	Aviatrans....................E5	12	Hotel House...............E4		Yerevan.......................F6
5	Bass............................C1	13	Hotel National.............D5	20	Yerevan State University
6	Center Hostel.............F5	14	Hrazdan.......................B3		Guest House.......................F2
7	Congress...................D6	15	Metropol......................B6		
8	Downtown Hostel.....G4	16	Penthouse Hostel........H3		

✕ Where to eat and drink

21	Ai Leoni.....................E2	34	Green Bean Coffee	46	Square One......................E5
22	Ankyun........................F5		Shop........................D5	47	Tashir Pizza...............E6, F3,
23	Aragast.......................G2	35	Jazzve.........................D3		F4, H5
24	Ararat.........................E5	36	Jingalov Hats...............G3	48	The Bell......................D3
25	Arya...........................E2	37	Karloff.........................E2	49	The Club.....................E2
26	Beerloga Pub.......................C3	38	Khinkalis......................F4	50	The Colour of
27	Black Angus Burger Bar......E5	39	Kilikia...........................G5		Pomegranates..............C5
28	Café Central......................G4	40	Marco Polo..................E5	51	Thomas Tea....................F4
29	Cantaloupe......................D3	41	Natura Gold.................F4	52	Tiziano...........................E5
30	Caucasus......................G5	42	Our Village...................F3	53	Tro's Pub.......................D2
31	Dolmama.........................F5	43	Pandok Yerevan..........D5	54	Van Gogh Art Café.........E3
32	Dvin............................G5	44	Pizza di Roma..............E5		
33	EcoPub......................E2	45	Segafredo.............D5, G3		

Another good option for the budget traveller is undoubtedly a homestay (bed and breakfast), particularly as dinner can be requested and will prove to be a much more authentically Armenian experience than most restaurants will provide. Homestays, invariably safe and usually very comfortable, can be arranged through Yerevan travel agents (see pages 63–4). It's best to buy a street plan beforehand and then ask the travel agent to show you where you are going as the biggest problem is often finding the right place. Take a note of the address in Armenian so that you can enquire of people, and also ask which minibus goes in the right direction: or 'splash out' on one of Yerevan's very inexpensive taxis. See page 86 for more information on homestays.

For a general overview of hotel prices, see box, page 86. Unless otherwise stated, all listings below accept cards and are included on one of the two Yerevan city maps.

CENTRAL AREA HOTELS

Map, pages 116–17.

⌂ **Ararat** (50 rooms) 7 Grigor Lusavorich St; ☏60 511000; e info@ararathotel.am; www.ararathotel.am. This pleasant, colourfully decorated hotel was built in 1990 & has helpful staff, disabled access & a roofed central courtyard with plants & water feature. Swimming pool. Restaurant. **$$$$$**

⌂ **Armenia Marriott** (256 rooms) 1 Amirian St; ☏599000; e armenia.marriott@marriot.com; www.marriottarmenia.com. Absolutely central with an attractive façade on Republic Square. The building dates from 1954 but has been completely modernised & the formerly small rooms have been greatly enlarged. All rooms have separate living & sleeping areas. Wi-Fi. Restaurant. Prices exclude the 20% tax & b/fast. B/fast AMD7,200–12,000pp. The most expensive accommodation in Armenia at AMD111,000/dbl + tax & b/fast. **$$$$$**

⌂ **Congress Hotel** (126 rooms) 1 Italy St; ☏591199; e sales@hotelcongressyerevan.com; www.congresshotelyerevan.com. A Best Western chain hotel built in 2001. Pleasant, brightly decorated hotel with 2 non-smoking floors. Wi-Fi. Fitness centre & sauna. Outdoor swimming pool. Restaurant. Tax & b/fast not inc. **$$$$$**

⌂ **Europe** (47 rooms) 38 Hanrapetutian St; ☏546060; e sales@europehotel.am; www.europehotel.am. Attractive central hotel opened in 2003. French spoken. Brochure states hotel is of French design. Wi-Fi. Non-smoking rooms available. **$$$$$**

⌂ **Hotel National** (55 rooms) 4 Amirian St; ☎574000; e reservation@hotelnational.am; www.hotelnational.am. A new luxury hotel in central Yerevan with 'Art Deco inspired décor'. Opened 2012. Restaurant, café, fitness centre & swimming pool. Wi-Fi. Same price for sgl or dbl occupancy AMD104,000 **$$$$$**

⌂ **Royal Tulip Yerevan** (104 rooms) 14 Abovian St; ☎591600; e marketing@hotelyerevan.com; www. royaltulipgrandhotelyerevan.com. Yerevan's oldest hotel. It was built in 1927 & refurbished in 1998 but the rooms are surprisingly small. On the main shopping street about 5 mins from the centre. Rooftop swimming pool. Restaurant. Wi-Fi. B/fast extra AMD7,000pp. AMD99,6000 (Mar–Aug); AMD109,560 (Sep & Oct) **$$$$$**

⌂ **Tufenkian Historic Yerevan Hotel** (86 rooms) 48 Hanrapetutian St; ☎60 501030, 60 501010; e hotels@tufenkian.am; www. tufenkian.am. Describes itself as 'a new building in the style of classic European & 20th-century Armenian style'. Opened 2012. Central; adjacent to Vernissage. Craft shop & carpet showroom. Restaurant offers 'classic West Armenian cuisine'. Wi-Fi. **$$$$$**

⌂ **Ani Plaza** (248 rooms) 19 Sayat Nova Av; ☎589500, 589700; e info@anihotel.com; www. anihotel.com. A 14-storey tower block, of which 9 floors in use as hotel, built in 1970 & partially renovated since 2002. Has non-smoking rooms. 10 mins' walk from the centre. Branch of Hyur travel agency in lobby. Restaurant. Swimming pool. Wi-Fi. Prices reflect the central location. **$$$$**

⌂ **Aviatrans Hotel** (55 rooms) 4 Abovian St; ☎60 484444, 60 484484; e hotel@aviatrans. am; www.hotelaviatrans.com. A comfortable, relatively small, central hotel with very helpful reception staff. Built in 1998, renovated 2008. Restaurant. Currency exchange, Avis car rental & gift shop within hotel. Wi-Fi. **$$$$**

⌂ **Hotel House** (13 rooms) 42 Arami St; ☎583800, 587900; m 099 583800; e info@ hotelhouse.am; www.hotelhouse.am. This small, well-appointed hotel in the city centre opened in 2010. Helpful reception with tourist information on display. Can arrange tours. Small garden &

outside swimming pool. Wi-Fi. B/fast inc; other meals not available. Accepts MasterCard & Visa. Feb–Aug **$$$**; Sep & Oct **$$$$**

⌂ **Metropol** (109 rooms) 2/2 Mesrop Mashtots Av; ☎510700; e metropol@metropol. am; www.metropol.am. Close to Victory Bridge about 20 mins' walk from the centre. Refurbished in 2010, it offers 'luxurious comfort & classic sophistication' & has a somewhat ponderous feel, reminiscent of Soviet luxury. Swimming pool, sauna, gym. Restaurant. Wi-Fi. **$$$$**

⌂ **Bass** (41 rooms) 3/1 Aigedzor St; ☎261080; e bassboutiquehotel@gmail.com; www.bass.am. Located on the west side of the city near the American University about 20 mins' walk or 5 mins by taxi from the centre. 100m from Marshal Baghramian metro station. Built in 1995, it was the first new hotel to be opened after independence. Originally small, it has expanded over the years. Pleasant staff & good food. Restaurant, café. Wi-Fi. **$$$**

⌂ **Erebuni** (38 rooms) 26/4 Vazgen Sargsian St; ☎564994, 580505; e info@erebunihotel. am; www.erebunihotel.am. Renovation has transformed this hotel which dates back to 1980, bringing it completely up to date. Helpful staff. Wi-Fi. Restaurant. **$$$**

⌂ **Hrazdan** (77 rooms) 72 Dzorapi St; ☎535332; e info@hotelhrazdan.am; www. hotelhrazdan.am. As the name implies, situated on the west side overlooking the gorge of the river. About 20 mins' walk or 5 mins by taxi to the centre. A 15-storey tower block built in 1976 & now renovated. The lift lobbies are box-like but the rooms themselves have lots of windows. A bright, cheerful, marble entrance hall. Outdoor swimming pool. Wi-Fi. **$$$**

⌂ **Shirak** (140 rooms) 13a Khorenatsi St; ☎529915; e info@shirakhotel.am; www. shirakhotel.am. Large 14-storey tower block built in 1981 with renovation continuing. Restaurant, café. Tour agency in hotel. Wi-Fi. **$$$**

⌂ **Yerevan State University Guest House** (45 rooms, various permutations of sgl, dbl, trpl & family) 52 Mesrop Mashtots Av; ☎560003; e ysuguesthouse@gmail. com. Accommodation for guests of the university; will accept others if rooms available. Refurbishment has turned it into pleasant, if basic, accommodation. 4 floors, no lifts. Restaurant & café. Wi-Fi. Cash only. **$$**

🏠 **Center Hostel** (3 rooms) Apt 31, 4 Vardanants St; ☎528639; m 093 444333; e info@center-hostel.com; www.center-hostel.com. Close to town centre. Renovated rooms. Lockers & storage inc. Wi-Fi. B/fast inc. Cash in advance. 6-bedded/4-bedded room AMD4,000/5,000pp. **$**

🏠 **Downtown Hostel** (can accommodate up to 45 ppl in sgl, dbl, trpl, quad rooms & 8-bedded single-sex dorms) 31/42 Nalbandian St; ☎564910; m 094 997794; e info@downtownhostel.org; www.downtownhostel.org. Run by the same people as Penthouse Hostel (see below) but a little nearer the city centre. Prices same as Penthouse. 24hr reception. Wi-Fi. Tea & coffee throughout the day; b/fast inc; other meals can be ordered. Cash only. **$**

🏠 **Envoy Hostel** (2 rooms with 8 beds, 6 rooms with 4 beds) 54 Pushkin St – entrance round the corner, from Parpetsi St; ☎530369; e info@envoyhostel.com; www.envoyhostel.com. Everything a hostel should be, although one visitor found it noisy. This clean, well-organised central hostel has 24hr reception, spacious toilet/shower rooms (separate male/female), common room, kitchen & Wi-Fi. Arranges tours to popular Armenian sites & to Nagorno Karabagh (*www.envoytour.am*) & free daily walking tours of Yerevan. B/fast inc. **$**

🏠 **Penthouse Hostel** (5 rooms: 3 dbl/twin, 1 trpl, 1 dorm with 9 beds) 5 Koriun St; m 094 997794; e info@penthousehostel.org; www.penthousehostel.org. On the 6th & 7th floor of Soviet era block of flats, on northeast section of outer ring road. Shared bathroom facilities. Communal areas spacious & clean. 24hr reception. English & Russian spoken. Tea & coffee always available. B/fast inc. Wi-Fi. No smoking apart from on the balcony, from where there are views over Yerevan to Mount Ararat. Dorm AMD5,500pp. Cash only. **$**

HOTELS OUTSIDE THE CENTRE
Map, pages 112–13.

🏠 **Golden Palace** (66 rooms) 2/2 Azatutian Av; ☎219999; e info@goldenpalacehotel.am; www.goldenpalacehotel.am. A luxury hotel in a pleasant location overlooking the city near the top of the Cascade: not a long way out but too far to walk – though you can use the Cascade escalator. Free taxi to city centre once daily. Opened in 2005.

Sauna, swimming pool, spa treatments, several restaurants. Live music every day; piano Mon–Thu; jazz Fri–Sun. Wi-Fi. **$$$$$**

🏠 **Aquatek Hotel** (28 rooms) 40 Miasnikian Av; ☎588888; m 091 500202; e info@aquatek.am; www.aquatek.am. In Nork district about 15 mins from the centre by taxi. The hotel is an integral part of the Aquatek building which also houses the aquapark (swimming pools, other water amusements, gym & sauna) to which hotel guests have free access. Rooms are bright, modern & overlook the swimming pool. All bedrooms are up stairs; no lift. Wi-Fi. Note that part of the cost is entry to aquapark. Accepts cards excluding MasterCard. **$$$**

🏠 **Nairi Hotel** (120 rooms) 121/7 Armenakian St; ☎652121, 655151; e reservations@hotelnairi.am, marketing@hotelnairi.am; www.hotelnairi.am. In Nork district, this new build, 8-floor hotel opened in 2012. Non-smoking rooms available. Restaurant, swimming pool & sauna. Wi-Fi. **$$$**

🏠 **Regineh** (57 rooms) 235/1 Norki Ayginer; ☎654020; e reservation@hotelregineh.am; www.hotelregineh.am. New, pleasantly airy & bright hotel. A stiff climb up from the city but with good views towards Mount Ararat. Dedicated to the memory of the owner's wife. Non-smoking rooms. Wi-Fi. Swimming pool. Accepts Visa & MasterCard. **$$$**

🏠 **Valensia Hotel** (37 rooms & cottages) 40 Miasnikian Av; ☎524000; e valensiareservation@xgroup.am; www.xgroup.am. In Nork district, 15 mins from centre by taxi. Rates inc 1 free admission to next-door-but-one Waterworld (not next door Aquatek) which has various facilities for cooling off during the summer inc a wave pool. This makes it a good option for families. Opened in 2001. Wi-Fi. Restaurant. Accepts Visa & MasterCard. **$$$**

🏠 **Areg** (14 rooms) 80 Bournazian St; ☎456213; e info@areghotel.com; www.areghotel.com. Located near the main railway station & hence easily accessible by metro. A pleasant small family-run hotel in a quiet suburban street. All rooms upgraded. Can arrange tours & cottages at Lake Sevan. Wi-Fi. **$$**

🏠 **Olympia** (30 rooms) 64 Barbyus St; ☎271850; e olympia2000@rambler.ru; www.olympia.am. Near the Kievian bridge, overlooking the Hrazdan River on the northwest side about 15 mins by taxi from the centre. Restaurant & summer outdoor café. Wi-Fi. **$$**

Theatre Hostel (7 rooms: sgl, dbl, trpl, 4-bedded, 8 bedded) 27 Tigran Mets Av (entrance at back of bldg; go through alley next to Beeline office); 545674; m 099 548676; e info@theatre. am; www.theatrehostel.com. Claims to be 5 mins' walk from Republic Square. This hostel has made significant improvements since it was first opened. Pleasantly decorated communal sitting area. Tea & coffee available all day. Hostel rules clearly stated. English spoken. Shared bathroom facilities. (Self-contained flat in next building also available, sgl/dbl occupancy AMD15,000/20,000.) Wi-Fi. B/fast inc. AMD4,500/5,500pp in 8/4-bedded room. $

WHERE TO EAT AND DRINK

Yerevan has innumerable eating places, many of which, especially away from the centre, are very cheap. The following is merely a selection of interesting and popular places. Apart from these it is worth looking at Proshian Street, known locally as Barbecue Street because it is lined with places to eat in the reasonably priced range. There are lots of open-air (summer) cafés along Yerevan's green belt (now less green because of their number) and also around the opera house. Note that some charge a premium for sitting in areas with comfortable armchairs. Northern Avenue has many cafés and restaurants; prices here tend to be a little higher than elsewhere. Several small restaurants are clustered at the foot of the Cascade.

Most restaurants open at noon and cafés about 10.00. The first exception was Artbridge which opens at 08.30, but an increasing number of cafés in central Yerevan are open by 09.00. Most will stay open until midnight or until the last customer has gone. Few restaurants have websites; those which do exist are often not informative. There are exceptions and websites which are useful have been listed. Outside the central area of Yerevan there are innumerable small places where you can get a cheap snack and most districts of town have an acceptable restaurant (which has three or four bedrooms attached, payable by the hour). If you need to find somewhere to eat, then ask anyone 'Where is there a restaurant?' (*Vorterr e restoran?*).

Note that **restaurants in hotels** are not included in the list below. Hotel restaurants listed on pages 118–20 are open to non-residents. On the whole, Armenia does not have separate bars, although large hotels have bars, and there are stand-alone pubs in Yerevan. Cafés are the places for a wide range of ages to drink as well as eat.

All listings below are included on one of two city maps unless otherwise noted.

IN THE CENTRE
Map, pages 116–17.

Ai Leoni 40 Tumanian St; 538331, 530892; www.aileoni.am. Expensive Italian cuisine.

Ankyun 4 Vardanants St; 544606; www.ankyun.am. A delightful small family-run restaurant. Prices are a little above average but are well worth it for the quality of the food. Meat & fish main courses AMD6,000–7,000; pasta dishes AMD4,500.

Aragast 41 Isahakian St; 545500. An imitation boat with a pleasant view over a small artificial lake with boats. Inexpensive. Jazz in evenings.

Ararat Republic Sq, Government Bldg #2; 527933, 527382, 567634. Yerevan's best restaurant in Soviet days. Live Armenian music in the cellar part in the evening.

Artbridge Bookshop Café 20 Abovian St; 581284, 521239; www.artbridge.am; 08.30–24.00 (see also page 134). One of the few places open early in the morning so useful for b/fast which is available all day. Also soups, salads & pastries.

Arya 1/17 Tamanian St (entrance from Isahakian St); 568013. Iranian restaurant with genuine Persian cuisine. Enjoyable.

Beerloga Pub 24 Sarian St; 527840. Typical pub menu which inc pizza, salads, *lahmadjoun* (see page 90) & main courses. One of its attractions is that it also serves crayfish (AMD500–1,500 each depending on size).

Black Angus Burger Bar 2/5 Abovian St. Has as its logo an image of an Aberdeen Angus

Main courses usually cost somewhere between AMD2,500 and AMD4,000 and it is easy to have a full meal (which in Armenia usually comprises salads and a main course) for AMD5,000. Usually there is not much of a price difference between cafés and restaurants. Restaurants which fall outside this price range are noted under their individual entries. A light course, such as an omelette, may well cost about AMD1,000 and a savoury street snack can be had for as little as AMD150.

bull, one of Scotland's best beef breeds. Describes its beef thus 'originated in Scotland, brought from Germany to be tasted by Armenian gourmets'. A price mark-up of AMD200 for 'Angus beef' over 'beef'. Burgers from AMD1,800–2,900. Also serves pizzas & salads. All beer is German.

✗ **Café Central** (pronounced the French way) 30 Abovian St; ☎ 583990; www.cafecentral.am. Deservedly popular. Good salads & interesting desserts, as well as main courses. Also sells coffee beans/ground coffee.

✗ **Caucasus** 82 Hanrapetutian St; ☎ 561177. Separate section for Armenian & Georgian food but not everything on the extensive menu is always available. Live folk music evenings in the side decorated in Armenian style; you can hear it wafting through to the Georgian side. Reservations advisable.

✗ **Dolmama** 10 Pushkin St; ☎ 568931; www. dolmama.am. Good but very expensive by Yerevan standards. Whether it's worth the money depends on who is paying. Main course AMD10,000.

✗ **Dvin** 14/1 Tumanian St; ☎ 560280, 60 545280. A very successful fusion of Middle Eastern & Armenian cuisines. One of the tastiest restaurant meals I've had in Yerevan.

✗ **Green Bean Coffee Shop** 10 Amirian St; ☎ 529279; www.thegreenbean.am. ⊕ 08.30–23.30. An attractive eco-friendly, non-smoking café which aims to source locally made, preservative-free products. Website informative. Excellent soups (*AMD1,000*) & real homemade lemonade (*AMD1,500*).

✗ **Jazzve** 35 Tumanian St; ☎ 533663; www. jazzve.am. Also at 2 Abovian St, 18 Abovian St (inside Moscow cinema), 8/1 Isahakian St, 16 Komitas St & among the open-air cafés in front of the opera house. Established in 2003, this chain of coffee shops is decorated in literary style, with menus in the form of newspapers. Reliably good

coffee, desserts & a full meals menu. There is no jazz, jazzve being the Armenian word for the long-handled copper pot in which Armenian coffee (*sev soorj*) is traditionally made.

✗ **Jingalov Hats** 62 Terian St; ☎ 582205. Nothing to do with headwear; *jingalov hats* (see page 331) is the typical herb bread from Nagorno Karabagh. This café, which serves only this 1 dish, is good for when you want a quick, filling, tasty snack without having to spend time deciding what to choose. The next best thing to eating it in Karabagh. Also good for vegetarians – no meat served at all. One *hats* costs AMD650 & is ample unless you are very hungry.

✗ **Khinkalis** 21/1 Tumanian St; ☎ 582352. This basement restaurant doesn't really have a name but is known by its speciality, Georgian *khinkali*, ravioli-like dumplings. Indeed the sign outside simply says 'Ravioli'. An extensive area, decorated in large country-house style. Especially busy in winter.

✗ **Kilikia** 78 Hanrapetutian St; ☎ 548808. Pleasant restaurant with traditional Armenian music played at a sensible volume. Reservations advisable.

✗ **Marco Polo** 1/3 Abovian St; ☎ 561926. A popular café with a wide range of dishes. It is possible to have a tasty snack for under AMD1,000.

✗ **Natura Gold** 11 Abovian St; ☎ 582184. Originally a tea house serving speciality teas & desserts, it now serves snacks & main courses too.

✗ **Our Village** 5 Sayat Nova Av; ☎ 548700. In a basement decorated with old coffee pots, radios, etc. Serves only Armenian produce & drinks. Live folk music in the evenings. Waiting staff wear traditional costume & menus (singed at edges) have carefully placed holes burnt in them. An experience. Reservations required.

✗ **Pandok Yerevan** 5 Amirian St (☎ 545545, m 099 545545, ⊕ 10.00–24.00); 7 Paronian St (☎ 530563, m 091 530563, ⊕ 10.00–24.00); 29/2 Khorenatsi St (☎ 582515, 562515, ⊕ 09.00–

24.00); www.pandokyerevan.am. A chain of 3 restaurants specialising in Armenian food. Serves dishes such as *khash* & *harissa* in winter, *dolma* in summer. Popular with locals.

✕ Pizza di Roma 1 Abovian St, with smaller branches elsewhere; ✆587175. Forget the name, this place serves a wide range of food, inc fixed price salad buffet. Excellent quality & value.

✕ Segafredo 36 Abovian St; m 077 566016; 3/37 Amirian St; m 093 545206; ⏰ 08.00–02.00. International chain of Italian coffee shops serving mainly coffees (*latte AMD1,600; hot chocolate AMD1,700*), pastries (*AMD2,200*) & ice cream. Also soup in colder weather. Non-smoking.

✕ Square One 1/3 Abovian St; ✆566169. Serves European & American food. Very popular both with diaspora & locals – perhaps it's the English b/fast or (more likely) the American-style apple pie & chocolate cake. Music can be loud.

✕ Tashir Pizza Branches at 29 Komitas St, 33 Khorenatsi St, 16/45 Gai St, 50 Mesrop Mashtots Av, 15 Tumanian St, 69 Terian St, 27/4 Nzhdeh St, 37 Hanrapetutian St (on the corner with Tigran Mets, not far from Republic Sq); ✆511111/2/3/4/5/6/7/8/9 respectively. A deservedly popular chain producing high-quality pizzas. It is possible to buy portions (*AMD250–400*) rather than a whole pizza. Also serves pasta (*AMD1,000*), salads (*AMD500–900*), soups (*AMD500*), etc. Eat in & take-away.

✕ The Club 40 Tumanian St; ✆531361; www. theclub.am. Extremely good food in this basement restaurant which also incorporates a souvenir shop & bookshop with some titles in English. Forget the name as it's not a club at all. Reservations advisable. Occasional concerts. Has probably the most informative website of any restaurant in Yerevan which includes the menu, with prices, plus details of concerts.

✕ The Colour of Pomegranates 6/44 Zakian St (corner of Zakian & Khorenatsi streets); ✆525095. Pleasant, small restaurant, named after the iconic 1968 film, directed by Sergei Parajanov. Georgian & Armenian cuisine. The proprietor makes his own apricot vodka which is very good & explosively alcoholic.

✕ Thomas Tea 22 Abovian St; ✆543330; www. thomastea.am. A busy, basement café cheerfully decorated with all the appurtenances of tea making. Also sells its teas. Serves a vast range of teas, all well described on the menu. Also snacks such as crêpes, savoury & sweet (*AMD900–1,400*), as well as main courses.

☕ Tiziano 10/10 Northern Av; ✆533780; m 094 808096. Attractive Italian-style café just off the lower end of Northern Avenue. Serves coffees, cakes & ice cream.

OUTSIDE THE CENTRE
Map, pages 112–13.

✕ Charentsi 28 28 Charents St; ✆572945; www.charentsi28.com. Just beyond the central area but worth seeking out. In a fully restored old house with an ambience, as they say, of 'casual elegance'. A very informative website.

✕ Gold Star 16 Komitas St, ✆274441. Not far from the Republic of Nagorno Karabagh office where visas are obtained (see page 327), so a useful café if you arrive before the office opens.

PUBS
Pubs in Yerevan are much like pubs elsewhere, places where people, mainly young, go to meet other people. They tend to be busy & have music, food, television, darts, Wi-Fi &, of course, drinks. Pubs seem to favour the area to the west of the opera house. The following is a small selection, recommended by a connoisseur of such venues. See map, pages 116–17, for listings.

♀ Cantaloupe 54/23 Pushkin St; m 095 055287
♀ EcoPub 6 Spendiarian St; ✆502524; facebook. com/ecoPUB.am. A non-smoking pub.
♀ Karloff 31 Moscovian St; ✆539780; facebook. com/Karloff.Czech.Brewery. Serves Czech beer & food.
♀ The Bell 41 Pushkin St; m 055 107061, 055 200019
♀ Tro's Pub 5 Sarian St; m 077 673775. 'There are no strangers here, only friends you haven't yet met.'
♀ Van Gogh Art Café 31/3 Tumanian St; m 091 415594, 055 415594; www.vangogh.am

ENTERTAINMENT AND NIGHTLIFE

Details of what is on are published in *Noyan Tapan Highlights* (page 100), in *TourInfo* magazine (page 115) and on billboards outside theatres and concert halls.

CINEMA Two cinemas show **films in English** most evenings. **Kino Nairi** [117 F2] (*50 Mesrop Mashtots Av;* ✆ *542829*) shows films in English at 22.00. **Kino Moscow** [117 F4] (*18 Abovian St;* ✆ *521210*) shows the same film in English and dubbed into Russian in separate auditoria. The week-long annual Golden Apricot International Film Festival (see page 99) takes place in Yerevan during July.

CASINOS All Yerevan's casinos have been closed and moved outside the city boundary. The road to the airport is thickly populated while there are quite a few on the Sevan highway.

CLASSICAL MUSIC The **Spendiarian Armenian Theatre of Opera and Ballet** [117 E3] (*54 Tumanian St;* ✆ *533391, 565803, 586311;* e *info@opera.am; www. opera.am*) stages regular opera and ballet except during July and August. However, it is worth seeing the building for its own sake although it can only be viewed during performances. Unfortunately schedules of performances are only ever announced two or three weeks in advance. Tickets (*AMD1,500–15,000*) are best bought in person from the ticket office (⊕ *Mon–Sat 11.00–19.00*) just behind the theatre, to the northeast. Although it is theoretically possible to book by phone and pick up the tickets just before the performance starts, it has been known for the tickets no longer to be available for collection. The **Aram Khachaturian Concert Hall** [117 E3] (*46 Mesrop Mashtots Av;* ✆ *560645;* e *philharmonic@apo. am; www.apo.am*), in the northern half of the building whose southern half is the opera and ballet theatre, is the home of the Armenian Philharmonic Orchestra and hosts concerts throughout the season. The **Komitas Chamber Music Hall** [117 H3] (*1 Isahakian St;* ✆ *526718*) presents regular concerts by the Armenian Chamber Orchestra.

Other theatres Apart from the Spendiarian Armenian Theatre of Opera and Ballet (see above) there are at least 15 other theatres in Yerevan. They are listed in the free publications *Yerevan Scope* and *TourInfo*. All, except the **Stanislavsky State Russian Drama Theatre** [117 F4] (*7 Abovian St;* ✆ *569199*), which performs in Russian, perform exclusively in Armenian. There are two puppet theatres which may appeal to non-Armenian speakers: the **Yerevan State Theatre of Marionettes** (*43 Mesrop Mashtots Av;* ✆ *562450*) and the **Hovhannes Tumanian State Puppet Theatre** (*4 Sayat Nova Av;* ✆ *563244*).

JAZZ The main jazz club is **Poplavok** [117 G2] (*41 Isahakian St;* ✆ *522303, in Aragast restaurant, see page 121*) where reservations are always required. It is well known for the murder of a Georgian Armenian by presidential bodyguards in the men's lavatories (see page 26). Quite good for food though drink prices are high. The **Malkhas Jazz Club** [116 D3] (*52 Pushkin St;* ✆ *531778*) is a bar/restaurant serving Armenian and European cuisine but which also stages live jazz. It is owned by Levon Malkhasian who is considered to be the godfather of Armenian jazz. **Cafesjian Centre** (see page 154) hosts concerts, including jazz and classical.

NIGHTCLUBS For those who wish to sample Armenian nightclubs, the old Armenia Information website (*www.armeniainfo.am*) still lists 28 such venues, giving contact details. More up-to-date information may be found in the advertisements in *Yerevan Scope* and *TourInfo*.

SPORT Although facilities are slowly increasing they remain limited. During good weather billiard and table-tennis tables appear in parks and can be hired by the hour. Tennis courts can be hired by the hour at the **Ararat Tennis Courts** [117 H4] (*2 Alek Manukian St;* ℡ *570648*) in Yerevan's green belt near Yerevan State University. Equipment can be hired and coaching is apparently always available. There is an adjacent clubhouse and café. Tennis, basketball, golf and minigolf are available at **Ararat Valley Country Club** [112 B2] (see below) next door to Vahakni Residential Community. At **Play City** [113 F2] (*35 Acharian St;* ℡ *288377;* e *info@playcity.am; www.playcity.am*), in Yerevan's northeast suburb of Avan, you can play bowling, karting, paintball, billiards and minigolf. There is a bar/restaurant in the complex.

Riding Riding lessons for all ages and abilities and hire of horses can be arranged at the **Hovik Hayrapetyan Equestrian Centre** [112 B6] (*39 Shirak St, Charbakh;* ℡ *465000;* m *099 465000;* e *info@hhec.am; www.hhec.am;* ⊕ *09.00–19.30 Tue–Fri, 10.00–16.00 w/end*) in the Shengavit district of southwest Yerevan.

Swimming Several of the larger city-centre hotels (including Ani Plaza, Congress, Golden Palace, Metropol, Regineh and Royal Tulip) have swimming pools to which non-residents are admitted for a fee. Among the other venues are:

Aquatek [113 F3] See page 120 for contact details. ⊕ 09.00–22.30, last entrance 21.00; Jun–Oct Mon–Fri adult/child: AMD6,000/3,000, Sat & Sun: AMD7,000/3,500. Prices about AMD1,000, lower Oct–Mar. Other facilities extra. Non-residents can visit the swimming pools & other water amusements.
Ararat Valley Country Club [112 B2] 50 Gevorg Chaush St; ℡394085; www.vahakni.com; ⊕ swimming pool: Jun–Sep 10.00–20.00; adult/child Mon–Fri AMD5,000/3,000, Sat & Sun AMD8,000/4,000. The Club has a very pleasant swimming pool area to which non-members are admitted. A couple of hours spent relaxing here can be recommended. The club also has facilities

for tennis, basketball, football, minigolf & golf (9 holes).
Erebuni Business Centre [117 E6] 26/1 Vazgen Sargsian St (off Republic Sq); ℡510451; e info@erebuni-plaza.am; www.erebuniplaza.am. The centre has a gym & swimming pool which are available to visitors. ⊕ 08.00–16.00. Single visit AMD4,000; 12 visits AMD30,000.
Waterworld [113 F3] 40 Miasnikian St; ℡638998; ⊕ Jun–Sep 13.00–20.00; admission price is by height, adult approx AMD5,000. It is popular with Yerevan residents during the heat of summer so it can be busy. It is especially suitable for families with children as there is much to keep them entertained.

SHOPPING

Yerevan has every type of retail outlet imaginable, from expensive shops on Northern Avenue selling internationally known designer brands, to that part of Vernissage specialising in secondhand nuts and bolts. Some pedestrian underpasses have a host of small shops. For cheap clothes try the Ararat covered clothing market (sometimes marked on maps as 'Rosia'), opposite the foot of the steps to the cathedral. The street market to the south of Rosia sells most things from budgerigars to coffee beans and is useful for any small item you may have forgotten to pack. For fresh food shopping (and dried fruits) it is worth visiting the Haikakan market on Khorenatsi Street off Tigran Mets Avenue about 500m south of the cathedral. The covered market on Mesrop Mashtots Avenue has been turned into a large supermarket (see pages 139–40) although there are still a few market stalls selling fresh fruit and vegetables at the entrance. Those with a sweet tooth may wish to patronise the Grand Candy store and pastry shops near the Matenadaran (page 137) or the Jazzve cake shop (*30 Tumanian St*). There are also plenty of vendors of ice cream on Yerevan's streets.

Craft items are best bought at **Vernissage** [117 F6] (see page 132) if in Yerevan at the weekend. Similar items, although a much smaller range, can be found on the first floor of **Disc Planet** (*1/3 Abovian St* [117 E5]; ❧ *542334; 33 Abovian St* [117 H2]; ❧ *582098*). **Made in Armenia Direct** (*www.madeinarmeniadirect.com*) has outlets in Marriott Armenia [116 D5] and Congress [116 D7] hotels. Another good souvenir shop is **Salt Sack** [117 F4] (*3/1 Abovian St*). One of Yerevan's biggest **bookshops** is **Noah's Ark** [117 E5], Republic Square. It has the range of Collage maps (see page 60) and a good selection of books in English. Some other titles not stocked here may instead be found at the city centre **Ejmiatsin Cathedral Bookshop** [116 D5] (*11 Amirian St;* ❧*501102;* ⊕*11.00–19.00*) which also has art books in English. **Artbridge bookshop/café** [117 F4] (*20 Abovian St;* ❧ *581284; www.artbridge.am;* ⊕ *08.30– midnight*), specialises in foreign-language publications and has a wide selection of English-language books on Armenia. It also sells handmade crafts and the café does a very good *café glacé*. **Bookworld** [116 D4] (*20 Mesrop Mashtots Av*) is a large bookshop mostly stocking books in Armenian and Russian but there is an English section. **Bureaucrat** bookshop [116 C3] (*51 Pushkin St (entrance on Sarian St);* ❧*500152;* m *091 018098; www.bureaucrat.am*) has a good selection of books in English, including books on art. **Secondhand books** are to be found at a group of stalls on the green belt just north of the statue of Aivazovsky and at Vernissage. **Brandy** can be bought from numerous outlets in markets and supermarkets but specialist dealers are to be found at 14 Abovian Street, 12 Amirian Street and at Yerevan brandy distillery [116 A6] (see page 145). If intending to take brandy home with you, remember airline regulations on liquids (see page 97). **InVino** [116 D2] (*6 Sarian St;* ❧ *521931; www.invino.am; facebook.com/InVinoEVN*) is a wine merchant and wine bar with a good range of the world's wines, including Armenian. It also functions as a wine club with special events. An attractive, non-smoking shop which also stocks cheeses and sausages and sells baguette sandwiches by the centimetre! A good **photographic** dealer with several branches is **Jupiter Photo Express** (*15 Vartanants St, 33 Khorenatsi St, 21 Baghramian Av & 50 Terian St; www.jupiter-photo.info*). Another is the **Zig Zag** chain (*24 Mesrop Mashtots Av & 20 Sayat Nova Av*).

Small **supermarket chains** have arisen in recent years and many branches are open 24 hours. They are well stocked and in addition have 24-hour currency exchange kiosks. One such chain is **SAS** (*18 Mesrop Mashtots Av, 31 Tumanian St, 85 Baghramian Av, 52 Komitas Av & 35 Isahakian St; www.sas-grp.com*).

OTHER PRACTICALITIES

BANKS AND EXCHANGING MONEY There are several banks in the centre of Yerevan, for example on Vazgen Sargsian and Nalbandian streets. HSBC, just round the corner from the Marriott Hotel, is popular but it is always busy and the queues move slowly. If all you want to do is change some cash it is much quicker to go to one of the currency exchanges in the small supermarkets (see above).

EMBASSIES AND CONSULATES IN YEREVAN For a list of Armenian embassies abroad, see pages 65–6.

❸ **Belarus** 12a Nikol Duman St; ❧220269; e armenia@belembassy.org

❸ **Brazil** 57 Simeon Yerevantzi St; ❧500210;
e embassy@brasil.am; www.brasil.am

❸ **Bulgaria** 16 Sofia St, Nor Aresh; ❧458233;
e embassy.yerevan@mfa.bg; www.mfa.bg/

embassies/armenia
Canada 10 Vazgen Sargsian St; ☎567990;
e concda@gmail.com
China 12 Marshal Baghramian Av; ☎560067;
e chiemb@arminco.com
Egypt 6a Sepuh St; ☎226755/220117;
e egyemb@arminco.com
Estonia 43 Gyulbekian St; ☎263973, 220138;
e aries@arminco.com
Finland 6 Tamanian St; ☎565587
France 8 Grigor Lusavorich St; ☎591950;
e cad.erivan-amba@diplomatie.gouv.fr; www.
ambafrance-am.org
Georgia 2/10 Babayan St; ☎200742;
e yerevan.emb@mfa.gov.ge; www.armenia.mfa.
gov.ge
Germany 29 Charents St; ☎523279; e info@
eriw.diplo.de; www.eriwan.diplo.de
Greece 6 Demirchian St; ☎530051, 536754;
e gremb.ere@mfa.gr; www.mfa.gr/armenia
India 50/2 Dzorapi St; ☎539173/4; e amb_
office@embassyofindia.am; www.indianembassy.am
Iran 1 Budaghian St; ☎280457; e iranemb.
evn@mfa.gov.ir; www.iranembassy.am
Italy 5 Italy St; ☎542335/6, 542301;
e segreteria.jerevan@esteri.it; www.ambjerevan.
esteri.it
Kazakhstan 153 Armenakian St, Nork
Marash; ☎652001; e erevan@mfa.kz
Kuwait 7/3 H Kochar St; ☎508050;
e kuwaitembassyyerevan@gmail.com
Lebanon 13/14 Dzoragyugh St;

☎501303/04; e info@lebanonembassy.am; www.
lebanonembassy.am
Lithuania 2/13 Babayan St; 297680;
☎297682; e amb.am@urm.lt; www.am.mfa.lt
Nagorno Karabagh 17a Zarian St; ☎249928;
e ankr@arminco.com
Poland 44a Hanrapetutian St; ☎542491/3/5;
e erewan.amb.sekretariat@msz.gov.pl; www.
erewan.polemb.net
Romania 15 Barbusse St; ☎275332, 277610;
e ambrom@netsys.am
Russia 13a Grigor Lusavorich St; ☎567427,
545218, 589843; e info@rusembassy.am; www.
armenia.mid.ru
Switzerland 2/1 Melik-Adamian St;
☎529860; e yer.vertretung@eda.admin.ch; www.
eda.admin.ch/yerevan
Syria 14 Marshal Baghramian Av; ☎524028,
524036; e syrem_ar@intertel.am
Thailand 4/1 Marshal Baghramian Av;
☎560410; e info@thaiconsulate.am; www.
thaiconsulate.am
Turkmenistan 52 Yerznkian St; ☎221029,
221039; e tmembassy@netsys.am
Ukraine 5/1 29 Arabkir St; ☎229727;
e emb_am@mfa.gov.ua
UK 34 Marshal Baghramian Av; ☎264301;
e enquiries.yerevan@fco.gov.uk; www.
ukinarmenia.fco.gov.uk
USA 1 American Av; ☎464700; e usinfo@usa.
am; www.usa.am

INTERNET With the huge expansion in laptop ownership and Wi-Fi access throughout Armenia, internet cafés are not as ubiquitous as they once were and do tend to come and go. To find one the best plan is to ask around. Expect to pay about AMD500 per hour. Many hotels make a computer available to guests.

MEDICAL ISSUES Most hotels can help with finding a **doctor** and embassies may have lists of specialists. **Hospitals** have 24-hour emergency departments; there is a rota for receiving patients. To call an **ambulance** in an emergency, dial ☎103; patients needing hospital admission will be taken to the receiving hospital.

Hospitals also have casualty departments where patients can self-refer if needing immediate treatment. Possible hospitals include:

✚ **Arabkir Medical Complex Children's Hospital** [113 E2] 30 Mamikoniants St; ☎231352, 236883
✚ **First Clinical Hospital of Heratsi Medical University** [113 E3] 58 Abovian St; ☎561778, 563508

✚ **Nairi Medical Centre** [116 A3] 21 Paronian St; ☎537742. Knows how to cope with visitors' insurance.
✚ **V Mikaelian Institute** [113 E2] 9 Hasratian St; ☎281790, 281990

There is also a 24-hour emergency **dental service** but apparently it is staffed by relatively inexperienced, newly qualified dentists so anyone with a problem may prefer to attend one of the many private dental clinics, some of which have 24-hour cover. Again embassies may hold lists of dentists. A clinic which has at least one dentist who speaks good English is **Agat-dental** (*33a Baghramian Av;* \272623 – *ask for Hasmik*). I have no personal experience of treatment at the clinic. **Pharmacies** abound and are indicated by a green cross and the (Russian) word '*apteka*'. **Natali Pharm** is a chain which has 24-hour branches throughout the city including, in central Yerevan, at 3 Mashtots Avenue [116 B5] and 10 Tigran Mets Avenue [117 E7] (a full list can be found at *www.spyur.am/natalipharm*).

POST OFFICE The most convenient post office is that on Republic Square [117 E6] (*see page 129;* ⊕ *08.00–19.00 Mon–Sat, 10.00–16.00 Sun*). It has a Philatelic Corner for anyone interested in stamp collecting. See also page 102.

WHAT TO SEE AND DO

A WALK AROUND YEREVAN
Around Republic Square Visitors to Yerevan are inevitably drawn to the large and imposing **Republic Square** [117 E5–E6] and it is an appropriate place to start this walk: in Soviet times the square was called Lenin Square. It is certainly one of the finest central squares created anywhere in the world during the 20th century. The building on the northeast side with fountains outside is the **State History Museum** [117 E5] (see pages 150–2) of 1926 with its white symmetrical colonnades to which the **National Gallery of Art** (see pages 152–3) storeys in a similar colour were added in 1950. It is sometimes claimed that Yerevan needed a large new art gallery after 1945 because many valuable works of art were brought here for safe keeping during the war years from other Soviet cities and never subsequently returned; the collection is almost certainly the finest in the former USSR apart from those of Moscow and St Petersburg. The water of the **three fountains** outside the museum sometimes dances in time to classical music on summer evenings while changes to the lighting are used to enhance the effect. This unusual spectacle was invented by Abraham Abrahamian, a professor in the electronics department of Yerevan University.

Underneath the square is a **large bunker** constructed during the Cold War to protect officials from danger in the event of a nuclear attack. Since independence, suggestions have been made that it could be handed over to the museum as an additional display area but lack of funding together with renewed tensions in the Middle East will probably ensure that it retains its original purpose for the time being.

To the left of the museum across Abovian Street on the northwest side of Republic Square is a **government building** designed by Samvel Safarian (1902–69) and built in the 1950s. It incorporates much Armenian detail but although built to harmonise with the earlier buildings it is somewhat more massive. It now houses the Ministry of Foreign Affairs. By contrast the ground floor is occupied by one of Yerevan's best bookshops called **Noah's Ark** [117 E5]. Continuing anticlockwise, across Amirian Street is the curving façade of the **Hotel Armenia** [116 D5] (page 118), possibly Yerevan's best hotel, certainly its most expensive, after its opening in 1954 and very popular with the diaspora. It has now been extensively refurbished by the Marriott chain. During the rebuilding work a secret floor was discovered with a 1.5m-high ceiling: it was used by the KGB to spy on the guests.

Still continuing anticlockwise, a broad street with fountains down the middle is crossed. In the centre of the street formerly stood the statue of Lenin designed by Sergei Merkurov (1881–1952), erected in 1940 to mark the 20th anniversary of Soviet power and speedily removed, along with its huge pedestal, after independence. Standing where the statue once stood and looking at the hillside behind the museum it is possible to see the statue of **Mother Armenia** [113 E3] on an even larger plinth, 34m high, constructed in 1950 as the Victory Memorial in memory of the Great Patriotic War. The forged copper statue of Mother Armenia, a heroic figure holding a sword, was designed by the sculptor Ara Harutyunian and erected in 1967. Very provocatively for this date, the statue with sword takes the shape of the cross. Mother Armenia actually stands in the space occupied from 1950 until 1962 by a 16.5m-tall statue of Stalin; at 21m Mother Armenia is, perhaps symbolically, taller than Stalin used to be. A Soviet writer in 1952, one year before Stalin's death, claimed:

> Topping the Memorial Building is a statue of Stalin in a long greatcoat of which one lap is thrown open, showing the figure caught in a forward stride. In this statue wrought in Armenian bronze, the sculptor S. Merkurov (NB: The same who was responsible for Lenin), has depicted Stalin in a characteristic pose of dynamic movement, supreme composure and confidence. Stalin stands with one hand in his coat-breast and the other slightly lowered as though his arm, swung in rhythm with his step, has for one brief moment become frozen in space. Stalin's gaze rests upon the splendour of the new Armenian socialist capital, upon its new handsome buildings, its wide green avenues, upon the central square in the opposite end of the town. There, Lenin, in his ordinary workday suit, has swung abruptly around in that characteristic, impetuous, sweeping way of his, so dear and familiar to every Soviet man, woman and child. The statues are very tall and the impression is that the two great leaders exchange glances of deep understanding as they survey the prospering life around them, so much of it the handiwork of their own genius, their self-abnegating labours, their perspicacity, the wisdom that enabled them to see far into the future.

A flower bed has replaced Lenin whose statue, with head detached, lies stored in the courtyard behind the History Museum. The sculptor of the vanished Lenin and Stalin as well as of Stepan Shahumian, Sergei Merkurov (see also page 230), was no incompetent hack who devoted his whole working life to immortalising (?) communist leaders. Born in Alexandropol (present-day Gyumri), Merkurov studied in Paris where he was much influenced by Rodin before going on to sculpt many of the leading figures of his day as well as to create striking monuments to such figures as Chekhov and Pushkin.

The next building on the square, also built in 1950 and with a curving façade, houses a **post office** [117 E6] which is accessible through the left-hand door. Although not the main post office of Yerevan this one has a pleasing stained-glass window behind the counter depicting a woman in Armenian costume holding a telegraph tape. The building also houses the Ministry of Transport and Communications.

The final building, on the southeast side of the square, was partly built under Tamanian's direction in 1926, though only completed in 1941. An irregular pentagonal structure with one curved side, it is possibly Tamanian's masterpiece. An elegant colonnade above arches forms a gallery along the whole façade and is combined with Armenian detail in the capitals. The archway to the inner courtyard is surmounted by a clock tower which usually flies the red, blue and orange Armenian flag; the building is home to the offices of government ministers.

To the cathedral Leave Republic Square along the street that runs between the post office and the government buildings. It is named **Tigran Mets Avenue** in honour of King Tigran II (the Great) who ruled Armenia from c95BC to 55BC. The street bends right after a few yards between buildings which mostly date from the 1920s and 1930s.

Emerging from Tigran Mets Avenue, to the left on the corner of **Khanjian Street** is a **bronze statue** [117 E7] dating from 1974 of Alexander Griboyedov (1795–1829), the satirical playwright whose best known play, *Woe from Wit*, was only performed and published posthumously. Its hero is branded a lunatic when he arrives in Moscow full of liberal and progressive ideas – a dangerous practice in either the Tsarist or the communist era. Griboyedov was also a diplomat and instrumental in Russia's peace negotiations with Turkey following the war of 1828–29 when Russia gained control of much of Armenia (see also page 246).

Just past the statue, the striking building on the right with a two-part roof is the former Russia cinema, now the **Ararat clothing bazaar** [117 E7] (sometimes marked as 'Rosia' on maps): the two parts of the roof symbolise the two peaks of Mount Ararat. Underneath it is the **metro station** originally called Hoktemberian ('October' in honour of the October revolution of 1917), but now renamed Zoravar Andranik ('Commander Andranik') in honour of Andranik Ozanian (1865–1927). Born in western Armenia, Ozanian became head of the Armenian self-defence troops in the 1890s until in 1905 he moved west to seek assistance for the Armenian cause. He subsequently participated in the liberation of Bulgaria from Ottoman rule in 1912–13 before organising Armenian units to fight alongside the Russian army against Turkey during World War I. Being more in sympathy with socialist ideals than the new Armenian government led by the Dashnak Party he left in 1918 for Bulgaria and then moved to the USA, dying in Fresno, California. His last expressed wish was to be buried in Armenia. Although he was originally interred in Fresno, after a few months his coffin was moved to Europe and he was reinterred among the renowned in the cemetery of Père Lachaise in Paris. He was finally brought to Armenia in 2000 and now rests in the Yerablur Cemetery in Yerevan where the dead from the Karabagh war are buried. His **statue** [117 E7], unveiled in 2003, can be seen at the foot of the slope leading up to the cathedral. It depicts him brandishing a sword while rather uncomfortably riding two horses at once, one of which is crushing a snake beneath its hoof. Continuing straight on for a block brings you to the traditional covered **Haikakan market** [113 E5], which spills out on to the surrounding streets. It is a good place to buy Armenian dried-fruit delicacies.

The **cathedral** [117 F7], straight ahead up the slope to the left, is dedicated to St Gregory the Illuminator (as he is always called, although St Gregory the Enlightener would be a better translation since his achievement was converting Armenia into a Christian country). It was consecrated in September 2001 to celebrate what was officially the 1,700th anniversary of Christianity becoming the state religion and to this end symbolically has seating for 1,700 people in the main church although a further 300 can be accommodated in the smaller chapels dedicated to St Trdat, the king who adopted Christianity as the state religion, and his wife St Ashken. There is also a *gavit* and a bell tower. The cathedral may well be the first church in Armenia which visitors see but, even apart from its modernity, it is in several respects atypical. It was one of the first churches in Armenia to introduce seats. Traditionally there were no seats in Armenian churches as the congregation stood throughout the service. Secondly, there are no candles. It is normal on entering an Armenian church to buy candles and then to light them. Here candles are forbidden and may only be lit in a separate building on the southeast side. Thirdly, there is an organ. Fourthly, the church is well lit, having many windows as well as a large metal chandelier. Fifthly, by Armenian standards it is enormous with a total area of 3,500m² and a height of 63m. It has been described as having more the atmosphere of a concert hall than a place of worship but it is conspicuously busy with numerous Armenians of all ages visiting and a constant succession of weddings, particularly at weekends. (See pages 37–8 for information about Armenian wedding customs.) Rather incongruously, near the entrance is a baldachin brought from the church of St Gayane at Ejmiatsin, underneath which is a casket containing some of the relics of St Gregory which were brought here from the church of San Gregorio Armeno, Naples, where they had been kept for more than 500 years. They were a gift from Pope John Paul II on the occasion of the cathedral's dedication. Other relics of the saint have been built into the cathedral's foundations.

Leave the cathedral by the main door through which you entered and walk back down the slope. At the foot of the slope do a U-turn to the right into the part of the **circular green belt** in Tamanian's 1926 plan which was actually created. This part in summer now holds a children's funfair; beyond it, walk through trees and cafés. The first **statue** encountered is of Taras Shevchenko (1814–61) [117 F7] the Ukrainian poet and artist whose literary works are regarded as the foundation of Ukrainian literature and the modern Ukrainian language. Armenia and Ukraine have educational links. Both, together with Moldova, are Eastern partners in the Athena project, co-ordinated by the European Universities Association, which aims to contribute to the development, reform and modernisation of the higher education systems in the three countries. The co-ordinator for Armenia is Yerevan State University and, for Ukraine, the Taras Shevchenko National University of Kiev. European Union partners include universities in Portugal, Finland and the Netherlands. Continue along the green belt until a radial road crosses it. Here there is another **statue** [117 G7] of a warrior on horseback. It is Vardan Mamikonian, the leader of the Armenian forces killed at the Battle of Avarayr (see pages 17–18) in AD451 when his troops were overcome by a much larger Persian force. Made of wrought copper and unveiled in 1975, it is by Ervand Kochar (1899–1979), other examples of whose work include the fine statue of David of Sassoun outside the main railway station and several paintings in the National Gallery of Armenia.

WALNUT *SUJUKH*

Visitors will recognise most of the dried fruits and nuts temptingly displayed on market stalls but they may be less certain of the long, brown knobbly strings hanging up in the markets and also on stalls at popular tourist sites such as Garni, Geghard and Haghpat. These are strings of walnut *sujukh*. Don't let the unusual appearance put you off; if you are fond of nuts and dried fruit, walnut *sujukh* can quickly become a favourite. Walnut halves, about 50, are strung together and then dipped into a thick grape syrup. The grape syrup is what remains after making grape vodka and it is usually sweet enough not to need extra sugar. The syrup is boiled until it becomes thick enough to coat the walnuts then small amounts of cinnamon, cloves and cardamom are added. The knack is to have the syrup thin enough to coat the strings of nuts but thick enough so that it does not drip when they are hung up to dry.

Thanks are due to Gayane and her husband at Haikakan market who told me how they make their excellent walnut *sujukh*.

Vernissage [117 F6] Instead of continuing along the green belt, turn left across Khanjian Street and take the left hand of the two streets, **Buzand Street**, heading back towards the art gallery. If you are here during the week you will see a broad street with some non-functioning fountains down the middle and a handful of stalls. At the weekend you will, by contrast, be confronted by the justly celebrated **market** of Vernissage. (*Vernissage* is a French word, literally meaning 'varnishing' or 'glazing' but also used in the sense of 'preview', or 'private viewing', at an art gallery.) Vernissage is unquestionably the best place in Armenia, and possibly in the Caucasus, to buy souvenirs and craft items with a huge range of items being sold, for the most part by the people who made them. The range covers carpets, embroideries, wood and stone carvings, paintings, metalwork, etc, and the quality ranges from the superb to the tacky. It is generally possible to pay in either drams or US dollars and, while bargaining is acceptable, you may feel that the low prices do not really reflect the work that has gone into some of the items for sale and that if a stallholder is only asking £100/US$150 in the first place for something which has clearly involved 200 hours of highly skilled work then it is unreasonable to demand any reduction in price. As well as craft items there are also stalls selling various antique items, from old radios and Soviet-era medals to secondhand books.

Continue the length of Vernissage, repeatedly doubling back so as to visit each of the aisles. Outside the **Centre for Contemporary Experimental Art** [117 F6] (*1/3 Buzand St;* ⊕ *exhibitions 11.00–17.00 Tue–Sat*) is another **statue** [117 F6] by Ervand Kochar, his bronze *Melancholy*. At the far end, on the left, is the side of the art gallery whose front is on Republic Square. To the right, down some steps, is **Hanrapetutian Hraparak** [117 E5] ('Republic Square') underground station. Depending on the weight or bulk of any purchases made at Vernissage, this may be a good place to break the walk.

Abovian Street from Republic Square to Tumanian Street If you decide to

keep going, continue straight on along the back of the art gallery. Before turning right into Abovian Street, look first at the two buildings to the left which are at the bottom end of Abovian Street adjoining Republic Square. **Abovian Street** is probably Yerevan's most important shopping street and also has its best Tsarist-era buildings. It is named after Khachatur Abovian (1805–48), a teacher and writer whose best known novel, *Armenia's Wounds*, is based around the events of the Russo-Persian war of 1826–28. **Number 2** Abovian Street, on the left-hand side as one faces Republic Square, is a red and black neo-Classical building constructed in 1880 as a boys' secondary school on a site where it had originally been planned to build Yerevan's cathedral. In Soviet times the building was adapted for chamber music concerts and is now the Arno Babajanian Concert Hall. **Number 1** on the opposite side is slightly newer having been built between 1900 and 1914 to house a trading business; it is also constructed of red and black tuff but is in the then fashionable Art Nouveau style.

Before continuing up Abovian Street it may still be worth walking about 300m down **Arami Street**, opposite to the road you have walked from Vernissage, although at the time of writing most of the old houses with balconies were in various stages of demolition to make way for tall blocks of flats. The object of the detour is a **stone-carvers' yard** [117 D4] on the left where khachkars and other items are still created from tuff in the traditional way. To see these carvers at work is to witness the successors to over 1,000 years of tradition and it will be sad if this workshop is, in its turn, removed. A little further along Arami Street on the right is the maternity hospital with four **bronze sculptures** of 1982, *Maternity* by

Yuri Minasian. Returning towards Abovian Street, a further detour left up Terian Street brings you, after three blocks, to the overgrown ruins of the **Astafian Brothel House** [117 E4]. The carvings on the outside of this 19th-century house are said to have indicated the pleasures awaiting inside. Return via Arami Street to Abovian Street and turn left up the hill. On the left is the start of the new **Northern Avenue** linking Republic Square with the Opera and Ballet Theatre, part of Tamanian's master plan of 1926 which was not then realised, but on which construction finally started amidst much controversy in 2002. Either walk up Northern Avenue at this stage or walk down later from the theatre. The eight- and nine-storey buildings on Northern Avenue built in tuff of various colours combine modernity with a definite Armenian character. Internationally known retailers occupy the ground-floor shops while overhead the screaming swifts have happily colonised the high buildings.

Formerly located in the middle of the intended path of the North Avenue, but now on the pavement of Abovian Street, south of the lower end of Northern Avenue, is a **statue** of an old man holding a bunch of roses. Created by the sculptor Levon Tokmajian and erected in 1991, it originally marked the exact spot where the old man it portrays used to stand in the 1930s. His real name was Karapet, but the

ARMENIAN EMBROIDERY

Visitors will probably be most aware of embroidery during their visit to Vernissage, Yerevan's weekend market (see page 132). Here many colourful hand-embroidered articles are on sale, ranging from small items such as handkerchiefs to larger-scale works such as tablecloths. Much of the embroidery is based on the celebrated Armenian illuminated manuscripts, one of the most popular subjects being letters of the Armenian alphabet in the form of birds. The technique used is known as free-style embroidery or needle painting and some of the results are exquisite. Other styles of Armenian embroidery, such as Aintab, are types of drawn thread work or cut work, akin to Hardanger embroidery. Yet another variety is an interlaced embroidery technique, also known as Marash or Maltese Cross embroidery.

One theory is that these various types were introduced into Europe from Armenia at the time of the Crusades (1096–1270) as a result of the known commercial, military and social contacts between the Armenian kingdom of Cilicia on the Aegean coast of Turkey and the Crusaders.

A technique which may be less familiar to visitors is Armenian knotted needle lace. Superficially this resembles crochet in appearance but the loops are knotted together rather than looped together, thus making it more robust because even if some threads are damaged the whole will not unravel. The stitches are made with an ordinary sewing needle, not with a crochet hook. Once the basic knotting technique is mastered, the skill lies in regulating the size and shape of the loops and many different patterns are known with evocative names such as Ararat, Yerevan and Arek, the last based on the circular sun design common in other Armenian art forms and often seen on khachkars.

There is a good display of Armenian embroidery in the Museum of Folk Art in Yerevan (page 155) and in the ethnographical museum at Sardarapat (pages 195–6). Ejmiatsin Cathedral Museum (page 190) houses examples of ecclesiastical embroidery.

locals gave him the name 'Kara Bala' [117 E5], Turkish for 'black boy', because of his dark complexion. See box, page 184.

Number 8 on the right-hand side of Abovian Street was built in the 1880s, again in neo-Classical style. After 1937 the building housed the Soviet Central Committee and the office of Comsomol, the Soviet youth organisation; there was formerly a red star in the top arch of the masonry. It retains one of its original wooden doors. On the opposite side of the street at number 1/4 is the dark façade (now incorporated into a new building) of the Gabrielian mansion, built in 1910 by the architect Meghrabian and combining Classical and Art Nouveau elements.

Continue uphill across Pushkin Street. The first building on the right, with salmon-coloured stucco and red trim, dates from the 1870s. A plaque on the wall commemorates the playwright Maxim Gorky's one-night stay in the building in 1928. Opposite it, on the left, is the red tuff Khanzatian mansion and just above that is the Hovhannisian mansion, a large building dating from 1915–16 which incorporated a hospital on the ground floor. Note the windows which incorporate a Star of David in the framework.

Slightly higher up the hill, still on the left, is the Stanislavsky State Russian Drama Theatre [117 F4] built in 1937 in Constructivist style but considerably altered in 1974 when it gained a façade of yellowish tuff. Its architect Karo Halabian (1897–1959) worked on several interesting Soviet-era projects including Krasnopresnenskaya metro station in Moscow and the post-war reconstruction of Stalingrad.

Opposite the Stanislavski Theatre is the small square, once called Zodiac Square because its fountain incorporates each sign of the zodiac. However, in 2001 it was renamed Charles Aznavour Square in honour of the composer, singer and actor who was born in Paris in 1924 to Armenian parents who had fled the Turkish massacres. The square was created in the 1920s by demolishing a 17th-century Persian mosque together with the church of Sts Peter and Paul which also dated to the 17th century. The Hotel Yerevan (now the Royal Tulip Hotel), designed by Nicoghayos Buniatian (1884–1943) has its entrance on the square. It dates from 1926. At one time Yerevan's most elegant hotel, it once again boasts five-star status. Its red tuff construction with wrought-iron balconies in traditional Armenian style contrasts oddly with the grey stonework of the entrance surmounted by white Ionic columns. Across the square is the Moscow Cinema [117 F4] which dates from 1933. Between the hotel and the cinema is the exhibition hall of the Painters' Union used for temporary shows. The square is host to statues of creatures made from bits of machinery – a surprisingly life-like bull and an enormous spider. There is also a giant chess set, popular with children.

Abovian Street from Tumanian Street to the green belt
Continue uphill across Tumanian Street beyond which Abovian Street widens considerably and is lined with trees. Most of the buildings here date from the 1940s. Artbridge bookshop/café [117 F4], on the right at number 20, has an excellent range of English-language books, guides, maps and newspapers. The café is a good place for coffee, especially as it is opens early, at 08.30. Higher up on the left is the Children's Art Gallery [117 F4] which is well worth visiting (see page 154). Continue across Sayat Nova Avenue.

In the first block on the right is the 16-storey Ani Plaza Hotel built in 1970. On the left is the remaining part of the only one of Yerevan's churches to have at least partially survived the 1679 earthquake. Known as the Katoghike [117 F3] (literally 'cathedral', singularly inappropriate for the tiny building still standing), its current form dates from 1936 when the main church, a substantial basilica without a dome

KARA BALA

Kara Bala was said to have come from a well-to-do family and was married to a beautiful wife; they had a son. Kara Bala grew roses. He would take his roses to Astafian Street (as Abovian Street was then known) where he would stand and give them to girls. In particular he was said to be passionately in love with the famous actress Arus Voskanian who used to walk along Abovian Street to the theatre, and he gave her one red rose every morning. However, she had another admirer, a Turkish man, and this made Kara Bala so jealous that he murdered his rival, for which he was subsequently tried and imprisoned.

On his eventual release he found that his wife and son had left him, that he didn't have a house and a garden any more and that his roses had been uprooted. 'I am not Kara Bala any more, I'm Dardy Bala' ('dard' means sorrow in Armenian), he kept saying, wandering sadly around the town with a bottle of wine. However, he didn't stop giving flowers. Whenever he came across flowers he gave them to women and many in Yerevan still remember him going up to young couples in the 1960s to present the girl with a bunch. Eventually he died and his frozen body was found one morning sitting on a rock.

rebuilt in 1693–94, was demolished in the name of urban redevelopment. It was known that there had been a church on this site since the 13th century but until the demolition was under way nobody realised that the apse and sanctuary actually comprised this old church. Inscriptions of 1229 and 1282 on the newly revealed southern façade as well as one of 1264 on the wall proved this to be the case. Public and scientific outcry won the newly revealed church a reprieve, although until recently it was tucked away behind the 1930s buildings for which the 17th-century church was demolished. These buildings have, in turn, now been demolished and at the time of writing a large church was under construction, although this time beside the small one rather than around it. Since independence Katoghike has resumed a religious function and services are now held there, although it is so tiny that there is hardly room for the officiating priest let alone any congregation. To either side of the *bema* are carvings, some of which appear to have been defaced.

Continue up the hill. Just beyond Katoghike is a **statue** of Alexander Mantashyants (1842–1911) [117 F3], an Armenian industrialist, financier, oil magnate and philanthropist. He was born in Tiflis and spent his childhood in Iran, entering his father's cotton business at an early age. In 1869–72 he visited England, staying in Manchester, then a world centre of the cotton and textile industries. Later he bought most of the shares of the Tiflis Central Bank and became the bank's chairman. He invested heavily and successfully in the developing oil industry and funded the Baku–Batumi pipeline, launched in 1907 and, at 835km, the world's then longest pipeline. At his death he was one of the richest individuals in the world. Among other philanthropic activities he helped to found the Armenian Charitable Society in the Caucasus, donated 250,000 roubles to build the residence of the Katholikos in Ejmiatsin, sent young Armenians (including the composer Komitas) to study at European universities and built the Pitoewski (now Rustaveli) Theatre in Tiflis. Perhaps his most famous donation was some 1½ million francs in 1904 to build the Armenian church of St John the Baptist in Paris. On the right, plaques on numbers 28, 30 and 32 commemorate residents of these buildings which were put up in the 1930s to house artists and intellectuals. Slightly higher up, also on the right, is a 1930s Art Deco building sporting the Russian word for bread.

Continuing uphill Abovian Street meets the circular green belt. Steps lead down to a pedestrian underpass, partially closed for reconstruction at the time of writing, beneath Moscovian Street. It used to house a large subterranean department store which may reopen after the reconstruction. The continuation of Abovian Street uphill is dealt with in the *Elsewhere in Yerevan* section on pages 143–4.

The green belt The walk round Yerevan continues by ascending the steps on the left-hand side halfway along the underpass to emerge into the circular green belt with Moscovian Street on the left and Isahakian Street on the right. The first **statue** [117 G3] encountered, an old man with a walking stick, dates from 1965 and is of the poet Avetik Isahakian (1875–1957) whose early work reflected sorrow and anguish for the fate of humankind. He left Armenia in 1911 as a result of Tsarist oppression but returned in 1936. The statue is by Sergei Bagdasarian. To the right just past the statue, the building which looks like a large upside-down spaceship is **Yeritasardakan** [117 G2] ('Youth') metro station which opened in 1981: the name reflects the number of students in this part of the city owing to the proximity of the university.

Further along is a large pair of **marble hands** [117 G3], a gift from Yerevan's twin city of Carrara in Tuscany; Yerevan achieved its first twinning in 1965 when it was linked with both Carrara and Kiev. Yerevan's response to the gift was to send in return a model of a spring of water carved in tuff and decorated with Armenian motifs – an exact copy stands a little further on across Terian Street. Just before crossing Terian Street the **statue** of a woman, *Demeanor of Eternity* by Msho Charntir [117 G2], was installed to mark both Yerevan's year as World Book Capital in 2012 and the 500th anniversary of Armenian printing. The apparently single figure actually shows two women, one on each side, holding a large book. It is dedicated to the history of the preservation of the *Homilies of Mush*, the largest Armenian manuscript in the world, now preserved in the Matenadaran. The manuscript, written in 1200–02 and historically associated with the Holy Apostles Monastery in Mush (now in eastern Turkey), was saved from destruction during the 1915 genocide (when historic artefacts were also destroyed) by two women. The huge parchment manuscript, weighing 28kg, was too heavy for one woman so they divided it into two parts and each aimed to carry her portion to eastern Armenia. One woman reached Ejmiatsin and handed hers to the church. The other woman died on the way but managed to bury her half in the grounds of the monastery at Erzurum (also now in eastern Turkey). Here it was found by a Russian soldier who took it to Tbilisi and handed it over to the Armenian community, whence it was transferred to Armenia in the 1920s, thus reuniting both parts of this priceless book. Immediately across **Terian Street** is a **memorial** [117 G2] to the victims of both the Jewish Holocaust and the Armenian genocide. Uniting the two khachkar-like halves of the memorial is a brass representation of the eternal flame. The Armenian inscription reads 'Live but do not forget', presumably the Hebrew reads likewise.

Continuing along the green belt, the next **statue** [117 G2] is of a pensive-looking individual. This was erected in 2000 of the poet Vahan Terian (1885–1920) after whom the street was named. A little further, on the right, is the copy of Yerevan's gift to Carrara (see above) and to the left a small memorial monument to the architect Karo Halabian (1897–1959) [117 G2] whose designs include the Sundukian (see page 140) and the Russian Stanislavski (see page 134) theatres in Yerevan. Next is a small lake on which it is possible to hire battery-operated boats: the Aragast restaurant on the north side is itself built in imitation of a boat (see page 121). Just beyond the lake is a fish-like *vishap* [117 G2]. One of the cafés here may be a pleasant place to break the walk, partly because, unlike most, they do not (yet?) blast excessively loud music at customers, and partly because the remaining section of Tamanian's planned circular green belt back to Republic Square was never built such that this tour must revert meanwhile to city streets. At the end of the green belt to the right across Isahakian Street is a **statue** of Hakob Meghapart (15th–16th century) [117 G2], the founder of Armenian printing who published the first Armenian books in Venice in 1512–13. Just beyond, in Kochar Street, is a delightful **statue** of a man playing draughts [117 G2].

A visit to the **Matenadaran** [117 G1] (page 153) can conveniently be made from here by turning right up **Mesrop Mashtots Avenue**, formerly Lenin Prospekt but renamed in honour of the inventor of the Armenian alphabet; the museum faces down the street with a **statue** of Mesrop Mashtots outside. At the bottom of the slope leading up to the Matenadaran, to the left as one faces the museum, is a group of **pastry shops** selling mouth-watering Armenian cakes and pastries. Also, for those with a sweet tooth, on the opposite corner is the shop of Grand Candy, Armenia's best known brand of sweets, plus the adjacent doughnut café.

The Cascade [117 F1] The walk continues straight on across Mesrop Mashtots Avenue as far as the park at the foot of the Cascade. The **Cascade** was designed to be a large artificial waterfall tumbling down from the monument commemorating 50 years of Soviet rule but it was left uncompleted at the demise of the Soviet Union. Funding from the Cafesjian Family Foundation has allowed revitalisation of the project and the establishment within the Cascade complex of the **Cafesjian Centre for the Arts** (see page 154). Renovation started in 2002, with the Centre for the Arts opening at the end of 2009. Work continues to extend the Cascade up to the plaza at the top, from where there is an excellent view of the city. The plaza can be reached by steps alongside the Cascade or by road from the city centre. There is also an escalator under the steps and this started to operate again in November 2002 after being out of use since 1997, thus saving the residents living at the top of the hill a climb of around 500 steps. It operates from 08.00 until 20.00. The occasion of the escalator's reinstatement was the unveiling of a **statue** [117 F1] of a fat cat. The self-satisfied-looking, well-fed (and to my mind rather ugly) cat, 2.5m high in bronze covered in black, is the work of the Colombian artist, Fernando Botero (b1932), and one of several of his cats located in capital cities. It was a gift from Gerard Cafesjian and was the first exhibit of the arts centre to arrive. It was reported in the local press that while the cat was greeted with smiles by the local residents, accustomed to statuary of Soviet dimensions, the loudest cheers were for the reactivation of the much-missed escalator. Another Botero **statue**, of a fat, naked, stunted gladiator wearing a helmet, has joined the collection of statues in the **Tamanian Sculpture Park** at the foot of the Cascade after originally being placed at the top when it arrived in 2005. A more recent Botero arrival is another fat, naked figure; a prone woman smoking a cigarette. Much more appealing are some sculptures by British artists. There are three works by Lynn Chadwick (1914–2003) – the one entitled *Stairs* is particularly appropriately located – and two by Barry Flanagan (1941–2009) including an especially attractive *Hare on Bell*.

On the **plaza** above the Cascade, the approach enlivened by some colourful sculptures, as well as the tall monument commemorating 50 years of Soviet rule, there is also a low square grey building, a monument to Stalin's victims. This has now acquired a pink tuff tambour-like hat. Across **Azatutian Avenue** is the entrance to **Victory (Haghtanak) Park** [113 E3], at the east end of which stands

Mother Armenia (see page 129). In the centre of the park is a statue inscribed 'No to war'. Within the park are various fairground amusements and a boating lake.

In the gardens below the Cascade is a **statue** [117 F2] of Alexander Tamanian, much of whose work has already been seen on this walk. Carved from a single block of basalt and mounted on a marble plinth, his hands are resting on a plan of the city in this work by Artashes Ovsepian. It has been suggested that this was the first statue of an architect in the entire world. Tamanian, author of the original plan for the Cascade, stands with his back to it and, rather surprisingly, he is facing the back of one of his finest buildings; opened in 1933 as the Yerevan State Opera House.

Between the statue of Tamanian and his opera house is **France Square**, so named following a visit in 2006 by the President of France. In 2011 a **statue** by Rodin of Jules Bastien-Lepage, a 19th-century naturalist painter, was gifted by France to Armenia and stands in the centre of France Square. Unfortunately the 1.75m statue is dwarfed by the vast size of the busy junction and the only way to see it without risking one's life is with binoculars or by visiting in the middle of the night when the traffic is less. The diagonal junction centred on the statue divides the park around the square into quadrants. At the northeast corner stands the **statue** of a rather consumptive-looking William Saroyan [117 F2] (see page 53). Opposite him, on the other side of Mashtots Avenue, is a bust of Sayat Nova (1712–95), composer and poet in the Armenian, Georgian and Persian languages. Also in the eastern quadrant of France Square is a 1986 **statue** of a man leaning back on a tree: he is the composer **Komitas** (1869–1935) [117 F3] whose career is outlined on page 48. Behind him is the **Armenian State Conservatory** [117 F2] with busts outside of Bach, Shostakovich, Khachaturian and Beethoven. The western quadrant of France Square has at its centre a **statue** of the painter Martiros Sarian (1880–1972) [117 E2]. Rather appropriately the park is used at weekends for the sale of paintings in a similar way to Vernissage. A little to the south is the **sculpture** *The Men* [117 E2] depicting well-known characters from a Soviet-era film of the same name directed by Edmond Keosayan and popular with Armenians.

Around the opera house The southern quadrant of France Square merges with the opera house and its surrounding recreational area. Opened in 1933 as the Yerevan State Opera House, it was renamed two years later as the **Spendiarian Armenian Theatre of Opera and Ballet** [117 F3] after Alexander Spendiarian (1871–1928), an Armenian composer who trained with Rimsky-Korsakov. (Note that the oval building also houses the **Khachaturian Concert Hall**; its entrance is on the north side of the building.) Spendiarian's most famous work is the opera *Almast*, based on the poem *The Capture of Tmkaberd* by the poet Hovhannes Tumanian (1869–1923), and set in 18th-century Crimea. The noble and beautiful Almast is betrothed to Tatul, ruler of the Armenian fortress of Tmkaberd which is under attack by Nadir, Shah of Iran. Nadir deceives Almast into betraying Tatul after which she is killed by the bored Nadir in the poem, but treated very differently in the opera, which has a denouement more in keeping with Soviet Armenia in the 1920s. In it the Armenian forces rise up, liberate the fortress and collectively sentence Almast to exile. Left uncompleted at Spendiarian's death *Almast* received its premiere at Moscow in 1930 and its first Yerevan performance shortly after the new opera house opened in 1933.

At the back of the opera house (ie: on the side nearer the Cascade) is a **statue** [117 F3] of the Armenian composer who is the best known outside the country, Aram Khachaturian (1903–78); see pages 47–8 for biographical details. Round the front, the **right-hand statue** [117 F3] is the eponymous Spendiarian while to the **left** [117 E3] is Tumanian, a second of whose poems was the source of the most famous Armenian opera, *Anoush*. With music by Armen Tigranian it is another gloom-laden tale typical of the time when it was composed although it does contain much attractive Armenian dance music; it was first seen at Alexandropol (Gyumri) in 1912. The piece ends with Anoush leaping off a precipice after her brother has killed her lover for breaking a village taboo.

A **sculpture** [117 F3] of composer and pianist Arno Babajanian (1921–83) was erected next to the small pond (known, rather appropriately, as Swan Lake) in front of the opera house in September 2002 but had to be removed before its official unveiling because its expressionistic style met with far from universal approval. Passers-by said that the work of sculptor David Bejanian was 'an insult' and even the Armenian president, Robert Kocharian, questioned whether it was appropriate. The main objections were to the exaggerated facial features and the long fingers which, it was claimed, made Babajanian look almost like a bird. Bejanian did agree to take the work away to make the hands more realistic and to 'correct' the face, but he said that his new and unrealistic approach had made his sculpture different from other monuments in the city. He said that 'All the monuments in Yerevan are done in a similar style and if we change heads of all the monuments within one night – for example replace Tumanian's head with Spendiarian's, Sarian's with Komitas's – perhaps only the subjects will feel the change. Arno was done to be in an expressive manner so that his head couldn't be placed on the shoulders of anyone else.' When the statue was returned after its 'correction' any changes were imperceptible.

Mesrop Mashtots Avenue From the opera house you can walk down Northern Avenue to return to Republic Square, completing the eastern half of the walk around Yerevan, or you can continue by walking down Mesrop Mashtots Avenue. At this point a detour can be made to visit **Zoravor Church** [116 D3] which is hidden behind Soviet apartment blocks. Turn right from Mashtots Avenue along Tumanian Street, then left along Parpetsi Street, then first right into narrow Parpetsi 9A street. The church is at the end of this small street, surrounded by trees. It dates from 1693 with renovations in the late 18th century and 1990s. It was built on the site of a 9th- to 13th-century monastery said to house the relics of St Anania (mentioned in chapter 9 of the Acts of the Apostles by the Greek form of his name, Ananias, as the Christian sent to Saul, later St Paul, to cure Saul's blindness after his conversion experience on the road to Damascus). The underground mausoleum of St Anania survives beneath the chapel immediately west of the church. If you're in need of refreshment, there is a Jazzve coffee shop at 35 Tumanian Street. Continue down tree-lined Mashtots Avenue. It is not for the most part architecturally interesting, being lined by office blocks containing shops at street level. The first interesting building encountered is in the fifth block from the opera house. Behind elaborate doors on the left lies the **Blue Mosque** [116 C5], built in 1765 and the only one surviving in Yerevan. During Soviet days it was the museum of the city of Yerevan but in 1999 it was renovated in Persian style at the expense of the Iranian government and is now functioning as a mosque once more. The grounds (⊕ *10.00–13.00 & 15.00–18.00*) with shrubs and trees form a peaceful oasis. Just past the mosque on the opposite side is a building which has caused great controversy. It is the 1940s-built **covered market** [116 B5] designed by Grigor Aghababian (1911–77). It is immediately recognisable by its arching entrance and Armenian decoration on the façade. Until 2012 it was a huge arched market hall bustling with traders selling every kind of foodstuff. Despite being on the Culture Ministry's list of historical buildings which cannot be redesigned without government permission, it was privatised and the arched roof and interior demolished by one of Armenia's richest businessmen who has links to the government and owns one of Armenia's largest supermarket chains. There were protests and clashes between those for and against the development. The building reopened in October 2013. While there are a few stalls for small market traders near the entrance over which the characteristic arched roof remains, most of the building has now been converted into a large supermarket. A few metres further along Mesrop Mashtots, beyond the market and mosque, go straight ahead through the underpass beneath Grigor Lusavorich ('Gregory the Illuminator') Street. You quickly reach the Hrazdan Gorge close to **St Sargis Church** [116 B6]. The present church replaces the one destroyed in the 1679 earthquake. It was built during the period 1691–1705 and rebuilt between 1835 and 1842. Further extensive rebuilding including a taller cupola took place from 1971 onwards and was completed in 2000. From the church there are good views over the Hrazdan to Victory Bridge, Ararat, the stadium and the Genocide Memorial.

Italy Street and Beirut Street Return to Grigor Lusavorich Street and turn right in the underpass to emerge on the east side of this street facing south. After one block there is a **park** on the left, formerly called Kirov Park (see page 243 for information on Kirov) and now **Children's Park** [116 C6]. Keep straight on past the park as far as the next street on the left. To the right across the road is a striking new building complete with a clock tower. Finished in 2005, it houses the municipal offices for the city government and the **History of Yerevan Museum** [116 B7] (see page 154). The carvings on the southern façade represent the 12 capitals of Greater Armenia, from Urartian Van to present-day Yerevan. The carving over the entrance to the museum is a plan of Yerevan, and that over the entrance to the municipal offices is the tree of life over the circular symbol of eternity.

Turn left from Grigor Lusavorich Street into what was in his lifetime called Stalin Street but is now called Beirut Street. In the middle of this street is a 1980 granite **statue** [116 C7] of Alexander Miasnikian (1886–1925), a professional Bolshevik revolutionary who was appointed Commissar for Armenia in 1921. He was reported to have died in an air crash although rumours arose that he had really been poisoned on the orders of Stalin because of disagreements over western Armenia. There are rose gardens and fountains in the middle of the street behind the statue. The opposite side of the street is actually called Italy Street rather than Beirut Street; the Italian embassy is on the corner.

Walk along **Beirut Street**. Cross over to **Italy Street** after a few metres to visit the **Theatre Park** [116 D7], formerly named the Park of the 26 Commissars in honour of the 26 Bolsheviks who set up a short-lived government in Baku which was deposed as the Turkish army approached. They fled to Turkmenistan but were captured and executed in September 1918. The park has been renamed Theatre Park, as it is home to the **Sundukian Drama Theatre** [116 C7]. Its company was created in 1925. The inaugural performance was of the play *Pepo* by Gabriel Sundukian (1825–1912), a story about love versus exploitation set in Tiflis (Tbilisi) and first performed in 1871. There is a statue dating from 1976 of the eponymous Pepo in the park as well as a bust of Sundukian which dates from 1972. The present 1,140-seat building was built in 1966 and was reopened after renovation in 2004. Just beyond the entrance to the park in the central reservation is a bronze **statue** erected in 1970 of a boy holding a large jug of water. It is a reminder of the days when such youths used to sell water along the dusty streets of the old town.

Continuing along Beirut Street or Italy Street, depending on which side you care to walk, just past the next intersection is another **statue** [116 D6], this time of Stepan

Shahumian, again created by the same Sergei Merkurov who was responsible for the now vanished Lenin and Stalin. Stepan Shahumian (1878–1918) was an Armenian who was instrumental in imposing Bolshevik rule in Azerbaijan and one of the 26 commissars after whom the park was named. He is further commemorated in having two towns named after him: Stepanavan in Lori province and Stepanakert in Nagorno Karabagh. The granite statue, erected in 1931, is the oldest on this walk. Behind it, in the middle of the street, is a **fountain** with 2,750 jets, one for every year of Yerevan's existence up to the time that the fountain was installed in 1968. Halfway up is a **statue** of Vazgen Sargsian [117 E6] (see pages 341–2) after whom the continuation of Beirut and Italy streets is named. It extends as far as Republic Square which is where the walk started and, when the fountain is operating, the cafés lining it make it another pleasant place to rest after walking the streets of central Yerevan.

The eastern part of the green belt The part of the green belt not already covered in this walk is perhaps not as attractive as the northern section but it nevertheless has some worthwhile sculptures and offers the opportunity to see a slightly less sophisticated side of Yerevan life – men playing chess or backgammon and children playing open-air table tennis, for example. From the **statue of Mamikonian** [117 G7] continue along the green belt instead of turning left to Vernissage as described on page 132. The first sculpture encountered is a **basalt statue** [117 G7], by Artashes Hovsepian, of the composer Armen Tigranian (see page 48), holding perhaps the musical score of his best known opera *Anoush*. The next, after walking through an area of cafés, past an incomplete (for several years) sports complex and across Sayat Nova Avenue, is a **bronze monument** [117 H5] by Nikoghayos Nikoghosian to the poet Eghishe Charents (see pages 51–2), the pain depicted in the sculpture echoing his life. On the left, next door to a branch of Tashir Pizza, is the **Yerevan Chess House** [117 H5] (*50a Khanjian St*) with stylised chessmen on its curved façade. Opened in 1970, it is home to the Chess Federation of Armenia (see page 55). Since 1984 it has been named after the former world chess champion, Tigran Petrosian, whose statue stands beside the building. It is also home to the Yerevan Olympic Chess School, named after Henrik Gasparian (1910–95), who won the National Chess Championship ten times, became an international master in 1950 and was an internationally renowned chess composer, especially of endgame studies. In good weather chess is played outside – you may be invited to join in a game!

Shortly after this on the right is the **Yerevan State University**. There are a number of **statues** on the square in front of the building. Centrally are Mesrop Mashtots (362–440), creator of the Armenian alphabet, and Sahak Partev (338–439). The latter was Katholikos 387–428. Active in promoting education he, with Mashtots, translated many works including the Bible into Armenian. To the right, as one faces the university, is Anania Shirakatsi (610–685), mathematician, astronomer and geographer. To the left is Movses Khorenatsi (410–480), author of the *History of Armenia*, the earliest historical account of Armenia. It is probably best to stay on the Khanjian Street side of the green belt and use the underpass to negotiate the new road which crosses the green belt before returning to it to find the **bronze statue** [117 H4], also by Nikoghayos Nikoghosian, of Mikayel Nalbandian (1829–66) who looks out across the street bearing his name. Nalbandian – writer, philosopher, journalist and poet (the words of Armenia's national anthem are adapted from one of his poems) – was a revolutionary democrat who travelled widely throughout Europe, visiting Warsaw, Berlin, Paris, London and Constantinople. Returning to Russia he was imprisoned in the Peter and Paul fortress in

3

St Petersburg by the Tsarist government, spending three years in solitary confinement. He was subsequently exiled to a remote area 500 miles southeast of Moscow and died of TB in prison aged 37. In *A Reference Guide to Modern Armenian Literature*, Kevork Bardakjian (Professor of Armenian Language and Literature, University of Michigan) described Nalbandian as 'an outspoken publicist whose lively and bold style, at times crude and arrogant, was almost invariably laced with irony'. The sculptor seems to have caught the essence of the man.

Across Nalbandian Street is a **memorial** entitled *To the Innocent Victims of the Assyrian People in 1915*. Like the Armenians, the Christian Assyrians suffered at the hands of the Ottoman Turks. It is estimated that 250,000–300,000 Assyrians were slaughtered by the Ottoman armies during World War II, about two-thirds of the entire Assyrian population. Some fled to the Caucasus. There are still villages in Armenia with a significant Assyrian population. The next **statue** [117 G3] is by Yuri Petrosian. Set in bronze it depicts the painter Hovhannes Aivazovsky (see page 53), well known for his dramatic seascapes. He stands, palette in hand, among the waves. Perhaps, therefore, it is appropriate that the final **statue** on this part of the green belt should be Fridtjof Nansen (1861–1930) [117 G3], the Norwegian polar explorer and diplomat who visited Soviet Armenia in his role as League of Nations Commissioner for Refugees. He tried to help Armenian refugees from the massacre in the Ottoman Empire, proposing to the League of Nations that 360km^2 within Soviet Armenia be irrigated allowing the settlement of 15,000 refugees. Although the plan failed because the money was not forthcoming, Nansen's reputation remains high in Armenia. The statue was erected in 2011 to mark the 150th anniversary of Nansen's birth. A stamp was also issued to mark the anniversary. It was the second time Nansen had been so honoured in Armenia, a previous stamp having been issued in 1996.

ELSEWHERE IN YEREVAN Some of the sights covered in this section can be easily reached on foot. Others probably require transport, unless you are a keen walker, and these are noted under individual entries.

Around the railway station [112 D5] (*The easiest way to get here is to catch the metro to Sasuntsi Davit ('David of Sassoun') station*) Tamanian's plan was for a new central railway terminus but this was never realised and the main station is in an industrial area south of the centre. The fine **station building** dates from 1956 and is a striking structure though it now sees much less traffic because of the closure of the border with Azerbaijan; there are now only seven departures each day and consequently few visitors ever come here. The long façade has, uniquely for Armenia, a tall central spire that would not be out of place in St Petersburg. The finial of this spire is, equally unusually, still topped by a purely Soviet symbol being a form of the design of the coat of arms of Soviet Armenia adopted in 1937 and replaced after independence in 1992. The coat of arms was based on a design by the well-known Armenian artist Martiros Sarian and depicts the five-pointed Soviet star above Mount Ararat with a bunch of grapes and ears of wheat below. The coat of arms also bore the well-known slogan 'Proletarians of all lands, unite!' but the railway station does not appear from ground level to enjoy this embellishment.

In front of the station is Ervand Kochar's very fine equestrian **statue of David of Sassoun** [113 E5] mounted on his horse Dzhalali (see pages 55–6 for further information on Ervand Kochar). The epic stories of David of Sassoun date back to the 10th century though they were not written down until 1873. They recount the fortunes of David's family over four generations, Sassoun symbolising Armenia in its struggle against Arab domination. The statue shows David brandishing a sword which is ready to fall on the invaders while water flows from a bowl over the pedestal, symbolising that when the patience of the people is at an end there will be no mercy for the oppressors. David's crest of honour was a sword of lightning, belt of gold, immortal flying horse and sacred cross.

More prosaically, on one of the tracks away from the station platform is positioned a steam engine. It is E^u class number 705–46, built in 1930 and one of around 11,000 E-class 0-10-0s built between 1912 and 1957 as the standard design for hauling heavy freight trains. This is the largest number of any steam locomotive design ever constructed. In the E^u variant, to which this particular example belongs, the superscript U stands for *usilennyi* – 'strengthened'. The last driver of the train, born in 1927, has a collection of personal memorabilia, including photographs of Stalin, in the train which he is happy to show anyone who is interested. Like many Armenians he is more than willing to pose for photographs: he insists on wearing his uniform jacket with his medals for the occasion. A small **railway museum** (⊕ *10.00–17.00*) has been established in the station building. Only railway enthusiasts would make a special journey to see it but it might be worth a quick look while waiting for a train. If it is closed, ask at Enquiries.

The far end of Abovian Street
Abovian Street has some worthwhile buildings beyond Isahakian Street where it crosses the green belt. On the left corner of Abovian and Isahakian is the **Armenergo building** [117 H2] housing Armenia's main electricity utility. Constructed in 1930 of black tuff, it was designed by Hovhannes Margarian (1901–63) who was also responsible for the Yerevan brandy distillery.

Crossing Koriun Street, the building of black tuff on the right corner is the **Yerevan Medical University**. Continuing uphill along Abovian Street, on the left side is a small park housing the **original university observatory** designed in the 1930s by Tamanian but superseded by the Byurakan astrophysics observatory (see pages 169–70) on Mount Aragats. At the entrance to the park is a **statue** of Victor Hambartsumian (1908–96) [117 E4], a prominent astrophysicist and one of the founders of the observatory. On the right-hand side of Abovian Street there is a **neo-Classical building** of 1880 which originally housed the Guyanian Mirzorian School for Girls but now houses the university faculty of theology. After an elaborate wrought-iron fence (still incorporating a hammer and sickle design, alternating with the staff of Aesculapius) complete with stone posts and flowerpots that encloses a hospital courtyard, is an interesting building. It is the **Mari Nubar children's eye clinic** [113 E3] which includes a series of pyramids in the frieze below the cornice. This building stems from an initiative in Egypt taken on Easter Sunday (15 April) 1906. Armenians had been prospering in Egypt, and particularly so since the British occupied the country in 1882. Numbers of Armenians there were also being swelled by refugees from Ottoman oppression as well as from the Armenian-Azeri conflicts. The driving force behind the initiative was Boghos Nubar Pasha (1851–1930), an Armenian whose father, Nubar Pasha, had been prime minister of Egypt on five separate occasions between 1872 and 1895. The initiative saw the founding of the Armenian General Benevolent Fund whose mission was to establish and subsidise schools, libraries, workshops, hospitals and orphanages for the benefit of Armenian communities throughout the Middle East and adjacent regions and the Yerevan children's eye hospital was built under the auspices of this organisation. Later Boghos Nubar Pasha was to be leader of the Armenian delegation at the Paris peace conference of 1919. The newly decorated building is still an eye clinic but no longer just for children.

Abovian Street opens out into **Abovian Square** [113 E3], in the centre of which is a statue of Abovian himself sculpted by Suren Stepanian and unveiled in 1950. This was not the statue of Abovian originally intended for this site. That statue, made of bronze, was sculpted in Paris in 1913 by Andreas Ter-Marukian, packed up for shipment, but then, owing to some misunderstanding, it was forgotten and lay undisturbed for 20 years. When it was finally delivered in 1935 it was first erected on Abovian Street near the Moscow Cinema, then moved to the children's park by the Hrazdan River, before finally in 1964 being taken to the Abovian House Museum where it remains.

The building on the right as you enter the square is a hospital of the 1930s. The Folk Art Museum is just beyond that (see page 155).

Marshal Baghramian Avenue to the American University (*It is convenient to walk up one side & back down the other side of this broad street*) The street has some striking buildings and provides a contrast to the centre of Yerevan. It is home to a number of foreign embassies as well as to Armenia's parliament building and presidential palace. (Note that it is not advisable to stop outside these two buildings; see below.) Starting from the northwest corner of **France Square** [117 F2] walk up the south side of the street. Near the bottom on the left is the **Union of Writers building**, renovated in 2010. Higher up is the imposing **parliament building** [116 D1] (designed by Mark Gregorian in 1950) set in beautifully kept grounds behind tall railings. Across the next side street is **Lovers' Park** [116 C1] (⊕ *Mar–Nov 07.00–02.00, Dec–Feb 07.00–01.00*) which has been renovated by the Boghossian Foundation. It is favoured not only by couples but also by young mothers and older folk enjoying a rest on one of the benches in the shade. There are also a couple of cafés so it is a good place for a drink before continuing. A little higher up, across the road, are the **British embassy**, steps leading up to the **American University** and the **bronze statue** [116 C1], by Norayr Karganian, of Marshal Baghramian after whom the street is named. Hovhannes Baghramian was born in Russia to Armenian parents. He fought in World War I; then in the Turkish-Armenian war, taking part in the Armenian victory at Sardarapat in 1918 (see page 22); and then in World War II commanding forces which expelled the Nazis from the Baltic states. He is buried at the Kremlin Wall Necropolis in Moscow. Turn round at this point to walk back down to the centre of town. Opposite Lovers' Park the **presidential palace** [112 D3] is on the left. Just within its grounds are **two marble statues** by Levon Tokmajian, Tigran the Great on the left and Noah on the right. Admire the statues as you walk. If you stop you will rapidly be told to move on by police guarding the palace. Apparently after the post-election protests in 2008 (see page 28) a ruling allows people to walk past the parliament and presidential palace but forbids them to stop there.

Kond The district of Kond, on the west side of central Yerevan, is the only place where it is still possible to see a few of the **old houses** which, until the early 20th century, were typical of the whole of Yerevan. The easiest way to find the remaining (as of 2013) old houses is to enter Kond up the steep cobbled slope from Sarian Street, just below building 24. For the church, turn right at the top of the slope, then left, and the church comes into view. The area of small houses with their flat roofs, narrow alleys and small courtyards was earmarked for conservation during Soviet times but little was done and much has now been demolished to make way for taller modern buildings. Within Kond is **St John the Baptist Church** [116 C3], a medieval church destroyed in the 1679 earthquake and rebuilt in 1710 and again

in the 1980s. The busy church has an interesting carving (presumably modern) over the north door.

By Victory Bridge [116 A6] The high-level Victory Bridge dates from 1945, its name celebrating victory in World War II. Victory Bridge, 200m long and 34m above the river, supersedes the red tuff bridge constructed following the collapse of its predecessor in the 1679 earthquake and rebuilt in 1830 after the Russian conquest of Yerevan. The four arches of the 1679 bridge, 80m long and 11m above the river, can be seen to the south of Victory Bridge, the central two arches spanning the river itself; the smaller side ones originally crossed irrigation canals. Most visitors see the **Hrazdan Gorge** through which the river flows only as they cross Victory Bridge. In spring, when all is green and the poppies are flowering, driving or walking in the gorge is pleasant, but in the summer it can be hot. Restaurants and cafés have taken over one stretch of the gorge but, thankfully, much remains unspoiled. The **Children's Railway** (see box, page 147) is down in the gorge (✆ 527263; ⏲ 10.30–23.30 daily summer only – from late Apr, depending on the weather; the train leaves when it is full – there is usually not long to wait; child or adult AMD300).

At each end of Victory Bridge are prominent buildings associated with Yerevan's alcohol business. At the west (airport) end is the **Yerevan brandy distillery** [116 A6] (2 Isakov Av; ✆ 510149/150; www.ybc.am; tours approx AMD4,500–10,000 depending on the types of brandy tasted) which stands on a plateau high above the bridge. The distillery was founded in 1887 but the present building was designed by Hovhannes Margarian, the same architect as was responsible for the Armenergo building in upper Abovian Street. Its façade displaying nine arches can be best appreciated when approached by the long flight of steps from the valley below. Guided tours of the storage facilities and museum, with sampling of the products, can be arranged but the actual production is not shown. It is now owned by the French Pernod Ricard company. Unfortunately its excellent products are difficult to obtain in western Europe; presumably its owners see little point in competing with their French products.

At the other (city) end of the bridge the large, rather forbidding building constructed of basalt which faces the bridge, houses the **Yerevan Wine Company** [116 A7]: built about 1930, its shape and dimensions are exactly those of the former citadel that occupied the site, which is the reason for its appearance. Its architect Rafael Israelian (1908–73) was also responsible for the very fine memorial commemorating the Battle of Sardarapat in Armavir province. It is often stated that the first performance of Griboyedov's Woe from Wit was actually given in a room of the fortress by Russian army officers in 1827 but this seems unlikely (see page 246).

The Genocide Memorial and Museum [112 D4] The Genocide Memorial and Museum at Tsitsernakaberd ('Swallow Castle') are among the few points of interest on the west side of the Hrazdan River. Visiting them is strongly recommended for anyone wishing to understand Armenia and its people. In 1965, Armenians throughout the world commemorated the 50th anniversary of the 1915 genocide, and the lack of any tangible symbol in Armenia itself was conspicuous to the extent that the Genocide Memorial was created and completed in 1967. The architects Kalashian and Mkrtchian have succeeded in creating a striking and appropriate monument. Although the ideal approach is to mount the flight of steps leading up to it, most visitors are likely to approach instead from the car park, in which case the first thing they will notice is the collection of trees, each of which has been planted by a distinguished visitor. Separating the museum from the monument is a 100m-long memorial wall of basalt carved with the names of villages and towns where massacres of Armenians by Turks are known to have taken place. The monument itself has two parts. There is a 44m-tall stele reaching to the sky symbolising the survival and spiritual rebirth of the Armenian people. It is riven, however, by a deep cleft which symbolises the separation of the peoples of western and eastern Armenia while at the same time emphasising the unity of all Armenian people. Adjoining the stele is a ring of 12 large inward-leaning basalt slabs whose shape is reminiscent of traditional Armenian khachkars. The 12 slabs represent the 12 lost provinces of western Armenia and their inward-leaning form suggests figures in mourning. At the centre of the circle, but 1.5m below, burns the eternal flame. The steps leading down are deliberately steep, thus requiring visitors approaching to bow their heads in reverence as they descend.

The **museum** (*www.genocide-museum.am;* ⊕ *11.00–16.00 Tue–Sun; free guided tour in Armenian, English, French or Russian*) was added in 1995 to commemorate the 80th anniversary of the massacres. The museum is a circular subterranean building and was designed by the same architects as the memorial. The museum is well labelled in Armenian, English, French and Russian. Much information is given on the number of victims in different parts of western Armenia and there are many photographs taken by German army photographers who were accompanying their allies the Turks during World War I. There are also examples of foreign publications about various aspects of the genocide including reports by British, American and German officials on the maltreatment of the Armenians by the Turks. One typical exhibit reproduces the letter sent by Leslie A Davis, the American consul at Harput (west of Lake Van) to his boss, the American ambassador at Constantinople on 24 July 1915. It reads:

> I do not believe that there has ever been a massacre in the history of the world so general and thorough as that which is now being perpetrated in this region, or that a more fiendish, diabolical scheme has ever been conceived in the mind of man.

Erebuni

Erebuni, on a hilltop in the southern part of the city, is the original site of Yerevan. It can be reached by *marshrutkas* 11 and 72 (see page 114). Visitors can see the partially excavated remains of the site of the city's citadel together with interesting objects found there which are now housed in the museum at the bottom of the hill. When visiting the site it is useful to go to the museum first as the model of Erebuni there gives a good idea of the general layout. A guidebook in Armenian, Russian and English is available which deals also with the sites of Teishebaini (Karmir Blur) and Shengavit (page 149). Note that the informative website (see opposite) also deals with all three sites but only the pages about Erebuni are in English. Erebuni was discovered by chance in 1950 during exploration of Arin Berd Monastery which had later been built on the site. A cuneiform inscription was uncovered which can be dated to 782BC. It states: 'By the greatness of [god] Khaldi, Argishti, son of Menua the powerful king of Biaini and ruler of Tushpa city built this splendid fortress and named it Erebuni, strength to Biaini.' (Biaini was the Urartian name for their country. Urartu is the Assyrian name.) Argishti was the Urartian king Argishti I (ruled c785–c762BC) who established a garrison here of 6,600 troops, the first Urartian settlement on this side of the Arax. Its heyday lasted for only about a century until the Urartian king Rusa II (ruled c685–c645BC) chose a different site, Teishebai Uru (literally City of [the God] Teisheba) overlooking the Hrazdan River which he believed would be less vulnerable to attack by the Scythians. However, Erebuni remained occupied as is testified by archaeological finds from later periods.

As well as the model of the citadel the **museum** (*38 Erebuni Av;* ✆ *432661; www.erebuni.am;* ⊕ *10.30–16.30 Tue–Sun; guided tour in Armenian AMD2,000; in English, Russian, French & German AMD2,500; adult/child AMD1,000/300*) gives much interesting information about many aspects of life in Erebuni in well-presented displays. Interesting items include three silver rythons (drinking horns in the form of animals), the helmet of King Sarduri II (ruled c763–c734BC) and a large jug, possibly a funerary urn, with bulls' heads. There is also a good selection of jewellery, ceramics and weapons found on the site. The central courtyard of the museum is a reconstruction of the palace courtyard. Of particular interest is the stone, actually found at Tanahat Monastery, Syunik (not the better known Tanahat Monastery, Vayots Dzor). It has a cuneiform inscription dedicated to the Urartian king Argishti II (ruled 714–685BC) but the stone was made into a khachkar in the 11th century by which time no-one of course could read the inscription. A tuff **statue** of Argishti I on his chariot, by Levon Tokmajian, stands on the street outside the museum.

The shape of the hill on which Erebuni is built necessitated a triangular shape for the **citadel**. It had walls around 12m high, the lower 6m being formed of two parallel walls of large stone blocks with rubble filling the space in between the rows and large buttresses providing additional strength. Above the stone blocks

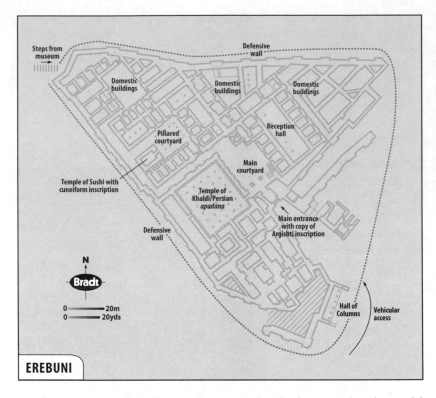

EREBUNI

clay bricks were used which were then covered with plaster. Within the citadel was the royal palace, temples and service premises, everything being connected by stairways because the slope of the hill necessitated the buildings being constructed at different levels. A **good view** of the walls can be had from below and it is worthwhile walking along the path which follows them right round the outside. It can be accessed from near the vehicle entrance to the site or from steps which lead up from the left side of the museum.

Entering the site from the access road and car park the first building on the left is the reconstructed **Hall of Columns** used to greet dignitaries. It has a blue wall with a frieze and the present roof is supported by six wooden columns. Continuing up the main entrance slope and steps, near the top of the steps is a copy of the **Argishti stone** (the original is kept in the museum) erected in 782BC and referred to on page 147. Just after going through the entrance way a narrow alley goes off right to the **necropolis**. To the southwest of the central square was the **temple of Khaldi**, the chief god. It was crowned by a tower with a flat top that was probably used for sending smoke signals which would have been visible from far across the plain. Following the collapse of the Urartian kingdom and the installation of a Persian vice-regent at Erebuni, the temple was converted for use as a 30-column *apadana* (**reception hall**). Part of this has been reconstructed and the design of frescoes can be seen generally with figures of gods between horizontal bands in contrasting colours.

Northwest of the Khaldi temple was a **pillared courtyard**, probably used by the king for important meetings, together with a **small temple** devoted to Sushi, another of Urartu's 79 gods, and used by the royal family. At its entrance is another cuneiform inscription. The palace's **main reception hall** was northeast of the central square. Surrounding the main buildings were living quarters for the garrison and for servants, together with buildings for storing produce such as meat, fruit, wine, sesame seed oil, and milk products in *pithoi* (large urns) sunk into the ground to keep them cool. Different parts of the site are stated to have had different functions but this is not obvious when walking round the ruins.

Karmir Blur [112 B5] The site of Teishebai Uru to which the Urartian king Rusa II moved his capital from Erebuni in the 7th century BC is now known as Karmir Blur (Red Hill) or Teishebaini. It is in the southwest suburb of Karmir Blur on the south side of the Hrazdan Gorge and is probably most easily found by taking a taxi. The site of the city, citadel and palace occupied about 0.45km². Today there is not a lot to see apart from the bases of the massive megalithic walls which surrounded the citadel and evidence of some excavated buildings of the town but the situation, on the edge of the gorge, is impressive. Walking around the hill not only gives an impression of how huge a city Teishebaini must have been but also affords excellent views of the gorge itself. Many of the articles unearthed during excavation are on display at the State History Museum (see pages 150–2). Archaeological evidence indicates that the city was destroyed by fire after a Scythian raid at the beginning of the 6th century BC, possibly at night, the large number of human remains suggesting that the inhabitants had no time to escape. The name derives from the reddish colour of the hill caused by the upper tuff walls of the citadel crumbling in the heat of the fire and turning a more intense shade of red. The ancient site was discovered in 1939, 2½ millennia after it was buried, following the finding of a cuneiform inscription of Rusa II.

Shengavit [112 C5] This important Early Bronze Age site, occupied from c3500 to c2000BC, now sits on a low mound on the south bank of the Yerevan Lake, an artificial reservoir formed by damming the Hrazdan River in the 1960s. Discovered in 1936 and excavated in 1958–83 it occupies some 10–12ha. In the 1970s the Soviet authorities erected a hospital on about half of the site, in spite of protests from local archaeologists. After independence there was no funding for maintenance of the site and its small museum. At one point almost half of the site was sold illegally to private individuals. After sustained lobbying by Shengavit's director the illegally privatised land was returned to the Shengavit Preserve in 2012. Some improvements to the maintenance of the site have been made, thanks to funding from outside donors, and further excavations undertaken. There are hopes that funding may one day be forthcoming to preserve the excavations, improve conditions in the museum and make the site attractive to visitors. Excavations show both round and rectangular dwellings and a surrounding cyclopean wall. Finds (some of which are on display in the State History Museum) include terracotta figurines, pottery, tools, domestic items, evidence of copper smelting and a gold pendant.

Avan and Kanaker Now suburbs in the northeast of Yerevan, Avan and Kanaker were originally villages; something of their old character can still be seen in their maze of small streets and low houses. Both contain minor sites for those who have time and want to see off-the-beaten-track Yerevan.

Avan Lying to the east of one of the main roads to Sevan, Avan is possibly most easily reached via Miasnikian Avenue from the centre of Yerevan. Turn right into Avan beyond the Botanical Garden then follow the main street through the suburb.

For **Avan Cathedral** [113 G2] turn left on to Khudyakov Street just before a large cemetery then immediately left again. (If lost, ask for Katoghike, or Tsiranavor as it is sometimes called locally.) Built in AD591 its present ruined state belies its immense architectural importance as the prototype of the much better known masterpiece, St Hripsime in Ejmiatsin. Avan Cathedral was the first four-apse church in Armenia to have western corner rooms in a centric composition. Uniquely, its corner rooms are circular (St Hripsime's are rectangular). As at St Hripsime they are reached via four three-quarter-circle niches. It is thought that the church had five domes: the main central dome and one over each corner room. A good example of a fish-shaped *vishap* has been used for the internal lintel of the west entrance. For the **church of St John** [113 G2] turn left at the far end of the cemetery. Dating from the 5th or 6th century and rebuilt in the 13th century, the black and red tuff church has been in ruins since the massive earthquake of 1679. A single nave basilica, it retains its original stepped base and has a Greek cross on the lintel of the entrance. Its most notable feature is the intricately carved *bema* front which has an open-work central boss clutched by the feet of birds (now headless) on each side. The **Botanical Garden** [113 F2] (*1 Atcharian St;* ⊕ *08.00–23.00; AMD300*) founded in 1935 both as a scientific institution and recreational area, has suffered badly from underfunding since the collapse of the Soviet Union. One can have a pleasant stroll but the educational aspect is limited.

Kanaker Situated a little west of Avan, Kanaker can be reached by taking Azatutian Avenue from the top of the Cascade. Where Azatutian Avenue becomes Tbilisian Road bear right on to 1st Street in Kanaker and then follow the winding street to reach the **Khachatur Abovian House Museum** [113 F2] (page 157). A little further along the main street, turn left on to 6th Street. This brings you first to **St Jacob Church** [113 E2] and then to **Mother of God Church** [113 F2]. Both churches were rebuilt after the 1679 earthquake (original dates unknown but probably early) and are very similar in style, being three-aisled barrel-vaulted basilicas with elaborate carving round doors and windows. St Jacob was restored in 1990 after being a barn in Soviet days; Mother of God was under renovation at the time of writing. Further along the main street is a **khachkar shrine** of 1265 in a stone frame with pointed roof. Carrying on, the **Russian church of St Pokrov** [113 F2] is reached, a striking contrast with its gold domes and bright white interior with iconostasis.

YEREVAN'S MUSEUMS AND GALLERIES Yerevan has many museums. There are some which most visitors agree are 'must-sees' and should be fitted in if at all possible. Others are very worthwhile even for those without a special interest in the subject covered. Yet others will probably appeal only to those with a special interest. I have tried to give some indication of these groups in the entries below although it is inevitably subjective. Non-Armenian speakers should note that some museums, particularly some of the smaller house museums, have information only in Armenian. For biographical details of persons whose house museums are listed, see individual entries in the index.

Most museums charge Western visitors around AMD500–1,000 per person although some (including the Genocide Museum and the Military Museum) are free. For more information on entry fees and opening hours, see page 98.

Must-sees
State History Museum [117 E5] (*Republic Sq;* ✎ *582761; www.historymuseum. am;* ⊕ *11.00–18.00 Tue–Sat, 11.00–17.00 Sun, last entry 1hr before closing; guided*

Haik Avenue (also known as Gai Avenue) in the northeast of Yerevan is the main road out towards Garni and visitors heading there frequently notice the four statues alongside the road. The **first**, on the left, made of copper and dating from 1975, is of a man wearing a lion skin and aiming his bow either at Turkey or at the block of flats opposite. This is Haik, great-great-grandson of Noah and legendary founder of the Armenian people. The **second** statue, a figure on horseback to the right of the road brandishing a sword and looking back towards Turkey, is another Haik, Haik Bzhshkian (1887–1937). Born in Tabriz (Persia) he was active in revolutionary movements and also in World War I when he commanded Armenian troops. Subsequently he supported the Bolshevik cause and after service in Siberia became commissar of the military forces in Soviet Armenia. His military career continued but he succumbed, along with 40,000 others, to Stalin's purge of the Red Army. The victims were variously accused of being 'spies', 'Fascists', or 'Trotskyite-Bukharinite'. The bronze statue was erected in 1977, a time when the true cause of death was not acknowledged.

The **third** statue, on the left and opposite a market, is a 2003 marble statue of King Tigran II (the Great) who ruled from c95BC to 55BC. It is by Levon Tokmajian who also sculpted the statue of Tigran the Great in front of the presidential palace (see page 144). The **fourth** statue, also on the left and dating from 1982, is of Tork Angegh ('Ugly Tork'). He is shown standing on a pile of boulders, carrying an enormous rock on his shoulders, and with a grotesque expressionistic face. In legend he was a very kind giant and a skilled artist. Eventually, despite his ugliness, he was able to marry the woman he loved after defeating her 20 other suitors.

tour in English, Russian, French & German AMD5,000; tours may have to be booked the previous day; adult AMD1,000) The museum displays are on three floors; it is difficult to do justice to it all in one visit. (As with many Armenian museums, one is expected to start at the top and work downwards.) The third floor houses the superb exposition 'Palaeolithic to Bronze Age' which opened in 2010 in four rooms and which has since been greatly expanded. The second and first floors cover the rest of Armenian history plus extensive displays of ceramics, national costumes, metalwork and carpets. Most sections have at least limited information in English, a few have none. The museum itself does not provide a floor plan but some years ago public-spirited individuals provided a **guide** which can be freely downloaded from www.tacentral.com. With the reordering of the museum much of it is out of date but it is still useful for those sections without English labelling (see page 152). It is difficult to know if it is better to save your visit to the museum until the end of your trip, when the most important exhibits can then be put into the context of sites with which you are already familiar, or whether to visit the museum first, the better to clothe the sometimes bare sites with the rich finds from them. Ideally of course one needs to do both!

The ticket office is to the right as you go in. Go up to the **third floor**, through the glass doors which lead to the art gallery, and up the stairs on your left to reach the display covering from two million to 1000BC. These rooms contain a fascinating collection of items showing the enormous wealth of historic objects unearthed in Armenia. The collection certainly brought to life for me the ancient

Yerevan has two cemeteries of interest. The **Pantheon** [112 D5], Arshakuniats Avenue in the south suburbs of Yerevan, is where Armenia's famous deceased are interred. The individuals most familiar to visitors are likely to be the composers Komitas and Aram Khachaturian together with the writer William Saroyan. Presumably the reason that only the upper half of Saroyan's body is shown in the 1984 sculpture on his tombstone, is that only half his ashes are here: the other half are in Fresno, California.

The cemetery of **Yerablur** [112 C5], Sebastia Avenue, to the right off the road to Zvartnots, houses the dead from the Nagorno Karabagh war together with Andranik Ozanian, fighter against Turkey in the late 19th and early 20th centuries, and Vazgen Sargsian, the prime minister who was assassinated in parliament in 1999. To visit this cemetery, particularly on one of the traditional Armenian days for visiting graves such as Easter Monday, is even more poignant than with most war cemeteries because the war in which they were killed is so recent (1989–94) and many of the figures tending the graves are the mothers or other close relatives of those who died. Most of the graves carry a picture of the deceased.

history of the country, with finds from so many well-visited sites such as Garni, Lake Sevan, Metsamor and Dvin, as well as less visited sites such as Artashat, Karmir Blur and Shengavit. There are introductory explanations in English although the English is often surprisingly poor, ending up with contortions such as 'The making of tools was a peaceful and trustworthy dialogue of the prehistoric man with materials to realise and obtain the spiritual energy of the image enclosed in stone.' Furthermore, whilst much is labelled in English, it's usually the obvious articles such as knives, beads, etc, and where labels would actually be useful they are often sadly lacking. Unfortunately details of some excavations are only in Armenian. Favourite items of mine include finds from Karmir Blur such as Argishti I's ritual helmet and decorative shield of the 8th century BC, jewellery from various pre-Christian sites, and the Bronze Age chariot burials from Lchashen, Lake Sevan. Also on display is the world's oldest shoe found in a cave near Areni and radiocarbon dated to about 3500BC by laboratories in Oxford in the UK, and California, USA.

On descending to the **second floor** English disappears completely in the rooms which cover Dvin and Ani: it is here the online guide (see page 151) is helpful. Thereafter English, occasionally high-flown, reappears with detailed information on all aspects of ceramics. Most following sections have an introduction in English although individual labels tend to be only Armenian. For some reason the rooms about the Soviet period and independence have no English. The **first floor** has items brought from churches including stonework from Zvartnots Cathedral, a carved wooden door from Tatev, khachkars and an extensive display of carpets and religious artefacts.

In the covered gallery outside the museum is an explanatory exhibition of stelae, an important category of stonework in Armenia, usually overshadowed by the abundance of khachkars.

National Gallery [117 E5] (*Republic Sq;* ☏ *580812;* e *galleryarmenia@yahoo.com; www.gallery.am;* ⏱ *11.00–17.30 Tue–Sat, 11.00–17.00 Sun; last admission 30 mins* *before closing; guided tour in English, Russian, French & Italian AMD5,000; adult AMD800)* The third-best collection in the former Soviet Union. Go straight ahead after entering the building and up the stairs to the **first floor** where the ticket office is on the left. (The ticket office on the ground floor is for the historical museum.) A **helpful floor plan** leaflet in English is available for AMD300, but you will have to ask for it; it is kept under the counter. Labels include English. After buying a ticket one is expected to take the lift to the **seventh floor** to start viewing but it is possible to go directly to other floors. The collection of Armenian works is on the fourth and fifth floors and includes all the major Armenian painters with a good collection of Aivazovsky's seascapes and works by Martiros Sarian.

The rest of the collection largely comprises paintings from the main European schools. Italian artists represented include Bicci di Lorenzo (*The Betrothal of St Catherine*); Benvenuto Garofalo (*Virgin Mary with the Christ Child*); Jacopo Tintoretto (*Apollo and Pan*); Jacopo Bassano (*Adoration of the Shepherds*); Leandro Bassano (*Good Samaritan*); and Francesco Guardi (*Courtyard with Stairs*). Flemish painters include: Hans Jordaens III (*The Jews Crossing the Red Sea*); and David Teniers the Younger (*Kegl Players and The Village Feast*). Dutch painters include Jan van Goyen (*View of Dordrecht*); Pieter Claesz (*Still Life*); and Jan Wijnants (*Landscape with Broken Tree*). French artists include Louis le Nain (*The Nest Robbers*); Jean Baptiste Greuze (*Head of a Girl*); and Eugène Boudin (*Sea Harbour*). Among the Russian works Ilya Repin's *Portrait of Teviashova* and Isaac Levitan's *Reaped Field* particularly stand out.

Matenadaran [117 H1] (*53 Mesrop Mashtots Av;* ☎ *562578; www.matenadaran. am (only in Armenian);* ⏰ *10.00–17.00 Tue–Sat; closed Sun & Mon; guided tour in Armenian AMD2,500; in English, French, German, Spanish, Italian or Russian AMD2,500–5,000 depending on group size; adult/child AMD1,000/100)* Enter the **ticket office** from the outside to the right of the main entrance steps. It is worth paying for the English-speaking guide. The Matenadaran was purpose built in 1957 to house 14,000 Armenian manuscripts but the original single display room could show fewer than 1% of them. The museum provides virtually the only opportunity in Armenia to see examples of this important art form. In 1997 the Mashtots Matenadaran Collection of Ancient Manuscripts was inscribed on UNESCO's Memory of the World Programme Register in recognition of its world significance. Following the construction in 2009–11 of an adjacent research institute, more space became available in the old building and there are now five display rooms. The original room displays the most valuable items. They include copies of histories (such as a *History of Armenia* by 5th-century Movses Khorenatsi), *Geography* by Anania Shirakatsi (6th-century), the *Book of Canons* by Hovhannes Odznetsi (one of the oldest works on church law), the *Homilies of Mush* (the largest manuscript in the collection, see page 136), the earliest Armenian printed book (printed in Venice in 1512) and translations of many important works into Armenian, the originals of which are, in some cases, lost. Other rooms display manuscripts from each of the three main Armenian manuscript centres (Cilicia, Vaspurakan and Karabagh), items given by Iran and maps. Armenians are particularly proud of the copy of Ptolemy's map which shows Armenia extending from the Black Sea to the Caspian.

Genocide Museum [112 D4] See page 146.

Erebuni Museum See page 147.

Cafesjian Centre for the Arts [117 F1] (*Cascade;* \ *567262;* e *info@cmf.am; www.cmf.am;* ☉ *10.00–17.00 Tue–Thu, 10.00–20.00 Fri–Sun; adult AMD1,000, 13–17yrs AMD700, children under 12 free; several categories of annual membership available*) The Centre, opened in 2009 within the Cascade, aims to bring the best of contemporary art to Armenia. The exhibits are from the personal collection of the founder, Gerard L Cafesjian, and include items from one of the most comprehensive glass collections in the world. The gallery is on six levels of the Cascade with a dedicated lift from each floor. The Cascade escalators between floors function between 08.00 and 20.00. A fascinating and eclectic collection of objects is displayed with excellent information labels in English. A visit here, together with the sculpture park in front of the Cascade, is strongly recommended. (For information on the Cascade itself and the sculpture park, see page 137.)

History of Yerevan Museum [116 B7] (*1 Argishti St;* \ *568185; www.yhm.am (website has useful links to other museums);* ☉ *11.00–17.30 Mon–Sat, closed Sun, national holidays & commemoration days; tour in Armenian AMD2,000, English AMD3,000; adult/child AMD500/250*) Located in the new City Hall (see page 140); enter by the far left-hand door. This well laid out museum on three floors traces the history of Yerevan from ancient times to the early 21st century. Most items are labelled in English. The first floor is ancient and medieval although the model in the centre shows 19th-century Yerevan, with archaeological sites (Shengavit, Erebuni, Avan, Teishebaini) at each corner; the second covers the 19th century whilst the third focuses on the 20th century.

Worthwhile
Aram Khachaturian House Museum [117 E2] (*3 Zarobian St;* \ *589418; www.akhachaturianmuseum.am;* ☉ *11.00–16.30 Mon–Fri, 11.00–16.00 Sat; guide in English, French or Russian AMD2,500; AMD500*) Contains personal memorabilia of Armenia's best known composer as well as props and costumes from his ballet *Spartacus* and photographs of Khachaturian with many well-known people including many non-musicians such as Che Guevara, Ernest Hemingway, Sophia Loren, U Thant and Charlie Chaplin. There is an astonishingly vivid painting by Edman Aivazian of Khachaturian conducting at the EMI studios in London. Painted in 1977, a year before Khachaturian's death, few paintings have ever captured so well the spirit of music making and the museum is worth visiting to see this alone. The museum makes no reference to the composer's falling foul of the Soviet authorities in the late 1940s.

Children's Art Gallery [117 G4] (*13 Abovian St;* \ *520951;* ☉ *11.00–16.00 Tue–Sat, 11.00–15.00 Sun; guided tours in English, German & Russian AMD2,500; adult/child AMD500/200*) This fascinating gallery has two parts to its exhibits. There is a permanent collection of works of art by children from around the world and there are temporary displays of work by Armenian children on various themes such as Europe, the Bible or Armenian folk stories. The standard of the exhibits, which include other art forms such as embroidery, metalwork and carving, is excellent. The children are given instruction in art and craft techniques and then assigned a theme to tackle. It is worth having a guide especially for the themed Armenian section. The gallery, which is on the corner of Abovian and Sayat Nova streets, has no sign although there are colourful posters in the window. The official entrance is on Abovian Street, the exit on Sayat Nova. If you want an English guide (recommended as there is no labelling in English) I suggest you go to the exit first which is where any members of staff who speak English are to be found. Attractive books of the children's work are on sale and they make excellent souvenirs.

Ervand Kochar Gallery [117 F2] (*39/12 Mesrop Mashtots Av;* ✆*580612, 529326;* ☉ *11.00–17.00 Tue–Sat, 11.00–16.00 Sun; guided tour in foreign languages inc English AMD2,000; AMD600*) As well as paintings from all parts of his career, including the Tiflis, Paris and Yerevan periods, there are also photographs of some of his monumental sculptures. This excellent museum gives a very good idea of the range of work of this interesting and talented artist who was persecuted in Stalinist times. A visit is strongly recommended.

Gallery of Modern Art [116 C5] (*7 Mesrop Mashtots Av;* ✆ *535359;* ☉ *11.00–18.00 Tue–Sun; AMD500*) On the northern corner of Mashtots and Sarian streets but not directly fronting Mashtots. There is a sign pointing to it on the building in front of it. Founded in 1972, it was the only such gallery in the entire USSR. With additional funds provided by the diaspora it has built up a representative collection of 20th-century Armenian painting and sculpture. This collection of thought-provoking art is well worth visiting even for those who think they don't like modern art.

Martiros Sarian House Museum [116 D2] (*3 Sarian St;* ✆*581762;* ☉ *10.00–17.00 Fri–Tue, 10.00–16.00 Wed, closed Thu; AMD600*) This three-storey house museum of one of Armenia's greatest 20th-century artists houses around 170 of his works and shows their brilliant colours reflecting a sunny climate. There is information in English about the painter's varied life and the paintings are labelled in English.

Mother Armenia Military Museum [113 E3] (*Victory Pk, 2 Azatutian;* ✆ *201400;* ☉ *10.00–17.00 Tue–Fri, 10.00–15.00 Sat & Sun*) The museum is located inside the structure, which from 1950 to 1962 supported the statue of Stalin, but now supports the statue of Mother Armenia. Originally the whole was devoted to World War II but the upper (ground) floor is now devoted to the Nagorno Karabagh conflict (labels in Armenian, Russian and English). The displays of uniforms, portraits of marshals, etc are not particularly interesting although camouflage netting is successfully used to create atmosphere on the lower floor (labels here only in Armenian). The museum is notable for succeeding, even in a Stalin-era building, in creating the atmosphere of a church as one enters and this is echoed in the statue of Mother Armenia, a young woman holding a sword horizontally and thus forming the shape of the cross.

Museum of Folk Art [113 E3] (*64 Abovian St;* ✆ *569387;* ☉ *11.00–17.00 Tue–Sun; English guide AMD2,500; AMD500*) A wide range of embroidery, lace, silver jewellery, stone carving, wood carving, carpets, ornamental metalwork and ceramics. There are numbers of salt containers in the shape of women, a traditional Armenian symbol of the woman as being the essence of the home. Other interesting exhibits include shawls from the Lake Van area (now in Turkey) which are similar in style to those from the Scottish Shetland Isles. The museum is particularly strong on wood carving.

Sergei Parajanov Museum [116 A5] (*15 Dzoragyugh St;* ✆ *538473; www. parajanovmuseum.am;* ☉ *10.30–17.00 daily; guided tours in English, French, German & Russian AMD2,500; AMD700*) Dedicated to the artist and film director known in Armenian as Sargis Yossifovich Paradjanian (1924–90), this museum is a must-visit for anyone with the slightest interest in 20th-century culture. It's best to get the English-speaking guide to show you round first, and afterwards to wander round on your own. Parajanov essayed a range of art forms from films (mostly silent, more like a series of still scenes one after another) to collages to pen drawings. He seems to have been either egocentric or megalomaniacal – witness his showing himself in the central place in *The Last Supper*. There is a fish made from broken combs and a representation of blue irises made from broken glass. Mosaics also feature prominently. All in all, it's an extraordinary museum.

And if there's still time ...

Alexander Spendiarian House Museum [117 G4] (*21 Nalbandian St;* ✎ *580783; www.spendiaryanmuseum.am;* ⊕ *11.00–16.30 Tue–Sat, 11.00–15.00 Sun; tour in Armenian AMD1,000, in Russian or English AMD1,500; AMD400)* Dedicated to the composer; as well as manuscripts and personal effects, there is a display about his best-known work, the opera *Almast*.

Avetik Isahakian House Museum [117 E1] (*20 Zarobian St;* ✎ *562424; www. isahakyanmuseum.am;* ⊕ *11.00–16.00 Tue–Sat, 11.00–15.00 Sun; AMD500)* Dedicated to the poet (1875–1957) who, after his return from study at Leipzig University, was arrested by the Tsarist police and banished because of his involvement in the Armenian freedom movement. Very much an establishment figure in Soviet days, he was awarded two Lenin prizes and became a deputy to the Armenian supreme soviet. The museum contains personal effects and memorabilia.

Derenik Demirchian House Museum [117 H2] (*29 Abovian St;* ✎ *527774;* ⊕ *10.30–16.00 Tue–Sun; AMD500)* Dedicated to the writer (1877–1956) who was best known for his play *Nazar the Brave* (1923). Among the personal effects is the writer's Stradivarius violin.

Eghishe Charents House Museum [116 D4] (*17 Mesrop Mashtots Av;* ✎ *535594;* ⊕ *10.00–17.00 Tue–Sat, 10.00–16.00 Sun; AMD500).* A well-presented museum containing the personal effects of the poet and public activist, whose picture will be familiar to visitors as it appears on the AMD1,000 banknote. Many will have stopped to photograph Mount Ararat from his memorial arch on the way to Garni. The English-speaking guide gave me an interesting tour. There is a separate **Charents Museum of Literature and Arts** [117 E5] (*1 Arami St;* ✎ *581651; www.gatmuseum.am)* which is an archive of Armenian literature, theatre, music and cinema for the last 300 years. Mainly a research centre, it apparently has a display of early printed books and newspapers.

Geological Museum [116 D1] (*24a Baghramian Av;* m *091 669061;* ⊕ *11.00–16.00 Mon–Fri, closed Sat & Sun)* Covers the geology and volcanic past of Armenia with displays on rocks, gems, minerals, etc together with palaeontology.

Hakob Kojoyan and Ara Sargsian House Museum [116 D3] (*70 Pushkin St;* ✎ *561160;* ⊕ *10.00–16.00 Tue–Sun; AMD300)* Dedicated to the artists (1883–1959 and 1902–69 respectively). Sargsian was a sculptor, producing works such as *Hiroshima* and *Mother Armenia*. The ground floor is dedicated to him and contains a reconstruction of his studio as well as examples of his work. It is Sargsian's granddaughter who shows visitors round. Upstairs is devoted to Kojoyan with examples of his work and personal effects. He was a talented book illustrator as well as a painter and is credited with the first Soviet Armenian painting *The Execution of the Communists at Tatev* (1930 – now in the National Gallery of Armenia). There is a striking painting of David of Sassoun on his horse in a style reminiscent of Russian fairy tales. The staff are very welcoming but don't speak any English.

Hovhannes Tumanian Museum [116 D2] (*40 Moscovian St;* ⊠ *560021;* ⊕ *11.00–16.00 Mon–Sat; AMD500*) An interesting museum even for those who do not know the works of this notable writer. There are good explanations in English; I particularly recommend reading the introductory board just inside the front door. As well as documenting his literary output the museum offers an insight into Tumanian's intellectual life and humanitarian activities in trying to help the plight of those caught up in the genocide. Upstairs is a recreation of his apartment, including his very large library and his study, where he had a notice saying 'please do not smoke and please do not ask for books'!

Khachatur Abovian Museum [113 F2] (*4 2nd St, Kanaker;* ⊠ *284686;* ⊕ *10.00–17.00 Mon–Sat; tour in Armenian AMD2,000, in English AMD2,500; adult/child AMD500/300*) This museum, set in pleasant gardens in the northern suburb of Kanaker, is dedicated to the novelist. The initial view is unusual; the small house in which Abovian was born is covered, umbrella fashion, with the 1978 display hall. The statue of Abovian originally intended for Abovian Square (see page 144) stands in the garden. The museum is well presented and labelled in Armenian, Russian and English so having a guide is not essential but it adds to a visit. Exhibits cover various parts of his life such as an ascent of Mount Ararat, the Russo-Persian war of 1828–30 and his sudden disappearance, possibly at the hands of Tsarist agents.

Middle East Museum [117 E5] (*1 Arami St;* ⊠ *563641;* ⊕ *11.00–17.00 Tue–Sat, 11.00–16.00 Sun; AMD300*) Based on the collection of the painter Marcos Grigorian, it has an excellent collection of Persian applied arts with pottery, bronzes and ritual figurines dating back five millennia. Included are exhibits from Persia's pre-Islamic Zoroastrian culture. Not always open when it should be.

Museum of Russian Art [117 F1] (*38 Isahakian St;* ⊠ *560872, 560331;* ⊕ *10.30–16.30 Tue–Sat, 11.00–14.30 Sun; guided tour in Armenian AMD1,500, in English, Russian or Persian AMD2,000; adult/child AMD500/300*) Mostly late 19th- and early 20th-century works. Founded in 1984 and based on the collections of Professor Aram Abrahamian. An attractive gallery and well worth a visit. Its marble floors make it a wonderfully cool oasis in the heat of summer.

Museum of Wood Carving [116 B5] (*2 & 4 Paronian St;* ⊠ *532461; www. artwood.am;* ⊕ *12.00–18.00 Tue–Sun; AMD400*) An interesting small museum. Separate sections cover the history of Armenian wood carving, applied carving and sculpture. The small sign outside is, somewhat perversely, carved in stone.

DAY TRIPS FROM YEREVAN See *Chapter 4, The Central Provinces,* for suggested day trips from Yerevan.

4

The Central Provinces

Any place in the five central provinces of Aragatsotn, Ararat, Armavir, Gegharkunik and Kotayk can be visited on a day trip from Yerevan except for the eastern parts of Gegharkunik. The most popular excursions are the **town of Ashtarak** together with the **fortress and monastery at Amberd** in Aragatsotn; the monastery of **Khor Virap** in Ararat with its stunning views of Mount Ararat in clear weather; the **churches of Ejmiatsin** and the **monument and museum at Sardarapat** in Armavir; **Lake Sevan** and the **Sevan Monastery** in Gegharkunik; and the temple at **Garni** and **monastery at Geghard** which are close to each other in Kotayk. All of these are standard places on most visitors' itineraries. The following pages make numerous other suggestions but, if I had to choose just one, it would be the amazing **field of khachkars at Noratus**.

ARAGATSOTN PROVINCE

The province whose name means 'foot of Aragats' comprises the land around **Mount Aragats**, at 4,090m (13,419ft) the highest mountain in the present-day republic. The province's geography is extremely varied and it is probably best thought of as being three separate zones: the mountain itself, arid steppe to the west, and the land bordering the gorge of the Kasakh River to the east. Each of these zones has its different attractions. Ashtarak ('Tower'), the provincial capital, is in the Kasakh Gorge in the southeast of the province and only 22km from Yerevan.

GETTING THERE AND AROUND There are **minibuses** from Yerevan to Ashtarak and Talin (see pages 80–2) and from Ashtarak local minibuses go to some villages, although it is probably easier to hire a taxi in Ashtarak, or even in Yerevan. See pages 82–3 for information about taxi fares. The main roads in the province are good. Most places are accessible by **car** and a 4x4 is only necessary if you are intending to explore very minor roads or are trying to reach Amberd before the snow has fully melted. Main roads have fuel stations, particularly plentiful between Yerevan and Agarak.

WHERE TO STAY AND EAT Accommodation in the province is limited apart from homestays, but since everywhere can be reached as a day trip from Yerevan this shouldn't prove a problem.

There are good **bakeries** at Aparan (page 168) and Mughni (page 162) which sell excellent snacks and a **café** at Amberd (page 171). There is also a café at Lake Kari (pages 169–70) which functions from about mid-June to early September, depending on snow melt. It serves mainly *khash*. The road out of Yerevan is lined with stalls

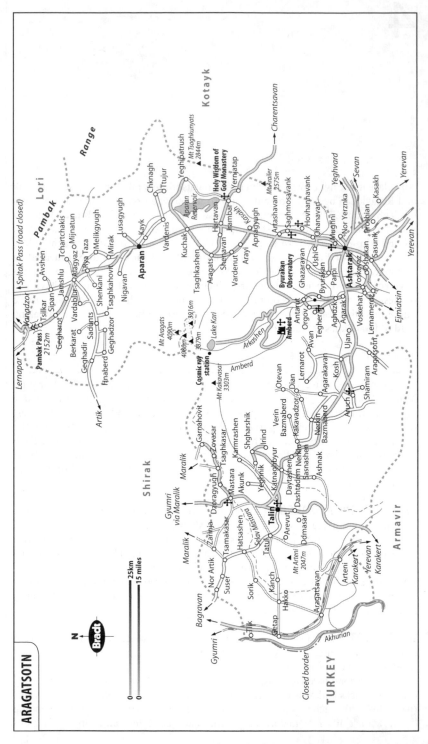

ARAGATSOTN

selling seasonal produce and with barbecue stalls. Some petrol and gas stations have small shops and cafés attached. Alternatively, take food from Yerevan for a picnic.

ASHTARAK (*Telephone code: 232*) Ashtarak is situated on the **Kasakh River**. This river rises in the southeastern corner of Shirak province and then flows south through Aragatsotn to join the Arax south of Yerevan. Ashtarak is a pleasant town with some older buildings including some fine medieval churches. It is now rather dominated by the modern bridge carrying the Yerevan to Gyumri main road high over the gorge, bypassing the city and considerably reducing traffic over the older **three-arch bridge** of 1664. This older bridge has a rather unusual appearance in that the three arches are unequal in size with the southernmost arch almost twice the height of the northernmost. Prominently perched atop an outcrop on the east bank of the river between the new and old bridges is the small red tuff **church of St Sargis**, a modern construction on early foundations. The main part of the city, however, is on the west bank.

Legend states that three sisters lived here who all loved the same prince – Sargis: the elder two decided to kill themselves to leave the way free for the youngest. One of the elder sisters dressed in an apricot-coloured dress and the other in a red dress and then they both threw themselves into the gorge. The youngest sister learned what had happened, put on a white dress, and threw herself into the gorge after them. The prince became a hermit but three churches appeared at the edge of the gorge: one apricot-coloured, one red and one white. The problem with this legend is that the present colour of these churches doesn't correspond with it, although the names do. Karmravor ('Reddish'), the church of the sister wearing the red dress, is apricot coloured (though it does have a red roof); Spitakavor ('White-ish'), the church of the sister wearing the white dress is red; while Tsiranavor ('Apricot-ish'), whose sister wore the apricot-coloured dress, is actually white!

By far the best preserved of the three is the small 7th-century **Karmravor Church** dedicated to the Mother of God. It is one of the few Armenian churches of this period to have survived unaltered, even retaining a roof of tuff tiles and a tiled octagonal cupola. A single aisle cross-dome church, it is one of Armenia's most appealing town churches. An extensive cemetery with khachkars lies to the north and east of the surrounding walls. The other two churches in the legend, 14th-century **Spitakavor** and 5th-century **Tsiranavor**, are both roofless and forsaken but are only a short walk away. Both are perched on the edge of the gorge; from outside their eastern walls there are good views of the gorge, the old bridge and St Sargis Church. **Tsiranavor**, on a three-step base, was a three-aisled basilica. There is evidence of the church having been fortified (see page 45) with remnants of an extra wall on the east, north and west and a rebuilt southern wall with castle-like windows and defensive shutes. **Spitakavor** is a small, almost square church, the apse occupying the full width of the eastern end. The large storage jars decorating the gardens passed on the walk are often unearthed in the district. The churches of the legend are on the northeast side of the city but Ashtarak's biggest church, **St Marina**, is in the city centre. Built in 1281, it is again a cross-dome church with octagonal tambour but the tambour and cupola here are unusually high. The tambour features attractive decoration in contrasting colours of tuff. Unfortunately the appearance of the whole is seriously marred by a, now dilapidated, late 19th-century addition which looks more like a large derelict shed than part of a church.

Eight kilometres southwest of Ashtarak is the village of **Oshakan** whose **5th-century church** was renovated in 1875 with frescoes added in 1960. A tall belfry rises at its east end. It is famous as the burial place of Mesrop Mashtots and the alphabet is spelled out in grass in front of the church. A new **stele** stands at the entrance to the church, commemorating the 1995 visit of Katholikos Karagen I. Near the top is a **sundial** with the traditional Armenian use of letters for numbers. However, whether due to unfamiliarity with the old letter/number system or because of Oshakan's association with the alphabet, the hours are uncharacteristically numbered with a continuous sequence of the first 12 letters of the alphabet (see box, page 41). In the grounds of the church is a collection of **modern khachkars** carved by Ruben Nalbandian. There are 36 of them, each a letter of Mashtots's original alphabet, carved with images appropriate to the letter as well as a typical Armenian cross and the circular symbol of eternity. A visit is enhanced by the company of an Armenian speaker but, armed with a copy of the Armenian alphabet (see page 346), it is possible to appreciate the ideas behind some of them. For example, the Armenian letter 'E' bears an image of Ejmiatsin, 'M' depicts Mesrop Mashtots, and on 'J' water flows from the eternity symbol, *joor* being the Armenian word for 'water'. The first rank of nine can be read as (Ch)rist, (E)jmiatsin, (S)aint, (M)(A) (SH)(T)(O)(TS).

In the **gorge** at Oshakan a **five-arch bridge** dating from 1706 spans the Kasakh. Any vehicles which look as if they are attempting an impossible fording beside the bridge are simply using the river as a free car-wash.

NORTHWARD ALONG THE KASAKH The main road north from Ashtarak towards Vanadzor and the Georgian border keeps, for the most part, to the west bank of the Kasakh. The section of road crossing directly over the Pambak range into Lori province by the **Spitak Pass** (2,378m) is now impassable owing to washouts, and the modern road deviates to the west over the slightly lower **Pambak Pass** (2,152m). The view from the road north from Ashtarak is dominated by Mount Aragats to the west; to the east **Mount Arailer** (2,575m) is prominent on the southern part of the route but further north the Pambak range rises to 3,101m at **Mount Tegh**. A whole succession of monasteries lie along the river, many of which are interesting and attractively sited.

Mughni The village of Mughni, nowadays within the Ashtarak city limits, lies just to the north of the main Yerevan to Gyumri road at the west end of the high viaduct over the Kasakh Gorge. The 14th-century **monastery of St George** was completely rebuilt between 1661 and 1669 during the period when eastern Armenia saw a revival of church building thanks to the stable conditions enjoyed under the Safavid shahs of Iran. It is unquestionably one of the finest buildings of this renaissance and it is now surrounded by well-tended gardens. It is notable that the church withstood the earthquake of 1679 which flattened Yerevan and badly damaged the monastery of Hovhannavank to the north. The main cross-dome church has a distinctively striped circular tambour supporting the conical umbrella cupola and different colours of tuff are also used to decorative effect on the gable ends. To the west is an arched gallery surmounted by a belfry whose cupola is supported by 12 columns. Both the west and south doorways are especially notable with elaborately carved tuff of different colours and fine carved wooden doors. Inside the church, fragments of early 19th-century murals survive, notably one showing the baptism of Trdat on the north wall. There is an altar screen, unusual in Armenian churches, also with paintings. The fortress wall of the monastery survives with small towers at the northwest and southwest corners. At the northeast corner the original service buildings have been restored: they originally housed the living quarters of the monks together with the refectory. St George's should be additionally commended for being the first church in

Armenia to produce for visitors a well-written useful guide in English. Presumably this commendable initiative was thanks to the Armenian Prelacy Ladies' Guild (New York) who funded the (well carried out) restoration.

Hovhannavank (monastery) Situated about 5km north of Mughni, Hovhannavank ('Monastery of John') is the southernmost of two sizeable monasteries that are perched on the edge of the gorge and linked by a path which makes a pleasant, though potentially rather hot, walk: it is about 5km from Hovhannavank to Saghmosavank and there is little shade. The oldest part of Hovhannavank, perhaps the more appealing of the two monasteries, is a barrel-vaulted **basilica** dating from the 5th century though extensively rebuilt since then. It has a painted wooden altar screen. On the south side of this early basilica stands the **main church**, dedicated to John the Baptist, and erected by Prince Vache Vachutian in 1216–21; the prince was Governor of Ani from c1213 until 1232. The corner rooms of this church are two-storey and those at the west have cantilevered steps. As at some other churches of this period, the front of the altar dais was originally decorated with stars, pentagons and diamonds and some of this decoration survives. The *gavit* was built in 1250 to serve both the churches and is consequently off-centre. Four pillars divide it into separate sections, each of which is differently decorated; the belfry supported by 12 columns was probably added in 1274.

The cupola of the main church collapsed following an earthquake in 1679 and then again, following another one, in 1919; the latter also damaged the south façade and still more damage resulted from the 1988 earthquake. However, the 12-sided tambour and umbrella cupola were reconstructed in 1999 and repairs are continuing. (The obliquely positioned **5th-century church** to the north of the *gavit* was under restoration at the time of writing.) Particularly strange is the tympanum of the door from the *gavit* into the main church. The bas-relief is always said to depict the parable of the wise and foolish virgins with Christ apparently blessing the five wise virgins with His right hand and rebuking the five foolish virgins with His left. Except that the virgins appear to have beards. Given the large sickle shape on Christ's left, I wonder if the scene actually depicts the last judgement. The church is surrounded by a fortified wall, originally constructed in the 13th century and rebuilt in the 17th. To the north is an extensive graveyard with khachkars.

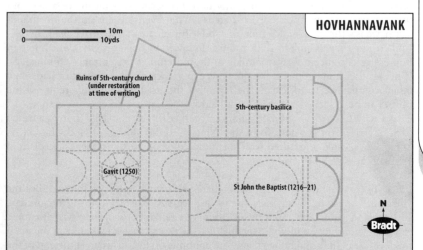

HOVHANNAVANK

0 — 10m
0 — 10yds

Ruins of 5th-century church
(under restoration
at time of writing)

5th-century basilica

Gavit (1250)

St John the Baptist (1216–21)

N

Bradt

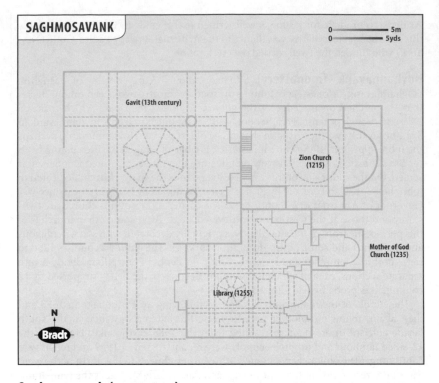

0 —— 5m
0 —— 5yds

Gavit (13th century)

Zion Church
(1215)

Mother of God
Church (1235)

Library (1255)

N

Bradt

Saghmosavank (monastery) This monastery was, like Hovhannavank, built by Prince Vache Vachutian. Not surprisingly the two monasteries have many similarities, not least in their situation on the rim of the gorge and in the stone used in their construction, although the architectural details are quite different. The oldest part of Saghmosavank ('Monastery of Psalms') is the **Zion Church** of 1215 with its round tambour and conical cupola. Inside there are four two-storey corner rooms; those in the west have cantilevered steps going up the west wall of the church, those in the east currently have no permanent means of access but there is a suggestion of cantilevered steps having been present up the north and south walls. The smaller **Mother of God Church** to the south, a plain barrel-vaulted church, was built in 1235 and was followed by the large *gavit* which has an impressive entrance doorway similar to those found at the entrance to mosques. Whether this simply reflects the previous experience of the architect or had some other significance is not clear. The layout of the existing buildings required the **library** to be L-shaped when it was added in 1255. It has an apse in its southeast corner with frescoes on the side pillars and carved angels above it. There is a fresco of St Gregory over the door from the library into the Mother of God Church. As at Hovhannavank, a **fortified wall** surrounds the complex and there are splendid views of the Kasakh Gorge.

Ushi To the west of the main road, where Hovhannavank is to the east, lies the village of Ushi with the massive site of **St Sargis Monastery** (5th–17th century). Although in ruins and rarely visited, enough remains to make a visit to these extensive monastery buildings worthwhile. The monastery is 1½km from the main road. Go straight through the village and continue on the dirt road at the end of the tarmac. It brings you to a picnic area below the southeast entrance to the monastery. The large complex (45x54m) up on the hillside is surrounded by a defensive wall of 1654 with round towers. The monastery suffered earthquake damage in 1679 and again in 1827. The small **church of St Sargis**, built in the 10th century, was the only structure left standing after the 1827 earthquake. It was restored in 2003–04. The church was built on the site of an earlier 5th-century chapel believed to house the tomb of St Sargis (see page 39). Executed by the Sassanid king in AD362 for his Christian beliefs, the saint was originally buried at Namyan, on the southern coast of the Caspian Sea. In the 5th century Mesrop Mashtots had the saint's remains reburied at Ushi.

The **Mother of God Church** (12th–13th century) lies to the south of St Sargis. It was a three-aisle domed basilica (stones from the tambour are laid out outside the monastery complex to the west). The remains of the eastern apse, with interesting carving on the front of the *bema* can be seen. Slightly more intact is the 1246 *gavit* to the south of Mother of God, its western portal and some walls still standing. Two large windows look out across the Arax plain and in clear weather there are good views of Mount Ararat. Enough of the intricate carving on the portal between the *gavit* and Mother of God Church remains, indicating what a magnificent doorway it must have been. A gallery and bell tower adjoined the western sides of the churches

MOUNT ARAILER – A BOTANICAL FORAY

The extinct volcano of Mount Arailer, about an hour's drive north of Yerevan, makes an ideal botanical excursion. The trip takes in semi-desert, mountain steppe, forest, meadows and agricultural ecosystems. There are several trails and tracks for a 4x4 but it is not necessary to climb to the 2km-diameter crater at the top; the lower slopes afford much of interest. More than 650 species of vascular plants grow on Arailer, almost 20% of the whole Armenian flora.

Timing a visit for flowers is always going to be a compromise. Arailer has snow cover from December which may not fully melt until late May. The first flowers to appear in February/March are *Merendera trigyna* and *Crocus adamii*. Irises, tulips and other spring flowers follow. The most luxuriant growth is in May/June including the scented white flowers of *Crambe orientale*, aromatic thyme, crimson poppies and the dark red bugloss *Echium russicum*. You should also see spectacular fields of agricultural weeds, cornflower, poppy, chamomile and blue larkspur. In the moister meadows are lovely violet-purple, almost black *Gladiolus atroviolaceus*, brilliant blue *Anchusa azurea*, white *Anthemis* daisies, the white foam of *Filipendula hexapetala*, various star of Bethlehem (*Ornithogalum*) species and much more.

Arailer's northern slopes have remnant forest, remains of much wider cover in the past. Over 40 species of shrubs and trees are present including Caucasian oak (*Quercus macranthera*), birch, maple, aspen, cherry, apple, pear and several species of *Sorbus*. There is also a subalpine crook-stem forest, where trees have been weighed down on their sides by heavy snow and then new growth has grown upwards before the snow melted. On the lower slopes can be found the orchid *Dactylorhiza romana*, an inflated cowslip *Primula megacalyx*, *Veronica gentianoides*, beloved by UK cottage gardeners, and a little later the large-flowered violet-blue *Iris demetri*.

For further information on Mount Arailer and details of how to get there, see pages 166–7.

and *gavit*. Domestic buildings line the south, west and north sides of the defensive wall and others run westwards from above St Sargis. Large as the monastery is, it is dwarfed by the size of a **Bronze Age fortress** on the slopes above. A good idea of the fortress and the monastery can be obtained from an aerial photograph (*rogpalmer.cantabphotos.com/081229205050/20*) taken during a project to identify archaeological sites in Armenia.

Mount Arailer (Mount Ara) As with the customary English version of some Armenian place names (see page 99), that of Mount Arailer is an example of tautology, with *ler* being Armenian for 'mountain'. Volcanic Mount Ara, on the border between Aragatsotn and Kotayk provinces, is a prominent landmark in eastern Aragatsotn. Its ridge is said to resemble the silhouette of a sleeping man, Ara the Handsome, lying on his back.

There is a popular **cave shrine**, dedicated to Kuys Varvara (Virgin Barbara), also known as Tsaghkavank (Flower Monastery), on the southern slopes of the mountain. (One of the hiking routes to the peaks passes the shrine.) From the Yerevan to Ashtarak highway take the Mughni turn-off and continue to Karbi village where, 2.3km from the highway, you turn right to wind down into the gorge of the Kasakh River. After winding up the other side of the gorge turn left after crossing a large irrigation channel, continue towards Mount Ara on the long, straight, asphalt road with the irrigation channel on your left. Where the asphalt ends turn right on to a dirt road. From here multiple tracks lead across the initially gentle-sloping foothills, all heading in the same direction towards an obvious cleft in the mountain. It is possible with a 4x4 to drive all the way to the cave shrine but the steeper later stages are along difficult rocky tracks.

It is a **pleasant walk** to the shrine (allow about an hour from the dirt road), especially in spring when it is not too hot and flowers cover the hillside. Later in the year the south-facing slopes can be extremely hot. If you don't feel like walking and don't have your own 4x4, you could use the jeep taxi service from the dirt road to the shrine run by a local man. His mobile number is on a board at his lower terminus. He charges AMD6,000 for the return trip which includes 30 minutes waiting time at the shrine. Inside the dripping cave the focus is the well in the centre of the floor. Its water is said to cure many ailments but only to be effective if you draw the water

THE LEGEND OF ARA THE HANDSOME

Legend relates how Semiramis, Queen of Assyria, was so enamoured by the beauty of Ara, King of Armenia, that she sent envoys to ask him to marry her. He refused: he was already married. Thereupon Semiramis sent her armies to Armenia, with orders to capture Ara alive but he was killed in the battle between the two armies. Grief-stricken, Semiramis, a sorceress, believed she could bring Ara back to life. Failing to do so, she dressed one of her lovers in Ara's clothes to convince the Armenians, who wanted to avenge his death, that Ara was still alive, thus preventing further war. Most versions of the legend agree that Ara was not revived but accounts vary as to how his outline appeared on the mountain. One tale says that when Semiramis buried Ara at the foot of the mountain his spirit rose and formed the mountain's top into his sleeping likeness. Another tale has Ara tied to the mountain and when Semiramis used her magic powers to try to fling him into the void his body landed on top of the mountain, giving it its present contour.

yourself. From the shrine it is possible to continue up the mountain – aim for the saddle, which is obvious from the foot of the shrine, between two peaks.

The 17th-century church in **Karbi** does not match its better known neighbours, Mughni and Hovhannavank, but the three-aisled Mother of God Church has a striking bell tower on the west side, its black and red tuff decoration reminiscent of Mughni's.

NORTH TO APARAN AND THE PAMBAK PASS With the four peaks of Mount Aragats to the west, the road continues north through fields of cabbages and past herds of cattle. In 2005, the 36 letters of the original Armenian alphabet carved out of tuff were placed on a hillside some 2km north of Saghmosavank, just north of the village of **Artashavan**. They are plain and, with their random positioning on the hillside, they compare unfavourably with the interesting and elaborately carved modern alphabet khachkars at Oshakan Church (see pages 161–2). Ten kilometres north from Saghmosavank at the village of Hartavan a road goes off right to **Yernjatap**: in about 4km the road starts to wind down towards the Kasakh. Turn left on to a minor dirt road which similarly winds down. (If you miss this left turn keep going along the main road as it crosses the river and climbs up the other side. From quite high up a road goes off left to wind back down into the valley and across a minor bridge to join the dirt road mentioned above.) Standing on a knoll above the river are the ruins of the **Monastery of the Holy Wisdom of God**, founded in the 5th century and renovated in 1244. It is a peaceful and isolated spot. The black tuff cross-dome church is swathed in wooden scaffolding within and without and a little work has been done on the roof to keep out the elements. Restoration continues slowly, the problem being shortage of funds. The *gavit* with its massive columns is roofless. Its west portal has elaborate carving as does the west entrance to the church with its black and red decoration. Some decoration survives on the altar dais and the remains of a red-painted frieze are discernible. Painted decoration can also be seen at the main entrance to the church and on adjacent khachkars. A door in the south wall leads to a small 4th-century barrel-vaulted church.

Returning to the main road at Hartavan and continuing north, **Aparan Reservoir** on the Kasakh may be glimpsed over to the east: it supplies Yerevan with drinking water. When the reservoir was created in the 1980s the village of **Zovuni** was submerged, with residents being moved to the suburb of Yerevan which now bears the same name. Three historic Zovuni monuments were threatened by the rising waters: the important 5th- or 6th-century church of Sts Peter and Paul, the Vardan Mamikonian mausoleum and a 4th-century chapel or Tukh Manuk (see box, page 184) shrine. The latter two were dismantled and reconstructed on higher ground on the east side of the reservoir above the church; the church was left and its ruins can be seen and reached when the water level is low. All three can be visited either from the south or north end of the lake and a loop can be done via Yeghipatrush with its 10th-century Mother of God Church (see page 168). (**Note:** the Sts Peter and Paul Church is misplaced on several Collage maps: it is actually about halfway along the eastern shore, not far from where the maps show the once direct road from Yeghipatrush to Kuchak entering the water.) For the southern end of the reservoir take the Jrambar turn-off from the main road just north of Hartavan. At the end of the asphalt turn left at the T-junction on to a dirt road. There is a police check-point here at the end of the reservoir dam; there should be no difficulty having the barrier raised if you say you want to visit the Zovuni monuments. It is a pleasant drive, first through wooded countryside (at a fork bear right; the left-hand track to a picnic place is exceedingly difficult after rain) and then across a flat grassy

4

plain where the Tukh Manuk shrine can be seen in the distance. The **mausoleum** of Vardan Mamikonian, hero of the Battle of Avarayr, AD451 (see pages 17–18), is encountered first. The now roofless mausoleum is reached by going down steps beside the entrance to the adjacent ruined church. Between the mausoleum and Tukh Manuk are some ancient khachkars; a dark pillar-like one may have been a *vishap*. The 4th-century **Tukh Manuk** is built of large blocks. Inside it is typical of such shrines, an array of votive offerings adorning the small apse. A large cemetery occupies the hillside below the shrine.

The **Sts Peter and Paul Church** is most easily reached, if the water level is low enough, by going straight down from the picnic table immediately to the west of the Tukh Manuk, keeping to the right of a small ravine. The church on its stepped pedestal is in a sadly ruined state, making it difficult to appreciate its importance in the development of Armenian church architecture. It was the first to be converted from a three-aisle basilica, with free-standing pillars supporting the roof, to a domed hall church in which the pillars adjoin the walls, thus creating a large unbroken space in front of the altar. The conversion at Zovuni was carried out in the early 6th century. The new pillars, adjacent to the walls but without structural cohesion, supported a dome positioned centrally over the original basilica. An eastern apse was added at the same reconstruction with the result that the dome is asymmetrically positioned in regard to the total length of the interior.

The dirt road continues north to **Yeghipatrush**. (The more direct route to the village and the north end of the reservoir leaves the main highway at the sign for leaving Kuchak.) The dome of the large 10th-century **Mother of God Church** can be seen on entering the village. Most of the interest lies with the roofless 13th-century *gavit* which is apparently unique in Armenia in having watchtowers at both its northeast and southeast corners. The *gavit's* west portal has a distinctly oriental appearance, its pointed arch decorated with shell shapes all surrounded by a decorated rectangular frame.

Just before reaching **Aparan** (*telephone code: 252*) town the appearance of the countryside changes with open stony grassland replacing cultivation. Aparan's main square is named after Tigran Petrosian (1929–84), World Chess Champion 1963–69, whose statue stands on the square. Aparan's **Holy Cross Church**, about 100m east of the road towards the north end of the town, is one of Armenia's oldest, dating from the earliest days of Christianity in Armenia in the 4th century. Perhaps more than anywhere else in Armenia it is really possible to feel the age of this church built of dark grey tuff and standing in its well-tended garden, It is a three-nave basilica without a cupola, the naves being divided by T-shaped pillars; the roof is barrel-vaulted. At the apse a modern stained-glass window is virtually the church's only decoration. An unusual feature is the row of four large stone blocks, a little like khachkars, which form a sort of half barrier across the chancel in front of the altar dais. The stepped base on which the church stands is larger than the present church and there are the outlines of two other churches to the north. Aparan has a second functioning church, the restored 4th-century **Teghenyats Church**. Set on a rocky knoll within its cemetery, it too feels old despite the obvious renovation. To reach it, take the first right from the main road north of the Holy Cross road. Continue until you see an old wall and follow the wall as it curves to the right. The metal gate in the wall is the entrance to the church grounds.

It is worth being in Aparan at lunchtime. On the right, immediately after entering the town from the south, a metallic grey building houses an immensely popular **bakery**; the smell of freshly baked bread will guide you there and tempt you to try one, or two, of their delicious snacks (eat-in or take-away).

Leaving Aparan a striking **monument** can be seen on a hill to the west. This commemorates three events: the Armenian victory over Turkey in 1918, the genocide of 1915 and the Great War (World War II) 1941–45. The monument is reached through park-like grounds and up a flight of steps. It resembles three apses, each containing a memorial to one of the events. The countryside becomes greener as rainfall in this area is higher than in the lower-lying areas further south. The road passes several villages inhabited by Yezidi people. Working mostly as shepherds, they are fire-worshipping Zoroastrians and recognisable (to the Armenians) as being racially different with darker skin; the women also tend to wear more colourful clothes and a scarf over the head. As they joined the Armenians in fighting the Turks they are seen as natural allies and there is no racial discord. Modern Yezidi cemeteries are distinctive with graves that look almost like small houses. An older cemetery is by the road in the village of **Rya Taza** where there are tombstones in the form of horses for the men though much simpler ones, sometimes depicting a cradle, for women. Constructing tombstones in the form of animals was not associated solely with Yezidis in Armenia as the tombstones of Armenian nobility were sometimes in the form of sheep.

The road climbs up through rolling hills and over the pass into Lori. Although the old road via the Spitak Pass is unusable by vehicles it would probably make an interesting walk. The whole distance from Alagyaz, where the new road branches off, to Spitak is about 25km but anyone with a driver could be taken as far as Sipan on the old road and then picked up at Lernatsk, about 5km south of Spitak, leaving about 16km to walk over the pass itself.

MOUNT ARAGATS Mount Aragats has four separate peaks, the highest being the northernmost one at 4,090m. The four summits are situated around the rim of a volcanic crater, broken between the southern and eastern peaks by an outflowing stream. Any reasonably fit person can walk to the southern peak once the snow has melted, although it is always necessary to remember that even those accustomed to walking at home will take longer here unless they are acclimatised to the altitude. It is obviously essential to take the same precautions here as are necessary when ascending any mountain. Do not consider going without walking boots, compass, waterproofs, warm clothing and water. The easiest approach is to take the road, often closed well into June, which ascends the southern slope of Aragats as far as the cosmic ray station situated by (artificial) **Lake Kari** at 3,190m. The cosmic ray station was inaugurated in 1943 to study astroparticle physics. According to the station's brochure, work currently concentrates on monitoring solar activity as well as on studying the physics of extensive air showers and measuring the incident flux of galactic cosmic rays.

From the end of the road it takes about two hours to walk up to the southern peak (3,879m) by heading for the northwest corner of the summit until a rough track is encountered which leads to the top. For those wishing to reach the highest point in Armenia it takes about four hours from the end of the road and should be attempted only by those accustomed to mountain walking. Because clouds often gather round the crater from mid-morning, an early start is recommended to maximise the potential for spectacular views and to minimise the risk of becoming disorientated in cloud. Apart from the break between the southern and eastern summits the peaks are linked by high saddles and a ridge descends south from the southern peak.

South of the cosmic ray station at an altitude of 1,405m is **Byurakan Astrophysical Observatory**, founded in 1946. Visits to the observatory and cosmic

4

ray station can be arranged (see page 63). The original equipment included a 45cm Cassegrainian telescope (a reflecting telescope in which incident light is reflected from a large concave mirror on to a smaller convex mirror and then back through a hole in the concave mirror to form an image) and a 52cm Schmidt telescope (a reflecting telescope incorporating a camera and consisting of a thin convex glass plate at the centre of curvature of a spherical mirror which thus corrects for spherical aberration, coma and astigmatism). Radio telescopes were added in 1950. In 1960, a larger Schmidt telescope with a 102cm glass plate and 132cm mirror was installed and, in 1965, an important programme began looking for UV-excess galaxies. It continued for 15 years and achieved considerable international renown with 1,500 such galaxies being identified. (In 1968, the observatory was awarded the Order of Lenin.) A larger 2.6m telescope was installed in 1976 and a second survey was started which was also to achieve major international recognition. The object this time was to obtain baseline data for an ongoing survey of 600 quasars, emission-line and UV-excess galaxies although the detailed work ended up providing information about 3,000 varied objects. Since independence the 2.6m telescope has been refurbished and in 1998 the observatory was named in honour of Viktor Hambartsumian (1908–96), its founder in 1946, whose face used to be familiar to visitors because his picture appeared on the AMD100 banknote until the note was replaced by a coin.

Reach **Lake Kari** (and Amberd; page 171) either by going north on the better surfaced road via Agarak from the Ashtarak to Gyumri road, or by turning west from the Kasakh Gorge road at the Armenian letters just north of Artashavan (see page 167). The roads meet 7km south of the turn-off for Amberd. Note that these mountain roads may be closed by snow into late May. It can be very cold and windy at Lake Kari however hot it is lower down. As the road climbs, temporary villages are encountered, large herds of cattle and flocks of sheep having been brought to the mountain pastures for summer grazing. Beehives are also brought for the bees to forage amidst the abundant wild flowers. Looking down on Amberd a clear impression is gained of the castle and church on their triangular plateau above the Amberd and Arkashen gorges. The extensive boulder fields are evidence of Mount Aragats's volcanic past. The road holds much of botanical interest. In early June, look out for *Draba, Crocus adami, Scilla siberica, Pushkinia scilloides* and the delightfully downy *Ajuga orientalis*. July and August see the alpine meadows in full flower. During the short summer months a **café** functions beside the lake. It serves mainly *khash*; you may wish to take your own picnic.

The southern slopes of Mount Aragats
The fortress and church of **Amberd** are beautifully situated on the southern slope of Aragats at an altitude of over 2,000m between the gorges of the Amberd and Arkashen rivers but may be inaccessible because of snow as late as May. In late May/June, the fortress and church are surrounded by expanses of bright red oriental poppies, geraniums, various peas including the Persian everlasting pea *Lathyrus rotundifolius*, a relative of the garden-popular perennial pea, and the tall *Nectaroscordum siculum*, an onion relatively rare in the wild but often grown in UK gardens. In nearby grassland grows the striking borage relative *Solenanthus circinatus* with its metre-high stems of bluish-purple flowers. From the Ashtarak to Gyumri highway the road to Amberd goes through **Byurakan** village, with its Astrophysical Observatory (pages 169–70).

Byurakan has **two early churches**: the interesting 5th-century church of St John within the village and the 7th-century Artavazik Church just outside the village in a small ravine. To reach **St John**: from the 'square' in the middle of the village take the right-hand fork, then first right again, then at the next fork take the upper road to the church. You will come across it quite suddenly, set above the road in beautifully tended grounds with a collection of interesting stones and khachkars. The south façade, which is the first to be seen, immediately suggests several periods of building. The western portion is plain apart from the horseshoe-shaped arch over the door and three high narrow windows, also with curved arches. The eastern portion is plain in its lower half but the upper half has blind arcades and two small round windows, in front of which hang two bells. The blind arcades continue on to the east façade where two of the narrow vertical windows have carved stone grilles (even better seen from inside the church). On the north side the distinction of round porthole-like windows to the east and vertical windows to the west continues. Wrapped around the northeast corner of the church is an extra wall, built externally of large tuff blocks and internally of an early type of concrete (see pages 42–4), most easily seen beside the west door. In the Middle Ages churches were sometimes used as fortresses and an extra wall was built round the outside of the church. Remnants of such walls still persist in places; the best example I have seen is the Tsiranavor Church in Parpi, not far away. Most such defensive walls have been demolished, as has part of the wall here at Byurakan; old photographs show that the wall once obscured the blind arcades on the south façade.

An intricately carved khachkar stands beside the west door. Inside the church there are massive wall piers supporting the arches of the high barrel-vaulted roof. The unusual *bema* is reached by six steps on each side. Not only is it unusually high but it is also rectangular, a rare shape for a *bema* in medieval Armenian churches. In spite of the windows being small and high up this peaceful church feels light and airy.

The second church, **Artavazik**, is much less notable than St John but it has a pretty setting. The tiny ruined cross-dome church is reached by continuing along the right-hand fork from the village square to the far end of the village then by taking the right fork down into the shallow ravine. The 13th-century belfry over the west door was damaged by lightning.

To reach Amberd, turn left off the road to the cosmic ray station about 14km north of Byurakan. In clear weather spectacular views of the church and fortress can be obtained from the approach road with Mount Ararat in the background, a view all the more impressive because the café does not obtrude when viewing from this direction. The owner of the **café** (⊕ *May–end Oct, depending on weather*) lives on site so opens the café when tourists arrive and closes when they have all gone. (*Snacks start at about AMD2,500; a mug of herbal tea is AMD200; the car-park attendant expects a discretionary tip & the toilets are AMD100pp.*) The **church**, a typical cross-dome structure with an umbrella cupola, is older than the present fortress, having been built in 1026 by Prince Vahram Pahlavuni, leader of the Armenian forces who fought against the incorporation of Ani into the Byzantine Empire. The present **fortress** dates from the 12th century although there had been a stronghold here since the 7th century which changed hands several times according to the fortunes of war. The final phase of building took place after the brothers Ivane and Zakare Zakarian captured it from the Seljuk Turks in 1196. Acquired by Prince Vache Vachutian in 1215, it withstood Mongol invaders in 1236 but was finally abandoned in 1408.

The approach to the fortress is from the west, the side least protected by natural defences, and the windowless west wall has defensive towers and steps inside the castle up to what would have been a walkway on top of the wall. The eastern side of the fortress is more domestic in appearance. Inside there is evidence of at least three storeys of small rooms and the many windows of differing styles, looking out towards the church, suggest various phases of rebuilding.

Three small buildings at the foot of the fortress on the east have been restored. That nearest the castle (the **cistern** on the site plan) certainly has evidence of a water-related function. The middle building is a small **chapel** while the easternmost, the 13th-century **bathhouse**, has two rooms each with a dome. Grooves in the wall would have held clay water pipes, similar to those visible at Lori Berd near Stepanavan. A path around the outside of the fortress affords good views of the gorge of the Amberd. It is possible to go inside the castle. Many people scramble up the steep scree-like slope visible from the car park but the easiest (and official) way in is through the door in the east wall; a path goes off between the chapel and cistern. (Note that, inside, some of the walls don't seem too stable.)

Another attractive and interesting monastery is **Tegher**, founded by Prince Vache Vachutian's wife Mamakhatun in 1213. Constructed of basalt and commanding extensive views over the plains below, it is south of Amberd. An alternative route between the two sites goes west from the Byurakan road at Antarut then via Orgov to join the road to Tegher, dropping down to cross the Amberd River (a popular spot for fishing) and back up the far side.

The oldest part is the **Mother of God Church** with round tambour and conical roof. The front of the altar dais shows seven arches (filled with new paintings depicting scenes from the life of Christ), said to symbolise that this was the seventh church built by the family. To its right is a now blocked-off secret passage down into the river gorge for water and escape. The large *gavit* of 1232 is particularly attractive with decoration around the base of its cupola: the pillars supporting the roof were brought from 10km away. Set into the floor is the grave of the founder and her husband and, more unusually, one grave depicting the deceased as having only one leg and another indicating that the deceased, a stillborn child, had been buried with feet pointing west rather than east. Two small chapels are perched on the west end of the roof of the *gavit*; entrance to them is only from the roof, presumably by ladder. Perhaps they were used as semi-secret storage areas. A suggestion has been made that the students slept here, the removable ladders being one way of curtailing night-time excursions! In the vicinity are the remains of other buildings including a **bread oven** just below the church. On the adjacent hillock are the ruins of the old Tegher village. Behind the church is a **picnic area** and some visitors **camp** here then walk the 12km over the hills to Amberd.

Continuing south from Tegher the road descends through **Aghdzk** village. On the east side of the village street are the ruins of a 4th-century three-aisle **basilica church**, to the south of which is a **mausoleum**, originally of two storeys but with only the subterranean part now intact. According to the early historians Movses Khorenatsi and Pavstos Buzand, the mausoleum was built in AD364, in the period of the Armenian-Persian war, to house the bones of the kings of the Arshakuni dynasty which had been seized by the Persians but were then recaptured by the Armenian leader Vasak Mamikonian. The carvings in the chamber date from the late 4th or early 5th century and are unique in early Armenian Christian art. On the north wall is Daniel in the lions' den while on the south is a boar hunt. A torch is essential for seeing the carvings.

THE WESTERN STEPPES OF ARAGATSOTN

The arid steppe which forms the western part of Aragatsotn is a complete contrast to the eastern and central parts of the province and is crossed by the main Yerevan to Gyumri road. For convenience the western slopes of Aragats are included here as they too are best accessed from that highway.

Parpi

Although some maps show the road to Parpi going off from the northbound Ashtarak to Aparan road, in fact it exits from the Yerevan to Gyumri road just west of the Aparan road. It is signposted if approaching from the east but not from the west. Parpi is an attractive village with three interesting churches. Once on the Parpi road turn left at a T-junction and then left again in the centre of the village in front of a statue of a seated man reading a book. This is Ghazar Parpetsi, chronicler and historian, who was born in Parpi around AD442. He is best known for his *History of Armenia* written in the 6th century. Having turned left, follow the road as it curves right; you will end up at someone's front gate and the 5th-century **Tsiranavor Church**, although this might not be immediately obvious. The massive high wall on the left is part of the north wall of the church. What is particularly interesting about this church is that it is very easy to appreciate the several conversions it has undergone. The 5th-century building was a hall church with relatively wide windows high up. It probably had a wooden roof. In the 7th century the roof was converted into a stone, barrel-vaulted one with the addition of wall piers and arches. Note how the arches supporting the roof have been built in front of older windows in the south and west walls. In the 10th century the church was fortified by building a second wall outside the first; it is this defensive wall which is the first to be seen on arriving. Outside, its construction can best be seen at the ruined east end of the church; inside, it is most obvious blocking the double west window. Entering the church on the west, one first goes through the low doorway in the defensive wall, with its heavy stone door pivoted above and below (a similar door can be seen at Aruch; page 174), and then through the doorway in the earlier wall.

You may have spotted **Targmanchats** (Holy Translator) **Church** up to the right, within a cemetery, on entering the village. Built in the 7th century, rebuilt in the 10th and 11th centuries and restored recently, this small tetraconch church has a wealth of carved detail, most notably on the capitals of the double columns flanking the doorway and the huge lintel with its trinity of large geometric shapes. In the angles between the wings of the church there are half columns with decorated capitals. Unfortunately the two birds over the east window have lost their heads.

From Targmanchats a third church, **St Gregory**, is visible just across the main road. The restored church may be locked but the grounds are worth exploring. A medieval cemetery spreads over the hill. Around the church excavations have uncovered what was obviously a large building within which the present church stands and on top of which are more recent graves. Carved stone fragments line the excavation.

Agarak Heading west along the main road, some 8km from Ashtarak, is Agarak village where a large site, dating from the 3rd millennium BC, was excavated during the first decade of this century. The site occupies 200ha on an extensive outcrop of tuff. Finds indicate occupation from the Early Bronze to Middle Iron ages, the Urartian period (8th–6th centuries BC), the early Christian era, the medieval period (12th–14th centuries AD) and a final phase from the 17th to 18th century. The foundations and walls of many buildings are visible around the periphery of the site which is signposted on the left just after leaving the village. After an information board the track veers right, uphill. Keeping close to the weather-beaten cliff-like rock on your right you reach a 1m³ cavity in the white tuff. At the bottom is a small passageway, 50cm long, which leads into an underground 2m³ chamber. Carved into the walls are large rectangular niches. Apparently a complete skeleton and weapons, thought to be Urartian, were found in this rock-cut sepulchre. A torch is essential if you wish to explore. On the top of the rocky outcrop removal of the thin layer of topsoil has revealed numerous pits carved into the rock. Some are deep and either rectangular or circular, others are shallow and have an obvious channel running from them. Some are now filled with water creating small ponds in which irises and frogs flourish. Yet others look very like the rock-hewn coffins in places such as Lmbatavank.

Kosh Some 20km from Ashtarak a road leads right to Kosh village. Behind the village is a cemetery dominated by a hill on which are the remains of a small **13th-century castle** built on an earlier foundation. It is rectangular in shape with round corner towers. In the cemetery itself are the 13th-century **church of St Gregory** complete with two sundials, and the 19th-century **church of St George**. In Kosh, turn right about 1½km from the highway on to the Sasunik road (the main road bears left – if you reach the prison you have missed the turning). After another 1½km you reach the Arzni–Shamiran irrigation canal, recently renovated. To reach the above sites turn right before crossing the canal then left across the canal into the cemetery. A track leads to the churches. More interesting than either, however, is the 7th-century **church of St Stephen**. It is reached by carrying on across the Arzni–Shamiran canal rather than turning right before crossing it. Follow the road for a short distance up the hill until the church is seen in a gorge to the right. A short track leads over to the church, passing old khachkars and caves apparently formerly used by the monks. The well-preserved church is perched on a ledge so narrow in the side of the gorge that the shape of the roof had to be adjusted to avoid an overhanging rock. One of the church's corners is supported by a pile of rocks, more dramatic before the recent path around the church was laid but still visible. Inside can be discerned the remains of frescoes.

Aruch Further west and just south off the main road is the much more important but much less appealingly situated monastery of **Aruchavank** in Aruch village. The large **cathedral church of St Gregory** was built of red and grey tuff in 666 when Aruch was the seat of Grigor Mamikonian, a prince who enjoyed local autonomy during the period of Arab rule. The cupola of the church has collapsed, remaining unrestored when some work was carried out between 1946 and 1948. Further work has been carried out recently and the church, having been locked for many years, is now open. The windows have been glazed but the cupola is still missing. The church is unusual for one so large in having only a single nave. There are the remains of the frescoes in the apse. A cemetery with recumbent 19th-century gravestones surrounds the church and in the south of the precinct are the remains of Grigor Mamikonian's palace. The main palace building is immediately south of the cathedral. It consists of a three-aisled hall with a row of rooms on its south side. On the north side was another row of rooms and beyond them a gallery. The bases of the columns which supported the roof of the hall are still in place and two carved capitals also survive. To the east of this complex is another separate three-aisled building, possibly a church, possibly a reception hall, the lower parts of its massive pillars still standing. In the Middle Ages the building was fortified, as were some churches, and the remains of the defensive wall built round the outside can be seen. At the east end is a large stone door which pivoted top and bottom, very like that in Parpi's Tsiranavor Church. To the northeast stands a 4th-century, single-nave church.

Away from the centre of the village Aruch also has a **ruined caravanserai**, possibly Armenia's most frequently noticed as it is just a few metres from the main Yerevan to Gyumri road on the south side. When built it was on the main route linking the then important Armenian cities of Tabriz (in present-day Iran), Dvin and Kars. The caravanserai is commended as a stop for birdwatchers as it is an excellent location for the larks, wheatears and other birds of this arid plain.

Irind Between the large cathedrals of Aruch and Talin is the important 7th-century **polygonal church** at Irind, north of the main road. (Note that whatever the Collage maps show there is now no direct turn-off from the main road for either Irind or Yeghnik. Instead, turn off at Katnaghbyur and take the good tarmac road to Shgharshik where there is a T-junction; right for Irind, left for Yeghnik.) In Irind bear right at an obvious white statue (a former prime minister). At the time of research restoration was under way and the church was swathed in scaffolding within and without. Inside there are seven apses of equal size, the eighth being replaced by the rectangular west entrance. The east apse houses the *bema* and from the two adjacent apses square corner rooms go off eastwards, making the exterior of the church rectangular at the east end as well as at the west. The octagonal tambour rests on the arches over the apses. Each apse has a window and in the tambour there is a window over each apse. Externally there are triangular niches between the apses and the whole rests on a stepped base which follows the church's contours.

Talin (*Telephone code: 2490*) The next point of interest heading west is **Talin** just south of the present main road. The semi-ruined **cathedral** here is more ornate than that at Aruch and impresses by its size. Like Aruchavank it was built in the 7th century. It has, however, three naves and three polygonal apses and is an altogether more impressive building of red and grey tuff with a 12-sided tambour decorated with arches into which windows are set. There is good 7th-century decoration around some of the windows. The remains of frescoes can be seen. The one in the apse probably depicts the Transfiguration while on the south wall can be seen a portion of the entry into Jerusalem. Talin lost its cupola in an earthquake in 1840 and was further damaged by another in 1931, although some restoration was carried out in 1947 and again between 1972 and 1976. The smaller church in a corner of the large site is roughly contemporaneous. An inscription records that Nerseh built it 'in the name of the Holy Mother of God for her intercession for me and my wife and Hrapat my son'. Unfortunately it isn't clear which of several Nersehs was involved. Near the small church are a number of stelae with Christian carvings, their shape harking back to pre-Christian *vishaps*.

Dashtadem A road runs south from Talin across the Talin Plateau eventually to drop down into the plains of Armavir province. Leaving Talin there is a very large **ruinous caravanserai** on the left, just after a forest of electricity transmission towers: its sheer size is testament to the importance of the trade routes across Armenia. In about 6km the road reaches the village of Dashtadem. In the centre is a large **fortress** whose perimeter walls are entered through an arched gateway over which are interesting carvings of animals. Built according to the best theories of castle building, the gateway requires anyone entering to turn through a right angle thus preventing horsemen charging the entry. Within is a keep of the 9th or 10th century to which half-round towers have been added at some later date and under which large cellars can be explored. An Arabic inscription of the month of Safar 570 (ie: September 1174) on the fortress records that it was then under the control of Sultan Ibn Mahmud, one of the Shaddadid Seljuk princes who ruled in Ani. In 2006 we wrote, 'amazingly this is not some preserved monument but home to several farmers who pile their hay up against medieval walls and also keep their livestock here. Dusk presents the extraordinary spectacle of the fortress's sheep arriving back from the fields to be followed by the fortress's cattle, a continuation of a routine seen throughout Europe in medieval days but where else now?' By 2010 most of the families had been rehoused in the village and there were grand plans to turn the fortress into a working museum and tourist attraction. However, funds have run out and work has stopped. The keep has been restored, not entirely felicitously, and the small 10th-century chapel against its inner wall has been rebuilt. If the door is not locked it is possible to scramble up on to the walls of the keep from where there are good views but care is needed; there are no safety precautions. There are also good views from the surrounding defensive wall, especially towards the south, across the extensive ruins of an old settlement, to the church of St Christopher. Two families still live within the fortress but most of the houses lie derelict, some half demolished. The still impressive fortress remains in limbo, no longer a living community but not an appealing ancient monument either. Good views of the fortress on its hill can be obtained by continuing past the village along the main road. About 2km along this main road a khachkar marks a track going off left which leads to the restored 7th-century **church of St Christopher**, built of rather forbidding grey stone. Nearby is a rectangular tower with sloping sides; a 13th-century bell tower according to the Soviet-era plaque.

Around the church is an extensive graveyard in use from the 6th century to the present day.

Mastara Mastara is yet another village now bypassed by the main road but the **church** here definitely warrants the short detour necessary to see it. Constructed of red tuff, most of the present structure dates from rebuilding carried out in the 7th century: it has never suffered significant earthquake damage. A surprisingly large construction, it has a massive octagonal tambour supporting a 12-panel cupola. The tambour in turn is supported by eight large arches, or squinches, and eight smaller ones. This unusual design is found in other 7th-century churches which are referred to as being of the Mastara type. Inside the church there is a great feeling of height – it is 21m from floor to cupola. Floor space for worshippers is larger than in plain cross-shaped churches, achieved by rectangular corners protruding between the apses. Thus, internally the church is square with four protruding apses; externally the alternating pentagonal apses and the square corners surround the tambour. The single-storey east corner rooms, built at the same time as the church, are tucked into the angle each side of the east apse. The tambour admits light by a window on each side, those on the cardinal points being wider. The rather incongruous balcony on the west side dates from the building's use as a grain store for the local collective farm from 1935 until 1993. The church is dedicated to St John the Baptist whose relics, brought back from Caesarea by St Gregory the Illuminator, are said to be buried at the site.

Garnahovit The road through Mastara continues northeast to another architecturally important church, that of St George, at Garnahovit. The round dome of the huge 7th-century **church of St George**, fully restored, looms over the village. It has the same composition as the much better known church of St Hripsime at Ejmiatsin (pages 190–1). Rectangular externally, inside there are four apses at the cardinal points and between the apses four three-quarter-circle niches, each of which in turn leads into a square corner room. There is a structurally important difference from St Hripsime. In the latter, the entrances to the round niches are set squarely across the right-angles of the basically square floor plan. Here at St George they are positioned asymmetrically: the two eastern ones turned a little to the east, the two western ones to the west. The transition to the octagonal tambour is by arches over the apses and by fan vaults over the round niches. The cardinal sides of the tambour have two large windows, the diagonal sides smaller ones. Externally, niches play an important part in the decoration as well as reducing the bulk of stone. St George has the common triangular niches each side of the apses, here rounded in their upper halves, but there are also niches below the gable on each side and at the corners of the tambour. The twin half-columns with a single capital in the niches of the west façade, typical of the second half of the 7th century, echo the portal frame.

ARARAT PROVINCE

Mount Ararat is now in Turkey but the name of this province recognises that it is the part of present-day Armenia which approaches nearest to the biblical mountain: it is only some 33km from Khor Virap Monastery to the 5,165m (16,946ft) peak, separated from the lower 3,925m summit by the Anahit Pass. The whole massif looms high and spectacular above the plain, which is only around 900m above sea level, and the views are particularly stunning during the months of early summer (late May and early June) and autumn (late September and October) when visibility is at its best. Mount Ararat is especially beautiful in early morning and late evening.

Ararat province has two distinct parts. There is fertile plain along the Arax Valley but most of the province is mountainous, rising to 2,445m at Mount Urts. Several fairly large areas within these mountains comprise the Khosrov Forest State Reserve (pages 181–4).To the south the province is bordered by the detached Azeri region of Nakhichevan; the main road and rail links are of course closed at the border. The much smaller (a mere 7km²) Azeri enclave of Karki, astride the main road linking Yerevan with the south, was the scene of fierce fighting in the early 1990s, but the Azeri population has gone and the village is now inhabited by Armenians dispossessed from Azerbaijan. Karki has since been renamed Tigranashen. The main road from Yerevan to southern Armenia follows the southern border of the province and crosses into neighbouring Vayots Dzor province over the Tukh Manuk Pass.

The provincial capital of **Artashat**, 29km from Yerevan, is on the edge of the plain. Modern Artashat is some 5km northwest of ancient Artashat, established in 185BC by King Artashes I as his capital and retaining that role until the reign of Khosrov III (AD330–38) when the capital was moved to Dvin. There is little in the modern city to warrant a visit.

GETTING THERE AND AROUND The towns and villages in the province are served by minibuses. The few train services are timed mainly for those working in Yerevan and are unlikely to be of much use to visitors. Taxis are also an option; see pages 82–3.

OTHER PRACTICALITIES There are no reasonable hotels in the province. Apart from visiting the main sights of Khor Virap and Dvin there is little to detain most visitors in Ararat. However, for those wishing to visit the southern part of the Khosrov Reserve and stay overnight in the reserve there is accommodation, which must be pre-booked, at its southern entrance near Vedi (see pages 181 and 183–4). The towns of Artashat and Ararat have shops and eating places, but none of note to warrant a detour.

The main road between Yerevan and Yeraskh is flat and uninteresting but it can be an excellent place to buy fresh local produce and the first apricots to appear for sale are often found here. Fish from the Armash fish ponds can be bought on the main road near Yeraskh.

DVIN (*The gate in the fence surrounding the site is usually open; whether this will change in future, given renewed excavation activity, is unknown. The small museum*

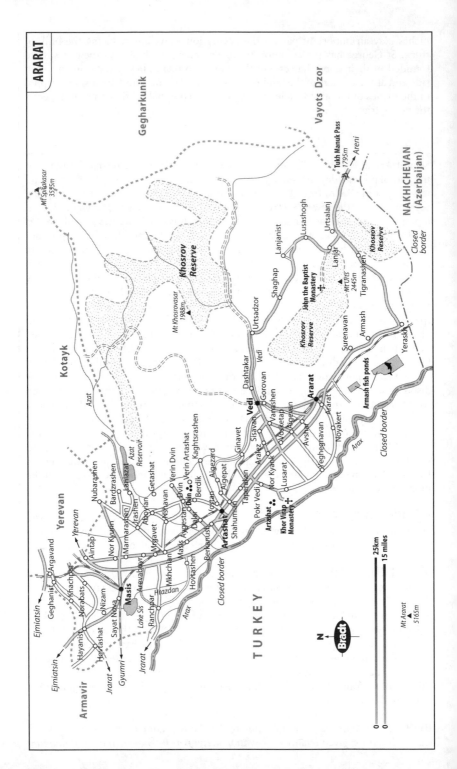

Gegharkunik

Vayots Dzor

Tukh Manuk Pass
1795m

Areni

NAKHICHEVAN
(Azerbaijan)

Mt Spitakasar
3555m

Urtsalanj

*Closed
border*

*Khosrov
Reserve*

*Khosrov
Reserve*

Lanjanist

Lusashogh

Lanjar

Tigranashen

Shaghap

John the Baptist
Monastery

Mt Urts
2445m

Khosrov
Reserve

Mt Khosrovasar
1988m.

Urtsadzor

Surenavan

Armash

Yeraskh

Dashtakar

Vedi

Kotayk

Azat

Gorovan

Vanashen

Ararat

Armash fish ponds

Vedi

Sisavan

Aralez

Yosketap

Ararat

Closed border

Dashtakar

Avshar

Noyakert

Arax

Yeghegnavan

Aigezard

Ginavet

Tapehakan

Nor Kyank

Aigepat

Lusarat

Yerevan

Nubarashen

Bardzrashen

Ghahazat

Azat
Reservoir

Getashat

Verin Dvin

Dvin

Berdik

Kaghtsrashen

Pokr Vedi

Nor Kyank

Yerevan

Trashen

Abovian

Aishavan

Verin Dvin

Dvin

Vostan

Shahumlan

Artashat

Khor Virap
Monastery

Kotayk

Marmarashen

Mygavet

Masis

Aigestan

Dalar

Berkanush

Mkhchian

Aintap

Nor Kyurin

Masis

Arevabuyr

Hovtashen

Armavir

Ejmiatsin

Geghanist

Argavand

Khachpar

Norabats

Nizam

Masis

Arax

Hrazdan

Lake Sis

Ranchpar

Yerevan

Ejmiatsin

Hayanist

Hovtashat

Sayat Nova

Jrarat

Gyumri

Jrarat

TURKEY

Closed border

N
Bradt

Mt Ararat
5165m

0 ——— 25km
0 ——— 15 miles

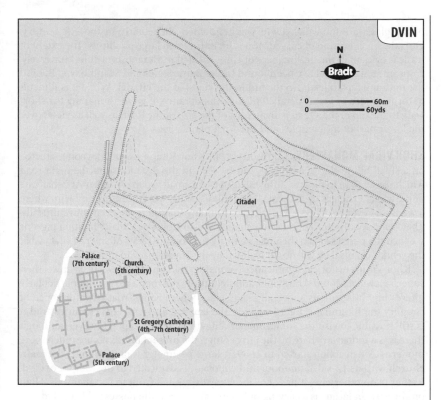

DVIN

N

Bradt

0 ———————— 60m
0 ———————— 60yds

Citadel

Palace
(7th century)   Church
(5th century)

St Gregory Cathedral
(4th–7th century)

Palace
(5th century)

can be opened whenever the resident caretaker is at home) Heading south from
Yerevan along the main road, the excavated ruins of the former capital Dvin lie
about 10km to the east. (**Note:** the site is not in Dvin village.) It is well signposted
from the Artashat turn-off on the main road (M2) south. Soon after leaving
Hnaberd village you come to a metal fence on the left. This is the fence around
the site of Dvin and the entrance gate is a little further on. If asking locally for
directions, be sure to ask for Hnaberd rather than Dvin. Simply push open the gate
in the boundary fence and walk into the site.

Dvin served as the capital until the Arab conquest in AD640 when it became
the seat of the governor. It was badly damaged by earthquakes in 863 and again in
893 but remained a significant town until the 13th century with a population, at its
peak, probably of the order of 100,000. The second of these earthquakes destroyed
what had been **Armenia's largest church**, dedicated to St Gregory and 58m long
by 30m wide. Its foundations can be clearly seen, including the layout from at least
two of its three rebuildings. Originally a pagan temple, it was rebuilt as a three-
nave basilica with an east apse in the late 4th century. It acquired external arcaded
galleries in the 5th century. Then in the 7th century it was rebuilt as a winged three-
nave domed basilica, with apses also on the north and south. This church was slightly
shorter, hence the double east apse seen today. Mosaics from its floor are now in the
museum. North of the church are the foundations of the 7th-century **palace of the
Katholikos** and a capital from one of its columns is now Dvin's best known exhibit.
East of this palace lay a single-nave **5th-century church**. An **earlier palace** (5th
century) lay southwest of the main church. The small museum is surrounded by the
caretaker's fruit trees. Its contents include finds from the site including examples

of the glassware for which Dvin was renowned particularly in the 7th century. Outside is a collection of carved stones including two large phalluses. The extent of trade is evident in the finding here of coins minted in Byzantium while, conversely, coins minted at Dvin have been found in the Baltic states and Scandinavia. Behind the museum a path leads up the hill to the ruins of the **citadel**. While it is difficult to form an idea of Dvin's detailed historic appearance, it is worth making the short walk to the top of the site to gain an idea of the size of the town as well as views over the lower part of the complex and the Arax plain.

KHOR VIRAP MONASTERY (⊕ *09.00–18.00*) Khor Virap ('Deep Dungeon'), situated on a small hill in the Ararat plain, can be seen in the distance from the main road which passes 5km to the east. (The hill is one of a small group on which Artashat, one of the ancient capitals of Armenia, was built – see below.) In contrast to Dvin, where few visitors ever go, Khor Virap receives so many that there are even souvenir stalls. They sell not only conventional souvenirs but also 'doves' – actually homing pigeons – which the purchaser can then release to 'fly to Mount Ararat'. At any rate that's what the vendor claims they will do. In reality they fly straight back to him.

Khor Virap's historical significance is considerable, and there are, in clear weather, superb views of Mount Ararat, but architecturally the monastery is not particularly interesting. It is famous above all as the place where King Trdat III imprisoned St Gregory the Illuminator for 13 years in the late 3rd and early 4th centuries, and it is still possible to visit the subterranean cell where he was kept. However, although there was a monastery here by the 5th century, the present buildings are much more modern. Construction started in 1669. A large perimeter wall surrounds the **main church** with its 12-sided tambour and cupola. It is dedicated to the Mother of God. Rather plain otherwise, it has an elaborately decorated front to the altar dais. High on the eastern façade is a carving of St Gregory curing the possessed King Trdat.

Access to the cell where Gregory was imprisoned is from the smaller **St Gregory's Church** which is the barrel-vaulted structure at the southwest corner of the walls. To the right of the altar dais is the entrance hole from which a long ladder with 27 steps leads 6.5m down to the surprisingly large underground chamber; the first 2m of descent is very narrow, after which the hole widens. It tends to be stuffy in the chamber because of a lack of air circulation combined with the number of burning candles. It should be shunned by the claustrophobic and those who do venture down should take a torch. (Do not be confused by a second hole to the right of the door of the church. This leads to a separate underground chamber, possibly another prison. The entrance shaft is even narrower than that of St Gregory's prison.) A path goes uphill on the north side of the monastery. From the top of the hill on which Khor Virap stands there is a good view of the monastery itself and of the irrigated Ararat plain to the border with Turkey in the south and to the mountains of the Khosrov Reserve in the north. It is also possible to appreciate something of the scale of ancient **Artashat** which was built on the group of hills near Khor Virap, including the hill on which the monastery was later established. The hills of Artashat can be reached by the track which runs between the Khor Virap mound and the cemetery at its base. Although it is now possible to see only minor evidence of the city (about which much detail is given on the USAID information boards) it was once a major centre of Hellenistic culture, described by Plutarch as a large and beautiful city, 'Armenia's Carthage', with villas, temples, statuary and an amphitheatre. It was founded as his capital in 185BC by King Artashes I, one of the Armenian kings who ruled with Roman consent after the defeat of Antiochus III at the Battle of Magnesia in 190BC (see page 16). Artashat retained its role as capital until the reign of Khosrov III (AD330–38) when it was moved to Dvin because the Arax River had changed its course, leaving Artashat without its former defence. The medieval historian, Movses Khoranatsi, described Artashat as being founded at the confluence of the Arax and Metsamor rivers. Such descriptions led to the location of the city being a mystery until the 1920s, the shifting of river beds giving a present-day confluence significantly further west than it was when Artashat was built. Excavations were carried out in the 1970s/80s.

On a hillock to the left of Khor Virap as one approaches is a statue of Gevorg Chaush (1870–1907) who led Armenian *fedayi* (armed volunteers) in their struggle against the Turks in Sassoun province, the area in western Armenia around the source of the Tigris. He was killed in battle.

KHOSROV FOREST STATE RESERVE Reserve regulations state that visitors must be accompanied by a member of the reserve staff. At the time of research it was necessary to apply, in writing, for a permit to visit the reserve either to the Ministry of Nature Protection in Yerevan (*Government Bldg 3, Republic Sq;* ✆ *10 521099, 519182;* e *info@ mnp.am; www.mnp.am. Neither this website nor the reserve's website, www.khosrov.am, gives useful practical information*) or to the reserve headquarters in Vedi (*79 Kasian St;* ✆*234 23247, 21352;* e *khosrov@mail.am. The reserve's deputy director, Hovik Tamazyan* m *093 228688, 055 228688, 099 006030;* e *officekhosrov@mail.ru, who is based in Vedi, can be contacted, preferably by email, to book accommodation, discuss activities/costs, etc. He can also be contacted for visits to the northern part of the reserve & is willing to act as a central contact point for other reserves in Armenia such as Shikahogh & Lake Arpi*). Permits take five days to be issued. These regulations may be changed as the authorities have found, not surprisingly, that there has been a drop in income from visitors. If you arrive at the reserve entrance without a permit the staff will phone the director; if you are lucky he will give permission over the phone but this cannot be guaranteed. You are not allowed to take your own vehicle into the reserve. A reserve vehicle may be available for transport.

Khosrov Reserve is one of the oldest protected reserves in the world, having been founded in the 4th century AD by King Khosrov III, after whom the reserve is named. The Soviet Union granted Khosrov reserve status in 1958 and it is currently 23,878km². Landscapes include semi-desert, mountain steppe, woodland and subalpine meadow, home to a unique range of European and Asian flora and fauna, including endemic, rare and endangered species, such as the Persian leopard, Bezoar ibex and marbled polecat. Lynx, brown bear and wolf also occur. Unless you are incredibly lucky you are unlikely to see any of the larger mammals, but the splendid scenery and sites of historic interest will make up for that. The Azat River flows west through the reserve to the Azat Reservoir (see page 217).

The reserve is probably best thought of in two parts as far as visiting is concerned, a northern part entered via Garni Gorge (see below) and a southern part entered via Vedi (page 183). Although the reserve is almost entirely in Ararat province most visitors enter via Garni in Kotayk province because the most interesting historical sites are in the north.

Northern entrance (🕘 *from approx 09.00; entrance AMD2,000pp, guide AMD5,000, the cost for the reserve vehicle depends on length of trip, up to AMD20,000. Horses can be arranged AMD10,000.*) Allow two full days to see the main sights in this part of the reserve. All involve walking, some of it strenuous so good footwear is essential. Trousers and long sleeves give some protection when the walk is through shoulder-high vegetation. Be sure to take a picnic.

To reach the **northern entrance** to the reserve **on foot** from Garni take the paved track to the left of the temple entrance down into the gorge. Near the end of the short paved section a path goes off to the left. This brings you to a metal gate, entrance to hydro-electric territory. (If you carry straight on down the track which later bears left you end up at the same metal gate by a longer, muddier route.) The guard is usually willing to let people through to walk down; you exit the hydro-electric site near the river. Turn left and continue along the river past the basalt columns to what was a medieval bridge. Having been rebuilt by the American Ambassador's Fund for Cultural Preservation (!) the only suggestion of the old original bridge is the shape of the arch. Cross it and go uphill, following the signs to the visitor centre. Allow about 45 minutes from Garni Temple to the reserve. If **driving**, turn right from the Garni Temple road, then left in front of the information office in the centre of Garni, then second right down to the river. At the river the right-hand turn leads to the basalt columns, the left to the reserve. Go left along the river for about 1km then do a U-turn over the river to wind up the hillside to the reserve gate.

Havuts Tar Monastery The nearest site to the reserve entrance (allow at least four hours to walk from Garni to Havuts Tar and back), is reached by an easy path which follows the side of the gorge and gives marvellous views both down into the gorge and also of Garni Temple. The monastery is about 3km along this path and, at an altitude of 1,590m, is some 200m higher than Garni Temple. The extensive site comprises two main groups of ruins, eastern and western, with evidence of other structures, or possibly graves, between them. The **western buildings** come into view first but the path approaches the eastern group. Although dating from the 11th–13th centuries the monastery was very badly damaged in the 1679 earthquake and much of what is now seen supposedly dates from its rebuilding in the early 1900s. It must be wondered how much rebuilding actually took place as the appearance of the site is such as to give the impression that Havuts Tar was effectively abandoned in 1679.

The **eastern buildings** were surrounded by a fortified wall which still stands to a considerable height on three sides. The entrance is an arched doorway at the southeast corner. The main church is relatively well preserved and once had a *gavit* – few traces remain. The western façade and the interior use a mixture of red and black tuff to striking effect and the interior is notable for its carved niches with birds appearing in several. On its north side work commenced in 1772 on the construction of a new church but it was never finished. Ruins of domestic buildings line the north and south fortified walls.

The west group is dominated by a cross-dome church whose walls are again constructed in a chessboard pattern of red and black tuff. This is probably the **Holy Saviour Church** founded in 1013 by Grigor Pahlavuni (c990–1058), founder also of Kecharis, although some sources state that Holy Saviour is the church in the east group. On the south side of this church is a small vaulted chapel built at a later date.

For the **other sites** having a guide makes it much easier to find them. The tracks are very rough in places; the reserve staff are expert drivers, very familiar with the terrain. If walking, remember it can be very hot. About 5km from the entrance the tracks to two of the most impressive sites, Aghjots Monastery and Kakavaberd Fortress, diverge at the bridge over a tributary of the Azat. The left track passes the deserted **Baberd** village where there is a 5th-century barrel-vaulted church. After a few more kilometres the reserve vehicle parks beside the Azat River for walks to Aghjots and Kakavaberd.

Aghjots Monastery Reach this monastery after a short but steep climb up rocky scree where the scent of thyme, lavender and other aromatic plants fills the air. It is well worth the effort. The monastery, which sometimes seems to merge with the hillside in its overgrown state, comprises the St Stephen Church with its *gavit*, the church of Sts Peter and Paul (whose carving is the gem of the monastery) with its ruined *gavit*, together with evidence of other buildings over a wide area. The monastery was sacked by the Persians in 1603, was restored but then damaged soon afterwards by the 1679 earthquake, despoiled again in the 18th century and finally ruined during Azeri-Armenian clashes in the early 20th century. The **church of St Stephen** was built in the early 13th century and, according to local legend, was founded by St Gregory the Illuminator on the site of the martyrdom of one of St Hripsime's companions, Stepanos by name. The church is a small cross-dome structure missing its tambour and dome. The front of the *bema* is decorated with carved octagons, all except two containing geometric patterns. Of the other two, one has a pair of birds, the other, wrongly orientated, two heads with tall hats. St Stephen's *gavit*, added in 1207, is wider than the church and at a lower level. It is ruined but what remains bears a wealth of carving. Ghosting on the west façade of the church shows the position of the *gavit* arches and how the *gavit* was added asymmetrically with respect to the church entrance. The **church of Sts Peter and Paul** stands to the north of St Stephen. The strikingly large bas-relief figures of St Peter, on the left, and St Paul, on the right, survive on the church's west façade. Such large figures are very unusual in present-day Armenia although they decorated the 10th-century Holy Cross Church on the island of Aghtamar on Lake Van, once part of Greater Armenia. Present-day examples are on the new church beside Katoghike on Abovian Street, Yerevan.

Kakavaberd (Geghiberd) (fortress)
This 9th–13th century fortress must be the most impressive in Armenia. It changed hands many times during its history and is last mentioned in 1224 in historical documents. Three sides of the ridge on which it stands are inaccessibly steep; the walls and towers, 8–10m high, guard the fourth side. From the bridge where the Aghjots and Kakavaberd tracks diverge it is about 8km to Kakavaberd, or 13km from the reserve entrance. From the Azat River it is a strenuous two-hour climb up to the fortress. The first stretch is uphill through meadows to the base of a high rocky knoll with sheer sides. Skirting the base one enters a ravine which climbs up to the ridge on which Kakavaberd was built. When the fortress first comes into view it looks totally inaccessible but continue up the ravine, sometimes walking along the bed of the stream. Fortunately, the last and steepest climb is through trees which mitigate the heat of the sun. The nearer one gets, the more impressive the high walls with their towers become. Entering the fortress, ingenious use has been made of a sheer rock face. The outer wall has been positioned so that anyone gaining entrance to the fortress had to turn right through a right-angle and then go along a narrow passage between wall and rock face, making them very vulnerable to attack from above. Within the fortress not much remains to be seen apart from grassy mounds marking the position of buildings, but the wild flowers are a joy – in early summer there were purple orchids, red poppies, yellow umbellifers, blue harebells, freesias, asphodels, purple vetches, saxifrages, thyme and many more. The panoramic views, especially from the highest point at the far end of the site, are magnificent. Near the entrance a tall ridge of rock forms a natural wall; in it has been carved a tiny chapel, complete with apse, *bema* and altar.

Southern entrance
(*All visitors must call at the reserve's headquarters, 79 Kasian St, Vedi; ☏ 234 23247, from where they will be escorted to the reserve entrance, some 18km beyond Vedi. The reserve* **hotel** *at the entrance has 4 dbl rooms: AMD5,000pp;*

b/fast AMD1,500; other meals AMD5,000. Camping (equipment provided): AMD1,000pp; sleeping bag AMD1,000pp. All meals can be provided with advance notice. Entrance fee: AMD1,500pp; guide AMD5,000/day; vehicle use AMD500/km – longest route is a round trip of 40km) The southern part of the reserve does not have the same wealth of historic sites as the north but it is probably better for wildlife, having fewer visitors. It contains important bird breeding sites and Armenia's only official desert, the Goravan sands, which is transformed into a mass of flowers in the spring. Most sights (deserted villages, ruined churches, caves) within the southern part of the reserve can be visited in one day unless wildlife watching is the main reason for a visit, in which case several days and nights may be necessary.

Gevorg Marzpetuni Castle (Tapi Berd) This is now a small renovated chapel within fortified walls set at the far end of a bowl-like plain surrounded by mountains. It is reached from the broken-asphalt road to the Khosrov Reserve entrance which goes off left from the Vedi to Urtsadzor road just after the Urtsadzor sign. After 6km on the broken-asphalt road turn left on to a dirt road. After 1km turn left for the Marzpetuni Castle (2km) or right for the Khosrov Reserve barrier (1½km).

The main road from Vedi through Urtsadzor is an attractive **alternative route** through spectacular scenery to Lanjar and the monastery of St John the Baptist (see below), avoiding a large part of the uninteresting highway along the Arax Valley and rejoining the highway at Urtsalanj as it climbs up to the Tukh Manuk Pass.

SOUTH FROM KHOR VIRAP The main road passes the town of **Ararat**, dominated by a large cement factory. Beyond Yeraskh the former main road and railway are both closed at the border and traffic must turn left at the roundabout to reach southern Armenia. From here the present-day road starts to climb northeast towards the **Tukh Manuk Pass** (1,795m) where it enters Vayots Dzor province and turns south. About 12km from Yeraskh the road crosses a former enclave of Azerbaijan: the Azeri village of Kharki, just south of the road, which is now the Armenian village of **Tigranashen**. Nineteen kilometres from Yeraskh a road branches left for **Lanjar**. Just beyond Lanjar

TUKH MANUK

Visitors to Armenia will probably best know the words Tukh Manuk as the name of the 1,795m pass between the Ararat and Vayots Dzor provinces. However, they may then become increasingly aware of the term in relation to numerous small chapels or shrines throughout the country, often in remote locations such as hilltops but also common in small villages. Sometimes a corner room of a larger church seems to fulfil the same function. Such shrines are obviously popular, having a multitude of offerings – religious pictures of Jesus Christ or the Virgin Mary, crosses, embroidered items, flowers and other small tokens. It is evident that candles are frequently lit and outside there may be signs of animal sacrifice (see page 36).

The shrines are nowadays ostensibly Christian but their roots are thought to originate in pre-Christian times. Literally, *tukh manuk* translates as 'dark youth', a somewhat mysterious figure who seems to hark back perhaps to Zoroastrian Mithra or even further back to a proto Indo-European deity related to Krishna, a manifestation of the Hindu god Vishnu. Interestingly, the name Krishna apparently comes from the Sanskrit for dark or black. No-one quite seems to know who this dark youth is.

tracks go left off this road as it crests a hill. Take the track which keeps to the right of the mountain, which in 7km reaches the remote **monastery of John the Baptist**. The track is poor; the last section needs a 4x4. The monastery is attractively situated among rolling hills. The **Mother of God Church**, built in 1254, has a tall circular tambour and umbrella dome. Over the door is a carving of the Madonna and Child flanked by two angels. Above this is a second carving of Christ with the symbols of the four evangelists at his side and two heads at his feet. Both carvings have a background of deeply incised, ornate, leafy swirls. Inside, the small cross-dome church has an unusual stone altar screen with its own small apse and belfry. The *gavit* to the west of the church and a mausoleum southwest of the church are both ruined. West of the mausoleum are the two remaining storeys of a three-tier building, the uppermost, a belfry, now lost. It must once have looked similar to the three-storey building at Noravank. The lower storey has no entrance and was probably another mausoleum. The remains of a fortified wall surround the monastery.

Shortly before the road reaches the Tukh Manuk Pass there is a sign to the **house museum of Paruyr Sevak** (page 52) (*Zangakatun village*; m *094 034448;* ◷ *10.00–17.00 Tue–Sun; closed for lunch 13.00–14.00; closed Jan/Feb – when closed there is a contact phone number on the door; AMD500*) For non-Armenian speakers who do not know the work of this much-loved Armenian poet there is unfortunately little of interest in the museum. Sevak and his wife are buried in the grounds of what was their home.

ARMAVIR PROVINCE

The province is named after its capital, Armavir city, which is 46km west of Yerevan along a good dual carriageway. It is unlikely that anyone would choose to stay here as the main concentration of sights is in **Ejmiatsin**, or Vagharshapat as the city is now officially called, only 20km from Yerevan. The churches of Ejmiatsin together with the ruins of Zvartnots Cathedral were added to the UNESCO World Heritage List in 2000. The eastern part of the province merges imperceptibly with Yerevan's western sprawl where it includes Zvartnots International Airport. To the west the province comprises part of the flat and, in summer, hot plain of the broad Arax Valley. The Arax forms the border with Turkey in the south of the province while to the west the border is formed by the Akhurian River. There are several important ancient sites in the province, usually on small hills rising above the flat plain. While there is now little more than low excavated walls to be seen, these sites do hint at the extent and importance of Armenia's distant past. Such sites in Armavir province include **Metsamor**, with its own small museum, Urartian **Argishtikhinili** and Hellenistic **Armavir**. The marshes along the Arax River in the south of the province are the only remaining Armenian breeding ground for the scale insect, *Porphyrophora hamelii*, from which was extracted the colourfast, brilliant red dye, *vordan karmir*, used in Armenian illustrated manuscripts. There is little good hotel accommodation in the province but limited reason to stay here rather than in Yerevan anyway.

GETTING THERE AND AROUND Minibuses ply frequently between Yerevan and the two main towns, Ejmiatsin and Armavir, and from these centres *marshrutkas* go to local villages. The main roads in the province are good. The few train services are unlikely to be of use to visitors. There is a daily train from Yerevan to Armavir at 15.50, returning to Yerevan at 16.50 (*ticket AMD300*). The train to Tbilisi stops at Armavir just before midnight. Slightly more useful is the morning train to Gyumri

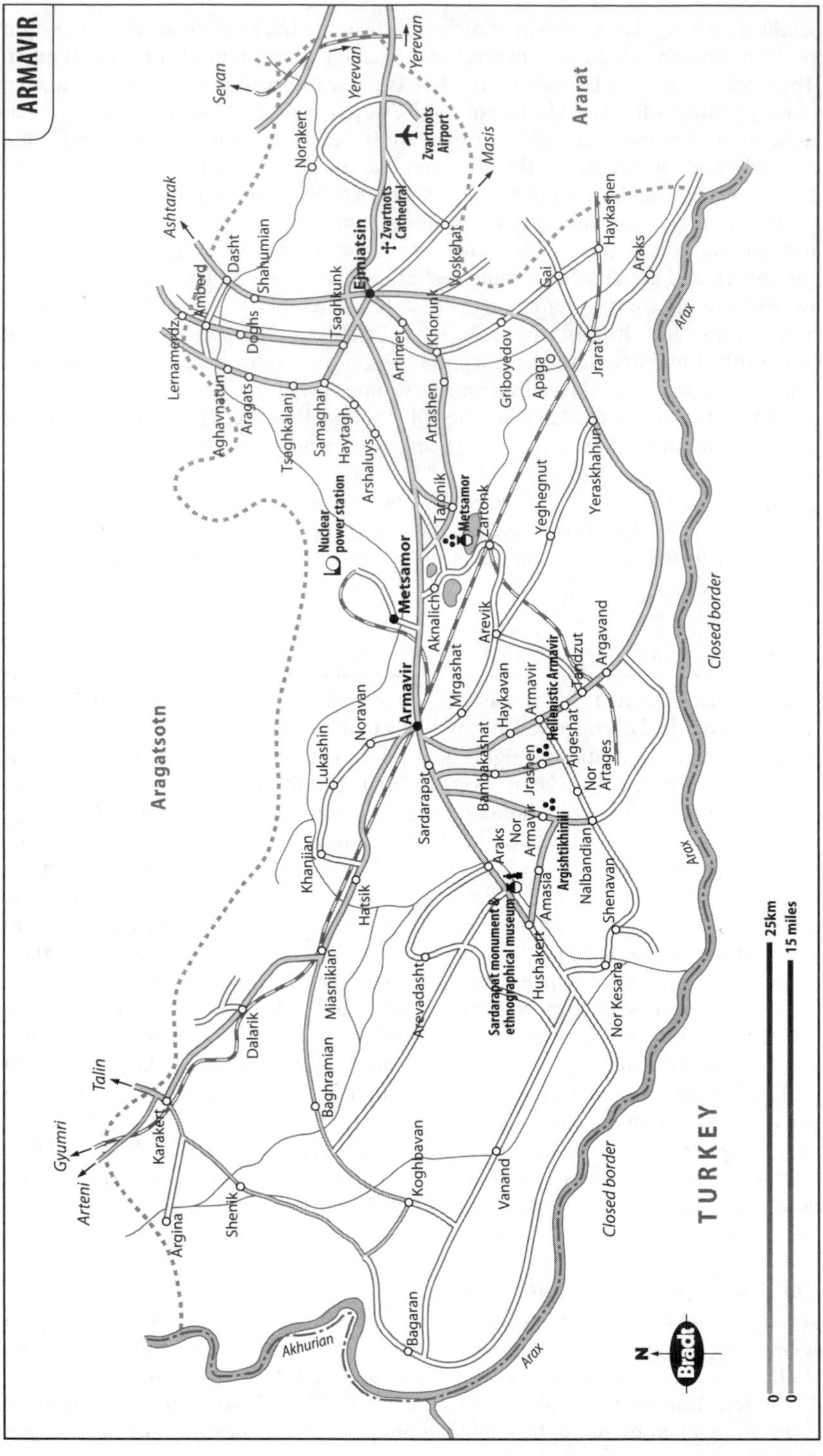

Aragatsotn

TURKEY

Closed border

Closed border

Ararat

Sevan
Yerevan
Yerevan
Norakert
Zvartnots Airport
Masis
Etchmiadzin
✝ Zvartnots Cathedral
Ashtarak
Dasht
Amberd
Shahumian
Shahumian
Tsaghkunk
Voskehat
Haykashen
Aragats
Doghs
Aghavnatun
Lernamedz
Aragats
Tsaghkalanj
Samaghar
Haytagh
Arshaluys
Artimet
Khorunk
Artashen
Griboyedov
Gai
Araks
Nuclear power station
Metsamor
Talunik
Metsamor
Zartonk
Yeghegnut
Apaga
Yeraskhahun
Metsamor
Aknalich
Arevik
Mrgashat
Haykavan
Haykavan
Armavir
Armavir
Tandzut
Argavand
Argishtikhinili
Hellenistic Armavir
Noravan
Bambakashat
Jrashen
Aigeshat
Nor Artages
Lukashin
Armavir
Sardarapat
Nor Armavir
Nalbandian
Khanjian
Hatsik
Sardarapat monument & ethnographical museum
Amasia
Hushakert
Shenavan
Nor Kesaria
Miasnikian
Arevadasht
Dalarik
Gyumri
Arteni
Talin
Karakert
Argina
Shenik
Baghramian
Koghbavan
Vanand
Bagaran
Akhurian
Arax
Arax
Arax
Arax

25km
15 miles

N
Bradt

0
0

186

which leaves Yerevan at 08.00, calls at Ejmiatsin at 08.30 and Armavir at 08.52, but going by road may be quicker.

OTHER PRACTICALITIES The sights in the province are usually visited as day trips from Yerevan. Ejmiatsin and Armavir have small cafés and in summer eating places appear along the highway and in the park near the cathedral precinct in Ejmiatsin. There are two restaurants at Sardarapat (page 196). If you are planning to spend time at Sardarapat or Metsamor in the heat of summer, remember that it can be very hot and there is not much shade at either site. It might be wise to take something to drink with you.

EASTERN ARMAVIR
Zvartnots Cathedral (⊕ *Tue–Sun: 10.00–19.00 Apr–Oct, 10.00–17.00 Nov–Mar; guided tour in English AMD2,500; car parking AMD100; adult AMD700*) Leaving Yerevan along a road lined with furniture shops whose wares are hauled outside each morning and then hauled back at the close of business, the first point of less commercial interest is the ruin of the huge **Zvartnots** ('Celestial Angels') **Cathedral** dedicated to St Gregory. It lies to the south of the road and the entrance driveway is marked by elaborate gates and an eagle with a ring in its beak gazing back over its shoulder, the work of the famous artist and sculptor Ervand Kochar. The complex comprises the cathedral, the royal palace of Nerses in the southwest and a winery to the south. Excavations revealed that the church was built on structures which date back to the reign of the Urartian king Rusa II (c685–645bc). The **church**, built between 643 and 652 by Katholikos Nerses III, is believed to have been a three-storey structure, built on a multi-step stylobate, but modern artists' impressions of its appearance are inevitably conjectural. Intended to surpass even Ejmiatsin Cathedral by its grandeur, it is usually thought of as having been circular but in reality had 32 equal sides. Decorated with frescoes, it was destroyed, probably by an earthquake in 930, to be lost under layers of dirt and debris and even the location was forgotten until its rediscovery in the early 20th century. Some limited reconstruction has been carried out, but protests have caused plans for a more thorough one to be held in abeyance.

The interior of the church consists of four apses; the eastern one housing the *bema* has a solid wall, the other three each have six columns forming open semicircles. The massive pillars between the apses supported the upper tiers, tambour and cupola. On the southern side of the *bema* are the remains of a pulpit and in front is what looks like a baptistery in the floor reached by going down some steps, although it is now labelled as the reliquary of St Gregory Lusovorich, ie: the Illuminator, for whom the church is named. Within the outer polygonal wall an ambulatory surrounds the whole inner quatrefoil. At the east end of the quadrilateral structure was the vestry, the equivalent of eastern corner rooms in other Armenian churches. To the east of the church, various stones are laid out according to which storey of the building they are thought to belong. There is some interesting sculptured decoration among the ruins, including one capital on the southeast pillar carved with a fine representation of an eagle. **Nerses's Palace** to the southwest consists of a labyrinth of rooms, well labelled, and a winery with vats sunk into the ground lies to the south. At the far southwest corner of the site is the **museum** (⊕ *10.00–17.00 when the cathedral complex is open, closes at 15.00 on Sun; inc in entrance ticket*) which after years of being under construction is now open and contains a wealth of information (in Armenian, Russian and English) with attractive displays. Outside the museum is a basalt stele with a cuneiform inscription recording the construction of a canal from the Hrazdan River by King Rusa II.

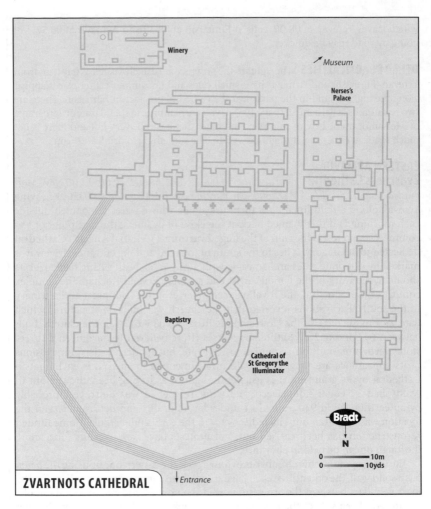

Winery

Museum

Nerses's
Palace

Baptistry

Cathedral of
St Gregory the
Illuminator

Bradt

N

0 ——————— 10m
0 ——————— 10yds

ZVARTNOTS CATHEDRAL   ↓Entrance

EJMIATSIN (*Telephone code: 231*) The central square of the town is Komitas Square and a statue of Komitas by the same Ervand Kochar responsible for the eagle at Zvartnots was erected here in 1969.

Cathedral precinct (In Armenian Mayrator or Mother See, literally 'Mother Seat') Ejmiatsin became the spiritual centre for Armenia's Christians shortly after the country's conversion in the early 4th century.

On the basis of archaeological evidence the first church at Ejmiatsin was of the basilica form but it was rebuilt in the 480s on a cruciform plan with four free-standing piers, four projecting apses which are circular on the interior and polygonal on the outside, and with a cupola. It was this second church, with cupola, which corresponds to Agathangelos's report of Gregory's vision (see page 191), a report which fixed in Armenian culture the idea that churches should be cruciform in shape and should have cupolas. Further rebuilding was carried out in the 7th century and Ejmiatsin remained the seat of the Katholikos until 1065 when the then Katholikos Gregory II was forced to flee by the Turkish Seljuk invaders who were ransacking monasteries. He moved to

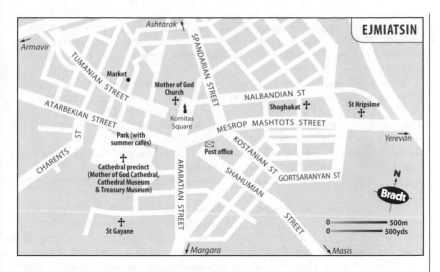

the Armenian principality of Cilicia (roughly the region of present-day Turkey around Adana and Tarsus at the extreme northeast corner of the Mediterranean Sea) and the seat of the Katholikos remained there even after Cilicia fell to the Egyptian Mamluks in 1375. Ultimately in 1441 a council decided that the seat of the Katholikos should return to Ejmiatsin. There are no records of any immediate reconstruction but the monastery was certainly in a very dilapidated state, with the roof in ruins and some facing stones having fallen, when in 1627 renovation eventually started. A wall was built around the precinct at this time and numerous service buildings were added. However, these were mostly destroyed in 1635–36 during the wars between Persia and Turkey for domination over Armenia and further rebuilding was required. The large three-storey bell tower was built in 1654 over the western doorway. Three smaller six-column rotundas were added at the beginning of the 18th century; that at the southern apse collapsed in 1921 to be replaced by a new structure.

Accordingly the **cathedral** (☉ *07.00–19.00*) which visitors see now is the site of a pagan temple used as the site for a new Christian church in the 4th century, rebuilt in a quite different style in the 5th century and then very extensively renovated in the 17th. The tambour with its decorative medallions and cupola, the elaborately carved bell tower and much of the exterior carving are pure 17th century, as are the surrounding wall and service buildings. The oldest wall of the cathedral is the northern, which is 5th-century original. The exterior retains two 5th-century figured reliefs with Greek inscriptions, one showing St Thecia and St Paul, the other a cross flanked by two doves. In 1720, frescoes were added inside the cathedral but they were removed in 1891 only to be reinstated in 1956. The interior is still, as in AD480, dominated by the four massive free-standing pillars supporting the tambour. In the very centre is a stepped holy table (the steps representing the hierarchy of angels) bearing many candlesticks and crosses. Surrounded by a framework from which hang lamps and incense burners, it is said to mark the spot where the 'Only Begotten' appeared to St Gregory, telling him to build a church. The frescoes, the use of marble for floor and balustrade, the embroidered curtains, and the candles and crosses on the holy table give a much more decorative feel to the building than exists in any other church in Armenia.

The cathedral is surrounded by gardens in which khachkars brought from different parts of greater Armenia have been erected. The **Treasury Museum** (as

The Central Provinces   ARMAVIR PROVINCE

4

opposed to the museum in the cathedral – see below) dates from 1869 and is one of the few Tsarist-era buildings here. The nearby seminary, closed during the Soviet period but reopened in 1997, is another. The carved wooden doors are also Tsarist-era and were made at Tbilisi in 1888.

In recent years there has been, and continues to be, a considerable building programme. The eastern, **main gateway** into the cathedral precinct commemorates the visit of Pope John Paul II in 2001. Its four tall pillars joined by arches, forming a rectangular space open at the top, suggests the shape of a church without a dome, perhaps representing St Gregory's vision (see opposite). On its eastern, outer aspect are the carved figures of St Gregory and King Trdat III facing each other, a central cross between them. On the west face are the figures of the two apostles, Thaddeus and Bartholomew, who are believed to have brought Christianity to Armenia in the 1st century AD.

An attractive new (2010) **baptismal chapel**, entered from the north perimeter wall, has provision for both infant and adult baptism (by immersion). Near the north gate of the precinct is a striking tall round (actually polygonal) building, the **Holy Archangels Church**. Polygonal churches have been a significant feature of Armenian architecture but this is an unusual, modern variant, albeit retaining many traditional features. Very tall for its area, with a tambour, topped by an umbrella cupola, almost the same diameter as the lower part of the building, the whole looks like a vertical cylinder. The many windows round the top are separated by crosses which, from a distance, also resemble a ring of people holding hands. The wall of the apse is carved with khachkars and at each side of the *bema* is a startling representation of a bishop's pastoral staff with serpent finials. The inscription above the entrance reads 'God is love'. On the north side of the exterior is a carving of the 'Descent of the Only Begotten' with a curly-haired Gregory looking on. A sundial adorns the south side. Across lawns and flower beds a long colonnaded white building at present houses a **library** and not much else. It was originally envisaged as a branch of the Matenadaran, allowing extra manuscripts to be displayed, but this has not (yet) come to pass.

The **Cathedral Museum** (⊕ *10.00–17.00 Tue–Sat, on Sun it opens only after the end of the service – usually around 13.30 but later if there is something special such as an ordination; guided tours only; AMD1,500*) is reached through a door to the right of the altar dais. The museum isn't well labelled but English-speaking deacons are available. The treasury contains some curious items including what is claimed to be the lance which pierced the side of Christ, brought to Armenia by the apostle Thaddeus and long kept at Geghard, the hand of St Gregory the Illuminator, wood from Noah's Ark (carbon-dated to 6,000 years old), a drop of St Hripsime's blood and similar relics as well as more ordinary ecclesiastical pieces. Interested visitors can also arrange in advance (through a tour operator in Yerevan; see pages 63–4) for admission to the separate Treasury Museum (pages 189–90) in the Old Residence where a similar collection of historic ecclesiastical items is displayed. Plans for the future include opening the Treasury Museum to the public rather than by special permission only.

The **cathedral shop** (⊕ *10.15–19.00 daily*), on the left as one approaches the cathedral, has a wide range of books and a selection of tasteful souvenirs.

The other churches at Ejmiatsin
St Hripsime St Hripsime was one of the refugee nuns from Rome in the late 3rd century who were persecuted under the rule of King Trdat III and the king himself tried to rape her. This 7th-century church dedicated to her is unquestionably one

top   Built in the 7th century, destroyed by earthquake in the 10th century and lost under layers of debris until the 20th century, Zvartnots Cathedral was a massive round church thought to have been three-storeys high (MV/S) page 187

above left   Sardarapat Memorial, a stylish red tuff monument, commemorates the Armenian military victory over Turkey at the Battle of Sardarapat in 1918 (DH) pages 194–6

above right   Although there are many groups of khachkars in Armenia, none can rival the 900 at Noratus (MM/S) page 205

below   Garni Temple, as it is called, is Armenia's only Graeco-Roman-style building (MN) pages 218–19

above The cathedral in Yerevan is dedicated to St Gregory the Illuminator (V/S) 130–1

left Tatev Monastery, in stunning mountain scenery, is one of Armenia's most popular sites (PS/S) pages 307–10

below Looking up at the dome of Akhtala's Mother of God Church with its superb frescoes (AC) pages 259–62

above left Geghard Monastery, partly hewn into the rock and with numerous carvings, is a UNESCO World Heritage Site (r/S) pages 219—22

above right The Holy Archangels Church in Ejmiatsin Cathedral precinct is an interesting and unusual modern Armenian church (DH) page 190

right The interior of the Sts Peter and Paul Church at Tatev during Lent, with the curtain across the *bema* closed (AC) page 309

below The monastery of Hayravank overlooks Lake Sevan, one of the world's largest high-altitude lakes (DH) page 204

top　　　Basalt columns in Garni Gorge (SS) page 219

above left　The vividly coloured Caucasian green lizard (*Lacerta strigata*) can be seen in a variety of habitats in Armenia (DH) page 7

above right　The Mediterranean tortoise (*Testudo graeca*) may occasionally be encountered as one crosses a track (DH) page 7

below　　Fishermen on Lake Sevan (MO) pages 199–202

above   The Spandarian Reservoir in the north of Syunik province (MO) page 299

right   A pleasant river valley in Dilijan National Park (MP/S) page 275

below   The cable-car to Tatev, the world's longest, opened in 2010 and carries passengers high above the valley of the Vorotan River (MO) pages 307–8

top   Women making *lavash*, Armenia's classic flatbread, in the traditional way (SS) page 90

above left   Stone carving remains a flourishing active art form in Armenia (SS)

above right   Traditionally women's dances are graceful with elaborate gestures while men's dances are martial and vigorous (SS) pages 48–9

below   Bringing the flock down from high summer pastures to winter quarters (MN)

above left   Although this famous statue in Stepanakert, Nagorno Karabagh, is officially called *We Are Our Mountains*, it is always affectionately known as *Tatik yev Papik* (Granny and Grandad) (S/D) page 336

above right   Ghazanchetsots Cathedral in Shushi, Nagorno Karabagh, is built of strikingly pale stone (G/D) pages 340–1

right   The thought-provoking Museum of Fallen Warriors in Stepanakert commemorates soldiers who died during the Nagorno Karabagh war (RK/A) page 334

below   Dadivank, one of the largest medieval monastery complexes, is on the northern route between Armenia and Nagorno Karabagh (MO) pages 338–9

above   The dormant volcano of Mount Aragats is the highest peak in Armenia at 4,090m (PC/A) page 169

LEGENDARY ORIGINS OF EJMIATSIN CATHEDRAL

According to Agathangelos's *History of the Armenians*, written in about 460, St Gregory the Illuminator saw a vision in which the heavens opened and a blaze of light shone upon the earth. Through the light a procession of angels came down to the earth headed by the tall and glorious figure of Christ. Carrying a golden hammer, he came down and struck the ground three times with it. A tall column of fire instantly arose, with a circular base of gold and a capital of cloud and cross of light. Similar visions appeared at three other sites where Hripsime, Gayane and another of their companions were martyred. The columns transformed themselves into churches covered by clouds whose shape was that of a cupola. After the vision faded, Gregory founded the monastery of Ejmiatsin ('Descent of the Only Begotten') on the spot where Christ had struck the hammer. In reality the monastery was founded, like many others in Armenia, on the site of a pagan temple whose altar still exists below the present altar.

of Armenia's architectural gems. Built by order of Katholikos Komitas in 618 it now unfortunately finds itself surrounded by undistinguished buildings between the main road in from Yerevan and the bypass. The present church is built over the mausoleum of the saint, which was constructed in 395. The church has proved more resistant to earthquake damage than many more modern buildings and its appearance has remained almost unchanged apart from the addition of a small portico on the west side and a cross on the roof in the 17th century. The belfry was added to the portico in 1790. Standing on a raised paved area above the road and with the old fortified wall (probably 15th–17th century) on the west side, the pinky-grey tuff church is essentially a cross-dome structure, with a 16-sided tambour. It has four apses and four rectangular corner rooms. Each corner room is, unusually for Armenia, separated from the central part of the church by a circular chamber. The large triangular niches seen on the exterior of each wall helped to reduce the bulk of stone which would otherwise have resulted where the apses and corner rooms join. The northeast corner room is reached by going down steps and further steps lead down to saint's mausoleum. The inside of the dome has decorative stonework and, unusually, a balcony runs round the base of the tambour, giving access to the small towers seen on the outside of the tambour. To the left as one enters the church the large 12th-century khachkar is a rare example of the open-cross type. A **souvenir shop** is to the left of the steps going up to the paved area which is likely to be open whenever there is the chance of a visitor buying something.

St Gayane St Gayane was the abbess of the fleeing nuns persecuted by Trdat III. Her church is slightly later, rather more pleasantly situated, and of quite different style. The present church was built by order of Katholikos Ezr in 630 on the site of Gayane's martyrium. By the early 17th century it was forlorn, the roof having collapsed to leave just the walls and piers standing. Major reconstruction was therefore carried out in 1651–53 and a chapel was constructed under the east apse for the saint's relics. Unlike St Hripsime's church, St Gayane's is of the longitudinal basilica style and with an apse and corner rooms only at the east end. Free-standing pillars support the octagonal tambour. In 1683, a gallery was added at the west end: the three central arches are open while the smaller side ones built to house the remains of dignitaries of the church are blanked off and topped with six-column belfries. This gallery, prominent as one walks from the gate, gives the church a 17th-century appearance even though the main part of the building is older. On Sundays St Gayane's church is a popular place for sacrifices; the *mataghatun* is in the southwest corner of the grounds.

Shoghakat This church was built in 1694 by Prince Aghamal Shorotetsi on the site of a chapel dedicated to one of Hripsime's and Gayane's anonymous companions. Coming here after visiting Ejmiatsin's other churches gives a clear picture of both continuity and change in Armenian church architecture. In particular the continued presence of a cupola atop a tambour, octagonal in this case, follows a tradition going back to the 5th century, but a prominent six-column belfry over the porch is evidence of 17th-century ideas. Similarly, the detailed ornamental carving in geometrical patterns could have been created at almost any time in the last 1,500 years. Few tourists ever go to Shoghakat, and certainly it does not compare to the main cathedral or St Hripsime, but it does provide interesting insights and locals claim that it marks the fourth place where St Gregory the Illuminator saw a vision of a column of fire.

Mother of God Church If few visitors go to Shoghakat, even fewer come here, yet it has an altar in an Italianate style which is unique in Armenia. The original church of 1767 was wooden and the present stone building dates from the 19th

METSAMOR NUCLEAR POWER STATION

Metsamor nuclear power station (not open to the public) is an early Soviet design, the first of its two 440 MW units being commissioned in 1976 and the second in 1980. In the immediate aftermath of the December 1988 earthquake there was concern lest Metsamor might have been damaged. It hadn't but nevertheless it was closed in March 1989 as a safety precaution. The energy blockade by Azerbaijan, imposed as part of the war over Nagorno Karabagh, resulted in catastrophic power shortages during the winters of 1992/93, 1993/94 and 1994/95. This was not only because electricity could not be imported but also the Armenian thermal power stations were dependent on imported gas supplies; those from Azerbaijan were cut off and the pipeline from Georgia was subjected to repeated guerrilla attacks within Georgia. Eventually in 1994 Armenia signed an agreement with Russia providing for Metsamor to be restarted with Russian help and one of the generating units was recommissioned in November 1995.

The main technical problem with Metsamor, apart from uncertainty over the quality of Soviet materials and workmanship, is the lack of a concrete containment vessel to contain radioactive leakage in the event of an accident. A plant spokesman is quoted as saying that it could withstand an earthquake of magnitude 9.0 on the Richter scale. The Armenian government, under considerable pressure from abroad, agreed to close it by 2004 provided other sources of generation could be developed. However, not surprisingly, other sources of generation did not materialise and the plant continues to function. A number of small hydro-electric stations are under construction throughout the country and the reliability of gas supplies has been increased by construction of a pipeline linking the Armenian and Iranian networks facilitating the import of gas not only from Iran but from Turkmenistan via Iran. The Armenian and Iranian electricity grids have also been linked. However, whether this will be sufficient to allow closure of Metsamor is century. The bell tower was added in 1982. It was built as the village church for the ordinary people of Ejmiatsin as opposed to the members of the Holy See or of the monasteries and seminaries. Even now it is near a small market and overlooked by blocks of flats. A three-aisle basilica, it has paintings on the square columns depicting Christ, the Holy family and saints. The stepped altar and the painting of the Madonna and Child within its marble frame are covered with a baldachin-like canopy, painted blue and decorated with gold, which is incorporated into the screen across the *bema*. The screen, including the two doors, one on each side of the altar, has further paintings.

CENTRAL ARMAVIR

Metsamor (Museum, archaeological site and ancient observatory) (⊕ *site always, but this may change; museum: see page 194*) After years of underfunding and decades of stagnation at this important site the situation at Metsamor museum is changing and there is hope of significant improvement. Already there is a secure water and electricity supply, both intermittent in the past. The new director has plans for improving the displays, including labelling in English, and there is the promise of a catalogue, which may be available during the lifetime of this guide. Pending these improvements a visit can be significantly enhanced by downloading beforehand the informative description of the site and museum from TourArmenia's website (*www.tacentral.com*). Heading west from Ejmiatsin across the fertile plain,

doubtful, particularly as Armenia's thermal generating plants are elderly and of low thermal efficiency. Metsamor was built with a 30-year design life and, since it had six years out of use, claims have been made that it could operate until 2016. Whether or not it does so may well depend on Armenia being able to fund a replacement able to supply the 40–45% of Armenia's electricity requirement which Metsamor currently satisfies.

Comparisons are sometimes made between Metsamor and the Chernobyl nuclear reactor in Ukraine which suffered a catastrophic accident with huge loss into the atmosphere of radioactive material while tests were being carried out in 1986. Such a comparison is misleading. Metsamor is a Pressurised Water Reactor (PWR) and uses light (ie: ordinary) water to cool the reactor and to generate steam. Water is also used as the moderator, the medium which slows down the neutrons to increase the chance of fission. It is therefore completely different in concept from the Graphite Moderated Water Cooled Reactor (RBMK is the Russian acronym) which failed at Chernobyl. The essential difference between the two is what happens if pockets of steam form in the coolant. In an RBMK reactor the excess steam does not lead directly to a change in the level of nuclear fission since that is controlled by the graphite moderator. Instead it leads to an increase in power generation which in turn leads to a further increase in steam, and a runaway cycle develops which is exacerbated because steam is also less effective as a coolant than water. (This is essentially what happened at Chernobyl when the normal link in the control system between thermal output and the degree of moderation had been temporarily disconnected for test purposes.) In the case of a reactor like Metsamor where water is the moderator as well as the coolant, the steam pockets increase the effect of the water in its role as moderator and so the level of nuclear fission declines.

Metsamor nuclear power station can be seen to the right (see box, pages 192–3). About 2km from the junction of the bypass with the turn-off for Ejmiatsin a conspicuous monument to the left marks the spot where a Yugoslav plane bringing relief supplies for the victims of the 1988 earthquake crashed as it approached Zvartnots Airport killing all seven on board. Four kilometres beyond that a road leads off left towards the village of Taronik, with its many stork nests. Take this road and continue through the village until a T-junction of surfaced roads. Turn right, continue through the village, then turn left immediately before the village cancellation sign. Follow this track through an area of fish ponds (and consequently quite good for little bittern, squacco heron and other birds favouring this habitat) towards the red tuff museum of Metsamor ('Black Swamp') which opened in 1971. The small **museum** (⊕ 10.00–17.00 Tue–Sat, 10.00–15.00 Sun; guided tour in Armenian AMD1,000; AMD700), although badly in need of the planned upgrading, is well worth visiting. It shows finds from the excavations at the site. At the time of writing, there was minimal labelling in English and the staff do not speak English. Of particular interest is the basement where there is an exact reconstruction of one of the excavated royal tombs. The excavation of royal tombs has shown that the deceased were buried with feet to the east, presumably to face the rising sun, and in the foetal position within a sarcophagus in the early tombs but later lying within a casket. Royalty was buried not only with their jewellery and a supply of food and wine, but also with the domestic animals and decapitated human beings, presumably their slaves, who were slaughtered for the occasion. Also exhibited are some superb examples of gold jewellery, belt decorations in the form of lions, and a weight in the form of a frog made from agate and onyx. This weight, found around the neck of a woman, bears an inscription in Babylonian cuneiform. The ground and upper floors of the museum show examples of ceramics, jewellery, tools and other items including a very large phallus.

The small hill on which the museum stands is the site of an important Bronze Age **citadel**, around 30% of which has been excavated. Although there was occupation here much earlier the important remains and finds date from around 2000BC. Excavations have revealed an important metalworking industry, a postulated astronomical observatory and considerable evidence of international trade.

The **excavated part of the site** lies just beyond the museum. The walls built in the second millennium BC can be seen; they were strengthened in the Urartian era. Up on the plateau are chambers and pits (those with runnels thought to be related to the metalworking industry) hewn into the rock. However, it is the ancient **observatory** where various markings can be seen on the stones which is likely to be of greatest interest. Archaeologists have suggested that it was used around 2800–2500BC to detect the appearance of Sirius, the brightest star in the sky, which may have been worshipped and which possibly marked the start of the year and indicated the time to start planting crops: at that epoch Sirius was visible in summer rather than in winter as it now is. It should be said that some authorities dispute this astronomical observatory claim. If there is no-one from the museum free to show you the markings, walk along the path beside the megalithic walls in the direction of the power station, heading for a small outcrop of reddish rocks. On the far side of the rocks you will come across steps carved into the rock and it is in their vicinity that the markings are to be found. The easiest ones to see comprise a series of converging lines.

Sardarapat (Monument and Ethnographical Museum) If using public transport the best option might be to travel to Armavir (see page 81) then take a taxi. There are no taxis at Sardarapat so you would have to negotiate a price for waiting. Allow

several hours. The monument is on a small hill; from the car park at the bottom there is a long flight of steps up to the monument and then a level walk through the gardens to the museum, a total distance of about 1km. For those unable to negotiate the steps or the distance, a road to the museum goes off left just before the car park. There are barriers on the road; if closed you may be able to ask for them to be opened.

The monument To reach Sardarapat continue along the main road westwards as far as Armavir city. Just after what used to be a large brandy factory on the right (taken over by the French Pernod Ricard company and then closed) is a flyover. It is necessary to turn left but to do so requires turning right and then right again over the flyover. Leaving the flyover the main road turns right at the T-junction. After leaving the suburbs of Armavir the road becomes a dual carriageway again as far as Sardarapat whose striking **red tuff monument**, in the form of two Assyrian bulls facing each other separated by a structure from which bells are hung, can be seen straight ahead. This 35m-tall structure, contrasting with the massive bulls, is built in a form inspired by the stelae at Odzun, Lori province, and Aghudi, Syunik province.

The monument commemorates the victory by Armenian troops and irregular forces commanded by Daniel-Bel Pirumian over attacking Turkish troops who were coming down the railway from Alexandropol (Gyumri). The Battle of Sardarapat lasted from 22 May to 26 May 1918 and was a decisive victory resulting in the declaration of an independent Armenia on 28 May 1918. The monument was unveiled in 1968 to commemorate the 50th anniversary and each year on 28 May celebrations are held here: the bells are tolled and there are performances by folk song and dance groups. Near the monument is a memorial for the dead of the Nagorno Karabagh conflict.

The area surrounding the monument is meticulously well kept, perhaps because it has since 1998 come under the control of the Ministry of Defence: older women sweep the paths with besoms while younger ones weed the rose beds. This commemorative monument is probably unique among those erected anywhere in the former Soviet Union in its appropriateness, stylishness and thankful absence of banal pseudo-heroic bombast. Its designer was the evidently gifted People's Architect of the USSR, Rafael Israelian (1909–73). At right angles to the approach slope, broad paths through gardens and flanked by eagles lead to a memorial wall covered with symbolic reliefs and penetrated by an arch. From here a path leads to the museum. Outside its entrance stands a convincing example of a *vishap* and representative examples of other stone monuments.

The ethnographical museum (⊕ 09.30–17.45 Tue–Sun; parking AMD100; guided tours in English, French, German & Russian AMD5,000; guidebook, with separate English supplement, AMD5,000; adult/child AMD700/300; admission to the war museum hall costs an extra AMD300) This is an excellent museum; a visit is highly recommended. The guidebook has a good selection of photographs with explanations of the exhibits and also of the memorial. The interesting material is well presented in pleasant surroundings with good labelling in Armenian, Russian and English. Symbolically the museum has only two windows facing outwards: one looking north towards Aragats and the other south towards Ararat. Instead there are large windows on to a central courtyard and skylights, in the tradition of the *yerdik* of medieval Armenian architecture.

The displays cover many aspects of life in the Arax Valley including finds from various archaeological sites; traditional farm and domestic implements; the tools of various occupations such as armourer, blacksmith, hatter and shoemaker;

crafts such as carpet weaving, embroidery and lace making; musical instruments; puppets; herbal and mineral medical remedies and much more. A hall of contemporary sculpture, nothing more than 15 years old, has many intriguing pieces. The separate war hall has material about the Battle of Sardarapat.

There are two restaurants within the Sardarapat complex. The **Hazarashen Restaurant** (🕐 *10.00–'until the last visitor has gone', closed Mon; serves the standard Armenian fare of salads & khorovats for about AMD5,000*) is, as its name suggests, built in the form of a traditional Armenian house with a central *hazarashen* roof under which large *tonirs* are set into the ground to cook the food about to be eaten. The **Vardevar Restaurant** (🕐 *12.00–18.00 in summer, approx late Apr/early May–Oct, depending on the weather*) is built in a style resembling a *gavit* with intersecting arches and also has a long room to accommodate traditional Armenian mountain dancing. The inscription at the dining hall entrance has elements of the sentiments inscribed on memorial khachkars and uttered during Armenian toasts – 'Bending down before the names of our great ancestors and inspired by their skilful works we, the grateful descendents, built this dining hall … when visiting this heroic site it is impossible not to raise a glass to the memory of heroes who sacrificed their lives for the homeland.'

Argishtikhinili To reach this Urartian site, continue south on the road past Sardarapat towards Hushakert, turning left for Amasia, then left again at a fork where Nalbandian is signposted right. From here the westernmost hill of Argishtikhinili is visible. Follow the road to the northern side of the hill from where a track goes up to its summit. The town was founded by Argishti I in 776BC and lasted for about 200 years. It is thought that it was an administrative rather than a military centre but it did have fortified walls as well as palaces, temples and dwellings. It occupied a ridge of low hills, its dimensions approximately 5km x 2km. Excavations were carried out from the 1920s to 1970s and many of the finds are now in the Sardarapat museum. The major digs were covered with earth to conserve them but some foundations and walls are still visible, hinting at what once existed. There is a plaster model of the site, now somewhat weathered, on the western hill.

Armavir Although only a short distance east of Argishtikhinili direct access to Hellenistic Armavir by vehicle is difficult. It is best to return via Sardarapat to present-day Armavir and approach from the north via Haykavan. After Haykavan and about 300m after the main road bears left, turn right to reach the southern side of the hill which the town occupied. A modern cemetery girdles the base of the hill. The site was occupied from antiquity but was most important as the capital of the Orontids from the 4th to the 2nd century BC. At that time the Arax River ran further north than it does now, its marshes helping to defend the town. When the river changed its course the capital was shifted but the site continued to be inhabited through the medieval period. The climb to the top of the hill, while short, is difficult because of loose scree. On top is evidence of the temple platform and various dwellings.

GEGHARKUNIK PROVINCE

Gegharkunik comprises the area surrounding **Lake Sevan**, a large high-altitude lake whose surface level was originally 1,915m above sea level, and which formerly occupied almost 5% of the total surface area of the country. It is 78km long and

56km wide at its broadest point. Historic Armenia was a land of three large lakes but Lake Van is now in Turkey and Lake Urmia in Iran. The province also includes the beautiful and little-known valley of the Getik River which lies to the north of the lake. The Getik rises close to the Azerbaijan border and then flows northwest, roughly parallel to the lake shore but separated from it by the Areguniats range of mountains whose highest peak is **Mount Karktasar** (2,743m). The Getik flows into the Aghtsev River about 15km east of Dilijan.

The name Gegharkunik recalls early legends. Gegham was the great-great-grandson of Haik, the legendary founder of Armenia (see pages 13–14). Gegham left Armavir and moved north to Lake Sevan where he established a city which he called Gegh. The lake he called Geghamalich ('Gegham's lake'). The name of the province translates as 'Gegham's seat' since this is where he established his capital. The whole area around the lake is rich in prehistoric and historic remains. It seems that almost every village has a nearby Bronze or Iron Age fortress, megalithic tomb, medieval settlement or something else of interest.

GETTING THERE AND AROUND The main road links are: to northern Lake Sevan, from Yerevan via Hrazdan, and from Dilijan, in Tavush province, via the Dilijan tunnel which bypasses the Sevan Pass (2,114m); to the south of the lake from

The Central Provinces   GEGHARKUNIK PROVINCE

4

Yeghegnadzor, in Vayots Dzor province, via the Selim Pass (2,410m). A mostly good road circumnavigates the lake; the southeast stretch south of Tsapatagh less so. Minibuses from Yerevan go to Sevan, Martuni, Chambarak and Vardenis (see pages 80–2). For general comments on transport see pages 79–82. In summer the train service from Yerevan to Hrazdan is extended to Sevan each day and to Shorzha on Saturdays and Sundays (see page 80), usually from July until mid-September although dates are decided annually so can change. It has been mooted that the service could be withdrawn due to low uptake but both the tracks and stations were being renovated throughout 2013. If you intend to use the service, check beforehand. Sevan station is some 4km from the Lake Sevan peninsula but there are plenty of taxis available.

WHERE TO STAY AND EAT There is a lot of accommodation, mostly at the northwestern end of the lake, ranging from large Soviet-era guesthouses and new hotels to small motel-type establishments. Some accommodation is only open in the summer holiday season. The Tufenkian hotel at Tsapatagh on the eastern shore is a very pleasant hotel but not well located for the main tourist sights, although improvement in the road on that side of the lake has made the journey there much easier than it was. Homestays are available and were the only real option for places like Martuni until the recent availability of a small number of rooms at the Khrchit restaurant (see opposite). They are also the only option in Sevan town, as opposed to around the lake. Apart from the hotels and restaurants listed below, summer sees many eating places opening around the lake, especially on the western side.

Avan Marak Tsapatagh (34 rooms) Tsapatagh, Lake Sevan; contact via Tufenkian central office in Yerevan, ☎60 501010; e hotels@ tufenkian.am; www.tufenkianheritage.com; ⊕ 1 May–15 Oct, high season Jul & Aug. Opened in Dec 2002 this luxurious Tufenkian hotel is situated on the east side of Lake Sevan, at Tsapatagh. Its construction incorporates old stone barns. Outdoor swimming pool. The restaurant is in a separate building a few mins' walk away round the edge of the village but transport is available. Very pleasant hotel but not well located. It is 57km from Sevan town. Wi-Fi. Cards accepted. Prices vary depending on size of room & view of lake. **$$$$–$$$**

Bohemian Resort (25 rooms, 18 cottages) 102 Yerevanian Rd, Sevan; ☎261 25885; e info@ bohemianresort.am; www.bohemianresort.am; ⊕ 1 Apr–31 Oct. Part of the Best Western chain, opened in 2006, on the west shore of Lake Sevan. Has 8 non-smoking rooms. Swimming pool. Wi-Fi. Cottages sleep 4 persons; all are 2 storeys with the bedrooms upstairs. Cards accepted. Reduced low season rates. High season 25 Jun–15 Sep. **$$$**

Harsnaqar (34 rooms) Tsamagaberd, Sevan; ☎261 20450, 20092, 22400; e reservation@harsnaqarhotel.am; www.

harsnaqarhotel.am. One of the few hotels at the west end of the lake open all year. Built in 2005, it has very pleasant rooms. Cottages (*AMD90,000–100,000*), which sleep up to 8 ppl, are also available. Entrance to Water World AMD1,500–2,000, depending on height. Private beach. Sports facilities. Wi-Fi. Cards accepted, excluding American Express. **$$$**

Ashot Yerkat Restaurant/Hotel Complex (8 rooms) Sevan Peninsula; ☎261 25000; m 091 025000, 091 500043. Near the car park for peninsula monasteries. Mainly a restaurant & still one of the best. Restaurant can seat 350 but it is so popular it is best to book ahead (*2hrs*) at busy times. Ideal for coffee & pastries (their baklava is delicious) when visiting Sevanavank. Their barbecued *sig* (see page 200) is also delicious. **$$**

Blue Sevan (49 rooms) Chambarak; m 098 288277, 091 288277; e bluesevan@gmail. com; www.blue-sevan.com; ⊕ May–Oct. Note that although the postal address is Chambarak, this hotel is actually on the north shore of Lake Sevan. A well-renovated pleasant hotel set in wooded grounds geared to families from Yerevan. Also has cottages, AMD150,000, which sleep up to 6 ppl. A word of caution if you decide to stay outwith the busy months of Jul & Aug: one Mon night in late Jun I discovered that all the staff in the hotel had gone home without warning me, presumably because I was the only guest. There was no b/fast the next morning, although the room rate inc b/fast, & no staff for me to pay my bill! (I did pay later via my travel agent in Yerevan.) The previous day, when the hotel was busy with w/end visitors, there was an excellent buffet b/fast. Lunch (⏰ *14.00–17.00*) can be ordered in advance AMD4,000pp. Evening meal not available. Price varies with floor (cheapest on ground floor) & view of lake. **$$**

🏠 **Arevik** (10 cottages: 6x4-person (2 dbl rooms), 4x2-person) Near Harsnaqar, Lake Sevan; m 094 210534; ⏰ closed in winter (Nov–Mar, weather depending). The en-suite cabin-like cottages provide satisfactory basic accommodation. B/fast extra AMD1,500pp. FB AMD5,000pp. Prices a little higher Jul & Aug. **$$–$**

🏠 **The Association Aregouni** 3 Baghramian St, Vardenis; m 093 323193; e varegouni@ yahoo.com, aslakaren@yahoo.fr. This is a group of 5 families in the town of Vardenis which has formed a link with people in the town of Romans in France. Children in Vardenis are taught French during the summer months & exchange visits are arranged. With the help of their French partners the Armenian families have been able to upgrade their bathroom & toilet facilities to enable them to take guests. Between them the families can accommodate up to 27 ppl in homestays in Vardenis. The author has stayed with 2 of the families in the association. Evening meals can be arranged AMD4,000pp. **$**

🏠 **Khrchit Restaurant/Hotel** (3 rooms) 100 Kamo St, Martuni (see comment on Martuni, pages 206–7); ☎ 262 42964; m 091 228881, 094 030810; ⏰ all year. The restaurant is on the main road just after entering Martuni from the west; a useful landmark is the pair of artificial storks on their nest at the front entrance. This restaurant, my favourite of several in Martuni, now has 3 very nice en-suite dbl rooms, with the advantage of readily available meals. B/fast extra, approx AMD1,000pp. **$**

✖ **Hrashk Ojakh Restaurant** Victor Hambartsumian St, Vardenis (1km from the main road on the road to Ayrk); ⏰ 10.00–midnight. Opened in 2012, they serve a good fish kebab.

OTHER PRACTICALITIES The towns in the province are small but like all small towns in Armenia they have all basic facilities. Lake Sevan's beaches are very popular with Armenians and in summer, particularly at weekends, it can be very busy.

Tourist information is available at the town hall (*164 Nairian St*; m 099 199555; e *davidtorosyan09@yahoo.com*; ⏰ *09.00–18.00 Mon–Fri*) in Sevan town. When I visited there was no information sign on the outside of the building (I did suggest one might be helpful for tourists!). Inside there is an *i* sign but no indication of where to go – ask. They hope to establish some sort of mobile information unit during summer in the parking area below Sevan Monastery.

LAKE SEVAN

History Lake Sevan, which now enjoys National Park status, is fed by 28 rivers but there is only one flowing out, the Hrazdan which exits the lake at the western end to become a tributary of the Arax. In 1910, the Armenian engineer Soukias Manasserian published a book entitled *The Evaporating Billions and the Stagnation of Russian Capital* in which he proposed reducing the depth of the lake from 95m to 45m, using the water for irrigation and hydro-electric generation. The reference to 'evaporating billions' is a comment on the fact that 90% of the lake's water is lost through evaporation. (Manasserian also produced a plan to reduce the level of the Aral Sea, a much better known environmental disaster.) Manasserian's scheme was developed in the Stalin era and approved by the then Armenian Soviet government though inevitably without any consultation with local people. The plan was later changed to reduce the level of the lake by 55m which would result in a reduction in its perimeter from 260km to 80km and its volume of water from 58km^3 to 5km^3. With breathtaking lack of realism it was planned that this drastic reduction in size would be accompanied by an equally drastic increase in the yield of fish caught in the lake of between eight and ten times to be achieved by releasing trout fry from hatcheries into the remains of the lake. A typical Stalin-era writer stated that Lake Sevan's 'scraggy, barren shores will be turned into sweet-smelling meadows, groves of nut trees and oak trees ... Around it beautiful roads and promenades will be laid ... There could be no objection to diminishing the size of the lake for it would merely mean diminishing the annual evaporation of a vast quantity of moisture that rose uselessly into the air.'

Work began in 1933 to implement the scheme when the Hrazdan was deepened to increase the discharge from the lake. A tunnel was also bored 40m below the original lake level but, because of delays caused by the war, it was not inaugurated until 1949 and was then trumpeted as a major achievement of the Soviet era. The lake level started to drop by more than 1m per year.

After Khrushchev's speech criticising Stalin at the 20th congress of the Communist Party of the Soviet Union in 1956, the wisdom of the Sevan venture started to be questioned. Already problems were starting to become manifest such as the difficulty of growing the promised nut trees and oak trees on the newly exposed shore together with a reduction in catch of the four subspecies of the endemic Sevan trout *Salmo ischchan*. In 1958, a 'Sevan Committee' was formed and the Soviet government decreed that the lake level was to be kept as high as possible with new thermal power stations replacing two of the originally projected eight hydro-electric ones. The new power stations were to be completed by 1970 but removing water for irrigation purposes was to cease by 1965. As a result of the action then taken the water level stabilised in 1962 at 18m below the original level but then eutrophic algal blooms started to occur, for the first time in 1964. A new tunnel, 49km long, was also constructed, intended to bring 200 million cubic metres of water each year north from the Arpa River into the lake. Completed in 1981 the tunnel only succeeded in raising the water level by 1.5m and a second tunnel 22km long was considered necessary to divert a further 165 million cubic metres each year from the Vorotan into the Arpa and thence to the lake. (This tunnel was only completed in 2003.) Matters deteriorated after 1988 as a consequence of the economic blockade of Armenia during the war over Nagorno Karabagh and the simultaneous closure of Metsamor nuclear power station. The Hrazdan River hydro-electric stations had to be operated more to maintain at least limited electricity supplies in Armenia and the level of the lake fell 20m below its original level with a surface area of 940km² in comparison with the former 1,360km².

Common whitefish *Coregonus lavaretus*, known as *sig* in Armenia, were introduced in the 1920s from Lake Ladoga. This species is also found as a relict species in various lakes in western Britain where it is called the powan, though another closely related fish also shares that name. The idea was that, as the whitefish were shallow-water feeders and the trout fed in deep water, the two could co-exist. In reality the whitefish did not at first thrive, but changes in the lake caused by the reduction in level with an associated rise in temperature, and the use of agricultural fertilisers in the area round the lake, gave rise to conditions which favoured the whitefish but not the trout. The trout are now on the verge of extinction in Armenia although they survive in Lake Issyk-kul in Kyrgyzstan where the species was introduced. Catching the endemic trout has been prohibited since 1976 but the ban is poorly enforced. It is also possible that the introduced crayfish *Astacus leptodactylus* is another competitor and goldfish *Carassius auratus* have also been accidentally introduced.

So far as the whitefish are concerned, falling numbers are giving cause for concern and the Ministry for Nature Protection now imposes a quota on the weight which can be caught each year together with a complete ban during the spawning season which runs from late November to mid-December. There is, however, no way of enforcing the quota, and the local fishermen say that there is no way they can afford to cease fishing for the three or four weeks of the spawning season. There is a proposal to ban the netting of fish completely for three to four years. Fish can still be bought on the lakeside but they are no longer openly displayed. Instead the fisherman indicates to likely passing cars that he has fish for sale with the same gesture usually used to show the size of the one that got away. If crayfish are for sale the hand is held in a mimetic position, thumb, ring and little fingers together with index and middle fingers wiggling like the antennae of the creature. The decline in numbers is largely caused by overfishing but common carp *Cyprinus carpio*, which appeared in the lake in the 1980s, also compete with the whitefish for food.

The Armenian government's policy is to raise the lake level to 1,904m (a level last seen in 1957 but still some 11m lower than the original 1,915m) by the year 2031. To take the level higher than this would cause great problems because of the building and construction which has taken place on the drained land. By early 2012 a level of 1,900m had been reached. The newly flooded areas are conspicuous at all points around the lake. If the government's target is reached some 1,697 buildings and structures on the lakeside will be submerged, according to the chairman of the Lake Sevan Commission. Only 481 of these buildings are legally authorised and for these compensation will be paid. The rest will be demolished without compensation. A 15km section of the main road around the lake has been submerged and rebuilt on higher ground. It is estimated that a total of 4,000ha of shoreline will have to cleared of trees by 2020/21 to mitigate problems caused by submerged vegetation. By 2012, 1,400ha had been cleared. Other factors contributing to the pollution of Lake Sevan include outdated waste-water treatment and sewage disposal, with raw sewage being discharged into rivers flowing into the lake. In 2012, to help the government of Armenia with the high cost of upgrading the water and sewerage systems, the European Bank for Reconstruction and Development provided a loan of €7m and the European Union a €5m capital expenditure grant. Upgrading work includes a new sewer network in Sevan and waste-water treatment plants for Gavar, Vardenis and Martuni. Another cause for concern is the pollution which could result from a proposed increase in gold mining at Sotk, east of Vardenis.

In June 2012 the government approved amendments to the law which limited the annual volume of water which can be taken from Lake Sevan. Previously set at 170 million cubic metres, they agreed an increase to 320 million cubic metres citing a need to protect supplies of irrigation water to agriculture in the Ararat Valley in the light of a predicted drought. Environmentalists dismissed that explanation, claiming that the real reason was the desire to save from inundation expensive properties on the shores of Lake Sevan, many of which are thought to be owned by members of Armenia's political and business elite. Environmentalists estimated that the increased outflow would result in a drop of 11cm to the lake surface. The State Committee for Water Management predicted a drop of only 2–3cm. The original aim of raising the level of the lake to 1,904m by 2031 envisaged an annual rise of 20cm.

Visiting the lake today To those accustomed to the lakes of Switzerland or the lochs of Scotland, Lake Sevan with no mountains tumbling down to the water's edge will initially seem bare and windswept. Its real attraction lies in the ever-changing colours of its surface and in the skies above it. It is also, particularly on its southern side, an area with a long history and with a great many interesting places to see. Even these historical sites bring forcibly home the problems of the lake: the best known, the monastery of Sevanavank, was formerly on an island but falling water levels have turned that island into a peninsula and visitors travel there by road rather than by boat. Other attractions of the lake, for Armenians at least, are the beaches, the only ones in Armenia. While Western visitors would be unlikely to consider landlocked Armenia as a possible destination for a beach holiday, the beaches do provide a unique experience within the country for Armenians. Privatisation has resulted in visitors having to pay to use some beaches adjacent to hotels but, in compensation, they are now looked after properly and kept clean.

Many buildings are springing up on the lakeside. There is no robust planning-permission system and an owner of land can build more or less anything regardless of how inappropriate it might be. Perhaps the owners hope to make enough of a profit before lake levels rise and their buildings are demolished. One hopes that the shores of Lake Sevan will not suffer the same fate as Yerevan's green belt.

Sevan (*Telephone code: 261*) Most visitors to Lake Sevan bypass the town of Sevan to go straight to the peninsula churches or to the beaches. Even those arriving by train probably spend minimal time in the town, hiring a taxi to take them the 4km to the lake. Certainly there is little of interest in the town itself. In spite of an increasing number of new shops and renovated buildings Sevan still has a somewhat run-down feel. It seems not to have benefited from the increasing number of visitors in the same way as the lakeside has. Most facilities are on or just off the main thoroughfare, Nairian Street. They include: the post office and market towards the west end; the town hall (with information office, see page 199) and the hospital towards the east end. Sayat Nova Street crosses Nairian Street about halfway along it. Both the railway station and the bus stance are on Sayat Nova, the railway station to the north, the bus stance to the south. (The bus ticket office is the inconspicuous small triangular building.) Just outside the town to the west is a **war cemetery** where German prisoners of war lie buried, one of several in Armenia (see pages 229 and 245). To get there go west along Nairian Street to a roundabout, turn right and cross the railway, then take the first left turn. Continue for about 1km looking out for the large plain cross of the war cemetery across fields to the left. Within the cemetery are four groups of three crosses as well as the large cross underneath which is the same inscription as the other German war cemeteries, *Hier ruhen Kriegesgefangene – Opfer des zweites Weltkrieges* ('Here rest prisoners of war – victims of World War II'). In early summer the cemetery is a meadow of colourful wild flowers.

Ddmashen The village of Ddmashen, 12km west of Sevan, though more easily reached from Hrazdan in Kotayk province, has the 7th-century **church of St Thaddeus**. This domed basilica church is considered to be the fourth most important of this type of construction after Talin, Ptghni and Aruch. It has survived without major alterations, although it received a new 16-sided tambour in 1907 following earthquake damage. The tambour has eight windows; the intermediate façades have niches. There is a single small window in the altar apse and much larger windows in the nave. It is very plain both inside and outside, the only external features being undecorated moulding at the windows. The window arches and the pattern of lighting is typical of early 7th-century churches. To the south of the church is a large cemetery, the grave stones mostly unmarked recumbent slabs.

THE WESTERN SIDE OF LAKE SEVAN
Sevanavank (monastery) This monastery is one of Armenia's most visited tourist sights. The reduction in the level of the lake has both reduced the picturesqueness of the setting – it is now on a peninsula rather than an island – and boosted the number of tourist buses arriving. Although worth visiting, it is not really one of Armenia's most appealing places and owes its popularity largely to its proximity to the lake and to its accessibility from Yerevan. It is on the southwest slope of a hill overlooking the north end of Lake Sevan. The surviving buildings comprise the Mother of God Church, the smaller Holy Apostles Church, together with a ruined *gavit*. (**Note:** most sources use the church names followed in this guidebook – the information boards at the monastery names them differently.) An inscription on the **Holy Apostles Church**, the oldest of the churches and the first to be encountered, states that the monastery was founded in 874 by Princess Miriam, wife of Prince Vasak of Syunik, and daughter of the Bagratid King Ashot I. This was a time when Armenia was emerging from subjugation under the Arab caliphate and the church was one of the first to be built in Armenia after more than 200 years of Arab Islamic domination. Not surprisingly the architects resorted to 7th-century practice in developing the design. Despite what the inscription says about Ashot being king, in 874 this was a little premature. By judicious exploitation of others' enforced absence at the caliph's court in Samarra, Ashot was able to amass great power and in 862 the caliph awarded him with the title Prince of Princes. Ashot managed to remain neutral in the wars between the caliph's Arab forces and the Byzantine Emperor Basil I which were being waged when Sevan Monastery was built. The caliph was only to give Ashot the title King in 884, ten years after the date of the inscription; he was later followed in doing so by the Byzantine emperor.

Holy Apostles is a typical and plain cross-dome church and, in the absence of corner rooms, its interior shape can be seen from the outside. There is a large doorway between the south and west arms and a small chapel with an apse between the south and east arms. The octagonal tambour has four small windows.

The larger **Mother of God Church** is in similar style and lies to the southeast of the Apostles Church; it too has an octagonal tambour. The small chapels were probably later additions. There are two features of particular interest. One is an extremely elaborate 13th-century basalt khachkar inside the church. At the top right is God the Father with right hand raised in the Armenian style of blessing – tips of thumb and ring finger touching with the other three fingers upright – representing the Trinity. He is surrounded by the winged symbols of the four evangelists – eagle, lion, ox and man. At the top left is God surrounded by angels. The central panel shows Jesus on the cross flanked by Mary and St John. To the right of Jesus are panels showing his birth, the ox and ass, and the three kings. To his left are panels showing scales weighing good and evil, three figures and abstract decoration. Below Jesus, God is shown expelling Adam and Eve from Eden. The other notable feature is the wooden altar screen, part carved and part painted. It is most un-Armenian, being a gift in 1824 from the monastery of St Thaddeus, south of Maku in present-day Iran.

Off the Mother of God Church is a ruined *gavit* in which are displayed pieces of khachkars found hidden in the cupola of the church. Its roof once rested on six wooden columns. The finely carved wooden capitals from the *gavit* depicting a chalice and the tree of life flanked by two doves are now in the Historical Museum in Yerevan, as are two carved walnut doors also from the *gavit*, one dating from 1176 and the other from 1486. Northeast and a little uphill from Mother of God Church is the low outline of a third church, **Holy Resurrection**.

The monastery was one of the first seminaries to reopen in Armenia after the Soviet period. In the past being here was not necessarily a matter of choice. The French expert on the Caucasus, Jean-Marie Chopin, who visited the island monastery in 1830, reported that the regime was extremely strict with no meat, no wine, no youths and no women. It therefore served as a reformatory for those monks banished for their misdemeanours from Ejmiatsin. Another visitor reported that as late as 1850 manuscripts here were still being copied by hand. Walking to the end of the peninsula affords good views across the lake as well as some escape from the multitude of visitors thronging the monastery at the height of the season. On the north side of the peninsula is the seminary, and at the tip, protected by a high metal fence, the guesthouse of the president.

Heading southeast from Sevan along the west side of the lake the road passes through **Lchashen**, site of the discovery of the Bronze Age burial chariots now on display in Yerevan's State History Museum. At **Norashen** is one of the world's largest breeding colonies of the Armenian gull (*Larus armenicus*), another being at Lake Arpi in northwest Armenia (pages 233–4). The gulls breed on islands in Lake Sevan and by the late 1990s the reduced water level had turned the islands into peninsulas. This allowed access to predators and domestic cattle, which trampled on the eggs. In addition human activity caused disturbance during the breeding season, all leading to a serious threat to the viability of the colony. In 1999 a project, led by the Acopian Center for the Environment (*www.acopiancenter. am*), dug a channel so that Gull Island was once again an island, thus allowing the birds to breed more successfully. An area of the lakeside at Norashen has been set aside as a reserve. It is also a good place to see a range of passerines, flowers and butterflies. Armenian Monuments Awareness Project (AMAP) boards provide information if your neck can cope with their height above the ground.

Hayravank (monastery) Just south of Berdkunk, and about 22km from Sevan, the monastery of Hayravank can be seen on a knoll to the left of the road overlooking the lake. The monastery and surrounding rocks are all conspicuously covered with reddish-orange lichen. The monastery consists of a domed four-apse church from the end of the 9th century, a *gavit* from the 12th and a small 10th-century chapel off the south wall of the church. The topography of the rather cramped site with the ground falling away quite steeply led to the *gavit*, at a lower level than the church, incorporating the western apse of the church, which now protrudes into the interior of the *gavit*. The east arch of the *gavit* spans the church asymmetrically in relation to the west door and crosses the top of the west apse window. The interior of the *gavit's* short octagonal tambour and dome are decorated with red and grey tuff, thought to be one of the earliest examples of polychrome decorative masonry. Every interior wall of the *gavit* is covered with carved crosses. The disposition of the buildings means that, of the original church, only the east apse and part of the north apse are visible from the outside. There are many attractive khachkars at the monastery.

Gavar (*Telephone code: 264*) Not far beyond Hayravank the main road bypasses the rather uninteresting provincial capital of Gavar which was founded as Nor Bayazit (ie: New Bayazit) in 1830 by Armenian migrants who had left Bayazit, Turkey, following the Turkish defeat by Russia. In 1959, it was renamed Kamo, the *nom de guerre* of Simon Ter-Petrosian (1882–1922), one of a number of Bolshevik supporters who raised money for the party by robbing banks in particular, but also post offices and railway ticket offices. He died in a road accident in Tbilisi. The city changed its name again following the Soviet collapse. Most of Gavar's industry has closed but the hosiery factory survives, exporting to the other CIS countries and seeking niche markets elsewhere. The big central square in Gavar has the large Mother of God Church (1900), a post office, the Culture Palace where taxis wait and from where minibuses depart and the tall building of the (now closed) Soviet-era Khaldi Hotel with the bus ticket office (✆ 264 26001) at its base. The area was once important. The ridge which runs through Gavar (perhaps best seen from the road to Karmirgyugh), now the modern cemetery, is the site of an early Iron Age fortress thought to be an Urartian royal capital. Tombs from 4000bc and medieval monuments have been found in Gavar.

For those who enjoy visiting small village churches there are a number of interest in and around Gavar. For more information on these and other off-the-beaten track sites such as the medieval settlement of **Kanagegh**, go to www.bradtguides.com/europe/armenia.

Noratus field of khachkars After the Gavar turn-off the main road heads south and skirts the edge of Noratus, home to one of Armenia's most amazing sights – the **field of khachkars**. Turn left off the main road at one of those preposterously over-engineered Soviet-era road junctions. On the eastern edge of the town is a huge **cemetery** with a modern section which is quite interesting but with an array of stones from the medieval period onwards where the range and fascination of the khachkars are overwhelming. Although there are many groups of khachkars in Armenia, nowhere can rival the impression made by the approximately 900 here. It is quite impossible to do justice to the carved stones on a single visit and one can merely wander across the site gazing in amazement at a row of 15 erect ones here, an area of recumbent ones there, no two alike. Stones with single crosses, stones with multiple crosses, geometric patterns, naturalistic ones: it is quite impossible to take in the riot of carved detail. Perhaps the sheep who graze here every day eventually learn to appreciate the detail but mere tourists don't have a chance. The AMAP information boards at the cemetery give much detail but visitors may find it useful to carry with them the description of the Noratus cemetery walking tour instituted by AMAP in 2010 (see their website: *www.armenianmonuments.org/en/monument/Noratus*). A small problem is that the numbers on the posts have disappeared: the suspicion is that this is the work of small boys who hope thereby to act as guides! Visitors should note that, like all khachkars which are still in their original positions, these face west and can therefore most easily be photographed in the afternoon.

On the southern edge of the village of Noratus stands the small white 9th- or 10th-century **church of St Gregory** with its relatively high cylindrical tambour. The narrow front of the church combines with the small projecting corner rooms, the high tambour and the conical dome to give the appearance of a space rocket. Behind the east end of the church is a row of ten interesting khachkars. In the centre of the village the larger 9th-century Mother of God Church has been under gradual restoration for several years.

Dzoragyugh and Nerkin Getashen These two villages which lie south of the main road have interesting historic churches and also provide a picture of Armenian village life in the 21st century. **Dzoragyugh** ('Gorge Village') is home to two churches, both of which were founded in the late 9th century shortly after Sevanavank. The larger, ruinous one, Shoghagavank, dedicated to St Peter, is situated on a hill at the western end of the village. The church was built between 877 and 886 and its founder was the same Princess Miriam who founded Sevanavank. The site again has a good array of khachkars, and is where local royalty are thought to be buried, but it is no rival for Noratus. Dzoragyugh's other church is harder to find. Coming from the main road into the village, bear left on to a dirt road about 3.8km from the main road, just after a large school/kindergarten on the right. Follow a wall round to the left. The dirt road does a big loop to cross a small river. Keep the wooded river gully on your left and eventually the church will be seen among houses. It still functions as the village church today and was one of the first to have carpets on the floor and on the altar dais. It is decorated with, among other things, a carpet hanging on the wall depicting the Last Supper (and owing its composition to Leonardo da Vinci) as well as various embroideries. A large wrought-iron chandelier hangs from the ceiling. Originally built as the Masruts Anapat ('Hermitage of Masru') it was subsequently extended and now presents a plain, square appearance. Today it is known as St John the Baptist. The lower, older parts of the building are constructed of dark grey, rough-hewn basalt blocks, and contrast rather startlingly with the upper parts and tambour which are formed of red tuff, and some modern repairs effected with dressed grey tuff. Khachkars are lined up beside the west and east walls and also occupy the orchard to the south of the church.

The next village, **Nerkin Getashen** ('Lower Getashen') was at one time the summer residence and administration centre of the Bagratid dynasty. It can be reached either from the Sevan–Martuni road or the road south from Martuni; it's more straightforward from the latter. On the road south turn first right in Martuni, at traffic lights, and continue straight ahead. In the village bear left up a smaller, less-used asphalt road just after passing a very ruined *zham* on the left (look out for the khachkars). This smaller road leads up to the cemetery. The large Mother of God Church (part of what was Kotavank) built of dark grey basalt was founded, again in the late 9th century, but this time by Miriam's son, Gregory Supan. It is almost square in external appearance thanks to the large corner rooms which conceal the internal cross shape. The dome and parts of the walls collapsed during the 17th century and only the east façade remains intact. Nonetheless the building still presents an impressive appearance today. Many interestingly carved tombstones and khachkars stand around the church including a row of 17 enormous ones. It is worth exploring the adjacent hill. It is covered with an array of khachkars to rival Noratus and from it one can see the ruins of Kot, the early medieval capital of the region.

THE SOUTHERN SIDE OF LAKE SEVAN

Martuni and beyond The main road passes through Martuni where the road over the **Selim Pass** (2,410m) branches off and goes south into Vayots Dzor province, being the only road linking northern and southern Armenia which avoids the capital. It has been upgraded and can now be used by all vehicles although at times it may be impassable in winter because of snow. Upgrading has taken away some of the pass's charm and has also reduced sightings of steppe eagles, black vultures and griffon vultures which were characteristic of the rolling uplands on this northern side. One of Armenia's most interesting sights, the intact 14th-century **Selim caravanserai**, is adjacent to the road but over the provincial border in Vayots Dzor. On the north side of the pass within Gegharkunik there is at the southern end of **Gegh'hovit**, the first village south from Martuni, a ruined 5th-century church dedicated to St George, surrounded by tombstones with much figure carving. There are **petroglyphs** on Mount Sev Sar to the east of the road.

Martuni acquired its present name in 1926: Martuni was the *nom de guerre* of Alexander Miasnikian, the first prime minister of Armenia in Soviet days. The renaming of towns here manages to create particular confusion as there is another Martuni, also in Gegharkunik province but in the Getik Valley north of the lake. It is always necessary therefore to specify which Martuni one means: the northern one seems usually to be called Martuni Krasnoselsk region even though Krasnoselsk (Russian for 'red village') has officially reverted to its former name of Chambarak. Just to add to the confusion there is a third Martuni in Nagorno Karabagh.

Beyond Martuni the road swings east. After about another 20km it crosses the short channel which links the hydro tunnel bringing the water from the Arpa River to Lake Sevan and immediately afterwards the village of **Artsvanist** lies to the south of the road. Of the two roads into Artsvanist, the easternmost one is better and shorter. In a gorge on the southern side of the village is the secluded and appealing **monastery of Vanevank**. It's probably best to park at the post office and walk down the track which is initially on the right-hand side of the river, then crosses to the left. The main church, dedicated to St Gregory and at the left-hand side, was built in 903 by Prince Shapuh Bagratuni together with his sister Miriam, the same Miriam who was also responsible for other churches in the district already mentioned. It was restored at the end of the 10th century by King Gagik I Bagratuni when the surrounding wall was built, parts of which can still be seen, notably on the hillside above and behind the monastery. The rather plain church building is itself basalt but the octagonal tambour is of contrasting red tuff. The right-hand church is barrel-vaulted and without a dome. It has a somewhat elongated appearance and is also built of basalt but has contrasting red tuff at the top of the gable ends. The *gavit* between the two churches was added at a later date. It has a bell tower and in the east part is what appears to be a burial vault.

Makenis Makenis is reached by continuing east from Artsvanist then turning right at Tsovik to head south for about 9km. The road to Makenis is in poor condition. Once in Makenis, bear left, then just before reaching the large school building turn sharp right and then left at the post office to reach the main gate of **Makenyats Monastery**, picturesquely situated at the edge of the village overlooking the Karchaghbur River. Quite apart from the monastery, Makenis is an evocative village with its livestock, dirt roads and dung drying for fuel. According to 13th-century chroniclers, the monastery was founded by Prince Gregory Supan in 851. It is a three-apse cross-dome church built of basalt with a circular tambour and surrounded by a substantial wall. There are large chapels on both sides of the altar dais with carved doorways. Carvings of horses decorate the base of the southern pillar and the inside of the lintel of the main door. At the west gable is a small belfry. The *gavit* is now ruined but there is a small chapel to the southwest. The river must have changed its course slightly since the monastery was built, as the conspicuous latrine in the perimeter wall is now a few metres from it. There is a good collection of khachkars, some of which have been incorporated into garden walls and one of which has been removed to act as a bridge over a modern irrigation channel.

Vardenis Vardenis is the principal town in the eastern part of Gegharkunik and looks as though it experienced better days before it became almost a dead end following the closure of the border with Azerbaijan. It is a convenient stopping place for those travelling to or from Nagorno Karabagh via the Sotk Pass but is of little interest. The prominent church is early 20th century. Until 2013, when the main road through the town was improved, all the roads of the town were in a bad condition. Even worse is the road running southeast to **Ayrk** which has two small medieval churches. Ayrk itself is pleasantly set in rolling countryside but looks poor and even more rundown than Vardenis with many empty houses, probably deserted by fleeing Azeris and, with little potential employment to attract Armenians fleeing in the opposite direction, they have remained unoccupied. The two churches are about 150m apart. Both have barrel-vaulted roofs and good collections of khachkars. The westernmost church, dedicated to the Mother of God, dates from 1181 and the easternmost, St George's, is slightly later. Between the two are remnants of massive Iron Age fortification walls and in the cliffs below the eastern church are caves, from which I disturbed a little owl (*Athene noctua*).

The road between Vardenis and the Sotk Pass across Geghakunik's flat eastern plain bypasses the town of **Sotk**, or Zod as it was (and often still is) called until 1991. (At the time of writing the eastern two-thirds of the road between Vardenis and the Sotk Pass, some 16km, was very poor.) Zod grew from village to town in the 1960s/70s with the industrialisation of the Zod gold mines. The predominantly Azeri inhabitants fled in 1988 during the Karabagh war. If passing, it is worth a short detour to see the **church of St Betghehem**. A long basilica, it has an old feel to it both inside and outside. Dating from the 7th century, there is evidence of several phases of rebuilding, including 13th-century khachkars incorporated into the walls, most notably a complete row in the west wall. The church, today standing in a farmyard, is mostly built of large blocks of stone and inside four massive free-standing pillars divide the barrel-vaulted church into a wide central aisle and two narrow side aisles.

THE EASTERN SIDE OF LAKE SEVAN

This side of the lake is much less developed than the west side. Although Vardenis is virtually a dead end so far as Armenians are concerned, this is not necessarily the case for tourists. They can either continue the circumnavigation of the lake or else continue across the difficult northern route to Nagorno Karabagh. Few tourists do either. The road on the eastern side of the lake is mostly in good condition although there are some poor stretches, particularly in the south. The flat area between Vardenis and the lake used to be the shallow Lake Gilli, a wetland complex of about 1,000ha and an important nesting area for more than 100 species of migratory water birds. In 1960 the Soviet government decided to drain Lake Gilli for agricultural land, mainly wheat and barley cultivation. Although initial crop yields were high, the fertility of the land soon decreased and productivity is now low. Although some small areas of wetland remained, many breeding birds were lost. The draining of Lake Gilli and the reduction in the level of Lake Sevan also destroyed important wintering grounds for wading birds. In autumn, however, greater flamingoes can still be seen. The eastern side of the lake has few specific tourist attractions although there are some pleasant beaches and, in early summer, an amazing, colourful profusion of wild flowers. A railway parallels the road: it was built to serve the gold mines at Zod but there are no longer passenger services beyond Hrazdan except in summer when the service is extended to Shorzha. The embankment can be spectacular with poppies, catmint, vetches and hypericum. On the shore of the lake salvias and iris can be found among the tamarisk trees. At the northern end, look out for the dark purple-pink mounds of *Onobrychis cornuta* and the pinkish-white carpets of rock jasmine (*Androsace* sp) in May/June. Between the villages of Artanish and Shorzha the rather square-shaped, hilly **Artanish peninsula** juts into the lake. Centrally Mount Artanish rises to 2,460m. A road goes down the flat west side of the peninsula from Shorzha and ends at a few houses and some beaches. A short road leads to Artanish bay on the east side. It is not possible to drive around the peninsula, but one can walk round.

The beautiful **Getik Valley**, quite different from the Sevan basin, can be reached by heading north from Shorzha over the **Chambarak (or Karmir) Pass** (2,176m) to the town of Chambarak. The road may be closed in winter by snow. In early summer colourful wild flowers carpet the hillsides. **Chambarak**, like Vardenis, looks as if it has seen better days. The shops, post office, bank, etc are on either September 21st Street (the road on which one enters the town), or Garegin Nzhdeh Street at right angles to it. These are the only tarmac roads in the town, all others being poor dirt roads. Some 8km north of Chambarak, at Ttujur village, the road over the spectacular Ttujur Pass (2,092m) goes off northwards (see page 270). The valley of the Getik itself is very pleasant, particularly further west, although it lacks any specific sights of interest.

KOTAYK PROVINCE

The Hrazdan River flowing south from Lake Sevan to Yerevan, ultimately to join the Arax in the south of the country, forms the north–south spine of Kotayk province. The main road and rail routes follow the river. A half-day excursion from Yerevan to **Garni Temple** and **Geghard Monastery** in the south of the province is probably Armenia's most popular trip for visitors and is well worth making. The provincial capital of Hrazdan is a slowly improving, rundown, postindustrial town. The northwest part of the province has long been a popular holiday destination for Armenians. The village of **Tsaghkadzor** is Armenia's principal ski resort and also offers pleasant walking in the surrounding wooded countryside. Mount Arailer is prominent in the west of the province while to the east, separating Kotayk from neighbouring Gegharkunik, are the peaks of the Geghama Mountains. The sights of the Hrazdan Gorge are not as well known as those of the Kasakh in Aragatsotn province, but are worth visiting if time permits.

GETTING THERE AND AROUND Most places can be reached by minibus from Yerevan and trains run from Yerevan to Hrazdan (see page 80). To reach Tsaghkadzor by public transport take either the train or minibus to Hrazdan, then a local minibus or taxi. There are minibuses to Garni village – note that they do not go as far as Geghard; take a taxi from Garni.

 WHERE TO STAY Everywhere in the province can be visited as a day trip from Yerevan. If planning a walking or winter skiing holiday Tsaghkadzor offers hotel and bed and breakfast accommodation. If you wish to spend several days exploring Khosrov Reserve (pages 181–4), mostly in Ararat province but usually entered from Garni, you may opt to stay in Garni, although for those with their own transport it can easily be done as several day trips from Yerevan.

Tsaghkadzor

Jupiter Hotel (32 rooms) Tsaghkunyats Sq; m 091 460617, 094 460617; e info@jupiter-hotel. info; www.jupiter-hotel.info. A new build, 4 floors, no lift. Wi-Fi. Accepts Visa & MasterCard. **$$**

Kecharis Hotel (34 rooms) 20 Orbeli Brothers St; ℓ 223 60409/509/609; e info@ kecharis.am; www.kecharis.am. A former department store, the space has been used imaginatively & attractively in this well-presented

hotel. Many facilities inc sauna. Disco w/end evenings in summer. Wi-Fi. Cards accepted. There is a Jazzve coffee shop in the hotel. Meals available, order in advance. **$$**

Tsaghkadzor General Sport Complex (182 rooms, of which 60 sgl) Tsaghkadzor City; ℓ 223 60524; e info@ sportcomplexhotel.com; www.sportcomplexhotel. com. 1½km uphill from town centre. Built to train Soviet athletes for 1968 Mexico Olympics,

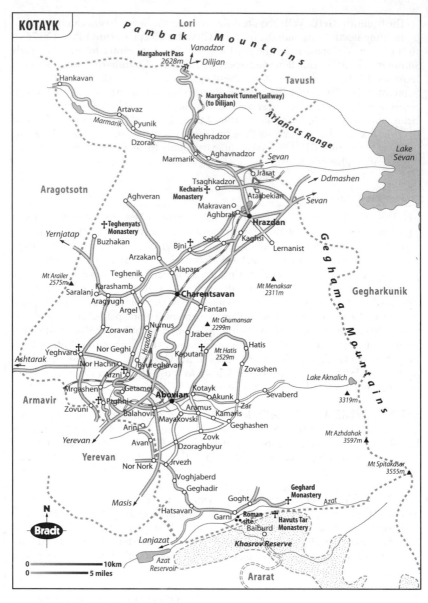

KOTAYK

Pambak Mountains
Lori
Vanadzor
Margahovit Pass 2628m → Dilijan
Hankavan
Tavush
Artavaz
Marmarik Pyunik
Dzorak
Meghradzor
Margahovit Tunnel (railway) (to Dilijan)
Atjanots Range
Aghavnadzor Sevan
Marmarik
Aragotsotn
Tsaghkadzor
Kecharis ✝ Monastery
Aghveran
Makravan
Aghbrak
Atarbekian
Ddmashen
Sevan
Lake Sevan
Hrazdan
✝ Teghenyats Monastery
Yernjatap
Buzhakan
Bjni ✝
Solak Kaghsi
Arzakan
Lernanist
Teghenik
Alapars
Mt Arailer 2575m ▲
Karashamb
Saralanj
Aragyugh
Argel
Charentsavan
Fantan
Mt Menaksar 2311m ▲
Gegharkunik
Zoravan
Nurnus
Mt Ghumansar 2299m ▲
Jraber
Hatis
Yeghvard ✝
Nor Geghi
Kaputan
Mt Hatis 2529m ▲
Ashtarak
Nor Hachn
Byureghavan
Zovashen
Arzni
Lake Aknalich
Mrgashen
Getamej
Kotayk
3319m ▲
Armavir
Ptghni ✝
Balahovit
Aramus
Akunk
Zar
Sevaberd
Zovuni
Arinj
Mayakovski
Kamaris
Mt Azhdahak 3597m ▲
Yerevan →
Avan
Zovk
Geghashen
Yerevan
Nor Nork
Jrvezh
Dzoraghbyur
Mt Spitaksar 3555m ▲
Voghjaberd
Geghadir
Geghard Monastery ✝
Masis →
Goght
Azat
Hatsavan
Garni
Roman site
Havuts Tar Monastery ✝
Lanjazat
Baiburd
Khosrov Reserve
N
Bradt
0 ———— 10km
0 ———— 5 miles
Azat Reservoir
Ararat
Geghama Mountains

this Soviet hotel has been well renovated. By Armenian standards the rooms are relatively small but look comfortable. Guests can use the ordinary swimming pool but not the Olympic pool, which is reserved for professional athletes only & has to be booked through the Armenian Sports Federation by the athlete's national organisation 3 months in advance. Wi-Fi. FB available. Cards accepted. **$$**

🏠 **Bagart Hotel Bistro** (6 rooms) Main Sq;

↳223 60295; m 093 594977, 091 439695. Opened 2007. Small but adequate rooms. B/fast inc but other meals not available. Guests can do their own cooking in the kitchen if they wish. Wi-Fi. Cards accepted. Price depends on size of room & whether there is a balcony. **$$–$**

🏠 **Writers Hotel** (77 rooms) Tsaghkadzor City; ↳223 60445; 10 281081 (Yerevan number); m 093 013044; e info@writershotel.am; www.

writershotel.am. A pleasant option, once called the House of Creativity of Writers. The statue in front of the guesthouse is of the writer Eghishe Charents. Set in attractive grounds & very clean. To stay here was until relatively recently a pure Soviet experience but modernisation has destroyed some of its period charm. It is very popular with conferences, & visitors may well find themselves talking to cardiologists or language teachers or some other professional group. They may also encounter spontaneous traditional singing & dancing on the part of the delegates. Most rooms have been fully & colourfully renovated but there remain a few cheaper rooms (*AMD13,000*) which have not yet been upgraded where visitors can still experience something of a Soviet-era bathroom. Wi-Fi. Cards accepted. B/fast extra AMD1,200pp; FB AMD4,000pp. **$**

Garni

🏠 **Garnietoun** (5 rooms) 30 Grigor Zohrab St, Garni; m 096 060470, 096 060480; e info@ garnitoun.com. The first hotel in Garni, opened 2013. A splendid situation on the edge of Garni Gorge; all rooms have balconies overlooking the gorge. Restaurant & café; they have their own bakery with tonir. Swimming pool. Wi-Fi. From

2014, the hotel hopes to organise hiking tours in Garni Gorge. Currently doesn't accept cards, but this may change. Even has its own small shrine, built on the site of an old sacred place & dedicated to St Thaddeus. **$$**

🏠 **The B&B of Narine Hovhannisian** 20 Charents St, Garni; m 091 528581. This homestay is a popular place to eat & stay. There are views of Garni Temple from the garden & back bedrooms. You don't have to stay here to get a meal but you must give 48hrs' notice to allow the food to be prepared. Groups can also be well fed here in the very pleasant garden. **$$**

Elsewhere in the province

🏠 **Arthurs Aghveran Resort Hotel** (60 rooms) Arzakan; 📞 226 61610; m 091 791227; e info@arthurs-hotel.am; www.arthurs-hotel. am. A new-build hotel, opened 2006, of the resort type (see page 85). In the hills at the far end of the Arzakan road, about 12km from Arzakan (northwest of Charentsavan). Suitable for those wanting either a restful few days away from everywhere or those wanting a comfortable base for walking. Swimming pools, indoor sport, gym, restaurant. Wi-Fi. Cards accepted. Accommodation in several separate buildings; steps up to them. **$$**

✕ **WHERE TO EAT AND DRINK** Apart from the eating possibilities mentioned above, such as the Jazzve café in the Kecharis Hotel at Tsaghkadzor, there is a pleasant café just below the temple at Garni, overlooking the gorge, and visitors will find plenty on offer for sale at both Garni Temple and Geghard Monastery. Why not try some of the dried-fruit sweetmeats or the round, freshly baked *gata* (see page 92).

OTHER PRACTICALITIES Entering the Khosrov Reserve at Garni requires advance permission (see page 181). There is free Wi-Fi for the whole of Tsaghkadzor. There is a local **tourist information office** (🕐 *10.00–17.00 daily*) on the main square in Garni village. It has few of the usual trappings but they can help with local accommodation, taxis or private car to Geghard.

NORTH FROM YEREVAN
Yeghvard and Kaputan These two villages in southern Kotayk, Yeghvard northwest of Yerevan, Kaputan northeast, have churches very similar in style to each other and to the much better known three-tier Mother of God Church at Noravank. The two churches, both also dedicated to the Mother of God, are small in floor area but disproportionately tall, have two storeys and are topped not by a tambour with cupola but by a belfry supported by columns. The lower storey of each is more or less square; the upper storey is a cross-shaped church. Access to the upper storey was by an external cantilevered staircase of which the top steps were stone while the lower were wooden and have now vanished. The only way now into the upper storey is by ladder. As well as these similarities there are also differences, in part accounted for

by the use of contrasting stone (warm pink tuff in the case of Yeghvard but a rather forbidding grey basalt, which is difficult to carve, at Kaputan).

To reach **Kaputan**, leave the main Yerevan to Sevan road at the Abovian turn-off and take the Kotayk road. At Kotayk take the left fork for Kaputan. The rather plain church, built in 1349, is on a hilltop above the village and the ground around it is strewn with shards of obsidian. The belfry has eight columns; the bell is missing. Among the votive offerings inside the church I was startled to see a reproduction of Salvador Dalí's *Christ of St John of the Cross*, the original of which hangs in my home country, in Glasgow's Kelvingrove Art Gallery!

After Kaputan the road goes on through the treeless upland to circumnavigate the eroded volcanic cone of **Mount Hatis** (2,529m). It is possible to do a loop back to Abovian although at the time of writing the road surface deteriorated after Zovashen.

Yeghvard is most easily reached direct from Yerevan although it may be convenient to combine it with the churches of the Kasakh Gorge (pages 162–7) and travel to Yeghvard via Ashtarak. Coming into Yeghvard a stretch of dual carriageway is reached. Keep on round the edge of the town until you see the church on the right above the houses. The church, which dates from 1301, is set in a well-kept garden in the middle of the village and is highly decorated both externally and inside. The upper church is particularly notable for its very fine carved animals: a lion and a bull on the west façade, an ibex on the north, a leopard killing an ibex on the east, and an eagle with a lamb in its talons on the south. Inside, the apse has radiating black and red tuff and there is geometrical carving around the *bema*'s two doors. The belfry has 16 columns and the bell has been rehung.

Elsewhere in the village are the remains of a (harder to find) basilica church of the 5th or 6th century. Turn left, just after a large shop, near to where you turned right for the two-storey church, and/or ask the way.

Some 6km north of Yeghvard is the ruined circular **Zoravar Church** at Zoravan. Like all so-called circular churches it is actually polygonal. Just north of the right turn for Zoravan village a track goes off left just beyond a cemetery. Follow the track along the side of the cemetery keeping an irrigation channel to your right. The church can be seen across the hillside. Standing on the lower slopes of Mount Ara looking across the Arax plain to Mount Ararat, the church was built in the second half of the 7th century by Prince Grigor Mamikonian. Some reconstruction was carried out in the 1970s. Standing on a circular base the church has eight apses, the east altar apse being wider than the others. The tambour, cylindrical inside but 12-sided externally, is carried on the apse arches and the pillars between apses. Externally the east apse is pentagonal, the other seven are three-sided. The church was lit by three windows in the east apse, one in each of the other seven apses and four windows in the tambour, at the cardinal points.

Further north **Teghenyats Monastery** is reached from the village of **Buzhakan**, a resort centre in Soviet days and an excellent centre for walking. Keep straight on through the village until the main asphalt road forks left and a dirt road continues straight ahead. In dry weather it is possible to drive all the way up to the monastery but parking at the start of the track and walking the last 3km to Teghenyats Monastery makes a very **beautiful walk**. The first section is between fields as far as a half-built guesthouse, construction of which was halted when the Soviet Union collapsed. The track then continues uphill through forest. There is a small river to the right down in the gorge and the track, after winding along the hillside, drops down to ford it. It is difficult to cross when the river is in spate. The track then climbs straight up to the monastery, with springs and places to picnic on the way. The monastery is evocatively situated with the Tsaghkunyats mountain range forming the backdrop.

The ruins occupy a large area. The ruinous 10th-century **church** looks as if it had a barrel-vaulted roof and the front of the *bema* has interesting carvings.

The massive red and black 12th- to 13th-century *gavit*, the best-preserved building, was domed; there is carved decoration on what remains of the base of the tambour. Northwest of the *gavit* low-walled ruins lead to the remains of the 13th to 14th-century **dining room**. One enters through the south doorway. Massive pillars on the north side supported what was probably a barrel-vaulted roof. At present the two doorways in the north wall lead only to an earth face. Immediately north of the *gavit* is a building with free-standing columns which has either been built into the hillside or excavated from it. There is evidence of other buildings to the west, south and northeast of the main complex. The graveyard, with tombstones shaped to look like sheep and horses, covers the hillside to the south of the monastery. Snow can linger up here well into late April; one visit in the spring revealed bear footprints in the snow while further down the valley an array of spring flowers rapidly succeeded the melting snow.

NORTHEAST FROM YEREVAN The main road from Yerevan to Sevan bisects the province from south to north, staying above and to the east of the Hrazdan River gorge. Leaving Yerevan it is notable for the number of casinos since they were banished from the city and also, in late summer, for the number of sheep herded into pens for sale. To the right of the road, on top of a hill, can be seen what looks like a Russian church. It is the mansion of the owner of the Kotayk brewery.

The first point of interest is the ruinous **church of Ptghni** in the middle of the village to the west of the highway. It is not permitted to turn left off the highway and Ptghni is not signposted on the northbound carriageway. It is necessary to go beyond the exit for Ptghni, do a U-turn at the next U-turn sign, travel south and then turn right down into the village. The road skirts the outside of the village; keep bearing right until you see the church through a gap in the houses. The church is a large basilica of the 6th century whose cupola and roof have collapsed. The north façade of the church and much of the west end are still standing and were stabilised in 1939–40. Further restoration was undertaken in 1964 which included demolishing a 19th-century church that had been built adjacent. The size of the building is impressive as is the massiveness of the one surviving arch of the four which once supported the cupola. Over the windows, most notably on the south façade, carvings depict angels, hunting scenes, saints, plants and fruits.

To continue north after exiting Ptghni it is necessary to turn right, travel south and then do a U-turn.

Probably the most noticeable feature of the industrialised town of **Abovian** (named after the writer Khachatur Abovian) is the enormous new red tuff **church of St John the Baptist**, dedicated in 2013. Inside there are four full-length murals of four St Johns: on the north wall St John the Evangelist and St John the Baptist, on the south wall St John Chrysostom and St John Mandakouni, Katholikos AD478–90. The church was funded by the leader of the Prosperous Armenia political party. With its lavish furnishing, mass of carvings (some of which are quite interesting) and columned turrets topped with gold crosses, some have seen it as a symbol of the huge gap between rich and poor in Armenia.

Arzni, which is signposted off the highway, has a tiny 5th- or 6th-century octagonal church, the **St Kiraki Baptistry**. Octagonal on the outside, four-apsed inside with round windows in the thick walls, it is built on a stepped square base, which is probably older than the church, perhaps pagan. These features make it unique among similar contemporary Armenian buildings. It resembles early

Christian baptistries and may be Armenia's only example of a separate baptistry building. Its red-painted metal roof is anachronistic, as is the house number (No 6) which has been assigned to it! Arzni is a large village and apparently has seven churches. To reach the baptistery continue on the main Arzni road (2nd Street) as it bears left into the village, then take the third turning on the right (5th Street). The baptistry is at the end of the street. Arzni's main claim to fame is that it was developed from 1925 onwards as the Soviet Union's first purpose-built spa. Coming from the highway, where the road into the village bears left, a road goes straight ahead and descends into the Hrazdan Gorge which is lined here with huge guesthouses, mostly derelict and spoiling what must once have been an attractive setting. The sheer number of people who could have been treated here simultaneously with water from the mineral springs is truly amazing. Building works suggest that rehabilitation of the spa may be envisaged. It is possible to continue north either on the main highway to the east of the gorge or on the gorge road which stays on the west side of the river (see opposite).

The **main road** north now climbs steeply upwards to reach the plateau. Shortly before the summit, more conspicuous when travelling southbound, Lenin's name is clearly legible spelled out in trees on the hillside. Up on the plateau the industrial town of **Charentsavan** can be seen to the left. Most of the industry is now closed. Leave the road by the Charentsavan exit just north of the town, turn first right (not signposted) just before a gas station, and head west bypassing Charentsavan to **Alapars** (page 215) and **Arzakan**. At Arzakan turn right, immediately after crossing a bridge over the Hrazdan River, for **Bjni** which has a fortress and two interesting churches. The dome of the main church in the village appears above trees on the left. It is dedicated to the **Mother of God** and dates from 1031. It has a disproportionately large circular tambour and umbrella cupola as well as some fine khachkars from the 13th to 15th centuries. The small belfry was added in 1275 and the fortified wall in the 17th century. Used as a byre in the Stalinist era, it was restored in 1956 with assistance from the Gulbenkian Foundation. Just below the church to the east is the 13th-century **St Gevorg Church** with older khachkars built into the walls. The **fortress**, up on the small plateau within the village, was built in the 9th or 10th century by the Pahlavuni family. Parts of the northern and western walls remain but there are only traces of other buildings in what is a fairly large area. The entrance to the secret passage down to the village can be seen but it is blocked after 40m. The best way up to the fortress is from the east. The **small church** at Bjni on top of a hill beyond the fortress is dedicated to St Sargis and dates from the 7th century. It has an octagonal tambour and retains a roof of tuff tiles. To reach it continue along the road then turn left just after crossing a tributary of the river. The track then winds up the right side of the hill to the church or you can park at the bottom and walk up the path round the left of the hill.

It is possible to continue from Bjni direct to **Hrazdan** town along the scenic Hrazdan River, rather than returning to the main highway, the road running first along the flat river valley, with rocky cliffs to the right and hills to the left, and then climbing above the river as the gorge narrows. Coming into Hrazdan the road (some bad pot-holes here) skirts the western half of the Hrazdan Reservoir to join the Hrazdan to Tsaghkadzor road. Hrazdan itself has minimal appeal. It was heavily industrialised in the Soviet period and still has a large thermal power station. Within the municipality of Hrazdan, to the west, is the village (sometimes called a suburb) of **Makravan** with the **monastery of Makravank**. It is not easy to find; keep asking. The 13th-century church dedicated to the Mother of God has a tall round tambour and a conical cupola. On its south side is the smaller 10th-century Holy Redeemer

Church and to the west a ruined 13th-century *gavit* with many khachkars piled up around the remaining walls. The cemetery has gravestones dating from the 10th to 14th centuries.

ARZNI TO HRAZDAN VIA THE HRAZDAN GORGE This is a slower route than the main highway but it gives a very different view of the region. Not only is one much more aware of the gorge itself but also of the surprisingly large villages or small towns, to which one is more or less oblivious when using the main highway. From **Argel**, about 10km north of Arzni, there is a choice of three roads to Arzakan. One continues on the west bank of the river. It is possible to cross the river at Argel and there is then a further choice, either to stay close to the east bank of the river and cross back at Arzakan or to climb up to Karenis and go via the outskirts of Charentsavan and Alapars, joining the east bank road to cross the river. (It is of course possible to join the main highway from Charentsavan.) Argel has one of Armenia's largest hydro-electric power plants, the **Argel Gyumush power station**, with a capacity of 224MW. The road across the river actually takes you into the power station grounds then out the other side, an arrangement which is presumably the result of another road bridge a little upstream having been lost. Before reaching the river a narrow alley off left leads to Argel's **St George Church**. Built in 1890, incorporating earlier remains, this restored basilica church is dwarfed by its bell tower. A crowded cemetery extends east from the church.

Charentsavan was founded in 1948 to house workers building the hydro-electric plant and then became heavily industrialised. With the collapse of the Soviet Union there are now vast areas of depressing derelict factories. Descending from Charentsavan one reaches the much pleasanter town of **Alapars**. As well as a large red and grey (19th-century?) three-aisled Mother of God basilica, Alapars has two much earlier churches, both on Vardan Mamikonian Square. The most obvious, because of its incongruous red bell tower, is the **Vardan Zoravar Church** built by Prince Grigor in 901, rebuilt in 1901 and recently renovated. Inside it now has a typical village *zham* appearance. Local legend says that one of the stones contains a drop of blood from Vardan Mamikonian, hero of the Battle of Avarayr, AD451 (see pages 17–18). Just east is the earlier three-apse cross-dome 7th-century **church of St John**. At first glance it is not obvious that it is a church, the restoration of 1997 having given it a square metal roof in place of what would originally have been a dome. However, it stands on a three-step base, has khachkars embedded in its walls and a new carving of a church over the entrance. On the walls of the south apse are fragments of frescoes. The churches are usually locked but the key-holder, Zina, lives next door at number six; she is willing to open the churches for visitors.

From **Arzakan** the gorge road continues to Bjni as described on page 214. A side road goes north from Arzakan for about 10km, climbing through the wooded hills to **Aghveran**. This is a favourite leisure area for Armenians and the attractive side gorge has holiday homes, former *pensionats* and picnic areas. At the end of the road, closed rusting gates indicate another derelict Soviet holiday complex.

Tsaghkadzor and Kecharis Monastery

Tsaghkadzor (*telephone code: 223*) is Armenia's principal ski resort and the number of guesthouses reflects this. It is also an excellent centre for walking and the scope for doing so is extended by using the chair lift, which operates all year. In summer thousands of anemones (*Pulsatilla armena*) can be seen in grassland a short distance above the chair-lift terminus. A useful brochure containing a map of the town, details of ski facilities and hotels is published by Collage Publishing House in Yerevan. The ski resort, used for Olympic

4

training in Soviet days, is located on the eastern slopes of Mount Tegenis. The main season is December to the end of February and the snow can be up to 1m deep. Instruction is available and equipment can be hired at the skiing complex, as can snowboards and sledges. In winter a **skating rink** is open in the town's main square. The **chair lift** (☉ *summer 09.45–17.45, shorter hrs in winter*), opened in 1967 and rebuilt in 2004 by an Italian company, operates in three sections from the base of the ski slopes to the top at 1,966m. Each section costs AMD1,500, thus AMD4,500 the whole way. Two other chair lifts operate at different points on the slopes. There is a **rescue service** (☏ *223 60030*) and any injuries requiring hospital treatment go to the hospital in Hrazdan. The Tsaghkadzor Sport Base, built to train Soviet athletes for the 1968 Mexico Summer Olympics, is now a hotel (see pages 209–10).

The **Orbeli Brothers' House Museum** (☏ *223 60552; www.orbelimuseum.am;* ☉ *11.00–18.00 Tue–Sun; adult/child AMD500/200*) is, appropriately, on Orbeli Brothers Street opposite Kecharis Hotel. Of the three brothers, Ruben (1880–1943) was a marine archaeologist, Levon (1882–1958) head of the Military Medical Academy and Joseph (1887–1961) an archaeologist who took part in the excavations of Ani as well as being director of the Hermitage Museum in Leningrad. The museum contains personal belongings of the brothers and copies of their publications. An information leaflet in English is available, as is a booklet, produced for the 1,050th anniversary of Ani, detailing Joseph Orbeli's work in Ani with Nicholas Marr, the Georgian-born (of Scottish father and Georgian mother) historian and linguist who undertook annual excavations in Ani 1904–17. Disappointingly, for non-Armenian visitors, there is little accessible detail of the brothers' work in the museum displays.

Kecharis Monastery is situated in the village of Tsaghkadzor, Kecharis being an earlier name for the village. The **main church**, dedicated to St Gregory the Illuminator, was erected in 1003 by Grigor Pahlavuni (990–1059). Given his age, his personal involvement must have been slight. Son of the Lord of Bjni, he was to become a distinguished theologian and writer acquiring the title Grigor Magistros from the Byzantine rulers after their takeover of the kingdom of Ani from Gagik II in 1045. The circular tambour and conical cupola were damaged by an earthquake in 1927 but were restored between 1997 and 2000. To the south of St Gregory's lies the small **Holy Cross Chapel** which dates from 1051. It too has a conical cupola but its circular tambour is decorated with six arcatures. After the construction of these buildings the Seljuk conquest put paid to any further work, the region remaining under their rule until their defeat by the Georgians with Armenian support in 1196. Work immediately restarted and by 1206 St Gregory's had acquired its large *gavit* whose roof is supported by four free-standing columns. The final church, the so-called **cathedral**, lies to the south of Holy Cross and was built immediately after the *gavit* by Prince Vasak Prosh, being completed in 1214. As in other churches of the period, the corner rooms at the west end have two storeys with the upper storey being accessed by cantilevered stairs. It too has a conical cupola, the circular tambour having 12 arcatures. The Mongol invasions in the late 1230s saw Kecharis badly damaged but it was restored by 1248. Presumably it was at this restoration that the tympanum of the doorway leading from the *gavit* into St Gregory's acquired its Georgian-style frescoes. The monastery is once more a functioning church with new furnishings and embroidered curtains in all three churches. The embroidered text on the north wall of Holy Cross is the Lord's Prayer. About 100m from the main group of buildings is the small **Chapel of the Holy Resurrection** with its high circular tambour and another conical cupola. It dates from 1220 and was probably used as the family burial vault for the founders of the cathedral.

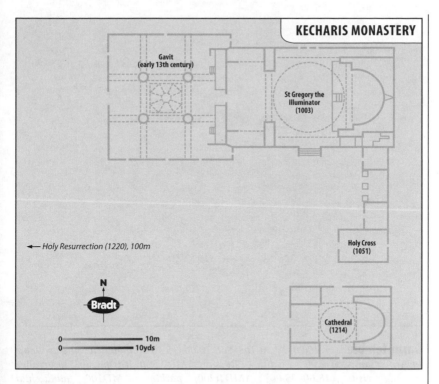

KECHARIS MONASTERY

Gavit
(early 13th century)

St Gregory the
Illuminator
(1003)

Holy Cross
(1051)

← Holy Resurrection (1220), 100m

N

Bradt

0 ——————— 10m
0 ——————— 10yds

Cathedral
(1214)

Hankavan
From a large roundabout in the Jrarat district of Hrazdan (from where the roads to Ddmashen and Tsaghkadzor also go off) a road goes northwest along the Marmarik River for 30km to Hankavan. This valley is another favoured holiday area for Armenians, but is rarely visited by tourists. There is nothing of historic interest but it is an attractive road with walking potential and the possibility of bathing in hot springs at the end. The road and railway follow the broad river valley for the first 15km or so. At Meghradzor the railway turns north to enter the Margahovit Tunnel through the Pambak range of mountains to reach Lori province. The road then climbs towards a renovated reservoir and beyond that to the village of Hankavan. *En route* are two enormous, mostly deserted Soviet-era buildings and the Hankavan sanatorium which is being renovated. The road finally ends in a clump of nettles in the middle of a large derelict Soviet holiday resort. Set in a superb position it is a sad sight with its ruined and overgrown accommodation, clinic and netball courts. Just south of Hankavan one of the hot springs in the area has been 'privatised' with the construction of three small and two larger hot water pools and changing cubicles. To book a soak in a pool call Benik (m *077 440828*). The cost is AMD4,000/hour/pool.

EAST FROM YEREVAN
A half-day excursion from Yerevan to **Garni Temple** and **Geghard Monastery** is probably Armenia's most popular trip for visitors and is well worth making. About halfway from Yerevan, near the village of Voghjaberd, it is worth stopping at the **memorial arch** to the writer Eghishe Charents (see pages 51–2) as it offers splendid views across the valley to Mount Ararat. During the descent to Garni the **Azat Reservoir** can be seen to the southwest; a right turn, signposted to Artashat, goes to the reservoir which is a favoured picnic spot in summer.

4

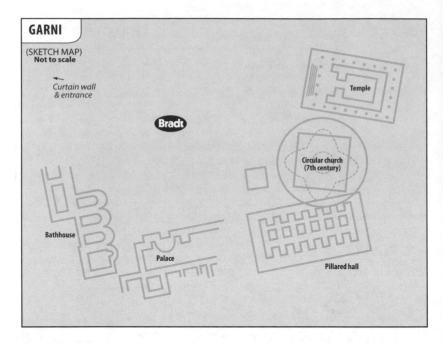

GARNI

(SKETCH MAP)
Not to scale

Curtain wall
& entrance

Bradt

Temple

Circular church
(7th century)

Bathhouse

Palace

Pillared hall

Garni Temple (⏲ *10.00–17.30 Tue–Sat, 10.00–15.30 Sun; guided tours available in Armenian AMD1,000, English & Russian AMD2,500; it is possible to arrange evening visits (18.00–23.00) AMD1,200; parking AMD100; adult/child AMD1,000/100*) Garni Temple, as it is called, is Armenia's only Graeco-Roman-style building and is one of the few historical monuments in Armenia for which there is an admission charge. Although usually said to be a 1st-century pagan temple, probably devoted to Mithra, more recently some historians have suggested that it is more likely to be the tomb built for a Romanised ruler, probably Sohaemus, in which case the construction would have been around AD175. It is the best known building on what is an extensive archaeological site, a triangle of readily defensible land jutting out into a bend of the Azat River far below. Archaeologists have discovered the remains of a Neolithic encampment; an inscription in cuneiform from the early 8th century BC on a *vishap* stone recording the capture of Garni Fortress by the Urartian king Argishti I; a Greek inscription on a huge basalt block recording the construction of a later fortress here by King Trdat I; a 3rd-century royal palace and bathhouse; churches from the 5th and 7th centuries; and the 9th-century palace of the Katholikos. Plainly the site has had a long and important history.

The 'temple' itself was destroyed in the great earthquake of 1679 but well restored between 1969 and 1975. It is easy to see which stones are the surviving originals and which are the modern replacements. The building looks rather like a miniature Parthenon and has 24 columns supporting the roof with Ionic capitals and Attic bases. The frieze depicts a variety of leaves and fruits while the cornice shows the heads of lions exhibiting a variety of expressions. Nine steep steps lead up to the interior in which are a reconstructed and probably inauthentic altar and sacrificial pit. The building differs from most other Graeco-Roman buildings in being constructed of basalt; the use of such a material probably required the employment of Armenian craftsmen skilled in the technique of carving so hard a rock.

Close to the temple are the remains of other buildings. The circular building next to the temple on the west side was a 7th-century church with four apses while northwest of the church was a palace and beyond it a bathhouse. The bathhouse has a mosaic floor which depicts sea gods framed by fish and nereids together with the ambiguous words: 'We worked but did not get anything'. Some further reconstruction was started in the early years of this century and the walls of the church and palace were built up slightly. This does give an idea of the original layout but work on the church in particular was most insensitively carried out using black and bright red stones which looked garish and out of place. There were understandable protests and work was suspended.

Other sights around Garni The area has several other sights, notably the churches of Mother of God and St Mashtots and the striking rock formations in Garni Gorge. **Khosrov State Reserve** is also accessed via the gorge (see below). The **Mother of God Church** in the centre of the town (just to the right and behind the information centre) is a red and grey 12th-century basilica with a small porch incorporating a belfry. Once inside allow a little time for your eyes to adapt to the dim interior, the better to appreciate the red and grey decoration and the unusual, for Armenia, red tuff altar screen in this atmospheric church. The smooth dressed stone of the four square, free-standing pillars contrasts with the rougher stone of the walls and barrel-vaulted roof. The more elaborate **St Mashtots Church** is in the eastern part of the town, set back on the left from the road down to the gorge (see page 182). It is a small square single-aisle church with a 12-sided tambour with much geometric carving and windows in four of its sides. The pink cupola and roofs contrast attractively with the grey stonework of the walls and tambour. There is more elaborate carving around the door and the windows.

There are two main ways down into the **gorge**, on foot by the path to the left of the temple entrance (see page 182 for directions) or by the road which goes down to the river past St Mashtots (see page 182 for directions). In the gorge are astonishing **rock formations** – regular columns of basalt which are similar to those of the Giant's Causeway, County Antrim, Northern Ireland and Fingal's Cave, Staffa, Scotland. They are also similar to those further east in Armenia along the Arpa Gorge near Gndevaz. The gorge has a flora of drought-tolerant shrubs including *Spirea crenata,* willow-leaved pear (*Pyrus salicifolia*) and the rare yellow *Rosa hemisphaerica.* Herbaceous plants include *Campanula, Verbascum* and spiny *Astragalus* (goat's thorn).

Geghard Monastery (⊕ *during usual church opening hrs 09.00–18.00*) One of the great sites of Armenia and on the UNESCO World Heritage List since 2000, Geghard ('Spear') Monastery in its gorge setting should ideally be seen when several of the country's less extraordinary churches have been visited. It is then easier to appreciate what makes this one different. Its unusual feature is that it is partly an ordinary surface structure and partly cut into the cliff. The name dates from the 13th century and reflects the bringing here of a spear said to have been the one which pierced the side of Christ at Calvary. This spear, a shaft with a diamond-shaped head into which a cross has been cut, can now be seen in the treasury at Ejmiatsin. It is inside a gilded silver case made for it in 1687. Visiting Geghard on a Sunday morning is an enthralling experience with beautiful singing from the choir, and beautifully groomed animals brought for sacrifice after the service.

The first monastery at this site was called Ayrivank ('Cave monastery'). It was founded as early as the 4th century but was burned down and plundered in 923

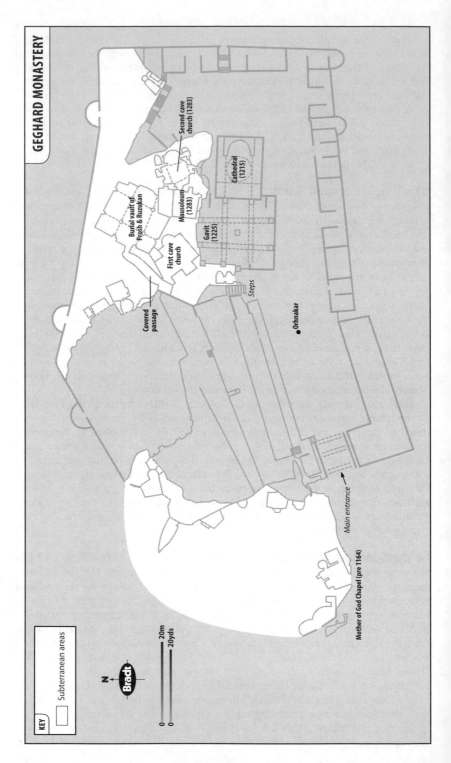

GEGHARD MONASTERY

KEY

Subterranean areas

N

Bradt

0   20m
0   20yds

Second cave
church (1283)

Burial vault of
Proshi & Ruzukan

Mausoleum
(1283)

Cathedral
(1215)

First cave
church

Gavit
(1225)

Covered
passage

Steps

● Orhnakar

Main entrance

Mother of God Chapel (pre 1164)

by Nasr, a subordinate of Yusuf, the caliph's Governor of Azerbaijan. Yusuf had just spent five years in prison for rebellion against the caliph. Nasr continued the rebellion, seeking to extend his own power and to enforce conversion of the Christian population to Islam.

Thereafter the monastery declined until the revival of monastery building in the late 12th century. The earliest surviving part, the **Chapel of the Mother of God**, dates from before 1164 and is situated above the road just before the gateway to the main monastery complex. It is partly a surface structure and partly hewn into the rock, rectangular in plan but with a semicircular apse. Adjoining it are other passages and small rooms in the rock.

In total, surrounding the main site are more than 20 other rock-hewn chapels and service premises, many of which have carvings. Also outside the gate are small ledges on to which visitors try to throw stones. If a stone remains on the ledge then the thrower's wish is supposed to come true.

The main buildings of the monastery are surrounded by walls on three sides and a cliff face on the other. Construction was started by the Zakarian family who came into possession of it after they had commanded Armenian forces which joined with the Georgians to defeat the Seljuks. The main cathedral was built in 1215 and is of the cross-dome type, the circular tambour being decorated with graceful arcature and narrow windows and topped by a conical cupola. Between the spans of arcature and on the portals and cornices are depicted a variety of birds and animals as well as floral and geometrical patterns. The southern façade is particularly interesting. Above the doorway with two doves facing each other is a lion attacking an ox, the emblem of the Zakarian family. The *gavit* at the west side which is attached to the rock face was completed by 1225. It is much plainer than the main church though the tympanum has an attractive floral design within an ogee arch.

The Zakarians sold the monastery to the Prosh family who constructed the subterranean part carved out of rock. In the **first cave church**, on the northwest side, is a spring. It bears the architect's name, Galdzag, and incorporates some fine khachkars as well as stalactite decoration around the roof opening. The Prosh family **mausoleum** and the second cave church at the northeast were probably by the same architect and completed by 1283. On the north wall of the mausoleum above the archways is a relief carving of a goat with a ring in its mouth to which is attached a rope whose two ends are round the necks of two lions which are looking outwards. The ends of the lions' tails are dragons looking upwards. Below all this, an eagle with spreading wings grasps a lamb in its talons. Both here and in the rock-cut churches there is much elaborate carving of crosses, geometrical shapes and khachkars. Rather surprisingly to the right of the entrance to the mausoleum are carved two sirens, mythical creatures with the crowned head of a woman and the body of a bird.

The **second cave church**, dedicated to the Mother of God, leads off from the mausoleum. Some of the khachkars show human figures including one who holds a spear pointing down while he blows an uplifted horn. To the right at the stairs leading to the altar dais is the figure of a goat. At the left side on the altar dais is a stone seat with a lion's head forming the end of the top of the back and to the right of the dais is a khachkar of two doves each side of a cross. The church, despite being underground, retains the same cross shape with tambour and cupola as other Armenian churches. There is an opening to the outside world at the top of the cupola which admits light.

The *gavit* which formed the burial vault of Prince Papak Prosh and his wife Ruzukan was hewn in 1288. It is at a higher level and to reach it, go up the steps at the west end of the complex and then follow the narrow subterranean passage to the right decorated with khachkars carved into the rock. The roof is supported by four pillars and in the floor is a hole looking down into the mausoleum below. The acoustics in this *gavit* are amazing. Anyone standing here and singing, particularly by the northeast pillar, sounds like an entire choir.

Other features of interest are the small **rock-hewn chapel** adjacent to the steps leading up to the *gavit*. Over the door is a carving of a figure wearing what appears to be a Mithraic-style hat. The *orhnakar* is in the middle of the paved area within the monastery walls but the *mataghatun* is outside the small eastern gateway. Around the boundary wall are various service buildings; that at the northeast corner is a **bakery** complete with *tonir*. Most date from the 17th century but those at the southwest corner only from 1968 to 1971.

After so much culture it is worth, on leaving Geghard, buying some freshly baked *gata* or some fruit *lavash* from the women who sell it near the entrance. The plum is particularly good.

Botanists may wish to explore the river valley with its wealth of herbaceous plants, including orchids, and trees. Oriental wild apple *Malus orientalis* and Caucasian pear *Pyrus caucasia* flourish on boulders in the middle of the fast-flowing river and wild grape vine *Vitis sylvestris* scrambles through trees, including *Euonymus*, *Cornus*, *Sorbus* and *Acer ibericum*, on the riverbank.

5

The Northern Provinces

The three northern provinces of Shirak, Lori and Tavush are very different from each other. **Shirak** is mostly a high plateau while **Lori** is characterised by its deep gorges; **Tavush** retains extensive forest cover. Most visitors who combine a visit to Armenia with one to Georgia cross Lori between Yerevan and the Georgian border, seeing some of the monasteries of the Debed Valley *en route*. Others cross Tavush via the town of Dilijan with its attractive wooden buildings, combining Tavush with a visit to Lake Sevan in neighbouring Gegharkunik province. The monasteries of Sanahin, Haghpat, Haghartsin and Goshavank are all much visited, and others such as Odzun receive a fair number of visitors, though such gems as Makaravank and Hnevank still see only a few. All three provinces have impressive scenery and contain interesting historical sites.

SHIRAK PROVINCE

Shirak province is bounded to the west by Turkey and to the north by Georgia. In the south the border with Turkey passes through the Akhurian Reservoir, the water being shared between Armenia and Turkey. Mostly a high plateau, it becomes increasingly hilly nearer the Georgian border and to the east where it borders Lori province. In the northwest corner is Lake Arpi National Park. Shirak is off the main tourist routes and even such fine monasteries as **Marmashen** and **Harichavank** are seen by few tourists. Those interested in churches should also visit **Anipemza** whose basilica church, although roofless, is one of the oldest in Armenia.

GETTING THERE AND AROUND   The only sizeable town in the province is **Gyumri**. It has road links to the south and east and there is a border crossing to Georgia in the north, at Bavra. One of the few **rail routes** in Armenia runs from Yerevan to Gyumri and thence eastwards across Lori province to enter Georgia at the Bagratashen border crossing in Tavush province. For trains to Gyumri and general comments on transport see pages 79–83. **Minibuses** depart from Gyumri's bus station (*avtokayan*) at the south end of Shahumian Street. This is one of Armenia's pleasanter bus stations and displays a timetable on the wall. Minibuses ply between Yerevan and Gyumri (*AMD1,500*) approximately half-hourly 07.00–19.00. For Yerevan there is no fixed schedule; the 15-seat vehicles leave when they are full. Minibuses go virtually everywhere. Other examples of longer routes are: buses or minibuses leave for Vanadzor (*AMD800*) at approximately hourly intervals between 10.00 and 16.30, for Bavra (*AMD500*) at roughly three-hour intervals between 08.45 and 17.30 and for Ejmiatsin (*AMD1,200*) at 10.00. **Taxis** also wait at the bus station. A taxi to Yerevan costs about AMD10,000 and, like the minibus, will usually leave when full (*AMD2,500pp*).

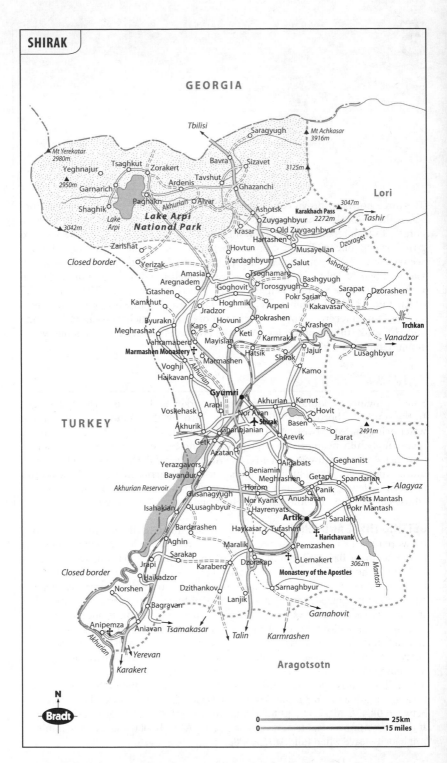

SHIRAK

GEORGIA

Mt Achkasar
3916m

Saragyugh

Tbilisi

Mt Yerekatar
2980m
Yeghnajur   Tsaghkut   Zorakert   Bavra   Sizavet   3125m▲
       ▲   Lori
        2950m   Garnarich   Ardenis   Tavshut   Ghazanchi
                                                                                            3047m
Shaghik   Paghakn   Akhurian   Alvar   Ashotsk   Karakhach Pass   2272m   Tashir
                                                          Zuygaghbyur
       3042m   Lake   Lake Arpi   Krasar   Old Zuygaghbyur   Dzoraget
                  Arpi   National Park   Hartashen
       Zarishat   Hovtun   Musayelian   Ashotsk
Closed border   Yerizak   Vardaghbyur   Salut
                Amasia   Tsoghamarg   Bashgyugh
              Aregnadem   Goghovit   Torosgyugh   Sarapat   Dzorashen
       Gtashen   Hoghmik   Pokr Sariar   Kakavasar
       Kamkhut   Jradzor   Arpeni
              Byurakn   Hovuni   Pokrashen   Trchkan
       Meghrashat   Kaps   Keti   Krashen   Vanadzor
            Vahramaberd Mayisian   Karmrakar   Jajur   Lusaghbyur
       Marmashen Monastery ✝   Hatsik   Shirak
              Voghji   Marmashen   Kamo
              Haikavan

                              Gyumri   Akhurian   Karnut
                     Arapi   Nor Avan   Hovit
       Voskehask   ✝ Shirak   Basen
TURKEY   Akhurik   Gharibjanian   Arevik   Jrarat   2491m
                     Getk   Azatan
       Yerazgavors   Aigabats   Geghanist
       Bayandur   Beniamin   Meghrashen Getapi Spandarian
Akhurian Reservoir   Horom   Panik   Alagyaz
       Isahakian   Gusanagyugh   Nor Kyank Anushavan   Mets Mantash
            Lusaghbyur   Hayrenyats   Pokr Mantash
            Bardzrashen   Artik   Saralanj
                     Haykasar Tufashen   Harichavank ✝
       Aghin   Maralik   Pemzashen
       Sarakap   Dzorakap ✝ Lernakert   3062m
Closed border   Jrapi   Karaberd   Monastery of the Apostles   Mantash
       Norshen   Haikadzor   Dzithankov   Sarnaghbyur
            Bagravan   Lanjik   Garnahovit
Anipemza ✝   Aniavan Tsamakasar
            Akhurian   Talin   Karmrashen
                  Yerevan
            Karakert   Aragotsotn

N

Bradt

0 _____ 25km
0 _____ 15 miles

WHERE TO STAY The only hotels that can be recommended are in Gyumri. In Artik there is a Soviet-era hotel which has a couple of renovated rooms. See pages 85–7 for general comments on accommodation.

Gyumri

Map, page 227.

Alexandrapol Hotel (19 rooms) 70 Mayakovski St; 312 50051; e info@ alexandrapolhotel.am; www.alexandrapolhotel. am. A new hotel of international standard not far from Gyumri's central square. Describes itself as a hotel palace. Heavy imperial-style decoration & furnishing. If you want to pretend you are a monarch this hotel might suit. Restaurant. Wi-Fi. Accepts cards. Has a range of suites up to presidential at AMD120,000. **$$$**

Araks Hotel (23 rooms) 25 Gorki St; 312 51199, 54435; e araks95@web.am; www. arakshotel.am. This handsome black building with an impressive marble entrance hall is a former police HQ. It has been fully restored & has well-appointed rooms. Wi-Fi. Meals other than b/fast must be ordered in advance. Accepts Visa & MasterCard. **$$**

Berlin Art Hotel (formerly Gästehaus Berlin) (15 rooms) 25 Haghtanak Av; 312 57659, 53148; e info@berlinhotel-gyumri.am; www.berlinarthotel.am. Opened by the German Red Cross after the earthquake – hence the former name. It is attached to a clinic although being ill is not a requisite of staying here. Small attractive hotel with helpful staff & displays of work by local artists & sculptors. Meals other than b/fast must be ordered in advance. Tours of the region can be organised for approx AMD10,000pp. Can also arrange homestays & cross-country skiing. Wi-Fi. Cards accepted. Discounts for members of humanitarian organisations & long-term guests. **$$**

Nane Hotel (formerly Hotel Isuz) (16 rooms) 1/5 Garegin Nzhdeh St; 312 33369; e info@nanehotel.am; www.nanehotel.am. This relatively new hotel underwent further complete renovation in 2010/11. Facilities are of a high standard. The façade preserves that of a former factory which was destroyed during the earthquake. Pleasant, well laid out garden with café. Restaurant. Wi-Fi. Cards accepted. A little

further from the town centre, approx 2km, than the website implies. **$$**

Kama Guesthouse (23 rooms) 3/2 Garegin Nzhdeh St; 312 52382, 30777; m 094 201208, 055 301208; e kamahotel@mail.ru. More like a very basic hostel than hotel. Near Nane Hotel (see below) round the back of the building. Wi-Fi. Prices range from AMD2,500pp in a trpl with separate shared toilets, to AMD16,000 for a cleaner dbl with shower. **$**

Elsewhere in the province

Homestay in Ardenis village Near Lake Arpi (see pages 233–4). This can be arranged through Berlin Art Hotel, Gyumri (see below) or contact Shakro, m 093 824005, the local manager of the Lake Arpi Important Bird Area. He & his wife offer B&B. I personally enjoyed my stay here. Facilities are basic but the beds are cosy in what can be a chilly part of Armenia for much of the year & the food is wonderful, the vast majority being their own produce. Evening meal available with advance notice. Shakro has a fund of knowledge & is also an expert taxidermist. I shared my bedroom with a large stuffed wild boar & a Eurasian eagle-owl. AMD9,000pp. **$$**

Lake Arpi National Park HQ Beside Lake Arpi at Paghakn village. One very basic dbl available. Can be arranged through Shakro (see above) or via the deputy director of Khosrov State Reserve (page 181). If no member of staff is around when you arrive, the security guard for the reservoir's dam will call someone for you. **$**

Ojakh Hotel (9 rooms) 3 Yekatughain St, Artik; 0244 51818. A Soviet-era 7-storey hotel of which 2 floors are in use. B/fast not inc, but available from the restaurant next door for AMD1,000pp. Unrenovated dbl rooms (no hot water, no shower) are decrepit but extremely cheap at AMD3,000. The 2 renovated dbl rooms (inc hot water, en-suite shower room) look satisfactory at AMD10,000. **$**

WHERE TO EAT AND DRINK Gyumri also has the pick of the province's eateries. Many small cafés have sprung up in Gyumri, mainly around Azatutian Square, Rizhkov Street and Kaghaghutian Ring, and also in Central Park (see page 229) during summer. The following is merely a selection, all of which have been included on the map opposite. There are also restaurants in the Alexandrapol and Nane hotels. See pages x and 92 for comments on prices.

✖ **Bonchik** On Azatutian Sq, opposite the town hall. A colourful café for a cheap filling snack. Bonchiks (*AMD200*) are light flat doughnuts which come with either a savoury or sweet filling.

✖ **Café Kalinka** Halfway up Rizhkov St; ✆312 61116. Cheerful café serving kebabs, pizzas & omelettes. One of the first to open as Gyumri started to recover from the earthquake.

✖ **Café Verona** 4/3 Kaghaghutian Ring; ✆312 50088. Service a bit slow but the food is freshly prepared & worth the wait.

✖ **Phaeton Alek** 47 Haghtanak St; ✆312 57988; m 094 344369; ⏰ 11.00–18.00. Evening meal for groups of 10 or more can be arranged, advance booking necessary. On the ground floor

of the local history museum where one can almost imagine oneself back in the days depicted upstairs. It is tastefully furnished with a mixture of old & reproduction furniture. Museum exhibits such as carpets & domestic utensils decorate the original stone walls. The eponymous horse-drawn carriage stands just inside the front door. Menu in English.

✖ **Tashir Pizza** 2 Sayat Nova St, near Ankakhutian Sq; ✆312 55005. A branch of the deservedly popular pizza chain (see page 332).

✖ **Vanatour** At the junction of Rizhkov & Gorki streets; ✆312 30192. Popular with locals. Serves Georgian dishes as well as Armenian; the cheese ones are tasty.

OTHER PRACTICALITIES Gyumri has all major facilities such as banks, post offices, shops, market, internet cafés, etc. Most are on the main Azatutian Square or Kaghaghutian and Ankakhutian squares. The two other towns, Artik and Maralik, also have facilities. There is no **tourist information office** in the province but Berlin Art Hotel (page 225) gives useful information and can help to organise homestays. Shirak Tours, run by the proprietor of the hotel, arranges tours of the region, including cross-country skiing in winter. In Gyumri numerous USAID information boards give details about what there is to see in the town centre. A detailed map of Gyumri (both Armenian and English script) is published by Collage (see page 60).

GYUMRI (*Telephone code: 312*) Gyumri is the principal city of northwest Armenia and the administrative centre of Shirak. At 11.41 on Wednesday 7 December 1988 – when most adults were at work and most children at school – around 60% of the buildings were destroyed by an earthquake. The epicentre of the earthquake, which measured 6.9 on the Richter scale, was 30km east of Gyumri in Lori province near the small town of Spitak (population then about 25,000) where every building was destroyed. In all, at least 25,000 people were killed and 500,000 made homeless in Gyumri and the surrounding region. (See box, page 232, for more information.) The problems Armenia has had in dealing with the aftermath of the earthquake have long made any visit to Gyumri a salutary experience. However, not to go there means missing an important aspect of modern Armenian history. Apart from the direct impact of the earthquake, an indirect consequence was the shutting of Metsamor nuclear power station because of its vulnerability to any further earthquakes. It was the closure of Metsamor, by far Armenia's biggest source of electricity, coupled with the blockade by Azerbaijan and Turkey as a result of the war over Nagorno Karabagh, which led to most Armenians having no electricity and hence no heat during the winters of 1992/93, 1993/94 and 1994/95 (see pages 324–7).

Gyumri was called Leninakan at the time of the earthquake and there is a certain irony in that Lenin's entire system of government was to collapse so soon after a city which had been named in his honour. Immediately after the earthquake, the Soviet prime minister Nikolai Ryzhkov promised the inhabitants that the city would be rebuilt within two years. That timetable was unachievable in the last days

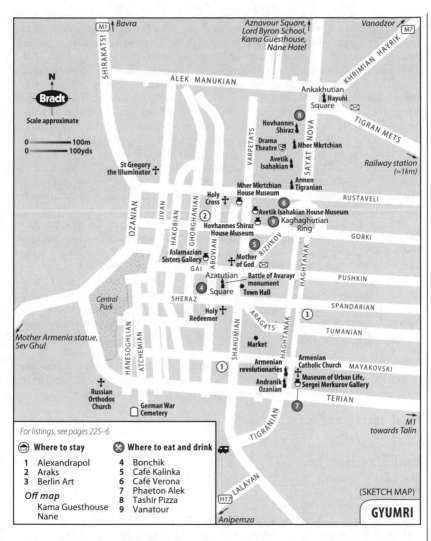

of the Soviet Union and, after the Armenian vote for independence in 1991, the Armenians ceased work on the partly completed buildings since they had not been designed with adequate earthquake protection. Nowadays, approaching the city from some directions (notably the northwest), visitors still see unfinished blocks of flats (known locally as the carcasses). Some of the blocks were almost finished. In others merely the foundations had been dug. They were being built on good agricultural land and farming continues between the buildings. In places, the rubble dumped from the many buildings which collapsed is still evident but nature is gradually taking over.

In 2001 around 40% of the population was still living in old railway containers into which windows had been cut. However, following substantial gifts from the American-Armenian Kirk Kerkorian from 1998 and USAID from 2000, progress was made and by 2002 it was possible to imagine that the air of depression was starting to lift and that eventually sufficient new housing might be built for those who had by then spent almost 15 years in those metal boxes. By autumn 2005 the number living in containers had fallen to 3,500, but an air of depression remained. Since then the rate of improvement has increased with rebuilding of much of the town centre either completed or in progress. However, there still remains much to be done. Behind the new buildings some of the old railway containers are still inhabited and there are historic buildings awaiting attention. (According to Armenian government data 7,000 families in northern Armenia who lost their homes in the earthquake still lived in shacks or other temporary accommodation in 2008. Some 5,300 of them were due to receive new accommodation by 2013.) On the whole, Gyumri is now a bustling city like any other. There are now adults who with their own children will have no personal memories of the earthquake itself but who will certainly remember the difficult aftermath. One can only wonder at the psychological damage to the inhabitants. There was not a single Gyumri resident who did not lose a family member in 1988.

The city itself is an ancient settlement, and was caught up in the long struggles for supremacy between the Persian and Ottoman empires. However, the older surviving buildings, mostly in the centre, date from the period after Russia gained control of the region following the Russo-Turkish war of 1828–29. A fortress was quickly built to defend the new border and in 1837, when Tsar Nicholas I visited Gyumri, the town was renamed Alexandropol after Nicholas's wife, Tsaritsa Alexandra Fedorovna. That name lasted until 1924 when it was again renamed, this time in honour of the recently deceased Lenin. The survival of the older buildings indicates that under Tsarist rule construction was to higher standards than in the Soviet era.

It is possible to imagine a time when Gyumri, with its mix of smart new buildings and renovated attractive old buildings, the shoddy Soviet-era constructions having been swept away by the earthquake, will once again be a pleasant place to live.

What to see and do Most sights are within walking distance of central Azatutian Square. A few are a longer walk or a short drive from the centre.

Central Gyumri There are more surviving Tsarist-era buildings here than in any other Armenian city and the older central streets offer an insight into 19th-century Russian provincial architecture. These buildings are concentrated in an area to the west of the main square. On the **main square** (Azatutian Square) two 19th-century churches face each other, **Mother of God** on the north side and **Holy Redeemer** on the south. Both were damaged by the earthquake, the latter suffering considerably when its large central cupola collapsed. Mother of God is functioning again and is busy with many people coming and going. While the church is definitely Armenian the blue altar screen with its painted pictures lends something of an Orthodox feel, perhaps not surprising given its date. Holy Redeemer is still under restoration. The new red and grey stone is being carefully matched to the colours of the old but some is being left plain to distinguish it from the older decorated stonework. The inscription on the monument to the south of Holy Redeemer Church reads 'To the innocent victims, to the merciful hearts', namely the victims of the earthquake and those who came to help. By contrast, Gyumri's largest 19th-century church, **Holy Cross**, which is situated to the north of the centre on Abovian Street, escaped lightly. For many years following the earthquake it housed families who had lost their homes but it too is now a functioning church again. By contrast again **St Gregory the Illuminator**, just a few streets northwest, was badly damaged in the earthquake and remains in a very ruined and precarious state. Its eastern façade can be seen on Jivan Street although it is entered from Rustaveli Street round the corner and through what is now the entrance to houses. The small **Russian Orthodox Church** (commonly called *Piplan Zham*, or Shimmering Chapel), in typical Orthodox style with a silver-coloured onion dome, appears to have suffered little damage but is now closed. None of these churches need detain the visitor long but they do combine with the older residential streets to provide one of the few extant pictures of the Tsarist era in Armenia.

The new pale tuff building occupying the whole of the east side of the main square is the **town hall**. Facing it, on the west side of the square, is a monument to those who fought Persian troops in AD451 at the Battle of Avarayr (see pages 17–18). Their leader, Mamikonian, is mounted and below him are four figures representing all ranks of society. Although the Armenians were defeated, subsequent events allowed the battle to be seen as a moral victory and one which preserved the Armenian language, hence the names of the first four letters of the Armenian alphabet carved on the tablet. From the northeast corner of the main square the popular pedestrianized Rizhkov Street (named after the person in charge of organising aid after the earthquake) with its many small shops leads to Kaghaghutian Ring, with its several cafés. From the southeast corner of the main square the colourful market stretches south. Near the end of the market, at the bottom of Haghtanak Street, is a **statue** of Andranik Ozanian (see page 130). Behind him, in the park-like central reservation of the dual carriageway, are busts of Armenian revolutionaries. They include Gevorg V (1847–1930), Katholikos during the Armenian genocide and early Soviet period; Garegin Nzhdeh (1886–1955), statesman and Armenian commander; and Nikol Duman (1867–1914), freedom fighter in Baku and Yerevan. Nearby, next door to the Museum of Urban Life of Gyumri (page 230), a new **Armenian Catholic church** was under construction at the time of writing.

Walk westwards from Azatutian Square to reach **Central Park**. It is a favourite place for Gyumri residents to stroll, its trees giving welcome respite from the summer heat. It has a number of statues including busts of Isahakian and Shiraz and a statue of Alexander Pushkin, the Russian poet, who visited Gyumri in 1829 on his way to Erzurum (see page 246). Near the southern entrance to the park the building with a somewhat dilapidated exterior was once a theatre which, in 1912, staged the première of the opera *Anoush* by Armen Tigranian (see page 48), another native of Gyumri. In the upper, western reaches of the park is the columned neo-Classical Rotunda which gives good views over the town to Mother Armenia and Sev Ghul (see page 231).

Tucked into an inconspicuous corner of Gyumri just south of the central area is a **German war cemetery** where prisoners of war from World War II lie buried. To reach it go to the southern end of Atchemian Street, which ends as a cul-de-sac with two large metal doors. Go through the left-hand door. You will see the large dark cross up to your right. I scrambled up the slope, there being no other obvious way in. The cemetery is very like the other German war cemeteries in Armenia (see pages 202 and 245). Not far away, next to the small Russian Orthodox Church, is the more formal memorial to the dead of the 19th-century Russo-Turkish war.

The three sons of Gyumri whose house museums are detailed overleaf are also commemorated by statues outside the **Vardan Ajemian Drama Theatre** (*Sayat Nova St north of Kaghaghutian Ring*). From north to south the statues are Shiraz, Mkrtchian and Isahakian. South of the drama theatre, also on Sayat Nova Street, there is a statue of the composer Tigranian, another son of Gyumri.

Museums
Museum of National Architecture and Urban Life of Gyumri (*47 Haghtanak St;* ⊕ *11.00–17.00 Tue–Sat, 11.00–16.00 Sun; guided tours in English, French & Russian AMD2,000; adult AMD500*) This museum certainly merits a visit. It is located in a restored 1872 town house, the façade of which comprises black and orange-red tuff blocks together with a wrought-iron balcony. Inside are paintings by local artists and rooms furnished as they would have been in Tsarist days. It is particularly conspicuous that virtually all items in the rooms for the wealthier inhabitants came from western Europe and little from Russia, eastern Europe or Asia. This presumably reflects the aspirations of prosperous Armenians under Tsarist rule. The museum is on the upper floor and on the ground floor is an attractive restaurant (see page 226).

The adjacent gallery, the **Sergei Merkurov Gallery** (*same ticket office & details as Museum of Urban Life of Gyumri, above*), was the home of Sergei Merkurov, a prominent Soviet sculptor-monumentalist and native of Gyumri. He was considered to be the greatest Soviet master of post-mortem masks, making death masks of Lenin, Tolstoy and Gorky among many others. The statue of Lenin which stood in Yerevan's Republic Square during Soviet times was his work (see pages 128–9). The gallery houses his work.

Aslamazian Sisters Gallery (*241 Abovian St;* ☏ *312 48205;* ⊕ *11.00–17.00 Tue–Sun; donations welcomed*) This gallery, which features the paintings and ceramics of Mariam (1907–2006) and Yeranuhi (1910–98) Aslamazian, born near Gyumri, is well worth a visit. The two-storey gallery is in a black tuff building of 1880 and is reached by going through the archway to an attractive garden overlooked by balconies with carved wooden railings: the entrance is on your immediate right. Yeranuhi's work is displayed on the first floor, Mariam's on the second. Many of the works on display are in strikingly bright colours. Unusually for Soviet times the two sisters were allowed to travel abroad and some of the paintings reflect this. Mariam is the better known of the two sisters. She died in Moscow, but is buried in Yerevan's Pantheon cemetery.

Hovhannes Shiraz House Museum (*101 Varpetats St;* ☏ *312 55142;* ⊕ *10.00–17.00 Tue–Sat, 10.00–16.00 Sun; donations welcomed*) The museum contains items from and about this writer (see page 52) of popular patriotic and love poems. A pleasant museum with friendly staff, it is perhaps of less interest to non-Armenians who do not know his work. However, it is worth visiting for the sake of the building itself, an attractive 19th-century, single-storey, black and red tuff house. One notable piece is a gift from Parajanov (see page 56). The red cloth, not quite filling the frame, symbolises that Armenia is now just a portion of what it once was but it still has its religion, symbolised by the cross of gold braid, and its language, a quill through the cross.

Avetik Isahakian House Museum (*91 Varpetats St;* ☏ *312 57291;* ⊕ *10.00–17.00 Tue–Sat, 10.00–15.00 Sun; guided tours in English, French & Russian; donations welcomed*) See page 52 for biographical details of this writer whose picture will be familiar from AMD10,000 notes. The single-storey black tuff house, where Isahakian was born, was built by his grandfather in 1829. The reconstruction of the living areas, with all artefacts belonging to the house, gives an interesting insight into the life of an affluent citizen in 19th-century Gyumri. The young English-speaking guide gave me an excellent tour.

Mher Mkrtchian House Museum (*30 Shota Rustaveli St;* ✆ *312 55174;* ◷ *10.00–17.00 Tue–Sun; donations welcomed*) Mher Mkrtchian (1930–93) was an actor well known within Armenia for his comic roles although his personal life contained much tragedy. The museum contains his personal belongings and also props from some of his best known films.

Outside the centre The enormous statue of **Mother Armenia** stands on a hill on the western edge of the town. It was erected in 1975 as a memorial to The Great War (World War II) 1941–45 and is reached by climbing a long flight of steps. The climb is rewarded by panoramic views over Gyumri and the surrounding countryside. From here one can walk across to the adjacent hill on which stands **Sev Ghul** (Black Fortress), a Russian fortress built in the 1830s after Russia gained control of the region. The circular fortress is usually locked but the key-holder is often there allowing access. Inside is a central well, sunk to a depth of 28m. Living quarters line the walls and from the ramparts there are good views. Russia still maintains a garrison in Gyumri, guarding the border with Turkey. The troops occupy the Red Fortress (closed to visitors) on the hill to the north of Sev Ghul.

Gyumri **railway station** on the eastern edge of the town is a vast edifice which looks typically Soviet from the outside (apart from its roof) but whose entrance hall is reminiscent of the *gavit* of a church with its central dome, from which hangs an enormous chandelier, and a mosaic of the Armenian symbol of eternity on the floor under the dome. One of the frescoes beside the stairs to the upper floor could, similarly, be given a religious meaning – interesting for a 1977 building.

The main route north from Gyumri town centre includes the large **Ankakhutian Square**, its central statue *Hayuhi* representing Armenian independence and freedom, and **Aznavour Square** with its rather ordinary statue of Charles Aznavour, the French singer of Armenian parents who, since the 1988 earthquake, has provided much humanitarian aid to Gyumri. Not far away on Tetcher Street (named after Margaret Thatcher, UK prime minister 1979–90) is the **Lord Byron School** which specialises in teaching English. It was built after the 1988 earthquake with funds provided by the British government and donations from the British public and was opened by Margaret Thatcher in 1990. It is named after Lord Byron (1788–1824), considered one of founders of Armenology, in recognition of his knowledge of and work on the Armenian language. A bust of Lord Byron stands in the school grounds.

Some 7km southeast of the city is **Shirak Airport** (see page 68). The wrought-iron sign indicating the principal road to the airport is easy to miss; coming from Gyumri the dual carriageway to the airport goes off left just after some rails cross the road. A little further south (1½km) is a more obvious sign but following this second sign will take you via a much poorer road. Opened in 1961, the airport was reportedly designed to look like an airport in provincial Turkey so that, in the event of a hijacking, a plane could be diverted here and the hijackers then deceived into thinking that they had made it to the West. Apparently the normal airport signs could be rapidly changed to ones in Turkish, there were stocks of Turkish uniforms for the staff, and suitable photographs of such people as the Turkish president.

NORTH FROM GYUMRI
Marmashen Monastery (*Main church* ◷ *09.00–20.00 in good weather, but if the door is locked when you arrive it is likely that the caretaker will soon appear, having seen visitors arriving*) The monastery of Marmashen is beautifully situated in the valley of the Akhurian River, unlike most Armenian monasteries which tend to

THE 1988 EARTHQUAKE

The first shock, of magnitude 6.9, was at 11.41 on Wednesday 7 December 1988. It lasted for 47 seconds. Four minutes later there was a second shock of magnitude 5.4 and within the first fortnight there were 1,500 tremors. Unfortunately most of the hospitals and schools were of modern Soviet construction and so collapsed immediately: urgent medical care for the survivors was difficult, not just because of the collapse of the hospitals but because over half of Gyumri's doctors died in their ruins. All 60 expectant mothers in the maternity hospital died, along with the newborn and their mothers. In one area of nine-storey flats only five or six of the original 49 blocks remained. (Flats similar in design to these are common even today throughout earthquake-prone Armenia.) Out in the villages the older peasant houses sometimes survived but the children had usually been in modern schools and hence died.

The wounded had to be evacuated by helicopter to hospitals in Yerevan and emergency supplies (including large numbers of coffins) had to be flown in. As well as useful items, numerous bureaucrats also arrived with no ability to organise anything but who, imagining themselves to be important people, decided they should be there. Gorbachev himself cut short a visit to the USA to visit the scene, though earned the contempt of the survivors and rescuers by having his Zil limousine brought in by transport plane so that he could inspect the ruins in comfort. Help came from abroad as well as other parts of the Soviet Union – even from Azerbaijan despite the growing tension over Nagorno Karabagh. However, Armenian television was able to show Muslim demonstrators on the streets of Baku with placards: 'Allah be praised, He has punished the infidel'; 'Hurrah for the earthquake'; 'God is just, He knows whom to punish'.

Electricity, telephone and water supplies all failed. The absence of electricity and telephones, coupled with the perpetual shortage of batteries (to power radios) in the Soviet Union, meant that people, especially in the villages, had no sources of information and there were many who believed for days that the entire world had been affected. As well as being bereaved, many survivors had lost most of their possessions and were financially ruined. Looting and pillage soon broke out and as a result cars leaving the region were searched by soldiers and the forces of the Ministry of the Interior.

Could the earthquake have been predicted? Probably not, at least so far as the exact date and location were concerned, although after the event some shepherds said that they had noticed changes in the preceding days: specifically that the water in the artesian wells had become several degrees warmer.

be sited in elevated positions. A significant feature of Marmashen's position has changed recently with the damming of the river for a small hydro-electric plant just downstream. Whereas the monastery once stood above an attractive river flowing through a small gorge it now stands above a calm lake. It is not on a main tourist route, so sees relatively few foreign visitors. However, it is a popular picnic site for locals. To reach it take the main north road out of Gyumri and then fork left on the road to Vahramaberd just after a Russian military base on the left. (The inconspicuous wrought-iron signpost to Marmashen is easy to miss, especially when driving.) In Vahramaberd (about 8km from the left fork) turn sharp left, on to a poor road, between fields where rubble and more recent rubbish has been dumped. The road descends into the valley of the Akhurian River. The monastery can be seen below the road, picturesquely situated by the river, now a lake, and surrounded by fruit trees.

Three churches survive, the foundations of a fourth have been uncovered and the remains of many more buildings can be seen, as can parts of the surrounding wall, particularly on the northwest side. The main church, St Stephen, was built between 986 and 1029 in red tuff and is in the style of those at Ani, the former capital. It is particularly elegant with decorative arcatures on each façade and columns supporting the corners of the umbrella cupola. Inside, the front of the altar has been restored using the original carved stones where possible but supplemented as necessary with other stones found on the site. Much restoration has been expertly carried out, funded by an Italian-Armenian couple who went to the length of having experiments carried out in Italy to find an ideal mortar to repair the stonework. The church had a 13th-century *gavit* on the west, its position clearly visible on the church's west façade. The 10th-century church, St Peter, to the north of the main church is now roofless. The church on the south side, Mother of God, is rather like a smaller version of the main one. The foundations of the fourth church, circular and much earlier, lie further west. It was a four-apse church with a small room off each apse. There is a good array of khachkars, those marking the graves of men in front of the main church, those of women to the sides and back. On the small hill to the north of the churches is an extensive cemetery and a ruined chapel.

Lake Arpi National Park (*www.lakearpi-nationalpark.com*) This national park in the far northwest of Armenia is on the high Javakhq-Shirak Plateau, a volcanic plateau shared by Armenia, Turkey and Georgia. It includes mountain steppe, subalpine grassland, wetlands and lakes. As the source of the Akhurian River, Lake Arpi increased in size in 1950 from 4½km² to 22km² when the river was dammed. The lake is fed by melt water and four streams. The national park was established in 2009 and is a Ramsar Convention (The Convention on Wetlands of International Importance) protected site. The park is a habitat for 670 species of vascular plants, including some Caucasian and Armenian endemics, and for 255 species of vertebrate animals of which more than ten are included in the IUCN Red List of Threatened Species. It is an important staging and breeding ground for migrating birds: over 140 species have been observed around the lake, of which 80–85 were nesting when observed. The park is home to the largest colony of the Armenian gull in the world, is the only Armenian nesting site of the Dalmatian pelican and is the only world habitat of Darevsky's viper. Funding to assist in setting up and running the national park included grants from bodies such as the Caucasus Nature Fund (*www.caucasus-naturefund.org*), WWF (*www.wwf.org.uk*) and the government of the Federal Republic of Germany. The area has a harsh climate with deep snow cover for up to six months. By the end of October the ground is usually frozen. The milder months are May, June and July. The breeding season for birds is mid-April to late June. It is possible to drive right round the lake although the road is poor (4x4 advised). Most of the villages around the lake used to be inhabited by Azeris as evidenced by the lakeside Azeri cemeteries.

Visiting Lake Arpi The lake can be visited as a day trip from Gyumri but for any serious exploration of the area an overnight stay is necessary. There is little tourism infrastructure; tours to Lake Arpi and local bed and breakfast accommodation can be arranged through Berlin Art Hotel in Gyumri (page 225). Avarayr Adventure

Tour Company (page 64) also offers tours to the lake. It is possible to do a loop, going north on the increasingly hilly main road via Pokrashen and Ghazanch (there is a Lake Arpi Visitor Centre in Ghazanch which may be open in midsummer), then westwards from Tavshut on a variable dirt road across a high, flat plain to Paghakn on the lakeside. Rather than return the same way an alternative route is via Amasia. The road between Lake Arpi and Amasia is very poor but the rolling grassy hills are impressively bleak and raptors abound. From Amasia the road improves dramatically and there is a choice of turning east to rejoin the main road at Tsoghamarg or of following the gorge of the Akhurian River south to Vahramaberd (and the turn-off for Marmashen) and thence to Gyumri.

Some of the villages in the Lake Arpi region play host to a number of interesting sites. For more information on these and how to reach them, go to www.bradtguides. com/europe/armenia.

SOUTHWEST FROM GYUMRI Heading southwest from Gyumri and parallel to the Turkish border, the road (very close to the border in places) crosses the only rail link between Armenia and Turkey at a level crossing. This rail link was opened in 1898 to provide a connection between Tiflis (present-day Tbilisi, Georgia) and Kars (in present-day Turkey) at a time when both cities were in the Russian Empire. By the latter days of the Soviet Union there was only one train each week across the border but even this has been suspended since 1992 because the border is officially closed. The military significance of the area, the frontier between the former Warsaw Pact and NATO, can be judged from the continued presence of Russian soldiers.

Gusanagyugh (some 15km south from Gyumri) has an 11th-century, three-aisled basilica church which, unlike an increasing number of churches, has seen no renovation and so still gives an idea of the state many churches were in following the break-up of the Soviet Union. Nearby are two surviving fragments of wall from a medieval castle. About 25km south of Gyumri the ruins of the 10th- or 11th-century **Jrapi caravanserai** can be seen on the left together with a small 7th-century church and the ruins of another, rebuilt as a castle in the 11th century. The road continues through pleasant hilly country and as it starts to descend again to the plain there is a small picnic spot with a natural spring on the east side. An early summer lunch break here might be enlivened by nesting crag martins, Isabelline wheatears and black-headed buntings.

Continuing south past the village of **Aniavan** a road branches off right (look out for rose-coloured starlings) to **Anipemza** whose Yereruyk Church, though roofless, is one of the most architecturally important in Armenia and often features in collections of photographs of the country. Its significance rests with its early date (5th–6th century) and the idea it gives of early Armenian church architecture which was modelled on the style of churches in the eastern provinces of the Roman Empire. The basilica-style building is erected on a large plinth approached by steps. The porches are framed by elaborately carved pediments of Graeco-Roman style, contrasting with the different style of the carved window arches and the plain pilasters. There were galleries on three sides, north, south and west, constructed between the eastern and western corner rooms which project beyond the nave. Unusually, the eastern corner rooms are elongated along a north–south axis. The whole site covers an enormous area. To the north are natural caves and pits carved into the rock, some of which may have been for storage: others are coffin-like. Even the name 'Anipemza' has particular significance for Armenians since it reminds them of their inaccessible capital Ani; the 'pemza' part of the name refers to pumice which is mined locally.

The Turkish border is only a few hundred metres from the church and, on a clear day, both Mount Aragats, the highest peak in present-day Armenia, and Mount Ararat, the highest peak in historic Armenia, can be seen. Until some years ago it was possible to obtain permission to go to a specially constructed viewpoint (at Norshen) over the abandoned capital of Ani which is immediately over the border in Turkey. Because access to this viewpoint is now so difficult, AMAP (see page 104) has established another at **Haikadzor**. It is further from Ani and the view is not as good but it has the merit of being free and easily accessible. Take binoculars and hope for a calm, clear day. Note that the signpost for the viewpoint is misleading: it reads 'Ani 20km' – one cannot of course go to Ani! The observation point is 3km from the main road. That the Armenians are cut off from their historic capital is a consequence of the Soviet-Turkish treaty of 1921 which ceded to Turkey areas including Kars and Ani even though they had been under Russian control since 1877 and had even been awarded to Armenia under the Treaty of Sèvres in 1920. (See the *History* section in *Chapter 1* for a discussion of this issue.) The possible return of Ani to Armenia in exchange for two Kurdish villages further north was raised in intergovernmental talks in 1968 but nothing resulted.

To reach **Anipemza from Yerevan** the quickest way is probably to go via Gyumri; the roads are good all the way. The route which leaves the main road at Talin and goes cross-country via Tatul, Hatsashen, Tsamakasar, Suser and Bagravan, where one turns left on to the road from Gyumri, is a scenic route passing through several very rural villages with village ponds, donkey carts and an interesting cemetery at Bagravan but there are stretches of very poor road. At the time of writing, the route via Armavir, following the railway line to Gyumri, was mostly good but had a very bad section between Karakert and Getap.

SOUTHEAST FROM GYUMRI The sights in southeast Shirak are most easily reached by heading south on the main road from Gyumri towards Yerevan.

At **Horom** (some 16km from Gyumri) are the remains of one of the largest Bronze Age/Urartian citadels in Armenia which cover two hills east of the village, opposite the reservoir. Climb up from the road beside the reservoir's dam. From the top the vast extent of the settlement becomes apparent with long stretches of the lower courses of cyclopean walls and evidence of other structures. As always with such sites imagination is needed to reconstruct it in the mind's eye but it is a good walk and the views from the top are splendid.

Around 25km south of Gyumri the main road bypasses **Maralik**. Turn left towards Artik just before the road crosses the railway. On the right, opposite the road junction, there is a gigantic example of Soviet central planning: an enormous cotton-spinning factory, now operating at a fraction of its original capacity. It was typical of Soviet economic policy to site a large cotton-spinning factory far from the sources of cotton (in Uzbekistan and Tajikistan), far from the markets for cloth (mostly in the western USSR), requiring a dedicated railway line to be built to transport materials in and out, and not even near significant sources of power.

Several interesting monasteries lie close to this road. The first, which can be seen across the fields to the right after rounding a hill, is the **Monastery of the Apostles**. A dirt track goes off right across the railway then runs parallel to the railway. Beside a rubbish dump, a grassy track goes off right and curves back to the church. The dome of the 11th-century red tuff church has long since collapsed and there was considerable further earthquake damage in 2009 but it is still possible to get an idea of how the building must have looked. Notwithstanding its damaged state, the building is still used; there are the remains of burnt candles and the cloths and handkerchiefs which believers leave when a special wish is expressed. The dirt road continues and eventually rejoins the tarmac road to Pemzashen. This dirt road is not marked on maps and it may be easier to return to the tarmac road before proceeding. Turning right about 7km from Maralik a road leads to Pemzashen and Lernakert. **Pemzashen** has a complex of three medieval churches at a lower ground level than the present village. The now domeless 6th-century **St Gevorg Church** has three apses within its rectangular walls and an octagonal tambour. The tambour is notable with its four windows alternating with niches and shell-like fan vaults allowing the transition from octagonal tambour to dome. The tympanum over the entrance shows the Virgin Mary holding Jesus with, on the right, an angel and another figure. There was a similar composition on the left, now defaced. The church has two-storey eastern corner rooms but, unusually, these appear to be accessed from outside rather than from inside the church. The small **chapel** to the south, reconsecrated in 2010 to act as the village church, is also 6th century. To the north of St Gevorg are the foundations of a 5th-century basilica. Continuing on towards Lernakert you pass the ruins of a **9th-century cross-dome church**, Holy Apostles, shortly after leaving Pemzashen. There is weathered cable-carving at the portal. The church stands above a small gorge in which is a 17th-century Mother of God Church. As you wind uphill to **Lernakert**, you pass a new church (2005). To reach the 4th-century **church of St John the Baptist** continue through the village to the end of the tarmac then turn left up a cobbled road. This large barrel-vaulted basilica, restored to a functioning church after its days as a barn in the Soviet era, has a new roof courtesy of the Women's Association of Lebanon. The trim village is said to be one of the oldest in Armenia. It has a khachkar-carver's workshop, on the right as you descend from the church.

Returning to the Artik road, carry on for another 7km to reach Artik. The main entry to **Artik** is from the north, crossing the railway line by an improbably large flyover. (Note that coming from Pemzashen the signpost takes you into Artik further south and negotiating the town can be difficult. If you do enter the town this way, turn left before reaching the fire station – there are no signs – and you will reach traffic lights. Turning right at the traffic lights brings you on to the flyover.) The centre of Artik is just beyond the flyover but to reach **Lmbatavank (monastery)**, partway up a hill to the southwest of the town, turn immediately right at the end of the flyover. At a T-junction turn right again. Where the buildings end take the left fork uphill then at the next fork take the right option. From here you can see the monastery on the hill. This small 7th-century monastery, whose single-aisle church is dedicated to St Stephen, is built of red tuff and, with its high dome, is very well preserved being particularly notable for its frescoes. There are good views to the north from the hillside location. Scattered around the church are old hollowed-out coffins, also made of tuff. Lmbatavank is a good place to see sousliks, a burrow-dwelling member of the squirrel family. If you stay quietly in the car park below the monastery, you may be rewarded by glimpses of them emerging from their burrows in the earthen slope.

Artik (*Telephone code: 244*) There are a few older buildings here, but most of the town obviously dates from the post-1945 Soviet period. It was developed as a centre of tuff mining and the recent upsurge in construction work means that unemployment has fallen slightly from its very high level after the collapse of the Soviet Union. The town centre, just beyond the flyover, is recovering from its depressed post-Soviet state with new shops, banks, etc. The town has two old churches adjacent to each other. From the flyover go straight ahead along a short stretch of dual carriageway to reach a square. Take Tonakian Street to the right of the building at the head of the square and continue straight ahead. The churches are on the left, near a new angular building with a belfry. Both churches were under restoration but work stopped with the collapse of the Soviet Union. A crane is still in position so perhaps one day work will resume. The 7th-century **church of St George** is a massive four-apse cross-dome church whose dome has collapsed. Unfortunately it is locked, presumably for safety, but a good idea can be obtained from the outside and from glimpses through the large windows. The exteriors of the south and west apses are pentagonal and are decorated with double-column blind arcades. The arches of the arcades and those over the windows have floral or basket-weave carving. The north apse is round and plain. The curvature of the main east apse is almost obscured from outside by the eastern corner rooms but can still be appreciated at the three large windows. **St Marine** (or Mother of God) to the northwest is even more ruinous. It is a 5th-century cross-shaped church on a three-step pedestal. Although the west door is blocked it is possible to enter by the north doorway, under a huge lintel. The east apse is wide and shallow and is flanked by a narrow apsidiole on each side. The external apsidioles on the west walls of the north and south wings, together with remnants of barrel vaulting, suggest there may have been a gallery round the west end of the church.

Harichavank (monastery) (⊕ *Harichavank is now a working monastery; the compound gates may be shut at night but the monastery & the churches will be open all day*) To reach the large and important monastery of Harichavank turn left in Artik after crossing the railway. The road bears right up the hill. Just after the brow of the hill, some 3½km from the town centre and just before the prison, turn right for the village of **Harich** – the monastery is at the far end of the main street. It is situated on the edge of a plateau where two small ravines meet.

The monastery was founded by the 7th century and expanded during the 13th. Most of the ancillary buildings were added after 1850 when the Katholikos moved his summer residence here. The original 7th-century church, St Gregory's, has a round dome. From the southwest corner room a secret passage leads down into the gorge and a secret room is concealed above the roof of the same room. Its bell tower, resting on large columns, is a 19th-century addition as are the small chapels which adjoin it. The much larger Mother of God Church of 1201 has an unusual 16-sided umbrella dome and much elaborate decoration around the tambour. Inside, cantilevered steps lead to the upper storeys of the western corner rooms which are unusual in having arcaded windows looking on to the nave. In between the two churches is a very large *gavit* whose porch is particularly finely decorated with small twisted columns and inlaid carved red and black stones which show a striking oriental influence. On the east façade of the Mother of God Church is a relief showing the founders of the church and also one of a lion. An unusual feature is the small chapel perched on top of a high pillar of rock in the gorge; it owes its present inaccessible location to an earthquake. It is possible to walk down into the gorge; a path goes off from the northwest corner of the entrance courtyard. It is quite an easy scramble up to the plateau opposite the monastery. From both gorge and plateau the views of the monastery and its defensive walls are refreshingly different from what one would normally see within the monastery complex.

EAST FROM GYUMRI About 12km east of Gyumri on the Vanadzor road is the village of **Jajur**, home to the **Minas Avetissian House Museum** (⊕ *11.00–18.00 Tue–Sun; AMD200*). This is by no means a typical house museum, rather an excellent small art gallery showing work by this popular art-dissident painter and his friends. Avetissian (1928–75) (see page 54) was born in Jajur; it was while he

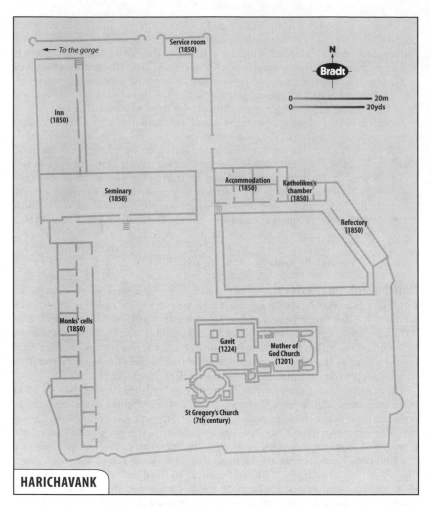

To the gorge ←

Service room (1850)

N

Bradt

0 ━━━━━ 20m
0 ━━━━━ 20yds

Inn (1850)

Seminary (1850)

Accommodation (1850)

Katholikos's chamber (1850)

Refectory (1850)

Monks' cells (1850)

Gavit (1224)

Mother of God Church (1201)

St Gregory's Church (7th century)

HARICHAVANK

was visiting his family here that his Yerevan studio was destroyed by fire in 1972. The rebuilt (after the 1988 earthquake) Jajur gallery opened in 2004. The paintings are colourful, attractive – even joyful – many depicting everyday village life. A visit is well worth the short detour. The gallery, with its cupola-like roof, is at the east end of the village and is signposted off the main road.

The excavated foundations of the **monastery of Chichkhanavank** at **Shirakamut** are actually in neighbouring Lori province but are probably more conveniently visited from Gyumri. They are the starting point for one of the routes to **Trchkan Waterfall** (*1,786m above sea level, height 23m*) on the Trchkan River, which flows into the Pambak River near Shirakamut. The waterfall is on the border of Shirak and Lori provinces and, although not large by world standards, is the largest in Armenia. In 2011, it was the focus of a successful campaign by environmental groups to save it after work had started to dam the river above the waterfall for a hydro-electric scheme (see pages 11–12). Preparatory work for the scheme included a dirt road (which forded the river several times) to the foot of the waterfall. This very difficult road (4x4 definitely needed) makes it just about possible to drive the 8km or so from

Shirakamut. Walking would probably be easier and certainly less scary. You can reach the top of the waterfall by rough dirt roads from Vardaghbyur 27km north of Gyumri.

LORI PROVINCE

Lori, Armenia's largest province in terms of land area, is very beautiful. Largely a high plateau with small mountain ranges, its outstanding features are the deep gorges which fissure the landscape. Apart from these river valleys, Lori is sparsely populated. The principal rivers are the Debed and the Dzoraget. The Debed rises in the southwest of the province where it is called the Pambak, flows east and then turns north towards the Georgian border. It ultimately joins the Kura whose delta is on the Caspian Sea south of Baku, Azerbaijan. The Debed Valley on the Georgian border is the lowest-lying part of Armenia with an altitude of 400m above sea level. The Dzoraget rises to the west in Shirak province and then flows east past Stepanavan to join the Debed halfway between Vanadzor and Alaverdi. The spectacular gorges of these rivers are excellent places to find eagles, vultures and also interesting smaller birds such as rock nuthatches. In addition, they are where Lori's most appealing sights, its ancient monasteries and fortresses, are to be found.

GETTING THERE AND AROUND The main **railway** line from Yerevan to the Georgian border at Bagratashen in neighbouring Tavush province crosses Lori and, while it is cheap, it is also slow. For train times and general comments on transport see pages 79–83. Vanadzor, the largest town in the province, is the main transport hub. The railway and bus stations are adjacent at the end of the short dual carriageway which runs from the main square. The bus station has timetables up beside the ticket windows. **Buses** or **minibuses** run almost everywhere. Most destinations have a once daily service with departures tending to be either in the morning between 08.30 and 11.00 or in the afternoon between 15.00 and 16.30. More important destinations, such as Alaverdi and Gyumri, have more departures. A bus goes daily to Yerevan at 10.30, the 120km journey taking 1½ hours (*AMD1,200*), and to Tbilisi at 08.30 (*AMD3,000*). The border crossing at Bagratashen is served by a minibus at 08.00 and a bus at 08.30. Times can change so it is wise to check in advance. Taxis wait at the bus station and can be a convenient way to travel both to local sights and intercity. They charge AMD100/km but for long trips obtain a price before leaving. A taxi from Vanadzor to Yerevan costs AMD8,000–10,000 and a round trip to Sanahin, Haghpat, Akhtala and Odzun costs much the same. While the most used border crossings to Georgia are Bavra in Shirak province and Bagratashen in Tavush province there is also a road crossing at Gogavan in Lori.

WHERE TO STAY Lori is a relatively cheap area of Armenia and very acceptable accommodation can be had for 'shoestring' or 'budget' prices. Because of the terrain there is no one place from which it is easy to visit all there is to see. Stepanavan is the best place to stay if wishing to visit Lori Berd or any of the remoter areas north of Stepanavan. For the monasteries of the Debed Gorge, the most popular sites, new accommodation in Haghpat and Odzun means that the Tufenkian at Dzoraget is no longer the only good, convenient hotel. A cheaper option, of course, would be a homestay in any of the towns or villages. Allow at least a full day to visit all the monasteries in the Debed Gorge. Vanadzor is a useful overnight stop when moving from one area to another. See pages 85–7 for general comments on accommodation. Where listings are plotted on a map, it is indicated overleaf.

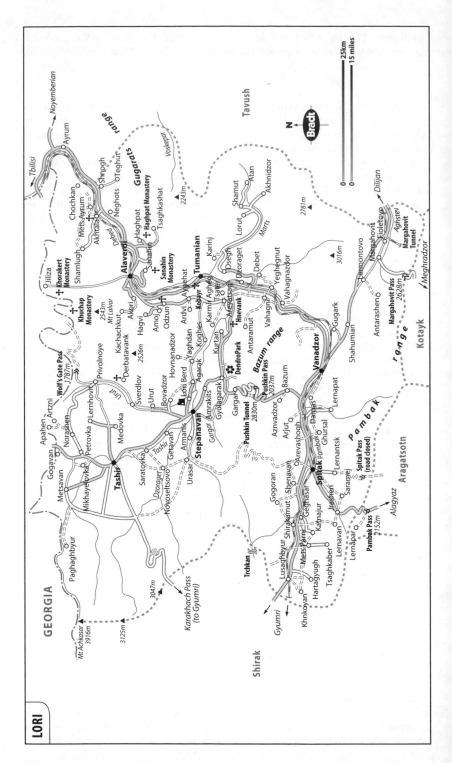

Stepanavan

🏠 **Lori Hotel** (12 rooms) 11 Nzhdeh St; ☎256 22323; e info@lorihotel.am: www.lorihotel.am. Conveniently situated in centre of town. Also has a café (⏰ *09.00–21.00*). Wi-Fi. B/fast not served until 09.00. Evening meal AMD2,500pp. **$**

🏠 **MM Hotel** (4 rooms) 9 Nzhdeh St; ☎256 24050; m 099 072414. A pleasant small hotel on the site of the pre-earthquake bus station, attached to a café (⏰ *from b/fast to 23.00*). Cheaper rate in winter. **$**

🏠 **SH Resort** (8 rooms) 145 Baghramian St; ☎256 22007; e h_israyelyan@yahoo.com; ⏰ 1 May–30 Nov & 10 days at Christmas. Outdoor swimming pool. Hotel opened 2009. Rooms on 3rd floor, no lift. Function suite for up to 400 ppl on 2nd floor so could be noisy during a wedding party. A pleasant hotel & quiet when I stayed there. **$**

🏠 **Stepanavan Information Centre Guest House** (2 rooms) See page 243 for details or contact Armine directly (m *093 196096;* e *armine5@yahoo.com*). Shared shower room. Wi-Fi. Dinner upon request. Good reports from those who have stayed there. **$**

Vanadzor

Map, page 243.

🏠 **Argishti** (22 rooms) 1 Batoumi St; ☎322 42556/7; m 095 442556; e argishti@freenet.am. A good hotel in the centre of town with attractive marble floors & stairs. Restaurant. Sauna. Discount for groups. **$$**

🏠 **Green House** (16 rooms) 8d Banaki St; ☎322 40015; m 091 310070 (Anahit); e greenhousehotel@yahoo.com. Banaki St is parallel to & 4 streets south of main Tigran Mets Av, between Miasnikian & Nzhdeh streets. A comfortable hotel but the soundproofing is poor. All rooms on ground floor. No evening meals. Wi-Fi. **$**

🏠 **Hotel Kirovakan** (20 rooms) 1 Mashtots; ☎322 47010; m 099 417010, 098 417010; e hotel.kirovakan@rambler.ru. This old Soviet hotel has had 3 floors renovated to a high standard & hopes to renovate more. Conveniently situated at the east end of the town centre with good views of the town from its elevated & highly visible position. By car it is reached by going off east from the Tumanian Sq roundabout on to Halabian St; it is well signposted from here. There is a more direct pedestrian access, inc steps, from the hotel to the town centre. Helpful reception. Wi-Fi. Accepts cards. Restaurant. B/fast extra AMD3,000pp, other meals AMD4,000pp. **$**

🏠 **Hotel Laguna** (6 rooms) 68a Yerevanian St; ☎322 50009; m 099 877222, 093 877222, 055 877222; e admin@laguna.am; www.laguna.am. Built in 2010. 2km from town centre. Behind Soviet-era flats, signposted. Wi-Fi. No dining room, meals taken either in rooms, in sitting areas on landings or in summer house in the garden. B/fast extra AMD1,500pp. Evening meal AMD3,000. Accepts cards. **$**

🏠 **Metropolina Hotel (formerly Gugark Hotel)** (17 rooms) 20 Tigran Mets Av; ☎322 41519. Very central. Occupies 3rd & 4th floors of the building; reception on 4th. A cheap, no frills option (although this may change in the future as renovation has begun). No restaurant. B/fast not available but plenty of nearby places to eat. Some rooms have no hot water. Rooms with no hot water & no TV AMD9,000 (*sgl occupancy AMD5,000*). With hot water & TV AMD11,000–15,000. **$**

Debed Gorge

🏠 **Tufenkian Avan Dzoraget** (54 rooms) Debed Gorge at Dzoraget. Bookings through the Tufenkian office in Yerevan; ☎60 501010; e hotels@tufenkian.am; www.tufenkianheritage.com. On the bank of the Debed River about halfway between Vanadzor & Alaverdi. Decorated in the attractive hallmark style of Tufenkian & serving locally sourced food. Wi-Fi. Cards accepted. Reduced rates Nov–Mar. Prices vary significantly with size of room. Stiff supplement for a view of the river. **$$$$–$$$**

🏠 **Hotel Gayane** (6 rooms & 4 cottages) Haghpat village; ☎0253 60618; m 091 611861 (Sophie). This deservedly popular hotel is expanding rapidly. Wi-Fi. Swimming pool. Sheltered BBQ area with an open fire for cooler evenings. A range of prices, all HB. **$$**

🏠 **Qefo Hotel** (16 rooms) Haghpat village; m 055 210210; e info@qefohotel.com. A comfortable new hotel which opened summer 2013 run by Armen's family (see page 242) so the food & friendliness is just as good as in the restaurant. Superb situation overlooking the Debed Gorge. Prices all HB. **$$**

🏠 **Agha Bek** (3 rooms) Dsegh village; m 094 660037 (Marineh Aghbekian). This B&B is one of several signposted in Dsegh village. Marineh is the church's key-holder & the house is next door to the church. Bedrooms are spacious. Can sleep up to 14. B/fast AMD2,000pp. **$**

🏠 **Hotel Debed** (12 rooms) 1 Gay St, Sanahin Sarahart, Alaverdi; m 099 953535; e debed_ hotel@mail.ru. A large Soviet hotel, closed for a number of years, now has some renovated rooms. Up on the plateau, excellent views & close to Sanahin Monastery. Those who have stayed speak well of the helpful staff, say that the rooms are clean & comfortable & that the food is good. **$**

🏠 **Hotel Odzun** (10 rooms & 2 cottages) Odzun village; m 091 717404, 095 717404. A Soviet holiday hotel of 1971 which is being excellently renovated to a high standard. On the hillside above Odzun 2.2km from the church (not 1.2km as it says on a sign beside the church). Turn right at the sign then left in 800m on to a tarmac road & keep going uphill. Ignore the first set of rusty gates & continue to the new gates. Set in extensive gardens with its own orchard, swimming pool & BBQ. Accommodation will increase as renovation progresses. Unrenovated rooms

cheaper. Cottages sleep 4. Would be a good centre for hiking. Restaurant & café. B/fast AMD2,000pp, FB AMD5,000pp. **$**

Elsewhere in the province

🏠 **Sochut Resort** (30 rooms) Gyulagarak, near DendroPark; m 095 411195; e info@sochut. am. Previously a Soviet sanatorium, built in 1955, impressively transformed into a modern hotel in 2009. Set in spacious, peaceful, well-tended gardens with the advantage of DendroPark (page 262) next door. Wi-Fi. Restaurant & café. Future plans inc spa facilities (swimming, sauna, massage). Cards accepted. FB. **$$**

🏠 **Hekyat Restaurant/Hotel** See below.

🏠 **Spitak YMCA** 4a Aygestan, Spitak 1802; ☎255 24083, 62901; e spitak @ymca.am; www. spitak.ymca.am. Built in 2010 the building is an important community centre running a wide range of facilities for children & adults. They have a few rooms which visitors may be able to use. Excellent reports from those who have stayed there – 'rooms very clean & comfy with good shower facilities'. **$$**

🍴 **WHERE TO EAT AND DRINK** Some of the larger hotels listed above have restaurants, noted under individual entries. MM and Lori hotels have cafés. The supermarket in Tashir has an in-store bakery which makes delicious bread.

🍴 **Armen's** Alaverdi; ☎0374 22474; m 0912 10624. One of Armenia's most pleasant restaurants & very highly recommended. It is reached by crossing the south bridge at Alaverdi (the one which is actually 2 separate bridges – one for each direction) & then turning immediately left. The restaurant is 1km along this road on the right on the east side of the river. The fare is the ubiquitous Armenian barbecued food, *khorovats*, but it is easily among the best. Armen, the proprietor, won 1st prize in a local BBQ competition to celebrate the removal of the wooden scaffolding from Akhtala Monastery (see pages 259–62) & was then invited to appear in a cookery programme on one of the major national TV channels. He now judges in what has become an annual BBQ competition. Vegetarians can eat well here. Armen can also arrange local homestays. AMD5,000.

🍴 **Hekyat Restaurant/Hotel** Gyulagarak, near DendroPark; m 093 303100 (Hrair), 094 424725. There is no sign outside this excellent restaurant whose name means 'fairy tale'

but it is the collection of buildings on the left just before entering the wooded hillside at DendroPark. Restaurant highly recommended. Also has accommodation (3 rooms & 2 cottages). Well-presented cottages, 3 floors, sleep up to 8 persons. AMD40,000/cottage. B/fast extra approx AMD3,000pp. A generous selection of salads, cheese, beer, jug of fresh homemade lemonade & tea/coffee cost about AMD5,000pp.

🍴 **Pazo'i mot** 11 Yeritasardakan St, Stepanavan; ☎0256 23777; m 093 428775, 094 173752; 🕐 10.00–24.00. Off (northwards) the main road south, about ½km from town centre, I can recommend this small restaurant with its wooden décor, tasty food & friendly staff. Most of the food is their own produce, inc the chicken. Can arrange take-away food for picnics. The restaurant doesn't actually have a name, everyone just calls it *Pazo'i mot*, which translates roughly as 'next door to Pazo's', Pazo being the name of the proprietress's late husband with whom she established the restaurant in 2008. Difficult to spend more than AMD5,000 pp on a full meal.

✖ **Soorjaran Ukranina** 9 Torosian St, Spitak;
☎0255 20708; m 055 282728. A delightful non-smoking restaurant & café which opened in 2013. Looks like a large Swiss chalet. Has a set business lunch for AMD2,000. Wi-Fi. Its name simply means

Ukrainian coffee-place, having been founded by the President of Ukraine.
✖ **Tashir Pizza** [map, below] 65 Tigran Mets Av, Vanadzor; ☎0322 44411/01. A branch of this popular chain (see page 332).

OTHER PRACTICALITIES Vanadzor, the largest town, has all facilities, with Stepanavan, Spitak and Alaverdi being reasonably provided. Stepanavan is the only place which has a **tourist information centre** (*11 Milion St;* ☎ *256 22158;* e *stepanavaninfo@gmail.com;* ⊕ *during the day Sat & Sun. At other times Armine who works nearby can be contacted on* m *093 196096*). The centre offers information on local minibus routes, places of interest and accommodation. They can provide a map of Stepanavan. There is also some accommodation within the centre (see page 241).

VANADZOR (*Telephone code: 322*) Vanadzor, the provincial capital, is situated on the Debed River at 1,350m above sea level between the Pambak mountain range to the south and the Bazum range to the north; both ranges exceed 3,000m in height. Prior to 1935 Vanadzor was called Kharaklisa. In 1935, it was renamed Kirovakan after Sergei Kirov (1886–1934), the head of the Communist Party in Leningrad, whom Stalin arranged to have assassinated because his popularity in the party made him a potential rival. In 1993, the city acquired its present name from the local Vanadzor River. Formerly the third-largest city in Armenia it was damaged by the 1988 earthquake but not to anything like the same extent as Gyumri and Spitak and its central square with buildings of pink tuff and its main shopping street survived more or less intact. Since then Gyumri's falling population means that Vanadzor is now Armenia's second city. An important industrial centre in Soviet times, most of the former chemical plants making products as diverse as glue and nail polish remover are now closed. The continued

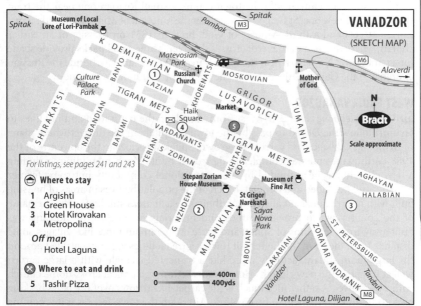

VANADZOR (SKETCH MAP)

For listings, see pages 241 and 243

🛏 **Where to stay**
1 Argishti
2 Green House
3 Hotel Kirovakan
4 Metropolina

Off map
Hotel Laguna

✖ **Where to eat and drink**
5 Tashir Pizza

0 — 400m
0 — 400yds

closure of most of the huge factories means that the city no longer lives under a dense pall of acrid smoke and the atmosphere is now clean and pleasant. Although there is little to tempt visitors to stay except as a transit stop on the way to Georgia or the monasteries further north or to the east in Tavush province, Vanadzor could also provide a suitable base for hiking in the surrounding hills. Banks, currency exchanges, tour operators, eateries, shops and most other facilities can be found on Tigran Mets Avenue, the main street. Parallel Lusavorich Street has the main markets while Miasnikian Street running between the two has clothes shops. From the main square, Haik Square, a short dual carriageway leads to the bus and train stations.

What to see and do If you are staying in Vanadzor or find you have a couple of hours to spare in the town, the most worthwhile place to visit is the **Vanadzor Museum of Fine Art** (*52 Tigran Mets Av;* ✆ *43938;* e *info@vanart.org; www.vanart. org;* ⊕ *10.00–18.30 Tue–Sat; for guided tour in English, AMD2,000, contact 1 day in advance; AMD200*). Founded as a branch of the national gallery in 1974, it concentrates on artists from Lori who often depict local subjects, including landscapes and some fine portraits, and who seem to me to capture something of the wistfulness of the Armenian soul. The labels include English. Start on the third floor of this spacious and light gallery and work downwards: floors three and two house the paintings; sculptures occupy the ground floor. There are a number of other places of minor interest. The **Stepan Zorian House Museum** (*24 Stepan Zorian St;* ✆ *43093;* ⊕ *10.00–17.00 Tue–Sat, 10.00–15.00 Sun; AMD100*) is bright and well presented with enough English to make it accessible. The writer Stepan Zorian (1889–1967) is best known for his novels and short stories based on Armenian village life. The small **Museum of Local Lore of Lori-Pambak** (*23/1 Karen Demirchian St;* ✆ *41751;* e *museumlori@mail.ru;* ⊕ *10.00–18.00 Tue– Sat; guided tour in English AMD500; AMD1,000*) has a new building displaying local artefacts including a good collection of decorative metalwork.

There are three **churches** in the town centre, a small Russian one near the train station, a large new one, St Grigor Narekatsi, at the junction of Miasnikian and Stepan Zorian streets and a third, Mother of God, built in 1831 on the site of an earlier church, where the road to Alaverdi crosses the river. Three small **parks** provide shade for a stroll, Sayat Nova Park near the new church, Matevosian Park beside the Russian church and the Culture Palace Park at the far end of Tigran Mets Avenue.

WEST FROM VANADZOR

Spitak (*Telephone code: 255*) West from Vanadzor, the main road and rail lines to Gyumri follow the Debed to pass by the town of Spitak, in the district where many of Armenia's cabbages and carrots are grown. Spitak was close to the epicentre of the 1988 earthquake and was completely destroyed by it. Much rebuilding, including a new church, has been funded by the international community but some former factories still lie ruined and derelict. Much of the population lives in areas of housing built with international aid after the earthquake, such areas still known by the name of the country which provided funds and materials. Inevitably the housing was built away from the ruins of Spitak and these areas remain more like villages some distance from the town. In the rebuilt town centre facilities are concentrated around the large **main square**, actually more like a truncated triangle with a large carved wall at its apex. The new church, **Holy Resurrection**, is a typical cross-dome church with a bell tower. A rather nice touch is the carpet-like throws over the pews harking back to traditional Armenian furnishings. Although the town feels as if it is coming to life again, the earthquake is not – indeed cannot – be forgotten. Apart from any personal memories of the inhabitants, the old Soviet memorial (see below) is visible from almost everywhere and there are memorials on Alek Manukian Street.

On a hill overlooking the town is the official **memorial to the victims of the earthquake**. Visiting it is thought-provoking. First, it is reached by a long flight of concrete steps, most of which have disintegrated and all of which are overgrown by a colourful range of weeds. At the top of the steps one reaches the rather grandiose memorial, now equally neglected with much of its marble cladding having fallen off, giving the appearance that total collapse may not be long delayed. Is there, in the memorial's neglect, implied criticism of the shoddy Soviet building standards which contributed so much to increasing the death toll? It is readily apparent that local residents never go there. There is no inscription in any language. Maybe the wild flowers gradually taking over the monument are a more fitting memorial.

Opposite the hill with the memorial is the town **graveyard**. Many of the victims are buried here. Some graves show not only a picture of the deceased but also a clock face with the hands pointing to 11.41, the time the earthquake struck. Those of younger people often show a flower with a broken stalk symbolising a life broken while in full bloom. The graveyard is less neglected than the monument but is clearly little frequented. Perhaps many of the deceased have no surviving relatives. Certainly some of the graves show three generations of victims from the baby a few weeks old to the grandparents. Still remaining in the graveyard is the prefabricated metal church which served in the immediate aftermath of the earthquake and which was erected within 40 days of the disaster.

There is another graveyard in Spitak round the other side of the hill. It is a **war cemetery** where German prisoners of war lie buried. It's a tranquil place – a flowery meadow with rows of metal crosses. Although the identity of each person is known, this is not marked on the grave with the sole exception of one grave where a relative has provided a stone tombstone. There is also a large cross bearing the words *Hier ruhen Kriegesgefangene – Opfer des zweites Weltkrieges* ('Here rest prisoners of war – victims of World War II'). The prisoners worked on the construction of a nearby sugar factory but that was destroyed in the earthquake. The German government pays a local man to look after the graves and to preserve the meadow by cutting the vegetation annually. To reach the war cemetery take the road which runs between the town graveyard and the earthquake memorial, signposted to Gyumri off the main road south to Yerevan. Stay close to the base of the graveyard then continue beyond it, keeping watch for the large black cross up on the hill to the left, behind some small houses. This is the largest of the German war cemeteries in Armenia. Others are at Sevan (see page 202), Gyumri (see page 229), Artashat and Abovian.

For the **monastery of Chichkhanavank** and **Trchkan Waterfall**, see page 238.

EAST FROM VANADZOR The road to Dilijan in Tavush province bypasses the three Russian villages of **Lermontovo**, **Margahovit** and **Fioletovo** in the valley south of the road. The villages are inhabited to varying degrees by Molokans, or as they call themselves, Spiritual Christians. The sect emerged in the 16th–17th century in Russia, refusing to obey the Russian Orthodox Church and rejecting the veneration of icons or the cross. True Christians, they believe, must worship only God and recognise the Bible as the Word of God. At the beginning of the 19th century the Russian government started to relocate those, including the Molokans, who did not accept Orthodoxy, exiling them to distant parts of the empire such as the Caucasus. The name 'Molokans' (milk-drinkers, *moloko* is Russian for 'milk') is most usually said to originate from their refusal to obey the dictates of the Orthodox Church which prohibited milk as well as meat during religious fasts. Another theory is that it derives from the name of the Molochnaya River (which translates as Milky River) in south Ukraine beside which the sect settled in 1820. They themselves prefer to think of their name as referring to 'spiritual milk'.

The Molokans maintain their traditional way of life and tend to marry within their own community. After marriage the men grow beards and the women cover their heads. Religious meetings are in houses rather than churches and men and women sit separately. Their economy is based on agriculture (their cabbages are well known) although many do seek work in towns, the men particularly in the building trade, and so speak some Armenian. Children receive their education in Russian. They are pacifists and are well known for being conscientious. They prefer not to be photographed. Lermontovo, with its typical two-story blue and white houses with balconies, is the most traditional of the three villages. Fioletovo appears to have a majority of Molokans, although with a significant Armenian presence, while Margahovit looks more Armenian and has an Armenian church. The roads down into the villages are poor, as are the roads within the villages.

NORTHWEST FROM VANADZOR

The Pushkin Pass There are two main roads north from Vanadzor, both of which continue to Georgia. The more westerly can be reached by heading west out of the city for about 6km along the main Gyumri road and then turning right. The present-day road avoids the Pushkin Pass (2,037m) by a 2km-long tunnel which has now been renovated and (dimly) lit.

The pass gets its name from Pushkin who, on a visit to the Caucasus, met there in 1829 a cart carrying the body of Alexander Griboyedov (1795–1829) who had been killed in Persia, an incident described in Pushkin's *Journey to Erzurum*. Griboyedov, whom Pushkin knew well, was a satirical playwright whose best known play, *Woe from Wit* (1824), was only performed and published posthumously – its hero is branded a lunatic when he arrives in Moscow full of liberal and progressive ideas, a dangerous practice there in either the Tsarist or the communist era. Griboyedov was also a diplomat and instrumental in Russia's peace negotiations with Turkey following the war of 1828–29 when Russia gained control of much of Armenia. After that he was appointed Russia's ambassador to Persia. Russia's defeats of Turkey and Persia and its consequent territorial expansion were followed by a change of tack in Russia's foreign policy as it was now considered important to ensure that both Turkey and Persia nevertheless survived as significant powers. Russia feared that dissolution of either might lead to the possible appearance of other, stronger powers on its borders. Both states accepted Russian control of the Caucasus but while Griboyedov was in Teheran negotiating with Persia an angry mob stormed the Russian embassy. His mangled body, barely recognisable, was being returned on the cart which Pushkin encountered.

There is a dramatic change of scenery as one emerges from the tunnel: gone are the bare stony hillsides and in their place are lush wooded ones. In early summer the fields as one descends are an amazing sight of yellows and reds with masses of buttercups and poppies. The road descends in a long series of zigzags towards the town of Stepanavan passing through the villages of **Gargar**, its black and white church visible on the left, and then through **Amrakits** with its fairy-tale but sadly ruined Russian church, its onion domes also visible from the road. A kilometre or so after Amrakits the road approaches closely the gorge of the Dzoraget River. It is worth stopping and walking the few metres to the edge of the gorge; from here there is a good view to the site of Lori Berd, the main reason for visiting Stepanavan.

Stepanavan (*Telephone code: 256*) Stepanavan suffered damage in 1988 but received little outside help and it has only relatively recently started to recover. Stepanavan is named in honour of Stepan Shahumian (1878–1918), an Armenian who was instrumental in imposing Bolshevik rule in Baku, Azerbaijan. Faced with an uprising he fled but was captured and executed by local anti-Bolsheviks, with some British involvement. The town is centred on the statue of Shahumian, near which can be found small shops, cafés, the museum, information centre (see page 243) and the bus station.

Stepanavan itself has a few places of minor interest. The **Stepan Shahumian Museum** (*housed in the square orange tuff building on Nzhdeh St; ⊕ 09.00–17.00 Mon–Fri; AMD100*) is actually built around the Shahumian homestead, an intriguing concept. The museum is labelled only in Armenian and no English is spoken. The house itself is of some interest, as is the model of the secret passage to the underground printing press where Shahumian printed communist leaflets. The **Communist Caves** (signposted on the left on the road south), where Shahumian and fellow revolutionaries met, can be visited. There is not much to see but the views of the Dzoraget Gorge are good. **St Sargis Church** is signposted left down one of the small side streets on the main road south shortly after leaving the town centre. Renovated in 2009, it dates from the 13th century. A khachkar, now on the east façade, gives the foundation date in Armenian letters (see box, page 41) as 666. Adding the 551 years needed for calendrical adjustment, this equates to AD1217. The **bottom of the gorge**, a popular place for picnics, can be accessed by vehicle on the north side of the gorge via a rough track which goes off from the start of the main road to Tashir and zigzags down to the river which it crosses on a rickety bridge.

Lori Berd (fortress) Just outside the town on the opposite side of the Dzoraget River, this is one of Armenia's most impressive medieval fortress sites. To reach it cross the large viaduct over the gorge of the Dzoraget ('Gorge River') at the north end of the town. At the far end of the viaduct, turn right and continue for about 2km, then turn right again on to an unmade road through the village of Lori Berd and continue for another 2km. (A taxi from Stepanavan costs AMD2,000 for a return trip plus waiting time.) The triangular site is spectacularly situated between two gorges: that of the Dzoraget and that of the Urut. The only side of the site not protected by these gorges, which are too steep-sided easily to scale, is the northern one and this was protected by a high stone wall with towers, at the foot of which there was a moat. A locked gate formerly prevented direct entry and it was necessary to climb over the ruined wall. However, the gate is now usually left open. As well as the area within the fortifications the town spread outside them and outlying districts also developed across the two gorges. Bridges were constructed to provide access from these outlying districts: that over the Urut survives and can be seen from the eastern part of the site. It can be reached either by a rocky path which descends from the top of the plateau just before the gate or by a steep path which winds down from just inside the gate and which is very slippery in wet weather.

The fortress was built by David Anghonin (ruled 989–1049), member of a junior branch of Ani's Bagratid dynasty, to be the new capital of the Tashir-Dzoraget kingdom: there were five Armenian kingdoms at the time. Though suffering heavy casualties, the Seljuk Emir Kizil managed to capture Lori Berd in 1105 and it subsequently came under Georgian rule following the Seljuk defeat by Davit IV Agmashenebelis (David the Builder) (ruled 1089–1121). Davit's great-granddaughter Queen Tamar transferred Lori to the ownership of the Armenian Prince Sargis Zakarian for his assistance in inflicting further defeats on the Seljuks between 1195 and 1204. The town subsequently flourished under his rule and that of his son, but in 1228 Shah Jala-Edin of Khoremsk captured the outlying districts and in 1238 the fortress itself fell to the Mongol Khan Jagat, allegedly because the captains charged with organising the defence spent too much time drinking and too little praying, or so their brother-in-law wrote. The town was ransacked and for over 200 years it passed through various hands only to fall to invaders again in 1430. Decline, however, continued and the last inhabitants left as recently as 1931, largely because of problems with the water supply.

The first building encountered is a **bathhouse** with two baths and evidence of pipes running in the walls. In the centre of the fortress can be seen a roofed **rectangular building** which, at first glance, looks like a church. However, it seems to have had a succession of uses, the exterior walls showing several phases of building. Inside, the six square-domed bays (with pillars supporting the arches dividing the bays) and the niche in the south wall facing Mecca, suggest that the building dates from sometime during the Muslim occupation which lasted until the 18th century. The building incorporates medieval tombstones and the doorway is flanked by two khachkars; there may have been an earlier church on the site and it is currently in use as a Christian chapel. Built on to the north side is what looks like a dwelling house with fireplace and chimney. Nowadays the building is home to a family of redstarts in the breeding season. In buildings on the side of the Dzoraget Gorge there is more evidence of pipes suggesting a **washroom** or latrine.

Northwest from Stepanavan
To head north from Stepanavan turn left after crossing the viaduct. For some length the road keeps east of the river at a distance of a few hundred metres. It is well worth stopping and walking across to look down into the immensely impressive gorge. The road passes through a series of Russian villages built by refugees who fled here to avoid religious persecution during the time of Catherine the Great. The houses typically have two storeys with living accommodation for the family being on the upper storey with its balcony, and the lower storey being used for storage. About 15km from Stepanavan the road reaches the small town now called **Tashir**. Founded in 1844, it was originally named Vorontsovka after Prince Mikhail Vorontsov (1785–1856), viceroy to Tsar Nicholas I, who had been brought up in Britain where his father was Russian ambassador. Vorontsov's role in the Caucasus was considerable. Appointed Governor General of New Russia with 'unlimited powers' during the reign of Tsar Alexander I he was so successful in integrating southern Ukraine into Russia that he was promoted to viceroy in 1845 and his mandate was extended to the newly acquired territories in the Caucasus. In 1935, Vorontsovka was renamed Kalinino after Mikhail Kalinin (1875–1946), the communist functionary who became titular head of the Soviet state. Tashir has the typical two-storey Russian houses, many still with their red roof tiles. It also has all facilities including a supermarket with an in-store bakery in the form of a large *tonir* where *puri*, a Georgian bread, is made in the same way as *lavash* (see box, page 90). Freshly baked and warm from the *tonir* it is delicious!

The main road continues north for 14km to the border crossing with Georgia at Gogavan. At the far end of Tashir a road branches left from the main road and heads northwest across marshy ground to the village of **Metsavan**. In the village go straight ahead at the roundabout in the main square, on the road to the right of the village hall, straight ahead at the next fork then turn left. This brings you to the first of the village churches, until 2012 a ruin with just four walls which was used as a rough football pitch. At the time of writing restoration was well under way. On the hillside at the far end of Metsavan (take the road to the left of the first church) is the small 10th-century **monastery of St John**. Church and graveyard are themselves surrounded by a wall made of gravestones. On the west façade of the church is an alcove, a much-used shrine, with what appears to be the upper part of a free-armed cross, unusual for Armenia. From Tashir it is possible to drive **cross-country to Privolnoye** (see below). The road is good as far as the crossroads for Medovka and Lernhovit. It then becomes a dirt road driveable in good weather (4x4 advised). It is an attractive route, climbing up through rolling grassy hills then down the other side to Privolnoye, the silver onion dome of its church visible among the red roofs of the village. It is then possible to return to Stepanavan via Sverdlov (see below). At the time of writing, the road south from Privolnoye was very poor (broken asphalt) as far as Urut. Privolnoye can also be reached directly from Stepanavan, as described below.

Northeast from Stepanavan Previously the main reason to tackle the poor roads in this part of northern Lori was to visit Khuchap Monastery (on the border with Georgia) via the Wolf's Gate Pass. Sadly this is not possible at present (see pages 260–1 for details).

Ten kilometres from Stepanavan, the Urut River is crossed at the village of **Sverdlov**, named after Yakov Sverdlov (1885–1919), a Bolshevik who was instrumental in overthrowing the elected Russian constitutional assembly in January 1918. He died from influenza the following year. The 7th to 12th-century St George Church with its red tile roof is visible on entering the village; keep going uphill. The church is a barrel-vaulted basilica; the arches supporting the roof spring from four pairs of piers in the side walls. The bell tower on the south wall of the church is roofed with stone tiles. Gravestones cover the hillock on which the church stands. Some 3km north of Sverdlov the **monastery of Derbatavank** can be seen across fields to the right. Dating from the 11th century it is a single-nave structure with barrel vaulting and rather tall for its size. Although attractively situated it was insensitively restored during the Soviet era.

Continuing up the narrowing valley the road reaches **Privolnoye**, a village with a Russian church and Russian-style houses. If you want to see inside the church ask for Vera (the 'e' is pronounced like the 'e' in vent and the 'r' is rolled), the keyholder, and she will be delighted to show you round and may even take you up the bell tower. The church was built in 1895 and the roof was renovated in 1991. Only the west end of the nave is in use forming a tiny Orthodox church complete with iconostasis and royal doors. Restoration of the remainder of the interior has been started but, like so many projects in Armenia, has run out of money. The church is dedicated to Archangel Michael.

NORTHEAST FROM VANADZOR
The Debed Gorge The other road north from Vanadzor, as well as the railway to Tbilisi, follows the scenic gorge of the Debed. The gorge is noteworthy for having five of Armenia's finest churches/monasteries, all of them worth visiting. Leave Vanadzor by Tumanian Street, cross the river and continue straight on. (**Note:** for anyone who is coming from Stepanavan and has 4x4 transport available it is much better to head east from there and visit Hnevank as well. See pages 262–3.) There are several short tunnels on this road, some of them curving and all unlit. Drive very carefully indeed through these tunnels – the official speed limit is 40km/h – as they are used by pedestrians and can have memorable pot-holes.

After 20km a road goes off right across the river to follow the valley of a tributary for a few kilometres before turning abruptly left to wind up the side of the valley to the plateau. It reaches the village of **Dsegh** where the **house museum** (🕒 *10.00–17.00 Tue–Sun; AMD100*) of the poet Hovhannes Tumanian (1869–1923) is situated (see page 51). Go through the village until you reach a square with a full-length statue of Tumanian and turn left to reach the museum. Although tourists who do not speak Armenian are unlikely to have encountered his works, the museum itself gives an interesting insight into living conditions in Tsarist days, notably the two older rooms with their rock floors and chest-like bed. The monument outside the museum was erected after the collapse of the Soviet Union when Vano Siradeghian, Minister of Internal Affairs, decided that the poet's heart should be buried here rather than kept in a jar in the anatomical museum of the medical university in Yerevan. Opposite the museum is the **church of St Gregory the Illuminator** (🕒 *09.00–18.00*), built in the 7th century, rebuilt in the 12th–13th centuries by the Mamikonians, restored in 1900 and again in 1969, when it became a museum. These two latter dates probably explain its *zham*-like appearance.

Just below the village of Dsegh is the ruin of a small cross-dome church known as **40 Children Church**. The explanation for this unusual name is the good news story that in the 17th century 40 children hid in the church from the invading Turks and were never found. The church is notable for an amazing variety of khachkars ranging from simple crosses to those with elaborate decoration. Interestingly a significant proportion of the khachkars show two equally sized crosses side by side. The views from the church over the gorge below are superb. Golden eagles and lammergeyers, Europe's largest vultures, are quite common here and alpine swifts nest in crevices in the valley side. The church can be reached either by a short steep descent (20 minutes) from Dsegh or a longer hike (about 1½ hours), with some steep stretches, up from the main road in the Debed Gorge near the Tufenkian Hotel. To get there from Dsegh, take the path to your right as you face the church of St Gregory the Illuminator then turn left beyond the house bearing the sign for 40 Children Church. This path takes you to the edge of the plateau. Walk along the edge to the obvious large khachkar from where a rocky path descends. From here you can see the church. At a suitable point leave the path and scramble down the boulder-strewn slope to the church. Returning to Dsegh the landmark to aim for is the last wooden electricity pole in the gorge (the next one is up on the plateau). This will bring you back to the path to the village.

To get there from the Debed Gorge, start from the bridge across the river to the Tufenkian Hotel and walk northwards along the main road for no more than 500m. The start of the path up to Dsegh is not very obvious; it goes off to the right just north of a café with a khachkar-like statue. The railway can be seen above the road crossing a small stream. Cross the railway line (beware of trains: this line is used) and the path becomes easier to see going up on the left of the stream. Continue up until you reach a small meadow a little below the plateau on which Dsegh stands. The church is across the meadow to your left. To continue up to Dsegh, see above.

Dsegh is also the starting point for visiting the ruined 13th-century **Bardzrakashi St Gregory Monastery** down on the side of the gorge. The monastery is signposted from the village and also at the edge of the plateau where the path into the gorge starts. It is about 2km from the village to the start of the path then a 20-minute walk down to the monastery. The path (slippery after rain) descends through the forest past collections of khachkars and a spring with a drinking trough before reaching the monastery in its peaceful setting.

The main buildings are the 13th-century Mother of God Church with a *gavit* on its south side and a second smaller church on its north side. All is in a tumbled down and overgrown state, but it is still possible to get an idea of what it must have looked like and there are some wonderful carved details both inside and out, such as the fish high on the eastern façade of the main church. The east façade of the *gavit* bears the Mamikonian family crest, a two-headed eagle with a lamb in its talons. The *gavit* is reached first and is entered from the south. The dome and roof, long since fallen, were supported by four free-standing columns and there is an eastern apse which has parted company from the rest of the wall. The Mother of God Church is entered on its south side from the *gavit*. It too is filled with fallen masonry but arches remain springing from a pillar with a decorated capital. The wide eastern apse has niches with scalloped carving. The second smaller church is difficult to enter, the doorway between the two churches being blocked by yet more fallen masonry. Back on the plateau, about 500m north of the start of the path to Bardzrakashi St Gregory Monastery is the **Siroun Khach** (Beautiful Cross), a large, intricately carved, 13th-century khachkar on a three-step pedestal.

Kobayr Monastery Back at the main road turn right to head north again. At the village of **Dzoraget** the road from Stepanavan via Hnevank comes in on the left shortly before the site of the Tufenkian Hotel. In about 5km the road passes the small industrial town of **Tumanian**, named after the poet and seriously marred by a huge abandoned brick factory. About 2km further north look out for a small railway station up above the road on the left. This is **Kobayr**, site of one of Armenia's most impressive ruins. About 400m south of the station a track goes off left, passing underneath the railway by a low bridge. Park here and walk up to the monastery. Take the path to the right as you face the bridge for a short distance then cross the railway line (beware of trains: this line is used) opposite some steps. Go up the steps then follow the path, which becomes steps, as it winds back and forth between small houses with their gardens, bearing right uphill at the spring and then left. The 15-minute climb is well worth it. The track underneath the bridge also leads to the monastery but it is steeper and can be muddy. The fortified monastery complex covered a large area.

According to an inscription, the **main church** was built in 1171 by Mariam, daughter of Kyurik II. At this time the Turkish Seljuks ruled Armenia but delegated control to local princes. Following Georgian victories over the Seljuk Turks in 1195 and 1202 the monastery came under Georgian rule, passing into the control of the Zakarian family who adhered to the Georgian Orthodox Church rather than the Armenian Church. (The Georgian Church differed in having accepted the views of the Council of Chalcedon, which took place in 451, over the duality of Christ's nature.) This explains the occurrence of Georgian features, notably the Georgian-style frescoes and carved inscriptions. Much of the south side of the complex has descended into the gorge below but the roofless apse and parts of the other walls survive with Georgian-style frescoes in the apse and chapel. The frescoes were well restored in 1971 but those in the apse have been exposed to the elements for years. Restoration of the church is now under way. While it will no doubt better protect the frescoes it is making the church darker and the dramatic view from inside the church down to the river in its gorge may eventually be blocked. In the apse the frescoes comprise three rows: in the top row the Virgin Mary and archangels; in the middle row Jesus and the Last Supper; in the bottom row figures of saints. The frescoes in the **chapel** on the north side of the church are in a similar style with vivid portrayals of Jesus and the disciples. At the time of writing the chapel was locked and even on peeping through the door the frescoes were not visible because the chapel was full of building material. Presumably at sometime in the future it will be possible to admire them again. Note that a torch is needed to see them.

Immediately southeast of the main church are two small chapels, one of which has a viewing balcony. The bell tower/mausoleum, north of the main church, in the centre of the monastery was built in 1279. The mausoleum houses the tombs of Shahnshah Mkhargryel and his wife Vaneni and has a spring flowing through it, a feature which may indicate that this has been a religious site since pagan times. The bell tower (under reconstruction at the time of writing) surmounting the mausoleum has eight pillars supporting the dome. The **13th-century refectory** is between the main church and the mausoleum slightly up the hill. Surrounding the whole complex was a fortified wall and the well-preserved gateway lies to the north of the main group of buildings together with a further small church dated 1223. It is possible for those suitably shod to climb further up the hillside and look down on the site. The views from there are even more impressive and there is another excellent chance of seeing lammergeyers.

Odzun and Ardvi Continuing north along the main road one reaches the left turn for Odzun in about 7km. **Odzun** itself is on the plateau and the road winds up the valley side to reach it. It is worth visiting for its **church** constructed of pink felsite (⊕ *usually in the tourist season 10.00–19.00. If shut, the caretaker can often be found & the priest lives nearby*). It is a large building, dating from the 6th century, reconstructed in the 8th, and one of Armenia's finest basilicas with a cupola. It stands on the site of an early 4th-century church (303–13) which was destroyed by an earthquake in the 5th century. Remnants of the 4th-century church were found under the apse of the present church. Tradition holds that the apostle Thomas ordained priests at Odzun on his way to India and that before he left he buried Christ's swaddling clothes where the present altar stands. A 6th-century inscription above the southern door of the church records this tradition. The two small bell towers at the east end were a much later addition in the late 19th century. The church had an exterior gallery on its north, west and south sides, those on the north and south were arcaded while that on the west had a blind wall with an arched entrance in the middle. The arcades on the north no longer exist but restoration, ongoing at the time of writing, may change this. The gallery ends on the southeast in a small chapel and on the northeast in an open apse. (See page 44 for the historical uses of galleries.) Inside the church there are three naves, the two side naves very narrow. The roof is barrel vaulted and the rib-vaulted octagonal tambour is supported by four free-standing columns. There are two additional supporting columns at the west end of the church. Carved stones from the 4th-century church were built into the wall of the church, most notably a carving of the Virgin Mary and Christ Child above the font in the north wall. The 2009 fresco in the apse depicts the Virgin and Child in the same postures. The most notable feature of the exterior carving is on the east façade above the central window where Christ can be seen holding open the Gospel of St John with angels below. At each side of the central window on the south side is an angel with traces of another figure, probably Christ. Above the central window on the north side is a weathered full length figure, possibly another image of the Virgin and Child. The west portal is surrounded by curving foliage and above the tympanum of the west entrance is an enigmatic fragment of a larger carving.

In the surrounding graveyard the clergy were buried near the church and were depicted on the gravestones holding staffs. Beside the church is a most unusual **funerary monument**, one of only two in this style in Armenia – the other is at Aghudi in Syunik province. It comprises a stepped platform supporting two slender obelisk-shaped carved stelae set between double arches. The carvings on the stelae are divided into panels depicting, on the east and west sides, biblical scenes together with the coming of Christianity to Armenia, and on the north and south sides, geometrical motifs and floral shapes. It has been suggested that the monument might commemorate Hovhannes Odznetsi (see below) who was Katholikos from 717 until 728 and undertook rebuilding work at Odzun, but its style suggests an earlier date and erection in the 6th century seems more likely.

Continuing through Odzun across the plateau the road heads south and then west towards Ardvi. It is worth stopping on a fine day and going across to the ruined **Horomigh Church** which is right on the edge of the gorge. It was built in the 7th century and rebuilt in the 13th using a darker stone which contrasts considerably with the warm honey-coloured older stone which has weathered badly. The darker stone, having scarcely weathered, almost has the appearance of concrete. A small central *gavit*, paved with gravestones, leads into the dark-stone barrel-vaulted church on the south and pale tuff chapel on the north. The view down into the gorge of the Debed is impressive. The tiny **Holy Cross Chapel** can be seen below and in spring the plateau is covered by an amazing carpet of flowers.

Continuing to **Ardvi** (not signposted from the main road: the turn-off is 3km after the leaving Odzun sign), the 10th-century **Holy Resurrection Church** is on the left as you enter the village, a small rectangular structure on a knoll. The roof of the barrel-vaulted nave has collapsed but that of the apse still stands. Two of the gravestones here depict a figure with a smaller figure within it, indicating the grave of a woman who had been pregnant when she died. Beyond the village, 5km after leaving the main road, is the small **monastery of St John** on a hillside. The 17th-century double church and its separate bell tower have very low doors, only a little over 1m high. The bell tower incorporates an unusual khachkar of a person wearing a hat and high-heeled shoes and carrying two unknown objects.

The small adjoining churches are both barrel-vaulted with thick walls and are entered from the south. In the second church is the tomb of **Hovhannes Odznetsi**. Odznetsi was born in Odzun and was Katholikos from 712 until his death in 728. He is revered in Armenia for his opposition to the influence of the Chalcedonic Byzantine Church and for his negotiations with the Arab rulers of the time to ensure the independence of the Armenian Church. In 719 he visited Omar Khalif in Damascus and secured exemption of the Armenian Church from certain taxes, freedom to profess the Christian faith and the cessation of persecution in Armenia. In return he

THE SNAKES OF ARDVI

Visitors to Ardvi are likely to have pointed out to them 'the snakes', a stratum of hard pink rock running more or less horizontally through softer pale rock where a spring issues from the cliff face in a gully near the monastery. Legend relates that one day when Odznetsi was praying two snakes (or dragons) appeared, terrifying his assistant. Odznetsi made the sign of the cross over the snakes (or dragons) and they immediately turned to stone, water gushing from them. There they remain to this day, petrified in the cliff face and with water still flowing from them. The water is considered an antidote to snake bites but I suggest following the advice on page 72 rather than relying on the efficacy of the spring. *Odz* is the Armenian for snake. The connection with the name Odzun is obvious. It is also interesting that the shape of the unusual funerary monument beside Odzun Church harks back to the shape of *vishaps*, or dragon stones (see page 46).

ODZUN TO KOBAYR

It is possible to walk from Odzun to Kobayr, though make an early start, or else choose an overcast day as there is no shade. Allow a long half day, with extra time to explore Kobayr. Continue for about 100m beyond the Odzun bus terminus and then turn left down a track to reach the gorge in less than 100m. The track descends slightly and then turns right. In reality it divides and redivides but keep going on a fairly level route never more than 50–70m from the cliff face on your right. If you descend more than this, you have gone too low. The path passes the Holy Cross Chapel (see page 253) and there are wonderful views down into the gorge. When you eventually come round a large outcrop and see an A-shaped electricity pole on the horizon ahead of you, then and only then is it time to descend. In theory it is possible to descend part way and then continue straight to Kobayr on the level, but the way is hard to find. It is much easier to walk down to the road, along it and back up as detailed on page 251.

promised the obedience of the Armenians. He convened the Council of Dvin in 720, to establish rules for church services and the moral conduct of believers, and the Council of Manazkert in 726 to settle a dispute between the Armenian and Syrian churches over differing interpretations of the nature of Christ. The Council agreed statements to ensure the unity of the churches and thus strengthen their Monophysite position against the Chalcedonic doctrine. His literary output was mainly on administrative, doctrinal and legal topics together with philosophical subjects which earned him the honorific *Imastaser*, Philosopher. He was the first to collect and systematise the canon law of the Armenian Church. His monumental work *Canon Law of the Armenians* is still used. He was canonised in 1774. The cemetery, on an adjoining hillock, has a very fine collection of khachkars; graves here span the centuries from the 6th to the 19th.

Alaverdi (*Telephone code: 253*) Returning through Odzun to the main road it is a short distance to the important copper-mining centre of **Alaverdi** ('Allah gave' in Turkish). This industrial city clings to the side of the gorge and is the commercial centre of the district. The copper-smelting plant still functions and casts a pall of smoke over the town but at least provides some desperately needed employment. While much of the town is down in the gorge there is also a district up on the plateau. Upper and lower districts are linked by road and by cable-car. The **cable-car** (*runs every 10 mins 07.15–10.00, 11.00–14.00, 15.00–19.30, 23.15–24.00; AMD100*) was opened in 1978 and had the steepest climb of any in the former Soviet Union. It has a drop of 200m and can carry a maximum of 15 persons. The lower terminus is close to the copper factory 500m north of the centre, the upper close to the Debed Hotel. There are two road crossings of the river, at the south and north ends of the town and a pedestrian-only medieval bridge (note the carved animals on top of the parapet), built in 1192, towards the north end of the town centre. From the east end of the southern road bridge (actually two separate bridges forming a dual carriageway) the road to Sanahin Monastery goes off right and winds up to the plateau. All the main facilities are in the centre of Alaverdi in the gorge.

Sedvu Monastery Visitors rarely reach this monastery near the end of the dead-end road to the village of Katchatchkut. It is a trip made for the breathtaking views, not for the monastery itself which in no way matches the splendours of the better known monasteries. The road from Alaverdi goes higher and higher, far above the well-known monasteries of the Debed Gorge. The views of those monasteries on their plateaux, themselves high above the Debed River, together with the main Debed Gorge and its subsidiaries, is stupendous. In Alaverdi take the road which goes off westwards under the railway bridge near the lower cable-car terminus. The road runs through the suburbs, turning to run southwards parallel to the river. Take the second right, beside a pharmacy. The road climbs up to the village of Akori then continues to climb to Katchatchkut with ever more impressive views. The monastery is hidden among trees some distance below the road. Go down through the cemetery by taking the track which goes off left 9km after leaving the main road in Alaverdi. The church and surrounding defensive wall are all that remains of the monastery. The very plain barrel-vaulted basilica church, built of dark grey stone, is somewhat sombre. With only a few small windows it looks as if it was built as much for defence as for worship.

Sanahin Monastery Added to UNESCO's World Heritage List in 1996, this famous monastery complex is just outside the city limits of Alaverdi. It can be reached by the cable-car (see opposite): from the upper terminus it is approximately 1km – walk away from the gorge to the main square, turn left and then right at a T-junction. To get there by road cross the river by the southern bridge in Alaverdi and continue up the hill past the Debed Hotel before bearing right to reach the monastery. Nowadays one of Armenia's most frequently visited sights, it was established in 966 by Queen Khosrovanush, wife of King Ashot III Bagratuni, on the site of two existing churches, St Jacob which dates from the 9th century and the Mother of God which was built sometime between 928 and 944. Sanahin became a centre of considerable cultural influence during the 10th and 11th centuries with its monastic school and important library where copyists worked to produce illuminated manuscripts. Sanahin's role declined as Armenia suffered waves of invaders although the local Argoutian family was exceptional in managing to retain its estates through to the 20th century.

The ensemble is very picturesque but does rather give the impression of having grown piecemeal. It is dominated by the **Church of the Holy Redeemer** with its conical dome; construction probably began in 966. This church, built of basalt, has its eastern façade decorated with arcature and the main window is similarly decorated. The gable of this façade has a sculptural relief depicting Smbat and Gurgen Bagratuni, two of the three sons of the founder, with a model of a church, the first appearance of such a scene in Armenia. Smbat became King Smbat II of the Bagratid dynasty, rulers of Ani, and Gurgen was the father of David Anghonin who constructed Lori Berd. The Church of the Holy Redeemer is separated from the smaller **Mother of God Church** by a gallery covered by a barrel vault, the **Academy of Gregory Magistros**, which is believed to have been used for teaching. Possibly the students sat in the niches between the monumental pillars.

On the west side of the churches are large *gavits* constructed in 1181 and 1211 and somewhat different from each other in style. The *gavit* of the Church of the Holy Redeemer is the earlier. It has four tall free-standing internal pillars supporting arches. The bases and capitals of the columns are decorated with carvings and reliefs depicting the heads of animals, fruits and geometric patterns. The *gavit* of the Mother of God Church is a three-nave hall with much lower arches than the earlier *gavit* and with less elaborate bases and capitals for the columns. Externally the western façade of this *gavit* has six arches, two to each gable. Abutting the *gavit* at its western end is the **bell tower**, crowned by a small rotunda, which is also early 13th century and thought to be Armenia's earliest. The floors of the *gavits* are paved

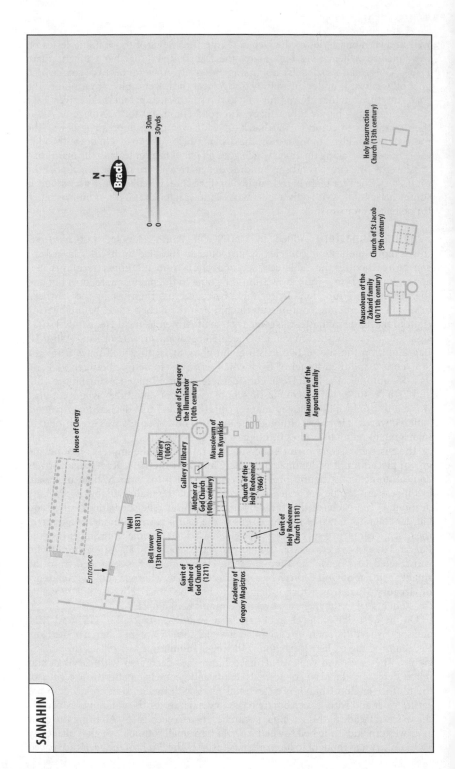

SANAHIN

House of Clergy

Well (1831)

Entrance

Bell tower (13th century)

Gavit of Mother of God Church (1211)

Academy of Gregory Magistros

Library (1063)

Gallery of library

Mausoleum of the Kyurikids

Mother of God Church (10th century)

Chapel of St Gregory the Illuminator (10th century)

Church of the Holy Redeemer (966)

Gavit of Holy Redeemer Church (1181)

Mausoleum of the Argoutian family

Mausoleum of the Zakarid family (10/11th century)

Church of St Jacob (9th century)

Holy Resurrection Church (13th century)

N

Bradt

30m
0

30yds
0

Sanahin's other claim to fame is as the birthplace of the brothers Anastas Mikoyan (1895–1978) and Artem Mikoyan (1905–70). A **museum** about them is located in a former school down the hill from the monastery (⏱ *10.00–18.00 daily, closed for lunch 13.00–14.00; guiding inc but only in Armenian AMD500*). Anastas achieved the distinction of being the longest-serving member of the Soviet Politburo. He survived a series of political upheavals to remain a member from 1935 to 1966 and was involved in many important events. In 1939, he was responsible for the discussions with Germany on trade prior to the signing of the Nazi-Soviet pact; in 1955 he was part of the delegation which sought to heal the rift with Tito in Yugoslavia; in 1962 he dealt with Cuba during the missile crisis (he spoke Spanish); in 1964 he was instrumental in ousting Khrushchev. Artem Mikoyan, by contrast, played a leading role in the development of Soviet fighter aircraft. He was named head of a new design bureau in 1939. His bureau collaborated with that headed by Mikhail Gurevich and at first produced a number of relatively unsuccessful planes. Then the turbojet-powered MiG-15, which first flew in 1947, proved a world-beating design and was the forerunner of a series of light fighter aircraft which saw extensive deployment during the Cold War era. MiG is actually an acronym for Mikoyan and Gurevich. In the museum itself, downstairs are everyday artefacts belonging to the family including furniture made by the illiterate father of the brothers. Upstairs is an exposition of their careers. In the forecourt is a MiG-21 fighter plane and a car belonging to Anastas.

with gravestones and throughout the site there is a wealth of khachkars, not all of them religious: one commemorates the building of the bridge at Alaverdi in 1192 and another the construction of an inn in 1205. Some particularly fine ones stand in front of the *gavits*.

On the complex's north side is the **library** of 1063 which has an octagonal tent roof resting on diagonally arranged arches which spring from four short pillars, one in the centre of each wall and each differently decorated. At the eastern end of the library is the small domed round **Chapel of St Gregory the Illuminator** built in the late 10th century. It is a two-storey structure with a pointed roof. To the northeast of the main complex are two **mausoleums** which date from the 10th and 11th centuries and beyond them are the 9th-century **church of St Jacob** (the nearer one) and the early 13th-century **Holy Resurrection Church** which has two identical apses. By the boundary wall on the north side is the monastery's **spring**. It is covered by a structure which dates to 1831.

Haghpat Monastery Haghpat is contemporaneous with Sanahin and very similar in style. Both were added to UNESCO's World Heritage List in 1996, the first Armenian sites to be so listed. Pilgrims in the monasteries' heyday were inevitably driven to compare the two and from this comparison derive the present names: Haghpat means 'huge wall' because that was one of its striking features, whereas Sanahin means 'older than the other'. Although Haghpat can be seen from Sanahin, to reach it requires a return to Alaverdi. Then head east along the main road for about 5km and turn right up the hill. A left fork leads to the monastery which can be seen high on the hillside. It is nowadays much more attractively sited than Sanahin, and consequently more pleasant to visit, as the approach is not through an

The Northern Provinces LORI PROVINCE

5

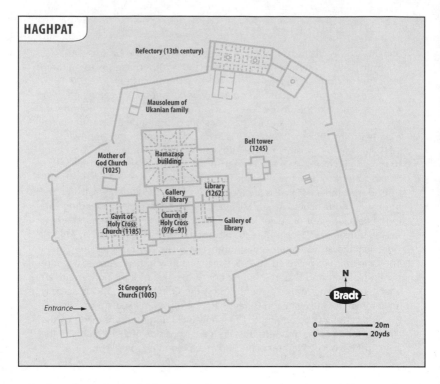

Refectory (13th century)

Mausoleum of
Ukanian family

Bell tower
(1245)

Mother of
God Church
(1025)

Hamazasp
building

Gallery
of library

Library
(1262)

Gavit of
Holy Cross
Church (1185)

Church of
Holy Cross
(976–91)

Gallery of
library

St Gregory's
Church (1005)

Entrance

N

Bradt

0   20m
0   20yds

area of rundown Soviet-era buildings. It is, however, also touristy. The **main church** with its huge dome is dedicated to the Holy Cross and was built between 976 and 991 at the behest of Queen Khosrovanush, also the founder of Sanahin. From the exterior it appears rectangular but internally is cross-shaped and, as at Sanahin, there is a relief of Smbat and Gurgen holding a model of a church on the east façade. Frescoes were added to the church in the 13th century; some are still faintly visible in the apse. Unlike Sanahin the buildings, which were gradually added, do not lead directly off each other. A smaller church, dedicated to **St Gregory the Illuminator**, was added in 1005 at the southwest side of the site and a domed **Mother of God Church** was added on the northwest side in 1025. The St Gregory Church lost its dome during rebuilding in 1211. A *gavit* was built in 1185 to the west of the cathedral and the cathedral itself gained a magnificent porch in 1201.

The three-storey **bell tower** was built in 1245, a much more substantial structure than at Sanahin. Its ground floor has the plan of a cross-dome church and serves as a chapel. The second storey by contrast is rectangular with the corners cut off thus turning into an octagonal shape. The transition between the two shapes is ingenious. The third storey, the belfry, is unusually seven sided and supported by seven columns. Another *gavit*, called the **Hamazasp building** after its donor, was built to the north of the cathedral in 1257 and is unusual for a *gavit* in being free-standing. The **library**, originally built with a wooden roof in the 10th century, was rebuilt with a stone roof in 1262. One of Armenia's most famous and beautiful khachkars, the **Holy Redeemer khachkar** of 1273, is in the passage leading to the library. This amazing work shows Christ crucified surrounded by saints and apostles with angels looking down and God the Father raising his hand in blessing. Haghpat's library became a storeroom after invaders had taken the manuscripts and the floor now has many storage jars sunk into it. The 13th-century **refectory** is an isolated building on the north side of the site. It is a long building whose tall roof is borne by intersecting arches supported by pairs of free-standing columns. The central section is crowned by octagonal domed vaults which admit light. This unusual structure adjoins the defensive wall of the monastery. Also notable to the west of the refectory is the **spring**. It is in a three-arched structure built in 1258. There are stone troughs along the back wall for watering cattle and a reservoir for general use.

Kayan Berd (fortress) The ruins of this small fortress are probably most often seen while coming down the road from Haghpat Monastery. There are also good views of it from parts of Haghpat village. Standing on a peninsula-like promontory of the plateau between Sanahin and Haghpat, the fortress is not as inaccessible as it looks and can be reached by a pleasant, relatively easy 30-minute walk from the bottom. The last few metres are up a rocky knoll but even this is quite easy as the rocks form natural steps. Starting from the lay-by on the road to Haghpat at the junction for Tsaghkashat, follow the path which goes down to the river and across a renovated medieval bridge then uphill to the right. After the first uphill stretch the path is mostly level along the side of the hill until it reaches the final short climb to the top. Much of the route is through woodland so there is some shade. There are the remains of defensive walls with semicircular towers round two sides of the triangular site. The best preserved building is the small black tuff Dsevank Mother of God Church built in 1233. Its black, red and white dome was damaged by an earthquake in 1827. The church is perched right on the edge of the site; one corner had to be built on boulders.

Akhtala Monastery (🕐 *site always; church all day*) Akhtala is further north towards the Georgian border and receives only a tiny fraction of the visitors who go to Sanahin and Haghpat. It is built in a quite different style but its setting is equally dramatic, perched up on a cliff. Unfortunately the view is marred by copper mining taking place on the opposite side of the valley, but the wooden scaffolding, which for decades obscured the view of Armenia's finest frescoes, has

---

THE 40 MARTYRS OF SEBASTE

Western visitors familiar with biblical narratives will have no difficulty in recognising what most of the frescoes depict at Akhtala, but they may be less familiar with the story of the 40 martyrs of Sebaste on the west wall of the south aisle. They were Roman soldiers martyred under Emperor Lucinius at Sebaste, Lesser Armenia, in AD320. Refusing to renounce their Christian faith, they were condemned to die by being exposed naked on a frozen lake with a north wind blowing. A warm bath nearby added to the temptation to renounce their faith. Only one succumbed and accounts vary as to what happened to him. Some say he expired immediately on entering the warm bath, others that he lived, repented and made amends for his apostasy by spending the rest of his life preaching the Gospel. The number of martyrs, however, remained at 40. A sentinel watching events was so impressed by a vision of the martyrs receiving their heavenly reward that he immediately became a Christian, stripped off his clothes and joined the 39 on the ice. The Feast of the 40 Martyrs of Sebaste is 9 March in the eastern churches, 10 March in the western.

Although maps still show Khuchap and Khorakert monasteries as being in Armenia, one is now in Georgia and the other in a disputed border region. **At present it is no longer possible safely to visit either of them from Armenia.** With the hope that one day it will again be possible to reach these fascinating monasteries from Armenia, descriptions of both are given, though they might not necessarily be fully up to date. The monasteries are only 5km apart.

RECENT HISTORY Khuchap and Khorakert monasteries have long been on the Armenia–Georgia border. When I first visited them in the early 2000s they were both in Armenia, although one had to cross slivers of Georgian territory to reach them. At that time this was no problem, the Armenian border guards simply phoned their Georgian counterparts for permission, which was readily given. Since then the exact position of the border appears to have changed, apparently without public announcement. Khorakert Monastery now seems to be definitely in Georgia and must be visited from Georgia. As far as I could ascertain, Khuchap remains in Armenia but is difficult to visit because of the border dispute. Apparently foreigners may be detained by the Georgian authorities if found by them in the disputed territory.

In 1918 Georgia and Armenia fought a short (17–31 December) war over disputed territory in the Lori, Javakheti and Borchalo districts which until 1917 had been part of the Tiflis Governate of the Russian Empire. A British-brokered ceasefire resulted in a neutral zone which was later divided between the Armenian SSR and the Georgian SSR, Lori going to Armenia, Javakheti (which has an ethnic Armenian majority) and Borchalo to Georgia. With the collapse of the USSR, the border dispute between the two independent countries resurfaced.

The whole of northern Lori has/had numerous minor crossing points to Georgia but even locals are now not allowed to go to and fro as was possible until 2008. Armenians living in the village of Jiliza, only 1km from the border with Georgia, are not allowed to cross the local checkpoint to visit either Khorakert Monastery, some 4km away, or their relatives on the other side of the border. Instead they must now travel about 100km via Alaverdi and the main international border crossing at Bagratashen.

KHUCHAP MONASTERY A 7km walk from Jiliza, Khuchap sits at the foot of Mount Lalvar. (A much more difficult route, one not permitted without special permission at the time of writing, is via the Wolf's Gate Pass (1,787m) north of Privolnoye. That road is closed in winter and absolutely dreadful in summer. Eventually after 15km a minor border crossing is reached from where it takes about an hour to walk to Khuchap. The beautiful walk along the river, through orchards and forest, involves wading across the river.)

now been removed making a visit to Akhtala even more worthwhile. To reach it take the main road east from Alaverdi for about 15km. The monastery is well signposted from the main road.

Akhtala is surrounded either by precipitous drops or by defensive walls. Entry is through the main gate in the defensive fortifications. Although this may be locked, entry can be achieved easily as there is an inconspicuous wicket gate within the main gate. Take very great care on the site as the long grass conceals drops into subterranean rooms of the original fortress whose roofs have collapsed. (The windows of some of these rooms can be seen in the defensive walls as one

The monastery is delightfully situated, hidden away in its small wooded valley. It was abandoned in the 1940s when the last nuns left, but the main church (13th century) is intact. Red felsite was used for the outer walls and forms an unusual and pleasing contrast with the yellow felsite used for the window surrounds, large crosses on two of the gable ends, and to produce a banded effect on the tall tambour. Inside, the church is rectangular with a very high cupola and two supporting octagonal pillars. There are separate naves at the west end of the church and vestibules were added at the east end sometime after construction. Outside, the decoration is amazingly varied with door and window surrounds being carved with a whole range of geometric patterns while carved figures of animals and projecting carved animal heads can be seen high up on the tambour. Every one of the 12 carved windows around the tambour has a different geometric pattern. On the west façade are the remains of a gallery-like addition with four arches. North of the main church are the remains of other monastic buildings, much plainer and built of grey andesite.

KHORAKERT MONASTERY Unless/until the minor border crossing at Jiliza opens and if non-locals are then allowed to use it, Khorakert can only be visited from Georgia (see below). Built in the late 12th and early 13th centuries, the really striking, unique, feature is that the tambour (which has ten sides – very rare in Armenia) is not a solid construction but comprises in the lower part 30 separate six-sided columns. The interior of the cupola is also most unusual: six intersecting arches form a six-pointed star in the centre of which is a hexagon which itself encloses another six-pointed star. The *gavit* of 1257 was also highly distinctive. It was roofed by another set of intersecting arches but unfortunately this collapsed in an earthquake in 1965. The whole ensemble gives the impression that it would not survive another. Outside the church on the south side is a stone frog which has been placed on a plinth. It looks as if the frog could originally have been mounted on a roof and there is certainly an unidentified animal on top of the cupola of the church. Traces of the main gateway, chapels and various other buildings also survive as does the well with its secret passage down to the river.

Note it is possible to visit Khorakert from the Georgian side of the Bagratashen/Sadakhlo crossing. I thank Dmitry Bosky for the following directions. Take the Sadakhlo–Tsobi–Aghkyorpi road to Aghkyorpi. The monastery is a few kilometres outside the village. When it is dry the minor roads are driveable in an ordinary car to within about 100m of the monastery. This is a border zone and locals say that strictly speaking a pass is needed to visit the area. Perhaps one could be obtained from the border post at Sadakhlo.

approaches the monastery.) The 10th-century fortifications, constructed of basalt, were built by the Kurikian branch of the Bagratid dynasty: Kurikian was a vassal state of the king at Ani. The fortress is contemporary with that at Lori (pages 247–8). Akhtala, like Lori, was a highly defensible site and one of the main strongholds of northern Armenia. The large round tower beside the entrance can be accessed with care. There are three partially remaining storeys each divided into sections by arches which radiated from a central column to the circumferential wall. Within the fortress stands the monastery, and the remains of other buildings can be seen. The **main existing church**, dedicated to the Mother of God, was built between 1212 and 1250 at the behest of Prince Ivan Zakarian who belonged to the same dynasty that obtained control of Lori Berd and Kobayr Monastery. It was therefore built as a Georgian Orthodox church but is on the site of an earlier Armenian one. It is of the domed basilica type with four massive pillars, two of which are free-standing. The dome collapsed in the 18th century and the existing small pyramidal roof dates from 1978. There are plans to rebuild the tambour and dome with work scheduled to begin sometime in 2014. Built, like the fortress, of basalt, the monastery is quite different in appearance from those at Sanahin and Haghpat, reflecting the Georgian influence on its design. The interior frescoes are absolutely magnificent. Especially notable is the Virgin Mary enthroned in the apse. Her face has been defaced either by the elements or by artillery (accounts vary); a hole in the wall can be seen in the centre of the cross high up on the exterior of the east façade. Beneath the Virgin Mary is a depiction of the Last Supper with Christ giving the bread to St Peter on the left and the wine to St Paul on the right. Two ranks of saints stand below. Other scenes include the Last Judgement over the west door, the trial and Crucifixion of Jesus and the Resurrection. Figures of saints adorn the pillars which divide the building into three naves.

Large relief crosses on each façade together with smaller more intricate crosses on the elaborate arcaded porch and the small chapel built on to the southwest corner of the church also show Georgian influence. Remains of domestic buildings line the inside of the east wall between the entrance gate and the main church; it is here that care must be taken to avoid falling into the underground rooms (see page 260). The small church in the west of the precinct is sometimes called the winter church – presumably it was easier to heat a smaller building.

JILIZA, KHUCHAP AND KHORAKERT MONASTERIES Although maps show these two monasteries to be in Armenia it is not, at the time of writing, possible to visit them safely from Armenia (see box, pages 260–1 for details). As the main point of travelling the 30km to Jiliza was to visit these fascinating monasteries there is now less reason to go there, although the route through the increasingly forested countryside affords many beautiful views. The village of Jiliza is only 1km from the Georgian border. Until 1992 no road linked Jiliza district with the rest of Armenia but following independence a new dirt road was constructed direct from Alaverdi. The road was upgraded in 2007 and, although still a dirt road, is reasonably good. The only public transport is a once-weekly *marshrutka*, from Jiliza to Alaverdi on Fridays, returning on Mondays. **To get to Jiliza**, leave Alaverdi by the Madan road which climbs out of the valley behind the copper plant. If you do find yourself in Jiliza there is one site nearby which it is possible to visit, the **fortress of Chakhalaberd**, close to the Georgian border. You need a local guide for the walk across grassy countryside and through woods to reach the ruined fortress on its elevated position overlooking Georgia.

FROM STEPANAVAN TO THE DEBED Rather than travelling via Vanadzor it is possible to travel via the **monastery of Hnevank**, a very worthwhile route but lacking public transport and unsuitable for larger vehicles at the eastern end. The road deteriorates east of Kurtan but is manageable by car as far as Hnevank. For the descent from Hnevank into the Debed Gorge a 4x4 is advisable. *En route* it is also possible to visit **DendroPark** (⊕ *10.00–19.00 daily*), an arboretum covering 35ha which was founded by a Pole in 1931 for the cultivation and acclimatisation of trees. The arboretum is well maintained; specimen trees are labelled. It is one of the most pleasant places in Armenia for a stroll. From Stepanavan head back towards Vanadzor for 10km as far as the village of **Gyulagarak**. In the village turn left. The road then passes the derelict village church of 1874 on the left with its black and red bell tower. If you wish to visit DendroPark turn right on to an unmade road (poor condition in places) signposted to the arboretum and bear left at the fork. The extremely ruinous 6th-century **monastery of Toromavank** is then passed on the right. Continue straight ahead for DendroPark.

If you do not wish to visit DendroPark keep left after the 1874 church. The road runs east through an area of strip farming with the Dzoraget River in its increasingly deep gorge to the north, the Herher River to the south and (often snow-capped) peaks in the distance. Just before **Kurtan** village the road to the Debed Gorge bears right to cross the Herher River and shortly after this there are some immensely impressive views down into the gorge on the left. Both booted eagles and golden eagles can be seen along the gorge. The highlight comes in a few minutes when, during the descent of some hairpin bends the extensive ruins of the **monastery of Hnevank** can be seen down in the gorge on a small hill close to the confluence of the Dzoraget and Herher rivers. In early summer this spectacularly beautiful site is enhanced further by the brilliance of the wild flowers. The monastery was founded in the 7th century but rebuilt with a much higher tambour in 1144. The *gavit* dates from the late 12th century and leads to both the small cross-dome main church on the east and a chapel to the west. Restoration may have diminished some of the charm of undisturbed ruins, but it does enable the visitor to make more sense of the layout. A barrel-vaulted building lies to the west and what was thought to be the refectory a short distance to the east. To the south of the *gavit* are the low remains of other monastic buildings, all but hidden when the vegetation grows waist-high.

Continuing east the unsurfaced road eventually leaves the plateau and descends countless zigzags to reach the Debed River at **Dzoraget** village, a short distance south of the confluence of the Dzoraget and the Debed.

TAVUSH PROVINCE

Armenia's heavily wooded and most northeasterly province is bounded to the north by Georgia and to the east by Azerbaijan. Land captured from Azerbaijan in 1994 has since been incorporated into Tavush: in particular the road from the provincial capital of Ijevan north to Noyemberian and on to Lori and the Georgian border crosses an area of Azerbaijan which, since 1994, has in practice been Armenian. It is most important here to use the new road which keeps a safe distance from the border: the old road passes dangerously close to the ceasefire line and is subject to attack by Azeri snipers.

The aftermath of the war is evident in other ways in Tavush: some sites close to the border, notably Khoranashat Monastery, are inaccessible because of the risk from Azeri snipers and the former main road and rail routes from Yerevan to Georgia and the rest of the former Soviet Union are closed at the border with Azerbaijan since they crossed Azeri territory to reach Tbilisi. The rail route is actually completely closed north of Haghartsin station (just north of Dilijan) and the overhead catenary has been dismantled. Freight trains do still operate from Yerevan as far as Haghartsin, passing under the Pambak range by the 8,311m-long Margahovit Tunnel, but passenger services have been withdrawn. Tavush's two largest towns, Ijevan and Dilijan, are sited on the Aghstev River whose valley broadens out as it flows northwards towards Azerbaijan. It rises in the southeast of Lori province in the Gugarats range and, as is the case with other north-flowing Armenian rivers, its waters join the Kura River ultimately to reach the Caspian Sea south of Baku.

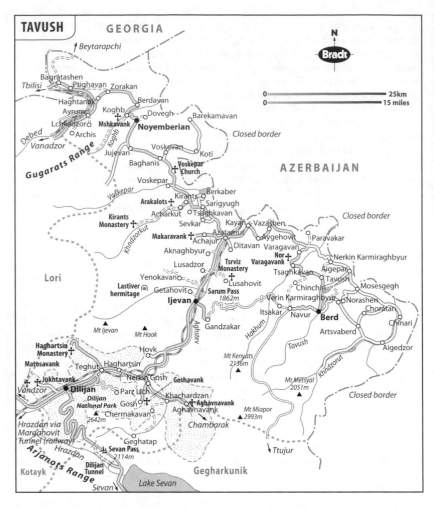

Travelling south from Dilijan to Sevan in Gegharkunik province became easier in 2003 as a new road tunnel (the **Dilijan tunnel**) was opened avoiding the **Sevan Pass** (2,114m). The most popular sights are the monasteries of Goshavank and Haghartsin near Dilijan and Makaravank north of Ijevan. The east of the province is understandably less visited but it is here that some of the most scenic roads are to be found.

GETTING THERE AND AROUND   Two main highways enter southern Tavush: one from Vanadzor to the east and one from Yerevan, via Sevan, from the south, these roads meeting in Dilijan. The main road through the province then runs north to link up with the Debed Gorge road in northern Lori and the road to the Georgian border at Bagratashen. For general comments on transport see pages 79–83. Ijevan, Dilijan and Noyemberian all have reasonable bus stations. **Minibuses** go more or less everywhere (check locally for details, always remembering that minibuses tend to depart when and if they are full). **Taxis** can be a convenient and relatively cheap way of reaching places of interest. For example, a round trip from Dilijan to Haghartsin and Goshavank monasteries costs about AMD8,000.

WHERE TO STAY The region can be explored from either Dilijan or Ijevan, the latter being more suitable for northern Tavush. Dilijan is nearer the more popular monastic sites and is convenient for those wishing to travel south to Lake Sevan. There is plentiful accommodation in the region, particularly so in Dilijan, from the upper end of the hotel range to a riverside campsite. See pages 85–7 for general comments on accommodation. Where listings are plotted on a map, this is indicated below.

Dilijan
Map, page 274.

Hotel Dilijan Resort & Spa (70 rooms & 12 cottages) 66 Getapnya St; ☎ 10 207755, 268 24303; m 055 047755 e info@hoteldilijan. am; www.hoteldilijan.am. This one-time Soviet hotel has undergone further renovation to transform itself into one of high international standard. Cottages sleep 4–8 persons. Sports facilities, swimming pool, children's play areas, spa treatments available. Disabled access. Restaurant. Reduced rates Nov–Apr excluding Christmas & New Year. Wi-Fi. Cards accepted. HB (b/fast & lunch). **$$$**

Villarest (8 rooms) 20 Parz Lich St; m 098 444409; e villarest@mail.ru: www.villarest.net. A new hotel (opened 2013) about 9km from Dilijan on the road up to Parz Lich. A hotel of international standard. Swimming pool, indoor sports, children's play area. Bright, airy restaurant with full menu. Average meal AMD6,000. Wi-Fi. Accepts cards. **$$$**

Tufenkian Old Dilijan (12 rooms & 2 apts) Sharambeyan St; book through the Tufenkian office in Yerevan, ☎ 60 501010; e hotels@tufenkian.am; www.tufenkianheritage. am. Has 12 rooms in the Old Dilijan Complex, some entered from pedestrianised Sharambeyan St, some from Miasnikian St above Sharambeyan. A restored 19th-century town house, Ananov Guesthouse, in the Complex has 2 floors, each forming an apt, with balcony, accommodating 2 persons. Lower floor AMD45,200, upper floor AMD50,800. All rooms decorated in hallmark Tufenkian style. B/fast taken in Tufenkian restaurant a short distance along the street. No room service. Reception open ⏰ 09.00–21.00. Wi-Fi. Cards accepted excluding American Express. Price varies according to size of room. Reduced rates Nov–Mar. **$$$–$$**

Daravand Guest House (7 rooms) 46 Abovian St; ☎ 268 27857; m 094 420965, 091 411766; e info@daravand.com; www.daravand. com. An attractive 3-storey house just outside the town on the way to Jukhtakvank monastery. Food prepared from fresh local produce. Restaurant recommended. English, Russian, German & Persian spoken. Wi-Fi. Not all rooms are en suite. **$$**

Getap Restaurant-Motel (9 rooms) Tbilisi highway; ☎ 268 25614; m 093 808642. Outside the town on the road north. Principally a restaurant (see page 267) which has expanded to include accommodation. Wi-Fi. B/fast extra AMD1,500pp. **$$**

Haghartsin Hotel-Restaurant Complex (31 rooms & 10 cottages) 121 Kamo St; ☎ 268 27770; m 093 044700; e info@haghartsin. com; www.haghartsin.com. Just outside the town on the road south. This pleasant stylish hotel continues to expand. All rooms finished to a high standard. Also has 10 motel rooms across the road for 2/4/6 persons at AMD20,000/30,000/40,000. Swimming pool. Restaurant. Wi-Fi. No room service. **$$**

Paradise Hotel (50 rooms) 156 Kamo St; ☎ 268 24016; m 077 299216; e info@ paradisehotel.am; www.paradisehotel.am. A Best Western chain hotel just outside town on the road south. A former Soviet hotel renovated to a high international standard. Swimming pool, sauna, 'kid's club', indoor sports. Restaurant has both à la carte & buffet. Standard rooms have 1 dbl bed (no twins), more expensive rooms have twin dbls (for 2 persons). Wi-Fi. Accepts cards. **$$**

Soonk Motel (10 rooms) Parz Lich St; m 093 414255. 5km from town centre on road to Parz Lich, off the road to Ijevan. A family business. Rooms basic but clean. B/fast extra AMD1,000pp. Other meals available, order in advance. **$$–$**

Hotel Seno (10 rooms) 5 Miasnikian St; m 094 763776. This newly built hotel in the centre of Dilijan was nearing completion at the time of research with some rooms ready to be occupied. Owned by the same family as Mkhitar Gosh Hotel, Gosh village (see page 266). Reception on 2nd floor, rooms on 3rd & 4th floors. No lift; 4th floor reached by outside spiral staircase from 3rd floor. Wi-Fi. Superb location, overlooking the town, just below Dilijan Museum & Art Gallery. Will also function as a restaurant. **$**

🏠 **Parz Lich Rest Area** ↘263 61011,
m 093 331144; e parz-lich@ararathotel.am;
www.ararathotel.am. Closed in winter. 10km
from main road. A destination mainly aimed at
Armenian family day trips or w/end holidays. (See
page 278 for details of Parz Lich & leisure facilities.)
Restaurant. Wi-Fi. Accommodation (b/fast not
inc) comprises 10 tents (bring own bedding, etc)
AMD2,000pp; 6 wooden huts (3 with 2 beds,
3 with 4 beds) AMD3,000pp. Separate toilet/
washing area. (*Also has 1 cottage, sleeps 8, b/fast
inc AMD60,000.*) **$**

Ijevan
Map, page 269.
🏠 **Dok Hotel** (7 rooms) 40 Ankakhutian St;
↘263 40171; m 094 515154, 091 301905;
e lusmel@yandex.ru. Can book online at
www.armhotels.am. This may be the best
available in the town centre but not particularly
recommended. My room smelt strongly of tobacco
smoke & the meal in the restaurant (supposed to
be the best in Ijevan) was disappointing. Wi-Fi.
B/fast not inc. **$$–$**
🏠 **Motel Elite** (5 rooms) Yerevanian St;
m 091 111300. A short distance outside the town
near the wine factory on the road south. Set in a
well-tended garden. The proprietors are on site
between 10.30 & 22.30; outside of these hours
the staff comprises a chap manning the security
gate. Note therefore that if you want to leave early
in the morning you will have to pay the previous
day. B/fast available with prior notice. B/fast extra
AMD1,000pp. FB AMD5,000pp. **$**
🏠 **Hotel Kantegh** (10 rooms) Yerevan–Tiflis
highway 137km from Yerevan; m 093 432632
(Sergei Ghazarian). Kantegh means 'lamp'. As the
address suggests this new hotel (opened 2010) is
just outside Ijevan on the road north. The hotel, the
clothing shop next door & the petrol station are
owned by the same family who live on the premises.
Reception & rooms on 2nd floor. 2 family rooms,
each of which sleeps 4 persons, at AMD20,000/room.
Wi-Fi. B/fast not inc, AMD2,000pp. Other meals
available. Very acceptable, pleasantly decorated
rooms. For those with transport this may well be the
best option in Ijevan. If the hotel entrance is locked
go through the shop. **$**
🏠 **Hotel Mosh** (8 rooms) 3 Yerevanian St;
↘263 35611; e moshhotel@mail.ru. Central, near
main market. A very acceptable basic hotel. Rooms

without bathroom are even cheaper. Wi-Fi. Cards
accepted. B/fast extra AMD1,200pp. **$**

Elsewhere in the province
🏠 **Apaga Tour** (See pages 272–3) Not a
tour operator but an enterprise near Yenokavan
mainly offering complete packages inc horseriding,
trekking & accommodation. Their own website
does not include information on purely hotel
accommodation, but it is possible to book
accommodation alone either directly or via www.
hotels.am/ijevan/apaga-gomer. **$$**
🏠 **Berd Hotel** (6 rooms) 1/1 Levon Bek
St, Berd; ↘267 24535; m 093 557424. Closed
Dec–Jan. Some renovation but still has a Soviet air
about it. Wi-Fi. B/fast not inc & not available. **$**
🏠 **Hotel Levon 2** (9 rooms) 29 Noyember St,
Noyemberian; m 091 201410 (Flora Antonian).
This hotel, a former office block, provides much-
needed accommodation in the north of Tavush.
On the right as one enters Noyemberian from the
north. Also functions as a very pleasant restaurant.
Own produce inc eggs & honey. Homemade jams.
BBQ & picnics available. B/fast extra AMD2,000pp.
Rooms without en suite AMD7,000, with en suite
AMD10,000. **$**
🏠 **Mkhitar Gosh Hotel** (10 rooms) Gosh
village; m 093 758595, 098 441019;
e hotelgosh@rambler.ru. Can book online at www.
armhotels.am. This delightful small hotel at the
head of the village square opened in 2010. En-
suite shower rooms are small but smart. Superb
views of the monastery from front bedrooms. **$**
🏠 **Utik Hotel** (9 rooms) 4 Haik Nahapat St,
Berd; m 093 373090, 094 739762. Of the 9 rooms
available, 4 (not recommended, but cheap at
AMD2,000 pp) share 2 bathrooms & b/fast is not
inc. B/fast AMD1,500pp. The other 5 rooms have
b/fast inc & are en suite; those with a pedestal
toilet AMD12,000, those with a squat toilet
AMD10,000. **$**
🏠 **Zikatar Environmental Centre** (7 rooms
(sgl, dbl & trpl) & 3 cottages) Koghb village;
↘266 62318; m 094 884355; e zikatar_center@
yahoo.com. Within the Caucasus Regional
Forestry Training Centre 10km from Koghb village.
Accommodation for training groups but can
provide rooms for visitors. Note that no food or
drink is available: visitors are expected to bring it
with them. Centre's kitchen can be used. There is a
service charge of approx AMD3,000 for using the

dining room. May suit those who wish to walk in the area. Bicycles for hire AMD1,000/hr. **$**

Å Anapat campsite Khachaghbyur River, near Yenokavan; facebook.com/anapatlastiver. For further details, see pages 272–3. **$**

✗ WHERE TO EAT AND DRINK Dilijan has better eating places than Ijevan but Ijevan is better provided with cafés for a snack late at night. It has a number of **riverside cafés** with canopied open-air tables, on both sides of the river, at the southern end of the town centre. The one on the east bank has quieter music. On the main roads there are numbers of barbecue and motel-style eateries, apart from those listed below. Some of the hotels listed opposite also function as restaurants as noted in individual entries.

✗ Café Cascade [map, page 269] Just up from Hotel Dok, Ijevan, off Ankakhutian St, in the open area with defunct fountains. ⏰ 10.30–24.00. Probably the most pleasant café in Ijevan with tasty food & friendly staff. Wi-Fi. Sandwiches AMD350–750, soups AMD600–1,000, pizza AMD2,500, *khorovats* AMD1,500–2,200, tea AMD250, Armenian coffee AMD200.

✗ Getap Restaurant-Motel Tbilisi highway; ✆268 25614; m 093 808642. Outside Dilijan on the road to Ijevan. Built in 2000 with later additions the restaurant consists of a number of chalets beside the river in restful gardens. One of several such complexes on this road. Also has accommodation (see page 265). Avg cost of meal AMD2,500.

✗ Haykanoush Restaurant [map, page 274] Sharambeyan St, Dilijan. Contact through Tufenkian office in Yerevan (✆60 501010; e info@tufenkian. am) or reception (⏰ 09.00–21.00) at Old Dilijan Complex; ⏰ 10.00–22.00 daily. Part of the restored Old Dilijan Complex. In the style of a late 19th- or early 20th-century Dilijan dining room. Wooden floors covered with handmade Tufenkian carpets. Typical Armenian dishes at the usual, relatively expensive, Tufenkian prices.

✗ Minimo Café [map, page 274] 50 Gorky St, Dilijan; ✆268 22440. A Georgian restaurant/café next to the bus station in the town centre. Food is fine but service slow. Soups AMD700–1,000, Georgian main courses AMD900–16,000, individual *khachapuri* AMD800–1,000.

OTHER PRACTICALITIES Ijevan has a large market as well as many small shops and is better for shopping than Dilijan. However, Dilijan has the tourist souvenir shops. None of the towns has a tourist information office but there is a private one-man, one-room information source in Dilijan (see page 273). Koghb village (page 272) offers good local information in the Culture Centre and some local information is available at Gandzakar municipal building (⏰ 09.00–17.00 Mon-Fri; for help with local guiding contact Zarmayil (Zarmo for short) Mardanyan m 094 469607; e zarmayilmardanyan@ymail.com).

SUMMER HOLIDAY IN DILIJAN, 1965

The province's more improbable visitors have included the English composer Benjamin Britten (1913–76) and the tenor Peter Pears (1910–86) who spent their summer holiday in Dilijan in August 1965 as guests of the Armenian Composers' Union along with the cellist Mstislav Rostropovich and his wife, the soprano Galina Vishnevskaya. Both Peter Pears and Galina Vishnevskaya have left accounts of the experience: while everybody seems to have enjoyed their visit, the English visitors had to listen to performances of the latest compositions of the Armenian composers, while headaches for the hosts included having to deal with Benjamin Britten wanting to buy a pair of shoes when his existing ones gave out – shoes were virtually unobtainable in the Soviet Union at the time.

IJEVAN (*Telephone code: 263*) The name of Ijevan, meaning 'inn', recalls the scarcely imaginable days when silk route traders passed through these forests. Ijevan is nowadays a pleasant though unremarkable town, its appearance enhanced by the extensive use of white felsite for building. The local dry red and white wines, made from grapes more usually associated with Georgia, are among Armenia's best.

The main street of Ijevan follows the west bank of the Aghstev River and the **market**, **post office** and **bus station** are all within a short distance of each other. The park along the east bank is a favourite place for locals to stroll. Also on the east side are the **banks** and the **sculpture park**. A relaxing hour or two can be had wandering around this park. Unfortunately the thought-provoking sculptures are not labelled. A catalogue was published and, if you can find one, it enhances any visit.

The local **historical-ethnographical museum** (⊕ *10.00–17.00 Mon–Fri*) is about 1km south of the town. It is a wide-ranging collection which includes geological specimens, wildlife, farming implements and domestic items. All the labels, now somewhat faded, are handwritten in Armenian. The elderly curator certainly knows his stuff and talks enthusiastically about each exhibit. For him one of the prized items is a radio given by Stalin to troops, together with a newspaper carrying Stalin's obituary.

Not far from the museum, on the opposite side of the road, is the **Ijevan Wine Factory**. Tours of the factory are possible (m *094 140018; cost AMD2,500–4,555 pp depending on length of tour & wines tasted*). It is also possible to visit the **Ijevan Carpet Factory** (*4 Vasilian St;* ✆*263 32498;* m *099 118484;* ⊕ *10.00–17.00*).

NORTHEAST FROM IJEVAN The former main rail and road routes to Azerbaijan follow the gradually broadening valley of the Aghstev. The first turn right after leaving Ijevan leads to the village of **Lusahovit** where the **Tsrviz or Moro-Dzor Monastery** is located. (The right turn is signposted for Khashtarak. In Khashtarak turn right 2km from the main road, almost a U-turn, and then continue straight ahead until Lusahovit is reached and you see the church below the village.) Established in the 5th century, the main **Mother of God Church** was rebuilt in the 12th and 13th centuries and has been restored fairly recently. It is a tiny four-apse church, one of only nine such early medieval churches in Armenia. Three of the four apses are seen externally, the fourth rectangular west wing concealing its internal apse. The four wings cluster closely round the relatively high tambour giving a somewhat curious appearance. The lower courses are of rough-hewn basalt, the upper of dressed stone. After 32km the main road now bears right at Kayan before reaching the border: even newer maps still show it going straight ahead into Azerbaijan. At the village of **Aygehovit** is a church called **Srvegh**, or (by locals) Srvis, high up on the hillside to the south. Its name, which means 'long pointed neck', is very apt. The ruined church, with its tall tambour and pointed dome, is very similar to Kirants Monastery (see page 272) both in style and the use of bricks for construction. To reach it, turn right in Aygehovit on to an unmade road which becomes a track going uphill through a field. Park here and walk the rest of the way, about 30 minutes up a steep rutted track. Or park in the village, in which case it would take about an hour to walk. The entrance to the monastery is through a gate on the left where there is a welcome spring. The path to the church goes from the far end of the barbecue shelter.

After Aygehovit the main road winds up and over a pass with numerous hairpin bends as far as the village of **Varagavan**. Turn right on to the main street of the village (Nor Varagavank is signposted 4.5km) and continue through it. A good road to the monastery winds up through attractive forest where both green and black woodpeckers can be found. The **monastery of Nor Varagavank** is very important historically. Having been in a sadly ruined state for a long time, work to renovate the façades and stabilise the

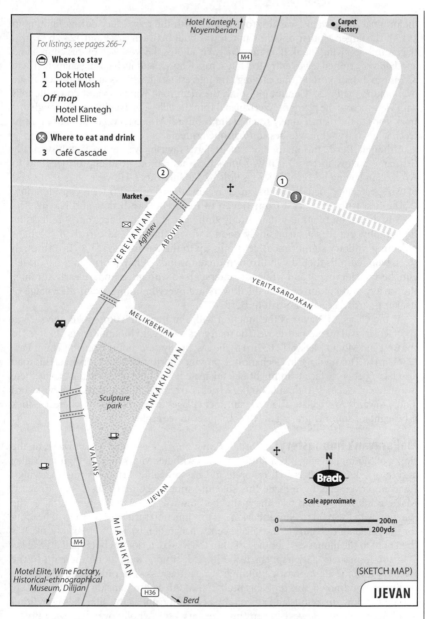

walls is under way. It was founded, as Anapat, by David Bagratuni, son of King Vasak I. The oldest part of the complex is the small Church of the Holy Cross built in 1198 at the southeast side. A two-storey burial vault was added at its north side in 1200. The monastery's importance, however, increased considerably in 1213 when it was chosen as the site for a relic, a piece of the True Cross brought to Armenia by Sts Hripsime and Gayane, which had been removed from the monastery of Varagavank, near Van in present-day Turkey, when that monastery was threatened by Mongol invaders. Hence the name Anapat was changed to Nor ('New') Varagavank. (The relic, back by then at the original Varagavank, was destroyed along with the monastery during fighting in 1915.) The larger Mother of God Church was built between 1224 and 1237 by David Bagratuni's son King Vasak II. A massive *gavit* adjoins the west wall of this church and another, very ruined, gives entry to Holy Cross Church and its flanking chapels. There are unusual door portals, fine carving and interesting khachkars at this attractive site overlooking the forest. Continuing south the main road winds up and down the hills with views across the plains of Azerbaijan. From the village of **Tsaghkavan,** a rough dirt track leads to the picturesquely situated **Shkhmuradi Monastery**. For details of how to reach it, go to www.bradtguides.com/europe/armenia.

Although **Berd**, the main town of eastern Tavush, was important historically (its name means 'fortress') it now suffers from its remote position, former links to Azerbaijan having been cut. There is little to detain visitors. However, it is at one end of two spectacular roads in Tavush and travelling them certainly merits consideration. The first is the road east from **Ijevan to Berd via Gandzakar and Navur**. The road is shown on maps as a dauntingly sinuous road, which accurately reflects its topography, but it is a surprisingly good and well-maintained dirt road (perhaps reflecting military significance). It climbs up to the Sarum Pass (1,862m) through steep wooded hills then down through mixed woods of hawthorn, oak, ash, hazel, elm, beech, elderberry and wild rose, interspersed with grassland. In early summer the variety and colour of the wild flowers are overwhelming. From the village of Itsakar the road is good asphalt to Berd.

At the village of **Navur** is the junction with the **Berd to Ttujur** road, the second spectacular road mentioned above. The road goes south with Mount Kenats (2,136m) to the west and Mount Metsyal (2,051m) to the east finally descending from the Ttujur Pass (2,092m) to Ttujur village in Gegharkunik province northwest of Chambarak. This road also has a better surface than might be anticipated. Not long after leaving Navur there is a statue of General Andranik, on horseback, carrying a child and holding his sword aloft – towards Azerbaijan. There are summer villages in the mountains where livestock is brought for summer grazing. It is a good place to see eagles.

Makaravank (monastery) (⊕ *site, always; church, every day*) Makaravank, on the slopes of Mount Paytatar, is beautifully situated with fine views over the Aghstev Valley and into Azerbaijan. It is well restored and has probably Armenia's finest carvings. Road improvements have made this splendid monastery more accessible. To reach Makaravank from Ijevan take the main road towards the Azeri border as far as the junction with the road to **Noyemberian**. At this junction turn left on to a road heading for the village of **Achajur**. In the village centre a sign points right to Makaravank. It is then 6km to the monastery; for the last 3km the road deteriorates but is still driveable.

If the monastery gate happens to be locked, simply walk along the path to the right, past domestic monastic buildings, to gain access. The **oldest church**, whose dedicatee is unknown, was probably built in the 10th century. Inside it has beautifully carved window surrounds and an equally beautiful front to the altar dais with floral and linear designs. However, even this fine carving is wholly overshadowed by the amazing carving of the main **Mother of God Church** built in 1204 by Vardan, son of Prince Bazaz. The carving here is wonderful. In particular the front of this altar dais is covered with eight-pointed stars separated by octagons in each of which is a different elaborate design: a man in a boat, sphinxes, sirens, birds, floral arrangements and other unusual designs. Outside there is more fine carving; the south façade has a sundial above the main window and a bird below it, while the smaller round windows each have a different intricate design. The *gavit* was added by Prince Vache Vachutian early in the 13th century. Plain outside except for a bull and lion fighting

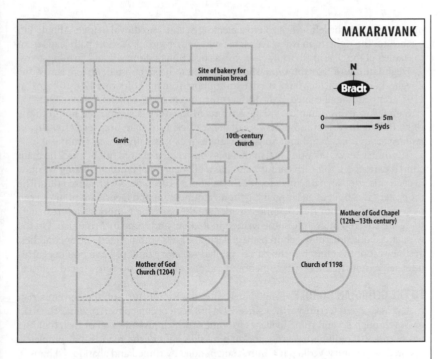

Site of bakery for communion bread

Gavit

10th-century church

N

Bradt

0 — 5m
0 — 5yds

Mother of God Chapel (12th–13th century)

Mother of God Church (1204)

Church of 1198

to the left of the door and a winged sphinx with a crown on its head to the right, it is a riot of carving inside. Adjoining the north side of the original church is the site of a **bakery** for making communion loaves. East of the main church is the small **Mother of God Chapel**, which is very unusual, being round in its lower part and octagonal in its upper part. It is surmounted by a round tambour. It was built in 1198 and like other parts of the complex has richly carved decoration.

NORTHWARD TOWARDS LORI Taking the Noyemberian road after the army barracks, Kirants village is reached after 10km. To go to **Kirants Monastery** and the other sites along the road turn left here and continue through the village of Acharkut for about 4km until the road ends at a barrier erected to stop illegal logging. It is possible to get the barrier opened but the track is so bad beyond here that walking is preferable, at least after the next kilometre or so. The walk through the forest with the Karahan River close by is extremely pleasant. At the barrier are information boards about the places and wildlife. Some of the sites are difficult to find; a local guide may be a good idea. It is 10km from Achakut to Kirants Monastery along a difficult, rutted and often very muddy track; allow 2½–3 hours to Kirants alone.

Arakalots Monastery is the first site to be signposted, off right. The 13th-century fortified monastery occupies an extensive area on a rock outcrop. The main church, a small basilica with a tall round tambour and dome, has remains of frescoes in the apse, sadly defaced by graffiti. The church is entered through the *gavit* on its west side. The open dome of the *gavit* is a good example of the *hazarashen* method of construction where stones are added across angles to make an aperture of decreasing size (*hazar* is Armenian for 'thousand'). The north wall of the church together with the north and west walls of the *gavit* form part of the defensive wall around the site. Outside the south wall of the church stands a notable khachkar. To the south through the trees are the substantial ruins of domestic buildings. A short distance beyond Arakalots a bridge over the river on the left brings you to a picnic area and a **medieval bridge**. About 2km further, on the right, is an extensive picnic area with a spring. A short path leads from the far left of the clearing to a low cave with a collection of domestic and farming items.

Deghdznut and Samson monasteries are next to be signposted, off left, across the Zayghoshan bridge which has a Persian inscription from the Hijra year 1207 (Gregorian 1792). Both are small ruined 12th–13th century monasteries which I failed to find.

Some 9km from Acharkut village **Kirants Monastery** is signposted uphill to the right. If there in early summer beware of dense thickets of giant hogweed (*Heracleum mantegazzianum*). Avoid touching the plant as it causes painful weals on the skin. The monastery is very unusual in that it is constructed of fired tuff bricks. The main church dates from the 13th century and has a tall octagonal tambour, a long window in each side, with an octagonal dome. The tambour is decorated with glazed tiles. The monastery was built as a Georgian Orthodox foundation and Georgian influence can be seen in the interior frescoes, most evident in the apse and tambour. Unfortunately these are covered in graffiti, some written in Russian and some in Armenian. On the west and south sides of the church are gallery-like halls with pointed entrance arches. To the west of the church is the barrel-vaulted refectory built of large boulders. This unusual, remote monastery is somehow a sad place: derelict, overgrown and defaced.

TO THE GEORGIAN BORDER Immediately after the Kirants turn-off the Noyemberian road crosses Azeri territory which since 1994 has been occupied by Armenia. The road passes through several ruined villages in some of which just one wall of each building has been left standing. A weird sight on a hillside right of the road is the completely restored 7th-century **Voskepar Church** surrounded by ruined and abandoned houses. The road re-enters Armenia proper and 35km from the junction with the former main road to Azerbaijan it reaches the town of **Noyemberian**, damaged by Azeri shells in the early 1990s and by an earthquake in July 1997. Some 4km north is **Koghb**. At the north end of the village, more or less opposite a big military base, is Koghb Culture Centre. On the second floor are two gems, an information centre and a museum. The very helpful director of the **information centre** (✆ *266 52599;* m *077 755755;* ⊕ *10.00–18.00 Mon– Fri*) can help with bus times, accommodation information, etc and can arrange a guide to local places such as Mshkavank (see below). He is also very happy to show visitors round the small but well-presented museum (⊕ *10.00–18.00*). Koghb does not have a petrol station – it is one of the few places where a mobile petrol station can still be seen, namely a van full of containers of petrol from which the fuel is transferred by bucket.

Mshkavank (monastery) lies about 6km southwest of Koghb. From the Culture Centre follow the blue signs to the Zikatar Environmental Centre. After about 3km a signposted track goes left to Mshkavank. The final 3km is a rocky track which needs a 4x4 to drive but it makes a pleasant walk up through the wooded countryside. I have seen tortoises on this track. The 12th-century *gavit* almost overwhelms the smaller 5th–6th century Mother of God basilica which is entered from the *gavit*. The *gavit* is on a stepped base and has remnants of decoration around the entrance. The roof is supported by two pairs of arches at right angles to each other and the open dome is constructed in a similar fashion. On the east façade of the church there is an unusual cross.

LASTIVER AND THE RIVER KHACHAGHBYUR Two very appealing holiday enterprises have been developed near the village of Yenokavan just north of Ijevan. There is a horseriding and trekking centre called Apaga Tour, and a local family has established a campsite with accommodation and meals available in an exceptionally beautiful spot by the tumbling waters of the Khachaghbyur ('Cross-spring') River. From Ijevan take the main road north for about 5km and, after crossing the

Khachaghbyur, turn left for **Yenokavan** which lies about 8km further on. The riding school only allows parking for its residents, so if making for the campsite either leave vehicles in Yenokavan or park on rough ground outside the school. There are about three *marshrutkas* a day from Ijevan, or take a taxi. **Apaga Tour** (❨ *263 60703;* m *091 290799; 099 250125;* e *info@apaga.info; www.apaga-tour.com*) offers packages which include full board, accommodation (in very attractive chalets) and riding or trekking with guides. They offer day excursions from the centre (*AMD30,000/day pp*) and longer camping trips (*AMD35,000/day pp*). It's a little over an hour's uphill walk from Yenokavan village to the school although anyone booked can be met with horses. The whole area on the slopes of the Mtnasar range is ideal for riding.

The **riverside campsite**, called 'Anapat' (*www.facebook.com/anapatlastiver*), is approached from the riding school along paths (3km) which ultimately give access to the high summer pastures and are ideal for walking. The flowers in the forest here are among the most attractive in Armenia and the paths winding along the steep sides of the gorge offer fantastic views. The (signposted) final scramble down to the campsite is steep. The camp with the waters cascading by has been developed by three brothers, Vahagn, Tatoul and Hovhannes Tananian (❨ *263 31465;* m *Vahagn 091 365437, 093 365437; Hovhannes 094 603010, 096 603010*) because they have such fond memories of coming to this place in their childhood. Rock climbing, hiking and fishing are also available (*guiding AMD5,000pp*). Accommodation for up to 50 people is in wooden chalets. Bedding, etc is provided. The campsite, including a bar, is open from May to November (*overnight stay AMD5,000pp inc b/fast; FB AMD15,000pp inc guiding to local caves*). In winter there is accommodation for up to 12 people (call in advance) in a cave which is well provided with bedding and a wood-burning stove. The campsite also caters for day visitors (*entrance AMD1,000pp inc tea/coffee & guiding to local caves; meals available*). The brothers will collect guests from Ijevan or Yenokavan.

Not far from the campsite is **Lastiver hermitage**. It comprises several rooms carved out of the rock on different levels, some of which are reached by ladder. In the caves there are carved faces and animals, strange enough that we wondered if they were modern but apparently they are very old, possibly Stone Age. Archaeological excavation has enlarged the cave opening enabling the carvings to be seen by daylight but a torch is useful too. There are also later Christian carvings.

DILIJAN (*Telephone code: 268*) Dilijan, a major holiday and health resort in Soviet days, lies 36km southwest of Ijevan. Considerable renovation is in progress and hotel accommodation is now plentiful. Roads into Dilijan converge at a roundabout in the centre of a large square on the Aghstev River. Nearby is a striking Soviet-era **monument** erected to mark the 50th anniversary of Soviet power in the Caucasus: its design was intended symbolically to represent the eternal union of Armenia, Georgia and Azerbaijan under Soviet rule. That it is still standing perhaps shows that the Armenians have a well-developed sense of irony. On the east side of the square is a statue of *The Men*, characters from a popular Soviet-era film of the same name. There is a one-man, one-room, private information office (⊕ *09.00–21.00*) on the main square just south of the roundabout. He can help with local tours, accommodation, etc. On this square is also the bus station, two small cafés, shops and a bakery. Many of Dilijan's surviving 19th-century buildings are built in a distinctive style: they have wooden balconies with carved handrails which are often supported by wooden struts. In the centre of the town the finely restored short **Sharambeyan Street** is home to the Tufenkian hotel and restaurant plus a number of craft shops; particularly appealing is that of the wood carver, who carves his wares on site. The **commercial centre** of Dilijan (banks, etc) is Miasnikian Street,

The Northern Provinces   TAVUSH PROVINCE

5

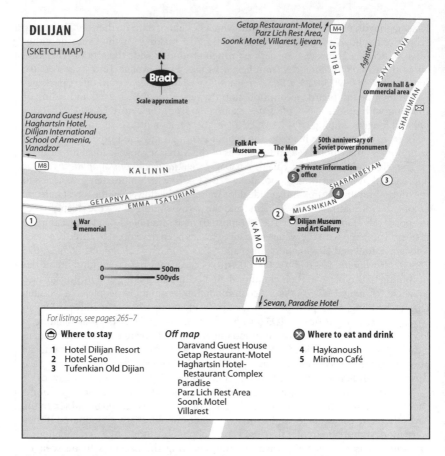

DILIJAN (SKETCH MAP)

Getap Restaurant-Motel, Parz Lich Rest Area, Soonk Motel, Villarest, Ijevan, [M4]

TBILISI · Aghstev · SAYAT NOVA

N

Bradt

Scale approximate

Town hall & commercial area

SHAHUMIAN ⊠

Daravand Guest House, Haghartsin Hotel, Dilijan International School of Armenia, Vanadzor

[M8]

KALININ

Folk Art Museum · The Men

50th anniversary of Soviet power monument

Private information office · 5

SHARAMBEYAN · 3

GETAPNYA · EMMA TSATURIAN

4

MIASNIKIAN · 2

① War memorial

Dilijan Museum and Art Gallery

KAMO

[M4]

0 ——— 500m
0 ——— 500yds

↓ Sevan, Paradise Hotel

For listings, see pages 265–7

🛏 **Where to stay**
1 Hotel Dilijan Resort
2 Hotel Seno
3 Tufenkian Old Dijian

Off map
Daravand Guest House
Getap Restaurant-Motel
Haghartsin Hotel-Restaurant Complex
Paradise
Parz Lich Rest Area
Soonk Motel
Villarest

✖ **Where to eat and drink**
4 Haykanoush
5 Minimo Café

above Sharambeyan Street. Also on Miasnikian Street is the **Dilijan Museum and Art Gallery** (*28 Miasnikian St;* ☏ *268 24450/1;* ⏲ *10.00–18.00 Tue–Sun; guided tour in English AMD2,000; AMD500*) which is worth a visit. Upstairs the paintings and sculptures are well displayed in light airy rooms; labels include English. The historical and ethnographical items are downstairs. Having been relocated here they were, at the time of writing, awaiting formal display. A guided tour of them was, however, still possible. Across the river is the **Folk Art Museum** (*1 Getapnya St;* m *094 433293;* ⏲ *10.00–16.00 Tue–Sun; guided tour in English AMD1,000; AMD500*) in a late 19th-century house, originally the summer house of Mariam Tamanian and latterly the home of the painter Hovhannes Sharambeyan (1926–86), whose *Early Spring* is in the National Gallery, Yerevan. Items from the 19th century to the present day are on display. It is a surprisingly interesting display. It is sometimes possible to buy locally made handicrafts there. Dilijan's well-known **spring** is to the west of the town and the mineral water bottled there is a familiar sight throughout Armenia.

The new **Dilijan International School of Armenia** (e *welcome@dilijanschool. org; www.dilijanschool.org*), also in the western part of the town, achieved United World Colleges (UWC) status in October 2013. An international co-educational boarding school teaching the International Baccalaureate, its first students are due to be admitted in September 2014. Ultimately it plans to accommodate some 650 students from an estimated 60 countries.

Some 23,400ha of the forest surrounding Dilijan were designated as a nature reserve in 1958 and then as **Dilijan National Park** from 2002, the change in designation being to take account of commercial activity in the area. The park stretches over the forested slopes of the Pambak, Areguni, Miapor, Ijevan and Halab mountain ranges, from 1,070 to 2,300m above sea level, the mountain meadows above this altitude being excluded.

As at Ijevan, there is considerable scope for walking over the forested hills or in the valley of the Aghstev River on which Dilijan lies. There are also **five monasteries** nearby each of which is in good walking country.

HAGHARTSIN MONASTERY (⊕ *site always; church all day*) Haghartsin lies in forest and was always one of Armenia's most visited monasteries. To reach it head east towards Ijevan for 7km and then turn left under a railway bridge and continue up the winding road for 9km. At the final bend in the road as one approaches the monastery are some small chapels (a good photographic vantage point) and both here and at the monastery are particularly fine khachkars.

In 2010 the ecclesiastical authorities, having decided that Haghartsin would once more become a working monastery, undertook renovation of the site, although rebuilding might be a more accurate term. Over the centuries Haghartsin has seen many such changes but for those who prefer historic medieval buildings to look their age, the reconstruction of Haghartsin is a disappointment. Externally much of the site now looks as if it is newly built although the interior of many of the churches is unchanged.

As at so many monasteries the original small church had buildings added over the centuries and is now rather dwarfed by its less ancient neighbours. The oldest part is the **St Gregory Church**, probably dating from the 10th century, and with octagonal tambour although the original building was damaged by Seljuk invaders and had to be reconstructed after the Georgian victories over them. This reconstruction was followed by a large increase in the monastery's size and an important school of church music became established here which developed a new system of notation for

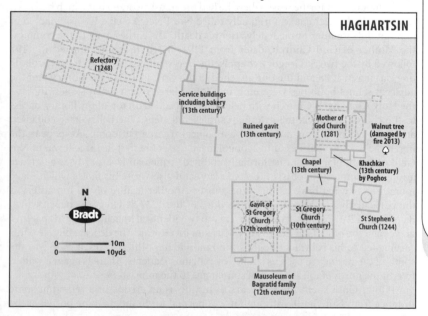

the Armenian liturgy. The original church acquired a *gavit* at a lower level reached by steps; it is unusual in that part of the pillar in the south wall to the east of the central arch rotated to provide a secret hiding place for use when the monastery was threatened. **St Stephen's Church** was built in 1244, the large **refectory** (divided into two parts by arches and with stone benches along its sides) in 1248 and the bigger **Mother of God Church** with a high 16-sided tambour, and also with *gavit*, was added in 1281. (Although most histories give this date I was shown a publication from the 1954 Ejmiatsin archives which stated that an inscription had been unearthed in the 1950s giving a date of 1071 for the church, the 1281 date referring to a renovation.) A relief of the donors with a dove (symbolising the Holy Spirit) above them can be seen on the east façade pointing to a model of the church. Finest of all the many khachkars in the monastery is the **khachkar** carved by Poghos in the 13th century which is outside the south door of the Mother of God Church. Among the other buildings which can be seen are the monastic **bakery** complete with oven. To the south of the *gavit* of St Gregory's are the reconstructed royal tombs of the Bagratid dynasty.

Perhaps even more upsetting for many Armenians than the renovation of the monastery was the destruction by fire in 2013 of the old walnut tree at the southeast corner of the Mother of God Church. Contemporaneous with the 13th-century spate of building it was estimated to be around 700 years old. Generations of Armenians enjoyed picnics in its shade and ate its nuts in autumn. Walnut trees are often found at the sites of monasteries: they were probably planted as a source of food.

GOSHAVANK (MONASTERY) (⊕ *site always, church all day; guided tour of the monastery AMD1,000 – ask at museum*) To reach the village of **Gosh** it is necessary to continue along the Ijevan road for another 8km beyond the turn-off for Haghartsin and then turn right towards **Chambarak**. The road to Gosh branches right off this road after about 2km. To reach Goshavank continue uphill into the centre of the village.

Goshavank was established in the late 12th century by the cleric Mkhitar Gosh (1130–1213) with the support of Prince Ivan Zakarian to replace the monastery of Getik, about 20km further east, where he had previously worked but which had been destroyed in an earthquake. Originally called Nor ('New') Getik, it was renamed in honour of its founder immediately after his death. The earliest part of the complex, the **Mother of God Church**, dates from 1191; its *gavit* was completed in 1197 followed by the two **St Gregory chapels**, the free-standing one with its particularly fine carving in 1208 and the one attached to the *gavit* in 1237. The **library** and the adjacent school buildings were built in 1241 of large rough-hewn stones. In 1291 the **Holy Archangels Church** with bell tower was added on top of the library, access to the church being via the external cantilevered steps. The belfry later collapsed and the building is now protected by a conical transparent dome. At its peak the library held 1,600 volumes until Mongol invaders set fire to it in 1375. It was at Nor Getik that Mkhitar Gosh first formally codified Armenian law (partly as a defence against the imposition of Islamic sharia law) and also wrote his fables which make moral points using birds as the protagonists. Another feature of the monastery is the particularly fine **khachkar,** by the door of the 1237 St Gregory chapel, which dates from 1291. Poghos, its sculptor, carved two identical khachkars for his parents' graves and the other is in the History Museum in Yerevan. The delicate filigree of his carving led to his sobriquet Poghos the Embroiderer. The two small rooms to the south of the *gavit* were used as studies by religious students. There is again a walnut tree, at the north of the site, and of similar age to the monastery.

Mkhitar Gosh spent the last years of his life as an ascetic in a retreat at some distance from Nor Getik. Although it was normal for founders to be buried at the

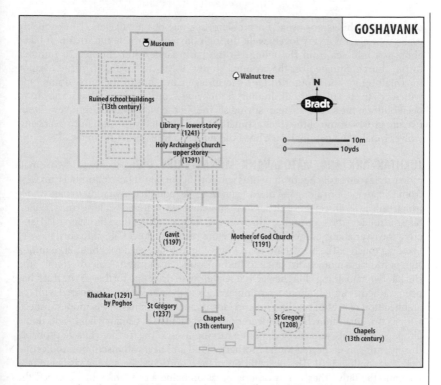

Museum

Walnut tree

N

Bradt

Ruined school buildings
(13th century)

Library – lower storey
(1241)

Holy Archangels Church –
upper storey
(1291)

0 ——————— 10m
0 ——————— 10yds

Gavit
(1197)

Mother of God Church
(1191)

Khachkar (1291)
by Poghos

St Gregory
(1237)

Chapels
(13th century)

St Gregory
(1208)

Chapels
(13th century)

monastery they had established, he requested that this should not be done and a mausoleum was built away from the site.

In the grounds of the monastery is a **small museum** (⊕ *09.00–17.00 Tue–Sun; AMD500*). By far the most interesting items there are large pottery bell-shaped objects which were hung from the dome with the open end downward to try to improve the acoustics by reflecting sound back downward into the church. The solution to the problems of some more recent concert halls such as the Royal Albert Hall, London, was clearly anticipated at Goshavank! After the monastery has been explored a variety of refreshing herbal teas, made with local mountain herbs, can be enjoyed on the veranda of the village's hotel.

A very pleasant walk (2½km) is to the small lake of Goshalich which lies deep in the forest. The path, which can be very muddy if wet, goes off (first right) from the road below the monastery. The trees offer welcome shade in the summer heat and the setting of the lake is very beautiful with trees rising on the hillside behind. Goshalich is home to some of Armenia's noisiest frogs.

AGHAVNAVANK (MONASTERY) This small 12th- or 13th-century church does not of itself merit a visit but the journey there, especially the last stretch through Dilijan National Park, is very enjoyable. It can easily be combined with a visit to Goshavank. Instead of turning right for Gosh village carry on towards Chambarak for another 8km. The village of Aghavnavank is signposted left. From the centre of the small village a sharp right hairpin bend takes you on to another dirt track which goes to the monastery (one of the white-on-green Armenian signs for Dilijan National Park points the way). A 4x4 is advised if driving up to the church as two streams have to be forded. Also the key to open the barrier into the national park has to be obtained but this is not usually a problem; ask one of the villagers. It is probably easier to walk; it is a very lovely walk through the woods beside the stream. It takes about ten minutes from the village to the park barrier and another 20 minutes to the church. Situated on the wooded slopes of Mount Tsaghkot in the Miapor mountain range the Mother of God Hermitage Church is of the cross-dome type with a relatively tall tambour. It abuts a rocky outcrop suggesting that it may have been built on the site of a pagan spring shrine. In the vicinity are virgin yew *Taxus baccata* groves, some of the trees estimated to be 300–400 years old. Both bears and wolves inhabit the national park but I did not encounter either on my walk.

JUKHTAKVANK AND MATOSAVANK MONASTERIES Visits to these two small monasteries can easily be combined, as you park at the same place for both. Head west from Dilijan for 3km along the main Vanadzor road and then turn right to pass under a high railway viaduct whose girders are painted in red ochre. (If walking from Dilijan, take the road on the south side of the river to start with, rather than the main road, and cross the river at one of the footbridges before reaching Hotel Dilijan Resort, thereby avoiding much of the busy main road.) Drive up the side road for about 2km until a sign points right along a dirt track to **Jukhtakvank** (*jukht* means 'pair' or 'couple': the site has two remaining churches). Do not attempt to drive any further as the track has been washed away. It is about ten minutes' walk to the monastery. Compared with the architectural glories of Haghartsin and Goshavank this monastery is modest indeed with its two small churches. The nearer one, dedicated to St Gregory, has lost its dome although it retains some very elaborate carving inside. The further church, probably the older one, is dedicated to the Mother of God and bears an inscription indicating that it was built in 1201. This peaceful site in the wooded valley makes a visit here very pleasant, the only other visitor on one occasion being a calf which had escaped the summer heat by lying down in front of the altar inside the Mother of God Church. **Matosavank** (Monastery of St Matthew) is less visited than Jukhtakvank but the walk is even more pleasant, although somewhat steep at first. A very short distance from the sign to Jukhtakvank a path goes off left down to a stream which is crossed on a low footbridge. The route to the monastery is clearly marked by red-paint waymarkers on trees and rocks. Follow them uphill and then left across open woodland which in spring is carpeted with cowslips, violets and blue anemones. One is almost upon the small monastery before seeing it, built as it is into the hillside and with its ruined roofs partially covered in vegetation. The undistinguished external appearance in no way prepares one for the wealth of attractive khachkars inside. The barrel-vaulted *gavit* leads into a small barrel-vaulted chapel to the east and into a domed chamber on the south. The walk takes about 25 minutes each way.

PARZ LICH (LAKE) A recreational centre with accommodation (see page 266) has been established on the bank of this small lake (*1,334m above sea level; 3ha*) in the hills northeast of Dilijan. It is aimed mainly at Armenian family day trips and weekend holidays and can be busy on summer weekends. The 10km-long bumpy road to Parz Lich leaves the main road about 7km north of Dilijan. There is a restaurant and activities include boating (*AMD2,000/½hr*), tennis (*AMD2,000/hr*), cycle hire (*AMD3,000/hr*), horseriding (*AMD1,500/10 mins pp*) and fishing (*AMD5,000/kg caught*). Swimming is forbidden for safety reasons. The name, which means 'clear lake', is a misnomer; the water is green.

6

The Southern Provinces

Southern Armenia is the least visited part of the country. That is a pity and is largely the consequence of visitors giving themselves inadequate time. There is spectacular scenery with roads zigzagging up and down over mountain passes. Two of Armenia's best known monasteries are here; **Noravank**, in Vayots Dzor province, visited by almost every tourist on a day trip from Yerevan and **Tatev**, in Syunik, requiring an overnight stay in the province. Other monasteries are to be found in remote settings allowing the possibility of walks through wonderful countryside to reach them. Petroglyphs, cave villages, Armenia's best known megalithic site and one of the world's best-preserved caravanserais are other gems. The south of Syunik is famed for the quality of its fruit. The main highway from Yerevan to Nagorno Karabagh traverses both of the southern provinces with the road to Iran branching off the highway to cross southern Syunik.

VAYOTS DZOR PROVINCE

Many visitors come to Vayots Dzor ('Gorge of Woes') on a day trip from Yerevan – principally to see the monastery of Noravank – but it is not really possible to see much else in this province unless you are prepared to stay for a few days. Vayots Dzor is crowded with interesting historic sites, all attractively situated, and a few days here are well justified.

For the most part, Vayots Dzor certainly lives up to the *dzor* ('gorge') part of its name. Visitors travelling from Yerevan cross the Tukh Manuk Pass and then descend to the Arpa River. The gorge here is at times narrow and spectacular, notably between Areni and Arpi and even more so beyond Gndevank. Even in autumn, after a long dry summer, the river is surprisingly full. Presumably this is because of water management at the hydro-electric power station, and despite the abstraction of the water which is being diverted in an attempt to raise the level of Lake Sevan (see pages 199–202). The Arpa rises in the northeast of the province between **Mount Sartsali** (3,446m) and **Mount Chaghat** (3,333m), flows south through Jermuk before assuming a more westerly course until it enters Nakhichevan after which it joins the Arax. There are many other gorges in the province, the more wooded ones being good places to see golden orioles in the breeding season, flocks of rose-coloured starlings, and also offering the occasional view of a Levant sparrowhawk.

GETTING THERE AND AROUND Most visitors coming to Vayots Dzor travel down the main road from Yerevan, entering the province at the **Tukh Manuk Pass** (1,795m). This route has been completely rebuilt and is in good condition throughout. It carries heavy lorry traffic, mainly Iranian vehicles travelling between Teheran and

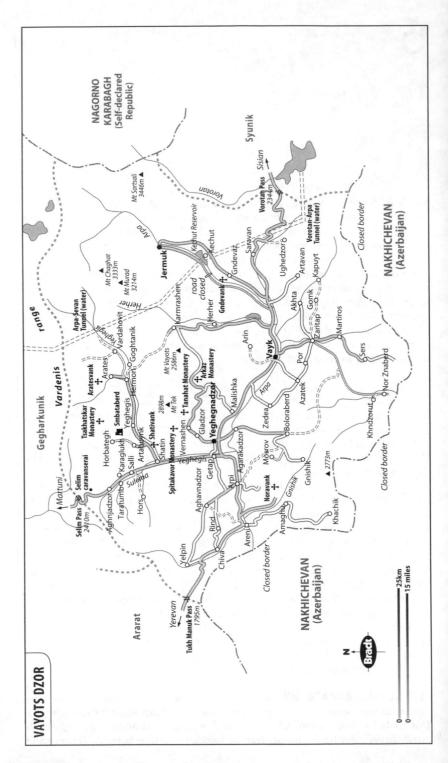

VAYOTS DZOR

NAGORNO
KARABAGH
(Self-declared
Republic)

Syunik

Mt Sartsali
3446m ▲

Vorotan

Sisian

Vorotan Pass
2344m

Vorotan-Arpa
Tunnel (water)

Closed border

NAKHICHEVAN
(Azerbaijan)

Kechut Reservoir

Kechut

Arpa

Sarovan

Ughedzor

Jermuk

Mt Chaghat
3333m ▲
Mt Murad
3214m ▲

Gndevaz

Artavan

Kapuyt

Arpa-Sevan
Tunnel (water)

Karmrashen

road
closed

Akhta

Gomk

Gndevank ✝

Herher

Herher

Zaritap

Martiros

Gegharkunik

range

Vardenis

Vardahovit

Goghtanik

Arin

Vayk

Por

Sers

Hermon

Yeghegis

Aratesvank ✝

Aratesi

Mt Voyots
2586m

Azatek

Nor Znaberd

Tsakhatskar
Monastery ✝

Arkaz
Monastery ✝

Malishka

Smbataberd

Tanahat Monastery ✝

Yeghegis

Zedea

Khndzorut

Shativank ✝

Mt Tek
2898m

Yeghegnadzor

Boloraberd

Horbategh

Artabuynk

Vernashen

Gladzor

Mosrov

Closed border

Selim
caravanserai

Karaglukh

Shatin

Spitakavor Monastery ✝

Getap

Agarakadzor

Gnishik

Salli

Yeghegis

▲ 2773m

Aghnjadzor

Taratumbo

Hors

Sulema

Aghavnadzor

Api

Noravank ✝

Gnishik

Khachik

Selim Pass
2410m

Martuni

Rind

Areni

Amaghu

Chiva

Yelpin

Yerevan

Tukh Manuk Pass
1795m

Ararat

NAKHICHEVAN
(Azerbaijan)

Closed border

N

Bradt

0   25km
0   15 miles

Yerevan. The other road from the north crosses the **Selim Pass** (2,410m) and may be closed in winter. Recent reconstruction means that it is accessible to all vehicles. **Minibuses** travel from Yerevan to Yeghegnadzor, Vayk and Jermuk (see pages 80–2). The minibus from Yerevan to Yeghegnadzor takes about two hours for the 120km trip, but a sensible driver might take somewhat longer. From these centres minibuses go to local villages but, to reach many of the sites mentioned, either a car or taxi is needed. The main roads in the province are good but some of the side roads are poor. A few sites can only be reached by walking or with a 4x4.

WHERE TO STAY The sights of Vayots Dzor itself can be seen during a stay of about four nights, although of course many visitors will combine it with either a visit to the Lake Sevan area, visiting Selim caravanserai *en route*, or to Syunik province, thus taking in some of the sights on the way south. Yeghegnadzor is central although the best hotel accommodation is in Jermuk. Homestays can be found everywhere (see page 86).

There is a pleasant hotel at Vayk, good hotel and guesthouse accommodation in Yeghegnadzor and plentiful accommodation in the spa town of Jermuk in hotels and sanatoria. It is possible for anyone to stay at the sanatoria but prices are usually inclusive of treatments regardless of whether you take them or not. Where listings are plotted on a map, this is indicated below.

Jermuk
Map, page 298.

Jermuk Armenia (60 rooms) 2 Miasnikian St; 287 21290, 10 281224 (Yerevan number); e jermukarmenia@yahoo.com; www.jermukarmenia.com. Next door to Jermuk's Mineral Water Gallery. Until recently this was the most comfortable establishment in Jermuk, but other hotels have now caught up with & even overtaken it. Splendidly refurbished to its former glory in the hope that patients will return, meals are still served in an unsigned room hidden in the basement called the canteen. By contrast, the large & prominent bar serves many non-residents whose tastes it presumably reflects by not selling beer that has been brewed in Armenia. Signage – except on a long corridor whose doors are marked 'gastroenterologist', 'proctologist', 'chief doctor', 'deputy chief doctor', etc – is non-existent. The hotel's medical complex offers a large range of investigations & therapies. Gym. Swimming pool. Price inc all meals & medical treatment, whether taken or not. Cards accepted. Wi-Fi. **$$$$**

Jermuk Olympia (52 rooms) 16 Shahumian St; 287 22366; m 094 444904; e info@jermukolympia.am; www.jermukolympia.am. This fully renovated sanatorium looks light & airy with carefully thought-out décor. Wheelchair access to hotel, but not to the pleasant dining room overlooking the grounds. Emergency evacuation routes marked. Indoor sports, bar, sauna, conference hall. Offers a range of medical investigations & spa therapies. FB & medical treatment inc. Wi-Fi. **$$$**

Ani Hotel (11 rooms) 26 Shahumian St; 287 21727; m 091/077/055 211727; e contact@jermukani.am; www.jermukani.am. Small, newly built hotel with good-quality interestingly shaped rooms. 4 floors, no lift. A brisk 10 min walk from the town. Wi-Fi. Cards accepted. FB. **$$**

Anush Hotel (16 rooms) 2 Vardanian St; 287 22441; m 094 444908/06; e info@jermukanush.am; www.jermukanush.am. A renovated Soviet building in the centre of town. Lots of steps up to front entrance. 4 floors, no lift. Wi-Fi. Cards accepted. **$$**

Ararat Health Spa (55 rooms) 18 Shahumian St; 287 22839, 22485, 23715; m 093 399355/951485; e arspa@inbox.ru; www.jermukararat.com. Another large Soviet-era sanatorium, partly renovated. Renovated rooms looked satisfactory, not all have hot water. A range of prices from AMD9,000pp for non-renovated rooms without hot water to AMD13,500pp for renovated rooms with hot water. All prices are FB. **$$**

Hotel Nairi (21 rooms) 7/1 Miasnikian St; 287 22008; m 098 101070; e info@jermuknairi.am; www.jermuknairi.am. Set on the edge of the Arpa Gorge with superb views. Very near town centre. Pleasant hotel with restaurant & bar. FB available. **$$**

🏠 **Central Guesthouse** (12 rooms) 12 Miasnikian St; ☎287 21607; m 093 177770, 055 840444. Entered from Shahumian St. New building in town centre, opened 2012. Rooms on floors 2, 3 & 4. Shops on 1st floor, dining room in basement. B/fast inc, other meals not available. **$$**

🏠 **Verona Rest House** (20 rooms) 9/1 Shahumian St; ☎287 22050; m 091/093 402615; e info@jermukverona.am; www.jermukverona.am. Within the Town Park at the side of one of the lakes. When entering Jermuk across the main bridge, turn right at the traffic lights, then left after 10m to enter the Town Park. Turn left in front of a huge derelict Sport Complex to reach the hotel. Do not be too put off by the Sport Complex, the hotel is pleasant & new in well-kept grounds with easy access to parks, the Mineral Water Gallery & the town centre. Wi-Fi. FB available. **$$**

🏠 **Cascade** At the southern end of Shahumian St; m 095 603007. Reception is the nearby portacabin. The luxe building is divided into two 2-storey apts each with 2 twin bedrooms, AMD30,000/apt. The other house is divided into quarters giving 4 2-storey apts, each with 1 twin bedroom, AMD20,000/apt. Prices in low season are AMD10,000/apt cheaper. **$$–$**

🏠 **Evmari** (pronounced Yevmarie) (1 dbl, 5 suites with 2 dbl rooms, 1 suite with 3 dbl rooms) 3 Shahumian St; ☎287 21814; m 099 011814; e hayro@inbox.ru. In town centre. Internet access inc. B/fast extra, approx AMD1,000pp. **$**

🏠 **Hotel Life** (4 rooms) 10/1 Shahumian St; ☎287 21256; m 055 811118, 093 721256; e info@jermuklife.am; www.jermuklife.am. More a self-catering hostel than hotel. In the town centre. All rooms en suite. Small shared kitchen. Wi-Fi. **$**

Yeghegnadzor

🏠 **Hotel Arpa** (14 rooms) 8/1 Narekatsi St; ☎281 20601; e hotel@arpatour.am. In the centre of town, this hotel which opened in 2010 provides much-needed high-standard hotel accommodation in the area. Taxi stance nearby. No sign outside. Evening meal for hotel guests available with notice. Wi-Fi. Cards accepted. **$$**

🏠 **Gohar Gevorgyan's Guesthouse** (7 rooms) 44 Spandarian St; ☎281 23324; m 094 332993; e sargisyan@hotmail.com. I can personally recommend this deservedly popular guesthouse, which combines the convenience of a small hotel with the experience of being part of an Armenian household. The food is excellent. All produce is either homegrown or produced locally by relatives. Coffee/tea always available & inc as part of Armenian family hospitality. Family members can arrange airport pick-up in Yerevan & can provide taxi-type transport, inc 4x4, to sites in Vayots Dzor & Syunik. Light meals (*AMD2,000pp*) can usually be provided without notice; a full dinner (*AMD5,000pp*) needs a day's notice. **$$**

Elsewhere in the province

🏠 **LucyTour Hotel Resort** (60 rooms) Hermon village; ☎281 21080; m 098 779778, 098 005829; e info@lucy-tour.com; www. lucy-tour.com. On the Yeghegis Valley road. This attractive new-build complex opened in 2012. Prices very reasonable for what is included – indoor swimming pool, bicycles, gym, volleyball & basketball. Detailed information leaflet about the province, inc map, provided. Can arrange tours with 4x4 & guides. Wi-Fi. Accepts cards. Hotel accommodation in chalet-like buildings. Also has hostel accommodation in 3/4 bedded rooms with separate toilet/showers AMD6,000pp. B/fast inc, other meals available. **$$**

🏠 **Vayk Hotel & Restaurant** (10 rooms) 10a Jermuk Rd; ☎282 92809; m 093 021170; e vaykhotel@gmail.com. This hotel cum private-initiative information centre has nice rooms with photographs of the region, taken by the owner. Very helpful staff. Information desk. Owner can arrange cultural, wine, camping tours & leads caving expeditions himself. Wi-Fi. Accepts cards. B/fast extra AMD2,000pp. **$**

✗ **WHERE TO EAT AND DRINK** The stalls at Arpi, open 24 hours to cater for the trucks from Iran, are a good place to buy food and some serve hot snacks. There is a restaurant at Noravank monastery (page 286) and a popular cave café (page 284) on the way up to the monastery. In summer there are many roadside eating places on the main road. There is a good restaurant at Vayk (see above) and a meal could be ordered in advance from Gohar Gevorgyan (see above) in Yeghegnadzor, where there is also a café in the central park in summer. In Jermuk it is possible to eat in the restaurants of any of the large sanatoria, but note that the evening meal is served early, presumably to allow their guests, who are there for a healthy spa holiday, to go to bed early. Unusually for Armenia, it can be quite difficult to find somewhere to eat in Jermuk in the evening apart from the restaurants listed below and they are often full. For listings, see map, page 298.

✕ **Gndevank Restaurant** Jermuk (next door to Jermuk Restaurant below). A more limited menu than the Jermuk Restaurant but the food is satisfactory. Has loud music.

✕ **Jermuk Restaurant** Jermuk (opposite the far end of the Town Park, on Shahumian St near the Ani Hotel). The food is very tasty; their homemade wine rather 'young'. Can be very busy. The decibel level from celebrations in the main dining room can be made less painful by choosing one of the individual rooms & keeping the door firmly shut.

OTHER PRACTICALITIES The towns in the province are small but have basic facilities such as shops, post offices, banks, cafés and taxis. Any special requirements should be brought from Yerevan. Vayk has a private **tourist information centre** within the Vayk Hotel (*see opposite; information desk* ⊕ *10.00–19.00 Mon–Fri, 10.00–16.00 Sat*) and the proprietor can help with arranging almost anything locally. Signposting to historic sites is generally good in Vayots Dzor.

ARENI Heading south from the provincial border the main road from Yerevan descends a side valley to join the gorge of the Arpa at the village of Areni, a centre of Armenia's wine industry. An annual wine festival is held on the first Saturday of October. It is part trade fair, part local celebration with wine tasting, dancing and an opportunity for young girls to tread grapes in the traditional barefoot manner. It is possible to visit the **winery** (*Areni Wine Factory, 1 Yerevanian St;* m *093 424406, 094 424476;* e *areniwines@gmail.com*) on the east side of the main road in the village. Visits can be arranged through tour operators in Yerevan (see pages 63–4) or by just turning up – you rarely have to wait more than 30 minutes for a tour. Tours are free but of course there is an opportunity to buy at the end. The price range for a bottle of (grape) wine is AMD1,500–10,000. They also produce a variety of fruit wines such as apricot, pomegranate and sour cherry. All the wines can be tasted at the factory's visitor centre. Areni gives its name to an indigenous grape variety mainly used for making dry red table wines. Roadside stalls in the Areni area prominently display for sale large bottles labelled Coca-Cola. Should you be feeling thirsty and tempted to buy one, then prepare for a shock. The usual purchasers are Iranian truck drivers and they are taking home to alcohol-free Iran a beverage with considerably more body and flavour than Coca-Cola.

In Areni village, but on the opposite bank of the Arpa, can be seen in the distance from the main road a **red cross-dome church** dedicated to the Mother of God and built in 1321. It was restored in 1997. At one side of the graveyard around the Mother of God Church there is a row of five modern graves belonging to young men killed in 1992 in the war with Azerbaijan, a reminder that the frontier is only 5km away.

The church's most remarkable feature is the tympanum of the west door which is a wonderfully carved effigy of the Virgin Mary created by Momik, one of Armenia's greatest stone carvers and also a great illustrator of manuscripts; he worked in this region in the late 13th and early 14th centuries. High on the west façade, the representation of a head gazing down is said to be that of a Mongolian, a reminder that at the time the church was constructed Armenia was under Mongol rule and that persecution of non-Muslims was increasing. Inside the church in the pendentives below the tambour are more fine carvings, again by Momik, of the symbols of the four evangelists. The graveyard too has some exceptional carving. One tombstone shows a horse and also a person playing a *saz*, a musical instrument rather like a lute and the ancestor of the Greek *bouzouki*. Other tombstones appear to demonstrate Areni's long winemaking history as they show a figure with a wine flask or wine glass. This long history is confirmed by excavations carried out by a team of Armenian and Irish archaeologists during 2007–10 in an Areni cave complex, Areni-1. The Areni-1 winery is 6,100 years old, making it the world's oldest known winery and showing that grapes had already been domesticated by 4000BC. Items found included a wine press, fermentation vats, storage jars and cups as well as grape seeds and the remains of pressed grapes and other fruit. It was in the same cave that the world's oldest shoe was found in 2008. It is on display in Yerevan's State History Museum (see page 152).

NORAVANK (MONASTERY) (⊕ *always although it may not be possible to reach it in winter*) Just south of Areni a road goes off west across a bridge and enters the narrow gorge of the Gnishik. It leads after 6km to one of Armenia's best known and most worthwhile tourist sights: Noravank ('New Monastery'). Some 2km up the road is a popular, cavern **café** (⊕ *10.00–dusk; no electricity*). Look for the wrought-iron railings and khachkar-like stones fronting the cave. Shortly beyond the café, Noravank can be seen high on the cliff face to the left. Its construction in red stone set against the similarly coloured rock of the mountainside is particularly evocative in the early morning or late evening light. If at all possible avoid coming here in the middle of the day as that is when the place is thronged with tourist buses from Yerevan and it is also stiflingly hot in the valley in summer. Approaching the monastery today the striking two-storey building that one reaches first is actually a mausoleum with another church on top of it and is the newest part of the establishment. The larger complex of buildings beyond is older; the oldest part of all is the ruined 9th- or 10th-century **church of John the Baptist** at the southeast corner.

The site was developed mainly in the 13th century by the Orbelian princes. They were a branch of the Mamikonian family, which had settled in Georgia in the 9th century and members of which had held the position of commander-in-chief of

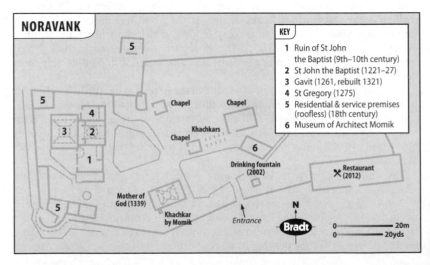

NORAVANK

KEY
1 Ruin of St John
   the Baptist (9th–10th century)
2 St John the Baptist (1221–27)
3 Gavit (1261, rebuilt 1321)
4 St Gregory (1275)
5 Residential & service premises
   (roofless) (18th century)
6 Museum of Architect Momik

Chapel   Chapel
Khachkars
Chapel
Drinking fountain
(2002)
× Restaurant
(2012)
Mother of
God (1339)
Khachkar
by Momik   *Entrance*
N
Bradt
0 ——— 20m
0 ——— 20yds

the Georgian forces in the 10th and 11th centuries. The Georgian army, which included many Armenians, defeated the sultan in 1204 and many families from Georgia moved into Armenia including the Orbelians who settled in Syunik. The Orbelians built several churches to act as burial places for the family and the see of the bishopric of Syunik was moved here to Noravank. The **oldest surviving church** is the one in the centre of the further complex of buildings. Erected in 1221–27, it is also dedicated to **John the Baptist** and is of the cross-dome type with two-storey corner rooms. To judge from a fragment of the church model which has survived, it originally had an octagonal tambour with an umbrella cupola but this collapsed during an earthquake in 1840 and has been replaced by a circular tambour and conical cupola. The more modest **church of St Gregory** was added on the north side in 1275 as the burial place of the Orbelians. In the floor are gravestones including one dated 1300 for Elikum, son of Prince Tarsayich Orbelian, who is represented by a lion figure resting its head on one paw. There are two carved doves by the altar dais, which is flanked by khachkars, and the remains of frescoes can be seen, the red colour of which is apparently the highly prized red dye, *vordan karmir* (see page 185), which was used in Armenia's illuminated manuscripts. The window of the church is set slanting in the east wall, probably so that on some particular day of the year the rays of the dawning sun will illuminate the grave of Prince Smbat who is also buried here.

The original *gavit* **of the John the Baptist Church** was built on the west side in 1261 by Prince Smbat Orbelian but it was completely rebuilt in 1321 following earthquake damage. Both the *gavit* and the Mother of God Church are the work of Momik who was also responsible for the fine carving at Areni (see pages 283–4) and the intricate khachkar in Yeghegnadzor Museum. The two tympana (one above the other, separated by a window opening) of the doorway are in every way remarkable. The carved relief of the upper, pointed one shows God, with his almond-shaped eyes looking straight ahead while a dove is entangled in his beard. He is raising his right hand in blessing while holding a head in his left. Whose head must remain a matter of speculation: possibly that of John the Baptist to whom the church is dedicated and who was decapitated, or perhaps it is the head of the Son or perhaps that of Adam. Above the head is a dove symbolising the Holy Spirit. To the right there is the winged head of a child, the medieval symbol of a seraph, while to the left the scene of Crucifixion. The lower tympanum is semicircular and depicts Mary, wearing a dress whose folds are accurately depicted, sitting with Jesus in her arms, on a patterned rug that is adorned with tassels. On the right is the Prophet Isaiah together with a banner that reads 'Holy Virgin Isaiah'. On the left is St John the Baptist with further words visible in the tracery. The whole is surrounded by an inscription which, according to a recent Armenian booklet describing Noravank, reads: 'Here is the blessed and awful name of my God from the beginnings to the verge of edges that is out of ends and ruptures.' Unfortunately the rest of the booklet achieves a similar level of obscurity although the illustrations are good. Inside the *gavit* there is further carving but nothing to rival the tympana.

The two-storey **Mother of God Church** also has very fine carving. Built by Prince Burtel Orbelian, it was completed in 1339, proving to be Momik's last work. Considerable damage was caused by the 1840 earthquake, and the church lost its tambour and cupola which were not restored until 1997, using fallen fragments as a pattern. The appearance of this church is very unusual: the lower storey is rectangular but the upper is of cross-dome form. The lower storey can be accessed by descending six steps at the west end and comprises the burial vault of the donor and his family. Over the doorway the tympanum depicts Mary with Jesus in her arms, but sitting on a throne this time, flanked by the archangels Gabriel and Michael. Inside the vault can be seen the figures of the evangelists. The church, in the upper storey, is accessed by narrow steps cantilevered up the outside face of the lower façade. Only those who are happy on narrow ledges should climb them. The tympanum over the upper doorway depicts a half-length Christ flanked by the apostles Peter and Paul. From the ceiling of the corner room to the right of the altar the head of a lion looks down.

The reinstated conical cupola is, unusually, not supported by a tambour but by 12 columns. On three of the columns at the western end can just be seen (binoculars help) carved figures of Mary with Jesus and of two donors of the church, one of whom is holding a model of it. There are still some very fine khachkars here although the finest of all have been moved to Ejmiatsin. One good and very intricate one which remains was carved by Momik in 1308. To the right of the entrance gate is the new **Museum of Architect Momik** (⊕ 10.00–19.30 *daily; closed mid-Nov–early Apr, depending on the weather; guide available; AMD500*) which depicts his work as a manuscript writer and illustrator. There is a 15-minute video presentation about Noravank generally and helpful casts of the important Noravank tympana enabling one to see the details close-up. Other displays show examples of 'vivifying flower teas'; the natural pigments used in manuscripts; and the 54 ingredients (herbs, spices and oil) used in the preparation of *meron*, the Armenian Church's chrism (consecrated oil for anointing).

The **Noravank restaurant** (⊕ 09.30–20.00 *Mar–Oct; contact Kristina,* m 093 368700) is highly recommended; belonging to the church and with something of a refectory feel, it has a simply furnished large dining hall, lined with the large clay pots found in the area. There is no background music and no alcohol is served. Prices are extremely reasonable. A full meal (such as chicken, four types of salad, bread, yoghurt, tea/coffee) costs just AMD3,500. Groups are advised to book in advance. They also serve some of the best *gata* I have tasted!

Descending into the gorge again, but then turning to the left once across the river, a track leads to the small **Chapel of St Pokas** (*recross the river at the sluice gate & continue up hill – about a 5 min walk*), in which is a 4th-century khachkar, oval with a simple cross, and a spring whose water is covered by a film of oil, supposedly oil from the saint's burial ground. According to Stepanos Orbelian writing in the late 13th century, surprising miracles formerly occurred here: all manner of pains, whose cure by men was impossible, such as leprosy and long-infected and gangrenous wounds, were cured when people came here, bathed in the water and were anointed with the oil. However, in cases where the diseases were incurable, the people died immediately upon drinking the water!

A **worthy detour** starts about 4km east of the Noravank turn-off on a road that goes north, signposted to **Aghavnadzor** and **Ulgyur** (13.5km). At Ulgyur, in the hills above the Arpa Valley, 5km northwest of Aghavnadzor, there are two fine *vishaps*. The road to Aghavnadzor village is tarmac, thereafter it becomes dirt and for the last 5km a 4x4 is definitely needed – and good weather. Leaving the vehicle at the end of Aghavnadzor and walking is a good option. From the highway the road first climbs up to a high plateau with extensive vineyards. The rough track then winds round the mountain, zigzagging higher and higher until a small chapel is reached in high mountain pasture. Ulgyur is well signposted throughout the route. The Mother of God Chapel (11th–14th century) was renovated in the Soviet period. Beside the chapel stand two impressive *vishaps*, the taller being over 3m high. The dragon heads can be seen clearly. Both had crosses added in the 11th–12th centuries. The gravestones of several family members of Momik, the architect of Noravank, were found in the chapel cemetery.

THE YEGHEGIS VALLEY After Areni the main road turns east to follow the Arpa and in about 15km it crosses the Yeghegis River. Turn left immediately after the bridge to see a number of interesting and attractively located sights – some walking is required to reach most of them, though Selim caravanserai is close to the road. The sights, from the village of Shatin eastwards, are the monastery of Shativank; Tsakhatskar Monastery and the fortress of Smbataberd; Yeghegis village (Zorats Church and the Jewish cemetery); and Arates Monastery.

Shativank (monastery) For 10km from its junction with the main road, the Selim road follows the Yeghegis River north but the river then turns east into the village of **Shatin**. Go into Shatin and ½km after turning off the Selim road, turn right where there is a shop on your *left* (ignore an earlier right turn with a shop on the right) and then take the road which *bears* right (not the sharp right turn). About 150m after crossing the river fork right, then after another 500m go left up a hill to the cemetery. If you get lost ask for the cemetery (*gerezman*); the road to the monastery goes through the cemetery. In a 4x4, in good weather and with an experienced driver, it is just about possible to drive beyond here to the **monastery of Shativank**, but it is a pleasant 7km walk along the track with fine views down into the valley on each side from the crest of the ridge. Note there is an alternative path direct up the gorge (left beyond the bridge where the track to the cemetery forks right). It is shorter but much steeper, frequently muddy, and there are no views. From the village cemetery the track to the monastery goes up between the graves and then bears left. After a few kilometres it is possible to see Shativank in the distance and the track winds down to it. Shativank was founded in 929 but was destroyed in the 14th century and then rebuilt. Like other Armenian churches in the late medieval period it was provided with massive fortified walls which are here well preserved, and the substantial remains of three round defensive towers can also be seen on the south side. The **Zion Church** itself, rebuilt again in 1665, is a three-aisle basilica built of basalt and of limited interest apart from its evocative site. There is evidence of a gallery on the church's west side and remains of other monastic buildings.

Tsakhatskar Monastery and Smbataberd (fortress) The next two sights along the Yeghegis can be combined to give a pleasant walk. Continuing east from Shatin village, take the left fork towards **Artabuynk**. About 1km beyond Artabuynk a track angles steeply down on the right-hand side, crossing an irrigation channel as it descends. At the bottom of the hill the track formerly crossed the Yeghegis by a bridge but this is questionably safe for vehicles, although it can be used by pedestrians. Vehicles with high ground clearance can ford the river although it is risky for others unless the river is exceptionally low. It is therefore better to park here and walk, especially as some of the track is in poor condition. **Tsakhatskar Monastery** should be visited first as this makes the navigation easier and gets the greater part of the climbing accomplished earlier in the day. A moderately fit person should allow 90 minutes to walk from the river up to Tsakhatskar, then 45 minutes from Tsakhatskar to Smbataberd, and 30 minutes back from Smbataberd to the river plus some time at each site and to admire the views. Follow the main track up from the far side of the ford or bridge. In about 500m there is a spring on the right where water bottles can be filled, although it may be dry towards the end of summer. There is another spring at Tsakhatskar itself. Continue up the main track always keeping left if in doubt. One junction in the track is signposted, left 2km to Tsakhatskar and right 1km to Smbataberd. The monastery can be seen high up on the mountainside to the left long before reaching it, but in practice it is hard to

6

detect, so similar is the colour of its basalt stone to the colour of the mountainside. The ruined monastery is reached after about 5km of continuous ascent and is astonishingly large for so isolated a place. According to a 13th-century historian, the monastery was built in the 5th century as the burial place for those who died in battles against the Persians (see pages 17–18) and rebuilt in the 10th and 11th centuries. There are two 11th-century churches, restored in 2010, and older ruined monastic buildings to the west.

The easternmost of the two churches, **Holy Cross**, dates from the 11th century and appears to have been a mausoleum. A square entrance area, above which is a second storey, leads through to a lower chapel. A large stone structure has been built across the original entrance for the full width of the building and on it stand large khachkars.

The more western of the two churches, **St John the Baptist**, was built in 1041. It is a cross-dome church with circular tambour and conical cupola. On the south façade there is a carving of an eagle clutching a lamb in its talons (symbol of the Proshians) and the doorway is elaborately decorated with geometric designs and inscriptions. The north wall has a carving of a lion tearing a bull (symbols of the Orbelians and Bagratunis); the west and east windows are surrounded by geometric carving. The front of the altar dais has a row of carved jugs. Outside there are many khachkars, including two very large ones near the entrance.

The main part of the **monastery** was at a distance from these churches on the west side. Extensive remains of buildings can be seen, most of them presumably the service buildings of the monastery, although including further churches dedicated to the Mother of God (10th century) and, at the southern end, to St John. The latter bears an inscription dated to 999. There are what appear to be the remains of cloisters and all of these buildings on the western side were once surrounded by a defensive wall, of which only the eastern part with its gateway survives. An inscription at the gateway records its restoration in 1221. The sheer scale of these remains, which stretch for over 200m, indicates clearly the former importance of this now forgotten place. From the site the view is over alpine meadows and apple trees down into the valley below but a mountain ridge stretches away to the south, on the furthest summit of which can be seen with binoculars the **fortress of Smbataberd**. It is fairly easy to work out a route, the key point being to determine how far to retrace the route up from the river before branching off left along the side of the ridge. The walk again provides magnificent views down into the valley on each side and is mostly downhill apart from the final slope up into the fortress. If visibility is poor it is safer to retrace your steps to the signposted junction and follow that track up to the fortress.

Stabilisation work has been carried out on the walls of the fortress and a paved path leads to one of the postern gates outside of which a small viewing platform has been built. Unfortunately the sensitivity evident in the work inside the fortress has not been shown in the prominent placing of a toilet block on one of the ridges looking down into the valleys. When I visited the state of the toilets could only be described as disgusting.

Smbataberd (fortress of Smbat, Prince of Syunik) was probably founded in the 5th century but considerably strengthened in the 10th and is one of Armenia's most impressive fortress. Few visitors can fail to be impressed by the gigantic ramparts built on the precipitous cliff face, especially those on the eastern side. Smbataberd is in a magnificent defensive position, crowning the southern end of the ridge and guarded by steep cliffs on three sides. Even on those sides, walls with frequent towers were built wherever the drop was less than precipitous and much of this survives. Inside the walls relatively little remains, although the outline of buildings can be discerned around the walls as well as the fortress's keep at the highest point of the site. According to local legend, Smbataberd fell to the Seljuk Turks when they employed a thirsty horse to sniff out the water supply: it came in an underground pipe from Tsakhatskar. This would indicate an 11th century date. However, other reports suggest that the castle was defended until the 13th century, which would imply that it was eventually captured by the Mongols rather than the Seljuks. See below for a route from Yeghegis to the fortress.

Yeghegis   Looking far down into the valley from the eastern rampart of Smbataberd you can see the ruins of the town of Yeghegis by the Yeghegis River. The town had two separate periods of prosperity: first, during the Syunik princedom (10th–11th century) at the end of which it was destroyed, possibly by an earthquake; and then under the Orbelians from the 13th century to the 15th. Present day Yeghegis is the village to the northeast. A visit there is worthwhile but can seem rather a let-down after a morning spent up on the ridge. A track leads down from Smbataberd to Yeghegis but it is very muddy after rain and it becomes less obvious nearer to the village. It may be easier simply to walk back to the car, retrace the route as far as the junction with the Yeghegis road, and then return up the parallel valley. Should one wish to walk up to **Smbataberd from the Yeghegis side** (the view of the fortress is actually better from this approach) the track goes off left just after the village sign when driving from Shatin. Walk up this track until it turns sharply right at some low cliffs and look for a metal pipe crossing a gully. The path to Smbataberd goes across the hillside just to the left of this pipe.

Yeghegis is a pleasant, unspoiled village with three churches and an old Jewish cemetery. The three-aisle basilica, the **Mother of God Church** with a grass-covered roof in the centre of the village, was built in 1708. Four massive pillars support the barrel-vaulted roof. The church is built into the hillside, a feature suggesting an earlier origin. Over the west door are carvings of two sirens. At the east end of the village the 13th-century **church of John the Baptist** is a small cross-dome church. However, the village's most notable church is the **Zorats (Army) Church** dedicated to St Stephen. It is highly unusual in that the congregation stood in the open air facing the altar. The roof was built to only cover the east end of the church and covers just the altar in the centre with a sacristy on each side. The name Zorats, and possibly the reason why it was an open-air structure, came from its use as the place where arms and horses were consecrated before battle. Obviously it would have been more convenient not to have the horses inside a building! The church was constructed in 1303 by a grandson of Prince Tarsayich Orbelian, governor of the province of Syunik. Excavations have uncovered medieval foundations on the north side of the church and to the east are many tombstones and an extensive area with large boulders forming walls and pathways around a plateau overlooking the valley. In season the walnut tree planted below the church still yields excellent fruit!

The **Jewish cemetery** here was rediscovered in 1996 by the Bishop of Syunik. It is one of the oldest known in the world and has been excavated since 2000 by a team from the Jewish University of Jerusalem under Professor Michael Stone. It is reached by a footbridge over the Yeghegis River. So far more than 60 gravestones have been identified including those used for the foundations of the footbridge and others used in the foundations of a mill. At the cemetery, some of the stones are positioned on open graves while others are on sealed graves. A number of the stones have magnificent ornamentation. Some of the symbols on the Jewish gravestones – like a spiral wheel – were also in use on Armenian Christian stonecrafts around the same time. It is most interesting that the same decorative motifs were shared by Jews and Christians. While some of the inscriptions were worn down over the centuries, a lot of them are decipherable. One stone dated the 18th of Tishrei of AD1266 is of 'the virgin maiden, the affianced Esther, daughter of Michael. May her portion be with our matriarch Sarah.' The opposite side quotes 'Grace is a lie and beauty is vanity' (Proverbs 31:20) and continues with a statement that Esther was 'God-fearing'. Another gravestone contains an emotional statement from a father mourning his son's passing in which the father claims that the soul is eternal and cites passages from the book of Isaiah that relate to the resurrection of the dead.

Comparing the style of the Jewish stones with those in Christian cemeteries of the period it seems likely that they were carved by the same craftsmen who served both communities. The evidence suggests that Jews were important members of the society at Yeghegis, probably engaged in flour milling, since the remains of three watermills have been uncovered in the Jewish district. On the evidence of the graves discovered, Jews probably arrived here in the 13th century during the period of Mongol rule, remained throughout the era of Turkmen control but left in the 15th, possibly around the time of Ottoman takeover.

Opposite the Jewish cemetery on the same side of the river as the road, there is a field where gravestones have been pushed over. This used to be an Azeri village before the war over Nagorno Karabagh.

Aratesvank (monastery) Some kilometres east of Yeghegis are the ruins of Arates Monastery. Few visitors reach it, apart from those with a particular penchant for monasteries. Beyond Yeghegis the road deteriorates but 4x4 is not required. Fork left in the centre of Hermon and then left again at the next fork. The road climbs uphill and reaches a disused military checkpoint. Continue on the asphalt road which bears right past the checkpoint until the village of Arates is reached. The monastery ruins are obvious, up on a knoll to the left. There are three small churches side by side – the 7th-century **St Sion Church** (probably the middle of the three), the 10th-century **Mother of God Church** and the 13th-century **St John the Baptist Church** – and a *gavit*, flagged with gravestones, built in 1265–70 by order of Prince Smbat Orbelian. Multiple small chapels lead off the churches. The village itself, having been an Azeri village, is deserted although the orchards are well tended. The steeply sided river gorge between Yeghegis and Hermon, the hills surrounding Arates and the wild flowers *en route* all make this an attractive extension to the visit of the Yeghegis Valley.

SELIM CARAVANSERAI Selim caravanserai is the best-preserved caravanserai in Armenia and one of the best preserved in the world; its formerly remote site high on the Selim Pass prevented its being quarried for building materials. There is now a good surface the whole way over the pass (2,410m). The caravanserai is situated just below the summit of the pass and affords wonderful views down along the valley.

Constructed of basalt and with a roof of flat tiles, it is a long building with a single entrance at one end: having only one entrance made the building more readily defensible against thieves. To the left of the doorway of the entrance vestibule is a griffin while to the right there is a lion. Above it is an inscription written in Persian using Arabic letters, while inside the vestibule to the right there is one in Armenian, recording that the caravanserai was built in 1332 by Chesar Orbelian during the reign of Khan Abu Said II. The main hall of the caravanserai is divided into three naves by means of seven pairs of pillars. The two narrower side naves were used for the merchants and their wares while the animals were kept in the central one. Stone troughs were provided for feedstuffs for the animals and there is a basalt trough in one corner to supply them with water. Light and ventilation were provided by small openings in the roof but the interior is dark and a torch is useful. Looking at all these arrangements it is possible to capture an image of the life of the 14th-century merchants who passed this way, to an extent which can rarely be experienced anywhere in Europe. The restoration carried out in 1956–59 did nothing to mar the atmosphere and it is only to be hoped that the greatly increased numbers of visitors will leave it similarly unscathed.

YEGHEGNADZOR (*Telephone code: 281*) The centre of the provincial capital lies to the north of the main road, the entrance to the town marked by a statue symbolising *Wisdom*. Apart from the Regional Museum (see below) Yeghegnadzor ('Valley of the reeds') is not in itself otherwise of any great interest except as a place to shop or change money.

Yeghegnadzor Regional Museum (*4 Shahumian St;* 281 23392; e *museum68@ rambler.ru;* ⊕ *09.00–17.00 Mon–Sat (if door is locked phone the number on the notice in the window beside the door); Sun visits possible if booked in advance; AMD500*) Through the striking horseshoe-shaped entrance this small museum contains a treasure trove of interest. The director, Kamo Sahakyan, is very happy to show visitors round. Pride of place goes to a 1330s khachkar by Momik, one of Armenia's greatest stone carvers. The two pieces of the broken khachkar were found quite separately and reunited in the museum. The whole stone is covered with unbelievably fine and intricate carving. Above the cross is the seated figure of Christ in Glory, his right hand raised in the typical Armenian position of blessing (see page 203), with the symbols of the four evangelists at his feet. The 12 apostles are beside the cross, six on each side. Other significant items in the museum include a stone altar with a Greek inscription from Areni, pottery from the second millennium BC, an Urartian bronze belt from the first millennium BC found in the town, and colourful glazed pottery from the 12th–13th centuries AD. A cradle displays an ingenious contraption to prevent bed-wetting by its (male) occupant and there are two stones said to be the female equivalent of phallic symbols. The storeroom has artefacts which can't be displayed for lack of space, including petrified sea urchins and starfish found in the vicinity showing that Yeghegnadzor, high as it now is (1,194m), was once below sea level.

AROUND YEGHEGNADZOR There are a number of interesting sights outside the town, in particular Spitakavor Monastery and Tanahat Monastery (with the related, but separately housed, Museum of Gladzor University). Just visible in the distance from the main road immediately east of its junction with the Selim road is a **13th-century bridge over the Arpa**. The bridge can be reached by taking the track which goes off between two metal posts about 100m east of the main road's junction with the Selim road and then crosses fields towards the river. Cross the new bridge over the river and turn left for ½km on the road which goes along the hillside parallel to the river. The old bridge, once upon a time on the main road to Julfa, consists of a single arch of 16m span. It is unlike other medieval Armenian bridges in being a lancet arch, an acutely pointed arch having two separate centres of equal radii. This gives it a pointed appearance with a high clearance over the river in the centre. The bridge is very picturesquely situated away from any main road and makes an ideal place for a picnic.

The Museum of Gladzor University (◔ *09.00–17.30 Tue–Sun; the key-holder lives next door; if she is at home she is happy to show visitors around even when the museum is officially closed; she speaks Armenian & Russian; AMD500*) From the centre of Yeghegnadzor a road leads northeast up the hill through residential areas. The Museum of Gladzor University is a few kilometres beyond the town in the village of Vernashen, on the left, housed in a former basilica church. This museum does not rank among Armenia's must-sees but it does explain why visitors may hear of Gladzor University at a number of sites they visit (it moved from place to place according to the wishes of the principal of the day). The former church in which it is housed has been well restored (there are some interesting carvings on stones incorporated into the walls) although the stone altar screen is not original. The seven modern stones outside the entrance represent the seven subjects of medieval learning: the trivium or lower part comprised grammar, rhetoric and logic while the quadrivium or higher part comprised arithmetic, geometry, astronomy and music. The museum has photographs of the various monasteries to which the university moved, illustrations of illuminated manuscripts produced at the university, and places where former students went to establish schools. In all, 350 *vardapets* graduated between 1282 when the university was established by Momik (see pages 283–4) and 1338 when it ceased to function. Throughout its working life the university was concerned with maintaining the independence of the Armenian Church and the rejection of papal authority.

Spitakavor Monastery The monastery of Spitakavor ('White-ish') can be reached from Gladzor University Museum (see above) either by car or on foot. Driving definitely needs a 4x4, good weather and a driver experienced in this sort of terrain. Even then it is a difficult 8.4km drive. The track to the monastery goes off left a few metres beyond the museum. If walking, park by the museum. The walk of about 6km is very pleasant, if rather steep at times. The first short section is through the village, after which the stream is crossed. The main track turns left but walkers should ignore the sign in Armenian instructing vehicular traffic for Spitakavor to turn left and should carry straight on while keeping the stream and a small dam on the right. The rocky path then ascends up the side of the ever-narrowing and dramatic gorge until it angles left and emerges into an alpine meadow as the gorge widens out. There are caves on the hillside in which presumably live the bears whose droppings can be seen along the path. The next section of the path is through a summer village where farmers from the villages below come to pasture their stock during the warmer months. The only way any visitor will ever be allowed to pass through here without accepting hospitality is by promising to stop on the way back. Beyond the summer village keep right and you will soon see Spitakavor high above you. In places the path has been washed away but it is fairly easy to follow the stream, which flows down the steep mountainside from the monastery. There is a very welcome spring at the top. Watch out for interesting reptiles on the way such as the nose-horned viper and Caucasian green lizard. Drivers will follow the main track left at the sign mentioned above. The track winds up round the hillside, giving magnificent views over the mountains and the valley in which Yeghegnadzor lies. It appears to go past the monastery but then doubles back to a small car park. Walkers can of course do a loop, walking up one way and down the other.

The **church**, dedicated to the Mother of God, dates from 1321 and was built by Prince Prosh of the Proshian family on the site of a 5th-century basilica. The bell tower was added in 1330. The *gavit* has seen some restoration. The church itself is a cross-dome church with tall cylindrical tambour and conical cupola. High up in the apex of the dome are carvings of the symbols of the four evangelists; the ox is

GAREGIN NZHDEH – THE SAVIOUR OF ARMENIA

Born Garegin Ter-Harutyunian in 1886, Garegin Nzhdeh was the son of a village priest in Nakhichevan. Later he led an Armenian band fighting alongside the Bulgarians in 1912 as Bulgaria battled for independence from the Ottoman Empire. During World War I he fought alongside the Russian troops against Turkey. By 1921, his guerrilla band was holding off both Bolshevik and Turkish forces in Syunik and Zangezur (southern Armenia) and he declared an independent Republic of Mountainous Armenia at Tatev Monastery in May 1921. This he used as a bargaining tool with Lenin to ensure that both Syunik and Zangezur were incorporated into Armenia, rather than into Azerbaijan as the Bolshevik government had at first agreed in its bid to achieve good relations with Turkey. After agreement with Lenin was reached, the tiny state capitulated in July 1921 and Nzhdeh went into exile via Persia. He later negotiated fruitlessly with Nazi Germany in a bid to recover the lost territories of western Armenia and in 1945 he was arrested in Bulgaria by Soviet troops. He was executed in 1955 for 'anti-Soviet activities'. He is regarded as the person who saved southern Armenia for the nation and, in the light of more recent events, he may almost be regarded as the saviour of Armenia since it is doubtful whether Armenia could have survived the early 1990s without the lifeline to Iran which those territories provided. His remains were secretly brought to Armenia in 1983 and kept in the cellar of one of those who had returned his remains. In 1987 he was reburied at Spitakavor. In his will, Nzhdeh had said that he wished to be buried on Mount Khustup so in 2005 parts of his body were taken from Spitakavor and buried for a third time on the slopes of Mount Khustup, near his memorial in Kapan. It is said that only his heart now remains buried in his grave at Spitakavor.

the easiest to see. There are interesting carvings outside. The tympanum is richly carved in a style similar to Areni and Noravank: stalactite decoration arches over a beautiful Madonna and Child and geometrical patterns surround the whole. On the east façade is a curious irregular and asymmetrical cross. The cross on the south façade is more regular but, rather like a tree of life, it seems to grow out of a pot and it has pentagonal stars within its arms. Outside the church the **modern grave** is that of Garegin Nzhdeh (see box above).

The track to the monastery continues uphill. At the crest of the track a path goes off right to the remains of the small **fortress of Proshaberd**, also built by Prince Prosh, on top of a rocky hill. The walk up is easy apart from a scramble at the end. Allow about an hour to walk up, look round and return. A rectangle of walls survives with a tower at each corner. Otherwise not much remains but the views are excellent. One thing which does survive is a deep, dungeon-like pit. Be careful not to fall into it – it would be very difficult to climb out again.

Tanahat Monastery Tanahat Monastery, where Gladzor University was probably first established, is 5km beyond the museum on the same road. A monastery was first established here in 753 but the present buildings date from 1273–79. Approaching it on a late summer day, its dark basalt is a striking and beautiful contrast to the arid hills with only the odd tree presenting any contrasting green colour. The lavishly laid out car parks and remains of other facilities were provided for celebrations which marked the 700th anniversary of the university's founding in 1982. The **main church**, St Stephen's,

After the Persians were defeated by the Byzantine emperor Heraclius (ruled AD610–41) they retreated from Egypt to their country. On their way back they passed through Jerusalem, and a Persian prince entered the Church of the Cross which had been built by Empress Helen, mother of the Roman emperor Constantine, to house the cross which she had discovered in 326. In the church he saw a bright light shining from a piece of wood. He reached for it and it burst forth with fire, which burnt his fingers. The Christians in the church told him that this was the base of the Holy Cross and that no-one was able to touch it except a Christian. The Persian deceived the two deacons who were standing guard over it and bribed them to carry this piece back with him to Persia. When Emperor Heraclius heard this, he went with his army to Persia and travelled about searching for this piece of the Holy Cross. However, the Persian prince had ordered the two deacons to bury the box containing the Holy Cross in his garden, after which he killed them. One of the captives of the Persian prince, the daughter of one of the priests, was looking out of the window by chance and saw what happened. She told Heraclius what she had seen so that Heraclius was able to recover it and take it in state to Constantinople in AD628. It is a portion of this relic which is supposedly buried in Arkaz Monastery, having been given to the wife of Burtel, Prince of Syunik, by Heraclius, whose mother was of Armenian descent.

is a cross-dome structure with a 12-sided tambour and umbrella cupola. Rather plain inside, there is much elaborate carving outside with a heavy preponderance of ones depicting animals and birds. Above the sundial on the south façade, two doves drink from a common cup. The crest of the Orbelian family (a lion and a bull) is high on the tambour; that of the Proshians (an eagle holding a lamb in its talons) is on the side over the door. Another eagle has a smaller bird in its claws and round the top of the tambour can be seen a whole range of animal heads. To the north of St Stephen's Church is the small 14th-century **Church of the Holy Cross**. There are more animals here – the tympanum depicts a mounted horseman attacking a lion. The reason for so much animal carving is not known. The foundations of numerous other buildings can be clearly seen, indicating that the monastery was once large and important.

Arkaz Monastery (*The church is usually locked*) About 3km beyond Tanahat Monastery along the same road is the church of the monastery of Arkaz dedicated to the Holy Cross. Rebuilding in 1870–71 and recent renovation has deprived it of interest, although it is a significant pilgrimage site in early October as under the walls is said to be a piece of the True Cross (see box above). From the church there are, in clear weather, some fine views of **Mount Ararat** towering high over Tanahat. Bears' droppings can be seen in the vicinity; the bears are partial to the bunches of ripe grapes in the autumn vineyards.

AROUND VAYK AND MARTIROS The main road south passes through **Vayk** (*telephone code: 282*), at the north end of which is the new **St Trdat III Church**, consecrated in 2000 and very much in the American-Armenian style with pews, and a balcony for the choir. The floor is of marble and the whole is lit by far more windows than are normal in Armenia. Despite all this modernity and obvious diaspora influence, it manages to embody the spirit of Armenian tradition.

Shortly beyond Vayk a road goes off right to **Martiros** which has a curious subterranean church, like a mini-Geghard. In the first village, **Zaritap** – a centre of tobacco growing – keep right at the fork and continue with the river on the left. To reach the church go through new Martiros and continue towards the old village several kilometres away by taking the dirt road which goes off left where the asphalt road bears right and where you can see a military installation on a hill. After about 2km the road goes downhill (it can be very muddy here when it is wet) and turns sharp left to the old village. At this point, take the rough track which turns right, runs along the base of a hill and then goes left towards a lone khachkar. From here a picnic table can be seen on the far side of the river, which marks the site of the cave church. Keep on the track as it winds around until you reach a short branch down to the river and an irrigation channel. The easiest way to the church is to park here, ford the river and walk up to the picnic table and a tree with handkerchiefs tied to it. The door in the hillside belongs to an entirely **subterranean church**, dedicated to the Mother of God, and built by the Proshian family in 1286. It comprises a small entrance *gavit*, the main church and a small separate chapel. There is a little light inside from windows high up in the hillside but a torch is useful. Standing inside this extraordinary excavation, the shape one sees is the same as if one were in the interior of any normal Armenian church.

From where the dirt road leaves the asphalt road, it is 3½km to the church. If walking a loop of the track can be bypassed by following the concrete irrigation channel encountered: it runs alongside the river to the crossing place described above.

NORTHEASTERN VAYOTS DZOR
About 6.5km beyond Vayk there is a left turn for **Herher**. The road follows the Herher River gorge and skirts a hydro-electric dam before reaching the village which has several churches. Their names seem to vary. On the road up a tiny hermitage (1297) with a square western façade is visible on top of a small hill to the east. This is **Chikivank** (or St George) – see page 296. Just after the entry sign for Herher the right-hand road goes into the village where there is the three-aisled, barrel-vaulted basilica of **St George** (except that locals call it St Karapet ie: John the Baptist). The 19th-century restoration is probably of a much earlier church, given the evidence of stones with eye-holes and chambered graves in the surrounding cemetery. Also the east end of the church is built into the hillside, a feature of originally pagan sites. Here it is easy to see the deliberate use of turf on top of stone roof slabs. Old khachkars have been used as building material. There is a rather nice touch on the west façade where the gable end has been shaped around someone's head. Others were not so lucky; having been cut in half, their heads point in all directions. Outside the village are the twin churches of **St Sion** and **Mother of God** (villagers call the site Goshavank) perched on the edge of the gorge and surrounded with interesting khachkars. They are well worth visiting but are not easy to find; it might be worth asking a villager to accompany you. From St George Church continue through the village until the dirt road meets tarmac; turn right on to the main road. (If driving, ignore the small sign in the square which points to St Sion round the back of a building. This is a rough short cut for walkers.) From the main road turn right on to a farm track just before the leaving Herher sign. Continue on this track, fording a stream, until you reach an orchard. Park here and walk left across a grassy area to the side of the gorge. From here a rocky path goes down into the gorge. The two churches will soon be seen above you. The monastery is first noted in the 8th century and was abandoned in 1604 at the time of the forced migration to Persia of thousands of Armenians, including those from Vayots Dzor, ordered by Shah Abbas during Persian-Ottoman clashes. **St Sion**, the older church,

is built of rough-cut stone and, very unusually for a basilica church, has an apse at both eastern and western ends. **Mother of God Church** (1283) is built of smoother stone and has a double eastern apse, another uncommon feature.

The tiny chapel of **Chikivank** is perched on top of a windswept rocky outcrop; why, one wonders, would anyone build a chapel here? To reach it (on foot is best although it is just about manageable in good weather with a serious off-road vehicle), having turned right for the village turn right again through a U-turn just before entering the village itself. From here it is about 3km to the chapel. When the track divides take the one which goes below the cemetery. It then climbs up to the rocky promontory on which Chikivank sits.

On the main road slightly beyond the Herher junction the Arpa River changes direction. It is well worth leaving the main road to explore its valley between here and Jermuk. There is a road each side of the river. The new road is up on the plateau on the east side of the river; it offers some splendid views down into the gorge, and is accessible to tourist buses. The old road follows the west bank of the river down in the gorge and is far more spectacular than the new road, but it is subject to rockfalls and a little way beyond the **monastery of Gndevank** it is completely blocked by a major landslide. Gndevank is just off this old road across a bridge about 11½km from the junction with the main road.

It is possible to walk down to Gndevank from the new road. It takes about 45 minutes though the walk back may take longer depending on your degree of fitness. Turn off into Gndevaz village, from which splendid views of Gndevank can be obtained by looking down on it in the ravine. To find one of the paths down bear left at a junction by a 30km/h sign 1km after leaving the main road, and follow this road round to the right. Just beyond the third house a path goes off left between houses, then turns right before going downhill. The inhabitants of the houses can direct you; they are also likely to invite you in for coffee.

Gndevank was founded in 936 by Princess Sophia of Syunik who claimed that 'Vayots Dzor was a ring without a jewel; but I built this monastery as the jewel for the ring'. The main church, dedicated to St Stephen, is of the cross-dome type with circular tambour and conical cupola. A *gavit* was added in 999. Unlike most *gavits* which are square this is more like a barrel-vaulted tunnel leading to the church. Encircling fortified walls were added later, the southern and western stretches lined with other buildings used by the monks. The complex was restored between 1965 and 1969 following earthquake damage and underwent further restoration in 2013. There are some particularly fine gravestones here: one shows ibex being hunted alongside falconry while another depicts a boar hunt. There are picnic tables at the monastery and a spring.

The northern part of the **old road** to Jermuk is the real gem of the district. It hugs the side of the narrow gorge underneath beetling cliffs with breathtaking views of the river and the ravine. Because of the landslide (see above) it is no longer possible to drive through from Gndevank and south of the Kechut Reservoir the road is closed by a barrier. However, it was always a better road to walk than to drive and this is still possible. Although the road is highly scenic, and thus strongly recommended for walking, there is ample evidence of numerous rockfalls and it would be unwise to use the road at times of high avalanche or landslide risk. The lack of traffic may increase the chance of seeing wildlife but a word of caution – once we were warned of a she-bear with her cubs in the vicinity. Also often in evidence in the gorge are European glass lizards *Ophisaurus apodus* which are legless, thus looking like snakes, and often quite sizeable at up to 1.2m long. They are harmless to human beings, eating nothing larger than mice. The old road starts at the west end of the Kechut Reservoir dam which can be reached most easily by continuing south from Jermuk town centre on Shahumian Street. The dam, across which a road has been built, can also be reached from the new main Jermuk road by a track which goes off downhill 2.2km south of the leaving Kechut sign. In spring the land overlooking the reservoir is covered with fritillaries. The Kechut Reservoir, although originally constructed for hydro-electric purposes, is now also the starting point for the tunnel which carries water from the Arpa River under the Vardenis range to help maintain the level of Lake Sevan.

JERMUK (*Telephone code: 287*) This is a town whose name every visitor to Armenia is likely to learn since it is the source of much of the country's mineral water. A useful small map of the town is published by Collage (see page 60). The town was a very large and popular Soviet spa resort and once more is attracting visitors. Some of the sanatoria have been renovated and are combining this role with that of a modern hotel. The town is gradually losing its previously rundown air although some unattractive concrete buildings remain. The **statue**, as one approaches the town just before the main bridge, is of Israel Ori (1659–1711), Armenia's first diplomat. From 1678 onwards, he travelled throughout Europe and Russia trying to establish contacts with the leaders of the Christian powers. Seeking protection for Armenia against the Persians and Turks, he met with Leopold I, Holy Roman Emperor, in 1700; Peter the Great, Tsar of Russia, in 1701; and Pope Clement XI in 1704. In 1709, he headed the Armenian delegation to the Persian shah. The bridge crosses the immensely impressive Arpa Gorge and enters the town at a T-junction with Shahumian Street, the main road of the town, more or less in the centre of the spa area. To right and left the large Soviet sanatoria perch on the top of the gorge. Straight ahead is the **Town Park** with many statues. Along its northern edge is a series of park lakes fed by streams from the slopes of the Jrasar Mountain, at the foot of which Jermuk sits. At the west end of the Town Park is the **Jermuk Drinking Gallery**, an attractive colonnaded building constructed in 1956 where there is a row of urns, each of which has natural mineral water of a different specified temperature pouring into it. In all there are five piped springs; the water temperatures range from 30° to 53°. Visitors bring their mugs, jugs and vacuum flasks to fill at the taps and in high season, late July to mid-September, queues build up. From the Gallery the Ghazarian Alley goes along the far side of the park lakes to the **Muradian sculptures**, a series of ten busts of Armenian revolutionaries, some of which are beside the path while others nestle among the rocks and trees of the hillside. The **commercial centre** of Jermuk is centred on the southern part of Shahumian Street. The bottom of the gorge is reached by a road which goes off just north of the Ani Hotel, zigzags down then up the other side to reach the statue of Israel Ori. From the bridge at the bottom of the gorge a road leads to a parking place near a water-pumping building. From here it is a short walk to a waterfall. It is very pleasant to stroll along the many paths in and around the spa area. Jermuk would be a good centre for more serious walking but there are no detailed maps or marked trails. Vayk tourist information centre might be able to help with guides (see page 283).

The small **Jermuk Art Gallery** (*1 Charents St;* ℡ *287 22132;* ⊕ *10.30–17.30 Tue–Sun; guide in Armenian or Russian AMD1,500; AMD200*) is well worth a visit. All the paintings are from the last 100 years and include evocative landscapes and portraits as well as abstract works.

A **ski lift** (⊕ *11.00–19.00 all year; return trip AMD1,000*) was built at the entry to the town in 2007. It goes from an altitude of 2,100m to 2,500m and the total length

6

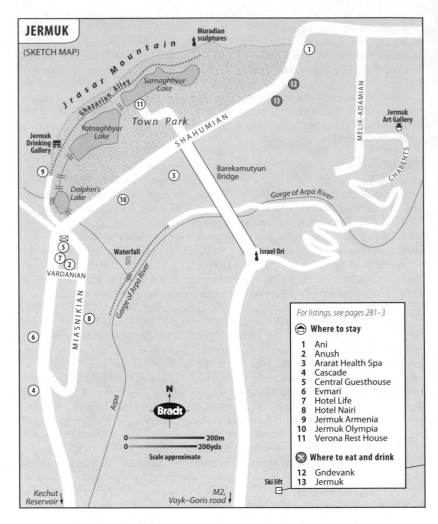

JERMUK

(SKETCH MAP)

Jrasar Mountain

Muradian sculptures

Ghazarian Alley

Sarnaghbyur Lake

Town Park

Yotnaghbyur Lake

Jermuk Drinking Gallery

SHAHUMIAN

Barekamutyun Bridge

Gorge of Arpa River

MELIK-ADAMIAN

CHARENTS

Jermuk Art Gallery

Dolphin's Lake

VARDANIAN

Waterfall

Gorge of Arpa River

Israel Ori

MIASNIKIAN

Arpa

N

Bradt

0 ———— 200m
0 ———— 200yds
Scale approximate

Ski lift

Kechut Reservoir ↓

M2, Vayk–Goris road ↓

For listings, see pages 281–3

🛏 **Where to stay**
1 Ani
2 Anush
3 Ararat Health Spa
4 Cascade
5 Central Guesthouse
6 Evmari
7 Hotel Life
8 Hotel Nairi
9 Jermuk Armenia
10 Jermuk Olympia
11 Verona Rest House

✕ **Where to eat and drink**
12 Gndevank
13 Jermuk

of ski slopes is 2.6km. The resort is low key and very much in its infancy. Skis and accessories can be hired at the building to the right of the ski lift terminal. There is a café (⏰ *same hrs as ski lift*) at both the lower and upper chair-lift terminals. The chair lift has 100 double seats. In summer the trip takes 12 minutes; in winter it is speeded up to seven minutes because it is so cold.

SYUNIK PROVINCE

Armenia's southernmost province has two well-known sites (Tatev and Karahunj) and one (Ughtasar) which, although much less well known, ranks as one of the most interesting in the country. Syunik's long western border with Nakhichevan is closed. The even longer eastern border with the self-declared Republic of Nagorno Karabagh has only one main road across it, between Goris and Stepanakert. There is a border crossing with Iran at Agarak. The far south along the Iranian border is, not surprisingly, the warmest part of Armenia and a centre of fruit growing.

The original road to the far south crossed Nakhichevan and the closure of the border required a difficult hill road to be considerably upgraded to take the heavy lorry traffic to and from Iran. An alternative road has now been built from Kapan to Meghri running through the Shikahogh Reserve in the east of the province. The routing of this road caused controversy because of fears about the impact on wildlife and also because it could open the area to illegal logging. Both roads traverse spectacular scenery and you may wish to do a loop, travelling south via one road and north via the other.

GETTING THERE AND AROUND Most visitors enter Syunik along the main road from Yerevan. The border with Vayots Dzor at the **Vorotan Pass** (2,344m) is marked by a large concrete structure on each side of the road: the symbolic Gates of Syunik. There is a good spring here at which water bottles can be filled. The road then descends past the Spandarian and Shaghat reservoirs running parallel to the Vorotan River which lies some distance to the south. After winter, pot-holes can be a significant problem on this stretch of road. **Minibuses** run from Yerevan to Sisian, Goris, Kapan and Meghri (see pages 80–2). Buses travel daily between Tehran and Yerevan (see page 69). From the main towns minibuses go to local villages but to reach many of the sites mentioned, either a car or taxi is needed. A few sites can only be reached by walking or with a 4x4. A **cable-car** to Tatev Monastery opened in 2010 cutting travelling time considerably. The road to Tatev has been improved although the final stretch from Satan's Bridge is still dirt. Allow the best part of a day if travelling all the way by road; it is not a fast road and there is much to see at Tatev.

WHERE TO STAY Sisian and Goris both have good accommodation and can act as a base from which to visit most of the province, with further overnight stays in Kapan and/or Kajaran if travelling to the far south. Unless you want to spend time walking in the Meghri area or visiting the Shikahogh Reserve, the sights of Meghri can be covered in a day trip from Kapan or Kajaran. Apart from the accommodation listed below, **homestays** can be arranged through tour operators in Yerevan (see pages 63–4) and the tourist information offices at Tatev Monastery and Goris (see pages 302–3). If really stuck for accommodation, asking around almost anywhere will probably produce someone who is willing to provide accommodation for the night but this is very much pot luck. Where listings are plotted on a map, this is indicated below.

Goris
Map, page 311.

Hotel Christy (20 rooms) 9 Mashtots St; m 055 019006, 077 000047; e christyhotel@ gmail.com; www.christyhotel.am. A welcoming, warm hotel with good hot showers. Very close to town centre. Rooms & dining room non-smoking. B/fast inc, order other meals 2hrs in advance. An excellent evening meal of *dolma*, salad, cheese, bread & a glass of wine cost AMD3,500. Swimming pool. Wi-Fi. **$$**

Hotel Mina (38 rooms) 169 Mashtots St; 284 30119; m 099 030119; e hotelminagoris@ gmail.com. A little further from the centre than most other hotels. Opened in 2009, this smart new

hotel has a swimming pool, gym & restaurant. Wi-Fi. Cards accepted. **$$**

Hotel Mira (6 rooms) 24/3 Ankakhutian St; 284 24880/1; m 093/096 595947; e mira. hotel@mail.ru; www.hotelmiragoris.com. A family-run hotel in a renovated house, opened in 2012. On 3 floors. Own fruit from garden. Restaurant. **$$**

Mirhav Hotel (31 rooms) 100 Mashtots St; 284 24612, 24632, 10 284402 (Yerevan number); e hotelmirhav@yahoo.com. This delightful hotel, run by an Iranian-Armenian retired neurosurgeon who speaks several languages, inc German & English, is tastefully decorated in natural materials. The restaurant serves excellent meals (the apricot

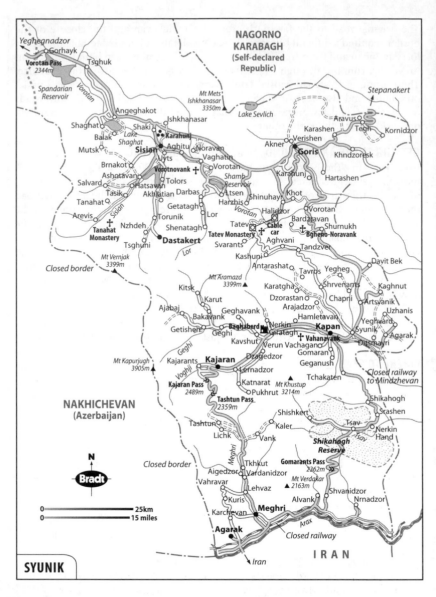

NAGORNO KARABAGH
(Self-declared Republic)

Yeghegnadzor
Gorhayk
Vorotan Pass
2344m
Tsghuk
Spandarian Reservoir
Angeghakot
Shaghat
Balak
Mutsk
Shaki
Lake Shaghat
Ishkhanasar
Mt Mets Ishkhanasar 3350m
Lake Sevlich
Stepanakert
Aravus
Tegh
Kornidzor
Karashen
Verishen
Akner
Khndzoresk
Goris
Brnakot
Ashotavan
Salvard
Tasik
Tanahat
Arevis
Tanahat Monastery
Sisian
Uyts
Aghitu
Noravan
Vaghatin
Vorotan
Shamb
Karahunj
Hartashen
Vorotnovank
Tolors
Hatsavan
Akhlatian
Darbas
Atsen
Shinuhayr
Khot
Reservoir
Harzhis
Vorotan
Halidzor
Vorotan
Getatagh
Lor
Bardzravan
Shurnukh
Nzhdeh
Torunik
Shenatagh
Tatev
Cable car
Bgheno-Noravank
Tatev Monastery
Aghvani
Tandzver
Dastakert
Tsghuni
Lor
Svarants
Mt Vernjak 3399m
Closed border
Kashuni
Antarashat
Davit Bek
Tavrus
Yegheg
Kitsk
Mt Aramazd 3399m
Karatgha
Shrvenants
Kaghnut
Karut
Geghavank
Dzorastan
Chapni
Artsvanik
Uzhanis
Ajabaj
Bakavank
Hamletavan
Arajadzor
Yeghward
Getishen
Geghi
Nerkin
Kilatagh
Kapan
Syunik
Agarak
Baghaberd
Kavshut
Verun Vachagan
Vahanavank
Ditsmayri
Mt Kapurjugh 3905m
Kajarants
Kajaran
Dzagedzor
Gomaran
Geganush
Closed railway to Mindzhevan
Lernadzor
Voghji
Kajaran Pass 2489m
Katnarat
Mt Khustup 3214m
Tchakaten
Shikahogh
Pukhrut
Tashtun Pass 2359m
Srashen
NAKHICHEVAN
(Azerbaijan)
Tashtun
Lichk
Shishkert
Kaler
Tsav
Nerkin Hand
Vank
Shikahogh Reserve
Tsav
Meghri
Closed border
Tkhkut
Aigedzor
Vardanidzor
Gomarants Pass 2362m
Shvanidzor
Nrnadzor
Vahravar
Lehvaz
Mt Verdakar 2163m
Alvank
Kuris
Meghri
Karchevan
Agarak
Arax
Closed railway
IRAN
Iran

N
Bradt
0 — 25km
0 — 15 miles

SYUNIK

pilaff is wonderful) – notice of 1–2hrs is required. Some of the smaller rooms are quite cramped for 2 ppl & 2 suitcases. The hotel stocks a good range of postcards & maps. Rooms are non-smoking. Wi-Fi. Cards accepted, 3% charge. Discounts for groups & children. **$$**

Goris Hotel (previously Hotel Olympia) (20 rooms) 53 Khorenatsi St; \ 284 30003; e olympia. goris@rambler.ru; www.hotelgoris.am. The approach to this Soviet building is not encouraging

but once inside one finds a warm, well-renovated hotel & helpful staff. Pleasant bar & restaurant. B/fast inc, order other meals in advance. Wi-Fi. The director of the Mirhav Hotel suggests this hotel to visitors when his own is full. **$$–$**

Hostel Goris (3 rooms) 55 Khorenatsi St; \ 284 21886; m 093 425220; e jirmar28@freenet. am. The 3 rooms (2 dbl, 1 trpl) share 1 bathroom. Extra guests can be accommodated in the owners' house next door. The host, J Martirosyan, is an artist & member of the Armenian Painters' Union. His gallery is in a rock cave & visitors are welcome. Guided tours of Goris, inc the Axel Bakunts House Museum, can be arranged (*AMD15,000 inc lunch*). Members of the family speak English, Russian & Turkish. Wi-Fi. Meals for those not staying can be arranged, 1 day's notice required. B/fast extra AMD1,500pp. **$**

🏠 **Hotel Vivas** (6 rooms) 65 Syunik St; ✆ 284 24812; m 093 746892; e info@vivas.am; www. vivas.am. One of the oldest B&Bs in Goris with cheerful, helpful proprietor. Only 2 rooms en suite, others share 1 bathroom. Wi-Fi. Restaurant, order in advance. Accepts cards. **$**

Kajaran

🏠 **Hotel Kajaran** (48 rooms) 3 Abovian St; ✆ 285 32055; m 098 575810, 077 180577; e kajaran.hotel@mail.ru. This satisfactorily renovated hotel is owned by the Zangezur Copper Molybdenum Combine. They coped well with unexpected guests arriving late at night. B/fast extra AMD1,500–2,000pp. Restaurant but order in advance. There is a 2nd building, possibly unrenovated, with cheaper rooms (*AMD5,000/ bed*). Cards accepted. **$**

Kapan

Map, page 315.

🏠 **Mi & Max Hotel** (15 rooms) 2 Demirchian St; ✆ 285 203000; m 091 192484; e mimaxhotel@ rambler.ru; the 8th & 9th floors of the same building as Hotel Lernagorts (see above). Well renovated to luxury standard. Minibar & AC in all rooms. No dining room, meals served in rooms, order 1hr in advance. B/fast extra AMD2,000pp. Reception on 9th floor. Lift doesn't stop at 8th floor; stairs between 8th & 9th floor. Door to main staircase of building locked to separate it from the rest of the building. Has another emergency exit staircase. Wi-Fi. Cards accepted. (*Luxe rooms* **$$$**) **$$**

🏠 **Hotel Darist** (32 rooms) 1a Aram Manukian St; ✆ 285 28262; e hotel_darist@yahoo.com. This hotel has now been fully refurbished & is probably still the best place to stay in central Kapan unless you want luxury. Reception on 4th floor, rooms on 3rd & 4th floors, restaurant 2nd floor. There is a lift. The restaurant serves tasty meals although the occasional live music is too loud for some tastes. The hotel prefers payment on arrival. Booklet

(*AMD1,000*) about Kapan & map (*AMD500*) of the town available. Wi-Fi. **$$**

🏠 **Hotel Dian** (12 rooms) 3 Gortsaranain St; ✆ 285 20120; m 098 886040; e dianhotel@gmail. com; www.dianhotel.com. A new-build hotel which opened in 2010. Probably aimed at business clientele. Not well situated for those without own transport. In an industrial area at east end of town, approx 2km to centre either via busy main road (inc a tunnel) or along a dusty back road. Comfortable in some respects but heating only from Nov to Mar so if weather turns cold early rooms are chilly. Hot water only from 07.30. No meals available apart from b/fast. Wi-Fi. **$$**

🏠 **Hotel Lernagorts** (32 rooms) 2 Demirchian St; ✆ 285 28039; e lernagorts@mail.ru. Occupies floors 1–7 of the same building as Mi & Max Hotel (see below). All rooms in this old Soviet hotel have been renovated. Price of rooms depends partly on size. Internet café attached. **$**

Meghri

Map, page 319.

🏠 **Arevik Guesthouse** (4 rooms: 1 twin, 1 dbl, 1 trpl, 1 quad with en suite) 20 Mejnouminan St, Pokr Tagh; m 077 305124 (Armine, the owner). Not easy to find. Follow the signs for the church in Pokr Tagh, which is a maze of small streets. Vehicles have to be left some distance away, beside a white garage door with green lettering. Then walk up to the left & follow steps & alleyway to dbl wooden doors. Pack a small bag & leave heavy luggage in the car. Delightful renovation of a 17th- or 18th-century house in the old district of Meghri, just below St Sargis Church. Rooms round an attractive courtyard. Dining room downstairs. Furnished with traditional materials. Quiet, no TV/radio. Has a monastic feel. Shower room & toilets across the courtyard (light left on at night but take a torch in case …). Food is wonderful! I had what was possibly the best meal of a trip; AMD10,000 for 2 ppl but the amount would have fed 6. Order meals in advance. I could recommend this guesthouse wholeheartedly but for 1 significant drawback: the only entrance to the guesthouse is padlocked shut at night on the outside, meaning that guests have no means of exit. The only other way out is via balconies in 2 of the bedrooms, to the garden of the house below (see page 318) & it is a long way down. If you do decide to stay here, & unless the arrangements have changed, make sure you have the key-holder's mobile number (but note she lives some distance away in the town). **$**

🏠 **Hotel Edem** (8 rooms) 31 Zoravar Andranik St; m 077 242526. Dbl, trpl & quad rooms. A basic hotel on the main road south opposite the turn-off into the town. Restaurant. Wi-Fi. **$**

Sisian

Map, page 305.

🏠 **Basen Hotel** (21 rooms) 2 Manukian St; ☎ 2832 4662; m 093 434685; e contact@ basenhotel.am; www.basenhotel.am. To reach it on foot from the town hall square go eastwards along Sisakan St, past Dina Hotel then left up steps opposite the next road junction. Once on Manukian St there is a large sign on the right. By road, you have to access the east half of Sisakan St (page 305) then go round three sides of a square. If no-one is in reception, try the restaurant. Excellent English spoken. The hotel comprises 3 separate, fully renovated, buildings each with 7 rooms. Restaurant (☎ 2832 5264) in separate building with small souvenir shop selling local handmade

articles. On the site of the original airport, it was a holiday complex in Soviet days & is now a family-owned fully upgraded establishment which also owns a nearby *tonir* bakery. Wi-Fi. **$$**

🏠 **Lalaner Hotel** (16 rooms) 29 Sisakan St; ☎ 2832 6600; restaurant ☎ 2832 5600; e info@ lalahotel.am; www.lalahotel.am. This previously comfortable hotel had a somewhat depressed air at the time of writing, possibly because it was under renovation. Restaurant. **$$**

🏠 **Dina Hotel** (16 rooms en suite, 15 rooms without) 35 Sisakan St; ☎ 2832 3333; m 093 334392; e sisiano@mail.ru; www.dinahotel.am. Useful access diagram on website. This remains my favourite hotel in Sisian. All rooms have now been renovated & the staff are as cheerful & friendly as ever. There is information about local sites of interest & staff can arrange transport to them, inc to the petroglyphs on Mount Ughtasar (see opposite). The small bright restaurant can provide meals, but larger groups need to give notice. Rooms without bathroom AMD3,000pp, b/fast AMD1,500pp. En-suite dbl rooms AMD12,000–14,000, b/fast inc. **$**

✗ **WHERE TO EAT AND DRINK** Many of the hotels listed can provide a full meal, some with advance notice, and probably coffee and a snack at short notice. Hotel Darist in Kapan, Lalaner Hotel in Sisian, Hotel Mina in Goris and Hotel Edem in Meghri have 'walk-in' restaurants. There are summer cafés on Sisakan Street in Sisian (page 305), Goris (page 310), at Khndzoresk (page 312) and at the Tatev cable-car terminals (pages 308–9). In summer, eating places spring up on the busier main roads and in town parks, but the roads south from Kapan to Meghri are less well provided.

✗ **Café Lord** [map, page 319] Meghri. On the main highway just north of the bridge over the river into the town. Sign visible only when travelling northwards. Rooms a bit smoky but in fine weather one can sit outside. A light meal of cheese, salads & chips AMD2,000.

✗ **Café Royal** [map, page 315] 2 Demirchian Sq, Kapan (next to Lernagorts Hotel); m 098 624006; ⊕ 10.00–22.00 daily. Convenient but smoky.

✗ **Elegant Restaurant** [map, page 315] 32/1 Shahumian St, Kapan; ☎ 285 21505. A busy place with loud music but good food. An efficient

ventilation system made the smoke not too troublesome.

✗ **Jrahars (Mermaid) Restaurant** [map, page 305] 39 Israelian St, Sisian; ☎ 2832 5386; m 094 866808. Down steps beside the bridge over the river. This cheerful restaurant serves the standard Armenian meal of barbecued meat & vegetables, salads, cheese, bread all for about AMD3,000. Also serves warming soup when the weather turns cold.

✗ **SKS Restaurant** [map, page 311] Narekatsi St, Goris; ⊕ 11.00–24.00. Bar downstairs, restaurant upstairs. Same menu in each. Eat in or out. No need to book. Loud music.

OTHER PRACTICALITIES Sisian, Goris and Kapan are the larger towns and have most facilities but bring any special requirements with you. There are tourist information offices at Goris and at Tatev Monastery. **Goris Tourist Information Office** (*3 Ankakhutian St;* ☎ *284 22690;* m *077 277765;* e *touristeoffice_goris@yahoo.fr;*

⊕ *10.00–17.00 Mon–Sat*) is staffed by volunteers so opening hours can vary. They have some information leaflets, can help to arrange homestays and offer a two-hour tour of Goris. **Tatev Information Centre** (see page 309) is near the cable-car terminal just outside the monastery. The centre can arrange homestays, guides for hikes and it runs the small café in the centre.

MOUNT METS ISHKHANASAR Mount Mets Ishkhanasar (3,550m), an extinct volcano, is the tallest peak of the Ishkhanasar range which lies to the northwest of Goris on what was the border with Azerbaijan and is now the *de facto* border with the self-declared Republic of Nagorno Karabagh. Visitors wishing to see the immensely worthwhile and fascinating **petroglyphs at Ughtasar** will need a local guide and probably transport; the 17km track, climbing 1,400m from the nearest settlement, requires a 4x4. The very helpful manager of the Hotel Dina (see opposite) in the centre of Sisian can organise a guide and transport or arrangements can be made in advance through a Yerevan agent; see pages 63–4. A guide and vehicle seating up to seven persons cost around AMD70,000. It takes about 90 minutes to drive to the site from Sisian although the last 500m has to be walked as the vehicle cannot make the steep ascent when fully laden. The petroglyphs are accessible only from mid-July to late September because of snow and it can be bitterly cold at the high site even in summer. To anyone who has seen supposed rock carvings in museums the petroglyphs here are an absolute revelation with numerous designs scattered on boulders over a large area. The 1.5km x 1km caldera is beautiful in itself with the eroded rim of the volcano towering above wide areas of natural grassland and seasonal pools. Most of the petroglyphs are on boulders around the permanent glacial lake within the caldera. It is also the haunt of bears and wolves, as is attested by the droppings and footprints.

Petroglyphs, called 'goat letters' in Armenian, are found in several parts of Armenia. They are scattered over tens of square kilometres at sites in the Syunik Mountains but these at Ughtasar are among the more accessible. The site itself is at 3,300m altitude and many thousands of petroglyphs have been recorded here. Some of the carvings depict animals, mostly the wild animals of the region but also domestic ones. Wild goats are especially common. There are carvings of hunting scenes and ones showing the impedimenta of hunting. Birds are rarely depicted, while snakes and leopards feature more frequently. People also feature in scenes depicting dancers, either two dancers together or communal dancing. Some rocks have just a single design but others have a whole collection of carvings, as many as 50 in extreme cases. The presence of hunting scenes and cattle has led to speculation that the people who carved the rocks lived partly by hunting and partly by animal husbandry, presumably pasturing their animals here in summer. They must have been at least semi-nomadic since it would not be possible to survive here in winter. The age of the carvings is difficult to ascertain but the majority of carvings at Ughtasar and elsewhere in Armenia probably date from the 5th to the 2nd millennium BC. A team of British and Armenian archaeologists is systematically surveying the petroglyphs at Ughtasar. Details of their work and results, including photographs, can be found at www.ughtasarrockartproject.org. Members of the team have provided advice (see box, page 304) on caring for rock art.

KARAHUNJ (*Note that Karahunj is off the main Sisian to Goris road, just west of the more easterly turn-off for Sisian; it is not near the village of Karahunj to the south of Goris.*) Much better known than the petroglyphs is another, slightly more recent site. **Karahunj** (also known as Zorats Karer) is sometimes called Armenia's

Although carved on rock the petroglyphs are fragile, many of them eroding in the harsh climate. They have also suffered damage from visitors walking on the carved surfaces (and from graffiti). Please help to prevent further damage to this wonderful rock art and the delicate balance of the site's rich natural environment.

NEVER
- Stand or walk on the carved surfaces
- Touch the panels unnecessarily
- Use any substance to enhance the carvings
- Use anything (including water) to 'clean' the rock surface; never try to remove graffiti
- Remove lichen from rock art panels
- Remove turf from buried or partially buried panels
- Scratch anything on or close to the carved panels
- Make fires close to rock carvings or light candles on the rocks

ALWAYS
- Take all litter away with you
- Take all food away; it is dangerous if the bears and other wild animals which frequent the site associate visitors with food
- Leave the carved rocks and other archaeological features as you find them
- Pass on this advice to others visiting the site

Stonehenge although the appellation is misleading since the two look very different. The whole site occupies about 7ha of plateau at the edge of a small ravine in the hills above the Vorotan River. The area is covered with numerous stone circles, cists and mounds as well as the best known arrangement of standing stones which comprises 204 rough-hewn stones. These are arranged in an elaborate layout and the most quoted theory is that they formed an ancient astronomical observatory dating from sometime prior to 2000BC. The stones are basalt and the largest, 3m tall, weighs 10 tonnes. Of the stones, 76 have apertures near the top. The configuration is of 39 stones laid in an oval formation with its main axis running east–west for a distance of 43m. Within this oval are some contemporary graves. Bisecting the oval is an arc comprising a further 20 stones. Three arms of stones lie off this central shape running to the north, south and southeast. The north and south arms are much longer than the southeast arm and bend west towards their tips. Stones with apertures occur only in the arms but not all stones in the arms have apertures.

There has been much theorising on how the monument was used. It certainly seems clear that the apertures must be significant but they are too large (at least 5cm diameter) to look through a single one in a precise direction and they don't seem to be lined up with each other for looking through pairs of apertures, which would have facilitated more precise observation. Conceivably the stones could have been used for observing the moon, but observation of stars seems difficult to imagine. Anyone looking at the sun would have risked severe damage to their central vision. In 2000 a team of archaeologists from the University of Munich in conjunction with the Armenian Academy of Sciences examined the site. Their opinion was that it is mainly a necropolis from the Middle Bronze Age to the Iron Age, citing the tombs found in the area. Later, they suggest, possibly in the Hellenistic/Roman period (c300BC–AD300), the site was used as a refuge with a wall of rocks and soil, the large vertical stones (today the only remaining elements) reinforcing the structure. Karahunj, on its rock-strewn site, is impressive but the lack of any convincing explanation makes a visit somewhat frustrating.

Some sizeable lizards (40cm in length) of rather prehistoric appearance clamber about on the stones. They are Caucasian agama (*Laudakia caucasia*), a species, despite its name, with a range from northeast Turkey to Pakistan.

SISIAN (*Telephone code: 2382*) Note that of the two access roads from the main highway the westernmost has a much better surface. Sisian is situated on the banks of the Vorotan River, surrounded by hills. One of the main streets, Sisakan Street, is no longer a through route, being interrupted by a park-like boulevard in front of the town hall. Sisakan Street and parallel Israelian Street, on the north side of the river have most of the facilities. The castle-like derelict building on Israelian Street was a bakery. Over the doorway, in Armenian script, is the word for bakery, *hatsatoun*, literally 'bread house'. South of the river there are more shops.

Some material excavated from Karahunj is in the **historical museum** (*Adonts National Historical Museum; 1 Adonts St; \ 2832 3331; ⊕ 10.00–17.00; guided tour in English AMD2,000; photographic fee AMD1,000; adult AMD400*) in the centre of Sisian. In recent years I have never found the museum open – others may be luckier. It is still worth visiting because outside is a good collection of gravestones in the form of sheep. There are also stones bearing petroglyphs.

It is much easier to get into **Sisavank**, the fine early church dedicated to St John which overlooks the town. Similar in style to the church of St Hripsime at Ejmiatsin, this was built of basalt by Prince Kohazat and Bishop Hovsep I between 670 and 689. Like St Hripsime it has three-quarter-circle ante-rooms leading into the corner rooms. It is notable for its regular geometrical composition; all four apses are of

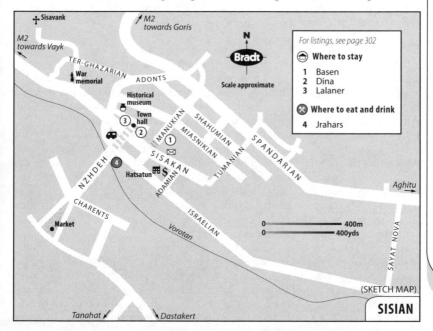

For listings, see page 302

🛏 **Where to stay**
1 Basen
2 Dina
3 Lalaner

✕ **Where to eat and drink**
4 Jrahars

(SKETCH MAP)

SISIAN

The Southern Provinces   SYUNIK PROVINCE

6

equal size, as are the ante-rooms; the volume under the dome is an exact square in plan; there are two deep triangular niches on all façades. Of cross-dome style, it has a conical cupola supported by a tambour, which is octagonal internally but 12-sided externally, decorated with 12 graceful arcatures with twin half-colonnettes: a window is positioned directly over each of the four apses. The interior of the church is decorated by a sort of frieze depicting vine leaves and grapes which runs round most of it, presumably a reference to Jesus being the true vine since this is not a district traditionally associated with winemaking. The altar table with a carved eagle on its front is new (2001) and was carved by the son of the present caretaker. The font, to the left of the *bema*, is also new (2008) and was carved by the caretaker's grandson. The old font, which is now in the southeast corner room, was unsatisfactory on two counts. The water did not drain away properly, so making the church damp, and the basin was in the form of a cross with sharp corners making it dangerous for the baby, given the baptismal practice of immersion. The church has a small collection of old books, the oldest dating from 1686, and also some miniatures by Eduard Ghazarian carved on items such as rice grains, which can be viewed through a microscope.

Some 7km west of the western entry road to Sisian lies **Angeghakot**, a large, maze-like village of low houses. For details of its interesting churches and how to reach them, go to www.bradtguides.com/europe/armenia.

AROUND SISIAN

North from Sisian A few kilometres northwest of Sisian is the **Shaki Waterfall** on a tributary of the Vorotan River. While not large by European standards it is quite pretty and the Armenians are very proud of it. From Sisian turn first left, under a yellow gas pipe, on Sisian's western approach road. From the Yerevan to Goris highway it is 3km to the turn-off. After about 2km you come to a hydro-electric station. Drive through the station's grounds to an open parking place. From there the path to the waterfall goes uphill along the river and continues up beside the waterfall and along the wall to the dammed river.

Southeast from Sisian To the southeast there are two worthwhile sights, Aghitu funerary monument and Vorotnavank Monastery. Stay on the north side of the river and take Sisakan Street, which runs in front of the Dina Hotel, making for the village of **Vorotan**. If asking for directions (the road out of Sisian is confusing at times) note that locals still refer to Vorotan by its old name, Urut. After about 5km the first village is **Aghitu** where there is an unusual 6th or 7th-century **funerary monument**, unlike anything else in the country apart from the monument at Odzun Church in Lori province. It is mounted on an arched base. Above that two rectangular columns support a two-tier structure. The lower tier has a circular central column and decorated capitals while the smaller upper tier has two carved round columns, again with decorated capitals. For whom such an elaborate monument was created is unknown and it is paradoxical that the efforts to ensure that he would be remembered have come to naught. Low ruins and tombstones show this was once an extensive site.

The road continues beyond Aghitu. Keep the Vorotan River on your right until, about 9km from Sisian, you encounter the **monastery of Vorotnavank** above the river. The oldest church, dedicated to **St Stephen**, was built in 1000 by Queen Shahandukht. It is barrel vaulted and has a much lower *gavit* on the west side. (Beware the extremely deep hole at the west end of the *gavit*.) In 1007 the queen's son, Sevada, built a second church, dedicated to **St John the Baptist**. There are remains of frescoes on the north wall and in the apse. It is a cross-dome construction and lies to the southeast of the first church. Both churches have arcaded galleries, but of different styles and presumably of different dates. A further smaller church, various service buildings and a fortified wall complete the complex. There was severe damage here in the 1931 earthquake but it has mostly been repaired. There is a plethora of gravestones which have rich figure carving. Some of them have at sometime (since restoration after the earthquake?) been incorporated into the buildings. The carvings depict both human beings, often in domestic scenes, and domesticated animals such as horses and cattle.

A little further on, 1.1km after crossing the river, are the scant remains of the **fortress of Vorotnaberd** on top of a steep hill to the left. This was a key site in Armenian history from AD450 when it was a stronghold of rebels under Vardan Mamikonian. It then changed hands many times; to the Seljuk Turks in 1104, recaptured by the Armenians in 1219, taken by the Mongols in 1386 who returned it to the Orbelians, conquered again by the Turks in 1407 then recovered by David Bek in 1724. It is a short but difficult climb to the top. There is not much to see of its momentous past apart from low remains spread over two hills – and the view. If you don't cross the river but continue to the village of **Vorotan**, turning right through some derelict Soviet buildings rather than left into the village, you come to a **hot spring** which is piped into a pool. The water is quite hot and were it not for the derelict buildings and litter it would be an idyllic place to soak outdoors amidst the mountains.

Southwest from Sisian
Heading southwest, a road follows the Sisian River. To reach it cross the bridge in the town and turn left at the T-junction, then right at traffic lights, then left and finally right again just after the large electricity substation. The ride along the valley is extremely beautiful and worth experiencing for its own sake. Just after a road branches off right for Tanahat village the remains of **Tanahat Monastery** can be seen on an outcrop on the valley side across the river. Unlike its namesake, Tanahat Monastery in Vayots Dzor, this monastery is very ruinous, but reaching it involves a pleasant walk with many flowers in early summer and myriads of butterflies in midsummer. There is a footbridge across the river some way past the monastery. It has partly collapsed but it is still possible to cross. A footpath leads across the hill to the monastery. (Wear sturdy footwear: in summer I saw several snakes in the area.) At times it may be possible to wade across or ford the river in a vehicle just after the road branches off to Tanahat village, but this is impossible when the river is in spate. The pink 5th-century single-nave church has remnants of carved tulip-like decoration – highly appropriate since wild white tulips are one of the earliest flowers to appear here after the snow has melted. Some of the graves in the cemetery look very like the chambered tombs of northwest Europe, the burial vault being covered by up to three large slabs. One 11th-century khachkar found here reused a stone with an earlier cuneiform inscription; it is now in the museum at Erebuni.

East from Sisian
Tatev Syunik's best known site, **Tatev Monastery**, is reached by continuing down the main road beyond the Sisian turn-off for a further 25km and then turning right. The road to Tatev (29km) is asphalt as far as Satan's Bridge then a good dirt road for the rest of the way. The journey time to Tatev, for those with a head for heights, has been still further shortened by a **cable-car** (⏱ *Jan & Feb 10.00–18.00 Sat & Sun only; Mar–Sep 10.00–20.00 Tue–Sun; Oct–Dec 10.00–18.00 Tue–Sun; closed Mon for maintenance; departures at approx 20 min intervals; last departure from Tatev approx 30 mins before closing; one-way ticket AMD3,000, return ticket AMD4,000;*

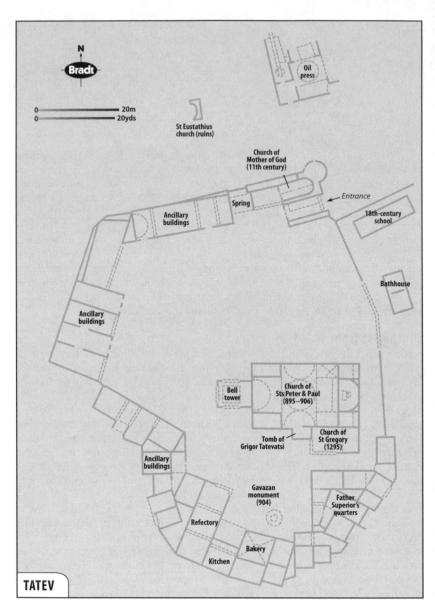

N

Bradt

0 ——————— 20m
0 ——————— 20yds

St Eustathius
church (ruins)

Oil
press

Church of
Mother of God
(11th century)

Spring

Ancillary
buildings

← *Entrance*

18th-century
school

Bathhouse

Ancillary
buildings

Bell
tower

Church of
Sts Peter & Paul
(895–906)

Ancillary
buildings

Tomb of
Grigor Tatevatsi

Church of
St Gregory
(1295)

Gavazan
monument
(904)

Father
Superior's
quarters

Refectory

Bakery

Kitchen

TATEV

*under 7s free. It is possible to phone (☎ 284 67507) & book tickets for later the same
day but it must be for a specific time)* which transports passengers from a terminal
near Halidzor village to Tatev village. The terminal at Halidzor is well laid out
with information boards, a children's play area, restaurant, café and car park with
attendants. At busy times you may have to queue. The longest cable-car ride in
the world, it spans the 5.7km between the two villages and was built by an Italian
company. It opened in October 2010. Each cabin carries 25 passengers for the
12-minute ride high above the valley of the Vorotan River. It is hoped that the 'aerial
tramway', as the Armenians like to call it, will make Tatev village and monastery

accessible even in winter, something which will certainly benefit the villagers who travel for AMD500. For those who prefer a less exalted form of transport there is a minibus between Goris and Tatev but it is timed for locals, not tourists. It runs only on Mondays and Fridays (*Tatev to Goris: 09.00; Goris to Tatev 15.00; the 30km takes 1½hrs; AMD700*). A taxi is more convenient. A return trip from Goris, including an hour's waiting time, costs about AMD10,000.

There is a legend about Tatev Monastery. It is said that the architect couldn't get down when he finished the cupola of the main church. He cried out: '*Togh astvats indz ta-tev*', which means 'May God give me wings'. And so the monastery got its name. An excellent distant view can be had from the left of the road where there is a small gazebo-type structure. The short path to the gazebo starts from the lay-by at the top of the climb from Halidzor. The gazebo is variously stated to mark the signalling point from which the monastery could be warned of the approach of possibly unwelcome visitors, or alternatively the spot from which a young lady threw herself into the gorge rather than submit to an unwelcome marriage with a local Muslim ruler. After the gazebo the road winds down to the Vorotan and crosses it adjacent to the so-called **Satan's Bridge**, a natural bridge over the swift-flowing river: a path leads down through eroded rock formations to a popular swimming pool. The road then winds up the far side of the valley to the monastery. Adjacent to the monastery is an **information centre** (⊕ *Apr–Oct 09.00–21.00 depending on the weather;* m *093 845632;* e *annshik14@yahoo.com; www.tatevinfo.com*). The centre can arrange homestays and hikes and it runs the small café in the centre.

The date of the now vanished first church at the **monastery** is unknown, but in 844 Bishop Davit persuaded the Princes of Syunik to grant lands which would support the founding of a monastery worthy to house the relics which the church in Syunik possessed. It was his successor, Bishop Ter-Hovhannes, who built the **main church**, dedicated to Sts Paul and Peter between 895 and 906. It was badly damaged by the earthquake in 1931 during which the cupola collapsed, but the whole has now been restored except for the bell tower which formerly had three storeys. Tatev's reconstruction has not always been sensitive – installing a marble floor rather than stone flags in the church and library rather jars, for example, but the restoration does give an excellent idea of how the monastery must have looked when it was a thriving centre of learning and 1,000 people lived here. Its greatest importance was in the 14th and 15th centuries under Hovnan Vorotnetsi (1315–88) and Grigor Tatevatsi (1346–1411). Tatevatsi was both a philosopher and a painter and is portrayed surrounded by his students in one of the few portraits in Armenian manuscript illustration. This is in the 1449 *Interpretation of the Psalms of David* and is presumably the work of one of his former pupils.

The complex is surrounded by a large fortified wall. The church is somewhat intermediate in style between the earlier domed basilica churches and the later cross-dome churches. The umbrella cupola is supported by an unusually tall decorated circular tambour. On the east façade, above the triangular niches, long snakes are looking at two heads while on the north façade, above a window, two shorter snakes are looking at a person: Armenians supposedly regarded snakes as protectors of their homes. On the north façade are also representations of the founders of the church – Prince Ashot, his wife Shushan, Grigor Supan, the ruler of Gegharkunik, and Prince Dzagik. In 930, the walls of the church were decorated with frescoes but these have almost totally vanished except for some scant remnants in the apse and the interior is now rather plain. Grigor Tatevatsi is buried inside the small chapel on the south side of the main church. His tomb is the highly decorated structure which abuts the church.

Outside the church on the south side is a monument erected in 904 called the *gavazan* (meaning a priest's or clergyman's pastoral staff). It is an octagonal pillar built of small stones with an elaborate cornice and a small khachkar on top. The pillar formerly detected earth tremors by rocking on the horizontal course of masonry on which it is constructed. It does not appear to have worked for some years, however, and the lower part is bound up by iron bands. The modest **St Gregory Church** adjoins the main church also on the south side. Dating from 1295, it replaced an earlier 9th-century building. To the west of the St Gregory Church there was a vaulted gallery with arched openings on the southern side. To the west of Paul and Peter Church the **bell tower** was built in the 17th century on the site of a *gavit* which had been destroyed in an earlier earthquake. Over the main entrance to the complex and the adjoining chapel is the unusual 11th-century **Mother of God Church**. It is a small cross-dome church with an octagonal tambour and umbrella cupola. The chambers of the clergy, the refectory with a kitchen and storerooms, and the dwelling and service premises form a rectangle around these structures within the fortified wall. They date from the 17th and 18th centuries. Outside the walls can be seen the ruins of various buildings including an **oil press** and the **school**. Wild red tulips *Tulipa julia* grow behind the monastery; unfortunately they often end up as cut flowers.

In the gorge of the Vorotan River, below Tatev Monastery, is the monastic complex of **Tatev Hermitage** (or Anapat). It can be seen from the road on the descent to the river or from the cable-car. A steep path from Tatev Monastery goes to Anapat (allow about 1½hrs); the information centre can provide a guide (*AMD2,000/hr*) and can arrange for a car to collect you from Satan's Bridge at the end of the walk. It can also be reached from Satan's Bridge. A track goes off the road to Tatev 800m north of Satan's Bridge. If you follow this path to the house of an elderly couple they will probably let you walk through their yard to a path which goes down to the river where you can cross on a simple suspension bridge high above the water. It takes you to the wrong side of the Tatev ravine for Anapat but there is a metal rail across this stream. Then follow the path through trees to reach the hermitage. If you can scramble down to the river some distance before the suspension bridge and wade across the river you can reach the correct side of the Tatev ravine.

The complex is surprisingly large. Built in the 17th and 18th centuries, it was both an educational and spiritual centre, accommodating 500 monks. The central **Mother of God Church**, dating from 1663, is a three-aisle barrel-vaulted basilica with a small central belfry. It has a gallery at its west end and a *gavit* was added on the north side in 1743. The rectangular site is surrounded by high defensive walls, built in the middle of the 18th century, with the main gateway to the northwest. An extensive range of domestic buildings lines the wall, including monks' cells, a kitchen with a large fireplace in the southeast corner, an adjacent dining room and possibly inn accommodation, with water troughs, for travellers.

Goris (*Telephone code: 284*) Goris, situated on the Goris River, is the most attractive town in southern Armenia with many two-storey houses built of grey stone, their design apparently influenced by a German architect who came to live here, and an absence of tall blocks of flats. The town is laid out on a regular grid pattern and some of the streets are lined with fruit trees: damson, mulberry, plum, cherry and apple. Most of the shops, banks, post office, etc are located towards the southern end of the town at the bottom of Mashtots and Ankakhutian streets and this is also where taxis and minibuses to local villages wait. The stance for long-distance buses is on the east–west highway in the north of the town. Also at the end of Ankakhutian Street is the arched entrance to **The Parc de Vienne**, a favourite place for strolling which has a children's funfair and, in summer, cafés, one of which, the **De Luxe Lounge Café** (⊕ *opens at 11.00*), has an indoor area for colder weather.

On the south façade of the **St Gregory Church** can be seen the trajectory of an artillery shell, which narrowly missed the building while the town was being bombarded during the conflict with Azerbaijan. The **house museum of Axel Bakunts** (*41 Mesrop Mashtots St;* ✆ *284 22966;* ⊕ *10.00–17.00 Tue–Sun; guide (French, Russian) AMD1,000; AMD300*), a writer who died in Stalin's purges, contains his personal belongings in a typical Goris villa with courtyard and veranda. Outside the **Historical Museum** (*28 Komitas St, within the Drama Theatre, museum entrance round to the left of theatre entrance;* ⊕ *10.00–17.00 Mon–Fri*) are some sheep gravestones which have been moved here from the church. The displays are mostly of domestic items. One notable artefact is a five-sided stone with a face carved on each side, thought to date from 4,000 years ago.

The setting of Goris is very pleasant and strikingly jagged rock formations can be seen on the opposite hillside. On the southeast edge of town an open-air **café** (*at the*

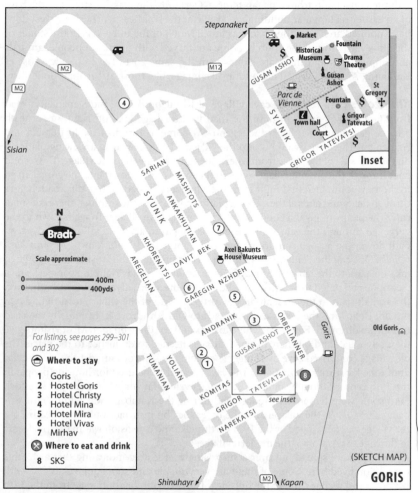

For listings, see pages 299–301 and 302

🛏 **Where to stay**

1 Goris
2 Hostel Goris
3 Hotel Christy
4 Hotel Mina
5 Hotel Mira
6 Hotel Vivas
7 Mirhav

✕ **Where to eat and drink**

8 SKS

(SKETCH MAP)

GORIS

eastern end of Tatevatsi St; ☺ when the weather is warm enough to sit outside, approx May–Oct, 10.00–late evening) overlooks these rocks and the caves of Old Goris. The café, once a quiet oasis, is now a popular, busy place which can be noisy.

Verishen The village of Verishen lies north of the main east–west highway, 2km northwest of Goris. It has two interesting churches and some cave dwellings still in use for storage or for housing livestock. On the hillside above the northern end of the village, with good views over the village to Goris and the surrounding hills, is the small church called **Nora Knunk** (New Baptistry). Its west end has been built on to a rocky outcrop, up the centre of which steps have been carved. If the church is open, you can see the bare rock at the west end inside the church. The easiest way to find the church is to go through the village until an area of cave dwellings can be seen to the right of the road, from where an obvious path leads uphill to the church. Within the village is the 5th-century **St Hripsime Church**, rebuilt in 1621. It can be spotted across gardens from the old town hall on the main street. It is a tall, relatively narrow barrel-vaulted basilica with thick walls built of rough stone. The eastern apse projects and looks as if it has been added later, a feature said to indicate conversion from a pagan temple. Certainly the massive stones of the base of an earlier rectangular building are visible at the southeast corner. The west door has a pointed arch over the khachkar lintel. Much of the interest is in the stones of the graveyard around the church. Some are carved with figures of people, animals and implements and there are stones with the same sort of eye holes as those at Karahunj. A carved capital has a tulip-like image, like those at Tanahat Monastery.

Khndzoresk To reach the **cave village** of Khndzoresk take the Stepanakert road from Goris for about 6km until the road to the village goes off right, underneath a metal gateway which bears the legend 'Welcome to Khndzoresk' in Russian and Armenian. There are two ways into the village. The first leads to a viewing platform on the west side of the gorge from where one can walk down to the village. The second goes through the present village to reach the eastern road down into the gorge. To go to the viewpoint, turn first right from the Khndzoresk road on to a dirt road. It goes through fields and ends at the viewing platform where, in the summer, there is a small café. The platform gives a good overall view of the cave village. To walk down to the gorge, go through the gate at the far end of the paved area and follow a fairly steep path down to a suspension bridge across the gorge (*5–10 mins down, 15 mins back uphill*). One can then either cross the suspension bridge to the far side of the gorge or take the path to the left of the bridge which ultimately leads right to Sparapet's grave (see opposite) or left to St Hripsime Church. For the alternative approach continue on the asphalt road to the present village. At the far end of the village, turn right down the hill (following the better asphalt road) to Old Khndzoresk. Eventually the road becomes a dirt road. Find somewhere to park and continue on foot. Most visitors give themselves half an hour here but half a day is needed to do justice to the place. The old village comprised cave dwellings hewn into the soft rock amidst the spectacular limestone karst rock formations. The caves ceased to be used for housing people in the 19th century though some are still used even today for storage and for livestock (and some were temporarily reoccupied during the Karabagh war while Goris was being shelled). As the villagers left the caves they built surface buildings nearby, but the village was devastated by the 1931 earthquake and a decision was made to relocate to the higher position of the modern village.

The caves are spread out over a surprisingly large area indicating that a sizeable population lived here. Some of them are very simple and some quite elaborate with windows and niches cut into the hillsides. The two churches both date from the 17th century and survived better than most of the other surface buildings. The upper one, St Thaddeus, is a single-nave church with a carved portal with remnants of red paint decoration. The lower one, St Hripsime, was in the centre of the village and dates from 1663. It is a three-aisled church, also with a carved portal. Across the stream at the bottom of the gorge and slightly further south is the 17th-century hermitage where Mkhitar Sparapet is buried along with his wife and followers. He succeeded David Bek as leader of the rebellion against Ottoman rule. In 1730 he was murdered by the villagers of Khndzoresk because of Turkish threats that they would be attacked if they harboured him. Apparently the Turkish pasha in Tabriz to whom they presented his head had the murderers beheaded for what he regarded as their treachery.

SOUTHERN SYUNIK
South to Kapan South from Goris the road follows the narrow gorge of the Goris River. In Soviet days the road more or less marked the boundary between Armenia and Azerbaijan and was actually on the Azerbaijan side of the border at times. Since 1994, however, the *de facto* border is further east. After leaving the gorge the road descends a long series of hairpin bends into the much deeper gorge of the Vorotan, which is eventually bridged close to a hydro-electric station. The ascent up the other side is even longer with innumerable hairpins and some fantastic views. The right turn signposted to **Bardzravan** leads after 3km to a track which goes off right to the remains of the **monastery of Bgheno-Noravank** in thick forest. Although the monastery is not far away it is invisible from the road. The only surviving part is a small, reconstructed basalt church of 1062 which incorporates several stones carved with human figures. There is also much geometric carving including swastika designs around the doorway and on the pillars.

On cliffs above **Artsvanik** village, about 10km north of Kapan, is the 6th-century **monastery of Yeritsavank**. From the main road turn off east for Artsvanik and follow the asphalt road (which eventually goes to a military base at Kaghnut). For Yeritsavank turn left 6.8km from the main road on to a rough track across grassland where the asphalt road bears right through about 90°. Where the rough track forks take the left fork for the monastery; the right leads to a large picnic area. The monastery is hidden among trees and does not present the startling appearance it once did according to ancient chronicles (although unfortunately they do not explain why it was so startling). The St Stephen Church, although ruined, is the best preserved building. There is a chapel to the south and between them evidence of a walled monastic precinct. **St Stephen** is a tall basilica with a pointed vaulted roof. The long north and south walls have three arches which were originally open. Nowadays it is difficult to know how the west and east ends of the church appeared, presumably there would have been an eastern apse. At one time a separate wall surrounded the whole church but this no longer exists. One theory is that the church was originally open to the outside on three sides, which might explain why it was so astonishing. The surrounding wall may have been built later as a defensive wall, a known feature of Armenian churches (see page 45). An alternative theory is that the church was never open to the elements but that the body of the nave, with its arches supporting the upper reaches of the walls and the roof, were built as one and that the external wall of the church was built as a shell – a device used to limit earthquake damage to the main hall. To the south is a cemetery and beyond that cliffs from which there are impressive views to Mount Khustup. Unfortunately the brilliant blue of the distant lake owes its colour to pollution from mining in the area.

Kapan Yet another watershed is crossed before the descent into the gorge of the Voghji. Kapan is a complete contrast to Goris. Formerly an industrial city whose workers lived in high-rise flats, the industry has now closed and the flats look as if they won't survive the next earth tremor. With an increasing amount of new building, Kapan is slowly catching up with other towns in Armenia. It is bisected by the eastward flowing Voghji River. The Vachagan River flows north from the slopes of Mount Khustup (3,214m) to enter the Voghji in the centre of Kapan at the main road bridge across the Voghji. Kapan does not have any sites of major interest and most of what there is to see can be covered in a walk of a couple of hours around the town. Most facilities are within a short distance of each other in the centre of the town on the south bank of the river. The market is on the north bank. The **statue** of a horseman by the bridge in the centre is of David Bek. Shahumian Street, which goes east from the main Karen Demirchian Square/Central Park, has many new shops including supermarkets and pharmacies. A renovated small park, the Peace Park, has a large black feline statue. The east end of Shahumian has restaurants and leading from it is the road which goes to the now closed **railway station**. In 1932, a branch line was opened to Kapan from Mindzhevan in Azerbaijan and it was operated by the Azerbaijan division of Soviet railways. The Nagorno Karabagh war meant that the line became isolated from both the Armenian and Azeri rail networks. As a consequence, a dozen Azeri diesel locomotives were marooned here along with an assortment of goods wagons and passenger coaches. Since then the rolling stock has gradually been removed and all that now remains are two coaches, stripped of everything including their wheels. The rails remain, as does the derelict station building, and livestock browse along the grass-grown tracks.

Demirchian Street, which becomes Stepanian Street, follows the east bank of the Vachagan River. The **church**, built in 2002 and dedicated to Mesrop Mashtots, is a large cross-dome church with a balcony at the west end for the choir. A short distance beyond the church Azatamartikneri Street goes off left, opposite the post office, and winds up the hill for about 1km to the **Baghaburj Memorial Complex**. (Turn left through a blue gate; the notice asks you to remember to shut the gate.) The memorial commemorates the Great Patriotic War (World War II), the 1915 genocide, the 1988 massacres in Sumgait and Baku, and the soldiers who died during the Karabagh war. It is a typical grandiose Soviet construction which now has a sadly neglected air. The two female figures of the 1940–45 memorial, one young and one old, are remarkable for the sadness they so vividly and poignantly portray.

The **Garegin Nzhdeh Memorial Park** is some 2km from the town centre up the same road on the east bank of the Vachagan. The memorial of the 'Saviour of Armenia' is set against the magnificent backdrop of Mount Khustup, where Nzdeh's remains were eventually buried, as he wished (see pages 23 and 293).

The **Historical Museum** (*24/41 Garegin Nzhdeh St;* \ *285 28591;* ⊕ *10.00–18.00 Tue–Sat*) has been partially renovated. One room is devoted to the Karabagh war. It displays photographs of the town during the war, a reminder that the border is not far away. As may be surmised from the address (see page 87) the museum is not directly on Nzhdeh Street but is in the block behind the first row of buildings.

The **Archaeological Museum** (*3/1 Mushegh Harutyunian St;* m *098 258018;* ⊕ *09.30–17.00 Mon–Fri; AMD1,000*) moved premises in 2013, to a building within the grounds of a kindergarten! The easiest approach is from the road on the south bank of the river Voghji (the cul-de-sac portion at the far east end) where the gates of the kindergarten can be spotted between buildings. At the time of research it was more ethnographical than archaeological.

Behind the Dina Hotel west of the main square is the **Children's Park**, with a funfair from May to October. It is a favourite place for evening strolls. The **statue** on the western edge of the park is a memorial to Hunan Avetisian, a local boy who died

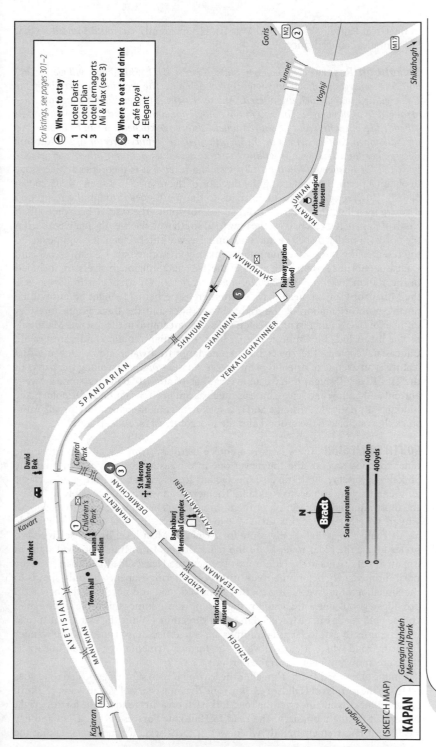

in the Great Patriotic War (World War II). He apparently sacrificed himself so that his comrades could advance.

Shikahogh Reserve (*Shikahogh State Reserve HQ, Shikahogh village;* \ 285 60655; e *office@shikahogh.am; www.shikahogh.am. The website has details of the 1-day guided tours which are offered. Any overnight stays required during tours are arranged in local villages. The HQ in Shikahogh has some limited accommodation (2 4-bedded rooms with separate shared toilets, shower & kitchen). It can be booked via the Shikahogh contact details or through the helpful deputy director of the Khosrov Reserve headquarters, who is willing to act as a contact point for other reserves. See page 181 for further information.*) To visit the reserve it is theoretically necessary to obtain a permit by contacting the director of the reserve in Kapan (\ 285 20064, 60655). However, one of the main roads to the south goes through the reserve so if you're travelling this way, the ruling does not apply. The reserve lies some 40km south of Kapan. It is reached via the new road south which leaves the main road from the north immediately before the road tunnel as you enter Kapan. It is signposted to the reserve. The forest-clad mountains (mainly Georgian oak, Caucasian oak and Caucasian hornbeam) on both sides of the Tsav and Shikahogh rivers are included in the 100km² reserve (*700–2,000m above sea level*). Of particular importance is the Mtnadzor Canyon, near Tsav, where there is perpetual twilight because of the north–south orientation of the high canyon sides and the thick virgin forest. A number of IUCN Red List of Threatened Species are found in the reserve. Mammals on the list include brown bear, Bezoar ibex, Armenian mouflon and, rarest of all, Caucasian leopard. The rivers have some large freshwater crabs. One unusual feature is an avenue of oriental plane trees (*Platanus orientalis*) along the banks of the Tsav River. Thought to have an average age of almost 500 years, some are very ancient and hollow and have a base as much as 5m in circumference. Oriental plane is doubtfully native to Armenia and it is speculated that merchants on the silk route stuck their staffs into the ground and then forgot them (see also page 320).

SOUTH TO MEGHRI There is now a choice of roads from Kapan to Meghri, the older road via Kajaran and the newer one in the east of the province through the Shikahogh Reserve. Both traverse spectacular scenery and both have good surfaces although they are subject to rockfalls. The new road was built ostensibly to bypass the most mountainous section of the old road, thus being less prone to closure in winter. Whether or not this turns out to be correct, the new road does provide an alternative to a vital supply route for Armenia. Most local drivers seem still to prefer to use the older road, as do the truck drivers from Iran. The road signs in Kapan direct drivers to the older road. The new road leaves the main road from the north immediately before the road tunnel on entering Kapan. The only sign is to the Shikahogh Reserve. Going south via the old road and north via the new road provides a good contrast. The following description assumes this route, although of course both roads can be travelled in either direction. (While the easternmost road itself is perfectly safe as far as landmines are concerned, it is prudent not to wander from the road where it runs close to the former Armenia–Azerbaijan border as there are known minefields on the border.)

On the older road south, 1km after the leaving Kapan sign a signposted road goes off left to the fortress of Halidzor (3.3km) and the monastery of Vahanavank (2.2km). Shortly after crossing the river the road forks; left on a dirt road for the fortress, right on asphalt for the monastery. The road to **Halidzor Fortress** needs a 4x4 and dry weather: it is extremely muddy when wet. It forks several times; keep taking the upper fork. (There is a shorter route for walkers. At a 'Silk Route' sign, near some small shops before leaving Kapan, the fortress can be seen on the side of the hill towards the west. A path goes up from the pedestrian bridge across the river.) Built as a convent in the 17th century, David Bek (page 19) used it as his headquarters. In 1725 Bek and 300 followers withstood a seven-day siege by an invading army of 70,000 Ottoman Turks. He led a charge downhill which so terrified the invaders that they fled. Bek died in the fortress in 1728 and is thought to be buried there. After his death the Ottoman army captured Halidzor. The heavily restored site has little atmosphere but does give an idea of the warren of rooms in the complex. To the right of the *bema* of St Minas Church is a large hole, perhaps the entrance to the secret 500m tunnel to the river which allowed the defenders to withstand the siege.

The **monastery of Vahanavank** was founded in 911 by Vahan, son of Prince Gagik of Kapan, who sought to become a monk in order to rid himself of the demons which possessed him. He built the main church, St Gregory the Illuminator, and is buried there. In the 11th century Queen Shahandukht of Syunik built the two-storey Mother of God Church to act as a burial site for her and her relatives. The monastery has undergone considerable restoration. Both St Gregory and its western *gavit* are entered through an arcaded gallery which runs along the south side of both buildings. Part of the gallery has been left unrestored so that the large arches for which the monastery is famous can still be seen. St Gregory is a cross-dome church with two free-standing pillars separating the main space from the two very narrow side aisles. The tall tambour is decorated with arcatures with twin half-colonnettes, similar to those at Sisavank.

After the turn to Vahanavank, by the river there is a **statue of a bear** with a ring and key in its mouth – the arms of Syunik. Some 3km west of the village of Hamletavan, on top of a hill is the **fortress of Baghaberd.** It is difficult to see the main part of the fortress when heading south (although much easier heading north) but a small fortification (and a square concrete construction) adjacent to the road on the right is conspicuous. A path leads up from the village school just beyond the site. It is extremely steep and difficult because of the loose scree. Baghaberd was briefly capital of the Syunik kingdom in the 12th century before it was sacked by the Seljuks in 1170. It was reoccupied by David Bek in the 18th century and has significant remains of the boundary wall but little else. The main gateway is near the northern end of the wall which defended the only side of the triangular hilltop with less than precipitous cliffs. Anyone gaining entrance through the gate then had to traverse a narrow passage between a vertical rock face and the outer wall. When descending, the path to the school can be difficult to find. Aim for the roadside tower otherwise you may end up, as I did, in someone's private garden with ferocious guard dogs.

Continuing south, the road follows the river as far as the molybdenum-mining town of **Kajaran** which was relocated here in the 1960s after earthquake damage on its former site further up the hill. In the town the main road south makes a U-turn over the river. Once across the bridge take the lower road to the left. It looks an unlikely road at first, as if you are going through back yards. The road climbs up over the **Kajaran** and **Tashtun Passes** (2,489m and 2,359m respectively) and then descends to the Iranian border.

Meghri (*Telephone code: 2860*) The principal town in the most southerly region of the country, Meghri has some attractive houses of the 18th and 19th centuries and is pleasantly situated amidst an arid mountainous landscape, the well-tended and watered gardens making a stark contrast with the surrounding barrenness. Meghri is well known for its fruit, particularly for its figs; in Yerevan, in late summer, Meghri figs are eagerly awaited – they are delicious! Walking around the narrow, cobbled alleys with their canopy of vines gives an insight into life in old Meghri. The wooden beams which were incorporated into the walls to give some protection against earthquakes can be seen in places, as can the cement of mud, straw and egg which was used. The houses were built in a terraced fashion on the hillside, the roofs of houses on a lower level forming the gardens of those on the level above. Apparently large slabs of stone were used in the roofs to keep the house below dry, but one wonders how successful this was. The town is divided into two districts by the Meghri River and the main road which runs alongside it. East of the river is **Mets Tagh** ('Big Quarter') with the central triangular 'square' housing most facilities; the Culture Centre and Town Hall face each other on opposite sides. The Culture Centre houses a Children's Art Gallery and a local museum; opening times are somewhat flexible!

The **Mother of God Church** in the centre of the town (take the small street to the left of the Culture Centre) was built in the 15th century and rebuilt in the 17th. It had the singular distinction of housing the first piano in Armenia, brought from Berlin to form part of the dowry of the daughter of a local family. The piano, in a somewhat sorry state, currently sits on a veranda of the house of the local priest. The pale-coloured stonework of the church contrasts with the very tall 12-sided pink tambour and cupola. The plain exterior in no way prepares visitors for the interior, which is covered with 19th-century murals. Those on the arches and cupola are mainly abstract or floral in design but the walls and pillars depict saints or Bible stories. In the Baptism of Jesus he is shown standing on a snake, and Hell looks suitably Brueghelish in the Last Judgement. The church was used as a store in the Soviet era and the murals were apparently painted over so it is pleasing to see how well they have survived.

There are two other churches in Meghri. **St John the Baptist Church** is reached by taking the street which leads north from the town square, from the right-hand side of the town hall as one faces it. The road runs parallel to and above the north–south highway. (The church can be spotted as one enters Meghri from the north, on a knoll at the base on the mountainside.) The church is tucked away behind a storage barn, built deliberately to obscure the church in Stalin's era. Keep to the path when walking on the south side of the church: straying off it could mean a fall through the roof of the adjacent property. The seriously ruined church is a domed basilica with three aisles and there are the remains of frescoes on the columns. The arches are all slightly pointed. Like the houses wooden beams were incorporated into the structure as seismic protection, but the church was damaged in the 1960s by the earthquake which led to the relocation of Kajaran and the huge cracks in the masonry do not bode well for the future.

Pokr Tagh ('Small Quarter') to the west of the river has **St Sargis Church** perched on top of a hill overlooking the town. It is reached by a tortuous narrow road in poor condition. The church is at the highest point. It was restored in the 1990s and is in good condition, the frescoes inside having been renovated in a sensitive way. Attached to the outside of the church is a small building, the morgue, in which the bodies of the dead were washed before being taken into the church. Such a building is unusual in Armenia, the ablution normally being performed at home. Pokr Tagh, the oldest part of the town, is a maze of narrow streets. The steepness of the gradient means that some houses are built on top of each other. In autumn black and green grapes hang from the canopies of vines and trees are laden with fruit: pomegranates, figs, peaches and persimmons.

Overlooking the town from a horseshoe-shaped ridge are the remains of several **small fortifications**, originally built in the 10th century but rebuilt in the 18th

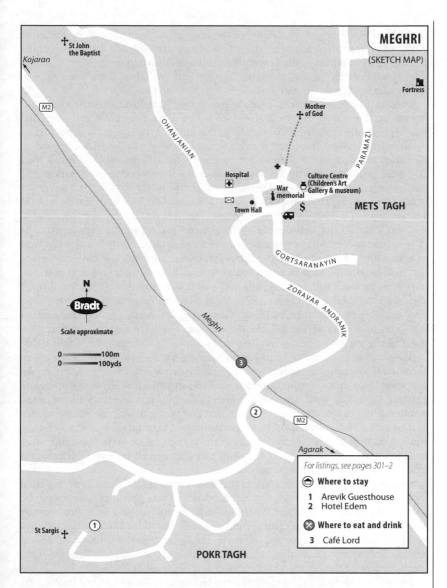

Kajaran

☨ St John
the Baptist

Fortress

M2

OHANJANIAN

Mother
☨ of God

PARAMAZI

Hospital
✚

Culture Centre
(Children's Art
Gallery & museum)

War
memorial

✉

METS TAGH

Town Hall

$

GORTSARANAYIN

N

Bradt

ZORAVAR ANDRANIK

Scale approximate

Meghri

0 ━━━━100m
0 ━━━●100yds

3

2

M2

Agarak ↘

For listings, see pages 301–2

🏠 **Where to stay**

1   Arevik Guesthouse
2   Hotel Edem

❌ **Where to eat and drink**

3   Café Lord

St Sargis ☨

1

POKR TAGH

by David Bek. It was the first fortress in Armenia built for artillery and the first impression on entering one of the towers is that of being in a dovecote. One of the towers can be reached by taking the road to the right of the Culture Centre. (This is also another, driveable, route to the Mother of God Church.) Just before the tarmac ends a dirt track goes off right. From here it is a short walk, albeit up scree-like terrain. It is an excellent viewpoint although not particularly interesting in itself.

Meghri to Kapan South from Meghri the road continues another 5km to the Iranian border. The new road to Kapan follows the border eastwards before turning north at the village of Andadzor. Even if the new road north is not being taken, it is worth driving east to Andadzor, and perhaps beyond (see page 320), and then west to the border crossing at Agarak to see the magnificent landscape along the River Arax, which forms the actual border. There is an alarmed fence on the Armenian side of the river, photography is forbidden and one is advised not to stop, although driving moderately slowly seems to be tolerated. Another abandoned railway follows the border: the former main line from Yerevan to Baku.

There is the option of a **scenic side trip** along the Arax River after the main road has turned north at Andadzor. A stretch of rail track has been lifted and converted into a good dirt road from Andadzor to the junction with a good asphalt road to Nrnadzor village. There are about 9.5km of railway road. Where the road to Nrnadzor turns north, an old and deteriorating – but still driveable – asphalt road continues east and climbs up for 6.5km to reach the former border post marking the border with Azerbaijan. Beyond the border the road worsens. Given the unknown situation regarding landmines (see pages 323 and 326) it would not be wise to venture beyond the border nor to stray from the road on the way up. The views to the Arax River flowing between the mountains of Armenia and Iran are superb. The railway road goes off just west of where the main road turns north. It is also just west of where the old road to Nrnadzor goes off. (**Note**: although the old single-track dirt road looks reasonable at first it soon becomes a steadily worsening, precarious, narrow rocky track with vertical cliffs to the left and a considerable vertical drop to the railway road below. For several kilometres there is no possibility of turning to go back and only a fool would even think of reversing. Eventually a gentler slope makes it possible to drive down the hillside to the railway road. The old road might make a good hiking route; I suspect it was only ever suitable for those on two or four feet.)

Shortly after the main road to Kapan turns north is **Shvanidzor** village where there is a 17th-century aqueduct which is still in use for irrigation. To reach it, take the Shvanidzor turn-off from the main road and then the first left turn, just before entering the village itself. There is a church in the village where, in Stalinist times, a cultural civic centre was built on to the west end thus blocking the main entrance and, as with St John the Baptist in Meghri, disguising the fact that it was a church. Embedded high up on the inside walls of the church are ceramic pots. They were used to improve the acoustics of the church by filling them with variable amounts of ash until the required result was obtained.

Shvanidzor, founded in the 13th century, has moved several times as necessitated by lack of water and poor soil fertility. Evidence of one previous location can be seen on the road north. Water continues to be a problem and work has recently started to re-establish an ancient system of supply based on *kakhrezes*, a series of wells connected by underground channels. The *kakhrez* system is found in areas of historic Persian influence, also in India and China. Shvanidzor has five *kakhrezes*, four dating from the 12th to 14th centuries and one built in 2005.

From Shvanidzor the road climbs to the **Gomarants Pass** (2,362m) then enters the wooded Shikahogh Reserve. This road feels much more remote than the older road through Kajaran, perhaps because of the absence of human habitation for much of the way and the lack of traffic. Near the village of **Nerkin Hand** is a relict **grove of oriental plane trees** (see page 316), along the Tsav River. The 'Plan [*sic*] Grove Sanctuary' is signposted at the junction for Nerkin Hand. Keep going down towards the river and turn right just before the large school building. There is a place to park and a small bridge over the river from where you can walk among the tall plane trees. Cuttings from the oriental plane root readily in moist conditions. New trees have been planted simply by sticking a length of wood in the ground, the same method by which, it is speculated, the plane trees first took root here, when merchants on the silk route stuck their staffs in the ground and then forgot them.

7

Nagorno Karabagh

Known by the name Artsakh to its present inhabitants and to Armenians, the alternative name Nagorno Karabagh dates from the Khanate of Karabagh's formal entry to the Russian Empire in 1813, *nagorno* being Russian for 'mountainous'; *karabagh* is Turkish for 'black garden'. Today Nagorno Karabagh is very predominantly inhabited by ethnic Armenians – they make up around 95% of the population. The language in the streets of its towns is Armenian – albeit with a strikingly different accent – and the banknotes are Armenian. However, it is not part of Armenia: it has its own government with its own foreign ministry, its own flag, its own stamps and its own national anthem. Despite all this, its existence as a state is unrecognised by any other state and no Western government can provide consular services there. It can only be entered from Armenia. Why go? One answer is that it has some magnificent scenery. It isn't called Nagorno for nothing: even within the pre-1994 boundaries the land rose to 2,725m at Mount Kirs but the incorporation of the territory which formerly separated Nagorno Karabagh from Armenia means that the highest point is now the 3,584m summit of Mount Tsghuk. Other reasons for going are that it has some very fine monasteries, and some thought-provoking damaged streets from which the ethnic Azeri population has fled. There are differences from Armenia. Inevitably, the military presence is more conspicuous. Additionally, Christian repression was greater here in Soviet days and all 220 churches which existed in Nagorno Karabagh during the Tsarist era had closed by the 1930s. Since 1989 there has been a steady reopening programme. A more mundane difference from Armenia is that the groups of men in the street are often playing cards rather than backgammon, which is the norm in Armenia.

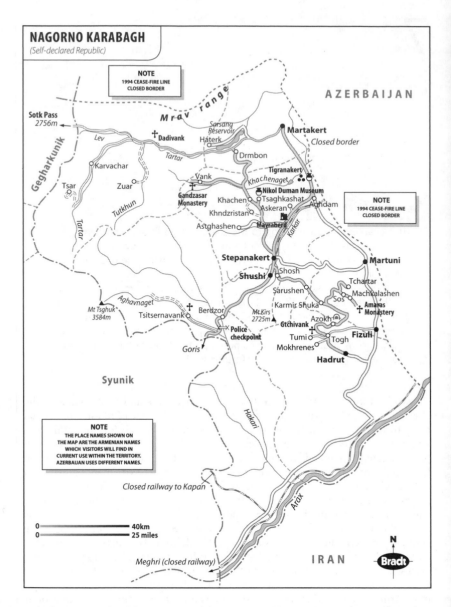

NAGORNO KARABAGH
(Self-declared Republic)

NOTE
1994 CEASE-FIRE LINE
CLOSED BORDER

AZERBAIJAN

Mrav range

Sotk Pass
2756m

Gegharkunik

Lev

Sarsang Reservoir

† Dadivank

Háterk

Martakert

Closed border

Karvachar

Tsar

Zuar

Tartar

Tutkhun

Tartar

Drmbon

Vank

Khachenaget

Tigranakert

Nikol Duman Museum

Gandzasar
Monastery

Khachen

Tsaghkashat

Askeran

Aghdam

Khndzristan

Astghashen

Mayraberd

Kartar

NOTE
1994 CEASE-FIRE LINE
CLOSED BORDER

Stepanakert

Shosh

Martuni

Shushi

Sarushen

Tchartar

Machkalashen

Karmir Shuka

Sos

Mt Tsghuk
3584m

Aghavnaget

† Berdzor

Tsitsernavank

Mt Kirs
2725m

Gtchivank

Azokh

† Amaras
Monastery

Fizuli

Tumi

Togh

Goris

Police
checkpoint

Mokhrenes

Hadrut

Syunik

Hakari

NOTE
THE PLACE NAMES SHOWN ON
THE MAP ARE THE ARMENIAN NAMES
WHICH VISITORS WILL FIND IN
CURRENT USE WITHIN THE TERRITORY.
AZERBAIJAN USES DIFFERENT NAMES.

Closed railway to Kapan

Arax

0 ———— 40km
0 ———— 25 miles

Meghri (closed railway)

IRAN

N

Bradt

Nagorno Karabagh has some interesting sights although they do tend to be rather spread out. Certain of the best sights are inaccessible because of their proximity to the ceasefire line and the risk from snipers. Hiking would be superb but should not be attempted without a local guide because of the continued existence of minefields (see box, page 323 and on page 326). Some of these have been cleared but local knowledge is vital before leaving obviously used routes. Some visitors consider the abandoned Azeri villages with their ruined houses to be of interest though they are hardly very appealing. Burnt-out military hardware can still be seen in places. The territory is under martial law: problems can arise with roads being closed for military manoeuvres.

Nagorno Karabagh was under Persian rule in 1805 when, along with other areas in eastern Transcaucasia, it was annexed to the 'everlasting rule' of the Russian Empire. The Gulistan Treaty of 1813 signed by Russia and Persia ratified this. The collapse of the Russian Empire in 1917 resulted in a changed arrangement of states in the Caucasus. The newly formed Republic of Armenia and the equally new Azerbaijan Democratic Republic both sought control over Nagorno Karabagh between 1918 and 1920. From the outset the Azerbaijan Democratic Republic made territorial demands for large areas of historic Armenia, even though the Tsarist census of the whole Karabagh region showed in 1917 a population which was 72% Armenian. (These figures are disputed by the Azeris who consider the Russian Imperial Census of 1897, showing an Armenian population of about 40%, to be more reliable.) Taking advantage of the confused state of affairs resulting from World War I, the collapse of the Russian Empire and continuing persecution of Armenians by Turks, Turkish forces along with Azeri military units destroyed hundreds of ethnically Armenian villages. (It was a feature of the whole region that all villages were dominated by one ethnic group: some Armenian, some Azeri, and elsewhere some Georgian and some Turkish.) Only in Nagorno Karabagh did the Armenian population succeed in repelling the attacks. In July 1918, the First Armenian Assembly of Nagorno Karabagh declared the region to be self-governing and created the Karabagh National Council. In August 1919, this National Council entered into a provisional treaty arrangement with the Azerbaijan government to try to halt the military conflict. This, however, did not prevent Azerbaijan's violation of the treaty, culminating on 28 March 1920 with the massacre of Armenians, accompanied by burning and plundering, in Shushi, the then capital. As a result the Karabagh Assembly nullified the treaty and declared union with Armenia.

The First League of Nations had its inaugural meeting in late 1920. Applications for membership were considered by the 5th committee, chaired by Chile, which recommended that Azerbaijan should not be admitted (mainly because of its Bolshevik government) while consideration of Armenia's admission should be postponed (because it was occupied). However, the League of Nations, before final resolution of the issue, recognised Nagorno Karabagh as a disputed territory since it had not in practice been ruled by any outside power since the Russian collapse

SAFETY – ADVICE ON AVOIDING MINES

The following list of points for travellers is provided by the HALO Trust (see box, page 326) which carries out mine clearance in Nagorno Karabagh:

- Mines and unexploded ordnance (UXO), including cluster munitions, litter the region and can be found in both remote areas and close to towns and villages
- Always speak to the local people before entering an area
- Keep to well-used tracks and paths
- If a track does not look used then avoid it
- Be aware that although a track may be used it could pass through a minefield or area contaminated with UXO
- Do not touch anything which looks like a mine or ordnance
- If you don't know what something is then don't touch it

in 1917. That only changed when Bolshevik forces occupied Nagorno Karabagh in 1920. Immediately following the establishment of the Soviet regime in Armenia, the Azerbaijan Revolutionary Committee on 30 November 1920 formally recognised Nagorno Karabagh, as well as Zangezur (southern Armenia) and Nakhichevan, to be parts of Armenia and in June 1921, Armenia itself declared Nagorno Karabagh to be part of Armenia.

Meanwhile the Bolshevik leaders in Russia were having visions of an imminent international communist revolution and believed that the new Turkish government under Ataturk was a believer in their cause. This resulted in a change of attitude regarding Turkey's ethnically close relations with Azerbaijan and the question of the disputed territories including Nagorno Karabagh. Stalin, Commissar of Nationalities in the Council of People's Commissars in Moscow, therefore persuaded the Caucasian Bureau of the Russian Communist Party to adopt on 5 July 1921 a policy of annexing Nagorno Karabagh to Azerbaijan rather than Armenia. This was despite the fact that both Armenia and Azerbaijan were still independent, albeit communist controlled, countries: the Soviet Union into which they would be incorporated along with Russia was not formed until December 1922 and it was no business of the Russian Communist Party to decide on the wishes of the Karabagh population. This Russian decision was put into effect but with the proviso that Nagorno Karabagh would be granted the status of an autonomous region.

On 7 July 1923, the Soviet Azerbaijan Revolutionary Committee resolved to dismember Nagorno Karabagh and to create – on only part of its territory amounting to 4,400km^2 – the promised autonomous region. A large part of the remainder, comprising the present-day districts of Lachin and Kelbajar, became the Kurdistan Autonomous Soviet Socialist Republic. Thus Armenia and Nagorno Karabagh were now separated by the territory of Kurdistan. In 1929, Kurdistan was abolished and the territory fully incorporated into Azerbaijan, so that from 1929 onwards, Armenia was separated from Nagorno Karabagh by Azerbaijan proper.

In 1935, there were protests in the region against Nagorno Karabagh remaining within Azerbaijan and these became an almost annual feature after 1960 following the Khrushchev thaw. Gorbachev's policy of openness, established after he came to power in 1985, merely served to bring matters further into the open. The year 1988 became a turning point in the history of Nagorno Karabagh. Mass demonstrations started there on 11 February 1988 demanding union with Armenia. On 20 February in an extraordinary session of the Nagorno Karabagh Autonomous Republic Council, the People's Deputies voted to secede from Azerbaijan and join Armenia and appealed to the Supreme Soviet of the USSR to recognise this decision. This was matched by massive demonstrations in Yerevan, accompanied by a petition signed by 75,000 Armenians, demanding the annexation of Nagorno Karabagh. A pogrom on 28 February at Sumgait, Azerbaijan, which was directed against ethnic Armenians, resulted in around 30 deaths (or some estimates claim up to 120) of Armenians by their Azeri neighbours. This unprecedented killing shocked the Soviet Union and the Soviet authorities arrested 400 rioters. Some 84 perpetrators were tried and sentenced in Moscow. (The incident which purportedly led directly to the Sumgait massacre was the death five days earlier of two Azeri young men, by youths reported by the press to be Armenians, in a skirmish between the two ethnic groups in the Aghdam region of Karabagh.) Thereafter ethnic tensions continued to rise and during the fighting over Nagorno Karabagh there were civilian deaths on both sides. (Perhaps the incident which gained most international notice and condemnation was the deaths of 161–613 (numbers are disputed) Azeri civilians, fired on by Armenian forces in February 1992, as they tried to leave Khojaly, near

Aghdam, as it was about to be occupied by Armenian forces. Khojaly was used as a military base by the Azeris to shell Stepanakert, or Khankendi as it is known by the Azeris.) The Sumgait massacre was followed by even bigger mass protests in Armenia itself when almost a million people were estimated to have participated. The inaction by Moscow produced massive unrest with an estimated 200,000 Azeris fleeing Armenia and 260,000 Armenians fleeing Azerbaijan. In July the Nagorno Karabagh Supreme Soviet, Nagorno Karabagh's supreme governing body, took the decision to secede from Azerbaijan and adopted measures to become part of Armenia.

The members of the Karabagh Committee, a group leading the fight for union with Armenia, were arrested in December 1988 and held in Moscow without trial whilst on 12 January 1989 direct rule of Nagorno Karabagh from Moscow was imposed. International protests eventually led to the Karabagh Committee members being freed on 31 May. Showing how little control of events Moscow had by now (the Soviet Empire in central and eastern Europe was fast disintegrating at the time) Azerbaijan started partially blockading Armenia in September. With a breathtaking disregard for the likely consequences, Moscow abandoned direct rule of Nagorno Karabagh on 28 November and handed control to Azerbaijan.

Armenia's response was swift and on 1 December the Armenian Supreme Soviet voted for unification with Nagorno Karabagh. The vote was declared illegal by the Supreme Soviet of the USSR to which Yerevan's response was to pass a new law giving it the right of veto over laws passed in Moscow. As of 10 January 1990 residents of Nagorno Karabagh were allowed to vote in Armenian elections. The year 1990 was to be a year of conflict between Armenians and central Soviet forces with massive protests over the Karabagh issue and often brutal police and military repression: six Armenians were killed in Yerevan by Soviet troops in a confrontation on 24 May. Eventually, after two changes of leadership, the appointment of Levon Ter-Petrosian as Chairman of the Supreme Soviet of Armenia on 4 August led to Armenia declaring independence within the USSR on 23 August.

The next year was to see momentous change. The failed coup against Gorbachev on 19 August 1991 led to the inevitable break-up of the Soviet Union at the end of the year. More immediately Azerbaijan's response on 27 August was to annul Nagorno Karabagh's status as an Autonomous Region which then led, on 2 September, to the declaration of the independent Republic of Nagorno Karabagh – the goal had changed and union with Armenia had ceased to be the objective. A plebiscite in Nagorno Karabagh on 10 December resulted in an overwhelming vote for independence. Azerbaijan began a blockade of the territory (which of course it completely encircled) and launched military attacks using the equipment of the USSR 4th army stationed in Azerbaijan. Meanwhile newly emergent Russia saw Armenia as a key ally – notably because of its long border with Turkey, a member of NATO. Accordingly Russia signed a treaty of friendship and co-operation with Armenia on 29 December, two days before the demise of the USSR. This was to be followed, much more crucially for Nagorno Karabagh, by a collective security pact signed by Russia and Armenia along with Kazakhstan, Kyrgyzstan, Tajikistan and Uzbekistan on 15 May 1992.

Azeri military attacks made initial territorial gains but by 8 May 1992 they had been driven back from Martakert and Shushi while on 18 May the Armenian army was able to force a corridor through the Azeri lines at Lachin and break the blockade of Nagorno Karabagh. This, however, was to be followed by a renewed Azeri offensive which resulted in considerable further Azeri gains so that by the end of July they had taken the whole of the Shahumian region, a great portion of the Martakert region, and portions of Martuni, Askeran and Hadrut controlling about 60% of the entire territory. These Azeri victories had several effects: there were demonstrations against Ter-Petrosian, by now the Armenian president, and he survived an assassination attempt on 17 August; the US Congress adopted a resolution condemning the actions of Azerbaijan and prohibited US government economic assistance; and Ter-Petrosian on 9 August invoked the less than three-month-old security pact asking for Russian help.

Russian support arrived in the form of supplies and equipment. By March 1993 the Armenian army was able once more to go on the offensive and it not only over the next few months recouped its losses but also gained almost all of Nagorno Karabagh, together with the former Kurdistan and a considerable swathe of Azeri territory bordering Iran. Finally on 5 May 1994 a ceasefire, brokered by Russia, Kyrgyzstan and the CIS Interparliamentary Council, was signed which took effect on 12 May. By this time Azerbaijan had lost control of a substantial area of its territory. Since then the self-declared Republic of Nagorno Karabagh has incorporated into its administrative districts even the occupied areas of Azerbaijan which were not in the former autonomous region, considerably increasing its size in the process.

The job of finding a solution to the conflict is in the hands of the Minsk Group of the Organisation for Security and Co-operation in Europe which was set up in 1992. It looks as far away as ever. Azerbaijan might be willing to hand over Nagorno Karabagh to Armenia in exchange for southern Armenia but that is unacceptable to Armenia since it would lose its important direct link to Iran. Armenia wants a resolution of the problem which it believes would help economic growth but Armenians feel that they cannot desert their kith and kin. Nagorno Karabagh is a key factor in the unwillingness of certain factions in Turkey to ratify the protocol, signed by the foreign ministers of Armenia and Turkey in October 2009 (see page 30), aimed at normalising relationships between the two countries. Turkey's prime minister has promised its ally, Azerbaijan, that it will not open its border with

MINE CLEARING

Landmines were used extensively (by both sides) during the war in Nagorno Karabagh, as were large amounts of cluster munitions and other explosive ordnance. Since the ceasefire in 1994, 328 people have been killed or maimed by landmines and unexploded ordnance (UXO). The presence of minefields leaves farmers unable to cultivate vast swathes of fertile agricultural land and also inhibits development and infrastructure projects. Towns and villages are alike affected.

The HALO Trust (see page 104), the largest humanitarian mine-clearance organisation in the world, has been active in Nagorno Karabagh since 2000. It provides the only large-scale mine-clearance capacity in Nagorno Karabagh. By October 2013 it had cleared 10,817 mines, 11,619 cluster bombs and 46,370 other items of UXO from 4,760ha (11,762 acres) of minefield and over 23,237ha (57,420 acres) of battlefield. Almost 85% of known minefields and about 77% of the area contaminated by cluster munitions have been cleared and most of this land has been returned to cultivation – mainly of wheat. At the 2010 funding levels, HALO believed that the remaining areas within the pre-1991 boundaries of Nagorno Karabagh could be cleared by 2016 but with the reduction in funding this timescale will inevitably stretch.

Armenia until the Nagorno Karabagh dispute is resolved and Armenian forces are withdrawn from what Azerbaijan regards as Azeri territory. This Armenia is not prepared to do. Meanwhile the ceasefire holds, despite occasional sniper fire across the ceasefire line with no war and no peace either.

GOVERNMENT

Although still part of Azerbaijan under international law, the self-declared Republic of Nagorno Karabagh is a *de facto* independent state with the necessary organs of government. The president, who is eligible to stand for not more than two five-year terms, and the 33 members of the chamber of deputies are directly elected by the population of around 150,000. Nagorno Karabagh has its own police, court system, education system and so on. The national flag of Nagorno Karabagh is basically the Armenian one but with a white five-toothed stepped arrow pattern on the right-hand side. In September 2005, the government announced that it would shortly start putting into circulation its own currency – the Nagorno Karabagh dram (NKD). Notes and coins have been produced and some are available from specialist numismatic dealers, but the currency in circulation continues to be that of Armenia.

The government has given assistance to the estimated 40,000 people who have settled in Nagorno Karabagh since 1991 (mostly ethnic Armenian refugees fleeing Azerbaijan) in the form of allocating housing, providing livestock and charging half the Armenian price for electricity. There are also incentives in place for couples to have larger families.

RED TAPE

Visitors require **visas**. Information and an application form (for use in Stepanakert) can be found at www.nkr.am. Visas can be obtained from the Republic of Nagorno Karabagh (NKR) Permanent Representation to the Republic of Armenia in Yerevan (where a slightly different form is used). Unfortunately this is in the inconvenient suburb of Arabkir to the north of the centre (*17a Nairi Zarian St;* \ *10 249705;* e *yerevancons@mfa.nkr.am;* ☉ *09.00–13.00 & 14.00–17.00 Mon–Fri*). It is advised that visa applications are made in the morning, especially if same-day visa service is requested. A 21-day tourist visa costs AMD3,000 if collected the following day. Same-day service costs AMD6,000. There are also permanent representations in Paris, Berlin, Moscow, Sydney (Australia) and Washington DC but they cannot issue visas. If there is any possibility of travelling in future to Azerbaijan then it is essential to obtain the visa on a separate piece of paper. A Nagorno Karabagh visa entered in a passport means that entry to Azerbaijan will be refused. It is also possible to obtain visas from the NKR Foreign Ministry (*28 Azatamartikneri St;* \ *47 941418*) after arrival in Stepanakert, provided visitors show the required identification documents at the border. This usually works well although the procedure can seem cumbersome and the waiting room something of a mêlée. Occasionally, however, travellers without visas have had trouble at the border and the Foreign Ministry staff advise that it is best to obtain visas before leaving Yerevan.

At the Foreign Ministry you queue (sort of) to go into the room where visas are issued; you are given a form and told to go outside and fill it in (it may speed the process if you have completed the form beforehand); you then queue to go back into the office where you hand in the form, your passport and the fee; you then go back outside and wait (about ten minutes) for your name to be called to go back into the room where you will be handed your passport, a receipt for the fee and a

- Nagorno Karabagh can only be entered from Armenia.
- A Nagorno Karabagh visa is required.
- Azerbaijan cannot be entered from Nagorno Karabagh.
- A Nagorno Karabagh visa is not valid in Azerbaijan and entry to Azerbaijan will be denied to anyone with a Nagorno Karabagh visa in their passport.
- The Republic of Nagorno Karabagh is not recognised internationally and no consular services of any kind are available.

form on which is written the places you are permitted to go. You should carry this form with you, although it is unheard of for it to be inspected; it has to be handed in at the border post when you leave Karabagh. (**Note:** although the visa application form asks you to state which *regions* of NKR you wish to visit, if you do write down the regions you will be sent outside again to fill in the towns and actual sites you want to visit. Note also that visiting Aghdam is not officially permitted. Although the form has a space for a passport photograph this has not been necessary in recent years but it might be prudent to take one in case requirements change.)

GETTING THERE AND AWAY

At present Nagorno Karabagh can only be entered by road and only from Armenia. Most visitors use the good asphalt highway from Goris to Stepanakert. There are several **minibuses** daily from Yerevan to Stepanakert, the capital, which leave hourly 07.00–10.00 from Yerevan's Central Bus Station, taking around eight hours for a fare of AMD5,000. If travelling by **car** the driver must stop at the **checkpoint at Lachin** on entering and leaving so as to register the vehicle. Visitors are usually asked for their passports and visas at the checkpoint.

The road from Goris crosses the so-called Lachin corridor through what had been, since 1929, part of Azerbaijan proper. After an impressive climb the road descends to the valley of the Aghavnaget where there is a new chapel up on the left dedicated to soldiers who died in battle in Karabagh. (The checkpoint is immediately after the river crossing.) The road continues and enters Nagorno Karabagh's pre-1994 boundaries just before the town of Berdzor (previously Lachin). This is the last sizeable place before Shushi 43km further on. Although over 50% of its houses were damaged in the war many, but not all, have been rebuilt. The houses not destroyed were largely occupied by refugees who chose to settle here. The road then climbs up and after the summit runs through sparsely populated country to bypass Shushi and descend rapidly into Stepanakert. Allow about seven hours to drive by car from Yerevan to Stepanakert.

There are **other roads** into Nagorno Karabagh from Armenia. Most of those marked on maps are minor mountain tracks which are likely to be in dire condition. See also the warning about landmines on pages 323 and 326. The only other one which should be considered is the northerly route from the east side of Lake Sevan from Sotk (or Zod as it was until 1991) over the **Sotk Pass** (2,756m). It has been upgraded to a reasonably good dirt road and is passable in summer, though a 4x4 is recommended. There is the possibility of further upgrading as the Hayastan All-Armenian Fund's 2013 fund-raising Telethon was devoted to raising finance for the construction of the Vardenis–Martakert highway. After the pass the road follows the beautiful valley of the Lev, at times with toweringly high cliffs on each side until its confluence with the Tartar where the road meets another coming along the Tartar Valley. It then follows the Tartar until Nagorno Karabagh's pre-1994 borders are entered just past the monastery of Dadivank. The road is extremely scenic all the way along the valley to Sarsang Reservoir. See also page 340.

Stepanakert Airport (*610m above sea level*) lies some 20km north of Stepanakert. Flights stopped in 1990 during the Karabagh war. Repair and upgrading started in 2009 and after several postponements it was announced that the airport would start to operate in the summer of 2012. Certainly in August of that year it looked as if opening was imminent with a new building, state-of-the-art security and passenger handling and all staff training having been completed. Initial flights would be to and from Yerevan only. However, flights have not yet resumed. The airport is on territory which under international law belongs to Azerbaijan and after the announcement by the NKR Civil Aviation Department of an opening date the director of Azerbaijan's Civil Aviation Administration warned that, according to aviation laws, flights from Yerevan to Stepanakert are not authorised and may be shot down. NKR responded by saying there would be 'an adequate response' from its armed forces. Armenia's president condemned the threat to shoot down a civilian aircraft saying he would be the first passenger on the inaugural flight. Azerbaijan condemned the Armenian president's statement as 'provocation', saying it did not and would not use force against civilian facilities. The Turkish government threatened to close its air space to Armenia if the opening went ahead. The airport, it seems, has become part of the bigger problem of the resolution of the Karabagh conflict under the auspices of the OSCE Minsk Group (see page 326) and there are no flights.

GETTING AROUND

The new **north–south highway** built with funds from the charitable Hayastan All-Armenian Fund (see page 105) has made travelling in Karabagh much easier than it was. As in Armenia it is possible to travel between most towns and villages by **minibus** (*marshrutka*). The best way to find out current times of departure is by asking at either the tourist office in Shushi (see page 333) or at your hotel or homestay. The well-organised bus station in Stepanakert has detailed information on departures from Stepanakert to places within Karabagh and to Armenia. **Taxis** are plentiful and cheap and are a reasonable and convenient alternative to the *marshrutkas*. **Car hire** can be arranged through Gala Tour based in Park Hotel (page 330) in Stepanakert.

WHERE TO STAY

It is best either to book into one of the modern hotels, concentrated in Stepanakert and nearby Shushi, or else to opt for a homestay. It takes about 15 minutes to drive from Shushi to Stepanakert. **Homestays** in different parts of Nagorno Karabagh can be booked via a Yerevan travel agent before leaving or through the tourist information offices in Shushi (see page 333). The website of the Karabakh Tourism Development Agency (see page 332) lists accommodation options in Karabagh. Most hotels offer lower rates in low season, approximately November to April. Double rooms are sometimes more expensive than twin. Note that hotel accommodation may be difficult to obtain 1–3 September as the government reserves it all for Independence Day celebrations on 2 September. Within price-code category, hotels are listed alphabetically.

At present Stepanakert has far more facilities than Shushi. Most places of interest to tourists can be visited as day trips from Stepanakert. The two most popular, Dadivank and Gandzasar, can be visited on the same day if travelling by car. Where listings are plotted on a map, this is indicated below.

STEPANAKERT
Map, page 335.

Armenia Hotel (55 rooms) Veratsnound Sq; 47 949400; e info@armeniahotel.am; www. armeniahotel.am. A hotel of international standard next door to the parliament building. Restaurant, bar. Gym. Wi-Fi. Cards accepted. **$$$**

Hotel Europe (32 rooms) 26 Azatamartikneri St; 47 975752, 975782; m 097 258033; e info@hoteleurope.am; www. hoteleurope.am. A new (2012) building with a curved façade next to the Ministry of Foreign Affairs. Swimming pool. Formal restaurant in basement; café on roof (*extra AMD2,000 for comfortable sofas*). Wi-Fi. **$$$**

Park Hotel (28 rooms) 10 Vazgen Sarsian St; 47 971971; e info@parkhotelartsakh.com; www.parkhotelartsakh.com. Opened in 2011 in a fully refurbished 19th-century building. Decorated & furnished in traditional style. Helpful staff. Restaurant, bar, summer café. Wi-Fi. Price varies with size of room & view. **$$$**

Vallex Garden Hotel (57 rooms) 35 Stepanian St; 47 973393/7; e info@vallexgarden. com; www.vallexgarden.com. A new hotel, opened 2013, of international standard in the centre of town. The designer of the building's exterior seems to have had imperial Rome in mind. Inside the décor is much more tasteful but illumination in the bedrooms is poor. The restaurant serves what is probably the best & most imaginative food in town. Fitness club, swimming pool. Wi-Fi. Accepts cards. Hotel is non-smoking apart from 4 rooms & the restaurant. All rates are for sgl occupancy; every additional person is AMD5,000. **$$$**

Hotel Heghnar (28 rooms) 39–41 Abovian St; 47 971221, 946626; m 097 266666; e heghnarhotel@yahoo.com; www.heghnarhotel. com. A fully renovated hotel tastefully decorated in natural materials, with healthy plants gracing lobby & landings. Attractive original modern paintings, many for sale, adorn the walls. B/fast inc, other meals can be provided if notice given. Wi-Fi. Own fruit trees; guests are welcome to sample the fruit. Summer café in garden. **$$**

Hotel Lotus (13 rooms) 81 Vagharshian St; 47 947802; e lotus-hotel@mail.ru. Was 1 of the 1st hotels to open (1997) after the Karabagh war & has now been overtaken by newer hotels in the town. Has a slightly unused feel. Rooms shabby but clean. A brisk 20 min walk or 5–10 min drive from the centre. There are a lot of stairs & no lift. B/fast extra AMD2,000pp. Cheaper rooms **$**. Better rooms **$$**

Hotel Nairi (46 rooms) 14a Ekimian St; 47 947802, 971502, 971503; e info@hotelnairi. com; www.hotelnairi.com. A clean, basic hotel north of the centre run by an enthusiastic Australian-Armenian who also runs tours. Corridors carpeted to reduce noise. No smoking inside building. Restaurant, café. Internet available. Accepts cards. **$$**

Yerevan Hotel (16 rooms) 62 Tumanian St; 47 977888, 60 277888; e yerevanhotel@gmail. com, info@yerevanhotel.travel. Opened in 2009 in part of a converted wine factory so there is lots of space. Reception on 2nd floor. B/fast inc; other meals have to be ordered 2 days in advance. Wi-Fi. Accepts cards. **$$**

Hotel Tiroun (9 rooms) 107 Tumanian St; 47 955996, 47 945996; m 097 223366. A small, friendly basic hotel. Has family rooms. Wi-Fi. B/fast extra AMD3,000pp. **$**

Olymp Plus (Recovery Complex) (5 rooms) 101 Toumanian St; 47 948401. Looks like an old Soviet hotel which has seen some renovation. Has a large swimming pool; residents get 50% discount on pool. Outside bar/café. Dinner available if order in advance. (*Luxe suite for 3–5 persons is en suite – shower extends from sink, b/fast inc. AMD25,000*). Rooms: 1 sgl, 3 dbl, have shared toilet/shower room. B/fast extra AMD1,000pp. **$**

SHUSHI
Map, page 341.

Avan Shushi Plaza Hotel (30 rooms) 29 Ghazanchetsots St; 47 731599, 733377; e avanplaza@hotmail.com; www.avanshushiplaza. com. A very well-renovated Soviet-era hotel in the centre of town. The tallest building in Shushi; 10 floors with a lift. Gym. Wi-Fi. Cards accepted. **$$**

Shushi Grand Hotel (45 rooms) 2B Manukian St; ✆47 733337; e info@ shushigrandhotel.com; www.shushigrandhotel. com. This was a sanatorium in Soviet days but is now purely a hotel. Very well renovated with pleasant rooms; 3 floors, no lift. Set in 2½ha of parkland near the green church. Restaurant, bar. Wi-Fi. Accepts cards. **$$**

Hotel Shushi (12 rooms) 3 Amirian St; ✆47 731357; e hotelshushi@yahoo.com; www. hotelshushi.com. In the centre of the town, close to the cathedral. Rooms warm & comfortable. Good reports from guests. 4 floors, no lift. Wi-Fi. **$**

Elsewhere in Karabagh

Sea Stone Hotel (14 rooms) Vank village, Martakert region; ✆10 500168 (Yerevan number); m 097 286285, 097 235072. This hotel is 3km outside Vank & is run by the same people as the Eclectica. It is a more luxurious hotel, with comfortable rooms, but is just as extraordinary. The large plaster casts of eyes, lips & mouths which decorate the outside of the hotel & are repeated inside, the statues of lions & nymphs guarding the front door & the huge representation of a lion's mouth, which roars as one passes, all seem out of place in the attractive riverside setting. Restaurant, café. Can arrange tours of Karabagh. Dbl without en suite **$**. En-suite dbl **$$**

Ani Paradise Hotel (8 rooms) 18km Stepanakert–Gandzasar highway, Khndzristan village, Askeran region; m 097 282000; e aniparadise@ktsurf.net. This small, pleasant hotel in a country house has a swimming pool & can arrange horseriding, fishing & hiking. B/fast inc, other meals can be provided with notice. **$**

Hotel Eclectica (18 rooms) Vank village, Martakert region; ✆10 500168 (Yerevan number); m 097 286285. Situated just below Gandzasar Monastery in Vank village. Rooms basic. The 6 rooms on the ground floor (1 dbl, 2 twin, 1 trpl, 1 quad, 1 for 5 persons) share 2 bathrooms. 13 rooms upstairs (9 dbl, 4 sgl) similarly. This hotel lives up to its name: the extraordinary entrance hall is decorated as an undersea world with perspex cases, containing models depicting Armenian life, set into the floor. The restaurant ceiling is held up by half a dozen Atlas-like figures & Corinthian columns, between which is a frieze embellished with casts of Armenian coins. The pictures on the wall are reproductions of Van Gogh. Outside, an open-air stage has tiered green & yellow plastic seats. Restaurant, bar, café. Internet café next door. No rooms en suite. **$**

✗ WHERE TO EAT AND DRINK

Some hotels have restaurants and/or cafés where non-residents can eat (see opposite). At the time of writing the best and most imaginative food was in the restaurant of the Vallex Garden Hotel (see opposite). Opening hours and prices are similar to those in Armenia (pages x and 92). Most villages have a well-stocked shop where food can be purchased and petrol stations sometimes have a small shop attached. The gas station on the edge of Stepanakert on the road north has a well-provisioned, clean, bright café. When spending a day away from the main towns, as when visiting Dadivank, a picnic is possibly the best option. The market on Sasuntsi

> ### JINGALOV HATS
>
> Food and drink in Nagorno Karabagh is similar to that in Armenia (see pages 88–95), but one local speciality is herb bread, *jingalov hats*. This is a classic flatbread into which are incorporated seven seasonal herbs. The dough is rolled out into a flat sheet, a generous pile of chopped herbs is placed on top, the sides of the dough are folded over the herbs and the whole is rolled out again. It is then cooked on a griddle brushed with oil. It's absolutely delicious though beware of some inferior imitations. You can watch it being made at the market in Stepanakert and buy it fresh and warm straight off the hotplate. It makes excellent picnic food.

Davit Street is a good place to buy provisions. Where listings are plotted on a map, this is indicated below.

STEPANAKERT
Map, page 335.

✘ **Café Aragil** Shahumian Sq. An outdoor summer café mainly for drinks. Armenian coffee AMD200, thyme tea AMD600.

✘ **Russia Restaurant** Sasuntsi Davit St, opposite the History Museum. ⊕ 12.00–02.00, all year. Free Wi-Fi. Possibly the 2nd best restaurant food in Stepanakert.

✘ **Sofia Complex** Opposite the market. Has a few outlets serving fast food such as beef burgers.

✘ **Tashir Pizza** 20 Azatamartikneri St; ✆47 971117. A branch of this deservedly popular chain. A wide variety of pizzas can be bought by the segment (*AMD250–400*) or as whole. Also serves

pasta (*AMD1,000*), salads (*AMD500–900*), soups (*AMD500*), etc.

✘ **Ureni Restaurant** 66 Tumanian St; ✆47 944544. Once the poshest restaurant in Stepanakert apart from those in hotels. Still popular with locals. Russian cuisine. AMD5,000.

ELSEWHERE IN KARABAGH
✘ **Mher Soorjaran** Hadrut. A small family-run restaurant/café between the 2 rivers, signposted in Armenian & Russian from both main streets. The building is 150 years old; inside dining rooms are barrel-vaulted stone rooms; outside one sits under a canopy of vines. Own fruit & vegetables. A simple but delicious meal for 2 cost AMD5,000.

SHOPPING

Most **shops, banks**, a **post office, internet cafés, currency exchanges**, etc are to be found on or near Vazgen Sargsian Street (formerly, and sometimes still, called Yerevanian Avenue) or Azatamartikneri Street in Stepanakert.

English-language books are rare. Maps can be bought at Kanzler, a **stationery shop** (*26 Vazgen Sargsian St, Stepanakert*). The **market** on Sasuntsi Davit Street sells household items and clothes as well as food.

For souvenirs **Nereni Arts and Crafts** (*10 Grigor Lusavorich St, Stepanakert;* ✆ *47 984711;* m *097 217711;* e *nereni_nk@yahoo.com; www.facebook.com/nereni. artsakh*) is the best option, with a good range of handmade local crafts. For handmade **carpets** try Artsakhgorg Carpet Museum and Showroom in Shushi (page 342).

OTHER PRACTICALITIES

Telephone and **internet** services are provided by Karabagh Telecom (*14 Nelson Stepanian St, Stepanakert;* ✆ *47 979702;* e *info@karabakhtelecom.com; www. karabakhtelecom.com*). **Emergency phone numbers** are the same as in Armenia: fire ✆101, police ✆102, ambulance ✆103. Anyone wishing to use a **mobile phone** in Nagorno Karabagh should note that Armenian SIM cards work as roaming cards and are thus relatively expensive. It may be cheaper to buy a Karabagh SIM card. Options available include prepaid and post-paid cards with tariffs dependent on whether NKR, Armenian or international access is desired. Information on cards and tariffs is available from Karabakh Telecom's website.

Nagorno Karabagh has attractive stamps. There is a philatelic corner in the main post office on Hakobian Street in Stepanakert. Staff here are efficient and pleasant. Postage rates are similar to Armenia's.

The **Karabakh Tourism Development Agency**, also known as the Government Tourism Department (*2 Knounyantsneri St, Stepanakert;* ✆ *47 949172;* e *info@ tourismdept.nkr.am; www.karabakh.travel*), website has much useful background information, in the midst of its flowery language, including details of the regions of Karabagh, accommodation, transport, museums and cuisine. It also publishes a guidebook, *Discovered Paradise*, which contains similar information, and a series of free booklets which contain background information and good photographs, but few practical details. Titles include *Karabakh*, *Stepanakert*, *Gandzasar*, *Tigranakert*, *Carpets* and *Nikol Duman*. I obtained mine from the tourist information office in Shushi. Some can be downloaded from the agency's website. Another good internet source is www.armeniapedia.org which has information on Nagorno Karabagh.

There is a useful, although old, **map** of Nagorno Karabagh, with street plans of Stepanakert and Shushi and notes on sites of interest. I found it at the stationery shop Kanzler (see opposite). A small folding map (you may need a magnifying glass) can be bought at Nereni Crafts (see opposite). The Collage maps of Armenia (page 60) also cover Nagorno Karabagh.

There is a **tourist information office** in Shushi (page 340) but none in Stepanakert. Gala Tour, based in Park Hotel (page 330) can help with some tourist information.

JANAPAR TRAIL For experienced walkers there is now a long-distance marked footpath from Hadrut in the south to Dadivank in the north. Markers are blue with a yellow footprint and it is said to take two weeks to walk the entire route. Detailed information, including maps, can be found at www.janapar.org. Anyone intending to walk the trail should also bear in mind the warnings given earlier in this chapter about mines and other unexploded ordnance.

WHAT TO SEE AND DO

Entrance to museums in Nagorno Karabagh is generally free. A contribution, and perhaps a tip to the guide, is always welcome. Historic sites which are ruinous are always open. Where there is a church which is now active it will be open every day, at least 09.00–18.00 and often longer. The rest of a monastery site is usually accessible at all times. The most popular historic sites for visitors in Nagorno Karabagh are the monasteries of **Gandzasar** (pages 337–8) and **Dadivank** (pages 338–9). The excavated site and museum of **Tigranakert** (pages 336–7) are well worth a visit. Shushi town (pages 340–2) provides thought-provoking evidence of the conflict over Karabagh, evidence which has now largely disappeared from Stepanakert.

STEPANAKERT Formerly Khankendi, the capital of Nagorno Karabagh (population 40,000) was renamed Stepanakert in 1923 in honour of the Armenian Bolshevik Stepan Shahumian (1878–1918) after whom Stepanavan is also named. His statue stands in Shahumian Square at the northern end of Vazgen Sargsian Street, one of the main shopping streets. Newly independent Azerbaijan renamed it back to Khankendi in 1992, but the name in use within Nagorno Karabagh today remains Stepanakert. The town suffered considerable damage in the war but this has now been repaired and the town centre has the feel and appearance of a capital city, albeit a small one. The town is clean and there are many notices saying 'Do not litter'. The new **parliament building** on Veratsnound (Renaissance) Square is topped by a transparent cupola reminiscent of Armenian church architecture. From Veratsnound Square steps go down to **Lovers' Alley** which has been renovated and given quirky lampstands. At the bottom is a sculpture of two hands with a wedding ring. Until recently Stepanakert had no churches but a new **cathedral**, dedicated to the Mother of God, is under construction south of the historical quarters. I was privileged to be given, by the builders, a guided tour of the partially built cathedral, including the crypt with all its wooden scaffolding, an experience which certainly would not have been vouchsafed under Western safety regulations! In the **market** (⊕ *07.00–18.00*) it is possible to see the herb bread being made (see box, page 331) and it is a good place to buy food for picnics and self-catering. **Artsakh State History Museum** (*4 Sasuntsi Davit St;* ✎ *47 941042;* e *tangaran@ktsurf.net; www.karabakh.travel;* ⊕ *09.00–17.00 Mon–Fri, 09.00–16.00 Sat, lunch break 13.00–14.00; Russian, English & French spoken*), is just up the hill from the market. It gives an interesting portrayal of Nagorno Karabagh from prehistoric times to the present day. The Soviet era is not totally ducked as sometimes happens but, World War II apart, the focus was on the positive side (industrialisation) rather than the negative (the purges). The two sides in the days of the First Armenian Republic, the Bolsheviks and the Dashnaks, are given complementary displays opposite each other. The final room covers the Karabagh war. Two museums related to the Karabagh war are close to each other on a small square between Nzhdeh and Hakobian streets: the **Museum of Fallen Warriors** (*25 Vazgen Sargsian St;* ✎ *47 950738;* ⊕ *09.00–18.00 Mon–Sat*) is devoted to soldiers who died during the war and whose graves are known. The **Museum of Missing Soldiers** remembers those who are missing, presumed dead (although their relatives still hope that they are alive as prisoners of war and that one day some will return). Both museums have collections of anything at all connected with those remembered (personal belongings, letters, flags, uniforms, medals, etc) as well as walls densely covered with portraits. What makes a visit even more poignant is that the volunteers who staff the museums, and show you round, are relatives of the dead or missing soldiers. One comment in the visitors' book reads 'To come to Karabagh and not visit these museums means not to have visited Karabagh'.

The **Vahram Papazian State Drama Theatre** (*18 Hakobian St*), founded in 1932, is an elegant theatre but in need of significant funds for restoration. There is still

PUBLIC HOLIDAYS

1 January	New Year
6 January	Christmas
8 March	International Women's Day
March/April	Good Friday
March/April	Easter Monday
7 April	Day of Motherhood and Beauty
24 April	Genocide Memorial Day
1 May	May Day
9 May	Victory and Peace Day
28 May	First Republic Day
2 September	Independence Day
10 December	Constitution Day
31 December	New Year's Eve

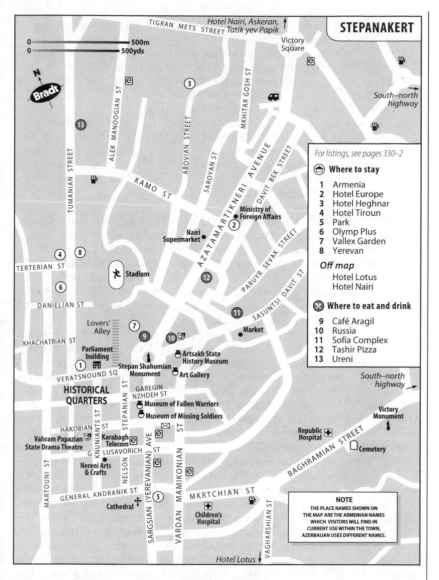

much beautiful plaster work. The season is usually May to October; it does not function during the winter because of the problem of heating it. The programme is advertised at the theatre and in the town. Tickets cost AMD500. The theatre seats 425. The crossed-off seats on the seating plan do not indicate those seats which are already booked, but rather those which are unusable at present. If you happen to call in when the manager is there he will probably be delighted to show you round and perhaps offer you a taste of his own mulberry vodka.

The delightful **Stepanakert Art Gallery** (*Vardan Mamikonian St, just before its junction with Sasuntsi Davit St;* ⊕ *09.00–18.00 daily; English spoken*) opened in late 2013 and is well worth a visit. Colourful, thought-provoking paintings by Karabagh artists are attractively displayed, with labels in Armenian, English and Russian. My one wish was that the dates of the artists/paintings had been included. Perhaps it was not thought necessary as many, if not all, are by living artists.

At the time of writing a large **memorial complex** was being built in the southwest of the town. Memorials envisaged are to the 1915 genocide, the Great Patriotic War (World War II), the 1988 earthquake, the Sumgait massacre of 1988 and the Karabagh war of 1991–94. Locals have dubbed the memorial 'the cobra' from the way in which the road snakes up and around the mound.

On the north side of Stepanakert is a **statue** reproduced in a thousand Karabagh souvenirs. The creation of the sculptor Sargis Baghdasarian in Soviet times, it is called *We Are Our Mountains*. Looking like an elderly couple in national costume, the statue is intended to symbolise the unity of the Karabagh people with their mountains. It is universally referred to as *Tatik yev Papik* (sometimes *Mamik yev Papik*) (Granny and Grandad).

NORTHEAST FROM STEPANAKERT Some 15km from Stepanakert just before the town of **Askeran** the main road passes right through the fortress known variously as **Mayraberd** ('Mother Fortress') or Zoraberd ('Powerful Fortress'). It was reinforced in 1788–89 by the Persians because of the increasing Russian threat and most of what can be seen today dates from then. The fortress is on both sides of the Karkar River. What survives is a triangle of walls breached by the road on the northern side plus a smaller fortification together with several towers and a length of wall with the remains of a walkway on top on the southern side.

Beyond Askeran the road continues another 5km to the ruins of **Aghdam**. Aghdam was a sizeable town, formerly inhabited by Azeris, but it was destroyed by the Karabagh army after they captured it to prevent it falling back into Azeri hands. To go there is either weird or depressing depending on perspective but many visitors do so, although official permission to visit will not be given.

Beyond Aghdam, on the Martakert road, is the **excavated site and State Archaeological Museum of Tigranakert** (*about 36km north of Stepanakert, halfway between Askeran & Martakert; www.tigranakert.am; ⊕ daily 09.00–19.00; English-speaking guide sometimes available; AMD250*). (The website's English pages were not active at the time of writing but photographs of this fascinating and impressive site can be viewed on the Armenian and Russian pages.) A medieval fortress sits at the foot of the dramatic site of the ancient city of Tigranakert, founded by Tigran the Great (ruled c95–55BC). Behind the medieval castle a wave-like escarpment on the southeastern slope of Mount Vankasar (879m) rises from the plain. The triangular fortified city, with the citadel at its apex, occupies the lower third of the slope above the castle. The site covers some 50ha and excavations, started in 2005, are continuing. Already two of the main walls of the city have been uncovered. Built of local white limestone, without mortar, the stone blocks were dove-tailed together by means of triangular joints. Also notable are the steps carved into the rock on the edge of the escarpment. The many finds, dating from the 5th century BC to the 17th century AD, are now displayed in the museum which opened in the medieval fortress in June 2010. Information is in Armenian, English and Russian. Note that, although the museum entrance is signed straight ahead of the entrance gate, to follow the exhibition chronologically either go in via the door to the left or make your way there once inside.

South of the castle the foundations of a 5th- to 7th-century basilica have been excavated. Beyond the fortified site a small renovated cross-dome church stands on the peak of Mount Vankasar. The church holds nothing of interest but it makes a good endpoint for a walk which gives a bird's eye view of Tigranakert and views across the Azerbaijan plain. It takes about an hour of moderately steep walking to reach the church, the first part made easier by the ancient steps carved into the rock. It is worth starting early in the day before it becomes too hot. Even if not wishing to reach the church, walking to the top of the excavated site is worth it for the overall impression of this important site.

Driving north to the town of **Martakert** there is much evidence of the war and the departed Azeri population: ruined houses, a well-preserved Islamic burial chamber, a toppled Azeri cemetery and a ruined Soviet memorial. Martakert centre looks surprisingly prosperous and has all the facilities expected of a town.

NORTHWEST FROM STEPANAKERT After passing *Tatik yev Papik* turn left, signposted Drmbon, and then bear right at the roundabout at Aygestan. About 40km from Stepanakert the road descends a hill into the valley of the Khachenaget River which it bridges. After the bridge the road to Gandzasar goes off left, the main road continuing to Drmbon, where the road for Dadivank goes off. From Drmbon the main road turns east to Martakert (at the time of writing, a very poor road but improvement may be in the offing; see page 328).

Some 22km north of Stepanakert, in the village of **Tsaghkashat** (Ghshlag), is the **house museum of freedom fighter Nikol Duman** (m 097 236327 for Mariam, the key-holder; ⊕ 10.00–18.00 Mon–Fri; donations welcomed). The lower floor of the restored 19th-century house is dedicated to the life and work of Nikol Duman (1867–1914) and includes collections of military and domestic items. The upper floor shows a typical living room of the era. Other ethnographical displays are nearby. Within the complex is a souvenir shop with local handicrafts and produce. Snacks are available and traditional meals can be organised (*contact Davit,* m *097 281281*).

Gandzasar Monastery Gandzasar is once more a working monastery and seminary and is open daily. Gandzasar ('Treasure Mountain') Monastery, dedicated to John the Baptist, is on a hilltop outside **Vank** ('Monastery') village, Martakert district. The name derives from the presence of silver deposits in the district. To reach it, turn left after crossing the bridge over the Khachenaget and continue a further 14km to Vank, following the river valley. Gandzasar has been fully restored since 1991. It is particularly notable for its exquisite carved detail. Surrounded by walls, it is a cross-dome church with its 16-sided tambour topped by an umbrella cupola. Owing to its inaccessibility, Nagorno Karabagh partly avoided the large-scale Seljuk invasion in the 11th and 12th centuries, as well as the Mongolian invasions in the 13th century. Consequently some of the finest church architecture of the period is found here. The monastery was founded in 1216, the church being built between 1232 and 1238, while the *gavit* was added in 1261. The founders were Melik Jalal-Dolan, ruler of Khachen, the most important of the principalities of the region, together with his wife Mamkan and son Atabeg. The monastery served as the burial place of the Khachen rulers, and until the 19th century as the seat of the Katholikos of Aghvank.

The tambour of the **church** is an outstanding work of art, decorated with numerous sculptured images between the triple columns separating each side. On the western side two bearded figures with long moustaches are sitting in an oriental posture with their feet tucked under them. On the south side are kneeling figures facing each other with arms outstretched and haloes round their heads while angels spread their wings over them in blessing. One side shows the Virgin and Child, there are two bulls' heads and an eagle with spreading wings. The *gavit* obscures another sculptural composition – a crucifix under the gable of the west façade with seraphs hovering over Jesus and Mary, and John the Baptist kneeling in prayer with outstretched hands. The north façade shows a bird in the west and the south façade has galloping horses. The west and east façades have large relief crosses. The *gavit* has an immense west portal which shows two birds as well as much varied abstract design. Over the north door are two lions, emblems of the Hassan Jalalian family. The six-pointed star in front of the right-hand creature is associated with Armenian royalty. The *gavit* is surmounted by a belfry supported by six columns. The interiors of both church and *gavit* have yet more carving including the finely carved front of the altar dais, the pattern of each triangle or square being different.

Compared with the tranquil traditional appearance of the monastery, Vank village is certainly a contrast. Someone with a fondness for yellow and green has painted all the gas pipes to match the tiered plastic seats of the outdoor theatre attached to one of the hotels, part of which is in the form of a ship.

Dadivank (monastery) Dadivank, one of the largest medieval monastery complexes, is on the northern route to Armenia from Nagorno Karabagh. Take a picnic (although most villages do now have a small shop) and, if your car is dual-fuel, fill up with gas before leaving Stepanakert – there are no gas stations between the one just beyond *Tatik yev Papik* and Drmbon (fill up at Drmbon if you are continuing beyond Dadivank). The road to Dadivank bears right after the junction with the Gandzasar road just after the Khachenaget bridge and continues north through the hills until eventually Sarsang Reservoir can be seen with the village of **Drmbon** in the foreground and the Mrav range forming a backdrop. Until Drmbon the road is mostly in good condition. Drmbon is an important mining area and the signposted road to Dadivank goes off left beside the large white and green building of the Base Metals Mining Company. The road from here is variable; mostly asphalt, poor condition at times, plus some stretches of dirt road. There are two petrol pumps at Getavan. Fill up with petrol: there are no more pumps for a long way. Initially mining activities are evident along the Sarsang Reservoir

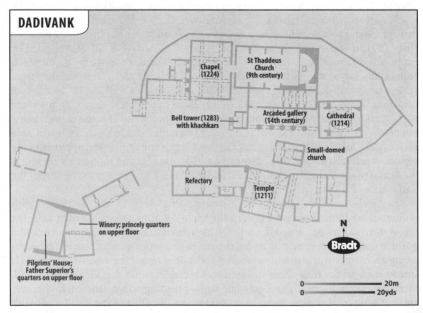

DADIVANK

Chapel (1224)

St Thaddeus Church (9th century)

Bell tower (1283) with khachkars

Arcaded gallery (14th century)

Cathedral (1214)

Small-domed church

Refectory

Temple (1211)

Winery; princely quarters on upper floor

N

Bradt

Pilgrims' House; Father Superior's quarters on upper floor

0   20m
0   20yds

but eventually these are left behind and then the rest of the journey is extremely beautiful along the gorge of the fast-flowing Tartar River as far as the monastery. It is possible to drive up to the monastery in a 4x4, the signposted road winding round what look like two slag heaps.

Dadivank is traditionally believed to be on the site of the grave of St Thaddeus who was martyred in the 1st century for preaching Christianity, 'Dadi' being a phonetic transposition of his name. Although there was probably a church here by the 4th century, the oldest surviving remains date from the 9th century. The church was pillaged in 1145–46 by the Persians but reconstruction started in the 1170s. The monastery went into decline in the 18th century and the monastery estates were only half occupied when the Khan of Shushi invited the Kurds to move on to them from Yerevan. The late 18th century saw further Persian military action, and plague and famine in 1798 saw the final abandonment of the site. There has been some restoration.

The layout is exceedingly complex and there are buildings on two levels. The 9th-century **church of St Thaddeus**, built over his grave, is at the north side of the complex. Less than ideal restoration work following excavations has resulted in some loss of atmosphere from this ancient church. To its west lies a **chapel** resembling a *gavit*, said to be the burial vault of a princely dynasty, built in 1224. There are further contemporary buildings to the west. Southeast of St Thaddeus is the main **cathedral** which dates from 1214. The 16-sided tambour has graceful arcatures and the cupola is conical. On both the south and east façades are two figures holding a model of the church. In front of it is a 14th-century **arcaded gallery** which extends as far as the **bell tower** of 1283. New steps at the bell tower enable the two intricately carved khachkars to be fully appreciated. To the south there is a **small-domed church** with circular tambour and a tiled dome; its date is uncertain. The restoration of this church is also somewhat insensitive but the remains of frescoes can still be seen high on the north wall. On the lower level are the **kitchen**, **refectory** and **wine press**, as well as various accommodation quarters. The building with four round pillars on square bases is, according to an inscription of 1211, the **temple**. There is a spring at Dadivank and picnic tables.

Some 7km west of Dadivank a road goes off south. After 17km, and one hour of driving on a very poor road, **Zuar**, with hot springs, is reached. Very hot water bubbles up then flows into a pool where the temperature is bearable and several people can soak, before it flows into the river.

The main road forks 10km beyond Dadivank. The right, northernmost, road follows the Lev River, then enters Armenia via the Sotk Pass (see page 340). The left fork goes south to the town of Karvatchar and thence to the isolated village of Tsar. In the Soviet period the road continued south for a further 12km to the hot springs resort of Istisu (now Jermajur) but the bridge over the river near the Tsar turn-off no longer exists. The road starts as a poor asphalt road then becomes a dirt road. **Karvatchar** is up on the plateau. It was mostly destroyed during the war but a few houses are now occupied and rebuilding of infrastructure has begun. Continuing on the road beside the river (signposted *Tak jur*, ie: hot water) takes one through a steep-sided valley, the lower slopes wooded beneath sheer cliffs with basalt columns and caves. One of the **hot springs** feeds into a manmade pool where it is possible to soak and enjoy the warm mineral water if you do not mind the rubbish which previous bathers have left behind.

Tsar village (*2,040m above sea level*) is on a triangular plateau above the confluence of the Tartar River and its tributary, the Tsaraget. The plateau formed an easily defensible site, the only side not so defended was a narrow (250m) strip of land which was fortified. (The short but narrow rocky track which zigzags up the side of the cliff to Tsar should only be driven in a 4x4 in good weather.) Tsar is mentioned in historical records from the medieval period onwards and once had four churches, two monasteries and cemeteries with numerous khachkars. With the changes in ruling powers (see pages 17–27) most Armenian Christians had left the Karvatchar area by the mid-18th century. For over a century villages such as Tsar were only occupied, by nomadic herdsmen, during the summer months. With the establishment of the USSR the area was incorporated first into Azerbaijan, then in 1923–29 into Kurdistan, then again into Azerbaijan. Only since the Karabagh war, when the region became part of the self-declared Republic of Nagorno Karabagh, have Armenian Christians again been the majority inhabitants. This chequered history has seen the destruction of much of Tsar's Christian heritage; only two small single-aisle barrel-vaulted churches remain among the ruined Azeri houses, St Gregory and St Sargis (both from 1274). Stone from destroyed buildings was reused as building material and many fragments of churches, monasteries and khachkars have been discovered in secular buildings of the region, such as the Azerbaijani school in Tsar, built in the 1950s. In 2013 14 families, some 65 persons, lived in Tsar.

Shortly after the Karvatchar turn-off the **northern route to Armenia** via the **Sotk Pass** (2,400m) enters an impressive narrow gorge where the cliffs tower high above the road beside the Lev River. The road then enters a broad valley where it crosses the river. The border post is passed at Nor Kharkhaput, some distance from the actual border, before the serious climb to the pass begins. (It is unusual for papers to be checked here which means that, according to official records, you have not left Karabagh, not having handed in the form which lists the places you are allowed to go.) The road zigzags up the mountain, exchanging the rocky, sparsely tree-clad slopes of Karabagh for the more rounded grass-covered slopes of the hills towards Lake Sevan. Before reaching the actual pass the enormous spoil heaps of the Sotk gold mines come into view and at times the summit is crossed on a short, muddy, one-track section through spoil. Descending through the gold mine on the Armenian side presents a desolate vista. The road descends to Sotk village and thence to Vardenis.

SOUTH FROM STEPANAKERT

Shushi The former capital of Shushi is about 15 minutes up the hill from Stepanakert and lies to the left just off the main Goris road. Unlike Stepanakert the scars of ethnic conflict are still very evident in Shushi with its many ruined buildings but there are signs of recovery. Shushi has a **tourist office** in the former bus station, off the north end of Nzhdeh Street (*3 Garegin Nzhdeh St;* \ *47 733296;* ⊕ *daily, 09.30–17.30 in winter, 09.30–18.30 in summer*). Prior to 1988 the town had a mixed Armenian and Azeri population, notwithstanding the destruction of many Armenian homes during fighting in 1920. Now the Azeri population has gone while the Armenians remain. Some of the blocks of flats are occupied, some are still burnt-out shells while others are in the process of being restored. In one way the place is more striking than the completely abandoned towns and villages because here life goes on around the destruction. The encroaching vegetation shows how long places have lain empty and unused.

The town itself, set on a precipice overlooking the impressive gorge of the Karkar, has several points of interest. Part of the medieval town wall remains and two 19th-century churches have been restored, both striking with their very pale stone. The massive, almost white **Ghazanchetsots Cathedral** (Ghazan refers to some very large vessels which were gifted to the church) was built between 1868 and 1887. Like all Karabagh churches it was closed during the Soviet period and saw service

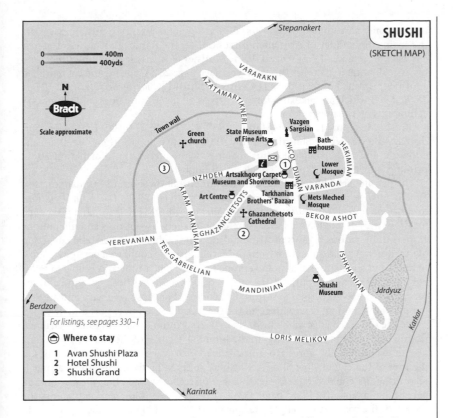

0 ———— 400m
0 ———— 400yds

N

Bradt

Scale approximate

Stepanakert

VARARAKN

AZATAMARTIKNERI

Town wall

Green
church

State Museum
of Fine Arts

Vazgen
Sargsian

Bath-
house

HEKIMIAN

NZHDEH

Artsakhgorg Carpet
Museum and Showroom

Nicol Duman

Lower
Mosque

VARANDA

Art Centre

Tarkhanian
Brothers' Bazaar

Mets Meched
Mosque

ARAM MANUKIAN

GHAZANCHETSOTS

Ghazanchetsots
Cathedral

BEKOR ASHOT

YEREVANIAN

TER-GABRIELIAN

MANDINIAN

ISHKHANIAN

Shushi
Museum

Jdrdyuz

Karkar

Berdzor

LORIS MELIKOV

Karintak

For listings, see pages 330–1

Where to stay

1 Avan Shushi Plaza
2 Hotel Shushi
3 Shushi Grand

variously as a granary, a garage and a munitions store. Oddly enough the bell tower, decorated with figures of angels playing musical instruments which stands beside it, was built earlier, in 1858. All but one of the angels decorating the bell tower were destroyed in the war, the remaining one being christened the 'guardian angel of Artsakh'. After renovation the church and bell tower, with new angels, were reconsecrated in 1998. The other church is the so-called **green church** (*kanach zham*), in the northwestern part of the town. It has a silver metallic cupola and was completed in 1847. Elsewhere in the town **mosques** survive: religious buildings were not destroyed after the war. The Church in 2005 took the most interesting one, the **Mets Meched Mosque** of 1883, under its protection and invited the Shiite authorities in Teheran to send specialists to restore it. In Soviet days it served as the town's historical museum. Across the square from the mosque the **Tarkhanian brothers' bazaar** has been rebuilt to its original design, with the hope it will function again as a market. Down the road opposite the bazaar is an overgrown second mosque, the **Lower Mosque**, of 1875. A *hammam*, or **bathhouse** (eastwards from the main square) has also been restored. On one side of the main square the old caravanserai has been magnificently converted to become the **State Museum of Fine Arts** (*24 Ghazanchetsots St;* ⊕ *09.00–18.00 Tue–Sun; AMD300*) which opened in 2013. A visit is highly recommended. All the works of art displayed have been gifted to the gallery either by the artist or by collectors. The splendid collection is well displayed and is labelled in Armenian, Russian and English (but unfortunately without dates for the artists or the works). A catalogue with excellent reproductions of the paintings is available for AMD5,000. The **statue** of the seated

Nagorno Karabagh WHAT TO SEE AND DO

7

341

man, usually surrounded by flowers, on the square is Vazgen Sargsian. Sargsian, the main commander of Armenian forces during the Karabagh war, was Defence Minister of Armenia 1995–99 and Prime Minister of Armenia from June 1999 until his assassination in October the same year (see page 26). Opposite the cathedral, in a former printing house, is the **Art Centre of Shushi** (*Ghazanchetsots St;* ⊕ *10.00–18.00 daily*) which has an exhibition of carpets on the ground floor and temporary exhibitions on the upper floor.

Shushi Museum (*17 Mesrop Mashtots St;* ☏ *47 731948;* ⊕ *09.00–17.00 Mon–Sat*) displays the history of Shushi in a mid-19th-century house. There are the usual domestic and archaeological items together with interesting information about printing, education and music. Labels are in English.

The private **Artsakhgorg Carpet Museum and Showroom** (*31 Ghazanchetsots St;* e *artsakhgorg@mail.ru; www.artsakh.com;* ⊕ *10.00–19.00 Tue–Sun; donations towards the upkeep/renovation of the building welcomed*) is well worth a visit, even for those who do not have a special interest in carpets. Two rooms contain antique carpets from various regions of Armenia and Karabagh, all the personal collection of the owner. A full explanation from the excellent guide could well occupy a couple of hours but she realises that not everyone has that much time and is able to tailor her information as appropriate. The attached showroom has both new and antique carpets for sale. New carpets cost from US$400/m². For those who wish and are able to buy, the showroom can manage all the red tape involved in export and delivery.

On the southeast edge of the town there is a recreational park-like area, **Jdrdyuz**, from where one can look down into the impressive gorge of the Karkar River. One way to experience the gorge from below is to visit **Karintak** village which lies at the foot of the cliffs below Shushi. Karintak suffered badly during the war but is recovering, its cobbled streets presenting a picture of village life. From Karintak part of the Janapar Trail (see page 333) can be followed (blue markers) across the river, past the *zontik* (umbrella) waterfall and the ruins of Hunot village (so deep in the gorge that no road could be built to it and abandoned in Soviet times) then back up into the eastern part of Shushi.

SOUTHEAST FROM STEPANAKERT Take the main Goris road as far as the city boundary but then turn left down the hill. The road heads out through **Shosh** where there are many plantations of mulberry trees, as silk was made here in Soviet days. There is a possibility that the industry might be revived but meanwhile the mulberries are used for producing mulberry vodka. The ruined 12th- to 13th-century **Pirumashen Church**, a single-aisle basilica, is passed on the right before the village of **Sarushen**. Restoration has started but seems to have stalled. The road winds down after Sarushen; at the bottom of the hill the 2,000-year-old **Platan Tree** is signposted left. This is a popular picnic site with locals and also acts as a shrine – witness the handkerchiefs tied to the tree. A fairly good 2½km dirt road leads to the tree. The hollow plane tree has a circumference of 27m (several people can stand inside it at once) and a height of 54m. The canopy arises either from boughs growing from the rim of the trunk or from new growth at its base.

The main road continues to the large village of **Karmir Shuka**. From Karmir Shuka it is possible to turn off the main road and travel eastwards along a good asphalt road to the **monastery of Amaras**, near the village of Matchkalashen. Amaras was founded by St Gregory the Illuminator in the early 4th century and Mesrop Mashtots is said to have taught there. It has been destroyed (by the Mongols in the 13th century, during Tamerlane's invasion in 1387 and again in the 16th century) and rebuilt several times. During the first half of the 19th century Russian troops used it as a frontier fortress.

The Armenian Church reclaimed it in 1848. The monastery was abandoned during the Soviet period but is once again a functioning church. The complex comprises a 17th-century fortified wall within which is the church of St Gregory built in 1858 and restored in 1996. Beneath the east end of the church is the tomb of a grandson of St Gregory the Illuminator, also St Gregory (322–48). One of the rooms which line the south side of the fortified wall has a marriage fireplace, the sides of the fireplace being in the form of two heads facing each other. Should you need fuel for the car, or other purchases, **Tchartar**, off the Amaras road, is a sizeable town which has a gas station and most other facilities. It also has a gem in the form of the **Sevak Ghouvakian Theatre**. The round, pink tuff building is modelled on Yerevan's opera house and has a delightful frieze of foliage, fruits and animals above its arcades as well as a lovely auditorium with comfortable seats. Local and Yerevan companies give a summer season with tickets costing AMD500–1,000.

South from Karmir Shuka and near Azokh village is **Azokh Cave**, reached by a scramble up the hillside. The eight linked caves have a total length of 600m and an area of 8,000m² with the largest chamber being 3,000m². The caves are equally famous for their stalactites and stalagmites as for the prehistoric finds which have been made there. These include the 1–1½ million-year-old remains of Palaeolithic and Mesolithic man together with more than 2,000 bones from 45 species of animal, some of them now extinct.

About 3km south of Azokh is **Togh** village through which the **monastery of Gtchivank** is reached. The monastery is signposted off the main road and at one further junction but not thereafter. It is possible to drive right up to the monastery, but the last 3km is extremely difficult. To avoid the risk of damage to one's vehicle it is better to walk the final stretch, either up the track or across the hillside (see below). At the Tumi/Mokhrenes junction (5.2km from the main road) at the far end of Togh bear right towards Tumi and continue bearing right, round the base of the mountain on your right. At the brow of the hill, just after a rocky spur has come down at right angles to the road (about 7.8km from main road), there is a small parking place on the right. Unless the cloud is low it is possible to see the tambour and cupola of Gtchivank breaking the skyline on the hill to the right. From the top of the parking area, near an electricity pole, a (faint in places) path leads up the hillside and then across left to the monastery. It is a very beautiful walk up the flower-covered hillside with wonderful views over the hilly countryside of southern Karabagh. (The alternative is to drive a further 2km then walk just over 3km up the track, see page 344.) The approach to the monastery is one of the finest imaginable but the monastery itself is an incredibly sad place. Where so many lived and worked to the glory of God vandals have spray-painted with graffiti every square inch inside, even climbing up to the most inaccessible parts of the cupola to cause as much desecration as possible. The graffiti comprise mostly people's names, written in Russian letters and often dated. The monastery was the seat of the archbishopric as early as the 5th century. The inscription records that the existing main cross-dome church was built between 1241 and 1248 by the brothers Sargis and Vrtanes, bishops at Amaras.

The church is entered through a barrel-vaulted *gavit* whose main hall is set asymmetrically to the church portal, perhaps to accommodate the large khachkar which stands to the right of the church entrance. The cross is supported by angels and above the cross, within the moulded frame, is the central figure of Jesus with six figures on each side representing the 12 disciples. The front of the church's *bema* is decorated with a geometrical design and a frieze of pomegranates. A very ruinous building lies to the north of the main church. Some restoration of the exterior of church and *gavit* has been undertaken. If work continues and includes removal of the graffiti the monastery may some day match its attractive setting.

The 3km 'jeep track' up to Gtchivank leaves the road 9.8km from the main road, through a 180° turn. As indicated on page 343 it is best to walk: it is a very difficult track to drive, even for a jeep in good weather. In wet weather it is impossibly muddy. I have seen tortoises on this track.

The main road continues south to the town of **Hadrut**, the southernmost town in the pre-war autonomous region of Nagorno Karabagh, through yet more impressive mountain scenery. The town has basic facilities (including a petrol station but no gas station), a restored church and a war memorial with a statue of a resigned, kneeling woman but there is little to interest visitors.

SOUTHWEST FROM STEPANAKERT
Tsitsernavank (monastery) This monastery is very close to the Armenian border. It can be visited as you enter Karabagh via the Lachin corridor if you have already, in Yerevan, obtained the permit listing places you are allowed to visit (see pages 327–8). If not, you will have to wait until after you have obtained it in Stepanakert. The signposted turn-off north is immediately west of the border post. Keeping the Aghavnaget River on your left, continue for 15km on a dirt road (4x4 necessary in bad weather) until the monastery can be seen on an outcrop between the Aghavnaget and its tributary the Khovnavar. At the fork take the lower track which crosses a bridge. It is better to park at the bottom of the steep final slope up to the monastery and walk the last few metres. The narrow, tall three-aisle **basilica** was built in the 4th century but renovated in the 5th and again in the 7th. Unusually, there are three arches above the apse. There is some decoration on the square pillars and on the front of the *bema*. Near the *bema* some of the 13th-century floor stones have been exposed to view. Outside, one of the gravestones in particular shows very fine figure carving. The 16th-century refectory is now a small **museum** which the priest will open and show you if he is around. Items on display include clay communion vessels dating from the 5th or 6th century, carpets and khachkars. One early khachkar originally bore two carved doves but one has been defaced, possibly by order of a cleric who believed that Christ had one nature, not two (see pages 35–6). Both the church and the later fortified wall have recently been restored. The name Tsitsernavank derives either from the Armenian for 'swallow' (the bird) or from the word for the tip of the little finger; St Peter's was reputed to have been brought to the monastery.

Appendix 1

LANGUAGE

Armenian is an Indo-European language but a significant number of words have been borrowed from the country's various occupiers, mostly Persian and Turkish. There are differences in grammar, vocabulary and pronunciation between eastern Armenian (as spoken in Armenia) and western Armenian (as formerly spoken in Anatolia and still spoken by the diaspora) although the two are mutually intelligible. An older form of the language called Grabar is still used by the Church.

SOME OF THE GRAMMATICAL RULES OF EASTERN ARMENIAN

- There is no gender and the same word is used for he, she and it. There are, however, separate masculine and feminine nouns where there is a clear difference, eg: man/woman; ram/ewe; male saint/female saint.
- The definite article appears as a suffix to the noun (as in a few other Indo-European languages such as Swedish and Norwegian). There is no indefinite article: a noun without the definite article suffix is assumed to be indefinite. (This is different in western Armenian where the indefinite article appears as a separate word after the noun.) If the following word starts with a vowel, then the definite article suffix is spoken as if it were the first syllable of the following word rather than the last syllable of the noun of which it is a suffix.
- The stress is on the last syllable of a word but the definite article suffix is not regarded as a syllable for this purpose and is never stressed.
- There is no interrogative form. Questions are indicated only by tone of voice in speech, and in writing by a special mark (ˀ) over the stressed vowel of the word about which the question is being asked. For example, in the question 'You have an apple?' the question mark in Armenian would be placed either over the word 'you' or over the stressed vowel of 'apple' depending on precisely what the questioner wanted to know.
- Nouns decline (as in Latin, Russian and German). There are seven cases.
- Pronouns also decline. Infinitives can act as nouns and then they similarly decline.
- Adjectives are placed before the noun; they do not change to agree with the noun.
- Most prepositions follow the noun rather than precede it (and are therefore sometimes called postpositions) and they govern the case which the noun takes.
- There are two main conjugations of verbs plus irregular verbs.
- Some Armenian words are never heard in spoken Armenian, the Russian equivalent being used instead.
- The second person singular is used when addressing close family members, close friends and also God in prayer.

THE ARMENIAN ALPHABET: PRONUNCIATION
(**Note:** letters may be pronounced slightly differently in spoken east Armenian in accordance with their position in the word.)

Ա ա As the a in father
Բ բ As the b in book
Գ գ As the g in go
Դ դ As the d in dog
Ե ե As the ye in yes at the beginning of a word; like the e in pen within a word
Զ զ As the z in zoo
Է է As the e in elf
Ը ը As the u in but
Թ թ As the t in today
Ժ ժ As the s in treasure
Ի ի As the ea in meat
Լ լ As the l in lip
Խ խ As the ch in Scottish loch
Ծ ծ As the tz in Ritz
Կ կ As the ck in tricky
Հ h As the h in healthy
Ձ ձ As the ds in lids
Ղ ղ As a French r
Ճ ճ As the j in job
Մ մ As the m in moon
Յ յ As the y in year

Ն ն As the n in nought
Շ շ As the sh in shoe
Ո ո As the vo in vocal at the beginning of a word; like the o in no within a word
Չ չ As the ch in children
Պ պ As the p in piece
Ջ ջ As the j in juice
Ռ ռ As the rolled Scottish r
Ս ս As the s in soft
Վ վ As the v in voice
Տ տ As the clipped t in but
Ր ր As an English r
Ց g As the ts in lots
Ու ու As the oo in fool
Փ փ As the p in pink
Ք p As the k in key
Օ o As the o in stone
Ֆ ֆ As the f in fool
և (Lower case only) Pronounced *yev* at the beginning of a word but otherwise *ev*; it also has the meaning *and*.

TRANSLITERATION OF FOREIGN WORDS As mentioned, extensive use is made of certain Russian words in preference to the Armenian. In this appendix Russian words have been given as transliterations direct from Russian into English although in some cases the transliteration into Armenian is also given, depending on how useful I thought it was likely to be. For simplicity, the Cyrillic alphabet, in which Russian is written, has not been used.

One hybrid expression you must not fail to understand If you ask an Armenian if he or she can do something for you, the usual answer is *Problem chka*. This is a Russo-Armenian hybrid expression which means 'NO problem'. It does NOT mean that there is any difficulty!

WORDS AND PHRASES
Essentials

Good morning	Բարի լույս	*Bari luys*
Good afternoon	Բարի օր	*Bari or* (Not much used in spoken Armenian)
Good evening	Բարի երեկո	*Bari yereko*
Goodnight	Բարի գիշեր	*Bari gisher*
Hello (formal)	Բարև	*Barev*
Hello (informal)	Բարև ձեզ	*Barev dzez*
Goodbye	Ցտեսություն	*Tstesootyoon*
My name is …	Իմ անունը … է	*Eem anoonu … e*
What is your name? (formal)	Ի՞նչ է ձեր անունը	*Inch e dser anoonu?*

What is your name? (informal)	Ի՞նչ է անունդ	*Inch e anoonut?*
Where are you from?	Որտեղի՞ց եք	*Vortereets ek?*
Australia	Ավստրալիա	*Avstralia*
Britain	Բրիտանիա	*Breetania*
Canada	Կանադա	*Canada*
Ireland	Իռլանդիա	*Eerlandia*
New Zealand	Նոր Զելանդիա	*Nor Zeelandia*
USA	Ամերիկա	*America*
I am from …	Expressed by saying եմ (pronounced *yes*) followed by the name of the country in the ablative case, followed by եմ (pronounced *em*). The ablative case is formed from the nominative case listed above by adding the suffix յից (pronounced *yeets*) if the name of the country ends in a vowel; or the suffix ից (pronounced *eets*) if the name of the country ends in a consonant. For example:	
I am from Scotland.	Ես Շոտլանդիայից եմ	*Yes Shotlandiayeets em*
How are you?	Ինչպե՞ս եք	*Inchpes ek?*
I'm fine	Լավ եմ	*Lav em*
Please	Խնդրում եմ	*Khndroom em*
Thank you	Շնորհակալություն	*Shnorhakalatyoon*
	(most people use the French *Merci* for the sake of brevity)	
Excuse me/Sorry	Ներողություն	*Nerorootyoon*
Pleased to meet you	Շատ ուրախ եմ	*Shat oorakh em*
Yes	Այո	*Ayo*
No	Ոչ	*Votsh*
	(Armenians often say *che* (literally, it is not) instead)	
I don't understand	Ես չեմ հասկանում	*Yes chem haskanoom*
Please speak more slowly	Խնդրում եմ ավելի դանդաղ խոսեք	*Khntroom em avelee dandagh khosek*
Do you understand?	This would be considered impolite in Armenian. Say instead:	
I hope it is clear	Հուսով եմ, որ պարզ է	*Hoosov em, vor parz e*

Questions

How?	Ինչպե՞ս	*Inchpes?*
What?	Ի՞նչ	*Inch?*
	(This is frequently used when you don't understand, haven't heard, or are surprised.)	
Where is …?	Որտե՞ղ է …	*Vorterr e …?*
What is it?	Ի՞նչ է սա	*Inch e sa?*
Which?	Ո՞ր	*Vor?*
	(Used when, for example, you've been shown several rooms in a hotel, to ascertain which of them you would prefer.)	
When?	Ե՞րբ	*Yerp?*
Why?	Ինչու՞	*Inchoo?*
Who?	Ո՞վ	*Ov?*
How much does it cost?	Ի՞նչ արժե	*Inch arzhe?*

Numbers

1	*mek*	11	*tasnmek*	21	*ksan mek*
2	*yerkoo*	12	*tasnerkoo*	30	*yeresoon*
3	*yerek*	13	*tasnerek*	40	*karasoon*
4	*chors*	14	*tasnchors*	50	*hisoon*
5	*hing*	15	*tasnhing*	60	*vatsoon*
6	*vets*	16	*tasnvets*	70	*yotanasoon*
7	*yot*	17	*tasnyot*	80	*ootsoon*
8	*oot*	18	*tasnoot*	90	*innusoon*
9	*innu*	19	*tasninnu*	100	*haryoor*
10	*tas*	20	*ksan*	1,000	*hazar*

Time

What time is it?	Ժամը քանի՞սն է	*Zhamu kanees ne?*
It's … AM/PM	(The expressions AM and PM are not used in Armenian. Say instead '… hours in the morning/in the afternoon/in the evening/in the night.')	
in the morning	առավոտյան	*aravotyan*
in the afternoon	ցերեկվա	*tserekva*
in the evening	երեկոյան	*yerekoyan*
in the night	գիշերվա	*geesherva*
	(Thus, 'It is 7.00AM' becomes 'առավոտյան ժամը յոթն է' – pronounced '*aravotyan zhamu yot ne*', literally meaning 'in the morning the hour seven is'. The suffix *n* on the word seven is the definite article, which is the letter *n* for all hours except two o'clock for which it is *sn*.)	
today	Այսօր	*Ice-or*
this morning	Այս առավոտ	*Ice aravot*
this afternoon	Այս ցերեկ	*Ice tserek*
this evening	Այս երեկո	*Ice yereko*
this night/tonight	Այս գիշեր	*Ice geesher*
tomorrow	Վաղը	*Varu*
yesterday	Երեկ	*Yerek*
Monday	Երկուշաբթի	*Yerkooshabtee*
Tuesday	Երեքշաբթի	*Yerekshabtee*
Wednesday	Չորեքշաբթի	*Chorekshabtee*
Thursday	Հինգշաբթի	*Heengshabtee*
Friday	Ուրբաթ	*Yoorbat*
Saturday	Շաբաթ	*Shabat*
Sunday	Կիրակի	*Kiraki*

(The names of months do not require initial capital letters in Armenian.)

January	հունվար	*hoonvar*
February	փետրվար	*petrvar*
March	մարտ	*mart*
April	ապրիլ	*apreel*
May	մայիս	*mayees*
June	հունիս	*hoonees*
July	հուլիս	*hoolees*
August	օգոստոս	*ogostos*

September	սեպտեմբեր	*september*
October	հոկտեմբեր	*hoktember*
November	նոյեմբեր	*noyember*
December	դեկտեմբեր	*dektember*

Getting around

I'd like ...	Ես կցանկանայի ...	*Yes ktsankanayee ...*
... a one-way ticket	... տոմս մեկ ուղղությամբ	*... toms mek oorrootyamp*
	(Return tickets are not issued for journeys within Armenia. Also trains and buses within Armenia are one class only. There are various categories of ticket on the overnight train to Tbilisi, Georgia. See page 68.)	
I want to go to ...	Ես ցանկանում եմ մեկնել ...	*Yes tsankanoom em meknel ...*
How much is it?	Ի՞նչ արժե	*Inch arzhe?*
	(In the following three sentences insert the word for bus, minibus, train or plane – given below – but with the suffix ը (pronounced like an unstressed *u*) to indicate the definite article.)	
What time does the ... depart?	ժամը քանիսի՞ն է ... մեկնում	*Zhamu kaneeseen e ... meknoom?*
The ... has been delayed	... ուշանում է	*... ooshanoom e*
The ... has been cancelled	... չի մեքնելու	*... chee mekneloo*
bus	Ավտոբուս	*Avtoboos*
train	Գնացք	*Gnatsk*
plane	Օդանավ	*Otanav*
minibus	(Use the Russian word pronounced *marshrootka*.)	
boat	Նավակ	*Navak*
platform	(Use the Russian word pronounced *platform*.)	
ticket office	Դրամարկղ	*Dramakurr*
	(Also used for the box office at a theatre.)	
timetable	Չվացուցակ	*Chvatsootsak*
bus station	Ավտոկայան	*Avtokayan*
railway station	Կայարան	*Kayaran*
airport	Օդանավակայան	*Otanavakayan*
car	(Ավտո)մեքենա	*(Avto)mekeena*
4x4	(Although 4x4 drive vehicles are common and useful in Armenia, there is no proper word for them. Use the word *Neeva* which is the commonest Russian make; or the word *Jeep* which is the commonest American make; or use the Armenian description *amenoor genats* (go-everywhere).)	
taxi	Տաքսի	*Taksee*
motorbike	Մոտոցիկլ	*Mototseekl*
moped	Մոպեդ	*Moped*
bicycle	Հեծանիվ	*Hetsaneev*
arrival/departure	ժամանում/Մեկնում	*Zhamanoom/Meknoom*
here/there	Այստեղ/Այնտեղ	*Ice-terr/Ine-terr*
Is this the road to ...?	Սա ... տանող ճանապա՞րհն է	*Sa ... tanorr janapar ne?*
Where can I buy petrol?	Որտե՞ղ կարող եմ գնել բենզին	*Vorterr karorr em gnel benzeen?*
... litres, please	... լիտր, խնդրում եմ	*... leetr, khntroom em*
... drams worth, please	... դրամի, խնդրում եմ	*... dramee, khntroom em*

diesel	(Use the Russian word pronounced *salyarka*)	
petrol	Բենզին	*Benzeen*
	(Unleaded petrol is not available in Armenia. So far as leaded petrol is concerned, see page 83.)	
My car has broken down	Մեքենաս փչացել է	*Mekenas pchatsel e*
danger	Վտանգ	*Vtang*
Go straight ahead	Ուղիղ գնաց եք	*Oorreer gnats ek*
left	Ձախ	*Dsakh*
right	Աջ	*Atch*
traffic lights	(Use the Russian word pronounced *svetafor*)	
north	Հյուսիս	*Hyoosees*
south	Հարավ	*Haraf*
east	Արևելք	*Aravelk*
west	Արևմուտք	*Aravmootk*
behind	Ետև	*Yetev*
in front of	Առջև	*Archev*
near	Մոտ	*Mot*
opposite	Դիմաց	*Deemats*

Street signs

entry	Մուտք	*Mootk*
no entry	Մուտքը արգելված է	*Mootku argelvats e*
exit	Ելք	*Yelk*
no parking	Կանգառն արգելված է	*Kangarn argelvats e*
open	Բաց է	*Bats e*
closed	Փակ է	*Pak e*
toilets	Զուգարան	*Zookaran*
information	Տեղեկատու	*Terrekatoo*

Accommodation

hotel	Հյուրանոց	*Hyooranots*
Where is there a cheap/good hotel?	Որտե՞ղ կա էժան/լավ հյուրանոց	*Vorterr ka ezhan/lav hyooranots*
Could you please write the address?	Խնդրում եմ հասցեն գրեք	*Khndroom em hastsen gurek*
Is there a vacant room?	Ազատ սենյակ կ՞ա	*Azat senyak ka*
I'd like ...	Ես կցանկանայի ...	*Yes ktsankanayee ...*
... a single room	... մեկտեղանոց սենյակ	*... mekterranots senyak*
... a double toom	... երկտեղանոց սենյակ	*... yerkterranots senyak*
... a room with two beds	... սենյակ երկու մահճակալով	*... senyak yerkoo mahjakalov*
... a room with a toilet and shower	... սենյակ զուգարանով և լոգարանով	*... senyak zookaranov yev logaranov*
How much is it per night?	Գիշերը ի՞նչ արժե	*Geesheru inch arzhe?*
How much is it per person?	Անձը ի՞նչ արժե	*Andsu inch arzhe?*
Where is the toilet?	Զուգարանը որտե՞ղ է	*Zookaranu vorterr e?*
Is there water?	Ջուր կ՞ա	*Joor ka?*
Is there hot water?	Տաք ջուր կ՞ա	*Tak joor ka?*
Is breakfast included in the price?	Նախաճաշը մտնու՞մ է գնի մեջ	*Nakhajashu mtnoom e gnee metch?*
I am leaving today	Ես մեկնում եմ այսor	*Yes meknoom em ice-ore*

Eating and drinking

restaurant	Ռեստորան	Restoran
breakfast	Նախաճաշ	Nakhajash
lunch	Ճաշ	Jash
dinner	Ընթրիք	Untreek

(On entering a restaurant one is usually asked: Քանի՞ հոգի եք (pronounced *Kanee hokee ek?*). It means 'How many of you are there?')

Is there a table for ... people?	... հոգու համար սեղան կա՞	... hokoo hamar serran ka?
Are there any vegetarian dishes?	Բուսական ուտեստներ կա՞ն	Boosakan ootestner kan?
Please bring me ...	Խնդրում եմ ... բերեք	Khntroom em ... berek
... a fork/knife/spoon	... պատարաքաղ/դանակ/գդալ	... patarakarr/danak/gtal
The bill, please	Հաշիվը բերեք, խնդրում եմ	Hasheevu berek, khntroom em
soup	Ապուր	Apoor
bread	Հաց	Hats
butter	Կարագ	Karag
lavash (Armenian flatbread)	Լավաշ	Lavash
cheese	Պանիր	Paneer
honey	Մեղր	Merr
oil	Ձեթ	Dset
vinegar	Քացախ	Katsakh
pepper	բիբար/պղպեղ	Beebar/peperr
salt	Աղ	Arr
sugar	Շաքարավազ	Shakaravaz
apple	Խնձոր	Khndsor
banana	(The correct word is Արամատուզ – pronounced *adamatooz*, but the word generally used is Բանան – pronounced *banan*.)	
grapes	Խաղող	Kharrorr
orange	Նարինջ	Nareenj
peach	Դեղձ	Derrds
pear	Տանձ	Tands
watermelon	Ձմերուկ	Dsmerook
apricot	Ծիրան	Tseeran
cherries	Կեռաս	Keras
strawberries	Ելակ	Yelak
plum	Սալոր	Salor
carrot	Գազար	Gazar
garlic	Սխտոր	Skhtor
onion	Սոխ	Sokh
sweet pepper	Բիբար	Beebar
potato	Կարտոֆիլ	Kartofeel
rice	Բրինձ	Brindz
tomato	Լոլիկ	Loleek
cucumber	Վարունգ	Varoong
salad	Սալաթ	Salat
salmon	Սարմոն	Sarrmon
tuna	Թյուննոս	Tyoonos
whitefish	Սիգ	Sig
smoked whitefish	Ծխացրած սիգ	Tskhatsrats sig
beef	Տավարի միս	Tavaree mees

lamb	Ոչխարի միս	*Vochkharee mees*
pork	Խոզի միս	*Khozee mees*
goat	Այծի միս	*Aytsee mees*
chicken	Հավ	*Hav*
barbecued	Խորոված	*Khorovats*
sausage	Նրբերշիկ	*Nrpersheek*
(white) ice cream	(Սպիտակ) պաղպաղակ	*(Spitak) parrparrak*
chocolate	Շոկոլադ	*Shocolad*
tea	Թեյ	*Tay*
coffee	Սուրճ	*Soorj*
juice	Հյութ	*Hyoot*
milk	Կաթ	*Kat*
water	Ջուր	*Joor*
mineral water	Հանքային ջուր	*Hankayeen joor*
wine	Գինի	*Ginee*
beer	Գարեջուր	*Garejoor*
brandy	Կոնյակ	*Konyak*

Shopping

I'd like to buy ...	Ես կցանկանայի գնել ...	*Yes ktsankanayee gnel ...*
How much is it?	Ի՞նչ արժե	*Inch arzhe?*
It's too expensive	Չափազանց թանկ է	*Chapazants tank e*
I'll take it	Ես սա կվերցնեմ	*Yes sa kvertsnem*
Do you accept credit cards?	Կրեդիտ քարտ ընդունու՞մ եք	*Kredeet kart untoonoom ek?*
A little more	Մի քիչ ավել	*Mee keech avel*
A little less	Ավելի քիչ	*Avelee keech*

Communications

Where is ... ?	Որտե՞ղ է ...	*Vorterr e ... ?*

(If any of the following nouns were used after *Vorterr e...?*, it would indicate the indefinite article: for example, 'where is there a church?'; 'where is there a museum?', etc. If the definite article is required, then add the unstressed suffix ը – pronounced *u* – when the noun ends with a consonant or the suffix ն – pronounced *n* – when the noun ends with a vowel. This results in the meanings: 'where is the church?'; 'where is the museum?', etc.)

church	Եկեղեցի	*Yekeretsee*
monastery	Վանք	*Vank*
castle	Բերդ, Ամրոց	*Berd, Amrots*
museum	Թանգարան	*Tangaran*
post office	Փոստ	*Post*
bank	Բանկ	*Bank*
market	Շուկա	*Shooka*
embassy	Դեսպանատուն	*Despanatoon*
exchange office	(Use the English word *change*.)	

Emergency

Help!	Օգնություն	*Oknootyoon*
Call a doctor!	Բժիշկ կանչեցեք	*Bzheeshk kanchetsek*
There's been a road accident	Ավտովթար է տեղի ունեցել	*Avtovtar e terree oonetsel*

There's been an accident (non-road)	Դժբախտ պատահար է	*Dzhbakht patahar e*
I'm lost	Ես մոլորվել եմ	*Yes molorvel em*
Go away!	Հեռու գնա	*Heroo gna*
police	Ոստիկանություն	*Vosteekarnootyoon*
fire service	Հրշեջ ծառայություն	*Hrshetch tsarayootyoon*
ambulance	Շտապ օգնություն	*Shtap oknootyoon*
thief	Կողոպուտ	*Korropoot*

Health

hospital	Հիվանդանոց	*Heevandanots*
I am ill	Ես հիվանդ եմ	*Yes heevand em*
diarrhoea	Լուծ	*Loots*
nausea	Սրտխառնոց	*Srtkharnots*
doctor	Բժիշկ	*Bzheeshk*
prescription	Դեղատոմս	*Derratoms*
pharmacy	Դեղատուն	*Derratoon*
paracetamol	Պարացետամոլ	*Paratsetamol*
antibiotic	Հակաբիոտիկ	*Hakabeeoteek*
antiseptic	Հականեխիչ	*Hakanekheech*
tampon	Վիրախծուծ	*Veerakhtsoots*
condom	Պահպանակ	*Pahpanak*
sunblock	Հակաարևահարման բույկ	*Haka-arevaharman ksook*
I have ...	Ես ... ունեմ	*Yes ... oonem*
... asthma	... աստմա ...	*... astma*
... epilepsy	... էպիլեպսիա ...	*... epilepsia*
... diabetes	... շաքարախտ ...	*... shakarakht*
I'm allergic to ...	Ես ալերգիկ եմ ...	*Yes alergeek em ...*
... penicillin	... պենիցիլինի	*... peneetseeleenee*
... bee stings	... մեղվի խայթոցի	*... merrvee khaytotsee*
... all kinds of nuts	... բոլոր տեսակի ընկույզների	*... bolor tesakee unkooyzneree*

Other

my/ours/yours	իմ/մեր/ձեր	*eem/mer/dser*
and	և (or) ու	*yev* (or) *oo*
some	մի քիչ	*mee keech*
this/that	այս/այն	*ice/ine* (as in nine)
expensive/cheap	թանկ/էժան	*tank/ezhan*
beautiful/ugly	գեղեցիկ/տգեղ	*gerretseek/tgerr*
old/new	հին/նոր	*heen/nor*
good/bad	լավ/վատ	*lav/vat*
early/late	շուտ/ուշ	*shoot/oosh*
hot/cold	տաք/սառը	*tak/saaru*
difficult/easy	բարդ/հեշտ	*bart/hesht*
boring/interesting	ձանձրալի/հետաքրքիր	*dsandsralee/hetakrkeer*

PLACE NAMES

ԵՐԵՎԱՆ	YEREVAN	ԷՋՄԻԱԾԻՆ	EJMIATSIN
ԳՅՈՒՄՐԻ	GYUMRI	ԵՂԵԳՆԱՁՈՐ	YEGHEGNADZOR
ՎԱՆԱՁՈՐ	VANADZOR	ՋԵՐՄՈՒԿ	JERMUK
ՍՏԵՓԱՆԱՎԱՆ	STEPANAVAN	ՍԻՍԻԱՆ	SISIAN
ԱԼԱՎԵՐԴԻ	ALAVERDI	ԳՈՐԻՍ	GORIS
ԴԻԼԻՋԱՆ	DILIJAN	ԿԱՊԱՆ	KAPAN
ԻՋԵՎԱՆ	IJEVAN	ՄԵՂՐԻ	MEGHRI
ՍԵՎԱՆ	SEVAN	ՍՏԵՓԱՆԱԿԵՐՏ	STEPANAKERT
ԾԱՂԿԱՁՈՐ	TSAGHKADZOR		

Appendix 2

FURTHER INFORMATION

Thanks largely to the diaspora, the current literature on Armenia is vast. There are also numerous out-of-print titles, many from Soviet days. It is clear that nobody could read more than a small fraction of the total. The following represents no more than some of the books which the author has found interesting or useful. NHBS (*www.nhbs.co.uk*) is a good source for books on natural history. Out-of-print books can often be found via AbeBooks (*www.abebooks.co.uk*). Amazon (*www.amazon.co.uk* or *www.amazon.com*) is a popular source of books.

HISTORY

A Question of Genocide Edited by Ronald Grigor Suny, Fatma Müge Göçek and Norman M Naimark; Oxford University Press 2011. Subtitled *Armenians and Turks at the End of the Ottoman Empire*, the book brings together essays by historians from both sides of the Armenian–Turkish divide, and from none, to examine in a non-nationalistic and non-partisan way the causes of the Armenian genocide in particular and communal violence in general.

Archaeological Heritage of Armenia Edited by Hakob Simonyan; Hushardzan Publishers, Yerevan 2013. A well-illustrated, bilingual (Armenian and English) introduction to the archaeology of Armenia. Also covers churches and monasteries from the 4th century to the 14th century.

Armenian Churches – Holy See of Echmiadzin Calouste Gulbenkian Foundation, 1970. Largely a book of black and white photographs with limited text, it is interesting to compare some of the 1960s photographs with the same church today and see the extent of reconstruction. Also covers a few churches in present-day Turkey.

Hasratian, Murad *Early Christian Architecture of Armenia* Inkombook, Moscow, 2000. Covers churches intact and ruined, large and small, well known and desperately obscure. Does not include churches from the later medieval period so some of the most famous are excluded. Detailed information explaining well the variety of forms found in Armenian churches. The absence of an index diminishes the usefulness of what is otherwise a well-produced book.

Hovannisian, Richard G *The Republic of Armenia* (4 volumes) University of California Press, 1996. An exhaustive and scholarly but readable account of Armenia in the crucial years from 1918 to 1921.

Karapetian, Samvel *Armenian Cultural Monuments in the Region of Karabakh* Gitutian Publishing House of NAS RAA, Yerevan, 2001. An interesting up-to-date account of what is to be found there. It includes territories occupied since 1994 but regrettably does not include all districts so that Nagorno Karabagh's best known sight – Gandzasar Monastery – is omitted.

Kevorkian, Raymond *The Armenian Genocide* I B Taurus, 2011. This weighty tome describes itself as 'a complete history' of the genocide. It traces the roots of the genocide, the impact on the Armenian community and the development of the Turkish state. The section comprising a region-by-region detailed documentation of deportations, massacres and resistance is an encyclopaedic work of reference.

Khalpakhchian, O *Architectural Ensembles of Armenia* Iskusstvo, Moscow, 1980. This thorough survey would have been more useful if only it had been better translated. It desperately needed review by a native English speaker. Standing with it in hand at the place being described it is, however, usually possible to work out what the author probably means. Covers only 19 sites but quite thorough.

Masih, Joseph and Krikorian, Robert *Armenia: At the Crossroads* Routledge, 1999. Although the English is occasionally curious the book does give a feel for Armenia's crossroad position – historically, geographically, politically and economically.

Nassibian, Akaby *Britain and the Armenian Question 1915–1923* Croom Helm, 1984. A good account of the British government's failure to help the Armenian people. Despite the title it includes the background to the events from the 1870s onwards.

Nersessian, Vrej *Treasures from the Ark* The British Library, 2001. The catalogue of the wonderful exhibition of Armenian art held in London that year. It is the best illustrated book of Armenian art treasures available.

Piotrovsky, Boris *Urartu* Nagel, 1969. Translated from the Russian by James Hogarth. Written by the director of Leningrad's Hermitage Museum and director of excavations at the Urartian site of Karmir Blur near Yerevan for over 20 years, this book brings to life the dry, both literally and metaphorically, remains of the kingdom of Urartu. Photographs of unearthed treasures, many of which are on display in the State History Museum, Yerevan.

Redgate, Anne E *The Armenians* Blackwell, 1998. A strongly recommended history of the Armenian people although rather sketchy on the period after 1100.

Rost, Yuri *Armenian Tragedy* Weidenfeld and Nicolson, 1990. A journalist's eyewitness accounts of the early stages of the conflict between Armenia and Azerbaijan and the devastating earthquake of 1988.

NATURAL HISTORY

Adamian, Martin S and Klem Jr, Daniel *A Field Guide to the Birds of Armenia* American University of Armenia, 1997. An invaluable well-illustrated field guide.

Baytaş Ahmet *A Field Guide to the Butterflies of Turkey* Ntv, 2007. Although it doesn't specifically cover the area of Armenia it would be generally useful and certainly more portable than Tuzov's *Guide to the Butterflies of Russia & Adjacent Territories* – see opposite.

Gabrielian, Eleonora and Fragman-Sapir, Ori *Flowers of the Transcaucasus and Adjacent Areas* Gantner Verlag, 2008. Available from NHBS. Expensive.

Greenhalgh, Malcolm *A Pocket Guide to the Freshwater Fish of Britain and Europe* Mitchell Beazley, 2001. Does not include all Armenian species but quite useful.

Holubec, Vojtech and Krivka, Pavel *The Caucasus and its Flowers* LOXIA, 2006. Available from NHBS. Expensive.

MacDonald, David *Collins Field Guide to the Mammals of Britain and Europe* HarperCollins, 2005. Omits a few species such as leopard, but useful.

Pils, Gerhard *Flowers of Turkey* published by the author, 2006. The most useful field guide for the average botanical traveller, but expensive. No text but lots of photographs, arranged by plant families. Available from NHBS.

Shetekauri, Shamil and Jacoby, Martin *Mountain Flowers and Trees of Caucasia* Martin Jacoby, 2009. Available from NHBS. Paperback and the cheapest of the botanical guides.

Szczerbak, N N *Guide to the Reptiles of the Eastern Palearctic* Krieger, 2003. One sees lots of reptiles in Armenia and this guide is useful although it does not always make it clear how to distinguish between related species.

Tuzov V K (ed) *Guide to the Butterflies of Russia and Adjacent Territories* (2 volumes) Pensoft, Sofia, 2000. A thorough guide illustrated with photographs of specimens and covering the whole of the former USSR but unfortunately not very portable.

GENERAL

Petrosian, Irina and Underwood, David *Armenian Food: Fact, Fiction and Folklore* Yerkir Publishing, 2006. This is not a cookery book! Written by an Armenian wife and American husband, it's a fascinating and revealing insight into Armenia as seen through the country's food. Entertainingly written and very informative. Highly recommended.

Solomon, Susan *Culture Smart! Armenia* Kuperard 2010. A guide to the customs and culture of Armenia. Helpful tips on social etiquette, dos and don'ts.

TRAVEL

Bachmann, Carine and Tufenkian, Jeffrey *Adventure Armenia – Hiking and Rock Climbing* Kanach, 2004. Describes 20 walks and five climbs. The first attempt to publish practical information about the country's potential though it only scratches the surface.

Hepworth, Revd George H *Through Armenia on Horseback* Isbister, 1898. In one of the best accounts of life among the Armenians of Anatolia shortly before the genocide, the evidently unbiased author gives an account of their hardships and oppression.

Kiesling, Brady and Kojian, Raffi *Rediscovering Armenia* Tigran Mets, 2001. A gazetteer which lists most of Armenia's villages and monuments and tells you how to find them. Not really a guidebook itself but it was often useful to the author of this one in indicating what exists.

Nansen, Fridtjof *Armenia and the Near East* George Allen & Unwin, 1928. The great Polar explorer was appointed League of Nations Commissioner for Refugees and in that capacity visited Soviet Armenia in its early days accompanied by Vidkun Quisling (later to become Norway's prime minister during the Nazi occupation and consequently executed for treason in 1945) who acted as his secretary. He was favourably impressed by the plans to use the water from Lake Sevan to irrigate the Ararat Valley.

PP (ie: Peter Pears) *Armenian Holiday August 1965* Privately published, 1965. The English tenor's account of his visit with Britten, Rostropovich and Galina Vishnevskaya. The Russian soprano, Rostropovich's wife, also gives an account in her autobiography *Galina – A Russian Story* (Hodder & Stoughton, 1985).

Shaginyan, Marietta *Journey through Soviet Armenia* Foreign Languages Publishing House, Moscow, 1954. A wonderful period piece of Stalin-era writing – the Russian original was published in 1952 before his death. Unfortunately out of print but eminently worth seeking a copy for anyone with a taste for the bizarre.

LITERATURE

Armenian Poetry Old and New Wayne State University Press, 1979. A bilingual anthology compiled and translated by Aram Tolegian. The English translations make available to non-Armenian speakers a selection from a wide range of poets, including some mentioned in the literature section of this guidebook. For those who have a little knowledge of the language the bilingual nature of the book allows a rare glimpse into Armenian poetry.

Folktales of Armenia Translated into English by Leon Surmelian. Nahapet Publishing House, Yerevan. A charming collection of Armenian fairy tales in which I discovered that the Armenian equivalent of 'Once upon a time ...' translates literally as 'There was and there was not ...'

Pushkin, Alexander *A Journey to Arzrum* (ie: Erzurum) 1835, English translation by Birgitta Ingemanson published by Ardis, 1974. An excellent translation with extremely useful notes explaining matters unlikely to be familiar to modern Western readers.

Saroyan, William *The Human Comedy* 1943 and *Boys and Girls Together* 1963. Two works suggested as an introduction to the Armenian-American author.

LANGUAGE A variety of teaching material is now offered on the internet although much is for western rather than eastern Armenian. Try www.armeniapedia.org or search via Google for Eastern Armenian courses.

Avetisyan, Anahit *Eastern Armenian* Comprehensive self-study language course published by the author, Yerevan, 2008. The most accessible eastern Armenian course I have found. Everything is provided in three forms: Armenian, Armenian transliteration and English translation. It also introduces the learner to cursive handwritten Armenian. The sort of teach yourself book now available in most languages but which has been lacking for Armenian until now. Far better than the books previously available. Apparently unavailable outside Armenia.

Eurotalk *Learn Armenian* CD-ROM (*www.eurotalk.com*) Introduces the reader to basic words and phrases in what it describes as a fun way. It has the advantage that one can hear as well as see the language and it provides an element of feedback.

Grigorian, Kh *English–Armenian/Armenian–English Dictionary* Ankyunacar Press, Yerevan, 2005. Compiled for English speakers. The best small dictionary I have found. Apparently unavailable outside Armenia.

Muradyan, Lusine *Learning Armenian Headstart* Edit Print, Yerevan, 2011. A manual for English-speaking, absolute beginners. Based on conversational skills with the introduction of basic grammar. Extensive vocabularies. Includes a copy book section to learn cursive writing. The separate grammar section is in tabular form without explanations in English. CD included. Paper edition apparently unavailable outside Armenia. Digital Kindle version available from Amazon.

RELIGION

Ghazarian, Jacob G *The Mediterranean Legacy in Early Celtic Christianity* Bennet & Bloom, 2006. Visitors to Armenia may well be struck by the similarities between the decoration on Armenian khachkars and illuminated manuscripts and that on the Celtic crosses and illuminated manuscripts of Ireland and Scotland. This book explores possible reasons for those similarities.

Ormanian, Archbishop Maghakia *The Church of Armenia* Ankyunacar Publishing, Yerevan, 2011. Translated by G Marcar Gregory. First published, in French, in 1910, the present English translation includes annotations reflecting changes in the century since it was written. An informative small book about the history, doctrine, clergy, hierarchy and liturgy of the Armenian Church. Clarifies some matters for those unfamiliar with the Armenian Church.

Speaking with God from the Depths of the Heart. The prayers of St Grigor Narekatsi (c950–1010) translated by Thomas J Samuelian. VEM Press, Yerevan, 2002. The prayers, or lamentations, of St Gregory of Narek have been compared to the psalms of David and occupy a unique place within the Armenian Church and Armenian literature. Gregory sought an intuitive communication with God; his prayers pile image upon image, metaphor upon metaphor.

USEFUL WEBSITES

www.armenianchurch.org The website of the Mother See of Ejmiatsin. Comprehensive information about the Armenian Church.

www.armeniainfo.am Although the once excellent tourist information office in Yerevan closed several years ago the website still exists. Much of it is seriously out of date, especially the practical information, but some useful snippets remain.

www.armenianmonuments.org An evolving website. Not the easiest of websites to find what one wants but has some very useful information, eg: a guide to Noratus field of khachkars which is worth downloading to take with you when visiting the site.

www.armenianow.com The weekly English-language web magazine, *Armenia Now*, gives a flavour of contemporary events.

www.armeniapedia.org The best internet source of information on all things Armenian. Patchy on practical information. This website also covers Nagorno Karabagh. Has an extensive language section.

www.armhotels.am Online information and booking for hotels in Armenia and Nagorno Karabagh. Said to be a relatively expensive way of booking.

www.azatutyun.am A good website for keeping up to date with Armenian news. Has an English section.

www.fco.gov.uk UK Foreign Office website. Has advice for travellers to Armenia.

www.gallery.am Website of the National Gallery of Armenia with information on the collections.

www.haypost.am Website of the Armenian Post Office. Has some useful practical information plus information on philately.

www.meoweather.com Gives a seven-day forecast for Yerevan with options for seven other towns in Armenia.

www.mfa.am The official website of the Armenian Foreign Ministry. Gives information on visa requirements and other official government announcements.

www.nkr.am The website of the Nagorno Karabagh Foreign Ministry. Has information on visas, including a downloadable visa application form for use in Stepanakert but not if applying in Yerevan (see page 327). Also has information on geography, flora, climate, etc.

www.nt.am The website of *Noyan Tapan Highlights*, the English-language newspaper.

www.spyur.am Armenia's Yellow Pages.

www.tacentral.com Useful practical information although some of the country is not covered and a bit out of date at times. Interesting articles on topics such as Armenian carpets, flowers, language and archaeology. Useful guides (the only ones) to the State History Museum (a little out of date after recent redevelopment) and to Metsamor Museum.

www.timeanddate.com/weather/armenia/yerevan Gives a useful two-week weather forecast.

www.uk.mfa.am The website of the Armenian embassy in London. Has much useful information about Armenia. Details of visa requirements and a link to the application process for e-visa.

www.usa.mfa.am The website of the Armenian embassy in Washington. Essentially the same information as above.

www.zvartnots.aero Has useful information about Zvartnots Airport.

Index

INDEX OF ADVERTISERS

OCT 3 2014